POLITICS, POETICS, AND THE PINDARIC ODE:

1450-1700

MEDIEVAL AND RENAISSANCE
TEXTS AND STUDIES
VOLUME 351

ARIZONA STUDIES IN THE
MIDDLE AGES AND THE RENAISSANCE

VOLUME 27

Politics, Poetics, and the Pindaric Ode: 1450-1700

Stella P. Revard

ACMRS
(Arizona Center for Medieval and Renaissance Studies)
Tempe, Arizona
in collaboration with
BREPOLS
2009

ASMAR Volume 27: ISBN 978-2-503-52896-0   D/2009/0095/79

Library of Congress Cataloging-in-Publication Data

Revard, Stella Purce.
  Politics, poetics, and the Pindaric ode : 1450-1700 / Stella P. Revard.
    p. cm. -- (Medieval and Renaissance texts and studies ; v. 351) (Arizona
studies in the Middle Ages and the Renaissance ; v. 27)
  Includes bibliographical references.
  ISBN 978-0-86698-399-0 (alk. paper)
  1. Laudatory poetry--History and criticism. 2. European poetry--Renais-
sance, 1450-1600--History and criticism. 3. European poetry--Renaissance,
1450-1600--Greek influences. I. Title.

PN4129.15.R48 2008
809.1'43093584021--dc22

                                                                2009006730

∞
This book is made to last.
It is set in Adobe Caslon Pro,
smyth-sewn and printed on acid-free paper
to library specifications.
Printed in the United States of America

*For Stephen Revard, Geoffrey Revard, Vanessa Revard,
and Lawrence Revard*

τὸ δὲ παθεῖν εὖ πρῶτον ἀέθλων·
εὖ δ᾽ ἀκούειν δευτέρα μοῖρ᾽· ἀμφοτέροισι δ᾽ ἀνὴρ
ὃς ἂν ἐγκύρσῃ καὶ ἕλῃ,
στέφανον ὕψιστον δέδεκται.
(Pythian 1. 99–100)

TABLE OF CONTENTS

Preface

"Half yet remains unsung." Since the publication in 2001 of *Pindar and the Renaissance Hymn-Ode* I have heard Milton's cautionary words about incomplete works ringing in my ears. The first book on Pindar comprised only half of my original manuscript, for I had literally cut the book in two in order to facilitate the publication of the first part. Therefore, like the divided creatures of Aristophanes' myth in *The Symposium*, the first book was in danger of being an entity forever in search of its other half. Fortunately, thanks to the generosity of MRTS and the encouragement of its editor Robert Bjork the second half of the proposed study joins the first book to complete what I had originally envisioned as a whole. In the process I have reshaped the second book as a complement to the first—to focus on Pindaric politics and patronage as the first book had on the Pindaric hymn tradition. Like the epinician poet I can say at last that I have kept my word and delivered what I had promised.

The two books were a long time in gestation since I delivered my first papers on Pindar and Pindaric imitation in the late 1970s. The work could not have been finished without the generous support of the National Endowment of the Humanities, research fellowships from Southern Illinois University, Edwardsville, grants from the Huntington and Folger Libraries, and assistance from the staffs of the Folger, the Huntington, and the Bodleian and British Libraries. I am grateful to the organizers of the Dearborn conferences on seventeenth-century literature—Claude Summers and Ted-Larry Pebworth—and the organizer of the Reading Literary and History conferences—Cedric Brown—for permitting me to try out theories of Pindaric politics and poetics in papers on Marvell, Cowley, Jonson, and Aphra Behn. Also the Congresses of the International Association for Neo-Latin Studies (IANLS) during this period fostered my investigations into Neo-Latin literature as the first vehicle of Pindaric imitation and practice. I wish to thank colleagues and friends in IANLS for their interest in and encouragement of my Pindaric pursuits, especially Julia Gaisser, Philip Ford, Marianne Pade, Ann Moss, Brenda Hosington, and Walther Ludwig. Similarly, friends and colleagues in sixteenth- and seventeenth-century English studies have shown great kindness and support of my research into Pindaric studies. Mario Di Cesare, the former editor of MRTS, encouraged me to submit the original manuscript to the press and has followed its progress. My thanks to Barbara Lewalski, Michael Lieb, Albert Labriola, David Loewenstein, Thomas

Corns, Achsah Guibbory, Arlene Stiebel, Joan Blythe, Diane McColley, and many others. Lastly, my thanks to the Classics Department at Washington University and to Carl Conrad, Kevin Herbert, George Pepe for nurturing my studies in Greek and my interest in Pindar. I am grateful to Roy Rukkila and to Dr. Leslie MacCoull for their invaluable assistance during the process of copy-editing and preparing the manuscript for publication. Dr. MacCoull has gone far beyond the responsibilities of a copy-editor in her meticulous attention to detail and her suggestions for improving the manuscript. The advice of two anonymous readers of the manuscript was also very helpful in helping me revise the book.

Parts of this manuscript have appeared in articles printed over the past twenty years. Material from the following has been revised and reshaped in chapters 2, 3, 4, 7, and 8: "Pindar and Jonson's Cary-Morison Ode," in *Classic and Cavalier: Essays on Jonson and the Sons of Ben*, ed. Claude J. Summers and Ted-Larry Pebworth (Pittsburgh: University of Pittsburgh Press, 1982), 17–29; "*Ad Joannem Rousium*: Elegiac Wit and Pindaric Mode," in *Urbane Milton: The Latin Poetry*, *Milton Studies*, ed. James A. Freeman and Anthony Low (Pittsburgh: University of Pittsburgh Press, 1984), 205–226; "Building the Foundations of the Good Commonwealth: Marvell, Pindar, and the Power of Music," in *The Muses Common-weale*, ed. Claude J. Summers and Ted-Larry Pebworth (Columbia: University of Missouri Press, 1988), 177–90; "Cowley's *Pindarique Odes* and the Politics of the Inter-regnum," *Criticism* 35 (Summer 1993): 391–418; "Alpheus, Arethusa, and the Pindaric Pursuit in *Lycidas*," in *Of Poetry and Politics: Essays on Milton and his World*, ed. P. G. Stanwood (Binghamton: MRTS, 1995), 35–45; "Katherine Philips, Aphra Behn, and the Female Pindaric," in *Representing Women in Renaissance England*, ed. Claude J. Summers and Ted-Larry Pebworth (Columbia: University of Missouri Press, 1997), 227–41; "Lampridio and the Poetic Sodalities in Rome in the 1510s and 1520s," in *Acta Conventus Neo-Latini Bariensis*, ed. R. Schnur et al. (MRTS 184. Tempe, AZ: ACMRS, 1998), 499–507; "The Latin Ode from Elizabeth I to Mary II: Political Approaches to Encomia," in *Britannia Latina: Latin in the Culture of Great Britain from the Middle Ages to the Twentieth Century*, ed. Charles Burnett and Nicholas Mann (London: Warburg Institute, 2005), 156–69.

The book is dedicated to my four children, three of whom undoubtedly remember when we stood beside the waters of Alpheus and looked on the ancient precincts of Pindar's own Olympia.

INTRODUCTION

The history of the recovery of Pindar and the imitation of his odes is a complex one, part of which I have already outlined in the companion volume of this study—*Pindar and the Renaissance Hymn-Ode: 1450–1700*. Imitation of Pindar began in Italy and France, first as a neo-Latin form and then as a flourishing vernacular medium. One dimension of Pindaric ode, often emulated, was its religious or hymnic aspect, recreated in both the classical and the Christian mode. However, from the beginnings Pindaric imitations could also assume secular encomiastic forms and be employed to address sovereigns or compliment friends and patrons, to explore abstract philosophical matters or simply to commemorate appropriate events, ranging from weddings to funerals. This kind of ode, later popularized by Cowley and his followers in England, had early been current with the first continental pindarists. Although the religious pindaric began to wane in favor in the late sixteenth century, the encomiastic pindaric continued to proliferate. Early modern poets understood that while Pindar composed hymns to the gods, he was also a highly successful political encomiast who had addressed odes to kings, tyrants, and aristocrats throughout the Mediterranean world. Therefore, poets on the continent and in England quickly grasped Pindaric ode's potential as the poetry of praise and converted Pindar's encomia to athletes and their patrons to praise of their own aristocratic lords and princes. Further, instead of celebrating athletic victories, they celebrated military victories and commemorated formal state occasions, such as the making of treaties or monarchs' state arrivals and departures. They also used pindarics to proclaim royal births and deaths and to sound the jubilee for weddings.

To mark an occasion of military triumph or dynastic expansion, a Pindaric poet stood ready to sing the praise of the winning forces. The fifteenth-century poet-statesman Francesco Filelfo composed pindarics both to address Charles VII of France and to compliment his Sforza patrons, being among the first to make "victory" odes the appropriate medium for congratulating princes on vanquishing their enemies.[1] Such odes quickly became the appropriate form for

---

[1] The poets who followed Filelfo—Giovanni Pontano, Michele Marullo, and Pietro Crinito—although accomplished in their imitations of Pindar's hymnic forms, also composed Pindaric encomia and victory odes. Giovanni Pontano blended Horatian and Pindaric ode to celebrate the Neapolitan victory over the Turks.

celebrating the repulse of the Turks or the victories of the Italian states over the French or the French over the Italians. Such odes continued to be composed for battle victories well into the eighteenth century when Marlborough's victory at Blenheim called forth Pindaric jubilees.[2] In some ways we can chart the history of western Europe from the mid-fifteenth to the early eighteenth century simply by following the progress of the Pindaric "victory" ode.

However, neither on the continent nor in England did Pindaric ode serve simply to celebrate the military feats of princes and their generals. It became, instead, the most elaborate medium for encomiastic praise of both kings and commoners. Both the French poet Salmon Macrin and the Italian poet Luigi Alamanni courted François I in pindarics and, following them, Ronsard and his followers adopted pindarics to compliment Henri II and his sons. Taking his cue from the French pindarists, the neo-Latin poet Paulus Melissus introduced Pindaric ode into England with his Latin odes to Queen Elizabeth and the members of her court. Although Drayton, Jonson, and Milton adapted Pindaric ode, it did not become a flourishing type in England until Abraham Cowley reinvented the type in the mid-1650s.

Cowley is usually called the father of the Pindaric ode in English, credited with bringing Pindar's odes to England with his printing of the collection *Pindarique Odes* in 1656 and his composition in 1660 of a triumphal ode to celebrate Charles II's return to England. For the rest of the seventeenth century and well into the next the chosen form of the Pindaric ode was the Cowleian ode — constructed not, as with continental imitations, in Pindaric triads with regular strophes, antistrophes, and epodes, but in a sequence of parts or stanzas of differing lengths and metrical patterns.[3] This type of ode was so common that William Congreve remarked in 1706 (in disgust and dismay) that there was "nothing more frequent among us, than a sort of Poems intituled Pindarique Odes: pretending to be written in Imitation of the Manner and Stile of Pindar."[4] So pervasive was

---

[2] Sixteenth-century Italian and French pindarists turned to Pindar to celebrate military victories. Antonio Minturno and Salmon Macrin composed odes for those rivals for international power — Charles V, the Holy Roman Emperor, and François I, the French king, and in England pindarists celebrated the victories of England's warrior-king, William III. Less celebratory political events also called forth pindarics. The so-called Popish Plot and the conspiracy of Monmouth against Charles II inspired not only Dryden's "Absalom and Achitophel" but also "A Pindarique Ode, Upon the late Horrid and Damnable Whiggish Plot" (London, 1684).

[3] In the "Preface" to *Pindarique Odes* (London, 1656) Cowley offers an apology for his metrical choice, arguing that "looseness" in meter and style, rather than exact rendering, best fits the spirit of Pindar (Aaa 2^r). Both Aphra Behn and John Dryden took up the Cowleian model.

[4] William Congreve, *A Pindarique Ode, Humbly Offer'd to the Queen, on the Victorious Progress of Her Majesty's Arms, under the Conduct of the Duke of Marlborough. To which is prefix'd, A Discourse on the Pindarique Ode* (London, 1706), 1. Congreve's complaint about

Cowley's influence that the Pindaric revolution in England would appear to have been the result of one man's rediscovery of and imitation of Pindar. Yet although Cowley's contribution to the history of Pindaric ode was enormous, Cowley was only one of many Pindaric imitators in the early modern period—albeit for the latter part of the seventeenth century in England the most successful one.

However useful Pindaric ode had been for complimenting monarchs and celebrating military victories, it was also quickly appropriated for other purposes. As Pindaric encomia had praised the accomplishments of the living, the funeral pindaric became a mode that summed up the achievements of the dead. In England funeral pindarics poured forth after the death of Charles II in 1684 and the untimely demise of Mary II in 1694, and, like the odes that complimented living rulers, these Pindaric threnodies had political work to do beyond summoning up the noteworthy deeds of the deceased. The poetry of praise always has an agenda, sometimes an obvious one of seeking patronage, sometimes a less obvious one of commenting subversively on persons or current events. While a death concludes a person's life, it leaves behind issues that the life generated and the death left unresolved. When the Italian Benedetto Lampridio composed an ode for Vittoria Colonna, condoling the death of her husband, the Marquis of Pescara, at the battle of Pavia in 1525, he was also indirectly commenting on the battle that changed the dynamic of power between François I and the Emperor Charles V. Similarly, Sainte-Marthe's Pindaric threnody for Jacques Faye, a counselor of Henri III, comments on the religious wars in France and the events that would lead to Henri IV's kingship. The pindarics produced in England on the occasion of Cromwell's funeral and later those composed at Charles II's death comment indirectly on the eras these leaders dominated and prepare for uneasy political transitions.[5]

Although the funeral pindaric became *de rigueur* in England as in France for odes commemorating the passing of monarchs, it also attained a place for memorializing less prominent figures, particularly those connected with the poet

---

the omnipresence of such odes is prefixed to his own offering in the genre—a "victory ode" in triads celebrating the accomplishments of the Duke of Marlborough. Despite this complaint about the omnipresence of irregular odes, Congreve had composed a Cowleian pindaric in 1695 on William III's taking of Namur.

[5] See *Three Poems upon the Death of his late Highnesse Oliver, Lord Protector of England, Scotland, and Ireland* (London: William Wilson, 1659). Like Cromwell, Charles II was celebrated in life with pindarics and escorted to his grave in 1684 with Pindaric odes. James II's coronation and the birth of his royal heir were both celebrated with pindarics. Aphra Behn published not only *A Pindarick on the Death of Our Late Sovereign* (London, 1685), but also in the same year a *Pindarick Poem on the Happy Coronation of His most Sacred Majesty James II. And His Illustrious Consort Queen Mary* (London, 1685). The same medium served after the Glorious Revolution of 1688 to hail William and Mary as new sovereigns and also to commemorate Mary's death in 1694 and William's in 1702.

and poetry. Pastoral elegy had been a time-honored tradition, used by poets since Theocritus, Bion, Moschus, and Vergil to commemorate the deaths of fellow poets. Now the funeral pindaric became an alternate medium, sometimes in fact combining with pastoral elegy to mourn the dead poet. Shortly before his own death, the young Dutch neo-Latin poet Joannes Secundus created an ode for the poet-politician Thomas More that blended the pastoral with the Pindaric. Milton's "Lycidas" is also a poem that depends on pastoral and Pindaric alike for its structure, its tone, and its peculiar marriage of praise to lament. Later Pindaric threnodies for poets include those Cowley produced for Katherine Philips, and Dryden for the female poet Anne Killigrew. It is perhaps ironic that Dryden's death called forth a satiric poem—*A Description of Mr. D [ryde] n's Funeral* (London, 1700)—that jeers at the omnipresence of pindarics on funerary occasions: "Around the Corps in State they wildly press; / In Notes unequal, like Pindarick Verse, / Each one does his sad Sentiments express" (5).

By the end of the seventeenth century, particularly in England, Pindaric ode had become a kind of catch-all medium to commemorate all sorts of events and all kinds of persons. Both Cowley and Milton composed Pindaric odes to accompany books they sent to the Bodleian Library. For the dedication of the Sheldonian Theater an enterprising Oxford poet thought it proper to produce a very long and elaborate Pindaric ode in Latin, which he dedicated to Charles II and to the Rev. D. Gilbert.[6] Similarly, Alexander Pope penned a perfunctory 'pindarique' to celebrate a commencement at Cambridge in 1730.[7] Odes could be addressed to cities as well as to individuals, as the dominant Pindaric type—the city ode—came into being. In mid-eighteenth-century England it must have appeared that everyone was writing pindarics. Colley Cibber employed pindarics to say "Happy Birthday" to monarchs and aristocrats in the most sublime form.[8] Moreover, on a lesser occasion, as Boswell reports in *The Life of Johnson*, Cibber, visiting Johnson, had the temerity to abuse Pindar and then to present Johnson

---

[6] Corbet Owen, *Carmen Pindaricum in Theatrum Sheldonianum in Solennibus Magnifici Operis Encaeniis Recitatum Julii die 9º Anno 1669* (Oxford, 1669). The epigraph for the ode is taken from Olympian 2, and the ode itself, drawing abundantly on myth, compares Wren's accomplishment to Amphion's raising of the walls of Thebes and to Hercules's labors.

[7] *An Ode Compos'd for the Publick Commencement, at Cambridge,* with words by Pope and music by Maurice Greene, Doctor of Music at Cambridge, was published in 1730. A translation of "The Eighth *Isthmian* of Pindar," attributed to Pope, is contained in a book of *Translations in Verse* (Oxford, 1752), now at the British Library (14–21). Ruben Quintero argues that Pope's "Windsor-Forest" is Pindaric in rhetorical design: see *Literate Culture: Pope's Rhetorical Art* (Newark, DE: University of Delaware Press, 1992), 40–64.

[8] Colley Cibber was famous for his birthday odes and odes to the new year, but the use of the Pindaric ode for birthday poems goes back at least to Matthew Prior, *A Pindarique on His Majesties birth-day . . . Sung before Their Majesties at Whitehall, the fourth of November 1690* (London, 1690).

with a pindaric of his own composition that he professed superior to those of the "Prince of Lyric Poets."[9] Also if we may credit Gulliver's testimony in *Gulliver's Travels*, Pindaric ode was even a form of poetry known among the Houyhnhnms.[10] Yet an even lower fate awaited Pindar, for, as eighteenth-century poets converted serious epic into mock epic, they also reduced the most sublime of lyrical types into mock-pindarics. One of the chief examples of the mock-pindaric is Anne Finch's witty ode "The Spleen" that literally turns the Pindaric mode on its head. Following her, Peter Pindar was to have his day. But neither the satiric pindaric nor these other eighteenth-century manifestations are part of my story.

The principal aim of this book is to look with some detail at how the Pindaric ode developed in sixteenth- and seventeenth-century Europe as the principal medium for political and patronage poetry, whether manifest as a formal or perfunctory mode or more significantly as a serious means for political introspection and commentary. Pursuant to this investigation will be an inquiry into how and why humanists throughout Europe, many already adept at writing patronage odes for princes, began to address friends and associates in the familiar Pindaric style as an alternative medium to the epigram or the familiar Horatian ode. I will consider how the familiar pindaric became a means for poets to blend the personal and the political and making use of the Pindaric "I" even to reveal their most intimate thoughts. Curiously enough, the development of the personal pindaric, as we shall see, may even have ensured the pindaric's survival as a serious poetic form when eighteenth-century satirists assaulted the genre. Eighteenth- and nineteenth-century poets would rediscover anew the potentials in Pindaric ode for subtle lyrical expression. Thus, after its apex at the end of the seventeenth century as a political genre, Pindaric ode could live on, although under different auspices.

---

[9] James Boswell, *Life of Johnson*, ed. G. B. Hill (Oxford: Oxford University Press, 1979), 3: 72–73.

[10] In Part 4, Chapter 8, Gulliver, describing the athletic competitions among the Houyhnhnms, says that "the victor is rewarded with a song made in his or her praise." See Jonathan Swift, *Gulliver's Travels*, ed. Louis A. Landa (Oxford: Oxford University Press, 1976), 218.

CHAPTER I
THE PRAISE OF GREAT MEN: POLITICS AND PATRONAGE IN RENAISSANCE ITALY

From the beginning the poets of Renaissance Italy most closely associated with the recovery of Pindar's odes recognized that Pindar was a political poet whose language and techniques might easily be adapted to serve their own political and patronage needs. Pindar had addressed not just victorious athletes but also the patrons who supported them—the powerful tyrants of Syracuse and Acragas, the king of Cyrene, as well as leading aristocrats and rulers in the city-states of mainland Greece and those far-flung island-states that were also part of the Hellenistic world. In the mid-fifteenth century the humanistic scholar-poet Frances-co Filelfo (1398–1481) reintroduced Pindaric ode into Europe as a contemporary medium for praise. Before the fall of the city in 1453 he had served the Venetian consul general in Constantinople. He brought back to Italy with him manuscripts of Pindar's odes.[1] Modeling his own Greek and Latin poetry on Pindar's odes, he became the earliest modern imitator of Pindar, handing down to his younger contemporaries—the poets Giovanni Pontano and Pietro Crinito—a tradition of Pindaric imitation. The political climate of Italy in the fifteenth century was ideal for the re-introduction of the encomiastic ode in the style of Pindar, and the political pindaric established itself in a short time as an essential form for poets whose livelihood depended on patronage. It could be addressed to heads of state or to military leaders; it could commemorate the occasion of victory in battle or some comparable achievement. Metaphors from Pindar's odes to Hieron and Theron could be readily transferred to the leaders whom Filelfo, Pontano, and Crinito served—to Charles VII and Charles VIII of France, to Ferdinand of Aragon, to King Alfonso of Naples, to the Gonzagas of Mantua and the Sforzas of Milan.

In Pindar's odes to Hieron and Theron the ferment in Sicilian politics is often just below the surface. Poets of early modern Italy, plagued by the political turbulence of their own era, could readily grasp what these ancient rulers faced. The civil uprisings of ancient Sicily and the ever-present danger of foreign invaders

---

[1] See Carol Maddison, *Apollo and the Nine: A History of the Ode* (London: Routledge and Kegan Paul, 1960), 39–43.

mirrored the problems of their own times. In fifteenth-century Italy, city-states were continually set in rivalry one against the other; they also faced foreign intervention, now from the Spanish, now the French. Moreover, the Turkish Empire from the east posed a looming threat. Conflict and conflicting allegiances were inevitably part of the political climate. Some poets merely praised the autonomous ruler who stood firm. Others advised, commented on, and even deplored the shifting and dangerous politics of Italy. For poets such as Pontano and Filelfo who took an active role in politics, Pindar was an invaluable mentor.

1.

Pindar composed odes for Sicily and Magna Graecia for almost twenty-five years, most of them commissioned by the tyrants of Syracuse and Acragas—Hieron and Theron respectively—or by their close relatives or associates.[2] The majority of these odes were composed to celebrate the Olympian or Pythian victories that occurred during the golden era of Sicily's classical history (480–468 B.C.), a period of brilliant artistic and literary achievement, marked, however, by great political stress—revolution and upheaval at home and threat of invasion from abroad. Not surprisingly, then, most of the odes executed during this period concern political themes that take up the very issue of good government, treat myths that deal with good and bad rulers, and question at large the fortunes of men and the states that they rule. Among these odes are Pindar's most admired and accomplished pieces. First and foremost is the ambitious Olympian 1 with its famous opening, "ἄριστον μὲν ὕδωρ" (water is best), which praises the Olympic games and Hieron's achievements as ruler of Syracuse, but also contains the problematical myths of Tantalus and Pelops. Next is the brilliant Pythian 1,

---

[2] Most of the Sicilian odes date from 476 B.C. to 468 B.C. Among his Sicilian odes, however, are some of Pindar's earliest pieces: Pythian 6, composed for a chariot race that took place in 490 B.C., and Pythian 12 to Midas of Acragas, composed either in the same year or in the next decade. 476 B.C. marks the second year after Hieron's ascent to power and the year his horse and rider were victorious at Olympia. In 468 B.C., the year before Hieron's death, Pindar wrote his last ode for the tyrants of Sicily. Pythian 3 was the last ode Pindar wrote for Hieron, and Olympian 6 (for Hagesias of Syracuse) one of the last odes that he wrote for a Sicilian victor. See Pindar, *The Olympian and Pythian Odes*, ed. Basil L. Gildersleeve (London: Macmillan, 1908). Also see William H. Race, "The Odes to Hieron," in Race, *Pindar* (Boston: Twayne, 1986), 36–66. On the Pythian odes to Hieron and to Sicilian victors, see R. W. B. Burton, *Pindar's Pythian Odes* (Oxford: Oxford University Press, 1962). For an overview of Olympian 2, see Pindar, *Victory Odes*, ed. M. M. Willcock (Cambridge: Cambridge University Press, 1995), 133–66. In general see Rosalind Thomas, "Fame, Memorial, and Choral Poetry: The Origins of Epinikian Poetry—An Historical Study," in *Pindar's Poetry, Patrons and Festivals*, ed. S. Hornflower C. Morgan (Oxford: Oxford University Press, 2007), 141–66.

which celebrates the founding by Hieron of the city of Aetna and uses its *exordium* to the golden lyre to praise metaphorically the harmony of good government. Finally, there is the renowned Olympian 2, composed for Theron and beginning with the much-imitated invocation to "man, hero, and god," an ode that both celebrates Theron's Dorian ancestry and recounts the disastrous history of Cadmean Thebes. These three odes are among the most difficult and the most subtle in the Pindaric canon, posing problems for modern as well as Renaissance readers, editors, and imitators. Although the primary focus for this study will be on the sixteenth- and seventeenth-century readings of Pindar's odes, I shall refer, whenever pertinent, to contemporary commentary, particularly when such commentary can throw light on issues vexing to Renaissance and modern audiences alike.

Pindar's patrons, Hieron and Theron, were fascinating figures in their own right. Eager to make their western city-states the equal of those on mainland Greece, they invited leading poets and intellectuals to their courts.[3] The elder poet Simonides, the younger Bacchylides, and Pindar were all resident in Sicily at some time during their reigns, all of them commissioned to compose odes to commemorate victories at Olympia and Delphi. A legend recounts that Aeschylus both visited and died in Sicily. Hieron promoted his image as a magnanimous ruler by making rich offerings at Delphi—the statue of a charioteer given by him to the sanctuary is still to be seen there. Not content with his prestige at Syracuse, he founded the new city of Aetna in 472 B. C., hiring Pindar to compose Pythian 1 to celebrate the occasion. Theron of Acragas, his rival for fame and power, commissioned the building of the temples that still adorn the heights of modern Agrigento, temples to which Pindar alludes in Olympian 2.

The brilliant period in ancient Sicily's history was initiated by a military victory. At the very time that the Persians were threatening the sovereignty of the city-states of Greece, the Carthaginians and their allies, the Phoenicians, were attempting to invade Sicily, coming ostensibly to the aid of Terillus, the tyrant of Himera, whom Theron had deposed in 481 B.C. Theron, summoning Gelon, then tyrant of Syracuse, and his brothers, Hieron and Polyzelus, put down the Carthaginians at Himera in 480 B.C., the battle occurring shortly before the Athenians were victorious at Salamis and the Spartans at Plataea in the year following. To the Greek mind the victories of the Dorian settlers in Sicily and the Greeks of the mainland were parallel, for both were opposing foreign or Asiatic expansionism. Both proved the superiority of the Greek stock and preserved the right of Greek independence. Having repulsed the Carthaginians, Hieron, who succeeded his brother in 478 B.C., faced yet another threat. The Etruscans were attempting to overcome the southern Italian city of Cyme (Cumae), from which point they could threaten Sicily. Hieron, coming to the assistance of the Cymeans, won an impressive naval victory off Cyme and dedicated helmets at

---

[3] See M. I. Finley, *Ancient Sicily* (London: Chatto & Windus, 1979), 51–61.

Delphi to celebrate that victory. Pindar in Pythian 1 congratulates Hieron on saving Sicily both at Cyme and at Himera.

Turbulent though their times were and authoritarian their methods, both Hieron and Theron were apparently effective and popular rulers. Allies at Himera, they were also themselves sometimes rivals for power.[4] With supreme tact, Pindar stays in the good graces of both, taking care to foster their reputations as generous patrons of the arts, sometimes with what seems effusive praise. In Olympian 1, for example, he compares rulers such as Hieron to the sun that in blazing majesty eclipses all other stars. Some men are great in one thing, others in another thing, but, says Pindar, the crown of all are kings. In Pythian 1 he describes Hieron as the good charioteer of his people. He praises both Theron and Hieron for their generosity to their people and to strangers, repeatedly referring to the great hospitality of Sicily. Naturally, he mentions also their piety to the gods, for no ruler is truly blessed unless he is favored by gods as well as men. Pindar pays particular attention to the honor, wealth, and high position both men had attained through their own efforts. Though Hieron, after he had consolidated his power, took on the title of king (βασιλεύς), neither he nor Theron was in the true sense a hereditary monarch. Both had come to power through personal prowess and kept their position through military might. The Homeric ideal of the speaker of words and doer of deeds still had meaning in the fifth century B.C., and Pindar is not slow to point out both in Pythian 1 and in Pythian 2 Hieron's exploits in counsel and in war.[5] In fact, it is perhaps the odes of Pindar and his fellow poets Simonides and Bacchylides that were responsible for perpetuating the reputations that Hieron and Theron enjoyed in their own time as enlightened monarchs—wise and generous, strong in war, magnanimous in peace. It is no wonder that their names came down to the Roman and the Renaissance world—to the dukes, princes, and kings of Italy, France, and England—as the epitome of royal splendor, wealth, and artistic cultivation. We need not marvel, moreover, that Renaissance poets when they wished to raise the paean for their noble or royal patrons found in Pindar's odes to these Sicilian tyrants proper models. Pindar set the tone for Horace's praise of Caesar, Alamanni's of François

---

[4] While Hieron was repulsing foreign enemies, relations at home between Hieron and Theron worsened. Polyzelus, having failed to seize power in Syracuse from his brother Hieron, fled to Acragas and enlisted the aid of his father-in-law, Theron. The allies of Himera were now on opposite sides, as the tyrants of Syracuse and Acragas prepared for war; the battle was only averted, reportedly, when the poet Simonides reconciled Hieron and Theron and when Hieron on making peace married Theron's niece, the daughter of Xenocrates and sister to Pindar's friend Thrasybulus. See C. M. Bowra, "Echoes of Politics," in Bowra, *Pindar* (Oxford: Clarendon Press, 1964, repr. 2000), 99–158. For Hieron and Theron see esp. 117–37.

[5] See William H. Race, *Style and Rhetoric in Pindar's Odes* (Atlanta: Scholars Press, 1990), 56–57.

I, Minturno's of Charles V, Ronsard's of Henri II, and the Elizabethan and Jacobean poets of England for their respective lords and princes.

Less celebrated than the odes to the Sicilian tyrants, Pindar's odes to Arcesilas of Cyrene are also important as models for Renaissance poets. They include Pindar's longest and most ambitious ode, Pythian 4, which employs the story of the Argonauts, and Pythian 5, which, like the former, celebrates the founding of the dynastic house of Cyrene and its first king, Battus. These odes with their founding "myths" became for some Renaissance poets the counterpart of the myth of Rome's founding that Vergil celebrated in the *Aeneid*. As Charles Segal has pointed out, there are problems with Pythian 4's celebration of the dynastic house of Battus and its use of Jason as an exemplary hero.[6] Not only is the central myth and its hero oblique to the history of the African colony, but also the theme of *eros* and its constraints is less heroic than the usual account of heroic struggle and military founding that characterized Troy's myth. Nonetheless, with his praise of the king Arcesilas and the city of Cyrene, Pindar demonstrated how the mythic account of a city's founding might be made one with the praise of its current ruler. That Arcesilas' ultimate fate was less than happy was out of Pindar's ken in 463 B.C. when he composed the ode. Yet the conclusion of the ode and the plea for the exiled Damophilus may hint, as Segal notes, at troubles to come.[7] As the longest of the odes, Pythian 4 became unavoidably a heroic model for the kind of praise that poets like Minturno wished to fashion for the Emperor Charles V or Ronsard for Henri II.

Yet beyond Pindar's lauding of his royal patrons is something else, something which some of the poets who follow him carefully attend to, others either ignore, dismiss, or completely overlook. In his most lavish praise of Hieron and Theron or of Arcesilas, Pindar is often cautionary, even aloof. On the one hand, he proclaims himself friend to his patrons and accepts the responsibility that the festive occasion and the genre of the victory ode demand—that he praise both athlete and patron. Moreover, as Bundy's ground-breaking *Studia Pindarica* has demonstrated, much in the structure and *topoi* of the odes depends on certain epinician conventions that the poet respects.[8] Nevertheless, as a poet Pindar is never predictable nor merely the hireling of a patron. He remains, as future generations describe him, the holy mouth of the Muses. His responsibility is first to the gods, for he is their voice on earth. As such, he can urge kings and tyrants to hold to justice, to remain magnanimous, and to take care not to go to extremes. Pindar was aware, of course, that however generous and high-minded Hieron and Theron might be, they could also be ruthless and cruel. After winning the battle at Himera they had executed their enemies. They used the spoil of battle to support the

[6] Charles Segal, *Pindar's Mythmaking: The Fourth Pythian Ode* (Princeton: Princeton University Press, 1986), 12. Also see Bowra, *Pindar*, 137–42; Race, *Pindar*, 73–79.

[7] Segal, *Mythmaking*, 13.

[8] Elroy L. Bundy, *Studia Pindarica* (Berkeley: University of California Press, 1986).

splendor of their courts. Though widely admired, they lived in fear, keeping in-
formers at court. When Theron's son, Thrasydaeus, succeeded him in 472 B.C., he
proved himself a ruthless dictator, throwing off the mildness of his father and ruling with such great cruelty that his subjects in both Acragas and Himera revolted.
Their revolt was supported by Hieron, who expelled Thrasydaeus and granted
democratic constitutions to the citizens of both cities. When Pindar in Pythian 1,
written two years later, urges Deinomenes, Hieron's son, to rule wisely as king of
Aetna, he is probably recalling the unwiseness of Thrasydaeus's tyranny.

Pindar has a reputation as not only the praiser but also the counselor of kings.
Both Ascham and Sidney remark that through his odes Pindar encouraged the
magnanimity and curbed the severity of Hieron and Theron.[9] Such counseling as
Pindar offers, he usually sets forth in the guise of the cautionary myth. Many of
the myths included in his odes recount stories of heroes and rulers who in their
arrogance offended the gods, forgetting that, however great they were, they were
still mere mortal men. Why else in Olympian 1 does Pindar couple the account
of Pelops' victory in the chariot race with the story of his father's impiety? Tantalus was a great sinner who brought not only disaster to himself but ruin to his
race and his people.[10] Similarly, Pythian 2 and 3 also contain cautionary myths,
the first recounting how Ixion attempted to deceive Zeus and was himself de-
ceived, the second recounting, together with the praise of Chiron and Asclepius,
the duplicity and folly of Apollo's would-be bride Coronis.[11] Pindar in Pythian

---

[9] Ascham also points out that Pindar's praise of Hieron's "stoutness in warre and
iust gouernment in peace" influenced Horace's praise of Augustus. See Roger Ascham,
"The Scholemaster" (1570) in *Elizabethan Critical Essays*, ed. G. Gregory Smith (Oxford:
Clarendon Press, 1904), 1:8; Sir Philip Sidney, "The Defence of Poesie," in Sidney, *The
Prose Works*, ed. Albert Feuillerat (Cambridge: Cambridge University Press, 1963), 33.
Landino makes a similar remark about Pindar's influence on rulers in his "Commentary"
to Dante's *Commedia*.

[10] For modern critics Pindar's revision of the Pelops myth is especially problematical, particularly how the treatment of Pelops is related to the praise of Hieron. Gerber,
for example, posits a close connection between Pelops and Hieron; Verdenius is critical of
Gerber's view. See Douglas E. Gerber, *Pindar's Olympian One: A Commentary* (Toronto:
University of Toronto Press, 1982), xiv, 129, 140, 155–56; W. J. Verdenius, *Commentaries
on Pindar* (Leiden: E. J. Brill, 1988), 2:2–3, 16, 22, 37, 43–45. Also see Dorthe Fisker,
Pindars Erste Olympische Ode (Odense: Universitetsforlag, 1990), 63–86. John T. Hamilton remarks that Olympian 1 depends on the achieving of *kairos*: see *Soliciting Darkness:
Pindar, Obscurity, and the Classical Tradition* (Cambridge, MA: Harvard University Press,
2003), 87–96. Bruno Currie remarks that Pelops is part of the Hellenic cult of heroes and
thus a fitting example for Hieron: see *Pindar and the Cult of Heroes* (Oxford: Oxford University Press, 2005), 74–75.

[11] Hamilton remarks that in Pythian 3 Zeus has to correct Apollo's presumption in
giving the healing arts to Asclepius, just as Apollo corrects Coronis's presumption: see
Soliciting Darkness, 51–55.

1 introduces not only the good example of Croesus as a generous king, but also the bad example of Phalaris as a hated and ruthless tyrant. Pindar refers to the miseries of kingship as well as its rewards.[12] As often as there are allusions to a king's honor, wealth, and good fortune, there are references also to the envy and spite that such happiness provokes. Further, there is the inevitable reminder that all human happiness is limited, subject to time and therefore ephemeral.[13] Olympian 2, addressed to Theron, provides one example after another of that grim truth. In recounting the story of the house of Cadmus, Theron's reputed ancestor, Pindar tells of those whose happiness was short-lived on earth—the beautiful daughters of Cadmus, who one by one suffered unkind fortunes; the hapless Oedipus and his sons, whose kindly fortunes turned to disaster. Only Thersander, grandson to Oedipus and son of Polyneices, seemed to reverse that fortune and to bring joy out of sorrow in being the founding father of the dynasty over which Theron ruled in Sicily.[14] In retelling the myths of ancient Thebes, is Pindar cautioning Theron against the mistakes of his ancestors, reflecting philosophically that life brings both joy and sorrow, or congratulating Theron on having escaped the hardships of the past? The Theban eagle cryptically tells his audience that the wise need no interpreters. Pindar concludes the ode both by praising the generosity of Theron and by regretting that praise always provokes envy.

Pindar was aware that he was handing down a record for future ages, and he was determined that it be a true one. Just as Hieron and Theron guarded their reputations, so did he, but in a different way. If he praised accomplishments, he must also write of adversities. Hence his odes to Hieron, especially Pythian 1 and Pythian 3, praise the ruler, but also allude to his troubles and his grievous illness. The poet is aware that though he can render praise, he cannot confer health. Even the praise that he gives is lasting only if it is honest. If the poet misrepresents, he gives a false report to future generations. Pindar accuses Homer of just such false report in Nemean 7, in bestowing fame on the unworthy Odysseus rather than the worthy Aias.[15] To fare well, as Pindar says in Pythian 1, is

---

[12] See George Huxley, *Pindar's Vision of the Past* (Belfast: George Huxley, 1975), 33. Also see V. Hinz, *Nunc Phalaris doctum protulit ecce caput: Antike Phalarislegende und Nachleben der Phalarisbriefe* (Munich: V. G. Saur, 2001).

[13] As Kevin Crotty remarks, Pindar continually reminds his audience that man's fate is not in his own control, that men are exalted or debased as the god wishes: see *Song and Action: The Victory Odes of Pindar* (Baltimore: Johns Hopkins University Press, 1982), 19–22.

[14] Crotty describes Olympian 2 as an elegant treatment of the ambiguities attending both *praxis* and *pathos*: see *Song and Action*, 53–54.

[15] This is a controversial passage over which, however, there has been disagreement among modern scholars. See Gretchen Kromer, "Homer and Odysseus in Nemean 7. 20–27," *Classical World* 68 (1975): 437–38; Glenn W. Most, *The Measures of Praise: Structure and Function in Pindar's Second Pythian and Seventh Nemean Odes* (Göttingen: Vandenhoeck & Ruprecht, 1985), 148–56. Also see Gregory Nagy on the relationship of Pindar

the first of garlands, but the second is to be well praised. To achieve both is the highest goal a man may reach. Pindar hands down the challenge to those classical Roman and Renaissance poets who follow him not only to praise well but also to praise truthfully, a challenge few encomiasts of great men had the courage to take up.

2.

Renaissance poets were not the first to adapt Pindar's Sicilian odes for other masters. Horace was an assiduous imitator of Pindar despite the fact that one of his most famous odes—*Carmina* 4.2 ("Pindarum quisquis studet aemulare")—criticizes the excesses of Pindar's poetics and cautions poets against using him as a model.[16] Whoever seeks to imitate Pindar, quips Horace, ventures on waxen wings and runs the risk, like Icarus, of giving his name to a sea. Denying Pindaric ambitions in another ode, he tells Maecenas that he was not one of those who joy in collecting Olympian dust or in directing his chariot wheels to lift him to the very gods of heaven (*Carmina* 1.1). He also vehemently declares in 1.7, let others sing of Rhodes or Mytilene, of Ephesus or Corinth, and of Thebes and Delphi—places redolent with Pindaric associations. But this very poet does not hesitate to raise his voice with Pindaric declamation when the occasion demands. Addressing Augustus Caesar, Horace echoes Pindar's Olympian 2, asking what man, what hero, what god he should praise: "Quem virum, aut heroa lyra vel acri / tibia sumis celebrare, Clio, / quem deum?" (1.12.1–3).[17] Associating by implication the accomplishments of Augustus with those of the munificent Theron, Horace invokes for his own lord of men the favor of the highest god—the Roman Jupiter. Although Horace's twelfth ode does not treat the same themes as Olympian 2 nor introduce comparable mythic digressions, it exploits a basic Pindaric movement and structure and resounds with Pindaric associations. Horace praises, as Pindar does, gods, heroes, and men. Though he reverses Pindar's "god, hero, man" paradigm at the beginning of the ode, giving prominence to Caesar, he follows Pindar in lauding Jupiter as the first of gods and assigning proper rank to Bacchus, Athene, and Apollo before praising Hercules and the Dioscuri, Pindar's own prime heroes, here Romanized. Praise of the worthies, past and

---

and Homer in *Pindar's Homer: The Lyric Possession of the Epic Past* (Baltimore: Johns Hopkins University Press, 1990), 422–27.

[16] See, for example, Hamilton's discussion of the relationship of Pindar and Horace in *Soliciting Darkness*, 97–109.

[17] Horace is cited from *Odes and Epodes*, ed. Charles E. Bennett (New Rochelle, NY: Aristide D. Caratzas, 1984). As critics often remark, Pindar names god, hero, man—with Theron the man in third position after the god and hero. Horace, however, names first the man, that is, Caesar.

present, of the Roman state follows, before Horace at last arrives at Augustus Caesar, for whom, assuredly, the ode was designed in the first place.

The ode was probably written on the occasion of Augustus's adoption of Marcellus as son and Marcellus's marriage to Augustus's daughter Julia, for Horace takes care to single out the Marcelli for praise.[18] Horace's relationship to his patron Augustus is complex, but, unlike Pindar, Horace neither counsels nor consoles nor alludes to anything that might detract from Caesar's magnificence. No allusions to figures such as Cadmus or Oedipus intrude, as in Pindar's Olympian 2, though Horace introduces a level of ambiguity into the ode with the list of figures he includes from Roman history—Romulus, Numa, the second Tarquin, Cato. Does imperial Rome perhaps, as Horace suggests more pointedly in 3.6, not live up to its illustrious past? Or do such figures as Tarquin and Cato interrogate that past in a different way? Horace refrains from comment and does not remind Caesar that he is a mortal man with a mortal fate; instead he boldly petitions Jove that Caesar reign with a power second only to Jove's—a request Pindar would never have made for his own munificent patron. Further, concluding the ode on an imperial note, Horace invokes for Caesar a god-like force with which to scatter his enemies—the Parthians and all others that threaten—and that he extend his empire to China and India. Though it pursues an independent agenda, Horace's twelfth ode is, like Pindar's original, generous in its celebration of its royal subject.

The twelfth ode is not the only instance of Pindaric imitation, however. Throughout his public odes Horace consciously echoes Pindar, sometimes in invocations, sometimes in similes or metaphors, sometimes in moralizing aphorisms. He echoes him with a Horatian difference, however, adapting Pindaric associations to Horatian contexts. In *Carmina* 4.4 and 3.5 Jupiter's lightning flashes in a Pindaric way to confirm Caesar's military victories; in 3.3 the Pindaric heroes Pollux and Hercules appear to support Roman virtue. In 3.6 his chastising of Roman slackness has a Pindaric ring, and in 3.7, in reproving vice, he alludes to Pindar's example of the chaste Peleus's rejection of Hippolyte (Nemean 5.25–34). The characters and references are familiar, but put to different uses. Repeatedly, Horace adapts Pindaric myths and mythic heroes to laud Caesar and his military victories. For example, in *Carmina* 3.4 he celebrates Caesar's triumphs over the Scythians, the Britons, and the Spanish by alluding to Jove's triumphs over his foes, namely, the giants who attempted to scale Olympus and other enemies who also threatened Jove's reign—Typhon, Porphyrion, and Enceladus. These, of course, are the very mythic figures Pindar had referred to in his odes

---

[18] For commentary on *Carmina* 1.12, see R. G. M. Nisbet and Margaret Hubbard, *A Commentary on Horace, Odes, Book I* (Oxford: Clarendon Press, 1970), 142–69. Citing Theocritus 16 and 17, Nisbet and Hubbard remark that "Horace was not the first to be impressed by the convenience of Pindar's question" (143–44).

to illustrate overweening pride and to warn of the dangers of political anarchy.[19] In Pythian 1 Pindar had described Zeus's defeat of Typhon in order to recall Hieron's victories over the Carthaginians and Etruscans. For Pindar Typhon was essentially a figure of primitive unchecked force. Thus, at the same time he was congratulating Hieron on his victory over his foes, Pindar was pointing out the dangers of violent misrule. By defeating Typhon and keeping him tamed, Zeus permits orderly government to take the place of anarchy and permits cities such as the new Aetna to thrive. Only with just government can Sicilians themselves avoid Typhonic misrule. Similarly, when he refers in Pythian 8 to Zeus's defeat of Porphyrion, Pindar is not just alluding to the defeat of the "giant" Athens by Thebes; he is teaching a lesson about arrogance in political affairs and supporting the imperatives of peace, including the peace treaty between Athens and Sparta.[20] His ode begins, after all, with an invocation of the goddesses Hesychia and Diké (Peace and Justice).

It is perfectly logical that Horace should apply such Pindaric examples to Caesar's conquests over the "barbarians" which threatened Rome. Horace had a political point to make, and depiction of foreign powers as monsters and Roman leaders as gods had a certain propagandistic value. Moreover, he uses a Pindar-like aphorism to exhort his audience that force without counsel is its own ruin: "Vis consilii expers mole ruit sua" (*Carmina* 3.4.65). He also argues, as Pindar had, for the imperatives of peace and justice. As the "just" gods came to Jove's assistance and hurled the giants into the underworld, they also aided Caesar in putting down and punishing his gigantic foes. Recalling Pindar's Pythian 1, Horace reminds us that the giant Typhon still rages under Aetna (3.4.75–76). Thus it is necessary for Caesar, like Hieron, to be ever vigilant of the dangers of Typhonic anarchy. The myth of gigantic rebellion continues to play an important part in the political pindarics that Renaissance poets were to compose for their own princes, representing sometimes, as in Pindar and Horace, the danger of anarchic foreign force and sometimes in a more sinister way the threat of intestine civil rebellion.

Horace does not merely echo Pindaric myth to celebrate Caesar; he also connects Caesar to certain key mythic figures whom Pindar had singled out—particularly Hercules and the divine twins, Pollux and Castor. In the proemium to *Carmina* 1.12 Horace invokes for Caesar and Rome the favor of Hercules and

---

[19] Both Hesiod in the *Theogony* and Pindar throughout his odes allude to the attempt of the Titans and giants to wrest power from Zeus. For them Zeus's rule signified stable government and order; the giants and Titans, chaos and anarchy. Not until he had defeated these enemies could Zeus establish the kind of rule by law that Hesiod and Pindar represented as the model for the desired government on earth.

[20] See Bowra, *Pindar*, 142–46, 155–58; also see the analysis of the historical background by Ilya Leonard Pfeijffer, *Three Aiginetan Odes of Pindar: A Commentary on Nemean V, Nemean III, & Pythian VIII* (Leiden: Brill, 1999), 426–34.

the Twins. In *Carmina* 4.5 he takes care to link Caesar with Hercules and Castor, whom Greece held in reverence as Rome now honors Caesar. In this ode Horace welcomes Caesar back to a grateful nation, from which he has been long absent, observing that like Hercules and Castor, Caesar is a benefactor of mankind and deserves a like reward. Horace no doubt remembered Pindar's Nemean 1, Isthmian 4, and Nemean 10, all of which contribute to the view of Hercules that Horace wishes to promulgate. Pindar's Nemean 1 celebrated Hieron's associate Chromius of Aetna by connecting him to Heracles and by recounting how Heracles, as an infant, strangled the serpents sent to kill him.[21] Thus, even in infancy, Heracles justified his future career as a queller of tyrants and monsters, and, as the prophet Teiresias predicted, would rid the earth of these scourges and so bring liberty, peace, and justice to human beings. Pindar directs the myth to Hieron and Chromius implicitly to urge the Sicilian lord and his master to espouse Heracles' libertarian principles. Nemean 1 is important for Horace, and its myth became for Renaissance poets a touchstone to compliment royal subjects and to predict Herculean success for newborn princes.

Although Horace repeatedly casts Caesar in the role of a benefactor, the Caesarean Hercules is not exactly the libertarian figure that Pindar had made him.[22]

---

[21] For commentary on Heracles and Chromius, see Race, *Pindar*, 79–81; Race, *Style and Rhetoric*, 33–34, 172.

[22] No hero is more prominent in Pindar's odes than Heracles, son of Zeus, born in Pindar's native city Thebes, the reputed founder of the Olympics and the patron of the city-states throughout the Hellenic world. Pindar alludes to his birth in Nemean 1 as well as in Isthmian 7. In Nemean 7 (94) Pindar refers to Heracles as blessed (μάκαρ), and alludes several times to his deification after death and his marriage with Hebe. He celebrates Heracles as the founder of the Olympic games—Olympian 3 and Olympian 10, where Heracles acts the part of a reverent son in offering the spoil of war to Zeus. Although he alludes now and then to Heracles's labors, these are not his principal focus. As a battle hero he is comrade-in-arms to the famous heroes of ancient tradition, particularly to Castor and Pollux, Zeus's other semi-divine children, and to the heroes of Aegina, Aeacus and Aeacus's sons Telamon and Peleus, the fathers respectively of Ajax and Achilles (see Nemean 4 and 6, Isthmian 6.27, Isthmian 7). Heracles stands beside Telamon as a warrior and predicts the birth of Telamon's son Ajax. Loyal as Heracles is to his friends, he is also unyielding to adversaries, particularly those adversaries who practice injustice. Heracles is the righter of wrongs, the queller of tyrants, and a friend to the gods. Pindar recounts in Olympian 10 Heracles' punishing of Augeas for perjury and double-dealing. Augeas had attempted to cheat Heracles of the agreed-upon wage for cleaning the Augean stables. He incited his nephews, Cteatus and Eurytas, to attack Heracles and his host from Tiryns. To avenge the treachery, Heracles lay in wait for the nephews, and, having killed them, put the uncle also to death. Another aspect of Heracles' role as upholder of justice is his quelling of the giants who presume to overthrow the gods (see Nemean 1, Nemean 4, Nemean 7.90). Defeating the giants Alcyoneus and Antaeus, he saves human beings from violence and tyranny. As George Huxley has remarked, Pindar in reverence for Heracles suppresses the stories that Heracles killed his sons by Megara

Like Vergil in the Cacus episode of the *Aeneid*, Horace Romanizes Pindar's Greek hero, adopting him as Rome's patron "god" and remaking his image into an imperialistic conqueror, who vanquishes his enemies.[23] Like Pindar, he refers sparingly to Hercules' labors. Caesar plays the part of the earthly god-man who wars with giants (2.12.6–9) or a Jove who puts down the Titans—Horace's Caesar rules earth as Jove rules heaven.[24] In 3.14 Caesar is a Herculean conqueror who returns triumphantly from Spain. Pindar's liberator who stood up to tyrants is all but forgotten in the wake of the conquests of the Roman hero-god; Horace's Hercules has exchanged the republican club for a regal scepter. Moreover, Horace often reminds us that Caesar is to be rewarded in heaven and will sit beside Jove's sons, Hercules and Pollux, at the Olympian feast and sip nectar with reddened lips (3. 3. 9–12).[25] Just as Pindar in Nemean 1 had foretold Heracles's heavenly reward, so Horace predicts Augustus's apotheosis.[26]

As an epinician poet Pindar had the responsibility to commemorate the achievements both of his patrons and of their winning athletes.[27] Horace takes on a similar task as he celebrates Caesar's "virtus" and records his generals' victories in battle. *Carmina* 4.14 records Drusus's and Tiberius's defeat of the Vindelici in 14 B.C., a victory which resulted, as he proclaims in the ode following (4.15), in the closing of the gates of war. Like Pindar in Olympian 1 and 2 or in Pythian 1, Horace makes paramount the praise of his patron (rather than that of the winning general or athlete); the exordium of 4.14 is addressed to Caesar and opens with a formal, almost Pindaric question—how may Rome reward Augustus?

---

in a fit of madness or that he fought against the gods. Yet the latter is a notable instance of Pindaric equivocation, for Pindar simply refrains from repeating a well-known mythic incident. See Huxley, *Pindar's Vision of the Past*, 17–18.

[23] See *Aeneid* 8. 193–305. Vergil also alludes to Hercules' having defeated Typhon as one of the accomplishments for which the priests hymn him.

[24] See the notes on Hercules and the warfare with the giants (*Carmina* 2.12, 6–7) in R. G. M. Nisbet and Margaret Hubbard, *A Commentary on Horace, Odes, Book II* (Oxford: Clarendon Press, 1978), 188–91. When Horace alludes to Hercules' struggle with the Hydra in *Carmina* 4.4, he makes Rome the many-headed serpent which resists Hannibal's assault (61–62) and Hannibal the stand-in for an unsuccessful Hercules.

[25] Horace may be flashing back to Pindar's Olympian 3.33–35 where Heracles attends the festival at Olympia with the Twins.

[26] In Isthmian 4 Pindar also predicts that Heracles will win the joys of heaven. Further, in Nemean 10 Pindar tells how Zeus granted Castor and Pollux immortality.

[27] Adapting some of Pindar's stratagems of praise, Horace emulates the epinician poet to guarantee that the emperor and his deeds be remembered. For Caesar, however, there is also another kind of immortality he has in mind beyond poetic remembrance; he also looks forward to the immortality that the Roman state would surely confer on its emperor after his death.

Quae cura patrum quaeve Quiritium
Plenis honorum muneribus tuas,
Auguste, virtutes in aevom
Per titulos memoresque fastus

Aeternet, o, qua sol habitabilis
Inlustrat oras, maxime principum, (4.14.1–6)

What care of senators or of citizens
with gifts full of honors, Augustus,
will make your virtues shine eternally
through titles and memorial records,

wherever, O greatest of princes, the habitable sun
traverses the shore?

However, Horace did not ignore the achievements of Caesar's victorious generals. Like Pindar, who alluded, sometimes briefly, sometimes at length, to the performance of his victor athletes, Horace praises the heroic brothers, Drusus and Tiberius. Drusus had defeated the Vindelici the year previous; now joined by his brother he must subdue them once again. Striking with Caesar's force, Horace tells us, Drusus drove the Gernaunians back to their Alpine stronghold, and, joined by his brother Tiberius, defeated their allies. As Michael Putnam has commented, Horace may wish us to connect the brothers' assault on their enemies with his earlier treatment of the battle of the Olympian gods with the giants Otus and Ephialtes. One of the most Pindaric touches in this ode, Putnam argues, is Horace's description of Tiberius swooping down like the blast of the south wind against the waves and breaking the enemy lines with deadly force.[28] Yet, however much Horace showcases Tiberius's heroism in this ode, he takes care to define Tiberius's and Drusus's victory in terms of Caesar's forces, Caesar's counsel, and Caesar's divine auspices.

Epinician formulas often inform Horace's odes. Pindar usually follows, as Bundy has demonstrated, certain set practices or formulas, one of which is to is to allude to an athlete's former victories, as well as those of his close relatives, as

---

[28] Michael C. J. Putnam, *Artifices of Eternity: Horace's Fourth Book of Odes* (Ithaca: Cornell University Press, 1986), 242; 257. Putnam remarks that Horace's grandest Pindarizing is in ode 14. He remarks further that to "embrace Pindar stylistically is to accept Augustus politically" (257–58). In the geographical catalogue, as Michèle Lowrie comments, the names of the peoples and rivers "add up to empire" or, in other words, the political emphasis of the narrative section appropriates the lyric mode's sense of time. See Michèle Lowrie, *Horace's Narrative Odes* (Oxford: Clarendon Press, 1997), 343.

he congratulates the athlete or his patron on the present victory.[29] Once again
Horace appears to take his cue from a Pindaric practice, using the occasion of the
victory over the Vindelici to recapitulate Caesar's former victories, remembering
Caesar's triumphs over the Spanish, the Medes, the Scythians, and the Cantabers as the victories that led up the present one. He also follows Pindaric practice
and adds a vividness to the ode by naming specific geographic features of the
places alluded to. In his athletic catalogues Pindar refers to the homelands of the
victors as well as to the places where the athletes won their victories.[30] In a similar fashion, Horace makes the rivers of the conquered territories render homage
to Caesar: "Te, fontium qui celat origines / Nilusque et Hister, te rapidus Tigris,
/ Te beluosus qui remotis / obstrepit Oceanus Britannis" (The Nile, the Ister, the
Tigris, and the ocean about Britain also acknowledge Caesar and Rome their
fountainhead) (*Carmina* 4.14.45–48). The Nile leads the rest of rivers, perhaps in
commemoration of the fact that on this very same day, years before, the port of
Alexandria submitted itself as a suppliant to Caesar, thus ending the civil wars
with Antony and Cleopatra. By adapting Pindar's formulas, Horace makes the
odes for Caesar's military victories resound with the excitement of Pindar's odes
of epinician triumph.[31]

   Carmina 4.15 imitates Pindaric ode in a different way. Probably written in
13 B.C., the year following, the ode centers on a specific event—Caesar's closing
of the gates of war. Acting as the coda to the preceding ode, it celebrates rather
than narrates Caesar's victories, rejoicing in the renewed prosperity of Rome and
proclaiming that Caesar's glory and Latium's name extend from the rising to the
setting of the sun. As a patriotic celebration of Italy's prosperity under Caesar,
ode 15 recalls some of the exuberance of Pindar's Sicilian odes.[32] As Pindar in

---

   [29] The citation of the athlete's present victory, together with a recapitulation of his
past victories, is a part of the formula of the epinician ode. See, for example, Bundy's discussion of the first Isthmian and how the praise of the victor, Herodotus, and his father,
Asopodoros, occupies the climactic position in the ode (Bundy, *Studia Pindarica*, 47–67).
Bundy demonstrates how "the brightness of the present is set against the darkness of the
past" (48).

   [30] For example, Pindar refers in Olympian 7 to the places where Diagoras won victories—at the Isthmus, in Nemea, in rocky Athens, and in Olympia beside the running
waters of Alpheus; he also refers to Diagoras's homeland, the island of Rhodes.

   [31] In these odes Caesar's battle victories are compared to and almost attain a status
similar to victories achieved in Greece's or Rome's mythic past. Here again he may be
emulating Pindar, who often subtly connects an athletic victory with a mythic event. For
example, Hieron's racing victory in Olympian 1 is inevitably connected with the mythic
account of Pelops' chariot victory. In Isthmian 1 Herodotus as a charioteer is connected
with the hero-charioteers Castor and Iolaos.

   [32] When Caesar closed the gates of war, says Horace, he brought back fertility to the
fields. Citizens may now reap the rewards of Bacchus, singing like a chorus of Bacchic
celebrants of leaders whose deeds match those of the heroes of Troy—Anchises and Ae-

Nemean 1 (14–18) cites the teeming fields and wealthy cities Zeus has bestowed on a Sicily now ruled by Hieron, Horace attributes Italy's fertility to the peace and stable rule Caesar has brought. As Pindar celebrates in Olympian 2 and 3 Theron's noble Dorian forebears, Horace recollects Caesar's heroic Trojan ancestors. Pindar invokes a well-disposed Zeus to preserve the fatherland of Sicily for future ages (Olympian 2.13–15); Horace prays that Caesar's glory will shine from sun to sun. The celebrations that once ensued upon athletic victory now in Horace's ode break forth to confer victorious laurels on a ruler who has successfully brought peace to Rome. Now adapting a metaphor, now a mythic reference, Horace adjusts Sicilian politics to Roman and the praise of a Hieron or Theron to the praise of "the greatest prince" the world has ever known (4.14.6).

Horace's Caesar-centered odes are important models for Renaissance poets, such as Filelfo, Pontano, and Minturno, who in odes to contemporary heads of state were attempting to imitate Pindar's odes. Horace provided them with a model of how to adapt Pindar's epinician odes for different occasions. He showed them how to adjust Pindar's exordia, how to transform Pindar's catalogues of athletic victory for battle victory, and how to make his mythic allusions and mythic heroes relevant to a different kind of epinician performance. As an encomiast, Horace sometimes seems far more straightforward than Pindar, less ambiguous and apparently more willing to serve Caesar and praise his *Pax Romana*. If Renaissance poets often found Horatian politics closer to their own, they also found his poetics easier to imitate. In their Latin odes Renaissance poets turned more frequently to Horace's Sapphic or Alcaic stanzas than to Pindar's triads. Perhaps they remembered that Horace had used Sapphics both for his imitation of Olympian 2 (*Carmina* 1.12) and for the ode addressed to Antonius on Pindaric imitation (*Carmina* 4.2). One of the earliest Latin translations of Pindar's Olympian 2 (by Menradus Motherus in 1527) employs Sapphics, perhaps in deference to Horace's imitation of the same ode.[33] Well into the seventeenth century, poets such as Casimire Sarbiewski, the 'Polish Pindar,' continued to employ Horatian stanzas for their Pindaric imitations. It was almost as though Horace himself had sanctioned his favorite stanza forms for Pindaric imitation.

---

neas himself. As Michèle Lowrie has commented, we find the last of Caesar's deeds told in the perfect tense, with Caesar's acts now dissolving the distinction between the man Augustus and the Augustan age (Lowrie, *Horace's Narrative Odes*, 344).

[33] Menradus Motherus, *Pindari Olympiorum Hymni Primus et Secundus Latinate Donati* (Haganoae, 1527), sig. B4^r–C3^v. Motherus uses an irregular iambic line for the translation of Olympian 1 (sig. A3^r–A7^r). A Latin translation of Pythian 3, published by Iacobus Laureus in 1550, chooses dactylic hexameter (see *Aeliani De Varia Historia Libros XIII, Adiuncta est et Ode Pindari, quae inscribitur in Hieronem Celete, ab eodem Heroico carmine donata* [Venice, 1550], fols. 96^v–99^v).

3.

When Francesco Filelfo (1398–1481) determined in the 1450s to compose two books of odes, one in Latin, one in Greek, for his patron Francesco Sforza, for Charles VII of France, and for friends and noblemen in many of the leading courts in Italy, he took Pindar's odes, especially those for Hieron and Theron, as his model.[34] He neither completed nor published the odes during his lifetime, the Latin odes having been printed posthumously in 1497, the Greek odes remaining unpublished until the twentieth century. Circulating privately, the odes had considerable influence, however, on other would-be Pindaric imitators and on the development of political encomia in Italy. By about 1456 Filelfo had finished five of the projected ten books of Latin odes and had them ready for dedication to Charles VII. Filelfo originally planned to dedicate the odes to Francesco Sforza, for most of the odes were a product of Filelfo's sojourn in Milan during the tumultuous years from 1447 to 1456 that saw the fall of the Visconti dynasty, the rise and fall of the Ambrosian Republic, and the establishment of the condottiere Francesco Sforza as Duke of Milan.[35]

Filelfo's odes follow a pattern similar to that laid down by Horace in his political odes. In the place of athletic victory, they celebrate comparable events—military victories, dynastic celebrations, or political alliances. Filelfo takes such occasions both to offer commentary and advice and also to draw comparisons in the Pindaric manner with historical and mythic deeds accomplished by heroes of the past. As Kevin Crotty has commented, Pindar regularly compares his athlete heroes to heroes of the past, emphasizing the present's connection with historical and mythic events.[36] The first three books of Filelfo's *Odae* concern events in Milan during the 1450s. A heterogeneous sequence, these books include encomiastic odes to patrons, "victory" odes describing Francesco Sforza's recent military accomplishments, and philosophical odes commenting on the evils of the era. The odes most Pindaric in tone and design are those in which Filelfo takes on the role of the *vates* to laud the virtue of a patron.[37] Whereas Filelfo's odes

---

[34] Filelfo's odes to patrons, would-be patrons, and friends throughout Italy include odes to Carlo and Ludovico Gonzaga, Alfonso I of Naples, Pope Nicholas V, and Don Federigo da Montefeltro. He had early served the Medicis and was actually planning to return to Florence at the time of his death. See Maddison, *Apollo and the Nine*, 40.

[35] See Diana Robin, *Filelfo in Milan: Writings 1451–1477* (Princeton: Princeton University Press, 1991); Gabriella Albanese, "Le raccolte poetiche latine di Francesco Filelfo," in *Francesco Filelfo nel quinto centenario della morte* (Padua: Editrice Antenore, 1986), 389–458. Albanese also prints the Greek odes.

[36] See Crotty, *Song and Action*, 4, 98.

[37] The political poems in Filelfo's collection of fifty occasional *odae* are of two sorts, both reflecting more or less Pindaric influence and intent. The first is a kind of verse epistle, often written in couplets, which comments on contemporary affairs—wars, al-

never approach close imitation of Pindar in poetic structure, metrical form, or language, we need not doubt Filelfo's intent nor the sincerity of his debt to Pindar. Pindar's example was important to him, because it pointed the way for the creation of a new kind of political poetry, in which a poet may comment, may reflect, and may advise, as well as praise.

Imitating Pindar's Olympian 2 and Horace's 1.12 and using Sapphic stanzas (as Horace had), Filelfo begins his ode to Charles VII of France and his political allies by asking the Pindaric question,

> Quem tibi pulchris capias canendum
> Laudibus dignum meritisque magnum?
> Quem virum nobis celebres supremo
> Carmine Clio? (2. 10. 1–4)[38]

> Whom would you choose to sing,
> worthy of lovely praises and great in merit?
> What man would you celebrate for us
> in supreme song, Clio?

The man, of course, is Charles VII, and Filelfo portrays his would-be patron, as Pindar had portrayed Hieron in Olympian 1, as the most splendid of stars, a king among kings, whom no poet may weary of praising. He readily recycles the star figure, which he had already employed in 2.3 for Francesco Sforza, there comparing the former condottiere to a star that displays its eminence before all Latium: "Sydus illustrans Latium corusca / Luce" (2.3.1–2). Star metaphors and sun figures, as we shall see, will proliferate in political odes of the next century, as other leaders are complimented as Pindar first complimented Hieron. Also in 2.10 we encounter one of Pindar's favorite mythic heroes, Achilles, to whom Gaspar, the general of the Sforzas, is compared. As Achilles had been prepared by the centaur and by his tutor Phoenix (in piety and arms) to lead the armies at Troy, so Gaspar came to Milan well prepared for battle. Like Achilles, Gaspar was essential, for without him, Filelfo suggests, Francesco Sforza could not have taken Milan.[39] The mythic allusion is brief and to the point, though perhaps not

---

liances, the plague—and offers both general reflections and sometimes specific advice. The second is a more formal encomium, probably what we would call an ode, often written in Sapphics or some other stanzaic form—Filelfo uses a variety of verse forms even within a single poem. For analysis of Filelfo's meters see Albanese, "Le raccolte poetiche latine," 428–32, esp. notes 88 and 89.

[38] Franciscus Philelfus, "Carmen Decimum," *Odae* (Brescia, 1497), sig. e iiii[r]–e vii[v].

[39] Most of Filelfo's mythic comparisons are brief. In the opening ode (1. 1) he wishes Francesco Sforza the wealth of Croesus, the success of Cyrus; he tells Ludovico Gonzaga (5. 9) that Nestor has lent him his honeyed tongue to praise him. There are a few examples, however, of the use of extended myths. To praise Carlo Gonzaga in 2.1 Filelfo

as apt as might first appear, for Achilles, unlike Gaspar, was absent from the fall of the besieged city.

Some critics portray Filelfo as an uncritical encomiast of the Sforzas. Both Diana Robin and Albanese argue, however, that Filelfo, even as he appears to laud Francesco Sforza, deplores the tragic situation of Milan, crippled by famine and war. This is nowhere more evident than in two odes, 2.3 and 3.4, the first of which (2.3) marks the conclusion of the siege and the city's admission of Sforza as a victor.[40] The second (3.4) celebrates Francesco Sforza's triumphant installation as Duke of Milan. Both odes are in popular Latin meters: 3.4 in hendecasyllables, 2.3 in the Sapphic stanzas Horace preferred for his odes to Augustus.

The second ode, 3.4, exploits in an interesting way the theme of gigantic warfare to depict the chaos that ensues in the wake of civil war. Filelfo depicts Francesco as a hero who has overthrown two tyrannical giants, War and Famine, and has brought peace to Milan. As a victor over metaphorical giants, Francesco seems to take on the garments of a conquering Caesar or Hieron.[41] But rather than developing the theme of gigantic warfare, Filelfo instead devotes the central sections of both odes to describing the unparalleled sufferings of the Milanese citizens at the hands of the leaders of the Ambrosian Republic and Sforza's besieging army. In 2.3 also he juxtaposes the extravagant praise of the victor Sforza with a graphic account of the brutality he imposed on the citizens before starvation forced the city to capitulate. In 3.4 he works in a comparable way by alluding to the cruelty of the tyrant Phalaris and the barbarity of Hannibal's siege of Saguntum. Without dispraising Francesco, the poet makes us understand how dangerously close the condottiere is to these ruthless leaders. Filelfo, who could be outspoken in political matters, here lets the ode form do the work for him.

In 2.3 Filelfo narrates another brutal episode: how Gaspar de Vimercate and the citizens occupied the Palazzo d'Arengo and murdered the Venetian ambassador. Throughout the city, he tells us, Furor and Rapine rage, as though the fury Megaera had been unleashed. Yet Filelfo keeps reminding us that this is the day that Phoebus reigns over, a day that brings liberty to the city. He compares Francesco to a strong lion, but a lion that is about to spring on a helpless deer. As in 3.4, he describes the celebrations that follow the liberation of the city and Sforza's arrival with grain for the starving citizens:

---

tells the history of Bianor, the mythical founder of Mantua, and alludes to Hercules, Carlo's reputed ancestor. See Albanese, "Le raccolte poetiche latine," 439, 443.

[40] See Robin, *Filelfo in Milan*, 82–104; Albanese, "Le raccolte poetiche latine," 425.

[41] In neither of these odes does Filelfo develop an extended myth such as he fashions for Carlo Gonzaga in 2.1, in which he compares Carlo's accomplishments to those of Hercules. See H. David Brumble, *Classical Myths and Legends in the Middle Ages and Renaissance* (Westport, CT: Greenwood Press, 1998), 138–39 (s.v. "Giants").

Moenia ingressus pater ipse tecum
Liber & laetae Cereris choreae.
Ludus, & Comus, iocus & uoluptas
Omnia complent.
. . . .
Pace nunc ciues hilari fruuntur.
Nunc meus tecum populus triumphat.
Nunc suas hostes timidi ruinas
Funditus horrent. (2.3.125–28, 133–36)
[sig. dv^v–dvi^r]

Entering the walls with you is Father Liber himself
and the happy choruses of Ceres;
Game and joking Comus and Pleasure
all join in.
. . . .
Happy citizens now enjoy peace.
Now my people triumph with you.
Now the fearful host shudders
completely at its ruin.

In 3.4 Filelfo describes Sforza as an Apollo who not only brings back light to the city, but also causes the arts once more to flourish with the banishment of the fury Megaera. At the sound of the lyre the Muses sing and the people assemble in joyful choruses to offer praise and thanks to Sforza. Beneath the rejoicing the ode delivers a mixed message.

"Sentence" is another Pindaric hallmark that Filelfo imitates, liberally interspersing moral commentary throughout his odes of praise. In 5.5, for example, while lauding Pope Nicholas V for his leadership of the new Rome against the Turks who threaten Christendom, he pauses to reflect on the fragility of the human condition. While the eternal mind reigns above in splendor, human beings walk in shadows (sig. l^{r-v}). Similarly, in 4.9 he praises Alfonso I's leadership in Naples, but at the same time sermonizes like the psalmist (Ps. 39:6) on the instability of the human heart, its desire for gold, and its longing for the furor of war. Of course, Pindar's spare and often oblique use of aphorism contrasts with Filelfo's prolix moral commentary. Yet, like Pindar, he uses his moral commentary to temper the extravagant praises he lavishes on his patrons. No doubt Filelfo felt that he was filling for the Gonzagas or the Sforzas the role of poet-adviser that Pindar in equally dangerous times had filled for Hieron and Theron. He both offers the kind of public praise Pindar bestowed in Pythian 1 and extends the sort of personal consolation Pindar lent to Hieron in Pythian 3. More than a formal celebrator, Filelfo looked on the poet as an intimate friend and advisor. Moreover, by example, Filelfo recommended Pindaric ode as a form for praise to future political encomiasts.

Although the humanist-poets Giovanni Pontano (1426–1503) and Pietro Crinito (1465?-c.1507) served patrons and were involved in the political affairs of their own city-states, they composed few political odes.[42] Assiduous imitators of classical poetry, they more often composed amatory verse on Latin models than encomia in the Greek lyric style. Pontano is now perhaps best known for his hendecasyllabics in imitation of Catullus and for his long astronomical poem *Urania*. The founder of the Neapolitan Academy and a man of letters prominent in the literary life of Naples, Pontano was at the same time a leading Neapolitan statesman, who served Alfonso I and his son Ferrante and remained active in the affairs of the city until, with the invasion of Naples in 1495 by Charles VIII of France, he lost favor after swearing fealty to the French.[43] The campaign against the Turks at Otranto (Hydruntum) in 1480–1481, led by Alfonso, Duke of Calabria, called forth two victory odes from Pontano's pen.[44] The work of a man astute in political affairs and practiced in classical imitation, both odes employ Sapphic stanzas and combine Pindaric and Horatian techniques to celebrate a military action that recalls some ancient precedents—Hieron's repulse of the Carthaginians and Caesar's securing of the Pax Romana.

In the first of these odes, Pontano, adopting the role of *vates*, calls upon the Muse as the offspring of Jove ("Mens Iouis proles, Ioue mens parente / Nata" 1–2), not to fail him as he sings of the glory of battle.[45] He celebrates the victory by describing the triumphal procession and alluding to trophies—bloody trophies—won in the battle. By alluding to these trophies, Pontano celebrates Duke Alfonso's accomplishments, while acknowledging the costly nature of his victory. After losing the stronghold of Otranto to the Turks in 1480, the Italians regained the city the next year, but sustained enormous losses before at last negotiating a peace treaty with the Turks. Italians throughout the peninsula rapturously rejoiced at the truce. Some of this extravagant rejoicing is reflected in Pontano's gloating over the defeated Turks and his call for celebration. Like Fifelfo, in his celebration of Francesco Sforza's entry into Milan, Pontano is deliberately hyperbolic, calling for the forum, temples, and buildings to be adorned in Alfonso's honor and for the sparkling Falernian wine to flow readily:

---

[42] See the discussion of Pontano and Crinito in Stella P. Revard, *Pindar and the Renaissance Hymn-Ode*, MRTS 221 (Tempe, AZ: ACMRS, 2001).

[43] See Carol Kidwell, *Pontano: Poet and Prime Minister* (London: Duckworth, 1991), 1–18, 33–52. Pontano was prime minister and political adviser to Alfonso of Naples and secretary to Ferrante I and tutor to his son. Under Alfonso I of Aragon (1443–1458), as Kidwell (Maddison) explains in her earlier book, there was a prosperous period in Naples with a flourishing of the arts. See Maddison, *Apollo and the Nine*, 66–67.

[44] See Kidwell's description of the battle at Otranto and Pontano's verses for the victory (Kidwell, *Pontano*, 137–41).

[45] Joannes Pontanus, "Laudes Alfonsi Ducis Calabriae de victoria Hydruntina," in "Versus Lyrici," in Pontano, *Opera* (Florence, 1514), fols. 145^r-146^r.

Ite dis nostris meritos honores
Soluite, ornentur fora, templa, & aedes.
Atria argento niteant, fluatque
Molle Falernum. (53–56)

Go, perform the honors due to the gods;
let the forums be adorned, the temples and public buildings;
let the atriums shine with silver, and let the
sweet Falernum flow.[46]

Pontano was well aware of what was expected in victory odes. His aim, as he states in the second ode—"Laudes Alfonsi Aragonei Ducis Calabriae Ferdinandi Regis filii, de clarissima eius victoria" (sig. 147^V–148^V)—is praise: in this case Pindaric praise, which, as he says, adorns the souls of men. Taking a stance like that of the epinician poet, he tells us that he has come (with the help of the Muses) to render praise that is merited. It is not just victory that he is celebrating, but a victory pleasing to the gods:

Et diis cultus placet, & deorum
Addecet cultus simulacra summos
Addecent montes nemora, & strepentem
Populus amnem.
("Laudes Alfonsi Aragonei Ducis Calabriae," 1–4)

Reverence is pleasing to the gods
and the reverence of the gods is fitting;
groves and images become high mountains and the poplar
a resounding stream.

The passage rings with Pindaric "reverence." The worship that the poet offers to the gods and the praise that poet and people offer to the returning hero is comparable, Pontano urges. By praising the victor, the poet is fulfilling an obligation much like that which the epinician poet at a festival consecrated to the gods fulfills when he offers praise to the athlete-victor.[47] In this second ode Pontano develops a sequence of mythic and historical comparisons, carefully interlinked and chosen to illustrate military prowess. Alfonso may be compared, Pontano

---

[46] Pontano cannot quite refrain from adding a personal coda in the final stanza of this triumphal ode in which he reflects how sweet it is, while lying in his lady's lap, to congratulate these men of arms on their bravery.

[47] Pontano's fellow Neapolitan, Jacopo Sannazaro, also wrote political poetry addressed to Alfonso II and Federico III that was probably influenced to an extent by both Pontano and Filelfo. Sannazaro's elegiac verses, however, have fewer Pindaric affinities than Pontano's and Filelfo's stanzas. See Iacobus Sannazarius, *Opera Omnia Latine Scripta* (Venice: Aldus, 1535).

tells us, to Hercules in his conquest over the Nemean lion or the Lernean hydra; to Alexander, winning trophies of battle from Africa through India; to Caesar in conquests over land and sea; and finally to Scipio as a guarantor of his country's liberty. This is not a casual or randomly chosen list of conquerors. Hercules, Alexander, and Caesar will reappear in the political odes of the next two centuries and allusions to the killing of the hydra will be plentiful, as one of the favorite metaphors for civic danger averted. Taking his cue perhaps from Pindar and Horace, Pontano concludes the ode by referring to Duke Alfonso not as a warrior, but as a bringer of peace, a proper appellation that recalls Pindar's praise of Hieron and Horace's of Caesar.

Pontano's Florentine contemporary, Pietro Crinito (1465?-c.1507), a pupil of Poliziano's and a member of Lorenzo de' Medici's circle, was, like Pontano, best known for love poetry, but he also wrote familiar Horatian odes and experimental odes in the Greek mode. His few political poems are important, however, since they comment in a deeply personal way on the havoc wreaked throughout Italy with the invasion in the 1490s of French armies led by Charles VIII. In an ode to a friend ("Ad Faustum, de Carolo Rege Francorum cum ad vrbem tenderet cum exercitu") Crinito recounts graphically the atrocities of the French as they sweep through Italy and finally take Naples. Offering a personal condolence to his friend and a warning to Naples ("Vae tibi, Caue Neapolis"), he calls upon the Roman Senate and Caesar to witness how a foreign army is devastating the land of the ancient Romans.[48]

In the odes for Francesco Gonzaga, the general who commanded the allied forces against the French, and for Ferdinand of Aragon, who expelled the French in 1503, Crinito assumes a more ceremonial voice, closer to the Pindaric or the Horatian mark. Both odes praise Roman-style victories; both laud Francesco and Ferdinand as Caesar-like conquerors who have reestablished the "antiquum imperium" of Rome. Crinito addresses Francesco in a manner similar to that Filelfo had employed for his warring ancestor Carlo, congratulating the duke on his victories over the French and saluting him as the savior of Italy. Alternating between encomium and allusion to the horrific bloodshed of battle, he praises Francesco as the glory of Mantua, who broke the chains of bondage and restored Italy's ancient empire.[49]

---

[48] See Petrus Crinitus, "Poematum Lib. II," in Crinitus, *Opera* (Paris, 1508), Lib. I, sig. Fiii[r]. He also addresses a familiar ode to a Neapolitan friend on the calamity of Naples. See "Ad Bernardum Carapham de malis atque Calamitate Neapolis," sig. Fiiii[v]–v[r].

[49] "De Laude Fr. Gonzagae Principis Illustrissimi Mantuani cum ad Tarrum: contra Gallos dimicauit," sig. Fiii[v]–iiii[r]. Crinito compares Francesco's assault against the French with Mars's ancient wars against the fierce Thracians. Other political odes include that which Crinito addressed to Ludovico Sforza, reminding him of his illustrious forbears and lamenting his betrayal by the Swiss (sig. Fiiii[v]).

Crinito's odes for Ferdinand of Aragon also concern the expelling of the French from Italy, but differ from his ode for Francesco Gonzaga. Besides congratulating the prince on defeating the Gallic host, Crinito must present a case for the restoration of the House of Aragon to Naples. Hence he frames his odes for Ferdinand on the model of Horace's *Carmina* 4.14 and 15, addressed to Caesar on his return from Spain and on his closing of the gates of war.[50] Nor does Crinito forget that in celebrating Ferdinand's ejection of two foreign foes—the French from Italy and the Moors from Spain—he harks back to Pindar's lauding of Hieron's victories over both Etruscans and Carthaginians in Pythian 1. Accordingly, Crinito adapts Pindar's metaphor for the sun-like Hieron from Olympian 1, exclaiming that Ferdinand is yet more brilliant than that shining orb ("Princeps chorusca lampade clarior" [1]); he also addresses him, as Horace had addressed Caesar in 4.14.6, as the greatest of princes, "maxime principum" (69). Although Crinito refers in both odes to Ferdinand's crushing of the French in battle, he reserves for Ferdinand, as Horace did for Caesar, the title of bringer of peace and lauds him as the savior of the Neapolitan kingdom. In arguing Ferdinand's right to the Kingdom of Naples, Crinito does some deft maneuvering, pointing out that the Calabrians had first petitioned him. He could not, after all, leave "Parthenope" desolate. Both Fortune and Jove support his victory, Crinito exclaims, appropriating, as humanist poets were wont to do, Jove's favor for a Christian cause. He draws a direct line between the victory God grants to Ferdinand and that Jove granted to Augustus Caesar when Caesar's general Agrippa defeated the Cantabrians, a victory to which Horace alludes (*Carmina* 4.14.41). To drive his point home, Crinito conflates the Moors, whom Ferdinand had recently defeated, with the Cantabers, a warlike race who lived in ancient times in eastern Spain and whom Caesar defeated. Moreover, Crinito connects both the Cantabers and the Moors with the mythic giants whom both Horace and Pindar describe Jove as having conquered. Therefore, both piety and patriotism favor Ferdinand's victory. To piety nothing is denied, insists Crinito, thanking the "native" gods, who supported the defeat of the infidel Moors in Spain and now the invading French in Italy. Pointedly, Crinito makes Ferdinand a god-favored ruler, whose *pietas* resembles that of the pious Caesar of Horace's odes and the reverent Hieron of Pindar's Pythian 1. Like them, the Aragonese prince had put down "barbarous" enemies; after many storms and countless ills, he has returned to assert his native right in Naples and restore the Aragonese in Italy.

Crinito's second ode for Ferdinand sets the scene for the festive celebrations, urging that the triumphal cup of Bacchus be raised: "Quis reposti pocula Liberi / Depromit?" (Who draws the cups of stored wine? [1–2]). Crinito is putting a bright face on a complex political situation, for though he was wholeheartedly in

---

[50] See Petrus Crinitus, "Ad Ferrandum Aragonium Neapolis & Siciliae Regem Inuictissimum" and "De Laude Consalui Ferrandi in victoria Lyriana contra Gallos," "Poematum Lib. II," in *Opera*, II: sig. Fv^v–Fvi^r.

favor of the expulsion of the French, Crinito must have regarded the restoration of the Spanish as a trade-off for the Neapolitans. True, he might have hoped that Ferdinand would be a magnanimous ruler like his predecessor Alfonso I. But, of course, that was not to be. Yet he concludes his second ode on a celebratory note, perhaps emulating the tactics of his predecessors Filelfo and Pontano and before them Horace by applying a cheerful and propitious seal to the political situation.

4.

The Pindaric odes that Benedetto Lampridio composed for political leaders both resemble and differ from those of his Italian predecessors. Like Pontano and Crinito, he wrote few political pindarics, but those he wrote address some leading figures in the sixteenth-century political scene: Pope Leo X and the English king, Henry VIII, and Francesco Sforza, the Duke of Milan. His odes for Francesco Sforza—"Ad Cremonam Patriam" and "Ad Franciscum Sfortiam"—are patriotic and dynastic celebrations, occasioned by the restoration of the Sforza family to power after Charles V's defeat of the French in 1522 at the battle of La Bicocca. The odes for Leo X and Henry VIII are more complex, for they consider the crisis in religion brought about by Luther's challenge to the Church of Rome.

Benedetto Lampridio (before 1500–1540) was a more thorough-going pindarist than either Pontano or Crinito. Like Filelfo, he declared his Pindaric ambitions; unlike him he was determined to imitate Pindar's triads as well as his epinician mode. The Pléiade poet Jean Dorat called Lampridio a second Pindar, claiming that Lampridio achieved what Horace hoped for—true Pindaric imitation in Latin verse.[51] Born in Cremona some time before 1500, Lampridio was probably educated in Padua by the Greek teacher Marco Musuro (with whom he was later associated in Rome) and probably came to Rome at Pope Leo X's accession in 1513 to teach at the Collegio dei Greci, which Leo founded.[52] Undoubtedly, he was also concerned with Leo's other project, the sponsorship of a printing press on the Quirinale, which was to print Greek texts. The first book

---

[51] Dorat's epigram was printed in *Carmina Illustrium Poetarum Italorum*, ed. J. M. Toscanus (Paris, 1576), 1: fol. 83[r]. Dorat, the first poet in France to compose Latin triads, named Lampridio a Latin Pindar, who ventured where Horace dared not go.

[52] Lampridio remained in Rome during the 1510s, teaching at the Greek College in Angelo Colocci's villa on the Quirinale. According to Paolo Giovio, Lampridio taught Latin as well as Greek at the Collegio dei Greci. On the Collegio dei Greci, see Vittorio Fanelli, "Il Ginnasio greco di Leone X a Roma," *Studi Romani* 9 (1961): 379–93; also see Paulus Jovius, *Elogia Doctorum Virorum* (Antwerp, 1557), 219. Paolo Giovio includes in *Elogia Doctorum Virorum* three commendatory epigrams on Lampridio (one by Marc-Antonio Flaminio), as well as a brief life and assessment of his odes (219–20).

to come forth from this press in 1515 was Zacharias Callierges' Pindar, for which Lampridio wrote a commendatory epigram.[53] Most of Lampridio's Pindaric odes are the products of his sojourn in Rome, but he continued to compose pindarics after he left Rome for Padua upon Leo X's death in 1521.[54]

We cannot be sure exactly what spurred Lampridio's composition of Pindaric triads in Latin, nor whether it was Lampridio or his contemporary, Giovan Giorgio Trissino (1478–1550), who was the first poet to compose modern triadic verse on the Pindaric model. Although his verse, including his triadic odes, circulated privately during his lifetime, it was not published until 1550 after his death.[55] Many of his triadic odes are familiar pieces to friends, scholars, and fellow poets (which we shall consider more fully later); others are formal odes that bear the defining signatures of the early modern political pindaric.

"Ad Cremonam Patriam" is Lampridio's most expansive ode, conflating praise of a political leader with praise for the history and traditions of Lampridio's birthplace, Cremona. It falls under a sub-category of pindarics, the so-called city-ode, a genre we shall be examining later in the final chapter. "Ad Franciscum Sfortiam," like the victory odes of Pontano, Filelfo, and Crinito, celebrates

---

[53] See Pindar, *Odes* (Rome, 1515). The Rome Pindar was printed from a Vatican copy of the odes (Cod. Vat. Gr. 1312) rather than from the Ambrosian recension, which Aldus Manutius had used for his earlier Pindar in 1513. Zacharias Callierges, a former associate of Aldus, came to Rome to oversee the printing press that Leo and his Roman associates hoped would rival Aldus's at Venice. Angelo Colocci and Cornelio Benigno of Viterbo not only sponsored the project, but also were probably involved in editing Pindar's text, as Lampridio almost certainly was. Lampridio's commendatory epigram to Cornelius Benignus appears on the verso of the title page of the 1515 edition of Pindar's odes and praises the project and its patrons. Cf. A. C. Hero, "Pindar," in *Oxford Dictionary of Byzantium* (Oxford: Oxford University Press, 1991), 3: 1678–79.

[54] Although Lampridio moved to Padua to teach Greek at the university, he remained in contact with his Roman friends. Pierius Valerianus refers to Lampridio both in his prose and in his poetry, addressing one witty epigram to the philosophic sodality of poets in Padua, in which he names Lampridio as among the eight Muses and asks that he himself be admitted as a ninth Muse. See "Ad Sodales Patauij philosophantes," in *Hexametri Odae et Epigrammata* (Venice, 1550), fols. 126ᵛ–127ʳ. Valerianus also addressed other poems to Lampridio on friendship and humanistic study. See Pierius Valerianus, "Eivsdem Pierii Valeriani Amicitia Romana"; "Ad Benedictum Lampridium de Mentis auocatione Daphnia rusticante," in *Amorum Libri V* (Venice, 1549), fols. 89ʳ–92ᵛ; 7ʳ–8ᵛ. Also see Julia Haig Gaisser, *Pierio Valeriano on the Ill Fortune of Learned Men: A Renaissance Humanist and His World* (Ann Arbor: University of Michigan Press, 1999), 6.

[55] Benedictus Lampridius, *Carmina* (Venice, 1550). Lampridio's verse was reprinted in the following anthologies: *Carmina Illustrium Poetarum Italorum*, ed. J. M. Toscanus (Paris, 1576), 1: fols. 83 ᵛ–152ᵛ; *Delitiae CC. Italorum Poetarum, Huius Superiorisque Ævi Illustrium*, ed. Janus Gruterus (Frankfurt, 1608), I. 2. 1271–1384. Unless otherwise noted, Lampridio's poetry will be cited from the 1550 edition of his poetry. Citations of Pindar's poetry are from, *Carmina* ed. C.M. Bowra (Oxford: Clarendon Press, 1935).

a political leader—here, Francesco Sforza—and the battle that restored him as Duke of Milan. Francesco bore the same Christian name as the condottiere-founder of the Sforza dynasty, whom Filelfo celebrated, and it is remarkable how closely Lampridio's ode in praise of the second Francesco follows the pattern of the victory ode Filelfo composed some seventy years earlier to the first Francesco. Lampridio not only recounts the conduct of battle but also makes the city witness Francesco's victory, its joyful citizens repeating his name and offering a thanksgiving mixed with joy and grief at the temples of the gods. Lampridio was living in Padua at the time and probably had firsthand accounts of the events. Like Filelfo, he cannot celebrate victory without reflecting on its cost, and remarks retrospectively in the second part of the ode how good fortune is rarely unaccompanied with bad. While seeming to praise Ludovico, Francesco's father, he alludes obliquely to a fame not unmixed with blame. A single house, such as the Sforzas, cannot perpetually be blessed, no matter how much God loves them, but must suffer vicissitudes. He compares the Sforzas' fortunes to those of Theban dynasty that Pindar celebrated in Olympian 2. As Jove finally spared Thebes after much trouble and gave the sign of the rainbow as a token of peace, so God, Lampridio declares, will spare the Milanese dynasty. Even the great Hercules, Lampridio reflects, rose stronger after his labors. The ode concludes with cautious optimism and a typical Pindaric aphorism. Jupiter spreads the rainbow; Apollo gives the sign for congratulation with his lyre; and Hercules completes his labors. Although fate may seem to deny favor, remarks Lampridio, neither industry nor strength will fail before its day: "Quod seuero pollice parca uoluit, / Non industria, non uis, / Ante diem refringet" (fol. 6ᵛ). In this ode Lampridio makes a real attempt to duplicate the expansiveness of Pindar's best odes. Like Pindar he places a single event in a complex frame, considering a family's history as he reflects on the larger pattern of a nation's and a people's fate. While he celebrates a military victory, comparable to those athletic celebrated in Pindar's dynastic odes—Olympian 1 and Olympian 2—he also reflects seriously on the vagaries of fate as he congratulates the last surviving family member on that "victory."

Lampridio's verses to Henry VIII and Leo X advance the cause of the political pindaric in a different way, for in lieu of military victory, Lampridio celebrates other kinds of contests. The ode to Henry VIII commemorates an important event: Henry's proclamation of faith against Luther, "Assertio septem sacramentorum adversus Martinum Lutherum," and the pope's naming Henry Defender of the Faith. Probably composed soon after 1521, the year the pope excommunicated Luther, the ode is written in irregular six-line stanzas rather than in triads.[56] Henry is portrayed as a contestant pitted against his opponent Luther, and his alleged victory is depicted alternately as an athletic and a military contest—worthy in either case of Pindaric commemoration, although accomplished in the scholastic arena rather than on the battlefield or in the Olympic palaestra. One of its most interesting features is the use of myth for propaganda purposes. The war of the giants against the gods, previously employed by Pindar and Horace, by Pontano and Crinito, is now transformed into a propagandistic metaphor for Luther's assault against Rome. Luther becomes a presumptuous giant, who attempts but fails to achieve ascendancy over Jove. Henry is Phoebus Apollo, defending the "father" of the gods and men—Lampridio has transferred Jove's title to the pope. Once the gods guarded Sicily, says Lampridio; now they guard England and its king, sanctioning Henry's rulership over England and his alliance with the pope against the French. Lampridio congratulates Henry on his learning and on his virtue triumphing in the contest over Luther's vice. As Pindar had contrasted the worthy and generous Hieron to the tyrant Phalaris, so Lampridio contrasts the magnanimous Henry to the degenerate Luther.

Both Lampridio and Trissino composed verses for contemporary popes—Popes Leo X and Clement VII, respectively. Although neither ode celebrates a specific occasion, both refer obliquely to the fervid political climate in Italy about these Medicean popes. Leo and Clement were cousins, and as scions of the powerful Medici family, both, as Lampridio and Trissino remark, combine Florentine sensibility with Roman solidarity, using their office to support the arts and to restore to Rome the splendors of the ancient empire. While Lampridio's verses to Leo are in iambics, rather than in triads, he celebrates Leo in the Pindaric manner, beginning by calling upon the Muses and asking the Pindaric question: "Cui sumpsi Citharam in manus? / Diraeis potius quem referam modis?" (For whom should I take my lyre in hand, / whom should I celebrate more potently with Dircean verses?).[57] Leo stands to Rome as Hieron and Theron to the Sicilian cities—a rich man and a ruler, whose fame rests not only on his strong government but also on his support of the arts. Like them, he entrusts his reputation to the poets who write for him, and poets such as Lampridio do not fail to render compliments to Leo and his family. Remembering Leo's Medicean heritage, Lampridio praises his father, Lorenzo de' Medici, the prince who first moved

---

[56] See "Henrico Ottavo," fols. 20ᵛ–22ʳ. Lampridio's ode to Baptista Cassalius, the papal legate to England, also praises Henry VIII, referring to him as the flower of men and also praising Thomas More (*Odes*, fol. 51ᵛ). Other continental poets celebrate Henry VIII of England. Salmon Macrin lauds Henry for a military victory, comparing him to Achilles (*Carminum Libri Quatvor* [Paris, 1530], fols. 5ᵛ–6ᵛ). Macrin also has an ode to Thomas More, Henry's chancellor (fol. 16ʳ⁻ᵛ). However, Francesco Maria Molsa directs elegies to Henry on quite a different occasion, condemning his repudiation of his wife, Catherine of Aragon: see *Carmina*, ed. Toscanus, 1: fols. 43ᵛ–47ʳ.

[57] See "Leoni Decimo," fol. 24ʳ.

Etruria to studies and made Florence flower. In coming to Rome as Leo X, Lampridio asserts, Lorenzo's son has become the Genius who pours the Florentine riches from his cornucopia. Lampridio was, after all, one of the poets-scholars who had benefited from Leo's patronage.[58]

However, Lampridio does not merely refer to Leo as a generous patron. Mindful that Pindar had described Zeus as the warrantor of Hieron's rule, Lampridio calls upon a Christianized Jove to support Leo's pontificate. The very king of heaven, he affirms, gave the scepter to the divine Leo to lead the race of Romulus and to raise Rome to its former glory. Perhaps echoing Vergil, though in a different context, Lampridio exclaims, "O happy race of Aeneas," and "Florence, thrice and four times happy!" (*Aeneid* 1. 94). Casting Leo in the role of an Augustus Caesar who succeeds the Julius Caesar of Pope Julius II, Lampridio predicts that after the military successes of his predecessor, Leo will institute a Pax Romana. Leo's Golden Age will be comparable to that which Vergil predicted for Augustus in his Messianic eclogue and Horace in his *Carmen Saeculare*. Evil will fail, Lampridio proclaims, and universal good prevail. All is not celebration, however. Lampridio glances nervously at the troubles in Italy, not the least of which were the renewed claims of the French to Naples and Milan, and the continuing menace of the Turks. Cautiously he offers political advice, urging Leo to lead a crusade against the Turks that would unite Italy's warring factions and put an end to intestine war. Lampridio's verses close, as they open, with a Pindaric device, an aphorism which alludes to the Olympic contests and is appropriate both for a successful ruler or a victorious athlete.

> Non quisquis spatijs sudat Olympicis,
> Veloces agitans equos,
> Pulchris iuncta refert tempora frondibus (fol. 26^V).

---

[58] Lampridio wrote an epigram for the possesso of Leo X in 1513, predicting the glories of the age of Leo that were to come. See "De suis temporibus" in *Carmina*, ed. Toscanus, 1: fol. 152^V: "Olim habuit Cypris sua tempora: tempora Mauors / Olim habuit: sua nunc tempora Pallas habet." (Once Venus had her era; then Mars had his; now Pallas has her era). Lampridio celebrated Leo's Medicean heritage in "In Diem Cosmi Medici" (fol. 17$^{r–v}$). Other odes by Lampridio also refer to the pope. See, for example, "Ad Gibertum" (in Pindaric triads) and "Giberto" (in stanzas). In "Giberto" Leo is described as the recipient of Olympian favor: "Te, magnus Leo, cui rector Olympicus / Caros Imperium detulit in greges" (fol. 20^r) (You, great Leo, to whom the Olympian ruler granted the empire over his dear flock). "Ad Gibertum" was perhaps written on the occasion of the victory in 1513 against the French and the formation of the League of Mecklin, marking the peace, for Lampridio rejoices that the enemy has been expelled and that Leo holds the Tarpeian scepter unharmed, protected and approved by the Olympian king: "Dum Leo Tarpeia sceptra incolumis teneret, / Vidimus expulsos hostes, felicia cuncta, / Usque adeo erubuit Leonem, / Rex Olympicae domus" (fol. 12^r).

> Not everyone who sweats on the Olympic tracks
> Driving swift horses
> Brings back brows bound with lovely garlands.

Lampridio concludes by extending the pope a temporal crown of glory.

Trissino's Italian canzone to Pope Clement VII is less warmly complimentary and more urgently hortatory than Lampridio's Latin verses to Leo.[59] But then Trissino wrote in troubled times when the security of the papal Rome was compromised. Much as he praises the pope as God's vicar on earth, Trissino recognizes the overwhelming difficulties that Clement faced at home and abroad. Like Lampridio, he urges the pope to take the political situation in hand and to use his influence to move Europe against the Turks—to effect the liberation of Greece, Rhodes, and Belgrade (fallen in 1521) and to keep control over territories menaced by the Turks. What is interesting about this ode is Trissino's comprehensive political awareness and his ability to connect the political landscape of Pindar's odes with that of modern Europe. Trissino seems to have identified the Turks who threatened European civilization as the counterparts to the Persians Pindar described as threatening Greece or the Carthaginians Sicily. As in ancient times a complex web of imperialism engulfed the Mediterranean world. Other lessons of history were not lost on Trissino. He might have observed with interest Pindar's allusions to the double game that his compatriots, the Thebans, were playing, now allying themselves with the Persians against their own native Greeks. Modern Rome's position was not unlike that of ancient Thebes. In the power game of François I with Charles V the pope continually juggled allegiances until Rome ultimately fell to Charles V's imperial forces in 1527. Trissino's canzone probably predates that disaster, for he closes with exhortations to the pope, not unlike those Pindar delivered to Sicily's troubled leaders, to be vigilant against threats at home and abroad. Trissino's concluding triad resounds fervently with warning, as he repeats the word "veggio" (wake up!). But Trissino, like Lampridio, doesn't go too far. Crowning Clement with flowers and laurel, Trissino forecasts a triumph that the pope was not to enjoy.

---

[59] "Canzωn del Tris. a Papa Clemente VII" in *Rime del Trissinω* (Vicenza, 1529), sig. llii[r]–lliv[r]. Trissino's canzoni are less obviously Pindaric, except, of course, in form, and resemble, as Carol Maddison observes, Trissino's other "odes"—his Petrarchan canzoni also arranged in triadic pattern (See *Apollo and the Nine*, 144). Together with the canzone to Pope Clement VII, the ode in praise of Cardinal Ridolphus (sig. lliv[r]–mmii[r]) also has a political subtext. The cardinal had been a peace emissary between Charles V and François I. Hence Trissino not only mourns his death, but also looks at the degenerating political situation in Italy caused by the rivalry of François I and Charles V, the latter of whom at the sack of Rome in 1527 kept Clement prisoner in the Castel Sant' Angelo.

5.

While Lampridio was developing the Latin pindaric, Luigi Alamanni (1495–1556) and Antonio Sebastiani Minturno (?-1574) were trying to transform the Italian canzone into a vernacular equivalent of Pindar's poems of praise. At the same time in France Salmon Macrin (1490–1557) was also imitating Pindar, using Horatian stanza forms for both political and religious odes. Luigi Alamanni was a Florentine expatriate, who spent most of his productive years at the French court; Salmon Macrin was a Frenchman and a precursor to the Pléiade poets. Both, however, addressed odes to the French king, François I. During the same period Minturno was celebrating François' political adversary, Charles V, the Holy Roman Emperor. Their odes to these political rivals chart the history of this turbulent era and demonstrate how the pindaric continued to be a tool for political propaganda.

Alamanni was a poetic experimenter, intent, like Lampridio, on imitating Pindar's verse but in the vernacular rather than in Latin. Inspired perhaps by Trissino's triadic canzoni, he sets the eight "Pindaric" *hymni* of his *Opere Toscane* (1531–1532) in triads — ballata, contra ballata, and stanza.[60] Three of these (1, 2, 8) are political odes that praise François I.[61] Salmon Macrin's odes to François I are dispersed throughout several collections of his poetry, and, though he makes no attempt to imitate Pindar's triads, he espouses other aspects of Pindar's poetics.[62] Both Macrin and Alamanni ostentatiously invoke the Pindaric muses and declare a poetics of inspiration that looks forward to that later embraced by Ronsard and his followers. In Hymno 1 Alamanni asks the Muses to lift him to glory comparable to that of the good Theban spirit, that is, Pindar: "Alme sorelle chiare / ch'à tanta gloria alzaste / Il buon Thebano spirto" (Ballata 1. 1–3). Macrin also calls on the Pindaric Muses to inspire his lyre to sing of heroes. Both poets plead a "Pindaric" relationship with the king they praise. Alamanni

---

[60] See Henri Hauvette, *Un Exilé Florentin à La Cour de France au XVIᵉ Siècle: Luigi Alamanni 1495–1555: Sa Vie et Son Oeuvre* (Paris: Hachette, 1903). Alamanni's *Opere Toscane* (Leiden, 1531–1532) is a heterogeneous collection that includes elegies, sonnets, eclogues, several *favole*, psalms, *selve*, a translation of Sophocles' *Antigone*, as well as the eight *hymni* or imitations of Pindar's odes in triadic form. The volume is dedicated to François I and many of the elegies, sonnets, and *selve*, besides the three Pindaric hymns, celebrate the king. *Selva* 1.i, for example, is essentially a panegyric on the king's military victories. See Hauvette's discussion of the *Hymni* (*Un Exilé Florentin*, 225–32).

[61] The third hymn praises Marguerite, the king's sister, in a way that anticipates Ronsard's praise of another royal Marguerite, the sister of Henri II. The other hymns (4, 5, 6, 7) praise Alamanni's lady Pianta and her Ligurean heritage. See the discussion of these hymns in chapter 9.

[62] Macrin published a number of books of verse in the 1520s, 1530s, and 1540s. See Maddison, *Apollo and the Nine*, 194–200.

announces that François' person inspires him with a divine fury ("l'alto furor diuino") (Contra Ballata 2.2). François' valor and virtue, he proclaims, have made him comparable to Mars and Phoebus, a god upon earth.[63] Unfortunately, however, this "god upon earth" is also a man much afflicted with adversity. Therefore it falls to Alamanni, as it had to Pindar before him, not only to praise, but also to offer counsel and consolation to his patron.

As he charts the course of François' political career, Alamanni makes use of an important feature of Pindar's Cyrenean odes: the elaboration of the foundation myth. By implication Alamanni compares François to the Trojan Francus, who, after great adversity, came finally to establish the great empire in France over which François reigns. Later in the century Ronsard and French pindarists who follow him were to call up the same foundation myth to honor François' son Henri II and Henri's heirs. In Pythian 4 Pindar had recounted the adventures of the unlikely hero Jason, whose success depended more on personal charm and luck than on traditional battle courage. Throughout the ode Pindar proceeds by using negative examples. Despite long delay, the Argonaut Euphemus succeeds in founding Cyrene and in fulfilling the prophecies of Medea and the Pythia. Jason succeeds in winning the fleece through a combination of persuasion and daring. Drawing an implicit parallel between the Argonauts and Arcesilas of Cyrene, Pindar advises the king to practice the kingly arts of patience and conciliation in order to mend the rift caused by civil strife.[64] These are not irrelevant lessons for Alamanni to recommend to François, who, despite his good courage, suffered a disastrous defeat at the battle of Pavia in 1525, and subsequently a humiliating imprisonment in Madrid. But Alamanni is too tactful to allude directly to these events.

Hymno 1 applies a moral aphorism—whether you win or lose, you will be blessed if the gods incline to you. Alamanni connects François with his alleged Trojan ancestor Francus, whose seed survived after Troy's walls were put to fire. Despite apparent defeat, Alamanni observes, Troy lives, the "losers" having prevailed at last because of their piety, but the winners, the Greeks, who were

---

[63] Alamanni's praise of François is effusive. Not surprisingly he compares François' brilliance to the sun's in Hymn 1, Ballata 2.1–3. Alamanni follows the Pindaric practice in this hymn of not naming his subject in the first strophe of the poem. Hence in the second ballata he announces: "Questo è Francesco primo / Ch'ogni altro lume auanza / Quel Gallico splendore; / Quel ch'è sola speranza / De i buon (s'io dritto estimo) / E de i dì nostri honore. / Quello al cui gran ualore / Non uà cosa mortale; / Che soura 'l cielo aggiunge" (Hymno 1, Ballata 2. 1–9) (197–98) [Such is Francis the First, that every other light advances, just like a Gallic splendor. He who is the sole hope of the good (if I judge rightly) and of the gods we honor, whose great valor is such that it goes beyond a mortal thing and reaches above the sky].

[64] See Segal's discussion of Pindar's interpolation of advice to Arcesilas in *Pindar's Mythmaking*, 9–14, 73.

apparently victorious, lost even in winning. Significantly, Alamanni alludes to the principal Greeks—Agamemnon, Ulysses, Diomedes, and Achilles—without naming them. These "nameless" Greek heroes become negative examples that represent François' opponents, Charles V and his allies. Their great leader (Agamemnon) lost his life when his impious wife killed him; (Ulysses), even though led by a wise goddess, suffered on sea and land; (Diomedes), having wounded the goddess of love, was deprived of every pleasure; and finally the great hero (Achilles), though protected by a great shield, was conquered. By reversing our expectations and showing how the universally admired Greek heroes had failed, Alamanni implies that François' enemies will also come to defeat and that François, despite adversity, will triumph. The reversals of fortune François experiences become for Alamanni virtuous trials. By implication François is associated not only with France's founder Francus but also with pious Aeneas (also unnamed), who bore his father on his back through the impious flames and went to distant shores to found a nation. Like Aeneas, François is the bright sun of our blind world, wise, pious, and just, a ruler worthy of the name Augustus: "il chiaro sole / Del nostro mondo cieco, / Saggio, pietoso, & giusto / Che sol di nome Augusto / Tra noi degno sarebbe, / Del tuo bel tronco crebbe" (Stanza 4. 4–9).

Alamanni's second hymn is a disquisition on the unpredictable nature of bad fortune—"ria fortuna" (Contra Ballata 1.1). Here Alamanni is probably looking back on Pindar's repeated commentary on how calumny, envy, and scorn can beset even the best of princes. In Olympian 2. 95–96 Pindar remarks that envy unrighteously attacks praise, attempting to obliterate the good works of men. He advises Hieron, in Pythian 3, that the good should turn to the fairer side of events ("ἀλλ᾽ ἀγαθοί, τὰ καλὰ τρέψαντες ἔξω" [83].[65] Similarly in Hymno 2 Alamanni draws a Pindaric moral—if a man holds fast to virtue, his fortune will change. Taking his examples from classical history rather than myth, Alamanni points out that fortune was sometimes friend, sometimes enemy to Alexander and to Julius Caesar, his Roman counterpart. If a man is virtuous, says Alamanni, applying the classical maxim for François, fortune will smile again on him. At the same time Alamanni is eager to offer Christian consolation: in heaven, not on earth, he remarks, we will find every good. The time of our mortal voyage is dark and evil; but for the valorous, the stars, fortune, and good luck conquer and revive after death. Alamanni could have found the counterpart to this Christian consolation in Olympian 2 where Pindar advises Theron that the courageous, who keep from all wrong, will take the path by the tower of Cronos to the islands of the blest, the classical equivalent of the Christian heaven. Alamanni's eighth hymn also takes a thorough-going Pindaric attitude towards poetic praise—Apollo will keep the king's honor green. Whereas the invidious

---

[65] Glenn Most observes that in Pythian 2 also Pindar vehemently attacks slanderers, supporting Hieron's good report and criticizing his detractors. See *The Measures of Praise*, 124–25.

times may not assure long life, Alamanni remarks philosophically, the poet's rich song will fly to heaven and assure the king the divine name he aspires to.[66] It is the closest that Alamanni comes to granting François I an Olympic crown.

Jean Salmon Macrin took a freer view than Alamanni of his role as a Pindaric encomiast. He had close ties to the royal establishment in France, to his patron, the powerful Cardinal Jean Du Bellay, as well as to François I, to whom he dedicates his 1531 volume of odes. Macrin also had associates among the Italian humanists, having studied Greek with both Girolamo Aleandro and Lampridio's mentor, Janus Lascaris, who, after leaving the Collegio dei Greci in Rome, resided at the French court.[67] Like Alamanni, Macrin calls on the Pindaric Muses to inspire his lyre to sing of the deeds of heroes.[68] He pleads a special relationship with François, professing that he is filled with a divine *furor* at the sight of the king: "Quis mouet pectus calor? unde tantae / Suppetunt uires animo furenti? / Quísue Parnasi bibulo uolucrem / Vertice sistit?" (1–4) (What warmth moves my heart? whence suffices such strength in my raging breast? And who at the thirsty top of Parnassus sets its flight?).[69] You alone, he tells François, command my lyre.

Like Alamanni, Macrin attempts to console as well as celebrate the French king. His aim, as he tells us, is to compare the exploits of his king with those of heroes and athletes whom Pindar honored: "Pindaric" heroes such as Hercules, Perseus, Adrastus, Hector, Achilles, and the children of Leda.[70] Among these

---

[66] At the end of the ode Alamanni adds the often expressed aphorism that though the accomplishments of kings are great, their names would not survive without the poets: "Che'l poetico ardore / Tanto hà uigore & forza / Che'l tempo non l'ammorza" [That poetic ardor has such vigor and power that time does not diminish it] (Hymno 8. Stanza 3. 7–9) (232).

[67] In the ode "Ad Sodales" (*Carminum Libellus* [Paris, 1528], sig. aiiij^v) Macrin addresses an affectionate tribute to Lascaris as a friend and teacher. See I. D. McFarlane, "Jean Salmon Macrin," *Bibliothèque d'Humanisme et Renaissance* 21 (1959): 55–84. Lampridio also wrote an ode for Lascaris. See "Iano Lascari" in *Carmina*, 57^r–60^r.

[68] In an ode to François I Macrin specifically calls upon the Pindaric muses ("Pindaricae Camoenae") to govern his song and help him praise the king: "Tu; si qua nostris gratia versibus / Aspersa forte est, splendida fortium / Cùm facta dicuntur uirorum / Pindaricae fidibus Camoenae, / Tu: si supinum quid iuuet ocium / Spissa iacentum sub nemorum coma, / Per prata, conuallesque puris / Sic ubi fons aquulis tremiscit, / Noctem minutis siue ubi poculis / Conuiuiorum festa celebritas / Extendet, Heroumque laudes / Crinigeri recinunt lyristae, / Tu solus esto, quem mea barbitos / Obliuioso uindicet a situ, / Non pace, non armis minorem / Moroueo, Carolóue magno." ("De Laudibus Francisci Regis Franciae," in *Lyricorum Libri Duo* [Paris, 1531], sig. Dviii^v).

[69] "De Laudibus Francisci Regis," *Lyricorum Libri Duo*, sig. Diiii^v–Dvi^r.

[70] Macrin appeals to the Muses, the Nymphs, and Phoebus for inspiration, anticipating Ronsard's account of the onset of poetic *furor* in the "Hymn to Eternity," and perhaps, like him, imitating the opening of Callimachus' Hymn to Apollo or Michele

Hercules—the virtuous but often unhappy hero of Greek legend—is particularly conspicuous. Hercules becomes a useful stand-in for the much tried François I, who also suffered greatly at the hands of the blind goddess Fortune. Indirectly Macrin is implying that Charles V, François' adversary, played the part of Eurystheus to the other's Hercules. Yet at the same time Macrin predicts that François will, like Hercules, ultimately experience a change to better fortune and be properly rewarded. He combines this reference to Hercules' translation to Olympus with an allusion (adapted from Vergil, *Eclogues* 4.6) to the return of Astraea to the earth and the establishment of the Golden Age: "Prouidas Astraea redux ministret / Iudice leges" (sig. Dviʳ). Pindar consistently describes Heracles as a hero who behaved as befits the son of Zeus and in this Macrin follows Pindar in making Hercules a model of proper restraint and steadfast virtue.[71] However, in alluding to Hercules and in recounting his deeds, Macrin often overshoots the Pindaric mark. In one ode, for example, Macrin runs through what appears to be a complete list of Hercules' labors and other adventures.[72]

As a pindarist Macrin often follows the practice that Ronsard was later to adopt: excerpting quotations from Pindar's most celebrated and brilliant proemia to begin his own odes.[73] In one such ode, Macrin takes his cue from the opening

---

Marullus' Hymn to the Sun ("Soli") from his *Hymni Naturales*. See the discussion of *furor poeticus* in Revard, *Pindar and the Renaissance Hymn-Ode,* esp. 159, 164.

[71] See William Fitzgerald's discussion of Pindar's relationship to Heracles in *Agonistic Poetry: The Pindaric Mode in Pindar, Horace, Hölderlin, and the English Ode* (Berkeley: University of California Press, 1987), 58–61.

[72] See "De Laudibus Francisci Regis," *Lyricorum Libri Duo* (1531), sig. Dvʳ–Dviʳ. Although Macrin follows the Pindaric model for Hercules' portrait, more likely he models the catalogue of Hercules' labors on the choruses of Euripides' *Heracles* or Seneca's *Hercules Furens*. Euripides and Seneca describe the hero's achievements. Pindar never recounts any of Heracles' labors as the central myth of an ode, though he alludes now and then to one or another of the labors. Pindar's odes feature Heracles as a righter of wrongs, the defender of justice and the man who sets the proper limits to *areté*, thus a proper model for the virtuous French king. Pindar also recounts several of Heracles' fabulous journeys—for example, his expedition to bring back from the land of the Hyperboreans olive trees for Olympia, a labor assigned him by Eurystheus (Olympian 3). At the end of Olympian 2, moreover, Pindar alludes to Heracles' pillars, commenting that Theron's *areté* reaches as far as those famed pillars. Like Pindar, Macrin alludes to Hercules' friendship with the Dioscuri. As Pfeijffer has noted, the praise of the victor athlete in Nemean 3 is implicitly linked to that of Heracles, both of whom strive to achieve the limit of what man or man-god is capable: see Pfeijffer, *Three Aiginetan Odes of Pindar,* 225. Also see Brumble, *Classical Myths and Legends,* 154–66 (s.v. "Hercules").

[73] For a consideration of Macrin's references to Pindar and his Pindaric borrowings, see Jean-Eudes Girot, *Pindare avant Ronsard: De l'émergence du grec à la publication des quatre premiers livres des Odes de Ronsard* (Geneva: Librairie Droz, 2002), 286–88, 290–300.

of Pindar's Nemean 5 to praise François and to plead for the return of peace. Pindar's original ode opens with an encomium to poetry: he contrasts the voiceless statue a sculptor sets on a pedestal with his own speaking odes, which proclaim the truth about honorable deeds.[74] Although he imitates Pindar's opening line ("Non ipse pictor, non statuarius" [I am not a painter nor a sculptor], sig. Bvi^v), Macrin develops a point quite different from Pindar's contrast of spoken and unspoken compliment. He implicitly compares the silence of the statue to the silencing of the Muses effected because of the wars throughout Europe. Invoking the favor of the gods and long life for the king, he appeals for peace and the return of free speech to poetry. With the restoration of peace and the return of a Golden Age, the dove need no longer flee from the eagle, and poetry and the arts—now silent as statues—may speak again. Macrin remakes Pindar's simile into a plea that the arts may again flourish under François I in France.

Macrin follows Pindar more closely in an ode to François that opens book 2. Not only does he imitate Pindar's opening strophe, virtually translating it into Latin, he also sets forth Pindar's theme—poetry's power to soothe. Nemean 4 was composed for a boy athlete, the child of a family of poets, whose dead father would ordinarily have composed the victory song. As ally to the Aiginetan family, Pindar now must do the honors, invoking song itself and the Graces and Muses who call it forth to soothe and charm.[75]

> Ἄριστος εὐφροσύνα πόνων κεκριμένων
> ἰατρός· αἱ δὲ σοφαὶ
> Μοισᾶν θύγατρες ἀοιδαὶ θέλξαν νιν ἁπτόμεναι.
> οὐδὲ θερμὸν ὕδωρ τόσον γε μαλθακὰ τέγγει
> γυῖα, τόσσον εὐλογία φόρμιγγι συνάορος.
> ῥῆμα δ᾽ ἐργμάτων χρονιώτερον βιοτεύει,
> ὅ τι κε σὺν Χαρίτων τύχα
> γλῶσσα φρενὸς ἐξέλοι βαθείας.
> (Nemean 4. 1–8)

---

[74] See Macrin, "De Laudibus Francisci Regis Franciae," in *Lyricorum Libri Duo* (1531), sig. Bvi^v–Bvii^v. In Nemean 5 Pindar says that his songs speak, and speech wins honor. The ode was written for a boy's pancratium and praises Peleus who won Thetis as a reward for his honest dealing. In contrasting the ode to the voiceless statue, Pindar had more in mind than simple praise of victor and hero. Indirectly he is commenting on when it is appropriate to speak or not to speak. He keeps his silence about Peleus's and Telamon's offense. He speaks out for Peleus, just as the hero had defended himself against Hippolyte's slander.

[75] The name of a Grace, Euphrosyne, is the second word of the ode. The Graces' favor permits the tongue to bring forth songs of praise—the "children" of the Muses which bring comfort to human beings. The myth of Nemean 4 connects the achievement of the Aeacids, Aegina's native heroes, with the process of making poetry.

> The best physician after wearisome toil
> is joy, when songs, the wise
> daughters of the Muses, touch and charm us.
> Not warm water to tired limbs soothes
> so much as praise, the friend to the lyre.
> The word lives longer than the deed
> when with the favor of the Graces
> the tongue draws it forth from the mind's depth.[76]

Pindar also invokes the lyre, the accompaniment to his song, urging it to weave the fabric of lovely song and commenting on how adversity often is necessary to bring forth beauty out of uncertainty and darkness. Unless trial bring it forth, he comments, making an analogy between the athlete and the poet, deeds would remain unaccomplished. So songs also are tested and brought forth only after a lapse of time, Pindar enjoins, returning to the theme of poetry at the end of the ode.[77]

Macrin's imitation of Nemean 4 extends Pindar's theme in order to praise François and link poetry, the poet, and the patron king.[78] Macrin claims for the poet, however, the power not just to soothe, but also to perform difficult tasks. Amphion animated stones to build the walls of Thebes and Orpheus soothed wild beasts. The poet's tongue, says Macrin, translating Pindar's Greek, draws words from the depths of the mind ("Verba, de mentis latebris profundae / Lingua reuoluit" [sig. Cʳ]). Pindar praises Heracles and Aeginetan heroes; Macrin chooses to draw his examples more widely from the ancient repertory—the battle of the Lapiths with the Centaurs, Perseus's winning of the gorgon's head, concluding with Phthian Achilles and his conquest of fierce Hector (sig. Cᵛ), all of which lead him quite naturally to his own heroic example, François.[79] In this tactic Macrin does not differ substantially from Pindar. Both poets allude to the deeds of the famous heroes of the past in order to praise present heroes and present victories. Macrin even remembers to join the praise of his king to praise of his kin: his sister (whom the Graces sprinkle with nectar), his father, his wife. To the

---

[76] Macrin translates Pindar's strophes into Sapphics, but the thrust of his Latin is analogous: "Absolutorum est medicus laborum / Aptas, illabens animis uoluptas, / Et ioci dulces, veniensque laeto è / Pectore risus. / Quin et argutis fidibus Camoenae / Floridos postque cecinere uersus / Corda permulcent, minuuntque edaces / Carmine cures. / Lapsa nec tantum sopor ipse membra, / Nec fouent thermas, liquor aut phalernus, / Blanda uox quantum tremuloque ductae / Pollice chordae" ("Ad Franciscum Valesium Huius Nominis Primum Franciae Regem," in *Lyricorum Libri Duo* [1531], sig. Bviiiᵛ–Cʳ).

[77] As M.M. Willcock outlines in his overview of the ode, Pindar's point is simple enough: the song of the poet is compensation for the strain and effort that both heroes and athletes expend (*Pindar's Victory Odes*, 95).

[78] See "Ad Franciscum Valesium," in Lyricorum Libri Duo (1531), sig. Bviiiv–Ciiv.

[79] Macrin probably adapts the epithet "Phthian" Achilles from Horace, *Carmina* 4.6.4, adding an Horatian element to this Pindaric song.

king himself he extends the Pindaric standard, measuring him as one who rules with just laws. Not all of Macrin's political odes follow so closely the Pindaric model, but this ode demonstrates his precise knowledge of a specific Greek ode and an awareness of how to adapt Pindaric themes and techniques for his own uses. Both he and Alamanni are important models for the Pléiade poets who in the next generation turn from the praise of François I to the praise of his son and grandsons.

7.

Macrin wrote few battle odes for François I, perhaps because François achieved so little of lasting importance on the field of battle. However, the two odes that he composed for François' victory over Charles V at Aquae Sextiae, in which Macrin compares François' victory to Jove's triumph over the giants, can claim both Pindaric and Horatian connections. Macrin pronounces the first ode a solemn epinician and the second a song that soars above Horace's Daunian lyre. Indeed, like earlier exempla these odes have a marked affininity to Horace's *Carmina* 4.14 and 15.[80] However, it is Macrin's contemporary, the Italian poet Antonio Sebastiani Minturno (d. 1574), who carries on the tradition of battle encomia from earlier poets such as Pontano and Crinito. Two ambitious odes, composed in 1536 to celebrate Charles V's victory over the Turks at Tunis in 1535 and perhaps commissioned by the Emperor himself, attempt to infuse epic fervor into Pindar's epinician design.[81] The first ode incorporates epic material from the *Aeneid* into the ode format. The second is a celebratory ode with a briefer myth, the aim of which is to celebrate Charles V as the conquering hero returning to Naples in victory. Both odes use Pindaric triads (volta, rivolta, stanza), employ Pindaric figures, and develop extended mythic digressions. Minturno's commentary on ancient and modern poetics, *L'Arte Poetica* (Venice, 1563), provides a useful guide to both odes.

If there is a general model for Minturno's first ode, it is Pindar's Pythian 4, which celebrates the founding of the North African kingdom of Cyrene by re-

---

[80] See Salmonius Macrinus, "De fuga Caesaris victoria Francisci Regis ad Aquas Sextias," and "De victoria Francisci Regis apud Aquas Sextias contra Car. Caesarem," in *Hymnorum Libri Sex* (Paris, 1537), 231–33, 233–36. Also see "De Victoria per Franciscum Regem Partainin Belgio," in *Lyricorum Libri Duo* (1531), sig. Cvii^r–Cviii^v. Macrin celebrated Charles V once in an ode to Charles on the defense of Vienna against the Turks (*Hymnorum Libri Sex* [1537], 148–50).

[81] For an overview of these two odes, as well as an account of the life and reputation of Minturno, see Raffaele Calderisi, *Antonio Sebastiano Minturno, Poeta e Trattatista del Cinquecento Dimenticato: Vita e Opere* (Aversa: Tipografia Fratelli Noviello, 1921), 64–67.

counting digressively the fortunes of Jason and his Argonaut comrades. Just as Pindar, celebrating the chariot victory of Arcesilas of Cyrene in 462 B.C., relates Arcesilas to the Argonaut Euphemus, the alleged founder of Cyrene and Arcesilas's ancestor, so Minturno relates Charles to his alleged Trojan forebear, none other than Aeneas.[82] The connection with Aeneas was obviously an important one for Charles V, for he commissioned a set of tapestries for the Alcazar in Seville (originally executed between 1548 and 1554) that in depicting the naval battle at Tunis cast Charles in the role of an Aeneas who brought glory to Hesperia.[83] A key quotation beneath the depiction of the naval battle is drawn from the *Aeneid* and offers praise for "arms and the man."

Minturno's first ode opens with an echo of Pindar's Olympian 2:

> Qual Semideo, anzi qual nouo Dio
> Tra gli huomini mortali,
> Qual supremo ualor, qual Gioue in terra,
> Qual Febo nel sauer, qual Marte in guerra,
> Qual' onor d'immortali
> Virtù, qual uincitor modesto, e pio
> Con ardente disio
> Di cantar lui m'infiamma.
> (Volta 1. 1–8)

---

[82] Pythian 4 focuses on the dynastic links between the present king and the heroes of the Argonauts, who also journeyed after glory and recognition. Its first section dramatizes Medea's prophecy spoken at Thera. Medea instructs Euphemus to found a city near the foundation of Zeus Ammon: he is to receive a marvelous clod of earth, which, when washed overboard, will lead him to the land promised to his descendants. The oracle resembles the kind of obscure prophecy that Odysseus receives in the *Odyssey* or that Aeneas, seeking his fortunes after leaving Troy, receives in the *Aeneid*. Having focused on Euphemus in the first part of the ode, Pindar turns to Jason, the principal hero of the Argonauts, and, beginning once more with oracular prophecy, traces the fortunes of Jason to Colchis and his successful winning of the fleece. Hence Pindar gives us in the ode not only a compliment to the founder of Cyrene, but also to a Hellenic hero who, like Arcesilas, has just been victorious.

[83] See Juan Carlos Hernández Núñez and Alfredo J. Morales, *The Royal Palace of Seville* (London: Scala Publishers, 1999), 74–75. Like Minturno's poem, the tapestries chronicle Charles's triumphant campaign against the Turks and the French, propagate a dynastic myth, and consolidate Charles's reputation as a military leader. As Hernández Núñez and Morales comment, the banderoles and inscriptions play a vital role in the tapestries, with quotations beneath the scenic representations. They depict the main events in the campaign, from the reviewing of the troops to the taking of Tunis and the boarding of the schooner. The set also includes a tapestry showing the map of the Western Mediterranean, the North African coasts, and the Iberian peninsula. The tapestries now in the Alcazar are copies and were commissioned by Philip V in the eighteenth century to replace the originals..

What demi-god or new god
Among mortal men,
What supreme valor, what Jove on earth,
What Phoebus in wisdom, what Mars in war,
What honor of immortal virtue,
What conqueror modest and pious
With ardent desire
Am I enflamed to sing of . . .? [84]

After this "Pindaric" invocation, Minturno turns immediately to developing the digression — the Vergilian myth. Alluding to Juno's ancient wrath, he tells us that it is now directed against the present generation of heroes in Italy. However, it is not Phoenicians or Carthaginians whom Juno employs against the Trojan seed, but the new power from the East, the Turks. Against the Turkish dragon, Charles is the Iberian Aeneas who valiantly resists. Proceeding sometimes with rhetorical questions, sometimes with allusions, and sometimes with direct narration, Minturno retells the story of Aeneas's departure from ancient Troy, pursued by Juno's unrelenting fury. The second triad takes us through the tempest that Neptune raises against the Trojan fleet to the wars in Italy and finally to Turnus's death — a mini-Aeneid. Triad 3 recounts the rise and fall of the Carthaginians and their assault on Rome under Hannibal, while the fourth triad brings us to the rise of the Ottoman dragon and the renewed spite of Juno toward the modern descendants of Anchises who can find no Aeneas to defend them. In the fourth triad, Charles, the rightful heir of the Dardan blood, appears to defend Italy, to sustain its eternal law, and to protect the high Trojan reign, now that Juno has spurred Italy's ancient enemies against new Troy. The final triad describes the battle massed on Neptune's plain. The description of the current storm of battle coordinates with the previous description of the Vergilian tempest referred to in rivolta 2. Swift eagles and fast dolphins bring victory to the new Aeneas. Like Pindar, Minturno telescopes the narrative material, returning to the present after the extended digression. He concludes the ode, as he began it, with praise of Charles, now triumphant over his foreign adversaries and adorned with victorious palms: "Africa è uinta or godi / Europa, e'l Re ne torna / Con palma, e te n'adorna" (175). [85]

Minturno's ode is a serious, if not a completely successful, attempt to reclaim a place and function for Pindaric ode in the Renaissance world. His commentary in *L'Arte Poetica* provides insight into his intentions. Organized as a dialogue be-

---

[84] Antonio Minturno, "À Carlo Quinto Imperadore, Vincitor Dell' Africa," in *Rime et Prose del Sig. Antonio Minturno* (Venice, 1559), 166. At the sea battle Charles V himself commanded the leading vessel, while Andrea Doria led the fleet.

[85] See Hilary Mackie's comments on Pindar's telescoping of epic material in *Graceful Errors: Pindar and the Performance of Praise* (Ann Arbor: University of Michigan Press, 2003), 60–62.

tween Minturno and several other poet-critics, it discusses the techniques Minturno uses to put together the canzone (as he calls it) for Charles V. Remarking on how Pindar developed the myth of Pelops in Olympian 1 in order to forward and support his praise of Hieron's chariot victory, Minturno maintains that he has applied the same principle in his own ode for Charles V. He tells us that Juno's anger against the Trojans provides the motivating force for the Turks' assault against Charles V and in turn justifies Charles's subsequent victory at Tunis. He compares his use of this long digressive section to Pindar's introduction of the Pelops myth in Olympian 1, explaining that as the praise of Hieron is directly related to the deeds of the heroic Pelops, so the praise of Charles V compares with the praise of Aeneas.[86] To support this view, Minturno adds the comments of Bernardino Rota, one of the principals in the dialogue, who provides another perspective on Minturno's digressions, arguing that in a lyric poem digressions are the equivalent of episodes in the heroic poem or scenes in comedy or tragedy, and thereby enrich the whole work and make it more magnificent.

To a significant degree, narrative rather than lyric devices, as Minturno himself acknowledges, dominate in the first ode. However, narrative and lyric are discrete genres, each with its own conventions. In narrative, as Michèle Lowrie has recently argued, the speaking voice steps backward in time from the discourse of the moment, whereas in lyric the speaker is directly involved in the

---

[86] In *L' Arte Poetica* Minturno explains how Pindar provides him with the model for his digression in the first canzone: "Dipartesi talhora dall' impresa materia; ma con digressione à lei conueniente, si come più d'ogni altro fà Pindaro, e specialmente nella prima Canzone: nella quale celebrando la uittoria, la qual' hebbe in Olympia il cauallo del Rè Hierone di Siragosa, discorre à laudar quella festa, & à narrare la fauola di Pelope lungamente." [Departing in such a way from the matter undertaken, but with a digression suitable to it, as Pindar does in like matter, not much otherwise, and especially in the first ode, in which, celebrating the victory which the horse of King Hieron of Syracuse had in Olympia, he discourses from praising that to narrating the fable of Pelops at length]. He continues to explain how he applies Pindar's practice to his own canzone: "Nella qual mi diparto à cercar di lontano le cagioni della impresa di Tunesi, attribuendo tutto all' odio di Giunone uerso i Troiani, e conseguentemente uerso tutti quelli, che da loro discendono; e uado infin' à Troia à trouar l'origine di Carlo Quinto Imperadore." [In which I departed to seek at length the causes for the expedition to Tunisia, attributing all to the hatred of Juno toward the Trojans and consequently toward all those who were descended from them; and I went at last to Troy to discover the origin of Charles the Fifth, the Emperor]. (*L'Arte Poetica del Sig. Antonio Minturno*, Libro Terzo, 177). Also see 183–84 where Minturno continues his explanation in greater detail. In his commentary on poetics, *De Poeta*, Minturno discourses at length on Pindar's poetics, explaining his use of triads and contrasting a monostrophic ode, such as Olympian 14, with the triadic odes. He comments specifically on how Pindar uses the epode and contrasts his odic strategies with those of Horace. Minturno includes a Latin translation of Olympian 1 to illustrate his remarks. See *De Poeta* (Venice, 1559), 393–401.

immediacy of the here and now, often directly addressing the subject or person to whom the lyric is directed. Ancient lyrics such as the odes of Pindar and Horace, Lowrie acknowledges, use narrative to a large degree, since they are governed by the rhetorical techniques of exhortation, prayer, praise, rebuke, and so forth. Certain narrative techniques in lyric poetry respond accordingly to these rhetorical needs and purposes.[87] By narrating Aeneas's exploits and following him from the fall of Troy to his advent to Italy, Minturno can suggest how Charles V has followed a comparable heroic career in building and maintaining his own empire. The narrative serves the lyric in preparing for the lyrical praise of Charles as a conqueror.

Historical precedent plays a part also in Minturno's odes. As a Neapolitan, he looks back at the victory odes that Pontano (a poet whom he much admires) composed for Alfonso of Naples's victory over the Turks. Like his predecessor, he composes a companion ode to his first ode in order to foreground the victory celebrations in Naples. Opening the ode with an apostrophe to Italy as the mother of heroes and the queen of the world, he elaborates on the mythic detail of the previous ode.[88] Minturno characterizes the Africans and the Turks collectively as horrible monsters, "orrendi monstri"(Rivolta 2.9), who oppose the new Ulysses, Charles (Rivolta 1.1). Like their classical prototypes described in Pindar's odes—the giants and Typhon—they are enemies to God and dwell under Ischia and Sicily, fixed in the ice of the abyss.[89] Further, Minturno compares

---

[87] See Lowrie, *Horace's Narrative Odes*, 31–33.

[88] See the opening volta of "À Carlo Quinto Imperadore Trionfante Dell' Africa," in *Rime et Prose*, 176–84. "Alma & antica madre / Di sommi duci, e d'onorato impero, / E del mondo Reina, / Che l'opre alte, e leggiadre / Vsata sì gradire, e'l ualor uero, / Quei, che portar diuina / Gloria, di pellegrina / Terra, a' soprani onori / Alzasti, or questa gloriosa proua, / Questa uittoria noua / Italia bella, quanto, e come onori? / Che trionfando torna / Di Libia, e tutto il bel Ponente adornà / Il uincitore, io parlo / Del Quinto inuitto Carlo" [Volta Prima, 1–15] (176). [Gracious and ancient mother of supreme leaders and of the honored empire, and Queen of the world, who used to welcome high and gracious works and true valor, who of the pilgrim earth have you raised to sovereign honors? For this glorious test, for this new victory, lovely Italy, how much and how do you honor the one who returns triumphant from Libya, and whom all the beautiful West adorns, I mean the invincible Charles the Fifth.]

[89] See Rivolta 2. 1–15. Pindar refers both to Typhon (Pythian 1) and to the other gigantic enemies of Zeus—Porphyrion (Pythian 8), the giants on the plain of Phlegra, whom the gods, together with Heracles, battled (Nemean 1. 67–69; Nemean 7. 90–91; and Isthmian 6. 33–36). Although Minturno could have drawn the giants' warfare from ancient sources, Pindar is particularly instructive. With the giants he represents politically and morally the insurrection within or without Hellenic culture. In Pythian 1 Typhon represents the disruptive Carthaginians, whom Hieron must oppose to institute the rule of law in Sicily. Typhon groaning under Aetna is kept in control by Zeus, lord of the thunderbolt and of the mountain, just as the Carthaginians are controlled by Hieron

FIGURE I.I
Charles V as Hercules leading his enemies in chains, see Francois I, the Pope, and
the Sultan to the left of Charles V. Caroli V Victoriae ex multis.
By kind permission of The British Library.

Charles's assault on Tunis to the assault of Mars and the other gods, together
with Hercules and his children, on the giants. The great hero Hercules becomes
inevitably a stand-in for Charles, as he had been for François I (see Figure 1.1).
The city of Naples was dear to Hercules and Minturno describes how it exulted
when Hercules joined Mars, Phoebus, and Pallas in battle to put down the giants
in Phlegra. So Naples now rejoices in Charles's victory.[90]

The very siren of Naples, Parthenope, whom Pontano, Sannazaro, and the
other Neapolitan poets had made famous in their poetry, is the "muse" of Minturno's ode. A place goddess not unlike those addressed in many of Pindar's
odes, she joins with the chorus and Apollo in the victory celebrations for Charles.
Minturno describes the song, dance, and festivities that ensue upon Charles's
victory as comparable to those that in Greece once attended the triumphant athlete-heroes after victory in the great athletic contests. As these athletes' names

and the Persians by the Greeks. At the time when Pindar was composing Pythian 1 the
Greeks had newly repulsed the Asiatic foe.
[90] In a contemporary engraving, Charles V is pictured between the pillars of Hercules, leading in chains the leaders he had conquered in battle, including François I, the
pope and the sultan. See illustration.

became immortal through Pindar's odes, so Charles's name will be enshrined in Minturno's. The concluding triad of the ode offers thanks and praise to God, who made possible the victory and who saved the women and children from ruin and barbarous sack.[91]

8.

Later Italian poets espouse the techniques of Pindaric encomia that Filelfo, Pontano, Crinito, and Minturno had pioneered. Among them were the Capilupi, their friend Bernardo Tasso, and their associate Giambattista Amalteo (1525–1573).[92] Especially interesting are the odes that Amalteo produced on the occasion of one of the most significant battles of the sixteenth century: the victory at Lepanto in 1571 of a coalition of Italian, Spanish, and Austrian forces over the Turks. Amalteo's set of Latin, Greek, and Italian odes, composed for the occasion, demonstrates just how far the victory ode had come in the one hundred years since Pontano had celebrated the repulse of the Turks at Otranto. To praise the respective leaders from Venice, the Vatican, and Spain, Amalteo shows

---

[91] As he suggests in *L'Arte Poetica*, Minturno looked on the Italian canzone as the vernacular equivalent to Pindaric ode and thus freely espoused its techniques in some of his other odes. Besides the two odes to Charles V, several of Minturno's canzone suggest Pindaric influence. His canzone to God Almighty ("Padre del Ciel") opens with an invocation to God that is both Pindaric and Christian, but develops as a political ode asking Charles V and the Colonna of Rome to defend Italy against the threat of the Turks. Minturno looks at the misery of a Greece enthralled, hoping to inspire Italy's western allies both to liberate the ancient lands and to defend Italy. Expressing apprehension at the progress of oriental armies against the west, Minturno asks God to assist the forces that oppose them, to protect the women and the children, and to give "antique valor" to Great Caesar—Charles V—and to the high Colonna of Rome. Like pindarics before it, the canzone includes a digressive passage, where Minturno imagines the rivers of the east—the Nile and the Euphrates—rising in force against the Rhine and the Tiber. The ode concludes with a prayer for peace. (See *Rime*, 91–99.)

[92] Ippolito Capilupo addresses Latin odes to men of the Church and State that comment on the political situation throughout Italy. The ode to Ercole Gonzaga contemplates affairs in Mantua (26–29); the ode to Cosimo de' Medici (43–44) consoles the prince on the death of his wife and at the same time praises him for his statecraft. Ippolito also addresses odes to Popes Pius IV (34–37) and Julius III (84–86) and to Charles V's son, Philip II of Spain (88). Although not a political poet in the strictest sense, Bernardo Tasso (1493–1569) addressed canzoni to Henri II, king of France (2. 56–62) and to Pope Clement VII (2. 113–18), expressing the kind of anxieties about the Orient, about the power struggle of princes, and about the fortunes of Italy that we have seen in the Pindaric odes of Lampridio, Minturno, and Macrin. See Hippolytus Capilupus in *Capiluporum Carmina* (Rome, 1590); Bernardo Tasso, *Rime* (Vinegia, 1560).

himself the master of Latin, vernacular, and Greek ode and also demonstrates his adeptness at using Pindaric techniques and references. His Latin ode, "De Victoria Naupactaea ad Sebastianum Venerium Ducem Classis Venetae," celebrates the Doge of Venice, Sebastiano Venerio, the leader of the Venetian fleet. He addresses the Doge as a Hercules, who crushed the Turkish Hydra, winning back the eastern empire for Rome.[93] Amalteo's Italian canzone, addressed to the leader of the pope's forces, Marcantonio Colonna, celebrates the victory in a comparable way. Near the place where Hercules won his victory over the river god Acheloos, this modern hero is also victorious. Like the Doge, he is a new Hercules, but he is also a modern Jason, whose destiny it is to command a new Argo and to win a victory comparable to that the Greeks won at Salamis.

> Ma'l Ciel, che a maggior gloria ui destina
> Altra Argo, altri guerrieri, & altre imprese
> Altro mar, u'apparecchia, & altri regni,
> Tosto c'haurà ripreso Salamina. (sig. Aiii^r)

> But Heaven, which destines a great glory for you,
> Another Argo, other warriors, and other enterprises,
> Another sea that appears to you, and other realms,
> So will have brought back [the victory of] Salamis.

Both Amalteo's Latin and Italian verses foresee a glorious future that this victory promises. Greece will be freed from the Turks, and the springs and caves and mountains restored to the Muses. The eastern reaches of the Mediterranean, including the Holy Land, will be liberated, and the Golden Age, often invoked in these victory odes, will revive. Amalteo tells Colonna: as you have conquered the sea, now conquer the land.[94]

Amalteo's Greek ode, triadic in form and Pindaric in concept, is briefer—a single triad only. While it employs elements similar to those of two previous odes, it accomplishes the feat of producing in miniature the essence of the Pindaric ode.[95] Addressed to Don John of Austria, Philip II's natural brother and

---

[93] See Ioannes Baptista Amaltheus, "De Victoria Naupactaea ad Sebastianum Venerium Ducem Classis Venetae," in *Trium Fratrum Amaltheorum, Hieronimi, Io. Baptistae. Cornelii Carmina* (Venice, 1627), 90–94.

[94] *Canzone di M. Giovanbattista Amaltheo. All' Illustr. Et Eccellent. Sig. Marcantonio Colonna. General dell' armata di Santa Chiesa, Sopra la Vittoria seguita contra l'armata Turchesca* (Venice, 1572), sig. Aij ^{r}–Aiij^v.

[95] See Amaltheus, *Carmina*, 149–50. The text is as follows:
Strophe: ΚΤΔΙΜΩΝ Εὔκλεια καλὸν φάος ἄθλων / σὰν ἐς αὐγὰν ἐκ πολέμου δέχεο / Καίσαρος παῖδ᾽ ἀντιθέου. / ὃν δὴ ἀγλαοῖς ἐν ἀγκώνεσσιν ἐνήνοχε νίκα, / Θραξὶ δεινὰς ναυμαχήσανθ᾽ ὑπὲρ / κόλπους Ἐχινάδων ἐπὶ Τρινακρίας
Antistrophe: πιστὸν ὅρμον. πῖνε δὲ νέκταρος εὐώ- /

the leader of the Spanish forces, it too, like the canzone to Colonna, alludes to the Argo, thus referring obliquely to the myth of Pindar's longest ode, Pythian 4. In the strophe Amalteo apostrophizes the naval victory John has just won as the most illustrious of contests. In the antistrophe Amalteo salutes the celebratory occasion and lifts a cup of nectar in John's honor, calling like Pindar on the favor of the Graces. Finally, in the epode Amalteo compares John to Jason, briefly summarizing Jason's voyage to Colchis, his subduing of the sleeping dragon, and his winning of the golden fleece. As the voyage of the far-sailing Argo brought glory to Greece, so, Amalteo suggests, John's victory shines forth to the citizens of Italy. The subduing of the sleeping dragon probably suggests the conquest of the Ottoman Empire, Minturno's eastern dragon. All three of Amalteo's odes demonstrate in different ways how pervasive Pindar's influence had become for sixteenth-century Italian poets ambitious to celebrate military victories.[96] However, although the contribution of Italian poets to the development of the political ode was great, by the time Amalteo composed his victory odes for Lepanto, Ronsard and his successors had already become the leading pindarists of Europe, and it was they, not the Italians, who would pass the Pindaric torch to the English poets of the next age.

δεις γλυκείας ἐκ κύλικος λιβάδας / ἄρτι κιρνωσᾶν χαρίτων. / ἀγλαΐζεται δ᾽ ἀεὶ κῦδος μετὰ κύκλον ἀέθλων / ἠλιοειδὲς , καὶ χρόνον μυρίον / ἀνθεῖ . πόνοι γὰρ εὔχεος ἐντὶ τροφοί.

Epode: ᾤχετο δ᾽ Ιονίας περάων θαλάσσας /

κύματα , καὶ πολὺν ἴθυνε στόλον / ἱερόν. οἷος ἔπλεεν Αἰσονίδας / Κολχίδος χρυσαυγέ᾽ ἐς πόλιν μολῶν , /

ἔνθ᾽ ἀριστεύων θεοστυγεῖ ταχὺν / ἔμβαλε στρατῷ μόρον . /

γηγενέων δὲ θανόντων , ὡς δράκονθ᾽ ὕπνος δάμε, /

χρύσεον εἶθαρ κῶας εἷλε. / κ᾽ αὐτοῦ εὔπλοος φαεινοῖς / ἐν ἄστροις λάμπει Ἀργώ

[96] The Hungarian humanist and poet Johannes Sambucus included a *carmen heroicum* (by Hugo Favolius), addressed to Don John of Austria, in a volume of sixteen emblems that celebrated the coalition of victors from Venice, the Vatican, and the Austro-Hungarian Empire. See "De Classica ad Naupactum contra Turcas Victoria," in *Arcus Aliquot Triumphal. Et Monimenta Victor. Classicae* (Antwerp: Philip Gallaeus, 1572), sig. D.2 r–D.5v.

CHAPTER 2
ROYAL ENCOMIA: RONSARD AND HIS
FOLLOWERS IN FRANCE AND ENGLAND

Inheriting the Pindaric mantle from Alamanni and Macrin, Ronsard assumed
the role of the leading pindarist in France, creating for Henri II and members of
the French court in the 1550s the most formal, most official, most ostentatiously
political of his odes.[1] Although later he himself abandoned formal Pindaric ode,
Ronsard set down the formulas for the French poets who followed him. Pindarics reigned uncontested in the latter part of the sixteenth century in France
as the favorite form for patronage poetry. In it praise was unbridled, and the
kings and the nobles were awarded a stature second only to the Olympian gods
to whom they were often compared. Pindarists in Italy and throughout Europe
were influenced by Ronsard, and it was the Ronsardian pindaric that first came
to England at the end of the sixteenth century.

1.

With supreme poetic tact, Ronsard directs both the opening hymn of his 1555
Hymnes and the opening ode of his 1552 *Odes* to the "Treschrestien Roy de
France Henry II."[2] Although hymn 1 of *Hymnes* is in *vers heroique* (hexameters),

---

[1] For a survey of Pindarism in France before Ronsard, see Girot, *Pindare avant Ronsard*. Girot briefly discusses both Alamanni (300–6) and Macrin (288–300), as well as
the Pindarism of Ronsard's first book of odes and its reception when published in 1550
(350–75).

[2] See *Hymnes de P. de Ronsard* (Paris, 1555); *Quatre Premiers Livres des Odes* (Paris,
1550); *Le Cinqiesme Livre des Odes de P. de Ronsard* (Paris, 1552). The 1552 *Livre* opens
with the ode, "Sur la paix faicte entre luy, & le Roy d'Angleterre l'an 1550." In subsequent editions Ronsard alters the sequence of odes. However, in all editions (except for
1560, where the long pindaric for Michel de L'Hospital has premier position), he carefully begins each book with an ode addressed to Henri II. Further, the odes of each of
the five books are carefully arranged to honor the different members of the court about
the king and to address those who offered special patronage to Ronsard. Hence the ode
to the king is followed by verses to the queen, Madame Marguerite (the king's sister),

rather than in the triads that Ronsard employs for many of the odes, it is as much indebted to Pindar as the triadic odes. Invoking Pindaric Muses, Ronsard adopts an aphorism from Pindar and Theocritus, proclaiming that as all true hymns begin and end with the name of Jupiter, so his hymn begins and ends with the name of Henri, who surpasses in honor all other kings and even the gods (ll. 1–8).[3] Like his classical predecessors, Ronsard remembers that the greatest compliment to a king is to link his name, if possible, with the god's name. Making use also of the Greek commonplace, employed by Pindar in Olympian 1, that kings belong to Jupiter and share in his dignity, he takes the compliment one step higher and places Henri above Jupiter. Over lesser mortals Henri soars like the eagle, Jupiter's bird, which was also the emblem for Pindar, the Theban eagle. Like poets, kings are born, not made.

Hymn 1 is an effusive poem of compliment that owes much to Pindar's and Horace's odes to their royal patrons. Ronsard chooses to compare the king to Pindar's principal heroes, likening Henri in battle to Achilles and Ajax and even remarking, as Pindar had, that just as Achilles and Ajax surpassed their fathers Peleus and Telamon in battle prowess, so Henri surpasses François I (ll. 331–336). Remembering Henri's pride in his horsemanship, Ronsard compares him to the twins Castor and Pollux, remarking that Henri may in fact be a better horseman than the renowned Castor. Ronsard concludes, perhaps tongue in cheek, that the magnificent court that surrounds the French king excels even the realm of the Greek gods. Whereas Jupiter had only one Mars to fight his battles, Henri had many, says Ronsard, naming the king's generals—and he also has just as many sage counselors to guide him.

Whereas Ronsard takes pains in Hymn 1 with mythic allusions and aphorism to emulate Pindar, Theocritus, and Horace, he neither follows the structure of their odes rhetorically nor develops their digressive patterns, as he sometimes does in his Pindaric odes. Hymn 1 moves through a very tightly organized pattern of praise, as Ronsard sets forth a list of Henri's virtues—wisdom, equity, liberality, valor, ambition, grace, piety—and then meticulously illustrates each. His apparent agenda is to demonstrate how Henri fulfills the pattern of the

---

Charles, Cardinal de Lorraine, Odet, Cardinal de Chastillon, Michel de L'Hospital, the son and daughters of the king, dukes, clergy, and other members of the nobility. Ronsard widens the number of associates that he includes in the hymnic praise of the king, including his sister, his wife, the dauphin, prominent members of the court, as well as the ministers—Lorraine, Montmorency, Chastillon. The odes range from serious political addresses that concern the state of the nation to mere compliment.

[3] Both Pindar's Nemean 2 and Theocritus's Ode 16 to Ptolemy Philadelphus are possible models. In Nemean 2 Pindar says that the Homeridae, the oldest and most respected of bards, always begin their songs with Zeus. Theocritus advises that one should begin and end an ode with the name of Zeus. In Olympian 2 Pindar indirectly links Theron with Zeus and Heracles as he names all three in the exordium.

warrior king, for we are regaled with a list of Henri's military victories, with a careful suppression of Henri's defeats or less than successful campaigns. Ronsard's purpose in showcasing the king's military accomplishments seems propagandistic, for in 1555 the king was about to embark on further campaigns. Therefore Ronsard even makes his king comparable to Julius Caesar and Octavian in their far-flung conquests in Europe and Asia. However, although some of Henri's wars had been popular, others were not. His challenge of the English to obey the terms of the treaty and surrender Boulogne was a popular cause, and the peace with the English that ensued Ronsard lauds in the first of his odes (1552). In contrast, Henri's forays into Italy and his continuing provocation of Charles V (which Ronsard defends) were less popular political policies. These wars depleted the treasury and brought French towns under Spanish siege. However, by selectively listing the king's battles and lauding his personal heroism, Ronsard creates in the hymn a patriotic aura that would have pleased his "warrior" king.[4]

We cannot overlook, however, Ronsard's own self-promotion, for he clearly wanted support for his projected *Franciade*. He sets himself as Apollo, Jupiter's son and the poet-musician, next to Henri-Jupiter, remarking that the king of the gods liked nothing better than to hear himself celebrated by Apollo's lyre, especially after he had triumphed over the giants who opposed him (ll. 19–21). If Ronsard has taken care to compliment the counselors who surrounded the king (see ll. 423–466), it is the poets for whom he reserves special praise, those multiple Apollos who share the stage with him—particularly Du Bellay, Jodelle, Baïf, Pelletier, Belleau, and Tiard. Though Henri II's reign began in 1547 with optimism, he was not a second François I in his support of the arts. Therefore Ronsard must remind the king that whereas his earthly conquests may secure him a temporal renown, only the poets will assure him glory after death: "ce renom ne peut / Venir après la mort, si la Muse ne veut / Le donner à celluy qui doucement l'inuite, / Et d'honneste faueur compense son merite" (ll. 733–736) (This renown cannot come after death, unless the Muse wishes to grant it to one who sweetly invites her and with honest favor recompenses his merit).[5] Curiously, Ronsard makes only a passing reference to Francus, Henri's putative ancestor and the intended hero of the *Franciade*, who figured so largely in his earlier ode to Henri. It

---

[4] See Philip Ford, *Ronsard's Hymnes: A Literary and Iconographical Study*, MRTS 157 (Tempe, AZ: ACMRS, 1997), 131–32. Ford proposes a different account of Ronsard's intentions in this hymn. Defending Ronsard against the usual charges of sycophancy, Ford argues that Ronsard's plan in the *Hymnes* is to contrast the king, the earthly Hercules of the first hymn, with Christ, the "Hercule Crestien" of the final hymn. Although God's anointed on earth, the king has brought on the chaos of war that he cannot cure. Only the divine Messiah can bring peace.

[5] Ronsard continued to revise the hymns after their first publication in *Les Hymnes de P. de Ronsard* (Paris, 1555), in which the Hymn to Henri II holds premier position. See Ronsard, *Hymnes*, ed. Albert Py (Geneva: Librairie Droz, 1978), 9–50.

is the warrior Henri that he congratulates on supporting the Protestant princes
who opposed Charles V. Accordingly the laurels that he lays at the king's feet in
the final verse paragraph are those of military victory: may the great goddess Victoire protect the king, he prays, and favor France with the trophies of Peace.

The survey of Henri's military and political problems both in hymn 1 and
in the odes Ronsard directed to Henri is cautious and restrained. Henri had
begun hoping to recover the lands his father had lost, but the very policies he
pursued, on which Ronsard congratulates him, led to a retrenchment and to the
loss of François' military gains, resulting shortly before Henri's untimely death
in the humiliating peace of 1559 with the Spanish. However, the ode Ronsard
composed to celebrate the peace of 1550 celebrates that peace in a way that the
saber-rattling hymn of 1555 does not, for it is Paix herself, and not Victoire, that
Ronsard invokes. True, as in the hymn, Ronsard begins with praises of the king's
exercise of reason, his precocious virtue, his battle courage. However, Ronsard
chooses the myths of the ode 1.1 (1552) to argue peace and not war. In the first,
the allegorical goddess Peace, a semi-Christian, semi-classical deity (whom Pindar had also invoked in several of his odes) institutes a debate with Chaos at the
beginning of things, proposing to bring order and light out of darkness and disorder. Ronsard salutes the goddess Peace almost as though she were his Muse:
"Ie te salue, heureuse paix, / Ie te salue, et resalue; / Toy seule Déesse tu fais
/ Que la vie soit mieux voulue" (antistr. 7. 7–10). At the same time, however,
Fortune is also present in the ode, a more ambiguous deity who either favors or
strikes down. Ronsard casts a cautious glance at the myth of Oedipus, depicting
Oedipus, as Pindar had in Olympian 2, as one not exempt from the reversals of
Fortune. On this occasion, however, Fortune smiles on Henri, who is now at the
summit of his power and whose star shines more brilliantly than ever. May he
never change good fortune for bad, Ronsard declares.

Congratulatory though Ronsard's ode may be, it is also, like his hymn, not
without self-interest. Ronsard reminds Henri that poets can confer immortality
on kings, adding a "Pindaric" plea for generosity on Henri's part. Generosity,
he observes, is the highest of kingly virtues, one liberally practiced by his father
François, who loved verse and rewarded the poets of his court. To reinforce this
point Ronsard alludes to the dynastic epic, the *Franciade*, which he was already
contemplating as a poem in Henri's honor. Tactfully, he introduces as the second myth of the ode a narrative of the exploits of Francus, Henri's alleged ancestor and the hero of this epic. As Minturno had made Aeneas the stand-in for
Charles V, Ronsard employs the legendary Francus in a similar way for Henri.
He links the fall of Troy with the founding of France, remarking that the destruction of Troy ironically guaranteed the survival of the Trojan race by dispers-
ing the remnant of its heroes to establish other cities. Francus was one such hero.
Ronsard tells how Cassandra predicted that Francus would found another Troy,
building a great city on the banks of the Seine and naming it in honor of his
fallen brother Paris. The long heroic passage that records the Trojan priestess's

prediction resembles perforce Medea's speech in Pythian 4 and fulfills a similar function by conferring honor on Henri and France as Pindar in Pythian 4 had conferred honor on Arcesilas and Cyrene. Ronsard concludes the ode by expressing the hope that as God has vouchsafed peace with England, he will grant Henri victory over Spain, promising to celebrate that victory with another ode. Neither the victory nor the ode was to be forthcoming.

Ronsard composed not one but two odes on the peace of 1550, the second ode appearing immediately after the first in the 1552 collection, but reserved in later editions as a final odic salute to the king: "Sur ses ordonnances faites l'an 1550." Although composed in strophes rather than triads, it is a full-scale "political" pindaric. Ronsard congratulates Henri on the success of his ordinances and the control he exercises over the neighboring English, Germans, and Spanish and compares him to the mythic Hercules. Ronsard's use of Hercules as a figure for Henri is unusual, for unlike his father François or his adversary Charles V, Henri was rarely compared to Hercules.[6] Ronsard has a particular point to make with the comparison, for it is not the strongman Hercules he alludes to, but the Pindaric hero, who displayed proper respect for the temple of God and was ready to offer sacrifices at his father's altar. Ronsard's Hercules, like Pindar's, is a purger of vices. Ronsard tells the king that his subjects celebrate him for this Herculean virtue: "O grand Prince, tes grand's pollices / Et les grandz faictz que tu conçois, / Te feront nommer des François / L'Hercule qui purge les vices!" (87–90) (O Prince, the holy policies and the great deeds that you conceive make you named among the French a Hercules who purges vices). What Ronsard is alluding to as Herculean piety, however, is hardly the equivalent of a Pindaric reverence for the gods. Ronsard is cloaking propaganda in classical dress. Henri was enforcing as "religious piety" strict policies against the Huguenots, and Ronsard by praising his Herculean piety was urging approval of these sanctions. It is not the last time we will find Pindar commandeered to justify sixteenth-century religious persecution.

Although Ronsard's other odes for Henri are replete with compliment and abundant Pindaric flourish, they are sparing of political commentary. Presenting himself as a Pindar to Henri's Hieron, Ronsard seems merely intent on advancing his own position as court poet. These odes are interesting, however, as some of the earliest of Ronsard's Pindaric experiments, and demonstrate his deliberate effort to adopt some of Pindar's poetic signatures.[7] For example, in 1.2, he adapts the Pindaric figure of the proffered cup from Olympian 7 and plays with

---

[6] See Marc-René Jung, *Hercule dans la Littérature Française du XVIᵉ siècle* (Geneva: Librairie Droz, 1966), 164. Also see the survey of kings from François I to Henri IV (159–85).

[7] For a chronology of Ronsard's odes see the Introduction, Tableau Chronologique, and notes on the different odes in *Les Odes de Ronsard*, ed. Charles Guérin (Paris: Edition du Cèdre, 1952). Unless otherwise indicated, Ronsard's odes are cited from this edition.

the idea that the different liquids—wine, dew, nectar—dispense different kinds of Theban or Doric grace.[8] To compliment the king, he echoes, moreover, the Pindaric aphorism that the heavens look on nothing greater than kings, joining, as he does in Hymn 1, the king's name with Jupiter's.[9] Ronsard's next two odes to Henri also begin with Pindaric figures. In ode 2.1 Ronsard modifies Pindar's architectural simile from Olympian 6 to compliment his own architecturally-built rhyme: "Je te veux bâtir une ode, / La maçonnant à la mode / De tes palais honorés" (I wish to build you an ode fit to the mode to honor your palace) (2.1.1–3). In Pindar's original ode poetry surpasses by implication all marble monuments or golden pilasters—not so in Ronsard's flattering lines. Palace and ode stand side by side, both enshrining the king's virtues. In ode 3.1 Ronsard proposes to emulate the steersman-poet and, like Pindar, to guide the bark of his verse into port, that is, if the king will favor him. Royal favor will ensure that he escape the dangerous rocks of antiquity—Scylla, Charybdis, the Symplegades. Once more Ronsard is pleading for royal patronage. By likening the king to the Trojan Francus and by comparing Henri's defiance of the German princes to Augustus's masterful empire building, he is equating Henri with the greatest of Rome's emperors. He is also tacitly proposing himself as the new Vergil who will preserve Henri's name from the eternal night of oblivion.[10]

Although Ronsard is quick to imitate Pindar's courtship of his royal patrons, he is hesitant to apply the strict limits Pindar imposed on flattery. Assuredly, Pindar placed kings at the top of the social order, to rule on earth as Jupiter in the heavens, but he does not make even the grandest of Sicilian tyrants the equivalent of the god. Far from it. He reminds the Sicilian tyrants that however high they soar, they must take care not to risk the fall that Tantalus, Ixion, or Bellerophon brought on themselves—myths that intrude into Pindar's odes to urge proper caution for even the most favored of kings. Kings must not trespass beyond the bronze threshold of Olympus nor tempt the gods. There is no need, however, for Ronsard to caution Henri. The "Treschrestien Roi" is God's anointed on earth.

---

[8] See Ode 1.2.1–2: "Comme un qui prend une coupe, / Seul honneur de son trésor" (As one who takes up a cup, the chief honor of his treasure). For a discussion of Ronsard's Pindaric borrowings, see Isidore Silver, *The Pindaric Odes of Ronsard* (Paris, 1937); idem, *Ronsard and the Grecian Lyre*, in Silver, *Ronsard and the Hellenic Renaissance in France* (Geneva: Librairie Droz, 1981–1987), 2: 1–3.

[9] See 1.2. strophe 2, 1–4: "De Jupiter les antiques / Leurs escrits embellissaient; / Par luy leurs chants poétiques / Commençaient et finessaient" (With Jupiter the ancients embellish their writing, for they commence and end their poetic songs with him).

[10] The fourth ode to the king (Ode 4.4) is only a brief strophic ode that offers compliments to Montmorency and the Duke of Guise as twin Achilles and to the Cardinal Lorraine as the defender of the Muses in France.

Often we feel that Ronsard, like Salmon Macrin, has merely ransacked Pindar's odes as quarries for decorative devices rather than studied them as structural or intellectual models. Like his predecessor, Ronsard is fond of appropriating Pindar's opening figures. He too imitates the opening aphorism from Nemean 4: "Le médicin de la peine / Est le plaisir" (1.13.1–2) (The physician for pain is Pleasure) without paying attention to the way that Pindar has coordinated the theme and structure of this ode with its dazzling opening.

Yet when he is freed from the necessity to offer effusive compliments to royalty, Ronsard demonstrates that he can do more than merely choose "bons mots" from Pindar. In the ode to the Seigneur de Carnavalet, Henri II's Master of the Horse (1.7), for example, he carefully coordinates figure and myth with theme. His opening lines echo Olympian 13, the ode that recounts Bellerophon's successful bridling of Pegasus. Like Pindar in Olympian 13, Ronsard is honoring an obligation with his ode to Carnavalet. Ronsard had been Carnavalet's pupil, and the ode thanks him for his teaching in the arts of horsemanship and of life. Ronsard takes pains to coordinate details about Carnavalet and his family with the myth of Bellerophon's taming of Pegasus. He uses the myth both to refer to Carnavalet's successful career as Master of the Horse and to his own poetic education. The two become inseparable: "Ou ta main qui sait l'adresse / D'acheminer la jeunesse / Par tes vertus à bon train? / Ou ton art qui admoneste / L'esprit de la fière beste / Se render docile au frein" (Epode 1. 7–12) (Whether your hand which knew how to lead youth by your virtues in good train or your art which admonished the spirit of the proud beast to render it docile to the harness). Carnavalet understood how to tame the fierce spirit both of his youthful pupil and of the horse. As Ronsard narrates the account of the bridling of Pegasus, it becomes clear that Carnavalet has assumed the role of Pallas, guiding Ronsard-Bellerophon in the knowledge of horsemanship and so ensuring his success. With his Pindaric Pegasus successfully bridled, Ronsard the poet can safely mount to heaven. Like Pindar, Ronsard passes over the more threatening aspects of the myth — Bellerophon's fall and death. He concludes, in his own typical fashion, with the praise of the lute. The poet has learned the secrets of the Muses and will use such art to render praise to his friend and mentor. Ronsard's ode for Carnavalet, while echoing Pindar's original, has a Gallic charm and grace of its own and manifests the light touch that is often the winning signature of Ronsard's best poetry.

2.

The political pindarics that followed in France in the next sixty years demonstrated the profound effect of the odes and hymns Ronsard composed for Henri II. The first encomia were written by members of the circle of poets closest to Ronsard: Olivier de Magny, Joachim Du Bellay, and the young poet Jacques Tahureau, who published his first collection of poetry in 1554. They follow closely both Ronsard's politics and his poetics. Although Tahureau imitates the triadic structure of Ronsard's odes, he declines to mount lengthy mythological digressions, either a gigantomachia or a song of Carthage or of Troy. Instead, he organizes his triadic ode, "Au Roy," about an elaboration of the king's virtues and accomplishments and takes pains to compare Henri to his alleged ancestor, Hercules.[11] Like Ronsard, Tahureau also lauds the king's Herculean piety; Henri has taken on holy arms, and like his great forebear, justly punishes impious vice—yet another reference to Henri's rigorous program against the Huguenots. The king is not only a second Hercules, but also the new Caesar. Alluding indirectly to Horace's odes on Caesar's conquests in Germany, Tahureau likens Henri's own military feats to Caesar's. Tahureau leaves off praising Henri only to render the ultimate compliment to his mentor, Ronsard, who, he asserts, will complete the king's praise in a proper *Iliad*—the promised *Franciade*. In another ode, "Contre quelques uns qui le blâmoyent de suyure la Poësie," Tahureau defends his espousal of Ronsardian poetics, mounting a passionate defense of the poets who imitate classical poets such as Horace, Vergil, and Pindar in order to praise France's worthies. Pindar lives ("Pindare vit"), he asserts, and thereby validates the art of poetry (sig. Dviij[r]). Who would have sung of Achilles, if Homer had not? Who would have admired Ulysses, if he had not been honored by the Greek? Like Ronsard, Tahureau is arguing for poetry as a "divine" art; but he also follows his mentor in urging the king and other recipients of poetic praise to support poetry as a "royal" art.[12]

---

[11] Jacques Tahureau, *Les Premieres Poësies* (Poitiers, 1554), sig. Aiiij[r]–Avii[v]. Tahureau died only a year after publishing his *Premières Poësies*. There is a certain amount of self-reference in "Au Roy," since Tahureau is quite conscious of his boldness in imitating Ronsard's pindarics. His opening figure depicts the terror of a storm at sea in order to suggest the distress the young poet feels in attempting to advance his little Pindaric bark of praise. He compares himself to a Prometheus, an Icarus in daring, even a Gallic Homer in his desire to honor the king. For Tahureau's association with Ronsard, see Marcel Raymond, *L'Influence de Ronsard sur la Poésie Française (1550–1585)* (Geneva: Librairie Droz, 1965), 196–216.

[12] Tahureau, *Les Premieres Poësies*, sig. Dviij[r]–Eij[r]. We later find similar sentiments espressed in another admirer of Ronsard who also died young, Jean-Édouard Du Monin (1569?-1586). Du Monin appeals to Henri III on similar grounds, arguing that poets are the oracles of the gods. See "Remonstrance, au Tres-Chretien Henri . III Roi de France

Like Tahureau, Olivier Magny imitates Ronsard's classicism, making brief classical allusions in his odes to the king and other noblemen and drawing on digressive myths from Homer, Ovid, or Vergil to provide poetical decoration, to render flattering compliment, and to further some discreet political observations. For Jean de Bourbon, Comte d'Anghiem, a warrior who was to fall in Henri's wars, he summons Pindaric Muses, comparing the count to Homeric types: he is both valiant as Hector and wise as Nestor as well as incorruptible as Achilles when he refuses Agamemnon's gold. Magny opens the ode for Cardinal Alessandro Farnese, the grandson of Pope Paul III, by alluding to this same Greek gold offered to Achilles, gold the wealthy cardinal would also refuse. Farnese was a man deeply involved in negotiations between Charles V and the French king, but to his political role Magny makes only passing reference, preferring to compliment the Cardinal on his wisdom and love of books.[13] Magny's patron was Jean D'Avanson, advisor to the king and president of the privy council, to whom he addresses the opening poem of his book, several other odes, as well as the long allegorical pindaric, "Ode de la Justice."[14] Composed probably just at the point when Henri was about to renew wars with Spain, the "Ode de la Justice" predicts the restoration of the golden age. In its extended myth Jupiter accedes to the pleas of Astraea and appoints the king and D'Avanson as his deputies to restore equity throughout France.[15] Magny's only real victory ode is a brief poem (without classical decoration or reference) in which he gloats over England's loss of Calais to France (*Les Odes*, fols. 92^v–96^r).

---

et De Pologne: Auquel l'Auteur prouue, que les Poëtes sont priuilegés touchant l'email & habits de soie communement defendus," in Du Monin, *Les Estoiles du Ciel* (Paris, 1583) printed with *L'Uranologie* (Paris, 1583). Du Monin cites the familiar example of Alexander and notes that Vergil has immortalized Augustus, as Du Monin would presumably Henri (fol. 203^{r-v}). In the letter to the reader that follows Du Monin expresses admiration for Ronsard ("seul imitable & seul inimitable" [alone imitable and inimitable]), Dorat, and Du Bartas (whose creation poem he translated into Latin), as well as the Scottish neo-Latinist George Buchanan ("Au bien veuilhant Lecteur," fols. 203^v–208^v).

[13] See *Les Odes d'Olivier de Magny* (Paris, 1559), fols. 7^v–11^r (Bourbon), fols. 15^v–17^v (Farnese). Magny's ode to Anthoine Fumée, the "grand Rapporteur de France" (fols. 52^v–65^v), exploits the Pindaric trope of the ode paying a debt; its extended account of Perseus's adventures, probably lifted from odes such as Pythian 12, serves no other apparent aim but to mark that France, like Greece, has had her great nationalistic heroes, born metaphorically of golden showers. For Magny's association with Ronsard, see Raymond, *L'Influence de Ronsard*, 217–38.

[14] D'Avanson was closely associated with Magny's patron, Hugues Salel. Salel had begun a translation of the *Iliad*, passages of which Magny cites in the poem to D'Avanson that praises Salel's country retreat. See "L'Ombre de Salel, A Monsieur D'Auanon," fols. 29^r–31^v.

[15] See Magny, *Les Odes*, fols. 38^r–47^r. See the discussion of this ode in Revard, *Pindar and the Renaissance Hymn-Ode*, 193–94.

Du Bellay celebrates the same victory that Ronsard had in his *Hymne au Roy Sur la Prise de Calais* (Paris, 1559), adopting a heroic tone similar to that of Ronsard's Hymne to Henri, but without its Pindaric flourish. However, the ode, printed the following year, *Lovange de la France et du Roy Treschrestien Henry II*, is more Pindaric. Du Bellay summons the Graces to predict that Henri will restore the golden age. Depicting the king as Jupiter himself, Du Bellay makes clear it will require Jupiter's thunder and lightning—the fury of Henri's combats—to put down those insolent giants who oppose him. But these enemies will be defeated, as well as Typhoeus, whose fall will affright the world. Moreover, at the finish of these battles, peace will reign and provinces and peoples will be brought together under this "grand Iuppiter des Princes" (fol. 4ʳ).[16] The predicted peace of 1559, which was to be presided over by Henri-Jupiter and his sister Marguerite, the new Minerva, came only at the price of unfavorable terms for France. Further, by the time Du Bellay's ode was published posthumously in 1660, both he and the king were dead.

The nature of the pindaric changed in the 1570s and 1580s when Henri's princely sons, Charles IX and Henri III, came of age. The poets who celebrate them both follow the tradition of pindaric that Ronsard had established and also attempt to deal in their odes with the changing political situation of the religious wars in France. The elder prince, Charles IX, was no warrior, but a prince of some literary taste, who had been educated by Ronsard and who, like his grandfather François I, generously patronized poetry and the arts. Henri III, who succeeded his brother in 1574, had made his reputation as a warrior prince with victories over the Huguenots at Jarnac and Montcontour in 1569. As king, however, facing the growing power of the Guises and the formation of the Catholic Ligue, he tried to make peace between Protestants and Catholics. Against a background of civil war and growing religious discord, the kind of extravagance that marked Ronsard's pindarics often rang hollow. Amadis Jamyn (1530–1585) and Isaac Habert (1560?–1615), both followers of Ronsard and excellent Hellenists, took up the Pindaric challenge, dedicating their books of poetry in 1575 and 1585, respectively, to Henri III.[17]

---

[16] See Ioachim Du Bellay, *Lovange de la France et du Roy Treschrestien Henry II* (Paris, 1560), fols. 2ʳ–5ᵛ. Du Bellay follows this poem of compliment with an appeal to the king to reward generously those writers who guarantee him immortal reputation ("Discours au Roy sur la Poësie," fols. 6ʳ–8ʳ). For the relationship of Ronsard and Du Bellay, see Raymond, *L'Influence de Ronsard*, 97–131.

[17] Amadis Jamyn had been Ronsard's page and had been instructed in Greek by Dorat and Turnèbe. He thought of himself as primarily a Hellenist, having completed the translation of the *Iliad* begun by Hugues Salel. He was secretary to Charles IX. Isaac Habert, also an admirer of Ronsard, was secretary to the Duc of Nevers. They both imitated Ronsard's poetics of inspiration with its heavy mythological machinery and

The odes that Jamyn addressed to Henri III on his return from Poland to assume the throne of France differ markedly from the first complimentary odes he addressed to his brother Charles IX and even from those victory odes he addressed to Prince Henri after his military successes at Jarnac and Montcontour. In these victory odes, Jamyn enrolls the sixteen-year-old Henri among the men of Mars, worthy to bear the name of Alexander (which indeed had been his baptismal name).[18] When Jamyn alludes in his odes to Henri's conquest of the Titans or giants, he is referring not to foreign foes, but to the king's adversaries in the civil wars. Although not altogether eschewing the military comparisons that proliferate in the odes to Henri, Jamyn's first odes to Charles IX are effusively complimentary in the style of the early Ronsard. He invokes both the king and Ronsard in his complimentary pindaric on Ronsard's laurel tree, predicting that Charles will crown the poet with this very laurel when Ronsard completes the much promised *Franciade* as the ultimate compliment to the kings of France (fols. 237^V–240^r). Jamyn's philosophical "Ode des Estoiles" also concludes with a compliment to the king, as Jamyn exhorts the stars to maintain Charles IX's glory and majesty and guide his destiny (fol. 51^r). The pindaric that follows ("Au Roy") is even more extravagant, opening with a declaration of transport at the prospect of singing the king's praises: "Une fureur me transporte / A chanter le plus grand Roy" (fol. 51^V), a declaration similar to that Habert later makes in the opening of his ode to Henri III. For Jamyn Charles is a Pindaric sun, who outshines even the brightest of stars, worthy to be a new deity in the sky—"Rien plus digne en cette terre / D'estre en Ciel un nouueau Dieu" (fol. 52^V). Jamyn introduces still another Pindaric flourish when he asks the Muses, as Pindar sometimes asked similar deities, to take a report to the deceased king François I that his grandson follows him in virtue, loves justice, corrects vice, and listens to the complaints of his subjects.[19] The compliment is double-edged, for in summoning up the example of François I and his era, Jamyn unavoidably contrasts it with the present. In urging the king to be, like Jupiter, the administrator of justice, Jamyn

---

reference. They proclaimed themselves "inspired" by Apollo to sing the king's praises. Both include Pindaric echoes in triadic and non-triadic odes.

[18] Amadis Jamyn, *Les Oeuvres Poétiques d'Amadis Jamyn* (Paris, 1575). See "Ode, Sur la bataille de Iarnac," fols. 26^r–27^r, and the ode following that celebrates Prince Henri's victory at Montcontour, fols. 27^r–28^V. (Ronsard's "Chant triomphal" also celebrates Prince Henri's victory at Montcontour.) Jamyn's hymn to Henri III, "Comparaison du Roy Henry troisieme & d'Alexandre le Grand" (fols. 38^V-42^r), extends the comparison between Henri and Alexander the Great. (After her husband's death Catherine had changed her son's name from Alexandre Edouard to Henri.) Jamyn concludes the hymn by congratulating Henri III on the crushing the mutiny at La Rochelle in 1573, likening him to a Jupiter who punished the giants on the field of Phlegra, to an Apollo slaying Python, and to Hercules killing Cacus.

[19] See, for example, the conclusion of Olympian 14 when Echo bears the news of the young athlete's success to his father in Hades.

lets us know (without offering anything but compliment) that Charles's adminis-
tration of justice leaves much to be desired.

Pindar was newly on the scene for many French aristocrats, for Nicolas Lesueur (Sudorius) had already begun to translate the odes into Latin, specially
recommending Pindar as an example for young men in the courts of Charles
and later his brother Henri.[20] In depicting Charles and his brother Henri as sun
kings, Jamyn and Habert echo Pindar's praise of the kingly state in Olympian
1. In one ode Jamyn proclaims that kings by function rule the earth, gathering
about them as courtiers an assembly of "gods" ("Ode," fols. 55ᵛ–57ʳ).[21] Another
pindaric to Charles IX opens with a direct recollection of Olympian 1: "Nos yeux
ne pourroyent contempler / Par le vuide espace de l'air, / Un Astre en ses rayons
plus beau / Que du grand Soleil le flambeau / Traisnant les iours en sa carriere"
(fols. 62ᵛ). Habert in his pindaric for Henri III also draws out the sun-metaphor
from Olympian 1, portraying Henri on his return from Poland as a splendid sun,
who as the sole sun of our age also wields the force of iron with his lance.[22]

Yet despite many similarities, the effect of Jamyn's Pindaric borrowings is
different from Habert's. Jamyn summons the sun king back from Poland less to
wield his military force than to cure the ills of France ("Au Roy, Sur son retour
de Pologne," fols.1ʳ–3ᵛ). Phoebus, says Jamyn, has refused to dispense his light

---

[20] See the discussion of Nicholas Sudor (Nicolas Lesueur) in Revard, *Pindar and
the Renaissance Hymn-Ode*, 28–29. Sudor's translations were first published in 1575 and
1576 (Olympians and Pythians), the complete odes in 1582. Pindar's odes were also available in Greek with facing Latin translations by Henri Estienne in editions published in
the 1560s. Scévole de Sainte-Marthe addresses an ode to Nicolas Lesueur. See Scaevola
Sammarthanus, *Poemata et Elogia* (Argustoriti Pictonum, 1606), 156–58.

[21] Jamyn makes a serious attempt in this ode to Charles IX to heroicize the young
king, comparing him to a young Hercules, renowned for virtue and the conquest of monsters, an Achilles in arms, a Ulysses in wisdom. Imitating Ronsard's compliments to
Henri II, he says in an ode addressed to Charles IX that the Cyclopes forge his aegis and
arms (fols. 55ᵛ–57ʳ). Before his accession to the throne, Charles's brother Henri had ac-
quired a reputation as a warrior. Thus Jamyn makes him a second Alexander in one hymn,
in another God's warrior for the people—a David, a Moses. Just as Jupiter relied on the
services of Vulcan, the smith of the gods, Henri commands a hundred Vulcans in France
to make his arms.

[22] See Isaac Habert, "Au Roy," in Habert, *Les Trois Livres de Meteores avecque autres
oeuures poëtiques, Seconde Partie* (Paris, 1585): "Comme le Soleil surmonte / Les Astres
de sa beauté, / Comme sa clarté fait honte / A leur plus viue clarté, / Ainsi d'un grand
aduantage, / O seul Soleil de nostre aage, / Tu luis sur les plus parfaicts, / Aussi ô grand
Roy de France / Les Dieus du fer de ta lance / Au Ciel ont graués tes faits" (fol. 3ᵛ). (As
the sun surpasses the stars in its beauty, as its brilliance shames their brightest brilliance,
thus to great advantage, O sole sun of our age, you shine on the most accomplished
things, also, O great king of France, the gods of iron on your lance have engraven your
deeds to the sky.)

in France during Henri's absence in Poland. Like Ulysses, he adds, the king has been hidden, captive to a Calypso who has denied him to his native land. Now he shines forth again with fresh promise. When he exhorts Henri to bind his brows with fresh green laurel, he is advising the king to enter a new era, one dominated not by war, but by peace. Let Venus flatter Mars and purge France of cruel war; let Minerva with her olive-branches displace Bellona. May the doors of the temple of Janus be closed, and may Phoebus, when he shines once more, see war quite extinguished. Other odes to Henri also offer compliment and advice with even hands. In the ode "Au Roy: De la Liberalité" Jamyn recalls the flourishing of the Muses under François I, adding that if Henri is as valiant as his warrior father Henri, may he also be as liberal as his grandfather. In the end Jamyn does not summon the war gods, but advises Henri to call back Bacchus and Pan (fols. 6^V–9^r). Though he still likens Henri to Alexander, he advises Henri to balance military exploits with prayer and concludes the ode with a prayer for peace ("Au Roy," fols. 11^V–14^r). Jamyn had learned that poetry could serve other purposes than merely to flatter the king and urge military exploits.[23]

Although published in 1585 at the height of the civil wars, Isaac Habert's collection of verse is more cautious than Jamyn's. It is true that Habert alludes, as his contemporaries had, to the troublesome myth of the gods' warfare with the giants, but he avoids direct controversy. His single triadic ode for Henri III—"Au Roy"—imitates the pindarics that Ronsard had composed for Henri II. For him the praise of the king supersedes all other subjects—the creation of Air, Water, and Earth, the quelling of the giants by Jove, the enumeration of the virtues of Hercules or Achilles. In singing of the king he soars like the pine over the flower.[24] Following Ronsard, Habert sums up the king's virtues with mythological comparisons: the king surpasses Pallas in prudence, Mars in war, Mercury in eloquence, and Ulysses in fortune and equals Jupiter in encompassing all virtues (fol. 4^r). Achilles is invoked to inspire Henri's martial prowess, Hercules to inspire his piety. Yet at the same time an aside in antistrophe 6 might lead us to suspect that all was not well. The poet calls upon Nestor, the Homeric counselor, to wish the king long life, sound body and mind, and subjects always obedient, gentle, and courteous, submissive to the king's laws. The summoning of this Homeric peacemaker lets us know that one still greater than Nestor was required to settle the quarrels between France's warring aristocrats.

Contemporary with Jamyn and Habert was the poet Clovis Hesteau, Sieur de Nuysement (1555?–16?), whose odes to the king and to his brother the Duc

---

[23] Jamyn's ode to Monsieur (François, Duc d' Alençon [1554–1584]) also urges peaceful pursuits, for Jamyn depicts Hercules as a defender of the Muses (fols. 16^V–18^V).

[24] See Isaac Habert, "Au Roy," in *Les Trois Livres de Meteores avecque autres oeuures poëtiques, Seconde Partie*, fols. 2^r–5^r. The opening of the ode owes much to Ronsard's pindarics. Habert summons Apollo and the Muses. His lute is ready to celebrate the king; he burns to pluck the poetic laurel and is filled with Apollonian "fureur."

d'Alençon reveal far more about the political situation in France at the time. Hesteau served as a royal secretary to Henri III, but his true patron was the politically ambitious François, Duc d'Alençon (or Monsieur, as he was called), who on Henri's accession to the throne headed a group called the "Malcontents" or "Politiques." Hesteau dedicated his *Oeuvres Poétiques* (1578) to Monsieur, whose military victories over the Protestants built him a reputation for soldiership that his brother Henri III had once possessed. In the late 1570s Henri III found himself challenged both by this youngest brother's growing popularity and by La Ligue, the Catholic coalition, formed in 1576 and headed by the Guise. After the "Paix de Monsieur" of 1576 at Beaulieu, which resulted in limited religious toleration for the Huguenots and gave Monsieur the duchy of Anjou, the Catholics of La Ligue felt increasingly threatened by the Protestants under Henri de Navarre. D'Alençon himself sought a *rapprochement* between Catholic and Protestant interests and a healing of the wounds of the Saint Bartholomew's massacre, and, but for his premature death in 1584, he might have been a force against the growing power of the Guise. He led the king's armies in 1577 when the sixth war of religion commenced, and it is against this background that Hesteau's "Hymne à la Fortune," his "Ode Pindarique, A Monsieur, sur ses victoires," and his "Hymne au Roy sur la Paix" were composed.[25]

Both "Hymne à la Fortune," Hesteau's imitation of the classical hymn genre, which Ronsard had revived, and "Les Gemissemens de la France, au Roy" describe the sufferings of a nation buffeted by civil war.[26] In "Les Gemissemens," Hesteau takes a historical approach, recounting the sufferings of France since Roman times in order to put the turmoil of the present era in context. In "Hymne à la Fortune" he invokes the favor of the unpredictable goddess Fortune, who indiscriminately spreads discord and permits the hydra-like serpents of rebellion to thrive. To counter this goddess and her rule Monsieur goes forth to battle against Antichrist, Discord, and Vice and to bring home Faith, Peace, and

---

[25] Clovis Hesteau, *Les Oevvres Poetiques de Clovis Hesteau* (Paris, 1578). The dedicatory letter is to Monsieur. Though Hesteau's volume contains poems addressed to both Monsieur and the king, it is clear that Hesteau favors Monsieur's interests. Hesteau's opening ode on Monsieur's victories (fols. 19^r–25^v), in six triads, is followed by another to Monsieur, in a single triad (fols. 25^r–25^v). The "Hymne au Roy, sur la Paix" (fols. 28^r–31^r) is in *vers heroiques*, the meter that Ronsard employed for his hymns. Several odes deal with the political situation: "Les Gemissemens de la France, au Roy" (fols. 4^r–11^v) and "Palas à Monsieur" (fols. 2^r–16^r), and "Hymne à la Fortune" (fols. 16^r–19^r). For commentary on the political situation behind Hesteau's poetry, see the "Introduction" to Hesteau's works: Clovis Hesteau de Nuysemont, *Les Œuvres Poétiques: Livres I et II*, ed. Roland Guillot (Geneva: Librairie Droz, 1994), 11–62.

[26] Although Ronsard's "Prière à la Fortune" (1555) anticipates many of the elements in Hesteau's "Hymne à la Fortune," Hesteau's "Gemissemens" contrasts with Ronsard's "L'Hymne de France" (1549), which had rejoiced in France's prosperity. See *Hymnes*, ed. Py, 179–88, 53–60.

Justice, initiating thereby, Hesteau hopes, the return of the Golden Age. Yet at the same time the poet prays to Fortune herself: to preserve Christianity and not to permit the proud who laugh at the nation's suffering to pour oil on the fire.

More optimistic are Hesteau's "Ode Pindarique, A Monsieur" and his "Hymne au Roy sur la Paix," both composed immediately before the peace of 1577 had temporarily halted the religious wars. The ode and hymn look back on odes composed by Jamyn and Ronsard to congratulate the young Henri III on his first military victories against the Protestants in 1569 and still further back on the odes Horace composed to congratulate Caesar on overcoming foreign foes.[27] The "Ode Pindarique" celebrates D'Alençon's victory at La Charité (2 May 1577) and elaborates on a single myth—Jupiter's conquest of the giants, which had fast become the most familiar mythic touchstone for the civil wars.[28] Hesteau refashions the myth in an interesting way. While Henri stands for Jupiter or Apollo, Monsieur takes the role of Mars. When Olympus is threatened, Hesteau tells us, Apollo calls on his brother Mars to assist him in putting down the giants. Hesteau mounts a Pindaric Pegasus in order to render praise to Monsieur, and compares his siege of La Charité to Achilles' siege of Troy. He takes advantage of so-called Pindaric license to develop figures and mount brief digressions. Monsieur is like a young bird or horse in first flight, a lion who frightens the flocks and makes them flee. Joined to the account of the siege of the giants and the shaking of Olympus is a reference to Jupiter's institution of law. If the king is Jupiter's stand-in on earth, Hesteau tells us, he must wield Jupiter's scepter justly, not merely use it to punish vice but also to institute law and to care for Jupiter's people in peace and justice. So frequent is the appeal among the French poets of this period for the king to reinstate law that we recognize implicitly that the law had been severely compromised.

Hesteau concludes the ode with a metaphor that he takes from Pindar and Horace by way of Ronsard: the building of the temple.[29] Likening himself to the

---

[27] See Ronsard, "Chant triomphal pour jouer sur la lyre sur l'insigne victoire qui a pleu à Dieu donner à Monseigneur, Frere du Roy" (1569) was later published as "Chant triomphal ou Hymne du Roy Henry III." Ronsard compares Prince Henri to a young eagle combating a dragon, a young lion conquering a savage bull. He calls Henri worthy as Alexander, a Pyrrhus to succeed his father Achilles (see *Hymnes*, ed. Py, 433–37). Also see Jamyn's odes on Jarnac and Montcoutour in *Les Oeuvres Poétiques d'Amadis Jamyn*, fols. 26ʳ–27ʳ, 27ʳ–28ᵛ.

[28] Like "Hymne à la Fortune," Hesteau's "Ode Pindarique" was influenced by Ronsard's hymns and odes to Henri II. Hesteau discourses on the effect of discord, remarking that peace, war, and concord are controlled by the same forces that control their opposites. Jupiter-God created all and is above all. The seeds of the world are fixed, but all is nourished by love.

[29] See Ronsard, "Le Temple des Messeigneurs le Connestable, et des Chastillons" (1555) in *Hymnes*, ed. Py, 151–58. Ronsard begins his hymn with an echo of Pindar's Olympian 6: "Je veux . . . te bastir . . . d'un Temple" (ll. 1–2).

Theban poet Amphion, who used his lyre to make the stones move and form the walls of Thebes, Hesteau sees himself building a temple of victory for Monsieur through his poetic art.[30] He aspires to be Monsieur's priest, worthy of his favor and exercising, as he says in another ode to Monsieur, his prophetic power to announce Monsieur's hour (25^r–25^v).

> Car ce temple sera fait
> D'une matiere si forte,
> Qu'il ne se verra deffait,
> Par le temps qui tout emporte.
> Ainsi s'y lira pour iamais:
> FRANÇOYS VRAY PRINCE DE FRANCE
> NOUS A SEUL PAR SA VAILLANCE,
> RAMENÉ LA SAINCTE PAIX.
> (fol. 25^r)

> For this temple will be made
> Of a material so strong
> That it will not see destruction
> By time that takes everything away.
> Thus it will read for ever:
> FRANÇOIS TRUE PRINCE OF FRANCE
> HAS ALONE BY HIS COURAGE
> BROUGHT US THIS HOLY PEACE.

Although addressed to Henri III, the "Hymne au Roy, sur la Paix" (fols. 28^r–31^r) in fact celebrates Monsieur and his victory at La Charité. In it Hesteau makes a curious use of both Pindar's sun metaphor and figures from Horace's ode, *Carmina* 4.5, which urges Caesar to return to Rome, and *Carmina* 4.14 and 4.15, which welcome him back to the city. Henri III had quitted Paris in November 1576 and did not to return to the capital until the following November, two months after the signing of the peace treaty. Hesteau anticipates the king's return, comparing him to the sun reappearing after night. However, this is not exactly the blazing metaphor for sun-kings that Italian and French poets were wont to frame in imitations of Olympian 1. Nor does Hesteau quite succeed in portraying Henri as the Jupiter who rules the universe, guaranteeing peace for his subjects. Adapting Pindar's aphorism about kingly rule, he attempts to present Henri as a divine lawgiver. If kings hold their laws from God, argues Hesteau, then mortals hold their laws from kings. However, in the chaos of civil war, lawlessness reigns with

---

[30] Pindar never mentions Amphion in his odes or takes him as an example, but Horace in an ode to Mercury (*Carmina* 3.11.1–2) notes that Mercury gave Amphion the lyre with which he raised the stones to build the walls of Thebes.

law, injustice with faith, the bad with the good, love with discord.[31] It was Monsieur, however, rather than the king who would pour vengeance on the ungodly, restore an unsoiled Faith to France, and disperse Chaos, snatching peace from its entrails and banishing cruel Mars. Echoing Horace's salute to Caesar at the beginning of *Carmina* 4.14, Hesteau asks what reward the sacred Parlement and the bourgeois of France may bestow on D'Alençon to eternize his virtue. The divine François, in arms redoubtable, has routed the serpents of rebellion. The baleful god Saturn has plunged the nation into mourning; France lies in the grips of a Hydra, awaiting an invincible conqueror to rescue her. Monsieur is the Hercules who alone can accomplish this task, a hero prophetically named Hercule-François, Hesteau reminds us, as a sign of the role he would undertake. If Henri is a Ulysses, ready to punish the impious who wish to usurp his place, Monsieur is the Telemachus who will assist him in the task. Optimistically Hesteau confers the title of Augustus on Henri, hopeful that his reign will be even happier than Augustus's and more fortunate: "affin que bien-heureux / Vous puissiez viure Roy vainqueur, paisible, & iuste, / L'âge mieux fortuné du plus heureux Auguste" (31ʳ).[32] It was a prophecy not to be fulfilled.

The next poet to assume the Pindaric mantle witnessed the bloody transition from the reign of Henri III to that of Henri IV. A great admirer of Ronsard, Scévole de Sainte-Marthe (1536–1623) composed both French and Latin verses, but attained greater eminence as a Latin poet.[33] He studied jurisprudence under Meurel, Turnèbe, and Ramus, held several offices under Henri III, and was also a mayor of Poitiers. After the assassination of Henri III in 1589, Sainte-Marthe transferred his allegiance to the Protestant Henri of Navarre, supporting

---

[31] It is likely that Hesteau borrowed this passage from the ode to Henri II that Ronsard composed after the 1550 peace. Both poets compare the bringing of peace out of war to the bringing of creative law from chaos.

[32] See, for example, the pindarics of Du Monin and of Gilles Durant, Sieur de la Bergerie. Jean-Édouard Du Monin addresses his patron, François de Vergy, the governor under Henri III of Bourgogne, in an elaborate triadic ode that celebrates Vergy's Burgundian heritage and likens his accomplishments as a warrior to those of Hercules and Scipio: "Ode Pindarique pour Hymne, A Monseignevr François de Vergi," in *Novvelles Oevvres de Ian Édovard Du Monin* (Paris, 1582?), 110–27. Durant composed numerous pindarics for French noblemen: see *Les Odes du Sieur de la Bergerie* (Paris, 1594). Also see Revard, *Pindar and the Renaissance Hymn-Ode*, 92.

[33] Sainte-Marthe first published his *Poemata* in Paris in 1570 with a long Latin poem on the education of children, *Paedotrophiae*. His son, Abel, also wrote poetry and published an edition of his father's poetry together with his own, after his father's death: see Scaevola et Abelius Sammarthani, *Opera Latina et Gallica* (Paris: Jacob Villery, 1633). As a classically-trained poet and a latter-day follower of Ronsard and the Pléiade, Sainte-Marthe takes care to follow not just French pindarics, but also Pindar himself. He pays tribute to the Greek poet in the preface to his poems and in the pindarics themselves. His pindarics are only one part of a much larger corpus of writing.

his struggle against the French Catholics of La Ligue.[34] Among his "Pindarica" is an ode to Henri IV, celebrating the crucial victory at Ivry on 14 March 1590 that would eventually secure Henri the crown. The battle of Ivry was a personal triumph for Henri, who exhorted his troops not to lose sight of his "panache blanc," and Sainte-Marthe's ode treats Henri like an epinician hero, to be crowned with laurel and celebrated in song as the highest son of Jove, "Iouis Optime propago" (81). Recapitulating Henri's successes on the field of battle, Sainte-Marthe describes him as both a Mars and a Jupiter who is armed with lightning and thunder with which to put down impious enemies. In the odes to the Valois kings, the impious enemies were the Protestant heretics. Now, however, they are the coalition of Spanish, Belgian, Italian, and Germanic forces, which have joined the French forces under Mayenne. Wary of celebrating the victory of French over French, Sainte-Marthe focuses on the defeat of the Ligue's foreign supporters. He presents an overview of the battle itself, singling out the individual leaders from the coalition who fall to Henri's onslaught, especially the Count d'Egmont, at whose death the battle turned and the enemy fled, pursued by Henri. He lauds the king as a victor, comparable to Caesar, whose conquests stretch from Euros, the river site of the battle, to Ganges—a leader, moreover, conspicuous both for piety as well as arms.

> Dicite Henricum pietate & armis
> Insignem, acerbis temporibus datum,
> Nulli labori non parem, fidei integrum,
> Virtute nec superabilem
> Nec arte, subiectis benignum
> Gentibus, indomitis tremendum . . .
> (stanza 17. 7–12)[35]

> Sing of Henri, noted in piety and arms,
> Given to these harsh times,
> Unequaled in labor, firm in faith,
> Surpassed neither in virtue
> Nor in art, gentle to his subjects,
> Fearsome to his foes . . .

---

[34] La Ligue was headed by the Count de Mayenne, the youngest Guise, who assumed his brother's place after the elder Guise was murdered at the instigation of Henri III.

[35] See Scaevola Sammarthanus, "Lyricorum Libri Duo," in *Poemata et Elogia* (Argustoriti Pictonum, 1606), 73–81. The ode opens in true Pindaric fashion with an appeal to the Muses.

Sainte-Marthe's second ode to Henri IV on this victory is a Horatian ode, which conspicuously presents Henri in a Caesarean role as a bringer of peace and a subduer of barbarians (134–36).

In the decades following, after Henri had assumed the throne, poets such as Nicolas Rapin, Jean Le Blanc, and François de Malherbe continued to praise him. Jean Le Blanc revives the triadic pindaric in the style of Ronsard in a collection of odes, first published in 1604, and then reprinted in 1610.[36] Closely modeled on Ronsard's 1550 book of odes, Le Blanc's book begins with an ode to the king, followed by odes to Marguerite de Valois and Marie de' Medici, to the Enfants of France, to the chancellor, secretaries of state, various dukes, and finally to Le Blanc's own associates, especially his poet-friends. Le Blanc is assuredly not a poet in the same class with Ronsard, but, given that qualification, it is remarkable how closely the attitudes toward poetry and politics of the one poet resemble those of the other. Le Blanc applies the compliments that Ronsard had once applied to the Valois king to the Bourbon Henri IV: Henri is quite simply the greatest king in the universe ("Roy le plus grand de l'univers" [Ode 1. 1]). Are we dealing with so-called "Pindaric" hyperbole pushed to the extreme, or are these extravagant compliments addressed to Henri IV in some way justified by the fact that he ended the wars of religion in France, reestablished French national pride in repulsing the Spanish, and attempted to bring order, peace, and justice to France? It is only ironic that Henri was assassinated in the same year that Le Blanc's collection of odes reappeared. Every king since François I had in some way played the roles of Jupiter and Hercules, and Henri IV no less. Le Blanc's contemporary, Nicolas Rapin, addresses Henri IV as "nostre Gallois Hercule."[37] Le Blanc imitates Horace in remarking that Henri divides the universe with the king of gods: Henri rules the earth, Jupiter heaven, and both rulers collect about them a royal court of splendid and handsome "gods." Given Henri's military accomplishments, does he deserve any less than to have Cyclopes forge his arms, those martial thunderbolts that make the rebellious tremble with fear? As Jupiter overturned the Titans with his thunder, Henri has driven the Spanish from the fields of France. Once more the Titans have become foreign and not native enemies. If the ode celebrates Henri's achievement as a warrior, it also celebrates his success in bringing peace. After war, the shepherds return to the hills, Diana

---

[36] See *La Néotémachie Poetique du Blanc, Odes* (Paris, 1610). It is in two parts, the first containing the *Odes*, the second *Rhapsodies Lyriques*. The copy I examined is in the Bibliothèque Nationale in Paris.

[37] See "Au Roy, sur son Retour de Bretaigne," in "Les Vers Mesurez de Nicolas Rapin," in *Les Oeuvres Latines et Francoises de Nicolas Rapin* (Paris: Olivier de Varennes, 1610), 5. Rapin also compares the newborn Dauphin (the future Louis XIII) to a Hercules, who can strangle serpents in his cradle and will grow up to take his father's place as a demi-god. See "Hymne sur la Naissance de Monseignevr Le Davphin, 1601," in "Les Vers Mesurez," in *Oeuvres*, 9–12.

revisits her forests, Ceres cultivates her crops and Bacchus his vines, and Pomona opens her horn of plenty. This is not mere mythological decoration, but describes the real effort of the king to revive French agriculture and to put the French economic state on a peacetime basis. Would a Pindaric ode in the Ronsardian style be complete without reference to the state of poetry? Like Ronsard's odes, Le Blanc's odes also celebrate the Muses and the Graces and call upon Minerva to revive the French academies. Le Blanc closes his ode by restoring Phoebus and the Muses to a land which can now once more hear the sound of the lyre. The odes that follow—to César, Duc de Vandosme (Henri's illegitimate son), and Jacques de Maillé de Brezé—though celebrating military accomplishment, also look forward to a France recovered from civil war.[38] It is astonishing that sixty years after Ronsard first published his odes a collection could be published that echoes Ronsard's book in form and content and in poetic tone.

Even though Le Blanc's contemporaries and successors continued to write triadic odes throughout the seventeenth century, already in 1610 Le Blanc's triadic verse was archaic.[39] One of the most eminent court poets of the Regency, François de Malherbe (1553–1629), never attempted formal Pindaric triads. Nevertheless, in other ways, Malherbe's odes for Henri IV and the Queen Regent demonstrate his knowledge of Ronsard's pindarics to Henri II and are full of Pindaric recollection.[40] Like Ronsard, Malherbe borrows an athletic metaphor from Pindar to describe his poetic endeavors:

> En cette hautaine enterprise,
> Commune à tous les beaux esprits,
> Plus ardant qu'un Athlete à Pise,
> Il me feray quitter le pris. [41]

> In this high enterprise,
> Common to all fine spirits,
> More eager than an athlete at Pisa,
> I will gain the prize for myself.

---

[38] The ode to César provides Le Blanc with an opportunity to include an extended Pindaric myth that recounts the story of Achilles from his first dip in the Styx to the appearance of that invincible warrior in Troy. The ode to Brezé compares Brezé not only to Achilles, but also to Charles VII who routed the English from Normandy. He is the Gallic Hercules who at last makes peace possible.

[39] Claude Garnier wrote pindarics on Louis XIII's majority, and Bernier de la Brousse included pindarics in his collection of poetry (see *Les Oevvres Poëtiques du Sievr Bernier de la Brousse* [Poictiers, 1618], fols. 99^r–113^v).

[40] See C. C. Humiston, *A Comparative Study of the Metrical Techniques of Ronsard and Malherbe* (Berkeley and Los Angeles: University of California Press, 1941).

[41] "A la Reine mere du Roy, sur les heureux succez de sa Regence," in "Les Poesies de Mr de Malherbe," in *Les Oevvres de Mre François de Malherbe* (Paris, 1630), 82.

He also adopts an opening figure for the ode "Au Roy Henry le Grand. Sur l'heureux succez du voyage de Sedan" that is reminiscent of Pindar's comparison of his verse to the completion of a voyage: "En fin aprés les tempestes / Nous voicy rendus au port" (29). Like Pindar, Horace, and Ronsard, he can also build his verses like an architect, though the Greek poet he alludes to is Amphion and not Pindar:

> Le fameux Amphion, dont la voix nonpareille
> Bastissant une ville étonna l'uniuers,
> Quelque bruit qu'il ait eu, n' point fait de merueille
> Que ne facent mes vers. (65)

> The famous Amphion, whose unparalleled voice
> Building a city astonished the universe,
> Such sound that he made was not more a marvel
> Than that which my verses make.

Still more to the point, Malherbe recollects how Ronsard and his followers compared their kings to Greek heroes and gods and alluded to their most famous feats. He likens Henri IV's undertaking of the religious wars to the young Hercules' assault on Troy (91–92). He also describes how Henri crushed rebellion just as Hercules beheaded the Hydra ("Priere pour le Roy Henry le Grand, allant en Limozin," 25). He compares Henri IV's taking of Marseilles to Hercules' punishment of tyrants ("Au Roy Henry le Grand, sur la prise de Marseille," 49–51). His ode to the young Louis XIII exhorts the king to arms, adopting the favorite myth of the French pindarists, the gods' defence of Olympus against the giants' assault. Typhon and Enceladus are the foes that the young king must conquer (62). Moreover, during the reign of Louis XIII Pindar's own odes were being rendered into French when the first French translations of Pindar appeared—by François Marin in 1617 and the Sieur de Lagausie in 1626. In the preface to his translation Marin remarks that Pindar has lessons to teach the princes of France.[42] Therefore, although few seventeenth-century French poets continued to compose triadic odes, Pindar remained a strong literary presence in France in the seventeenth century.

3.

Pierre de Ronsard had Pindaric followers not only in France, but also in Italy, the land that had given birth to the Renaissance pindaric. Hailed as the new Pindar, Gabriello Chiabrera (1550–1638) was a contemporary of Ronsard's French

---

[42] See Revard, *Pindar and the Renaissance Hymn-Ode*, 30–31.

followers and attained a reputation in Italy as a poet accomplished in canzoni and anacreontics, in dramatic and epic poetry as well as pindarics.[43] Although he wrote different kinds of pindarics (including sacred odes to saints), Chiabrera was especially proficient in the encomiastic ode. He celebrated the accessions of Urban VII and Urban VIII to the papacy in 1590 and 1623 respectively with sets of Pindaric odes.[44] The collection of "Heroic Odes" that he published in 1586, 1587, and 1588, although composed in stanzas rather than triads, were inspired by Pindar's example. His aim, as he explains in the prefatory letter to Ambrosio Salnero prefixed to the 1586 collection, was to honor great men as Pindar had honored athletes.[45] By great men Chiabrera meant the warriors and noblemen who had defended their homeland from foreign foes in the previous centuries. These "cavallieri" of Italy, he asserts, are as deserving of praise as those young men of Greece who had won victories in contests for their swiftness of foot or for their strength. As Pindar had been the encomiast for Hellenic athletes, Chiabrera aspired to be the poet for Italy's men of arms.

Chiabrera's book of odes is in its way as coherent and well planned as the collections of Ronsard or Le Blanc. The men of the century past who had impact on Italian history he treats as the counterparts not only to Pindar's athletes but also to mythic heroes such as Achilles or Ajax, also celebrated in Pindar's odes. While the first two books memorialize military men, Chiabrera adds in 1588 to his list

---

[43] In a letter written to Milton in 1647 Carlo Dati, Milton's Florentine friend, praises Chiabrera's accomplishments as a lyric poet. See S. P. Revard, "Milton and Chiabrera" in *Milton in Italy*, ed. M. Di Cesare, MRTS 90 (Binghamton, NY: MRTS, 1991), 505–20. Also see the discussion of Chiabrera's odes to saints in Revard, *Pindar and the Renaissance Hymn-Ode*, 265–69. For Chiabrera's connection with the French Pléiade, see Ferdinando Neri, *Il Chiabrera e la Pleiade Francese* (Turin: Fratelli Bocca, 1920), esp. 104–20.

[44] Chiabrera's odes to Urban VIII feature incidents from sacred rather than mythic history. Chiabrera makes the pope a second Moses rather than a second Hercules, recounting Moses' challenge to Pharaoh, his parting of the Red Sea, and the miraculous gift of manna which saved the children of Israel in the wilderness. In one ode he goes so far as to connect Pope Urban VIII with Pindar's patrons, Hieron and Theron of Sicily and Arcesilas of Cyrene. For the pindaric to Urban VIII, see "Canzoni in Lode del Sommo Pontefice Papa Urbano VIII, Per lo Giorno della sua Creatione," in *Canzonette, Rime Varie Dialoghi di Gabriello Chiabrera*, ed. Luigi Negri (Turin: Unione Tipografico-Editrice Torinese, 1952), 309–14.

[45] See the Prefatory letter to *Delle Canzoni del Signor Gabriello Chiabrera, Libro I* (Genoa, 1586), sig. A2^{r-v}. Until the end of his life Chiabrera held the view that Pindar was the standard for praise of great men. In a letter written in 1634, he maintains that although Horace is excellent in the art of the ode, his odes to the great men of Rome do not bear comparison with Pindar's when set side by side. See *Lettere di Gabriello Chiabrera Nobile Savonese, Date in luce da Giacomo Filippo Porrata Della Comparnia de Gesù* (Bologna, 1762), 35–36. Chiabrera's *Rime* (Venice, 1605) reprints many of the earlier odes and adds others to the collection of "Le Lodi di Diuersi Eroi."

of "great men" San Francesco and San Stefano and in 1591 Christopher Columbus. In his odes Chiabrera praises Italy's warriors, not only for defending their native cities from foreign armies and consolidating their kingdoms or dukedoms, but also for bringing peace and security to the Italian people. By honoring the great men of the past, Chiabrera departs from the usual pattern of the political pindaric. He does not eschew, however, addresses to present patrons and leaders, who warm to the patriotic message in his odes to past "heroes," who are, of course, their forebears. As Nagy and others have commented, the *kleos* of Pindar links the heroes of the past with the men of the present.[46]

Chiabrera opens the first book with an ode to Francesco Maria della Rovere, Il Vecchio (1491–1538), nephew of Pope Julius II, who with his uncle engaged the French to regain his dukedom in Urbino. Calling on Apollo as archer-god and as king of Parnassus, Chiabrera pays tribute not only to the Duke's eminence in arms, but also to his patronage of the arts. In choosing the myth of Bellerophon for this ode Chiabrera can celebrate Bellerophon as the slayer of the chimera, the victor over the Amazons and the Solymi as well as the rider of a poetic Pegasus. Bellerophon's mounting on Pegasus, the horse of the Muses, had already become a paradigm for the poet, who flies above the clouds on his own Pegasus.[47] Chiabrera also echoes a typical Pindaric aphorism in remarking that the Duke has achieved a victory "not without sweat," triumphing over envy and hate. To conclude, he transforms the classical observation about the happiness of the gods into the Christian assurance that in heaven alone is happiness secure.

The ode to Alfonso I of Este, the contemporary of della Rovere and his sometime adversary, is similar. Alfonso defended his state at the battle of Ravenna, winning a peace that made possible the flourishing of the arts at the court of Ferrara at that splendid time in Italian history—1505–1534—when Ariosto was composing *Orlando Furioso* for the D'Este.[48] Chiabrera notes that Ariosto's portrait of the warrior Ruggiero, the so-called ancestor of the D'Este, compliments the duke and the other "cavallieri" of the D'Este family. Chiabrera lists their exploits in arms just as Pindar would have listed the epinician victories of his athletes and the members of their family.

---

[46] See Nagy, *Pindar's Homer*, 192. Also see Mackie, *Graceful Errors*, 39–64. Mackie comments that trials of the athletes are raised to a level of heroic labors, thus connecting them with the heroes of the past (40).

[47] Perhaps Chiabrera is looking back at Ronsard's use of the myth. For us, however, it is an ironic look forward to Milton's use of Bellerophon as a cautionary myth in the proem to book 7 of *Paradise Lost*.

[48] See Albert Russell Ascoli, "Ariosto's 'Fier Pastor': Historical Meaning in *Orlando Furioso*," in *Phaethon's Children: The Este Court and its Culture in Early Modern Ferrara*, ed. Dennis Looney and Deanna Shemek, MRTS 286 (Tempe, AZ: ACMRS, 2002), 189–224.

The odes of Book One range from celebration of the recent duke of the house of Savoy, Emanuele Filiberto (1528–1580), who defeated the French at San Quentin, to praise of other defenders of Italian city-states, such as Francesco Gonzaga (1466–1519) who led the Venetian army and defeated the invading French under Charles VIII.[49] Setting Italy's heroic warriors beside the heroes of the Greek past—Achilles, Hercules, Jason, Perseus—Chiabrera commemorates their "virtù" of battle, but also alludes often to the Theban lyre, thereby reminding his readers of his Pindaric model. Chiabrera praises Enrico Dandolo, the renowned doge of Venice, who organized the Fourth Crusade and sacked the city of Constantinople, comparing him to two legendary heroes.[50] Because of his advanced age, Dandolo is compared to Nestor, but he is also likened to Jason questing for the fleece. But the most important mythic analogy for Dandolo's Venetian expedition is the Athenian attempt under Adrastus to take Thebes. Pindar had told the mythic tale of Thebes's fall to the Athenians with a certain ambivalence, referring in Olympian 2 to Polyneices' heroic struggle to save his city and in Pythian 8 to the seer Amphiaraus's prediction of Adrastus's final victory over Thebes. Chiabrera tempers his account of Dandolo's extraordinary feat in taking Constantinople in 1204 with a certain tragic foreboding that the city would later fall in 1453 to the Turks. Moreover, as Chiabrera was well aware, the Turks would lead an expedition from Constantinople against the Venetians, who saved their own city in 1571 only by the loss of many brave men at Lepanto. Like those odes in which Pindar alludes to the fall of Thebes, Chiabrera's ode to Dandolo resounds with ambiguities: past victory leads to defeat and later to a narrowly achieved victory.

Other odes in this first book also praise Italian soldiership. Giovanni Medici (1498–1526) was a professional soldier, who served, as Chiabrera's note tells us, in many of the military expeditions early in the century, even serving the French kings in a campaign against his native Milan. In arms Giovanni possessed Herculean strength, daring, and resourcefulness, accomplishing, as Chiabrera recounts, extraordinary military feats, such as leading expeditions over the Alps. Chiabrera borrows the myth from Pindar's Nemean 1, praising Giovanni's early promise as a soldier by asserting that like Hercules he strangled serpents in his cradle. He also describes Giovanni as a Jupiter, who defended Christianity against impious adversaries, mindful, no doubt, of how often the myth of the

---

[49] Other odes in the first book include those to Marc-Antonio Colonna il Vecchio, the defender of Verona; Nicola Orsino, the defender of Padua; Giouan-Giacopo Trivulzio, a celebrated condottiere who was the leader in the battle of Ghiara d'Adda; and Bartolomeo Liuiano, the victor over the Germans at Friulio.

[50] See C.M. Brand, "Dandolo, Enrico," in *Oxford Dictionary of Byzantium*, 1: 583.

assault of the Titans and the giants on Olympus had been employed in French pindarics to describe the religious wars.[51]

It is not Giovanni Medici alone who is characterized by Chiabrera as a Hercules. As in Pindar's own odes, Hercules appears and reappears in Chiabrera's poetry as a paradigm for native heroes or leaders. A Herculean Francesco Sforza killed the Nemean lion; Alfonso d'Este, like Hercules, had to contend with an Antaeus; and Francesco Gonzaga (1466–1519), who resisted Charles VIII, replicated the exploits of Hercules. Giouan-Giacopo Trivulzio (1447–1518) is both a Milanese Ulysses and a Hercules whose triumphant feats include the conquest of Geryon and the capture of Cerberus. For Emanuele Filiberto di Savoia (1528–1580) Chiabrera renders an even fuller account of Hercules' labors. Chiabrera's native city, Savona, had close ties to Savoy, and Chiabrera was the encomiast not only of the father, Emanuele Filiberto, but also of the son, Carlo Emanuele di Savoia (1562–1630). In his second ode for the former (Book One, 1586) he recounts how Hercules as a young pilgrim left Thebes and went on to conquer Antaeus in Libya, Geryon in Spain, and Cacus in Italy, before being glorified on Olympus as the spouse of Jove's own daughter Hebe. The reference to Hercules' marriage to Hebe had particular resonance for the Savoy dynasty, for after defeating the French under Henri II at St. Quentin, the Duke of Savoy married Henri II's sister Marguerite (the very Marguerite so often celebrated in Ronsard's odes). Thus in celebrating Hercules' virtue and his marriage to Hebe, Chiabrera is rendering compliments to the house of Savoy.[52]

Significantly, Chiabrera imitates the Pindaric ode not only for celebration, but also for dirge. The odes of the second book features those heroes who died defending a cause, notably Ercole Pio and Agostino Barbarico, who led the Venetian resistance to the Turks at the Battle of Lepanto in 1571. Thus Chiabrera rejoices in a victory at the same time he mourns the dead, perhaps remembering that in Isthmian 8 Pindar had celebrated an athletic victory at the same time he remembered those who had recently died repulsing the Persian invasion. Like Pindar in Isthmian 8, Chiabrera also uses the example of Achilles to make his point, recounting the details of Achilles' heroic warfaring with a modern

---

[51] Chiabrera includes one ode to Giovanni Medici in the 1586 collection, but others are contained in a later collection: see "Per Giovanni Medici" in "Le Lodi di Diuersi Eroi," 21–23; "Rime Varie," 32–34, in *Rime* (Venice, 1605). In alluding to Jupiter'conquest of the giants, Chiabrera is probably referring back to Horace's use of this battle to celebrate Augustus's triumphs in the east (*Carmina* 3. 14). However, he may also be referring to Pindar's reference in Pythian 8 to the conquest of Porphyrion and Typhoeus as a celebration of Hieron's defeat of the Carthaginians and Etruscans.

[52] Chiabrera also wrote odes and sonnets to the present duke, Carlo Emanuele di Savoia (1562–1630), Emanuele Filiberto's son. In his heroic sonnets, Chiabrera compares Carlo Emanuele to Hercules, encouraging him in his struggle against Genoa to persevere, like Hercules, who not without labor defeated the Hydra or put down Antaeus.

example in mind. Pindar praised Achilles for laying down his life in order to build for his warrior-friends the bridge of return to Greece. He thereby alludes to the sacrifice of Greek lives at Marathon. Chiabrera recounts how Achilles, on seeing the dead body of Patroclus bloody from Hector's sword, urges the making of his shield and armor, then fills the river Xanthus with enemy bodies to avenge his friend. Finally, though he later is himself killed, he kills Hector. Chiabrera applies the parallel to Ercole Pio, unhappy in his death, but happy in his victory. Only the Turkish blood consoles his countrymen for his death.

Chiabrera's achievement in these odes is significant. Writing at the same time as the French pindarists who celebrated Henri III or Henri IV, Chiabrera widens the perspective of the political pindaric to reflect not just on the politics of his day, but also the politics of yesterday. In connecting present leaders with those of the past, he makes the ode a universal sounding board, very like epic in its scope.

4.

At the same time that Chiabrera was imitating Ronsard's vernacular pindarics in Italy, a German and a Dutch poet were bringing the first Latin pindarics across the Channel to England. The Dutch had been among the earliest students of the Latin pindaric, the precocious Dutch poet Joannes Secundus having in fact begun to rival the Italians in the practice of neo-Latin poetry and in experimentation with the Pindaric ode. Two important practitioners, born in the decade after Secundus's premature death, were Paulus Melissus (Paul Schede), a German neo-Latin poet (1539–1602), and Janus Dousa (Jan van der Does), a Dutch neo-Latinist (1545–1604). Almost exact contemporaries, both studied in France and were much influenced by the encomiastic style of French poets such as Ronsard, Du Bellay, and Dorat—full of mythological fancy and devoted to the Muses and the Graces. Both also traveled to England in the 1580s and addressed odes to Queen Elizabeth and to her courtiers.

On the continent and in England Melissus was much admired and was called, as Lampridio and Ronsard also had been, a new Pindar—the Pindar of the Germans. His fame extended from his native Franconia to Vienna, where he had been crowned poet laureate by Ferdinand I, to Italy where he was created Count Palatine and *Civis Romanus*, to France where he was intimate with Ramus, Dorat, Ronsard, and Lambin, and to Geneva, where he cultivated Franciscus Portus (the Greek professor and commentator on Pindar), Henri Estienne (the publisher of Pindar's odes), and Joseph Scaliger (the editor of Pindar). Melissus addressed epigrams to all of them.[53] He was in Geneva at the crucial

---

[53] Melissus left us a poetic record of these friendships, for he addressed epigrams or odes to all of his illustrious acquaintances. See, for example, the epigrams included in *Melissi Schediasmatum Reliquiae* (Frankfurt, 1575).

period when Portus and Estienne brought forth commentaries, translations, and editions of Pindar's odes. Influenced perhaps by Jean Dorat's Latin pindarics, he undertook triadic verses in Latin, which he called "emmetra," and was the first to introduce Latin pindarics into England. One of his initial emmetra was a Latin Pindaric ode to Elizabeth that was printed in an elaborate presentation copy for the queen.[54]

Both as a pindaric and as a complimentary ode to Elizabeth, the "Oda Pindarica" is important, and may have served as a model for Dousa's later ode to Elizabeth.[55] The ode is in four triads and, although addressed to a sovereign, has some affinities with the French pindarics of the period to aristocratic ladies. Opening with a formal invocation to "Eliza," Melissus salutes the queen with the standard mythic comparisons that had become almost *de rigueur* for courtly ladies. Elizabeth is wise in heart as Pallas, sweet-tongued as Persuasion, lovely as Euphrosyne, regal as Themis—and endowed also with Christian purity and faith. Not surprisingly the queen joins the Muses to the Graces, as she had in Spenser's ode, "Aprill," and shines like Hyperion in the sky. Both her wit and her learning are praised.[56] What nation, what soil, what race, what people could boast such a monarch? What poet—Pindar, Vergil, Homer—could grant her greater fame than she has? Is she not to be compared even to the divine Solomon? Indeed, says Melissus, it is not fitting to sing of her as a human being, but as a goddess. However, amidst this effusive praise, some real political commentary

---

[54] See *Oda Pindarica ad Serenissimam Potentissimamque Dominam Elisabetham Britanniae, Franciae, Hiberniaeque Reginam* (Augustae Vindelicorum, 1578). The presentation copy of this Latin pindaric to Elizabeth is in the British Library and contains manuscript verses to George Gilpin complimenting both him and Elizabeth. Melissus reprints the Pindaric ode to Elizabeth as the first poem in the collection he dedicated to Elizabeth: *Schediasmata Poetica* (Paris, 1586). When Gherus [Guterus] collects Melissus's poetry for his anthology of German Latin verse, *Delitiae Poetarum Germanorum Huius Superiorisque Aevi Illustrium, Part IV* (Frankfurt, 1612), he also publishes the pindarics first, giving the Elizabeth ode pride of place (4:342–46). (The British Library's copy of *Schediasmata Poetica* is imperfect: the pindarics and melic odes are not affected, however. The Folger Shakespeare Library has a perfect copy of the volume.)

[55] Melissus first addressed poetry to Elizabeth in his 1575 collection: see *Melissi Schediasmatum Reliquiae* (Frankfurt, 1575), 5, 6, 151. In 1580 he interspersed epigrams to the queen with poetry addressed to others: see *Epigrammata* in *Mele sive odae ad Noribergam et Septemviros Reipub. Norib.* (Noribergae, 1580), 42, 47, 49, 57, 65, 71, 72. Melissus even prints Elizabeth's epigram ("Reginae Responsum") after the epigram to which the queen responds (72). An English translation of Melissus's epigram and the queen's response are included in *Elizabeth I, Collected Works*, ed. Leah S. Marcus, Janel Mueller, and Mary Beth Rose (Chicago and London: University of Chicago Press, 2000), 301–2.

[56] In one melic ode Melissus tells Elizabeth that he has collected his Latin verses especially for her, knowing that she is proficient in all languages and an accomplished Latinist ("Melicorum Lib. II," 110).

quietly intrudes. Characterizing Elizabeth as a monarch who keeps her people safe, Melissus demonstrates that he is an astute observer of the shifting political scene and values Elizabeth's role as a peace-keeper in sixteenth-century Europe. At Elizabeth's invitation Melissus went to England in 1585, staying at the court in Richmond and visiting both Oxford and Cambridge. He dedicated his 1586 volume of verse, *Schediasmata Poetica*, to Elizabeth, reprinting the "Oda Pindarica" as the first poem in the book. Elizabeth urged him to remain in England. He preferred, however, to return to Germany, eventually becoming the curator at the Palatine Library in Wittenberg, a post he held until his death in 1602.

Like Melissus, Dousa courted Elizabeth I both in poetry and in person, having come to England in 1584 and again in 1585. Like Melissus he also dedicated in 1586 a collection of Latin odes, *Odarum Britannicarum Liber*, to the queen, which included odes both to her and to members of the English aristocracy, as well as a friendly set of iambics to Melissus, complimenting him on the publication of his poems and alluding to his association with the English queen. Unlike Melissus, Dousa was not seeking the queen's patronage; his principal concern was to persuade Elizabeth to assist the States General in the struggle against Spain and to send an army to the Low Countries, as, of course, Elizabeth eventually did in 1585. His book, printed in the following year, is a fascinating study of the progress of Dousa's campaign to win support.[57] But even before his journey to England, Dousa had been appealing to Elizabeth to aid the Dutch cause. Dousa may have gained access to Elizabeth, as Jan van Dorsten has argued, not through his diplomatic status but through his renown as a poet. Elizabeth was notoriously reluctant to intervene in affairs on the continent and also to commit monetary resources. By adapting Horace's ode to Maecenas (*Carmina* 1.1) for her, Dousa won her ear: "Regina magnis edita regibus / Ipsa erudita ô Pieridum manu, / O Gratijs secunda nulli" (Queen descended from great kings, educated at the very hand of the Muses, O, in graces second to none).[58]

---

[57] Janus Dousa, *Odarum Britannicarum Liber, Ad D. Elisabetham Britanniarum Franciae Hiberniaeque Reginam* (Leiden, 1586). For commentary on Dousa see Chris L. Heesakkers, "Introduction," in *Iani Douzae a Noortwyck Epigrammatum Lib. II* (Leiden: Brill, 1976), 1–4. See the discussion of Melissus's and Dousa's odes to Queen Elizabeth in S. P. Revard, "The Latin Ode from Elizabeth I to Mary II: Political Approaches to Encomia," in *Britannia Latina: Latin in the Culture of Great Britain from the Middle Ages to the Twentieth Century*, ed. Charles Burnett and Nicholas Mann (London: Warburg Institute, 2005), 156–64.

[58] Dousa sent the ode to England with William Cecil, the queen's principal minister, hoping that the personally dispatched poem would win Elizabeth to the Dutch cause. In this ode he alludes to the Council of Trent and the Spanish Inquisition, reminding Elizabeth of her position as "Defender of the Faith" in England and passionately urging England's assistance against Spanish oppression. See J. A. van Dorsten, "Janus Dousa: Spokesman of the Dutch Revolt," in *Acta Conventus Neo-Latini Amstelodamenis* (Munich:

The first ode in Dousa's 1586 volume is addressed directly to Elizabeth, and is, like Melissus's pindaric to the queen, heavy with mythological reference. The odes that follow are addressed to Elizabeth's advisors and courtiers—Cecil, Heneage, in fact anyone who might sway the queen to his cause. As a kind of coda to the book, the elder Dousa appended the odes that his son Janus addressed to the queen as well as to Leicester and Sidney. Even though Dousa's odes are not triadic, they employ Pindaric techniques, and like Melissus, Dousa was frequently compared to Pindar.[59] All of the odes in the collection to Queen Elizabeth are effusive in compliment, but at the same time Dousa is not reluctant to speak openly about the plight of the Low Countries and to petition directly for aid. After the assassination of William of Orange and Spain's reconquest of the Low Countries, the situation had become desperate.[60] Dousa's opening ode on the birth of Elizabeth seems at first to consist principally of lists of goddesses who like fairy godmothers bestowed on Elizabeth at her nativity gifts of beauty, wisdom, and grace.

> Quisque certatim sua conferentes
> Dona, opes PLVTVS, CYTHERAEA formam,
> At mares PALLAS animos, suamque
> Suada medullam.
> SVADA, quae mentes hominum reuincit (sig. A2^{r-v})

> Each one competes to confer his gifts on her:
> Plutus riches, Cytherea beauty,
> But Pallas manly spirits and
> Persuasion her inner heart,
> Persuasion who conquers the minds of men.

However, by deftly including Persuasion among the goddesses, Dousa implies that it is Elizabeth's greatest ornament, the divine quality which insures that Elizabeth will in the future assist Flanders. After complimenting the queen,

---

Wilhelm Fink Verlag, 1979), 336–37. For the poem to Elizabeth, see *Iani Duzae Nordovicis Novorum Poematum . . . Editio* (Leiden, 1576), sig. G^{v}–Giiij^{v}.

[59] See the poems that Justus Lipsius and Franciscus Kammius addressed to Dousa in *Elegiarum Lib. II. Epigrammatum Lib.* (Leiden, 1586). Lipsius says, "Tange lyram; rari consurget carmen honoris, / Altáque Pindaricis Musa feretur equis" (75) (Touch the lyre and a song of rare honor will swell, and the lofty Muse will be borne by Pindaric horses). Kammius notes, "Mox tua Pindarico carmine gesta canis" (90) (Presently, you sing your deeds in Pindaric song).

[60] For background on Elizabeth's war policies, see Wallace T. MacCaffrey, *Elizabeth I* (London: Edward Arnold, 1993); idem, *Queen Elizabeth and the Making of Policy, 1572–1588* (Princeton: Princeton University Press, 1981); idem, *Elizabeth I, War and Politics, 1588–1603* (Princeton: Princeton University Press, 1992).

Dousa alludes to the tyranny Spain exercises over the Low Countries, which suffer under Parma's brutal yoke. Elizabeth, he asserts, was ordained from her birth as the tutelary deity who will bring relief. When, he asks, may I see Leicester come to pursue war in Batavia? He concludes with a direct supplication for assistance.

The odes that follow are similarly pointed in their mythic allusions. Cecil is likened to Nestor in wisdom and counsel and to Ulysses in steadfastness. Just as Ulysses resisted the blandishments of Calypso and Circe to return to his native Ithaca, so may the wise Cecil, Dousa suggests, be likewise steadfast and faithful. By implication Spain's wasting of the Low Countries is compared to the visitation of the Harpies. Through these allusions Dousa urges Cecil to lift these devastating plagues from the Low Countries. Dousa's odes negotiate skillfully between compliment and diplomatic maneuvering. His ode to Thomas Heneage proceeds, with salutations to Leicester and Sidney, to request aid for the Low Countries, painting, as in the previous ode, a vivid picture of the devastation on the continent. He contrasts the storm of war that afflicts Flanders with the idyllic picture of rural England, devoted to the Muses, and urges Englishmen as the heirs of Henry VIII to take care for Belga.

The odes of Janus Dousa Filius, appended to the collection, were composed after Elizabeth had already dispatched Leicester and Sidney to the continent, and accordingly they give thanks for assistance provided. The younger Dousa is also effusive in his praise of the queen, wishing for the skill of a Homer or Vergil so that his song might equal the songs of Phoebus. Elizabeth is worthy, he says, to rule not merely Britain, but also all of Europe, and to give laws to Asia. Mindful that the States General had offered Elizabeth the governance over the Low Countries, Dousa's son subtly forwards his father's diplomatic designs by praising Elizabeth's regal qualities. No woman was ever comparable to her in justice, in doctrine, and in religion, as well as in all the other arts. Hopeful that she might consent to enlarge her kingdom, Dousa Filius concludes by wishing that she might not only rule the English people in peace but also add new peoples to her empire. Like his father, he praises Elizabeth not as a woman, but as a goddess, who will be conveyed to the heavens after her death, to shine among the stars.

The final odes are addressed to Leicester and Sidney. Dousa Filius gives thanks to Leicester for assisting a people not his own and describes the joy among the Belgians at Leicester's arrival in the Low Countries and at his appointment as governor by the States General. For Sidney he reserves a special salute, greeting him, as his father also had, as a fellow poet, wise as Pallas, eloquent as Hermes, in heart a Mars, in song an Apollo.[61] If Homer should make a new *Iliad* or Vergil return from the shades of Elysium, they would propose Sidney as

---

[61] The elder Dousa had given Sidney a copy of the Petronius Arbiter that he had edited. He addressed a short ode to Sidney in which he alludes to the gift and exchanges literary compliments with Sidney (see *Odarum Britannicarum Liber*, 21–22).

another Aeneas, another Ulysses. Dousa's valediction has an unexpected poignancy. He wishes that even as Sidney surpasses these in virtue, so might he surpass them in years.[62] In the hands of Dousa, both father and son, the Latin ode becomes not just the medium for extravagant praise, but also the instrument for international diplomacy.

Although less directly political in intent than Dousa's book of odes, Melissus's *Schediasmata Poetica* (printed in the same year) is not without a deliberate design. It opens with a letter of compliment and an epigram to Elizabeth, and commences every section of the extensive volume with poetic addresses to the queen—in pindarics, lyric, epigram, elegy, and so forth. Melissus courts no other monarch, indeed no other person, so assiduously. The Pindaric ode that he first presented to Elizabeth in 1578 is given pride of place in this volume as the first of the fourteen triadic odes or *emmetra*. Melissus's pindarics include odes both to leaders of state and friends, as well as odes on occasional subjects. Although Melissus opens the "Emmetra" of his 1586 collection with the ode to Elizabeth, he closes it with an ode to Pope Gregory XII—a remarkable conjunction since Elizabeth and Pope Gregory, who encouraged Spain's aggressive policies against England, could hardly be called political allies. However, the ode to the pope is circumspect, witty, and just as full of gracious compliment as the ode to Elizabeth.[63]

Melissus's melic odes, although not in triads, also use Pindaric techniques, and, like his *emmetra*, allude circumspectly to the delicate situation that Elizabeth found herself in as the ruler of a country surrounded by well-armed enemies. He even refers in one ode to the assassination attempt on the queen.[64] He

---

[62] "His etenim cunctis & VLYSSEM & NESTORA vincis, / Aetate atque annis tantùm superaris, at ipse / Omnibus in rebus superabis utrosque, si eorum / Virtutem vt superas, sic & superaueris annos" (*Odarum Britannicarum Liber*, 55). The younger Dousa, who himself died young, had a special regard for Sidney, for whom he wrote an eclogue after his death. He also composed a poem on the defeat of the Spanish Armada and in praise of a fountain in London. See Janus Dousa Filius, *Poemata* (Leiden, 1607), 75–78, 100–9, 199.

[63] See "A Hugonem Boncompagnium, Grigorium XIII. P. M." in "Emmetra," in *Schediasmata Poetica*, 55–57. The Pindaric ode to Pope Gregory XIII had already been published in *Epigrammata in Urbes Italiae. Cum Eiusdem Odis, Ad Romam, Pont. Max. & Ducem Venetum* (Argentinae, 1585). Melissus compares the pope to the dragon who guards the golden apples of the Hesperides, and cleverly works in a Pindaric digression on Gregory's reformation of the Julian calendar. Melissus also indulges in a Pindaric roll-call of dynastic titles, connecting the present pope to Aeneas Silvius the Pious (Pope Pius II), to the former popes, the Piccolomini, as well as to illustrious members of his own family, the Boncompagni.

[64] See "Melicorum Lib. I," 92–93. Calling upon the classical deities, Melissus exclaims, what fury moved those brigands to plot against the queen, whom the divine care of God protected against such violence?

was aware of the pressure on Elizabeth to give assistance to the Netherlands, but, unlike Dousa, he makes no specific plea, remaining more a commentator on than a mover of the political situation. In a later ode, however, he goes so far as to contrast the tranquillity of England, where people can cultivate the arts, with the troubles in the Low Countries, remarking, "Unhappy is that people whose sleep is continually interrupted by the fearful drums of war, ever beating."[65] Melissus does not let Elizabeth forget entirely the plight of Protestants on the continent.

Odes to foreign dignitaries and European princes sometimes also allude to politics. With diplomatic tact, Melissus encourages Nicolas Ponteus, the Doge of Venice, to forge good relations between Italy and Germany, indulging (curiously) in a digression in which he recounts Attila's ravages of Italian soil to assure Venice of the present friendship of the German people.[66] Although composed in stanzas rather than triads, Melissus's melic odes are similar in technique and reference.[67] Melissus's ode to Charles IX of France (69–70) negotiates between compliment and political observation, for while he congratulates the king on his marriage, he also regrets the devastation of the civil wars in France. In his ode to the Duke of Saxony he pleads for the release of the humanist scholar-doctor Kasper Peucer from prison (93–95). But he discreetly refrains from further political comment, demonstrating the tact that won him the titles of Count Palatine and *Civis Romanus*.

---

[65] "O infelices populos, quibus horrida somnum / Obturbant crebrâ tympana pulsa manu!" ("Elegiarum Lib. V," in *Schediasmata Poetica, Pars altera*, 134). In another ode he also contrasts the splendors of England, especially its universities, Cambridge and Oxford, the double lights of the kingdom, with the devastation on the Continent—with hostile arms oppressing the people of the Low Countries, their cities burnt, the temples of the gods profaned, the fields streaming with blood, and the citizens weeping. While he sorrows for these, he tactfully praises the peace and prosperity the queen has assured to England ("Melicorum Lib. VI," 353–55).

[66] "Emmetra," in *Schediasmata Poetica*, 10. The ode to the Doge uses the usual Pindaric devices. Melissus summons Calliope and asks the Pindaric question: whom should he celebrate? How would it be fitting to praise so dexterous, so singular a prince? He uses maritime imagery to praise Venice's mastery over the sea and also refers to Venice's academies. Melissus even summons up a reference to the family of the Dandoli, one of whom Petrarch had praised as a friend.

[67] In a number of his stanzaic odes, Melissus refers to Pindar and imitates Pindaric devices. See, for example, his ode (VII) to Bartholomaeus Poemerius, the prefect of the city of Nuremberg. The Muses, Apollo, and Pallas appear and Melissus alludes specifically to Pindar's lyre. He addresses Poemerius, as Pindar had Theron, as the bulwark of his city (28). He also borrows from Pindar specific myths, as he compares the prefect to Perseus, conquering the gorgon, and to Bellerophon, mounted on the winged horse. The ode to Philip Geuderus in the same volume also invokes Pindar's Dircean lyre (13). See *Mele sive odae ad Noribergam et Septemviros Repub. Norib.*, 26–29; 12–16.

After his departure from England, Melissus continued to address poetry to Elizabeth and to members of her court and to compose odes about England that compliment the queen.[68] Two such pieces in the "English collection" combine lyric description with political innuendo: Melissus's poem on his journey to England, "Navigaturus in Angliam," and his strophic ode to the river Thames, "Ad Thamesim Flumen" ("Melicorum Lib. II," 151–53, 153–55). Ostensibly, we have no more here than the description of a journey and the celebration of a river, but Melissus had the knack, like Pindar, of addressing one subject while quietly commenting on another. As he recalls in the first ode his channel crossing to see England's famous queen, Melissus develops mythic digressions on Cassiopeia and on Perseus, which, given the time, may refer in a coded way to some important persons. Is Cassiopeia, who must cede her golden chair and the prize for beauty to Elizabeth, the ill-fated Mary Stuart, whose rivalry with Elizabeth was shortly to have fatal consequences? Is Perseus, who rescued Cassiopeia's daughter with the gorgon's head and his sword, Leicester or perhaps the much-wished-for heir who would follow Elizabeth? The myths are so circumspectly introduced that we can do no more than offer educated guesses. In the second ode to the river Thames the myth is more elaborate, and the handling of the mythic material demonstrates how skillfully Melissus had mastered the techniques of the Pindaric ode. The ostensible aim of the ode is to offer compliments to the queen by celebrating the Thames—the principal river of Elizabeth's realm—and its swans, the swan also being the traditional bird of Apollo and hence of the poet. Melissus devotes most of the ode to the elaboration of several interconnected myths on these most poetic birds. Beginning with an apostrophe to the river as the parent of swans, Melissus asks a Pindaric question: how did these birds, whiter than snow and milk, come to frequent the waters of the Thames? According to ancient fame, says Melissus, conflating several myths, it occurred when his sister-nymphs made lament over the fall of Phaethon, friend to Cycnus, the ruler of Ligurium, who was himself killed by Achilles. Determining that his son should not die, Cycnus's father Poseidon changed him into a swan and then to glorify the bird made its race multiply in great numbers on the streams of the Thames.[69] To compliment the swan further, Melissus recounts yet another myth, telling how the twins Castor and Pollux and the sisters Clytemnestra and Helen

---

[68] Among the addressees are Edward Stafford, Thomas Bromley, William Cecil, Charles Howard, the Earl of Leicester, Philip and Robert Sidney, Francis Walsingham, and Daniel Rogers. Many of these are purely complimentary pieces. We expect Phoebus and the Muses to adorn the ode to the Sidneys, and for Leicester to be endowed with the sinews of Hercules, and for Walsingham to be wished good fortune and not bad.

[69] There are at least three myths about the transformation of Cycnus into a swan. The first Cycnus was the friend of Phaethon, whose grief for the fallen Phaethon brought about the transformation. The second Cycnus was the ruler of Ligurium. The third Cycnus was the son of Poseidon, made invulnerable to weapons by his father, but who was

were born of one egg from Leda (who had been wooed by Jupiter in the form of a swan). Thus the race of swans won still more eminence. These rather heady dynastic references may be read as shallow compliments or as subtle political commentary. The much admired Philip Sidney was a swan, whose poetic fame was to survive his death. Elizabeth herself was the daughter of a Ledean Anne Boleyn and a Jupiter-Swan, Henry VIII. As he describes the Thames's swans, Melissus assumes the mantle of the Theban swan, Pindar, wishing for the swan's voice to honor the queen and her courtiers, even if, he wittily adds, he shares the swan's fate and dies in singing.

These odes of graceful compliment and mythic allusiveness are not without effect on the poets of the English court, particularly on Edmund Spenser, whose *Prothalamion* (as we shall see) celebrates the Thames and its swans while also honoring his patron Essex and the queen. Even as he displayed his virtuosity in Latin verse, Melissus demonstrated to English writers how Pindaric techniques could be successfully transferred from the Latin to the developing vernacular ode.

5.

If John Soowthern had been a better poet, the complimentary verses to the Earl of Oxford that he published in halting triads in *Pandora* (1584), while bragging that he was the first in England to pindarize, might have initiated a Pindaric revolution in England half a century earlier. Soowthern was after all translating a form to England that in France had abundant contemporary practitioners—Jamyn, Hesteau, Habert, Du Monin, Sainte-Marthe—and also had the magic name of Ronsard to recommend it. Soowthern's verses, moreover, though clumsy, echo those of the French school of pindarists. Further, even as he compliments Oxford, Soowthern raises poetic issues similar to those Spenser raises in his verses to English noblemen. Like Ronsard and the French pindarists, Soowthern is as much concerned with poetry and poetics as he is with the praise of his patron. He opens the ode with an apostrophe to earth, contrasting earth's role as a nourisher of man's immortality with poetry's: earth may nourish man while alive, but when dead furnishes him only with a grave. Muses, not marbles, guarantee immortality and keep alive the fair renown a man has won by his virtues. These opening strophes demonstrate Soowthern's knowledge of the Pindaric legacy in verse. At this point, however, perhaps following Pindar (whose name he invokes) or perhaps Ronsard, Soowthern excuses himself for wandering from his subject and returns to praise Oxford, enrolling Deuer's name among "our well renowmed men," a man who deserves the praises of a "syluer pen" (epode 2. 1–2).

---

strangled by Achilles. See "Cycnus" in *Brill's New Pauly*, ed. H. Caucik and H. Schneider (Leiden: Brill, 2003).

For who marketh better than hée,
The seuen turning flames of the Skie:
Or hath read more of the antique,
Hath greater knowledge in the tongues:
Or understandes sooner the sownes,
Of the learner to loue Musique (antistrophe 3. 1–6)[70]

Who, he continues, is better in horsemanship or other arts; who in sum in England is more "lyke *Deuer*, but hée," an "ornament of England," honored "both of the Muses and mée." To conclude, Soowthern promises that when he gets the spoil of Thebes he will build the Earl "a glorie, / That shall euer liue in memorie" (antistrophe 3. 16; epode 3. 4–14). Unlike the French pindarists, Soowthern cultivates no elaborate mythic comparisons to adorn the Earl further.

Although only a dim reflection of Pindar or even of the French imitations of Pindar, Soowthern's ode introduces English readers and the English scene to a different kind of encomiastic verse. Following Soowthern's lead, Michael Drayton and Ben Jonson respond to the possibilities for personal or political encomium that the new ode form offers, Jonson in two odes to noblemen, Drayton in two semi-heroic odes. Like Soowthern's ode to Oxford, Jonson's odes to the Earl of Desmond and to Lucius Cary and Henry Morison exploit the pindaric as a vehicle for encomiastic praise. Although we can take for granted that Jonson knew Pindar's odes at first hand, he was also widely read in continental literature and undoubtedly was conversant with both French and neo-Latin imitations. Jonson owned many neo-Latin books, among them a copy of Melissus, whose odes to Elizabeth and members of the English court he could hardly have escaped knowing as recent neo-Latin imitations.[71] As a poet Jonson was consistently interested both in Latin and Greek originals and in imitations. Perhaps the very existence of Soowthern's imitations of French pindarics (attacked by Puttenham in *The Arte of English Poesie* [London, 1589]) was enough to give Ben Jonson the impetus to write a real pindaric of his own, perhaps even to rival Ronsard and to revive a form Ronsard had so firmly made his own.

Jonson's ode to James, the Earl of Desmond, was probably written around 1600, shortly before the Earl's release from the tower by Elizabeth's order. The ode was not published, however, until the posthumous 1640 volume, *The Underwood*, an indication probably of Jonson's political discretion.[72] The Desmond ode

---

[70] John Soowthern, *Pandora, The Musyque of the beautie of his mistresse Diana* (London, 1584).

[71] See David McPherson, "Ben Jonson's Library and Marginalia: An Annotated Catalogue," *Studies in Philology* 71 (1974): 3–106.

[72] The headnote to the ode (presumably Jonson's) indicates that the ode was written during Queen Elizabeth's reign. See "*An Ode to Iames Earle of Desmond, writ in Queene Elizabeths time, since lost, and recovered*," in *The Poems*, in Jonson, *The Works of Ben Jonson*, ed. C. H. Herford and Percy and Evelyn Simpson (Oxford: Clarendon Press,

is closer to the French and neo-Latin political odes than the triadic Cary-Morison ode, composed about thirty years later and also published in *The Underwood*. Although written in regular thirteen-line stanzas, its alternating long and short lines, as well as its exploitation of Pindaric devices, mark it as a pindaric. Like the French pindarists, Jonson begins his poem with a direct invocation to Apollo and the Muses and an appeal to the so-called Pindaric "fureur."

> Where art thou *Genius*? I should use
> Thy present Aide: Arise Invention,
> Wake, and put on the wings of *Pindars* Muse. (ll. 1–3)

He asks to be enrolled as Apollo's priest, to be inspired by "strange rapture," and to have his brain heated with "*Delphick* fire" (ll. 11–12). Like the French pindarists, he is almost as much interested in the process by which his verses are inspired as in the verses' subject. He also makes the typical pindarist's claim that the verses will stand by their own virtue as well as by the virtue of the hero they praise. The earl's "Rich beame of honour" shines, Jonson exclaims, in his verse, and the verse itself will with its strong charms break the stony walls that hold his "True noblêsse" from view (ll. 14–26).

The very Pindaric form also licenses Jonson's consolatory tone and urges him to enter into a familiar dialogue with his noble subject. Here his deft and cautious compliments skirt a rather delicate political situation. The earl's father had been executed as a rebel, and the difficult relations between Ireland and England during this period required that the queen retain the earl under house arrest first in Ireland and then in the Tower despite the fact that he himself had never committed a treasonous act.[73] Jonson's commendation of the young man's virtue in effect interrogates the political system that has wronged that virtue: "the jealous errors / Of politique pretext, that wryes a State" (ll. 28–29). Further, in commiserating with the earl on his unhappy situation and in projecting his coming release from prison, Jonson covertly incorporates into his ode the kind of political commentary that Pindar's own odes so often contained. He never actually criticizes the monarch; yet his commendation of Desmond implies a criticism. It is perhaps the reason Jonson did not publish the ode during his lifetime.

The ode also exploits a theme dear to Jonson's heart and prominent both in Pindar and in his Renaissance followers, namely, that virtue is proved under trial. The theme is in essence a development of an athletic metaphor frequent in Pindar's odes. The young athletes who win the Olympian or Pythian contests

---

1947), 8: 176–80. Expectation of Desmond's release is obliquely referred to: "(As my hope tells) that our fair *Phoeb(e)'s* shine, / Shall light those places / With lustrous Graces" (ll. 58–60).

[73] See Annabel Patterson's comments on the Desmond ode in *Censorship and Interpretation* (Madison: University of Wisconsin Press, 1984), 132–35.

demonstrate their winning "metal"—metal tried under stress proves true, hence proves itself gold. In Pythian 10 Pindar remarks that as gold is tested and proved true by a touchstone, so is the true mind (ll. 67–68).[74] In Jonson's version Desmond's virtue, like metal, is tried and proved. The entire central stanza of Jonson's poem develops the metaphor, taking the place in Jonson's ode of the Pindaric digression. Like Jove's thunderbolts, like Aeneas's arms, Desmond's virtue has been "forged" in an Aetnean foundry. True gold will prove itself gold only when it has been heated and tried—and only true gold, like true virtue, will last the testing: "Gold, that is perfect, will out-live the fire" (l. 45).[75] With the arrival of the third of the Cyclopes who forges the arms, Jonson tells us, the period of Desmond's testing is coming to an end. Jonson's ode congratulates the earl on virtuously surviving the test imposed on him. Although Jonson profits in this ode from continental precedents, at the same time he tries to draw closer than continental pindarists had to Pindar's originals.

Drayton's heroic odes, first printed in 1606 and reprinted in 1619, also deal with the Pindaric theme of virtue tested. Like the continental pindarists, Drayton understood that one of the uses of the Pindaric ode was to combine lyric celebration with epic or heroic occasion. The occasion for the ode might be to celebrate a battle or a comparable event, which tested virtue or endurance as Pindar's epinician contests tested athletic prowess. Two of Drayton's odes concern precisely this sort of occasion: the first on the Virginian voyage and the second on the historical battle of Agincourt. "To a Virginian Voyage" addresses the young aristocrats of England who are on the verge of embarkation to the New World to found a new colony and to plant "English" virtue there. As virtue and honor were bywords for Jonson, so are they for Drayton, who celebrates aristocratic youths just at the very moment of achievement—the Pindaric καιρός:

> You brave Heroique Minds,
> Worthy your Countries Name,
> That Honour still pursue,
> Goe, and subdue . . . (1–4)[76]

Drayton's tribute to aristocratic honor and achievement is organized as a narrative into three sections that dramatize the embarkation, the voyage, and the arrival in Virginia. What prompts this ode—as it prompted some of the continental pindarics—is Pindar's celebration of dynasty. As Pindar in Pythian 4

---

[74] The maxim in Pythian 10 applies not only to Perseus, whose myth Pindar recounts, but also to the boy victor, Hippocleas. Composed when he was about twenty, this is probably Pindar's earliest ode.

[75] Zechariah 13:9 makes a similar point.

[76] *The Works of Michael Drayton*, ed. William Hebel (Oxford: Shakespeare Head Press, 1932), 2: 363–64.

chose to recount episodes from the voyage of the Argonauts to laud Arcesilas and his Cyrenian homeland, as he recalled Apollo's wooing of the nymph Cyrene in Pythian 5 in order to celebrate the begetting of the kingdom by the founding king Battus, so in "To a Virginian Voyage" Drayton chose a moment in English history to celebrate the spirit of English noblemen. The young heroes, like the Argonauts, embark on a "merry Gale" with a jaunty spirit of adventure, avoiding "Rocks, Lee-shores, [and] Sholes" (ll. 9, 15). They are accompanied by good omens: like Pindar's Jason they are seeking the golden fleece, like Hercules the Hesperides. Drayton depicts Virginia as "Earth's onely Paradise" (l. 24) and its attainment promises the return to the golden age. Virginia combines the classical and the Christian paradises—Eden and the archetypal golden-age garden. Significantly, this paradise is to be won through leaving the Old World and its society of warrior kings—rulers who had promised through their policies to accomplish the return of the golden age. In his ode Drayton invokes neither Augustus nor his English surrogate, James I, but those noblemen who have set out on their own. The New World, free from the Old World's political ethos, awaits them, where they will find pearl and gold abundant, plentiful fowl, venison, and fish, fruitful soil, and lofty trees. Drayton crowns no prince with laurel or vine leaves—in the new land the "ambitious Vine" is crowned with "his Purple Masse" (ll. 31–32). Even before they reach the shore, the voyagers are greeted with a "Lushious Smell / Of that delicious Land" that makes their hearts swell, "Approching the deare Strand" (ll. 43–48).[77]

The final section of the ode dramatizes the arrival in America and offers Drayton the opportunity to reflect of the aims of his heroic young voyagers. Part of what Drayton is doing in "To a Virginian Voyage" is revisiting the colonization myth that Pindar had set forth in Pythian 4 and which Italian and French pindarists tried to reinvent to compliment Renaissance monarchs. When Minturno narrated Aeneas's voyage in his victory ode for Charles V or Ronsard recollected Francus's exploits in his odes for Henri II, they were flattering the dynastic ambitions of the Spanish and French monarchs respectively. They were empire-building and using Pythian 4 to support their agenda. Drayton's odic Americiad is something different. For though he suggests that English virtue is being tested by the voyage, that Englishmen were to be replanted in a new land, he does not design the colonization necessarily to recreate in America the image of the European dynasties left behind. English virtue is translated to the new land, not England per se. The English adventurers beget something new, as Drayton's metaphor suggests:

> And in Regions farre
> Such *Heroes* bring yee foorth,

---

[77] Milton recollects these lines in *Paradise Lost*: as Satan approaches Eden, he smells the delicious scent of the spicy paradise (4. 153–165).

> As those from whom We came,
> And plant Our name
> Under that Starre
> Not knowne unto our North. (55–60)

New heroes and new heroic virtue are to be born in the New World. So Drayton makes clear as he turns from his colonial to his poetic vision. His vision of the Pindaric ideal is different from that of the French pindarists or Ronsard. They projected their poetic undertakings as means to foster their position in the Augustan court as court poets. Drayton, however, as the concluding lines of his ode make clear, envisions a new poetics flourishing in Virginia. "APOLLO's Sacred tree" will thrive and furnish branches with which to crown a "Poets Browes" (ll. 63, 65). His aim is to take on the role of the Pindaric poet-priest, but with a difference. Burning with Delphic fire, he will create a new poetic in a new land.

Drayton's ode "To the Cambro-Britons, and their Harpe, his Battle of Agincourt" (375–78) is a more conventional tribute to English nationalism, one which uses the tradition of the Pindaric battle ode to look hopefully to the future. In it Henry V's historic battle of Agincourt, rather than a contemporary battle, is celebrated, yet the ode is no less a celebration of contemporary patriotism than was Ronsard's commemoration of the achievements of Henri II or Sainte-Marthe's of Henri IV. Implicit in the commendation of Henry V (the first Prince of Wales) is the compliment to Prince Henry (the current Prince of Wales), Drayton's patron, to whom he dedicated *Poly-Olbion* in 1612. The last line of the ballad looks forward to such another "King Harry," an expectation that Prince Henry's early death thwarted.[78] As Hilary Mackie has commented, one of the functions of Pindaric ode is to do verbally what the hero or athlete does physically, to "make the past continuous with the present by reviving or renewing it."[79] Drayton extends the limits of the pindaric to include a ballad-like account of a battle. Like "To a Virginian Voyage," the ode begins with an embarkation — King Henry's departure for France — and continues to describe the expedition up through the time of the battle of Agincourt. The two main sections of the ode give us the king's speech before the battle and an actual description of the battle itself, both features that have warrant in Pindaric ode as well as in Renaissance battle poems. Many of Pindar's heroes speak: Pelops in Olympian 1, Pollux in Nemean 10, Heracles in Isthmian 6, usually in pivotal situations in which they request something or they look forward to some critical achievement. Pelops asks for his chariot victory, Pollux for his brother's life, Heracles for the birth of a hero-son for Telamon. So King Harry in the lyric-ballad-ode asks for victory in battle. In

---

[78] See Bernard Newdigate, *Michael Drayton and his Circle* (Oxford: Shakespeare Head Press, 1961), 152, 169–71. Newdigate notes how Drayton connects the Cambro-Britons with the Prince of Wales in *Poly-Olbion*.

[79] See Mackie, *Graceful Errors*, 41.

recounting the battle, Drayton is doing something that previous pindarists often did: he adopts the language of epic to describe the battle.

> They now to fight are gone,
> Armour on Armour shone,
> Drumme now to Drumme did grone,
> To heare, was wonder;
> That with Cryes they make,
> The very Earth did shake,
> Trumpet to Trumpet spake,
> Thunder to Thunder. (ll. 57–64)

Both Pindar's original odes and the battle odes of continental poets of the past century validate Drayton's practice, his impulse graphically to record heroic events in ode form. Pindar refers to the battle deeds of Achilles, Heracles, Ajax, and other legendary heroes and affirms that the purpose of poetry is to memorialize the heroic deeds of heroic men. However, Pindar never concentrates on or narrates, as Drayton does, the course of a single battle. It is the Italian and French pindarists who do that. We should remember that at the very time that Drayton was writing his ballad of Agincourt, Le Blanc in France was memorializing still another Henry and his deeds in battle—Henri IV.

Drayton and Jonson often invoke Pindar for inspiration, but they are also guided and directed by the French pindarists to whom they owe a largely unacknowledged debt. Ronsard and his followers served as mentors for Jonson and Drayton who were attempting to develop the English vernacular pindaric. Despite their efforts, however, the vernacular pindaric failed to take root in England until later in the seventeenth century, almost a hundred years after its apex in France. Jonson and Drayton serve as both pioneers for the English ode and as reminders of how much they as English poets owe to the French who came before them.

CHAPTER 3
THE POLITICAL PINDARIC IN ENGLAND
IN THE COMMONWEALTH ERA

Although both Ben Jonson and Michael Drayton produced under Stuart kings odes that were not without political relevance, it was during the Commonwealth period that the political pindaric came of age, to blossom in England under Cromwell and Charles II, as it had in France under the Valois kings. The men responsible belonged to opposite political parties: Andrew Marvell, the Puritan assistant to Cromwell's Latin secretary John Milton, and Abraham Cowley, secret agent for Charles I and a former member of the expatriate circle about Lord Jermyn and the young Prince Charles in Paris. Marvell wrote a series of odes during the 1650s on Horatian and Pindaric models that commented on Cromwell's rise to power, the success of his Protectorate, and his death. Cowley, who did not return to England until the mid-1650s, published the *Pindarique Odes* in 1656 as part of a folio volume of poetry, taking credit for introducing Pindaric ode into England. Further, in 1660 Cowley composed a Pindaric Ode on Charles II's restoration and return from France that was to become the model for the odes of political compliment that flooded England during the next half century. Cowley was responsible for the Pindaric revolution, but Marvell in his three odes produced some of the best examples in English of the political pindaric. Both men knew and to an extent were influenced by the example of a Catholic writer of Horatian and Pindaric odes, Casimire Sarbiewski.[1] Although a translation of some of Casimire's odes appeared in 1646 and although critics recognize his influence in Commonwealth England, he is usually regarded only as a poetic model. His influence on the emerging political pindaric has been all but ignored.

---

[1] See Jerzy Starnawski, "Sarbievius (Mathias Casimirus) (Maciej Kazimierz Sarbiewski) (1595–1640)," in *Centuriae Latinae*, ed. Colette Nativel (Geneva: Droz, 1997), 719–23.

1.

At the same time that Jonson was composing the Cary-Morison ode and Milton was experimenting with his first odes, Casimire Sarbiewski (1595–1640) was addressing neo-Latin odes on contemporary topics to important continental figures and using the Horatian and Pindaric modes to do so.[2] Admirers of his verse dubbed him both the Polish Pindar and the Polish Horace, for though he employed only Horatian verse forms for his odes, he clearly had Pindaric aspirations.[3] A Jesuit with intimate ties to Rome and to the courts of eastern Europe, Casimire addressed odes to Pope Urban VIII and his nephew Cardinal Francesco Barberini, as well as to the leaders of his native Poland, Sigismund III and his son Wladislaw, the Holy Roman Emperor, Ferdinand II, and also to their generals and counselors. Casimire held firm convictions about the politico-religious controversies of his time, employing the ode not just to compliment princes and popes, but also to comment on the political situation in Europe.[4] His collections of poetry, which appeared in 1625, 1628, 1632, and 1634, are heterogeneous, containing not only political and encomiastic odes, but also familiar odes,

---

[2] See the "Epicitharisma" in Mathias Casimirus Sarbievius, *Lyricorum Libri IV. Epodon. Lib. Vnus Alterque Epigrammatum* (Antwerp: Plantin, 1632), 289–336. Among the poets who compare Casimire to Pindar and Horace are Jacob Hortensius, Joannes Bollandus, Michael Mortierus, Jacob Wallius, and Sidronius Hoschius. See, for example, Hortensius' epigram : "O ter felicem nimiùm CASIMIRE Poëtam! / Sic tibi propensum qui CAPVT ORBIS habes. / Hunc Lyra non meruit Venusini Vatis honorem, / Non ita Dircaeum Pindarus vrget ebur" (297); also "Nec tua sufficiet lyra Pindare, nec tua Flacce / Sufficiet, quantus dicere, quantus hic est" (299). Other poets compare Casimire's verse to the pindarics of Pope Urban VIII. See, for example, Erycius Puteanus, in "Epicitharisma," 289–90. Quotations from Casimire's poetry, unless otherwise noted, are from the 1632 volume. I have also consulted other volumes of Casimire's poetry, including the posthumous *Lyricorum Libri IV. Epodon Liber Vnus, Alterque Epigrammatum* (Paris, 1647).

[3] Casimire never attempts triadic verse. All of Casimire's poems are in verse forms common in Horace: stanzaic odes, iambics, and so forth. Both he and his admirers allude to Pindar and the Pindaric strain in his poetry. See, for example, his odes to Pope Urban VIII (I.3; I.22), in which he professes a devotion to Apollo and the Pindaric plectrum. Casimire can joke about his Pindaric aspirations, as, for example, in his ode to Albertus Turscius [sic] (4.32). He says that he heeds his friend's and Horace's advice whenever he is tempted with too high flight, lest he fall like Icarus and give his name to a lake (l. 198).

[4] On Casimire's place in Polish literature, see Czeslaw Milosz, *The History of Polish Literature* (Berkeley: University of California Press, 1983), 119–22; Julian Krzyzanowski, *The History of Polish Literature* (Warsaw: Polish Scientific Publishers, 1978), 115–16. Also see Jozef IJsewijn, *Companion to Neo-Latin Studies* (Leuven: Leuven University Press, 1990–98), 1:239–53, esp. 242–43. Casimire was well known in England. Copies of his 1625 and 1634 poems were in the library of Christ's College, Cambridge. See Harris Fletcher, *The Intellectual Development of John Milton* (Urbana: University of Illinois Press, 1956–1961), 2: 662.

epigrams, biblical paraphrases, and other religious verse—and even trifles, such as the odes "To a Cicada" and "On the Barberini Bees."

Casimire's odes to the pope and to princes and potentates closely associated with the east central European milieu demonstrate his serious engagement with European politics.[5] His odes to Pope Urban VIII assume a place in his collection that those composed by Ronsard for Henri II and by Melissus for Queen Elizabeth have in their works. The 1632 volume has a dedicatory letter to Urban and, like his other books of poetry, contains poems addressed to the pope and to Cardinal Francesco Barberini. Casimire was in Rome in the early 1620s when Urban became pope and when the young Francesco Barberini, who was approximately Casimire's own age, was invested as cardinal. Although Casimire's odes to Pope Urban are adorned with graceful compliment, political references are unavoidable, since Urban was actively seeking to consolidate the papal lands in Italy and was involved in the European effort to keep the Turks in check. An observer of the intricacies of Polish politics, Casimire was not indifferent to the Polish king's expeditions against Sweden and Russia, undertaken to secure his right to the Swedish crown and that of his son Wladislaw to the crown of Russia (see, for example, 3.13). Uppermost in Casimire's mind, however, was anxiety about Turkish aggression. Situated closer to Turkey than other European nations, Poland had a history of border warfare with the Turks. After the failure of the truce in 1617, Polish encounters with the armies of the sultan became more frequent. Casimire records the devastating defeat Poland suffered in 1620, but celebrates with a rapturous ode a victory and a renewed truce in 1621.[6] Casimire's ode to Sigismund, "Laudes Invictissimi Potentissimique Sigismundi III" (2.20), exults in Sigismund's victory over the Turks. He comments ironically that the unfruitful Bosphorus now streams with Turkish blood. Two of Casimire's odes, addressed to Urban VIII (1.1) and Ferdinand II (2.1) respectively, deal with the withdrawal of the forces of the Turks (called Thracians in the ode) from Pannonia (here designating Hungary and the eastern regions of the Austro-Hungarian empire). Many other odes urge the princes of Europe to recapture the provinces of Greece held by the Turks and even to launch an attack against Turkey itself in

---

[5] Not all the odes addressed to leaders engage political subjects. Some odes to Sigismund, the king of Poland, or to Ferdinand II, the Holy Roman Emperor, are merely laudatory. One ode, ostensibly addressed to Apollo (2.15), concerns truly, as its subtitle confesses, the "necessity" of singing of the emperor's liberality, surely a theme "necessary" to poets from Pindar on. Ode 2. 26 ("Ad Famam") to Wladislaw is in a similar vein, as is 3. 17 ("Ad Tiberim") to Urban VIII.

[6] See Aleksander Gieysztor et al. *The History of Poland* (Warsaw: Polish Scientific Publisher, 1968); also *The Cambridge History of Poland*, ed. W.F. Reddaway et al. (Cambridge: Cambridge University Press, 1950), 1: 451–501; Norman Davies, *God's Playground: A History of Poland* (New York: Columbia University Press, 1982).

order to reclaim the Eastern Empire, once the stronghold of Christianity.[7] Curiously enough, Casimire's allusions to the Thirty Years' War occur in the context of the struggle with the Turks. He deplores what he calls the German civil war (2.21), regretting the Germans' revolt from the "mild" rule of Ferdinand II, commenting that it is one thing for Germans to fight Turks, quite another for Germans to be pitted against one another. Of course, Casimire is speaking as a Roman Catholic, not as a Lutheran.

In employing the ode form to celebrate military victory, Casimire is following a well-established tradition. It is hardly surprising that many of his odes resemble those produced in the previous century, or that Polish warriors and kings are praised in terms once applied to Charles V, François I, and Henri II. Like the pindarists before him, Casimire liberally exploits myth to celebrate his victor kings and princes. The hero Hercules comes forth wearing the laurels of the Christian hero. Casimire exults in the victory of Christendom over "paganism" and predicts in his ode to the pope (1.1) the renewal of a golden age. Faith, Truth, and Plenty have returned, says the poet, and the streams of Italy flow with milk and honey. Now that peace has returned, God has set the pope to rule over the earth as a Saturnian father-ruler. In a personal tribute to the Barberini pope, Casimire proclaims that all the trees of the country now pay tribute to the Barberini laurel.

It is clear that Casimire's victory odes share more than a little of the military fervor that characterizes Horace's odes to Caesar Augustus. The odes to Ferdinand II in fact appropriate the title Caesar Augustus for the Austro-Hungarian emperor and liberally mix the Horatian with the Pindaric strains. In 2.1 Casimire proclaims: what realm, what nation does not resound with praises to Caesar? Celebrating the defeat of the Turks in 2.12, Casimire invokes Horace's dictum for Caesar (*Carmina* 4.14)—the Rhine and the Danube and the regions beyond proclaim Ferdinand II Augustus. Like the Medici in Florence, the Valois princes of France, and the Farnese in Rome, the Hapsburgs of the Austro-Hungarian

---

[7] See, for example, 1.6, "Ad Principes Europae, De recuperando Orientis Imperio"; 1.8; 1.10 (to Urban); 1.11, "Ad Stephanum Pacium"; 1.12 "Ad Principes Romani Imperii, De recuperandis Graeciae Prouinciis"; 1.15, "Ad Equites Polonos"; 1.16, "Temporum nostrorum ignauiam reprehendit"; 1.20, "Ad Principes Italiae. De recuperando Orientis Imperio"; 2.11, "Ad D. Virginem Matrem, Cùm illi templum Ioannes Carolus Chodkevicius, signa contra Osmanum Byzantinum Imperatorem moturus, exstrueret"; 3.19, "Ad Militares Europae Ordines. De Prouinciis Graecis recuperandis"; 3.20. "Ad Aulum Laevinium"; 3.27, "In Primi Lapidis Iactv, cùm Ioannes Carolus Chodkevicius contra Osmanum Turcarum [sic] Imperatorem signa moturus, Templum Virgini Matri . . . extrueret"; 4.6, "Palinodia ad Parodiam Ioannis Kochanowii, Cùm Victoria de Turcis parta renuntiaretur, ac paulò pòst Stanislavs Koniecpolivs Exercituum Regni Poloniarum Ductor Campestris Scythas prosperis praeliis fudisset." The odes from the first three books were probably composed before 1625.

Empire claimed Hercules as an ancestor and were fond of adorning their palaces with sculpture and with painting that depict his labors. Naturally enough, in both 2.12 and 2.1 Casimire clothes the emperor in Herculean garments, comparing Ferdinand II's exploits to Hercules' conquests of the Cretan bull and the Nemean lion, his spoiling of the shades of Orcus, and his defeat of Memnon.

Even when praising the pope and Ferdinand with extravagant comparisons, Casimire also has subtler purposes in mind. His odes are not merely celebratory but also hortatory. As the "Epicitharisma" of the 1632 edition testifies, his contemporaries apparently valued him as an astute political advisor and even compared him to Pindar in this role. Jacob Wallius, for example, declares that Casimire's lyre partakes not just of Pindar's sweetness but also Pindar's ability to incite heroic striving.[8] Casimire even surpasses Pindar, declares Wallius, for he sings of sacred arms with such urgency that he moves princes to undertake even more heroic struggles than Pindar could have imagined. In another way also he is a worthy successor to the great Greek *vates* and can also be called, like Pindar, the priest of the Heliconian sisters. Casimire uses his lyre to urge action against the Turks who now hold in bondage those realms of ancient Greece that Pindar once celebrated. In pressing his countrymen on to victory in the east, Casimire proves his mettle as both a political poet and a Pindaric bard.

Though an ardent polemicist, Casimire was also a deeply religious and a philosophical poet as well—a Jesuit who looked at the history of his time from the perspective of other-worldly as well as worldly gains. Hence, if he urges men of his time to take up arms to recover the Eastern Empire, he also reflects on the moral and philosophical consequences of such action. Both Odes 1.6 and 1.8 explore the question of this prospective undertaking from different vantage points. Ode 1.6 opens with an affecting mythological figure depicting how the Turkish princes have put in bondage the gods of the sea, hence the sea itself. Neptune and Tethys and the Hebrus weep over their enslavement. Rousing the warriors of Europe to arms, Casimire tells them that they are ignominious to remain at their hearths when military exertion is needed. He recalls how the Romans marched against the tribes of the East and how they conquered Hannibal or Antiochus. Historical and mythic examples join to urge (as it were) the warriors of Europe to take immediate action.[9] Having made his point directly in the first part of this

---

[8] See Jacobus Wallius, "Ad Lyram Sarbievianam," in "Epicitharisma" in *Lyricorum Libri IV* (1632), 311–15: Wallius connects Casimire with Pindar: "Non solus olim lusit Olympicâ / Digno palaestrâ carmine Pindarus" (313). The Polish poet Szymon Szymonowic Bendonski (Simon Simonides, 1558–1629) was also addressed as a Polish Pindar. He composed odes both in stanzas and in triads. For his triadic verse see Simon Simonides Bendonski, *Opera omnia quae reperiri potuerunt olim sparsim edita, nunc in unum collecta*, ed. Angelo Maria Durini (Varsaviae, 1772), 77–115.

[9] Odes on the threat of or on the repulse of the Turks were common in the sixteenth and seventeenth centuries, particularly after the liberation of Vienna. See Bene-

ode, Casimire moves from exhortation to moral commentary and mounts a sermon against the debilitating effects of luxury and gold, urging the young warrior addressed in the first part of the ode to espouse heroic virtue.

The chastisement of love of gold at the expense of honor is part and parcel of the heroic ethos that ancient poets such as Pindar espoused. Ode 1.8, the companion ode to 1.6, sermonizes on the ill effects of gold, while it also urges human beings to be resolute in the face of fickle fortune, to prefer good deeds over long life. Casimire's philosophical odes are not without political application, for ultimately their moral is directed at the political end: the necessity of recovering the Eastern Empire, that is, of adding the kingdoms of Dawn to those of Sunset.

The selection of Casimire's poetry that George Hils translated and published in 1646 comprises mostly the philosophical and moral odes and the biblical paraphrases.[10] However, one important political ode is included in Hils's translation, 1.1 (2–9), "When the hatefull forces of the Thracians departed out of Pannonia," the ode that celebrated the withdrawal of the Turks from Hungary. Two of the philosophical odes that Hils translates—"E Rebus Humanis Excessus" (2.5 [16–25]) and "The kingdome of a wise man" (4. 3 [52–59])—also take up political issues, giving English audiences some indication of the hortatory quality of Casimire's Pindarism. They do so, however, in the context of philosophical discussion. Abraham Cowley certainly recognized the Pindaric potential of 2. 5 ("E Rebus Humanis Excessus"), for he adapted it for his Pindarique ode "The Ecstasie," minimizing, however, the political comments of the original. Casimire's ode dwells on the political crises in Europe, on the fury of human armies, on the fleets scattered over the oceans. The allusions to the woes of an embattled Europe are very specific. Although "The Ecstasie" seems to be a poetic flight from the world's troubles,

---

detto Menzini's odes to Cosimo III of Florence in *Opere di Benedetto [Menzini] Fiorentino* (Florence, 1680), 65–68, 97–100. Also see Vincenzio da Felicaia's odes to Cosimo II and to the leaders of the expedition against the Turks in *Poesie Toscane* (Florence: Conti, 1819), 57–61, 62–66, 73–80. Felicaia (1642–1707) wrote a series of canzoni on the liberation of Vienna. He coordinates references to the Turk's impiety with classical and biblical allusions: the impiety of the giants who warred against Jove is compared with that of the Canaanites who warred against Israel. *Poesie Toscane* was first published in 1707.

[10] *The Odes of Casimire*, translated by G. H. (London: Humphrey Moseley, 1646). Also see Maren-Sofie Røstvig's facsimile of the 1646 edition, as well as her "Introduction" commenting on Casimire and the odes: *The Odes of Casimire, translated by G. Hils* (London, 1646), Augustan Reprint Society 44 (Los Angeles: University of California Press, 1953), i–iv. Other seventeenth-century translators of Casimire include Henry Vaughan, *Olor Iscanus* (London, 1651) and Edward Sherburne, *Poems and Translations* (London, 1651). See David Money, "Aspects of the Reception of Sarbiewski in England: From Hils, Vaughan and Watts to Coleridge, Bowring, Walker, and Coxe," in *Pietas Humanistica: Neo-Latin Religious Poetry in Poland in European Context*, ed. Piotr Urbanski (Frankfurt-am-Main, Bern, and Berlin: Peter Lang, 2006), 157–87.

Cowley does glance in the course of his ode at the political scene in England, ask-ing, "For this will any *sin* or *Bleed*, / Of Civil Wars is this the Meed?" (2. 6).

Ode 4.3 in Hils's translation also has a specific political context, even though it is developed philosophically. We cannot mistake the immediacy of the open-ing lines: "The large-commanding Thracians wee / Have fear'd" (53); Casimire is referring directly to the Turkish forces that Poland engaged. Contrasting with this political terror is the praise of the equanimity that the wise man attains when he rules the inner kingdom of his mind. What is it, Casimire seems to ask, to be a king? His answer is that it is to have control over oneself. In his first three books of lyrics, Casimire addressed extravagant compliments to the pope, the cardinal, the emperor, and other dignitaries. This late ode of the fourth book, however, does not lavish attention on those possessed of power and mag-nificence. Instead, like Pindar, Casimire praises in it the kingdom of the mind, recommending above kings and conquerors the man who controls his fears and curbs his ambitions. The very existence of Hils's translation places Casimire and his odes on the English scene at a crucial moment, just at the period when the pindaric was about to assume a central place in the work of Cowley and Marvell. We can assume that men such as Cowley and Marvell, who were well read in the neo-Latin literature of Europe, would have known Casimire's books of odes in the original Latin, as well as in Hils's translations. During the period of the civil wars in England, they were looking for a new kind of ode that would mix the philosophical with the political. In Casimire, the leading exemplar of the Pin-daric and the Horatian style, they would have found a poet who was a master of just such a political-philosophical vein.

2.

The role of English universities and their publications in forwarding the devel-opment of the ode in seventeenth-century England is not to be underestimated. From the latter part of the sixteenth century scholars and fellows of both Ox-ford and Cambridge Universities wrote Latin, Greek, and vernacular odes to commemorate important state occasions: the death of Elizabeth in 1603 and the succession of James I, the death of Prince Henry in 1612, and the death of James I in 1625 and the succession of Charles I, as well as the births of Charles I's children. Poets such as Cowley, Crashaw, and Marvell made their literary de-buts in university volumes with poems that look forward to later more mature performances.[11] Among the occasions that elicited university publication were

---

[11] Crashaw published poems in the 1630s in several Cambridge collections. Cow-ley wrote odes for the 1633 and 1641 Cambridge volumes on Charles I's returns from Scotland. Marvell contributed a Greek epigram on the birth of one of Charles's children to a university volume.

those of royal return—for example, the monarch's return home after a period abroad on a visit or after the conclusion of a treaty with a foreign power. James I's return from Scotland in 1617, Prince Charles's return from Spain in 1623 (without a royal bride), and Charles I's returns from Scotland in 1633 and 1641 all called forth odes from university scholars. The poems produced for such occasions possess a character close to that of the classical "victory" odes, for the university poets readily imitated Horace and Pindar to celebrate the return of their own Caesar Augustus "in triumph."[12] In the 1650s university poets composed similar odes for the Protector, particularly on the occasion of Cromwell's negotiation of a peace treaty with Holland at the end of the naval wars. It is inevitable that the style and content of the university odes should affect poets such as Marvell and Cowley when they were called upon to compose encomia or odes of royal return for Cromwell or for Charles I and Charles II.

In 1641, to mark Charles I's return from Scotland at the conclusion of the second of the Bishops' Wars against the Scottish Covenanters, both Cambridge and Oxford issued volumes of poetry: *Irenodia Cantabrigiensis* and *Eucharistica Oxoniensia* respectively. These "odes of peace" or thanksgiving were meant to congratulate Charles I on his treaty with the Scots—on presumably bringing the blessing of peace to Britain without actually going to outright war. The volumes could not have appeared at a more politically explosive time, for 1641 was the very year when the crisis with Parliament was coming to a head. The university poets had the ungrateful task of presenting the sovereign in the role of a gracious victor and peacemaker when he had in fact been forced to give in to the Covenanters' demands and when the nation was on the verge of a civil war exacerbated by Charles's policies. Yet the poetic epithets chosen for the king differ little from those conferred on other monarchs on happier occasions. Such is the compulsion of poetic imitation. The king is compared to the sun-god Apollo—"sol noster" or "Phoebus pater"—returned from dark Scotia to bring the light back to his own land.[13] One extravagant poet compares him to Jupiter returned from Ethiopia

---

[12] See *Rex Redux* (Cambridge, 1633) and *Solis Britannici Perigaeum* (Oxford, 1633) for Charles's return from Scotland in 1633; *Irenodia Cantabrigiensis* (Cambridge, 1641) and *Eucharistica Oxoniensia in Caroli . . . Regis Nostri E Scotia Reditum Gratulatoria* (Oxford, 1641) for Charles's return in 1641. The odes contained in these volumes were in Latin, English, Greek, and even sometimes in more recondite languages such as Arabic, Hebrew, and Anglo-Saxon.

[13] See *Irenodia* (1641), sigs. A2^r, A3^r, D3^{r-v}, C4^v. In the Latin ode Cowley refers to Charles as a greater Apollo, who drives away the shadows: "Sic vigil aeterno regnator Phoebus Olympo / Circumfert subitam, quà volat ipse, diem. / Nil illi prodest stellarum Exercitus ingens; / Ut possit tenebras pellere, solus adest" (*Irenodia* [1641], B4^v, ll. 31–34). Similar comparisons of Charles to a sun returned to its proper sphere occur in the Oxford volume. Also see the poems by James Tichborne and Henry Berkely in *Eucharistica*, sig. b4^v–c^r and d2^{r-v}, respectively.

(*Irenodia*, sig. E3ʳ). The young Abraham Cowley wrote two poems for the Cambridge volume, one in Latin (sig. B4ᵛ), the second in English (sig. Kʳ⁻ᵛ), the latter reprinted in a revised version in his "Miscellanies" of 1656. In his English ode ("An Ode upon the return of his Majestie") Cowley congratulates the king on the peace he has negotiated: "Others by warre their conquests gain, / You like a God your ends obtain" (ll. 5–6). The divine Charles has only to call Chaos to his command, only to speak, "and sweetly order'd all" (ll. 7–8). Cowley even goes so far as to query (unprophetically): "What will the triumphs of his battels be, / Whose very peace it self is victorie" (ll. 59–60).

Some poets in the Cambridge volume confer the name Caesar or Augustus on the king, thereby commending him as a conqueror. The royalist divine Charles Mason addresses Charles I as the "Great Prince of peace, more Conquerour then all / The Cesars that o'rspread Rome's Capitoll" (sig. K3ʳ, ll. 1–2).[14] Charles's powerful word, Mason says, "As lightning, through the scabbard melts the sword" (l. 10). It is a metaphor that Marvell will more successfully apply to Cromwell. He also compares Charles's delaying tactics with the Scots to those of the Roman Fabius 'Cunctator,' the general who defeated the Carthaginians under Hannibal. Divine providence also had a hand in the Scots' defeat, he maintains, echoing Judges 5:20; as the unjust wars of Sisera were checked by the stars, so were those of Scotland against the crown.[15] Jacques Duport, Professor of Latin and Greek from Trinity College, who was later to compose odes for Cromwell, draws on Pindaric and Horatian models in a stanzaic ode. He commences with an expansive figure drawn from the *Aeneid* (1. 154–156): Neptune rises from the waves to bring order, so Charles soothes the quarrelsome waters of the fierce age (sig. Fʳ–F2ʳ). The Roman analogy recurs, as Charles I is likened to Scipio conquering Hannibal, thereby saving his country from civil wars and bringing peace. Charles is also a Jupiter-Augustus, who subdues the familiar giants of civil strife, but, notes Mason, without thunder (sig. F1ʳ⁻ᵛ). Another poet, Charles Rich, succinctly sums up the king's so-called battle tactics: without conquering, you conquer, the palm of victory is yours ("Sed non vincendo vincere, palma tua est" [sig. I2ᵛ]).

As he summoned classical models and figures for his 1641 ode for Charles I, Duport chooses similar models for his ode for Cromwell that appeared in the volume entitled *Oliva Pacis* that Cambridge issued in 1654 on Cromwell's successful conclusion of the Dutch naval wars. Oxford issued Ἐλαιοφορία at the

---

[14] Charles Mason (1616–1677) had been a contributor to other Cambridge commemorative volumes, among them the volume on the birth of Princess Elizabeth in 1635 and *Justa Edovardo King* in 1638, the volume in which Milton's "Lycidas" appeared.

[15] N. Hobart in "Caroli Caduceum" also compares Charles to Caesar: "Nec Tibi Cæsareis fas invidisse trophaeis, / Partaéve lauro sanguine: / Marte alii victis, Tu victo Marte triumphes. / Pax laude major bellicá" (*Irenodia*, sig. Bʳ). Charles is even greater than Caesar, however, since he conquers without bloodshed.

same time.[16] Here the military figures conferred are more appropriate, for even though Cromwell assigned the generalship of the Dutch wars to others, he was renowned as commander and victor in the civil wars. 1654 marked the conclusion of Cromwell's first year as Protector, a year to be assessed by Marvell in "The First Anniversary." As Charles I had been dubbed in 1641 a bringer of peace and the savior of his country, so Cromwell was adorned with similar laurels and named the new Apollo. The Age of Gold that Casimire had predicted for Urban VIII on his accession to the papacy and the university poets for Charles on his return from Scotland is now to commence for Cromwell as he closes the gates of war.[17] The poets call forth tributes such as Horace conferred on Caesar in *Carmina* 4.14 and 15.

> So when *Augustus* with his Warlike hand
> Had brought home Triumphs both from Sea and Land,
> And (*Janus* Temple shut) now conquer'd more
> By arts of Peace, then feats of Armes before;
> (R. B., "To the Lord Protector," in Ἐλαιοφορία, 59)[18]

Accordingly, the abstract deity Pax is invoked to come and confer the laurels. Samuel Rowe celebrates Cromwell's victory as a "Pax Augustalis" ("Paci Gratulatorium," in Ἐλαιοφορία, 52–53). His ode has an uncanny resemblance to those composed during the during the wars of religion in France. Like the French pindarists, Rowe alludes to the defeat of the giants at Phlegra and calls for the return of Astraea with Pallas and the Charites.

The classical prototypes that earlier poets had employed for Charles I now adorn Cromwell, but with some significant differences. Like Charles, Cromwell is Augustus Caesar, but then he is also Julius Caesar, the great general, and Alexander the conqueror, and Hannibal. In contrast, Charles I was merely Scipio. One poet of the Oxford volume compares Cromwell with Achilles; another contrasts him with the Grecian warrior, remarking that Achilles was a "wild Invader of Mankind," who conquered men's bodies, not their minds (ll. 9–12).

---

[16] *Oliva Pacis Ad Illustrissimum Celsissimumque Oliverum, Reipub. Angliae, Scotiae, & Hiberniae Dominum Protectorem; De Pace Cum Fœderatis Belgis feliciter sancta, Carmen Cantabrigiense* (Cambridge, 1654); *Musarum Oxoniensium* Ἐλαιοφορία, *Sive Ob Fœdera, Auspiciis serenissimi Oliveri, Reipub. Ang. Scot. & Hiber. Domini Protectoris* (Oxford, 1654).

[17] With Cromwell's victory, comments another poet: "The Golden Age returns, that ancient Blisse" (1.1). Cromwell is cited as a combination of Ulysses and Achilles: "'Twas not b' *Ulysses* or *Achilles* done: / I'le tell you how, 'Twas by both these in One"(ll. 21–22). (N. Hodges in Ἐλαιοφορία, 67).

[18] Another poet comments that Cromwell as new Apollo is not less than Caesar: "Qui Jani reddit Templum, simul & Mare Clausum, / Non minor Augusto Caesare Caesar erit" (ll. 11–12) (G.O. in Ἐλαιοφορία, 7).

Cromwell, on the other hand, "can Cement Kingdomes: / And whom Seas / Divide assunder Can Unite in Peace" (ll. 13–14). He is the surgeon to the state, who can staunch a bloody flux (W. Hatley in ʾΕλαιοφορία, 65). As the victories of his generals were always attributed to Caesar, so the victory in the Dutch wars redounds to Cromwell. Moreover, this victory becomes the occasion to remember Cromwell's earlier military accomplishments. John Ailmer lists the famous generals of antiquity from Alexander and Hannibal through Julius Caesar to Charlemagne and Tamburlaine, suggesting that their battles in comparison with Cromwell's were mere skirmishes (in ʾΕλαιοφορία, 96–97). Other poets use the occasion to adorn Cromwell with the trappings of his own former victories for the Commonwealth. As Pindar preserved the historical record by listing the previous victories of athletes, these poets remember and record Cromwell's earlier conquests. The ode "Vox Britanniae" recapitulates Cromwell's career as a soldier, calling the battle of Naseby as witness to Cromwell's courage in battle. Even Ireland, forgetful of blood that was shed, praises Cromwell as a redeemer. The Scots are compared to savage giants that Cromwell quelled on the fields of Dunbar (*Oliva Pacis*, sig. C4^r–D1^v). Another ode rehearses Cromwell's triumphs as a soldier at Marston Moor, Dublin, and Dunbar (H. Beeston in ʾΕλαιοφορία, 101). The peace with Holland is treated as a final triumph in a career marked by victory (*Oliva Pacis*, sig D1$^{r–v}$). Although the Protector during this period was beset with civil strife at home and abroad, he is remembered tactfully in these odes as the triumphant general of the civil wars.

Descriptions of battle are prominent in these odes, just as they had been in the odes that commemorated Charles V's victory over the sultan at Tunis or Henri IV's triumph at Ivry. Cromwell is named the master of the trident, as he dispatches the ships to battle.[19] Poets of both university volumes adopt techniques from epic to narrate the progress of the naval battle and to congratulate the victors. After a brief description of the battle, R. Gorges lauds those who effected the victory: "*Blake, Deane*, and *Monke*, the *Trident* of the Seas" (1.27).[20] The ashes of battle are still aglow, declares another poet, describing the course of the naval battle from the navies' first meeting to its successful conclusion. Exploiting the vocabulary of battle epic, he describes how horrid noises resound, flames leap up, waves surge, as the contending winds meet. The nymphs of the sea and even Neptune hide when Jove with his thunder and lightning appears and Mars

---

[19] See Thomas Fuller, "ʾΕΙΡΗΝΩΔΙΑ ad Protectorem," in *Oliva Pacis*, sig. E2^v–E3^v. Also see Gu. Groone, "Ad Dominum *PROTECTOREM*, De pace cum *Belgis*, ipsius nuper auspiciis inita," *Oliva Pacis*, F4^r–G^r. Groone gives an overview of the battle and renders thanks for the victory.

[20] The poem goes on to congratulate Cromwell on the peace: "Thus Thou like that Great *Conq'rour*, who Calcin'd / The *Barbarous World* to *Ashes*, straight refin'd / The *Stagirit's soyle*, Betrothing her to be, / The sole *Espousall of his Victory*" (ll. 39–42) (R. Gorges, in ʾΕλαιοφορία, 61).

threatens. When the battle is over, the nymphs return and the sea is safe once more for merchant ships. Jupiter—almost a Cromwellian figure—makes peace and nature assumes once more her peaceful aspect.[21] The propaganda effect of these peace odes is not to be underestimated, for the victory over the Dutch bolstered the Protector's reputation at home and abroad.

Only one ode in the Cambridge collection makes a direct reference to Pindar, and that ode concerns the displacement of poetry in time of war.[22] Rather than celebrating the battle or the glory of the victor, the poet pleads for peace to return so that the arts of Apollo can be nurtured. The theme is Miltonic, as is the example that the poet calls forth. Although the walls of Thebes were razed, he tells us, Pindar's house remained standing, at the order of Alexander: "Doricus intactas servavit Pindarus aedes." During the time London was besieged Milton alluded to the same story in his sonnet "Captain or Colonel or Knight at arms." The Cambridge poet, like Milton, calls up the name of Pindar to make a plea for the restoration of peace:

> Sis bonus, ô felíxque locis, quos sacra Minervae
> Turba colit, quos & non unus Pindarus ornans
> Gratum propitio meditatur Apolline carmen.
>
> Be good, O happy one, and in the places where
> the sacred band of Minerva dwell, not Pindar alone
> will sing, adorning a pleasing song for propitious Apollo.

Amid the songs of congratulation on the warlike achievement, one poet, remembering Pindar's timely advice to Hieron and Theron, reminds Cromwell that kings and tyrants also have the responsibility to cultivate the arts of peace.

3.

In his three odes for Cromwell—"An Horatian Ode," "The First Anniversary of the Government under O. C.," and "A Poem upon the Death of O. C."—Marvell imitates many of the strategies for praise that the university poets had employed. Like them, he alludes to Cromwell's lightning swiftness; he names Cromwell a Hannibal, and bestows the title of Caesar on both Charles I and Cromwell alike. However, unlike the university poets who regale their audience with a list of Cromwell's victories, Marvell chooses sparingly. In "An Horatian

---

[21] G. Bright, "De pacis foedere inter *Belgas* et *Anglos* icto," in *Oliva Pacis*, sig. G2^r–G3^r.

[22] G.W., "Ad invictissimum Oliverum magnae Britanniae & Hiberniae Protectorem carmen gratulatorem," in *Oliva Pacis*, sig. D4^v–E^v.

Ode," he selects only two classical prototypes for Cromwell: "A *Caesar* he ere long to *Gaul*, / To *Italy* an *Hannibal*" (ll. 102–103).[23] He also succinctly sums up Cromwell's victories over the Irish and predicts the victory over the Scots: "And now the *Irish* are asham'd / To see themselves in one Year tam'd . . . The *Pict* no shelter now shall find / Within his party-colour'd Mind" (ll. 73–74, 105–106). In "The First Anniversary" Marvell turns to Cromwell's foreign achievements, citing how the princes of Europe grudgingly praise Cromwell's martial expertise. As a final tribute to his generalship, Marvell notes in "A Poem upon the Death of O. C." that Cromwell died on the very day that witnessed in a past year his greatest military victory, as though the stars had determined when he breathed his last to recall the day when "up the armed Mountains of *Dunbar* / He march'd, and through deep *Severn* ending war" (ll. 145–146). In comparison with the university poets, however, Marvell is reticent, even leaving unrecorded the victory at Naseby that made Cromwell's career possible.

Marvell's three Cromwell poems are deliberate exercises that attempt to make contemporary ode the equivalent of its classical predecessors. To achieve this, he imitates not only Horace and Pindar and prominent sixteenth- and seventeenth-century pindarists, but also contemporary encomiasts of Cromwell, such as Payne Fisher. Immediately after Cromwell's Irish and Scottish campaigns and his victory at Worcester, Fisher had published *Irenodia Gratulatoria* and a Horatian ode "Ad Illustrissimum Britanniarum Polemarchum, Oliverum Cromwellum."[24] Like Marvell's "An Horatian Ode," these are odes of military return that have in mind Horace's odes for Augustus. In them, as in an earlier mini-epic, he depicts Cromwell as a Roman victor, who prevailed with lightning force, bringing like Julius Caesar swift victory and like Augustus peace.[25] Although he employs Latin hexameters for *Irenodia Gratulatoria*, Fisher clearly has both Pindar's and Horace's strophic odes in mind, calling attention to the

---

[23] First published in *Miscellaneous Poems by Andrew Marvell* (London, 1681). "An Horatian Ode" and the other poems by Marvell are cited from *The Poems and Letters of Andrew Marvell*, ed. H. M. Margoliouth. 3rd ed. rev. Pierre Legouis and E. E. Duncan-Jones (Oxford: Clarendon Press, 1971), 1: 91–94.

[24] The two odes were printed together in the same volume with a frontispiece consisting of a dramatic portrait of Cromwell mounted on a horse. See [Payne Fisher], *Irenodia Gratulatoria, Sive Illustrissimi amplissimique Viri Oliveri Cromwelli, &c, Epinikion* (London, 1652). Payne Fisher published under the pseudonyms Fitzpaganus or Paganus Piscator. Both odes were englished by Thomas Manly as *Veni; Vidi; Vici: The Triumphs of the Most Excellent and Illustrious Oliver Cromwell* (London, 1652).

[25] After the battle of Marston Moor Payne Fisher (1616–1693), forsaking the royalist cause, had celebrated Cromwell in a mini-epic in the style of Lucan. See Paganus Piscator [Payne Fisher], *Marston-Moor: Sive de Obsidione Praelioque Eboracensi Carmen* (London, 1650).

classical design by dubbing his poem an epinikion.[26] Like the neo-Latin pindarists of the sixteenth century, Fisher divides his epinikion into parts, beginning by hailing Cromwell as general and savior, "Anglorum venerande Parens!"
(Revered father of the English) and comparing him to Fabius and Hannibal and
even affirming that he surpasses Aeneas in his pious commitment to fighting
for country and religion. The central parts of the epinikion recount in some detail the events of the Scottish campaign; Fisher calls upon the Muses to narrate
Cromwell's victories at Dunbar, Edinburgh, and Worcester: "Dicite vos Musae,
vos Æoniaeque sorores" (sig. C4r). However, like the Italian poet Filelfo, who
had described the devastation of siege of Milan, Fisher pays attention both to
the sufferings of the Scottish people under siege as well as to the determination
of the besieging army to break through (sig. D4r). Also, he includes within the
scope of his victory ode not only narrative but also other devices such as epic
speech, as when, for example, a victorious Englishman jeers at the Scots who flee
at Worcester (sig. E4r–F1v). At the same time Fisher evinces moments of Pindaric intimacy; like Pindar, he breaks off to address his Muse, urging her not to
hasten away too fast: "Sed calamum quo Clio rapis temeraria?" (sig. B2v).

The Horatian ode that follows is shorter, but, like the previous ode, it also
lauds Cromwell in extravagant terms. Fisher addresses him as the gracious light
of the city; like the choragus of an epic quire he promises to celebrate him with
drum and lyre (sig. Kv). At the same time, however, Fisher attempts not just to
congratulate Cromwell, but also to assess the nature of the victories he has won,
and, like Marvell in "An Horatian Ode," to apply classical lessons to England's
present crisis. Fisher investigates, as does Marvell, how Cromwell negotiated the
perilous interval between the execution of the unfortunate Charles I and the set-
tling of the Commonwealth, praising Cromwell for plucking the nation from a
storm without further letting of blood and for putting down the Irish and Scottish rebellions (sig. K2r). Hence he awards Cromwell a moral as well as a military victory, crediting him with reviving banished Truth and crowning him with
both Mars's bays and Pallas's peaceful olive branches (sig. K2v–K3r). In the final
stanza of the ode Fisher even identifies for us the three classical models he has
followed: Pindar's dithyrambs, Archilochus's odes, and Vergil's heroic verse.

> Sic *Pindarus* (Dux) ecstaticis furens
> Te Dithyrambis *Archilochus* suis,
> Redux Iambis te *Maronis*
> Atque Epicum celebrabit oestrum. (sig. K3r)

---

[26] See Laura Lunger Knoppers's discussion of Fisher's odes in *Historicizing Milton*
(Athens, GA: Universtiy of Georgia Press, 1994), 119; also see Knoppers, *Constructing
Cromwell: Ceremony, Portrait, and Print, 1645–1661* (Cambridge: Cambridge University
Press, 2000), 32, 63, 89–93. Knoppers also discusses Marvell's "An Horatian Ode" in
Constructing Cromwell, 52–56.

> Thus Pindar (O leader), raging with his
> Ecstatic dithyrambs, and Archilochus
> Leading his iambs, and Vergil
> Also with epic heat will celebrate you.

Like Payne Fisher, Marvell combines Horatian and Pindaric devices in his three Cromwell poems to celebrate Cromwell first in his military victories, then in his protectorate, and finally at his death.[27] Of the three poems, "The First Anniversary" is perhaps most closely constructed on the Pindaric model, but none of the poems employ Pindaric triads to signal their debt to the Greek poet. Unlike his contemporary Cowley, who made a point of associating himself with Pindar by naming his collection *Pindarique Odes*, Marvell does not call attention to Pindar by direct comment. However, like Cowley Marvell also eschews triadic verse, preferring English meters, so we must identify Pindaric influences in other ways. Cowley took care in the preface to *Pindarique Odes* to point out the nature of his Pindaric imitation and also to explain why he had not attempted Pindaric metrics. With the inscrutable Marvell we are on our own, left to discover in the poems themselves the traces of Pindar's poetics and his political sensibility.

The classical models for "An Horatian Ode upon Cromwell's Return from Ireland," as critics have recognized, are multiple.[28] The ode was not designated "Horatian" until its publication in the posthumous 1681 volume. Further, it is not clear whether the term "Horatian" refers to its military subject, to its style, to its stanzaic pattern—the four-line strophes in tetrameter and trimeter— or perhaps even to a specific ode of Horace's that it is meant to imitate.[29] Critics

---

[27] Fisher's "Irenodia Gratularia" and his other odes to Cromwell are public performances. Like Marvell, he also celebrates Cromwell's Protectorate. In 1654 Fisher published his "Inauguratio Oliveriana"; in 1655, like Marvell, he published an anniversary ode, "Oratio Anniversarius." His concluding poems for Cromwell were a "Paean Triumphalis" in 1657 and a final ode in 1658 on Cromwell's death, "Threnodia Triumphalis in Obitum Serenissimi Nostri Principis Oliveri Angliae, Scotiae, Hiberniae." In the "Threnodia" Fisher, like Marvell, combines a tribute to the dead leader with a salute to the victorious general, noting that Cromwell's death occurred on the anniversary of his triumph at Dunbar.

[28] David Norbrook, "Marvell's Horatian Ode and the Politics of Genre," in *Literature and the English Civil War*, ed. Thomas Healy and Jonathan Sawday (Cambridge: Cambridge University Press, 1990), 147–69, here 149. Norbrook draws attention to some, but not all, of these.

[29] Critics have in fact as often turned to Lucan as to Horace for Marvell's political underpinnings, and when they have turned to Horace it has been to the brief portrait of Cleopatra in *Carmina* 1.37 as the precedent for Marvell's heroic portrait of the martyr Charles and to *Carmina* 3.4 for Augustus's triumphal return from his campaigns in the East as the ostensible precedent for celebrating Cromwell's return from Ireland. See Rosemary Syfret, "Marvell's 'Horatian Ode'," *Review of English Studies* 12 (1961):

have most often cited as Marvell's primary model Horace's *Carmina* 3.4, the ode that celebrates Augustus's triumphal return from the East. If indeed this ode is his basic model, Marvell could scarcely have avoided Pindaric precedent, since, as Steele Commager and other critics have argued, 3.4 is one of the most Pindaric of Horace's odes.[30] In 3.4 Horace names Augustus the friend of the Muses, a title that also applies to Hieron, Pindar's patron and supporter, as well as to Cromwell. Moreover, in Augustus's triumph over the hordes of the East, Horace obliquely recalls Hieron's successful containment of the Carthaginians and the Etruscans. Horace and Pindar stand side by side in Marvell's ode, poetic partners as they are in so many neo-Latin pindarics. Indeed, the association of the two poets was inevitable once Renaissance poets had identified Pindar as a model for Horace's odes to Caesar.

Sublimity is a well-known marker of the Pindaric style. David Norbrook has observed that Marvell aims in his portrayal of Cromwell at a "kind of sublimity—a height, indeed, somewhat above Horace himself."[31] Horace often characterized himself as a humble poet who shrank from the lofty flight associated with Pindar. Far from shrinking from loftiness, Marvell in "An Horatian Ode" quests persistently after the high style. Yet sublimity is only one aspect of Pindar's poetics. Also characteristic of his odes is their intricate structural design, their use of figures, the application of aphorism, the episodic arrangement of parts, and the basic rhetorical movement from introduction through digressions to conclusion. Marvell makes use of all of these devices.

Marvell opens his ode with a Pindaric flourish—a figure that is both striking and objective in its restraint, which both seems to define Cromwell and yet is distinct from him:

> The forward Youth that would appear
> Must now forsake his *Muses* dear,

160–72; John Coolidge, "Marvell and Horace," *Modern Philology* 63 (1965): 111–20; A. J. N. Wilson, "Andrew Marvell: An Horatian Ode upon Cromwell's Return from Ireland: The Thread of the Poem and its Use of Classical Allusion," *Critical Quarterly* 11 (1969): 325–41. Also see Rosalie Colie, *"My Ecchoing Song": Andrew Marvell's Poetry of Criticism* (Princeton: Princeton University Press, 1970), 66–68; Christopher Wortham, "Marvell's Cromwell Poems: An Accidental Triptych," in *The Political Identity of Andrew Marvell*, ed. Conal Condren and A. D. Cousins (Aldershot: Scolar Press, 1990), 16–52; Thomas M. Greene, "The Balance of Power in Marvell's 'Horatian Ode,'," *English Literary History* 60 (1993): 379–96.

[30] Steele Commager, "The Political Odes," in *The Odes of Horace, A Critical Study* (New Haven: Yale University Press, 1962), 160–234. Among the odes in which Horace pursues the Pindaric model, however, it is hard to judge which is the most Pindaric. Michael Putnam argues, for example, that 4.14 evinces Horace's "grandest Pindarizing" (*Artifices of Eternity*, 257).

[31] Norbrook, "Marvell's Horatian Ode and the Politics of Genre," 155.

Nor in the Shadows sing
His Numbers languishing,
'Tis time to leave the Books in dust,
And oyl th' unused Armours rust,
Removing from the Wall,
The Corslet of the Hall. (ll. 1–8)

Although striking, Marvell's figure poses a problem, for, as with so many of Pindar's opening figures, we as readers must work out the connection between the figure and the central person or theme of the ode. Cromwell is not named or directly connected with the "forward youth" of the opening figure except that he, like the youth, possesses a restless energy and like him "could not cease / In the inglorious Arts of Peace" (ll. 9–10). Moreover, Marvell moves on immediately to characterize Cromwell in other ways, comparing him to "three-forked Lightning," concurring in this with earlier poets, who describe Cromwell as "the Worlds great wonder," the "Best son of *Mars*," whose "Sword, like fatall Lightning flies."[32]

Lightning flashes throughout Marvell's ode and becomes its thematic motif as well as the essential quality of the Cromwellian *persona*. In Pindar's odes lightning is Zeus's signature, the force that makes possible his ascendancy over his enemies.[33] In Pindar lightning is also connected with the primal establishment of law and justice in nature. In Pythian 1 as well as in Olympians 9 and 10 and in Nemean 10, Zeus the thunderer is also Zeus the dispenser of order. This concept is carried over into Marvell's ode where lightning as a divine force distinguishes Cromwell as the dispenser of divine justice. Lightning stirs Cromwell to act as a divine agent; it strikes through Caesar's laurels to establish a new, heavenly-destined order. Lightning is the violent force by which Zeus decrees change, but it is not for human beings to understand just how and why Zeus dispenses his rule. In Pythian 8—an ode that figures as source not only for Marvell's ode but also for Horace's *Carmina* 3.4—Pindar uses lightning as the symbol of Zeus's absolute, though incomprehensible, law. In it Pindar tells how Zeus's lightning cleaves the ground and swallows alive the seer Amphiaraus, even at the moment when, anticipating his own fate, Amphiaraus predicts the successful capture of Thebes by a new generation of warriors. Pythian 8 itself is an ode to Hesychia, the daughter of Justice, who makes cities prosper, but, as Pindar demonstrates, the establishment of justice cannot take place without divine lightning exacting

---

[32] See Ἐλαιοφορία, 66, 64, 60.

[33] One of the Oxford poets compares Cromwell's sword to lightning, but with different effect: "'Tis true your Sword, like fatall Lightning flies: / But 'tis to purge *ill Ayre* and cleare the Skies" (R. Gorges, in Ἐλαιοφορία, 60). Also see Thad Bower, "Sacred Violence in Marvell's Horatian Ode," *Renaissance* 52 (1999): 75–88. Bower calls Cromwell both an incarnation of divine violence and a creature of mimetic desire.

its toll. In this Pindar contrasts with Horace. Horace's *Carmina* 3.4 celebrates the establishment of Augustus's peace after war, whereas Pindar's Pythian 8 celebrates the unknowable and often unpredictable ways of Zeus's justice. In Horace's ode Jove ordains Augustus as the instrument of his divine power and will. Pindar's Zeus works in a different way: he sends the just seer Amphiaraus to the underworld, but confers a later blessing on his son. It is not just the giant Porphyrion and the monstrous Typhon who must fear Zeus, but also ordinary men who must bend to his will.

If figure is important in Marvell's ode to define the nature of Cromwell as subject, digressive myth or narrative functions in a different way to forward intellectually and thematically the larger design of the ode. In Marvell's ode the digressive myth recounts Cromwell's pursuit and capture of Charles I—juxtaposed are Cromwell's rise and Charles's fall. Cromwell, the mythic hunter, forges a net and hunts down his adversary, and Charles, his prey, as a "Royal Actor" plays out the final tragic scenes of his life on the scaffold-stage. Marvell deepens his characterization of Cromwell by using a narrative myth to contrast him with Charles.

Marvell's view of Cromwell also owes something to Pindar's attitude toward the winning athletes of his odes. Pindar's athletes are men chosen by the god, who prevail because of a combination of their own skill or art, their courage, and the god-given καιρός that favors them. When a godly force enters human life, it raises divinely-ordained men above themselves. Human life is uncertain, ephemeral, but athletes in their moment of victory briefly rise above the laws of human fate. Victory does not lie with a man but, as Pindar notes in Pythian 8, with the gods who grant it. For a brief moment a divine light falls on a man—but not on every man, only on the man who, chosen by the god, perseveres to his goal. Here the classical and the Christian poet share a concept, for Marvell also believes that a man moved by will and favored by grace can perform extraordinary deeds. Cromwell is such a man. Marvell's ode functions as not so much a panegyric in honor of Cromwell's victorious return from Ireland as an intellectual analysis of the underpinnings of that victory—a consideration of the man and the forces that made the man. Cromwell shares a restless energy with the Pindaric athletes who also make their own destiny. He moves onward, he cannot rest, he urges his "active Star," controlled by the energy or force within him that presses him onward to victory—the "Courage high," "industrious Valor" (ll. 12, 17, 33). He resembles not only Pindar's athletes, but also his mythic heroes. In Olympian 1 Pelops focuses his energy on winning the chariot race that will shape his destiny, a race, which he cannot win, however, without Poseidon's assistance. The god assures his victory, but his own "Courage high" secures it. In Olympian 13 Pindar's Bellerophon is also a man of destiny, who, when guided by Pallas, bridles Pegasus and masters the chimera. In Pythian 10 Pindar's Perseus, urged by the same goddess, kills Medusa and avenges his mother. These heroes are figures of destiny, who succeed when divine forces stir their own extraordinary spirit—and in Pindar human beings never succeed without the coalescence of the divine with the human. Although the moment and the man coalesce in Horace's ode to Caesar, is it through the power of the divine? Or does Horace's conquering Caesar merely act confidently the part of Jove or Hercules on earth? Marvell here seems closer to Pindar's ineffable mysteries than to Horace's confident assurance that "Caesar" is taking destiny's part.

Marvell's abundant use of *sententiae* throughout the ode is also a sign of Pindaric influence. In antiquity and throughout the Renaissance Pindar was singled out as the poet of gnomic sayings.[34] In Nemean 4.32, when Pindar wishes to comment on Heracles' accomplishment of a difficult feat, he says succinctly "ῥέ-ζοντά τι καὶ παθεῖν ἔοικεν" (to accomplish one must suffer). He sums up the athlete's victory at the end of Pythian 12 (28–29) by saying that happiness does not come about without work. In Pythian 10, commenting upon righteous men, he tells us that touchstones tell character in men just as in gold (67–68). Pindar does not apply these comments at random; he uses them deftly and sparingly to sum up what the ode has illustrated. Pindar aims at the universal, but he applies it to the specific. Like Pindar, Marvell is looking not just at how things happen, but at the essential dynamic law of why—and he is always ready to comment. Consider the pithy observations that he introduces at crucial points in the ode. To explain why Cromwell succeeds as he does, Marvell is at our elbow to note that in coming to power, "[Nature] must make room / Where greater Spirits come" (ll. 43–44). In reflecting on the turn of events, he puts in, "But those do hold or break / As Men are strong or weak" (ll. 39–40). But particularly, his *sententiae* apply to the fitness of Cromwell as a man. Repeatedly he tells us: "He had of wiser art," and "How fit he is to sway / That can so well obey," and further, "So much one Man can do / That does both act and know" (ll. 48, 83–84, 75–76). Although Marvell could have found similar *sententiae* in Renaissance books of gnomic sayings, the Renaissance texts did not tell a poet how and where to apply such sayings. Pindar, more than any other ancient poet, was renowned for the use of *sententiae* strategically within his odes, for his astute summing up of persons and situations.

Finally, the concluding section of Marvell's ode has more than a few hints of Pindar's famous equivocations. Marvell refrains from the celebratory tone of Horace's "Nunc est bibendum" (*Carmina* 1.37.1). He uses the figure of the falcon to define the restraint with which Cromwell acted. Like the eagle that rests on Zeus's staff (Pythian 1.6) and symbolizes the sleeping power of the king of the gods, the falcon is the symbol of Cromwell's power and discretion. Having killed, the falcon rests on the next green bough. Obeying the "falconer," Cromwell as servant of the state lays his victory at the Commons' feet.

---

[34] See Hanna Boeke, *The Vale of Victory in Pindar's Odes* (Leiden: Brill, 2007), esp. chap. 3, "The Gnomic Expression of Cosmology in Pindar," 29–101.

Marvell does not overlook what the victory cost or what it will take to maintain it. We are reminded of the fact that Pindar never congratulates his Sicilian patrons without subtle intimations of the limits of mortal victory. Olympian 3 ends as Pindar reminds Theron that when Heracles reached the pillars at the end of the world he wisely did not travel beyond. He cautions the monarch not to venture further than discretion advises. Olympian 2 concludes as Pindar comments that men are always willing to spoil praise by spite. Olympian 1 tells Hieron that kings are the highest of all men, but then warns him not to reach higher. Few imitators of Pindar have imitated his cautionary conclusions, especially in odes that address leaders of state. At the end of "An Horatian Ode," however, Marvell operates in the cautionary mode. Marvell tells the ruler that, however triumphant his victory, he must keep erect the sword that won that victory:

> The same *Arts* that did *gain*
> A *Pow'r* must it *maintain*. (ll. 119–120)

Like the ancient Greek poet, Marvell tells a prince that he must know his limits.

4.

From the time Pindar first struck the golden lyre at the command of Hieron, the tyrant of Sicily, and presented him with an ode to commemorate both his victory in the chariot race at Delphi and the founding of the city of Aetna, Pythian 1 became one of the most popular of Pindar's odes. In Pythian 1 Pindar created a poem that praises the power of music and also discusses the ideal of good government on earth.[35] Just as Hieron had asked Pindar for a celebratory ode, so Cromwell on a comparable occasion had a commission for the poet Andrew Marvell. Responding in 1654 to Cromwell's mandate, Marvell, like Pindar, struck the metaphorical lyre and composed a poem to celebrate a ruler's success. With "The First Anniversary of the Government under O. C." Marvell likened Amphion's raising of the Theban walls by the power of his music to Cromwell's establishment of the Protectorate.[36] In "The First Anniversary" Marvell demonstrates that the poet still possessed the power to use his speaking harmonies to describe both the building of a free commonwealth and the construction of an artful ode.

---

[35] For a discussion of the connection of music and government, see, for example, Charles Segal, "Poetry, Performance, and Society in Early Greek Literature," in *idem*, *Aglaia* (Lanham, MD: Rowan and Littlefield, 1998), 9–24.

[36] Marvell's ode celebrating the first anniversary of the Protectorate should be considered in context with Waller's panegyric to Cromwell that appeared in 1655.

The concurrence in Pythian 1 and "The First Anniversary" of occasion, subject, and thematic treatment is not, I think, accidental.[37] Poets during the Renaissance often modeled odes to kings and princes on Pythian l, prizing the ode for its compliment to music as well as to monarchs. Marvell understood very well that in the Renaissance the ode to rulers of state ran the gamut from poems of pure flattery to poems that delicately but astutely commented on the political situation. Marvell was attempting something in between. Just as he had assessed Cromwell's role as a military leader in "An Horatian Ode," he wished in "The First Anniversary" to assess the quality of the man as ruler.

Marvell composed "The First Anniversary" in heroic couplets, a weightier meter than his usual tetrameters. We can be sure it was a conscious choice, for like Cowley in the *Pindarique Odes*, he aspires to catch Pindar's spirit, not to duplicate his complex metrical design in English.[38] Cowley's metrical compromise was to create a pattern of stanzas of differing lengths and meters. Marvell aims at a more disciplined meter, but, like Cowley, he works in sectional blocks of material that unfold episodically and often digress abruptly. Critics have often remarked on the stylistic peculiarities of "The First Anniversary." Parts of the poem seem to develop thematically, often without attention to strict chronological order. One critic of Marvell, John Wallace, has even argued that Marvell used a rhetorical model and made "The First Anniversary" develop like an oration in seven parts: *exordium, narratio, divisio, confirmatio, refutatio*, digression, conclusion.[39] It is not amiss to point out that the seventeenth-century editors had applied these very rhetorical terms to the respective parts of Pindar's odes. Benedictus's 1620 edition of Pindar's odes, together with Schmidt's 1616 edition, were widely used, and the commentaries of Franciscus Portus and Benedictus Aretius, which had appeared in the 1580s, were also readily available and often consulted. Both Schmidt and Portus printed rhetorical diagrams of Pindar's odes. Their analysis of Pythian 1, for example, divided the ode into seven

---

[37] Fitzgerald connects Pythian 1 with Horace's Cleopatra ode as well as Marvell's Horatian ode (*Agonistic Poetry*, 139–69). Also see S. P. Revard, "Building the Foundations of the Good Commonwealth: Marvell, Pindar, and the Power of Music," in *The Muses Common-weale*, ed. Claude J. Summers and Ted-Larry Pebworth (Columbia: University of Missouri Press, 1988), 177–90.

[38] In his "Preface" to the *Pindarique Odes* Cowley had set forth his aims in imitating Pindar, assuring his prospective reader that he would not translate Pindar word for word but would find English equivalents for the complexities of Pindar's style.

[39] John M. Wallace, *Destiny his Choice* (Cambridge: Cambridge University Press, 1968). For comments on the design of "The First Anniversary," also see Annabel Patterson, *Marvell and the Civic Crown* (Princeton: Princeton University Press, 1978); John Klause, *The Unfortunate Fall: Theodicy and the Moral Imagination of Andrew Marvell* (Hamden, CT: Archon Books, 1983); Barbara Everett, "The Shooting of the Bears: Poetry and Politics in Andrew Marvell," in *Andrew Marvell: Essays on the Tercentenary of His Death*, ed. R. L. Brett (Oxford: Oxford University Press, 1979), 62–103.

parts. The rhetorical ordering that Marvell adopts for "The First Anniversary" may well have been influenced by the rhetorical patternings posed by editors of Pindar's odes. Just as the seven gates of London call to mind the seven gates of classical Thebes, the city which was created by the power of Amphion's lyre, so the seven parts of "The First Anniversary" would almost seem to look back on the seven parts of Pythian 1 that contemporary editors had posited. (See Figures 3.1, 3.2, and 3.3).

Yet prosodic correspondences are only empty architecture without deeper intellectual structure. When Pindar composed Pythian 1, he was doing more than celebrating an occasion for the tyrant of Syracuse; he was commenting on the essential problems of government that Hieron faced at a crucial moment in his governing history. While celebrating the accomplishments of Hieron's reign, Pindar was also analyzing what had made that reign successful up to that moment and what was likely to keep it so. Connected as he had been with Sicily and Sicilian politics for over twenty years, Pindar was an interested observer of the workings of government in the Sicilian states. Together with being a enlightened ruler in Syracuse, Hieron had founded the city of Aetna as a limited monarchy with a democratic constitution and handed its rule over to his son Deinomenes. Pindar was aware of the difference between ideal and real rulership, particularly in a newly-founded state, and his ode subtly comments on the difference.

Marvell was also an astute observer of political cross-currents, as well as a student of history. If he noted in "An Horatian Ode" a likeness of Cromwell to Caesar, he might also have marked a likeness between the careers of Cromwell the Englishman and Hieron the Syracusan. Both sought to be enlightened dictators. Like Hieron, Cromwell came to power suddenly, was a non-hereditary leader, and was one whose power was constantly threatened. Neither Hieron's nor Cromwell's rule lasted, but then their poets, when they composed their celebratory odes, could only guess at that. Hieron had to deal continually with unrest at home and rebellion close at hand in the city-states of Sicily and southern Italy; Cromwell had the Scots to control and the Irish to quell. Then there was trouble abroad for both, for Hieron and his fellow Sicilian tyrants from the Carthaginians to the south, the Phoenicians and Persians in the east, and the Etruscans to the north, the last of whom he had met in a sea battle off Cumae in 477 B.C. For Cromwell, there were the naval wars with Holland as well as the continual pressure from the Catholic monarchies of Europe. Both also faced dissidents at home. In fact, Cromwell's profile as a political leader far more resembles Hieron's than it does Caesar's, to whom he had been compared in "An Horatian Ode."

Pythian 1 was one of the last odes Pindar composed for Hieron, then at the height of his power. Hieron's victory at the prestigious chariot race at Delphi and his dedication of Aetna were triumphs that the tyrant would not repeat. Pindar catches in the ode a sense both of exultation and of uncertainty, praising Hieron's extraordinary accomplishments, but reflecting how transitory human achievement often is. Among the Renaissance imitations of Pindar's ode is Ronsard's

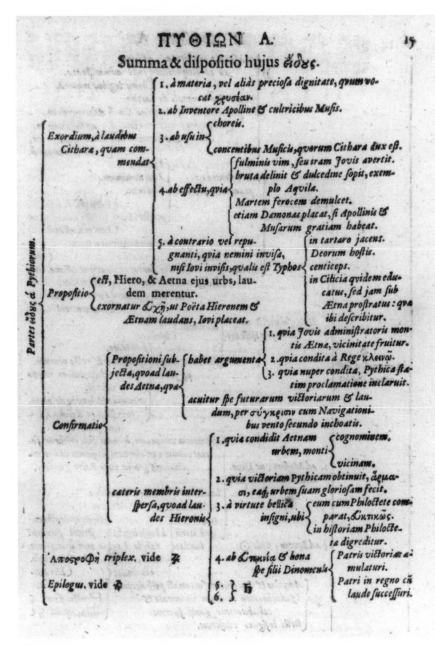

Figure 3.1
Page from *Periodos*, ed. Erasmus Schmidius (Wittenberg, 1616) illustrating the diagram of Pythian 1.

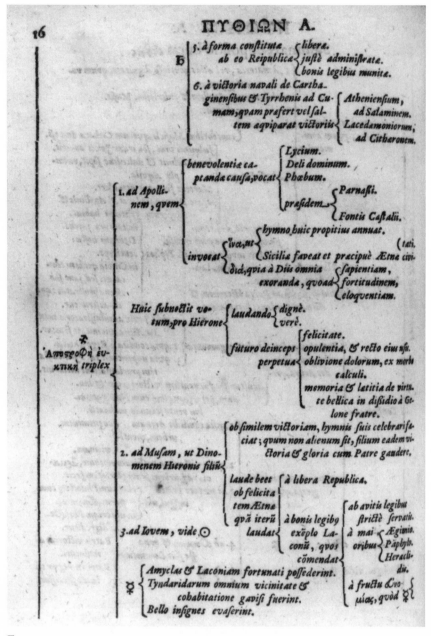

FIGURE 3.2
Page from *Periodos*, ed. Erasmus Schmidius (Wittenberg, 1616) illustrating the diagram of Pythian 1.
By kind permission of The Brithsh Library

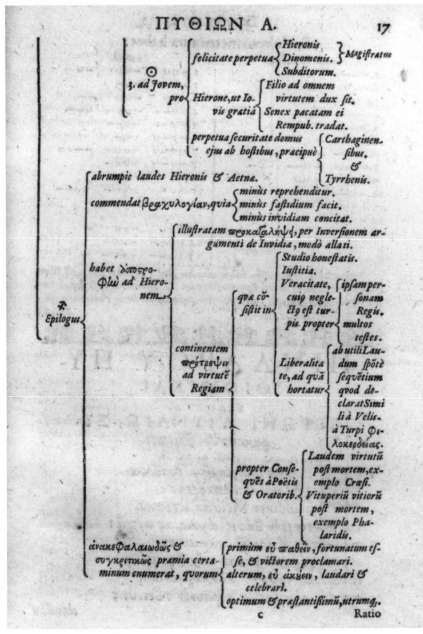

FIGURE 3.3
Page from *Periodos*, ed. Erasmus Schmidius (Wittenberg, 1616) illustrating the diagram of Pythian 1.

By kind permission of The British Library

hymn for Henri II, a poem that Marvell might very well have known. But Ronsard's imitation, eloquent though it is, hardly penetrates the complexities of Pythian 1. Ronsard was content merely to present himself as a bard striking the golden lyre and celebrating his Jupiter-king's triumph over his Typhonian foes.[40] Prominent as these motifs are in Pindar's original ode, they are not, as in Ronsard's hymn, mere complimentary flourishes with which to salute a ruler. Pindar takes the responsibilities of the poet to Apollo and the ruler to Zeus as religious duties. How the poet and the ruler fulfill these is essential to the poet's art and the ruler's successful governance. In comparing in "The First Anniversary" the poet's governing of his art with the ruler's governance of the state, Marvell also demonstrates a profound understanding of the correspondence between poetry and political rule.

For Marvell, as for Pindar, government comes from the divine and is part of the cosmic ordering of the universe. A true governor is the deity's power on earth—virtuous, high-minded, godly in his purpose, omnipotent like God, because like God he wields his power righteously. He commands respect for his iron hand and for the justice of his ways. Zeus, according to the Greeks, had established government through ordinance, after putting down Typhon and the rebellious Titans through his thunderbolt. According to Christians, the account of Zeus's defeat of his enemies was a thinly veiled allegory of Christian history; for the Christian God, wielding the thunderbolt and supported by angelic warriors, had defeated Satan and cast him into Hell. Through Zeus, said Homer, kings reign, a saying parallel to the biblical maxim (Proverbs 8:15). Zeus both dispenses power to Hieron and serves as a example of the righteous ruler, teaching him that he must keep his enemies in check. The hordes of Africa, Asia, and northern Italy that threaten Sicily resemble Zeus's "brutish" foes; unless they are kept in check, no free and enlightened government will be possible on earth.[41] Paradoxically, Pindar pleads that force must be used to guarantee freedom, for unless the strong and just wield force for good ends, the unjust will use force to enslave. Neither Pindar nor Marvell had any respect for true "tyrants."

Even though Pindar's historico-religious traditions are different from Marvell's, the argument for necessary force that underlies Pythian 1 and "The First Anniversary" is remarkably similar in both poems. Like Hieron, Cromwell holds his dispensation as a leader from a deity, who through force has defeated his own foes. Further, Jehovah's patriarchal law grants to Cromwell the right to resist by force dissenters at home and enemies abroad. The God of "The First

---

[40] *Hymnes de Pierre de Ronsard* (Paris, 1555). See the discussion of this hymn in chapter 2 above.

[41] When Theron constructed the temple of Zeus at Acragas (the modern Agrigento), he placed figures of conquered Africans as the colossi who support the temple. The temple was reduced to ruins by these same Africans when they at last defeated the Sicilian tyrants.

Anniversary" controls the locusts from the pit and the Great Dragon (Revelation 9: 3–11). He authorizes "angelic" Cromwell to defend England against the enemies that attempt to deprive her of her freedom. The force he uses to resist his enemies paradoxically will keep the Commonwealth free.

> 'Tis not a Freedome, that where All command,
> Nor Tyranny, where One does them withstand;
> (ll. 279–280)

To argue that force is justified when wielded by the deity's deputy on earth is not an original position for a poet-apologist to take. What Pindar says of Hieron and Marvell of Cromwell, Horace said of Augustus. Pindar's royalist imitators in sixteenth-century Italy and France used similar arguments to defend Ferdinand of Aragon, the French kings, Charles VII and VIII and François I, as well as the Henrys of both France and England. Why then is Marvell's treatment of the issue different or in any way more persuasive? And how may it be said to relate more closely to Pindar's view than that of his other imitators? Partly it is, I think, that Pindar and Marvell connect the enlightened autocrat not merely with a divine ruler, be it Zeus or Jehovah, but also with the poet-musician. Both Pythian 1 and "The First Anniversary" employ musical metaphors to define the good governor and good government. In the process the ruler becomes the cosmic musician who moves in harmony with the very nature of things and tunes his state accordingly. Hence Pindar's opening address to the golden lyre, held in common right by Apollo and the Muses, is more than a graceful compliment to the affective powers of music. It is a leading concept in the poem:

> Χρυσέα φόρμιγξ, Ἀπόλλωνος καὶ ἰοπλοκάμων
> σύνδικον Μοισᾶν κτέανον· τᾶς ἀκούει
>   μὲν βάσις ἀγλαίας ἀρχά,
> πείθονται δ᾽ ἀοιδοὶ σάμασιν
> ἀγησιχόρων ὁπόταν προοιμίων
>   ἀμβολὰς τεύχῃς ἐλελιζομένα.
> (ll. 1–4)

> Golden lyre, possession in common right
> Of Apollo and the violet-tressed Muses, which
> The step, the onset of revelry, heeds;
> The singers obey the signals,
> Whenever you with your quivering sound
> Lead the chorus with your prelude
> To lift up the dancing feet.

When the poet strikes the lyre, the chorus moves in response. The poet-composer who metaphorically or actually strikes the lyre "rules" the chorus, rehearsing them in their steps. They, in turn, bring the poet's composition into performance.

The poet-composer himself is ruled by the divine forces within him: Apollo and the Muses who inspire his poetry. Thus the poet takes the place of the deity on earth and is the one who controls the many. He is a "ruler" through the god Apollo, just as the prince or tyrant is a ruler through Zeus. The lyre itself is a cosmic symbol: the *phorminx* or lyre was a constellation of the Greek sky, itself made up of a group of stars that move in consort with other stars in the heavens. The *phorminx* is a continual reminder of the cosmic or divine power of music. It moves with the spheres of heaven and orders or rules them, as the harmonies of music order both heaven and earth. Pindar was well acquainted with the Pythagorean theories about the governing power of music. Music, like the good governor, has the power both to order and to control: to subdue violence and to bring all under a beneficent rule. Pindar tells us, therefore, that music's charms can quench Zeus's thunderbolt, can keep his powerful eagle subdued, and can even make the warlike Ares drop his arms (See Figure 3.4). All respond to music—all, that is, but those, like Typhon, who reject the principle of law and social contract inherent in musical harmony.

In the first long section of "The First Anniversary," Marvell develops the notion of time, as Pindar has developed music, into a symbol of good government. As the poet in Pythian 1 controls the lyre, so Cromwell controls time, bringing it under his hand and forging a cosmic harmony and power through it, like that the musician-poet effects. While the opening image of the stone dropped in water does not directly imitate Pindar's struck lyre, it works in the poem in a comparable fashion. Marvell employs this highly developed figure to convey his argument, transforming, as Pindar had, a physical phenomenon into a cosmic principle. By likening the passage of time to the circles of water—"the vain Curlings of the Watry Maze" (l. 1)—that form about a dropped object, Marvell explains how a just ruler, such as Cromwell, can control the passage of time. Others are merely overwhelmed by time, not, however, the just ruler, who understands how time's circuits are the earthly pattern of something higher. Time moves in an orderly sequence of days, months, years, a circuit which is controlled by the orbiting of the spheres that move the universe, move it *musically* as the creator God ordains. Cromwell, like Pindar's poet-musician, in tune with God's purposes, "tunes" these spheres; he "cuts his way still nearer to the Skyes, / Learning a Musique in the Region clear, / To tune this lower to that higher Sphere" (ll. 46–48). The ordering of time, then, produced by the musicianly Cromwell, is analogous to the ordering of the chorus by the poet in Pythian 1. Musical references so permeate the first section of Marvell's poem that time almost becomes music. Cromwell's orbit is not dull and saturnine. Like the "Jewel of the yearly Ring," he contracts the "force of scatter'd Time," producing in one year "the work of Ages" (ll. 12–14). Unlike the heavy monarchs governed by malignant Saturn, who have no musical instinct and are only like the "wooden Heads unto the Violls strings" (l. 44), Cromwell commands music within the state.

FIGURE 3.4
Photograph of two aspects of Jupiter, as thunderer and as musician from Vincenzo
Cartari, *Le Imagini de i dei de gli antichi* (Venice, 1587).
Photograph by Stella Revard.

The central musical metaphor in "The First Anniversary"—a metaphor
for the construction of good government—is Amphion's raising of the walls of
Thebes by the playing of his lyre. It is not one that Pindar employs, for he never
alludes to Amphion, even though he was the musician most closely connected
with Thebes, Pindar's native city.[42] However, allusion to Amphion's feat of mu-
sicianship is common in ancient and modern poetry, and poets often employ
it as a metaphor for good government. In an ode to the rulers of Poland (4.26)

---

[42] Although Pindar does not allude to Amphion in his epinician odes, this is perhaps not a significant omission: he alludes only once (in Pythian 4) to Orpheus, the other
archetypal mythic poet.

Casimire Sarbiewski alludes to Amphion, making an analogy between the poet's
ordering his poem and rulers constructing the order of the state. In a similar
fashion Edmund Waller in his ode "Upon His Majesty's Repairing of St. Paul's"
compliments Charles I on his kingship by likening his rebuilding of St. Paul's to
Amphion's raising the walls of Thebes.[43] By extension both Waller and Casimire
are expressing a Pindaric notion: good government is like good music. Similarly,
Marvell, making use of the metaphor, describes how Cromwell emulates Amphion's lyrings by "tuning" the ruling instrument of the state with "wondrous
Order and Consent" (ll. 67–68). The word "instrument" designated both a musical instrument and the so-called "Instrument of State" by which Cromwell insti-
tuted the Protectorate in 1653.

> And still new Stopps to various Time apply'd:
> Now through the Strings a Martial rage he throws,
> And joyning streight the *Theban* Tow'r arose;
> Then as he strokes them with a Touch more sweet,
> The flocking Marbles in a Palace meet;
> But, for he most the graver Notes did try,
> Therefore the Temples rear'd their Columns high:
> Thus, ere he ceas'd his sacred Lute creates
> Th'harmonious City of the seven Gates. (ll. 58–66)

The poet's creation of the city walls with his sacred lute imitates the archetypal
creation of God himself. Prompted by the god, the divinely-ordained ruler in
turn creates order within the state, the state being as much his creation as the
ode is the poet's or the world God's. In likening Cromwell's accomplishments
as state-builder to those of the builder-poet, Marvell acknowledges music as the
ultimate civilizing force. Further, as the millennium approaches, there is still
greater need for a ruler who can bring the discordant elements that strive against
harmony into a final concord and consent. At this point the earthly poet-musi-
cian-architect becomes heavenly, and the music we hear is not just creative but
also apocalyptic. Cromwell becomes "angelic Cromwell," that is, Michael, the
punisher of the dragon and the herald of the last age (Revelation 12:7–9).[44]

---

[43] "He [Charles I], like Amphion, makes those quarries leap / Into fair figures from
a confused heap; / For in his art of regiment is found / A power like that of harmony in
sound" (ll. 11–14): in *The Poetical Works of Edmund Waller and Sir John Denham*, ed. Rev.
George Gilfillan (Edinburgh: James Nichol, 1857), 9–11.

[44] Whereas some early Christian theologians interpreted the war in Heaven described in Revelation 12:7–9 as a past war in which Michael and his angels fought with
the Dragon (Satan) and his angels, defeated them, and cast them out of Heaven, Puritans
such as Marvell would have interpreted Revelation 12:7–9 as a future war that would lead
to the millennium, the establishment of Christ's kingdom on earth, and the chaining of
Satan in Hell for one thousand years. Throughout "The First Anniversary" Marvell char-

In Pythian 1, the dragonish Typhon represents the primeval anarchy that resists the establishment of justice (*dikē*) not only at the beginning but also at the end of things. This monster child of Earth is the irreconcilable foe of Zeus, who cannot be civilized and made a part of Zeus's commonwealth. Although overthrown and pinioned under Aetna, he is never entirely silenced. Pindar describes him at the beginning of the first epode: a hundred-headed beast, sprawled full length under the mountain, the pillar of Aetna piercing his spine and causing him to bellow in pain and send forth clouds of smoke and rivers of fire from the volcano. This monster enemy of Zeus is also an enemy of the Muses, whose beauty and harmony he hates. Pindar includes in Pythian 1 a prayer of blessing on the new city of Aetna, which, he tells us, cannot flourish unless its enemies are controlled. He implores the Zeus who conquered Typhon to keep the Carthaginians at home and silence the battle cry of the Etruscans. Hoping that the battle force that Hieron evinced at Cumae will dissuade his enemies from pursuing war, Pindar rejoices not only in the prowess of the Syracusan leader, but also in that of the Athenians and the Spartans, who scattered the hundred-headed Persian galleys in the sea at Salamis and defeated the Persian army at Plataea, preserving good government and a home in Greece as in Sicily for the Muses. These hundred-headed galleys are but one more evocation of the monster Typhon.

Like the ancient Sicilian ruler, Cromwell takes a firm stance toward his enemies, reconciling those he can, strongly resisting the others. Some opponents may be useful to the government, their opposition serving to make the fabric of the state stronger, as opposing pressure in an arch serves to uphold the single center stone: "The crossest Spirits here do take their part, / Fast'ning the Contignation which they thwart" (ll. 89–90). Other antagonists, however, must be more strictly dealt with, or their dissonant voices will drown all harmony: they "sing Hosanna to the Whore, / And her whom they should Massacre adore" (ll. 113–114). Here Marvell alludes to the danger of the subversive Catholics to the state, the Whore of Babylon of Revelation 17:5 being the symbol among Protestants for the Roman Catholic Church.

Throughout the Renaissance the gigantic and monster enemies of Zeus were connected with the heretical enemies of continental kings and rulers — no less so in Marvell's ode, where they represent, however, Catholic rather than Protestant insurgents. Connecting the dragon of Revelation both with those foes of the Olympian deities and with the foes of Cromwell, Marvell develops the biblical analogy further. "Angelique *Cromwell*" (l. 126), like the biblical Michael or the heroic Zeus, must pursue "the Monster thorough every Throne: / Which

---

acterizes Cromwell as a divine agent, an "angel" who will be instrumental in establishing the climate for the millennium. See the commentary on Revelation in Revard, *The War in Heaven: Paradise Lost and the Tradition of Satan's Rebellion* (Ithaca: Cornell University Press, 1980); also eadem, "Milton and Millenarianism," in *Milton and the Ends of Time*, ed. Juliet Cummins (Cambridge: Cambridge University Press, 2003), 42–81.

shrinking to her *Roman* Den impure, / Gnashes her Goary teeth; nor there secure" (ll. 128–130). The Whore's partner, the dragonish Satan, though defeated
and dispossessed of the kingdom of Heaven, remains, like Typhon, a menace:
"Stars still fall, and still the Dragons Tail / Swindges the Volumes of its horrid
Flail" (ll. 151–152).[45] Satan controls the thrones on earth and attempts through
Rome to topple those states headed by just, god-like rulers. Like Hieron, Cromwell cannot relax his guard. Still more "paganish" foes oppose Cromwell at
home—the dissident sects that Marvell, drawing another biblical parallel, describes as "Accursed Locusts" from the pit (Revelation 9: 3–10).

Perhaps following Pindar, Marvell describes Cromwell as the "Peoples
Charioteer," a man who must steer cautiously and hold the reins securely, guided
by God. The image of the charioteer is important in Pindar, for it describes not
only the victorious athlete who governs his horses well but also the ruler of the
state who leads his people. In Pythian 1 Pindar describes Hieron as a skillful
charioteer, perhaps because he was celebrating Hieron's chariot victory at Delphi,
perhaps because the image of the charioteer was one of his favorites. Pindar often
likens the poet to a charioteer or steersman and prays that, like the athlete, he
steer his course straight. Hieron the ruler is the steersman for the state, and for
him Pindar makes analogous prayers—that he steer his people with a just tiller
(l. 86), keeping Sicily free and plotting a course for his son as the king of Aetna
to follow. Hieron had in fact commissioned a bronze statue of a charioteer and
made a gift of it to Delphi in honor of his chariot victory. Marvell's portrayal of
Cromwell as the "Peoples Charioteer" (l. 224) is similar in concept, for it honors
Cromwell as the leader of the democratic state, who is responsible to its people.
As chosen leader he is superior to a hereditary king: "For to be *Cromwell* was a
greater thing, / Then ought below, or yet above a King" (ll. 225–226).

In "The First Anniversary" Cromwell remains the man of destiny, whose
fate has been plotted by God: a man at "whose happy birth / A Mold was chosen
out of better Earth" (ll. 159–160). Marvell also continues to represent him, as
he did at the end of "An Horatian Ode," as a soldier, who stands with his sword
ready: "knowing not where Heavens choice may light, / Girds yet his Sword,
and ready stands to fight" (ll. 147–148). Yet at this apocalyptic moment when the
millennium is approaching, Cromwell is also the "angel" who guards England,
preparing the land for Christ's assumption of kingship on earth.

In the first part of Pythian 1, Pindar argues Hieron's right by connecting
him with the divine musician and with Zeus himself. In the second, he alludes to
types closer to the ruler—human leaders who justly or unjustly discharged their
rule. The effect in one sense is to bring Hieron down to earth, to remind him he is
a man, not a god, and to urge him to rule generously and justly. The first of these
types is a hero of the Trojan War, not Achilles or Ajax, whom elsewhere in his

---

[45] Probably an allusion to Revelation 12:4: the third part of the stars that fell from
Heaven was often interpreted as the angels who fell with Satan.

odes Pindar cites as supreme warriors, but the archer Philoctetes, a man mortal
and limited, afflicted with a foul and grievous wound, yet a man who was courted
by the Greek leaders, since his presence was necessary to effect Troy's final ca-
pitulation. Of Philoctetes Pindar says that though he walked on feeble flesh, he
was a thing governed by fate: "ἀσθενεῖ μὲν χρωτὶ βαίνων, ἀλλὰ μοιρίδιον ἦν"
(l. 55). Perhaps, as some commentators believe, Pindar is referring to Hieron's
illness and commending his courage in persevering despite it. Yet he is also indirectly reminding the tyrant that he is still a man, subject to human limitation,
however high he has been raised. Marvell effects a similar reminder when he
alludes to Cromwell's recent coaching accident: "When thou hadst almost quit
thy Mortal cares, / And soyl'd in Dust thy Crown of silver Hairs" (ll. 179–180).
On the one hand Marvell can rejoice that providence saved Cromwell's life; on
the other, he can read in the episode the inexorable truth that as a mortal man
Cromwell must one day die. No ruler, however angel- or god-like, may escape
man's destiny. Both he and his accomplishments must be measured by the human yardstick.

The final sections of Pythian 1 and "The First Anniversary" apply this human
yardstick yet more rigorously. While offering words of praise, Pindar and Marvell also assess for posterity how the still-living rulers have fulfilled the require-
ments of good leadership. Both poets measure the rulers, Hieron and Cromwell,
against human models, taking prototypes from Greek and Hebraic history. The
ideal of the good leader may be laid up in Heaven, but its fulfillment must be on
earth by mortal men. Pindar prays that Deinomenes, Hieron's son, may follow
his father's example and be a constitutional monarch in the Dorian tradition, attentive to the needs and views of his people. May he steer his course with justice,
having forged his tongue, as Pindar says, on an unlying anvil. If he prove a faithful steward, not seeking his own profit but generous to his people, the people in
turn will testify to his worth, a testimony the poet will echo.

For Pindar the poet is the custodian of the future, who will decide whether a
ruler will be remembered as a Croesus, the most generous of kings, or a Phalaris,
the most hated of tyrants.[46] The Sicilian tyrant Phalaris was famous for burning his victims in a brazen bull, thus making the heatened brass bellow harshly.
The allusion to bellowing recalls for the last time the bull-like prototype of the
bad ruler, Typhon, whose angry cries resound under Aetna, producing the dissonance that contrasts with the music of good governance. Hence, Pindar reminds
us, neither lyres nor youthful choruses greet the tyrant (ll. 94–98), but are reserved for a generous ruler such as Croesus or Hieron. Curiously, Pindar's allusion to the contrasting rulers, Croesus and Phalaris, is double-edged. Certainly
by implication he is comparing Hieron to Croesus and urging him to continue
to be generous and indulgent to his subjects. But he is also perforce cautioning

---

[46] Segal comments that the voice of moral order, good song, honors Croesus, but is
denied to Phalaris. See Segal, *Aglaia*, 15–16.

him about the sting to his future fame should he be less magnanimous. Thus, by alluding to the choruses of praise that greet the just ruler, the poet in a sense has the last word in the poem, just as he has had the first in the proemium. The poet, after all, as he advises Hieron, is the one who confers the garland of praise, which crowns all achievement.

τὸ δὲ παθεῖν εὖ πρῶτον ἀέθλων·
εὖ δ᾽ ἀκούειν δευτέρα μοῖρ᾽· ἀμφοτέροισι δ᾽ ἀνὴρ
ὃς ἂν ἐγκύρσῃ καὶ ἕλῃ,
στέφανον ὕψιστον δέδεκται.
(ll. 99a–100b)

The first of prizes is to fare well,
but the second is to be well praised;
He who meets with both and holds them
has won the highest garland.

Marvell also alludes to the shifting nature of reputation, and his allusion to contrasting types is yet more cautionary. The types he alludes to are pre-Davidic figures: the prophet Elijah, the soldier Gideon, the patriarch Noah.[47] At first glance these are successful leaders, but, as Marvell's account illustrates, they did not rule without problems. Elijah the prophet refreshed a thirsty land (1 Kings 18: 41–45), but, like Cromwell, brought on a storm that "wet" a king. Gideon defeated two kings with a small band of followers, yet lost the support of the elders (Judges 8). Noah survived the deluge and as a husbandman planted the vine of liberty, but, even as he brought the ark to safety, caused the division among his sons when they saw him drunken and naked (Genesis 9: 20–27). With these types Marvell alludes indirectly to Cromwell's difficulties, demonstrating that a strong leader may alienate even as he attempts to bring the ship of state to safety. A strong leader cannot always rule with equity and praise. The voice of the future may not be a chorus of approval.

For this reason, perhaps, Marvell puts the final praise of Cromwell's achievements into the mouths of his adversaries, the grudging choir of European kings who collectively "complain" of the Lord Protector's virtues and acknowledge the infant Commonwealth's successes. The European kings enumerate the feats that

---

[47] The connection of the good Christian ruler with David had almost become proverbial, but Marvell refrains from connecting Cromwell with him, perhaps because, as some critics argue, David was one of the first of Israel's kings and Cromwell had, as Marvell comments in the ode, refused the kingship. See Steven N. Zwicker, "Models of Governance in Marvell's 'The First Anniversary'," *Criticism* 16 (1974): 1–12; Derek Hirst, "'That Sober Liberty': Marvell's Cromwell in 1654," in *The Golden & the Brazen World*, ed. John M. Wallace (Berkeley: University of California Press, 1985), 17–53.

Cromwell as Captain of the Wars performed: razing and rebuilding the state, reconstructing the British navies, commanding the traffic of the oceans. Marvell's tribute in "The First Anniversary" to Cromwell as the victor of the Dutch wars is comparable to that which the university poets offered to him in the volumes of peace odes. However, by having the encomium of the good leader spoken by his enemies Marvell hopes to place Cromwell's accomplishments into perspective:

> The Nation had been ours, but his one Soul
> Moves the great Bulk, and animates the whole.
> He Secrecy with Number hath inchas'd,
> Courage with Age, Maturity with Haste:
> The Valiants Terror, Riddle of the Wise;
> And still his Fauchion all our Knots unties.
> (ll. 379–384)

Ironically the foreign kings remark that Cromwell has succeeded in both being and not being a king:

> He seems a King by long Succession born,
> And yet the same to be a King does scorn,
> Abroad a King he seems, and something more,
> At Home a Subject on the equal Floor.
> (ll. 387–390)

By recording what the fear and spite of his enemies report of the man, Marvell hopes to strike a true note and avoid merely echoing what his supporters might say through love and duty. Perhaps he remembered the advice that Pindar gave to Hieron, who was also beset with spiteful enemies: "Envy is better than pity" (Pythian 1. 85). In creating a poem on the Pindaric model, Marvell both celebrated Cromwell and grappled with the hard issues of his leadership. He looks at Cromwell warts and all and, while praising him as a man of destiny, acknowledges that he walks, like the Philoctetan Hieron, in mortal flesh.

5.

Marvell's final ode for Cromwell, "A Poem upon the Death of O. C.," is a Pindaric hybrid, for it is both a political ode that praises the dead Protector and a Pindaric elegy that mourns that death. The poem was intended for a small collection of odes on Cromwell's death to be published by Henry Herringman. It was removed from the collection and an ode by Waller put in its place when William Wilson, rather than Herringman, brought out the volume with two other odes by

John Dryden and by Thomas Sprat.[48] Marvell's poem functions in some way very like the odes in the collection for which it was intended. As a funeral elegy, it is like Dryden's heroic stanzas, which summarizes the Protector's achievements. It also has some affinities with Sprat's ode, "To the Happie Memory of the most Renowned Prince, Oliver Lord Protector," which was dubbed a "Pindarick ode" and is one of the earliest odes (after the publication of Cowley's *Pindarique Odes* in 1656) to adopt the Cowleian format.[49] Sprat, however, is more expansive than Marvell. His pindaric attempts to sum up the achievements of Cromwell as the "Great Name"—now consigned to the judgment of history—and it takes sixteen Pindaric sections to do so. Sprat runs the gamut, beginning with Cromwell's private years before "England did thy Armes intreat" (6. 3), treating cautiously of the wounds of the Civil War (which Cromwell finally assuaged), and concluding with praise of Cromwell's military successes abroad. Although Sprat now and then uses a technique improvised by Cowley, his ode has more striking affinities with the celebratory odes of the university volumes than with Cowley's pindarics or Marvell's Cromwell poems. The final brief ode that concludes the collection, Waller's "Upon the Late Storme and Death of his Highnesse Ensuing the same," is, like the ode of Marvell that it displaced, a funeral ode which focuses upon the death of Cromwell. Like Marvell, Waller sees the storm that occurred on the night of Cromwell's death as in some way heaven's judgment on the man. Comparing the storm to the tempest that shook Rome when Romulus was lost or to the fury on Oeta that preceded the death of Hercules, Waller defines Cromwell's legacy in terms of the commotion in nature that he caused. Waller's ode is hardly as impressive a performance as his earlier ode to Cromwell, "A Panegyrick to my Lord Protector," composed, as was Marvell's "First Anniversary," to commemorate the first year of the Protectorate and published in 1655.

In his own ode on Cromwell's death, Marvell, who in his earlier poems had viewed Cromwell as a cosmic force, now focuses upon the man himself. His ode falls somewhere between the political pindaric and the personal ode-elegy, a genre that Cowley practiced in the 'pindariques' to private men in the 1656 *Odes* and one that we shall later be considering. Curiously, Marvell's ode has much in common with Pythian 3, the consolatory letter-ode that Pindar wrote for Hieron. Pindar's ode is unique among the epinicians in that, although it alludes to former victories, it celebrates no current victory. Instead, Pindar employs the

---

[48] Waller's "Panegyrick" for Cromwell, originally composed, like Marvell's "First Anniversary," to celebrate the success of Cromwell's Protectorate, was reprinted with the three odes on Cromwell's death in 1709. See *A Panegyrick on Oliver Cromwell, and his Victories, with Three Poems on his Death* (London, 1709).

[49] *Three Poems upon the Death of his late Highnesse Oliver, Lord Protector of England, Scotland, and Ireland* (London: William Wilson, 1659). My thanks to David Norbrook for drawing my attention to the Sprat ode.

ode form to express his regrets that he cannot confer on Hieron the blessings of golden health. The ode opens with an extravagant figure: Pindar wishes that Chiron were still alive so that he might dispatch his famous pupil, the physician Asclepius himself, to heal Hieron. The ode is full of contrary-to-fact reflections. Not only is Chiron not living, but Asclepius, after healing many, has been struck down by Zeus, who punished him for bringing a man back to life. Unlike Pythian 1, Pythian 3 consoles rather than praises. The misfortunes of life rather than its successes command Pindar's lyre. He even concludes with a dirge on the death of the great hero Achilles, mourned by his father Peleus as well as his Greek comrades.

Marvell's poem is marked with a similar kind of regret. Again and again he acknowledges that praise cannot soothe and even grief is impotent. Although the ode records Cromwell's accomplishments as a general and leader of the Parliamentary armies, it approaches him as the private man of private sorrows, who, overcome by the death of his daughter Elizabeth, followed her to the grave. It is almost as though in addressing the dead Cromwell Marvell confesses that the heroic figure of his two earlier poems had now ceded his extraordinary status as commander to that of mere man. Marvell praises the humility with which Cromwell accepts his death: "he no duty by his height excus'd, / Nor, though a *Prince*, to be a *Man* refus'd" (ll. 83–84). In his death Cromwell eschews the spectacular flourishes that marked his life; he cedes himself to private griefs: "To *Love* and *Griefe* the fatal Writ was sign'd; / (Those nobler weaknesses of humane Kinde)" (ll. 21–22). As man he accomplishes a private end: "He without noise still travell'd to his End, / As silent Suns to meet the Night descend" (ll. 135–136). Yet, despite his emphasis on Cromwell's modesty and quiet demise, Marvell cannot leave Cromwell simply to sleep "in Peace under the *Laurel shade*" (l. 156). The paradoxes of the two previous poems give way at last to panegyric. In death Marvell lauds Cromwell more extravagantly than he had in life. Extolling him as "*Heavens Favorite*," and proclaiming that "to none / Have such high honours from above been showne" (ll. 157–158), Marvell raises Cromwell above Moses as a leader and above Gideon as a warrior. Valor, Religion, Friendship and Prudence combine in him, and we are perforce reminded how Ronsard in his hymn to Henri II made his king the epitome of all virtues. Looking on his pale corpse, Marvell at first declaims on the transitory nature of all things before affirming Cromwell's greatness: "Yet dwelt that Greatnesse in his shape decay'd / That still, though dead, greater than death he layd" (ll. 257–258). Yet, restraining such hyperbole, he reflects that only in future ages will proper praise for Cromwell be possible when "Truth shall be allow'd and Faction cease" (l. 272).

Ode-elegies for deceased rulers, as we shall see more fully in chapter 5, predictably look not only backward but also forward. In this aspect, Marvell's ode for Cromwell is no different. He concludes by praising Richard Cromwell, Oliver's heir, but does so with a Marvellian conceit, forecasting calm in Richard's succession, rainbows after the storm of Oliver's death. With the return of Charles II in 1660, however, this prediction would be revised and with it the character of the Pindaric ode that Cowley would present to the restored monarch.

CHAPTER 4
COWLEY AND THE *PINDARIQUE ODES*: POLITICAL TEXT AND SUBTEXT

Cowley's *Pindarique Odes* are the product of the same decade as Marvell's Cromwell poems, but their essential impulse must be differentiated from that of Marvell's poems. Marvell deals directly with Cromwell and his Protectorate; Cowley's pindarics—while they seem (ostensibly) to address other subjects—indirectly concern the dead Charles I and his son, the future Charles II. Earlier in his career, Cowley had written odes that directly lauded Charles I, poetry published in the university collection *Irenodia*; later he would write a celebratory pindaric to mark Charles II's return from France.[1] In 1656, however, Cromwell and not Charles II held power in England. Therefore, any celebration of the Stuart royalty had to be covert rather than open. After the Restoration, Cowley would claim that he never wavered in allegiance to the Stuarts, even during the period of Cromwell's protectorate when he had returned to England seeking amnesty and with the design to see his 1656 *Poems* into print. To examine that claim and to look at the political subtext of those poems, particularly the *Pindarique Odes*, is essential to our understanding of Cowley as a political writer.

Both Cowley and Sprat—the former in his "Preface" to the 1656 *Poems*, the latter in his "Introduction" to Cowley's 1668 *Works*—describe the *Pindarique Odes* as innocent of political intentions. In his "Life of Cowley" Sprat tells us that the "occasion of [Cowley's] falling on the Pindaric way of Writing, was his accidental meeting with *Pindars* Works, in a place, where he had no other Books to direct him" and where "having then considered at leisure the height of his

---

[1] Cowley had produced several odes in honor of Charles I's returns. In *Sylva, or Divers Copies of Verses, Made upon sundry occasions by A. C.* (London, 1636) he included two English odes to Charles I on his return from Scotland: "On his Majesties returne out of Scotland" (sig. Er–v) and "A Song on the same" (E2r), Two odes of his on the king's return from Scotland in 1641, one in English, one in Latin, were included in *Irenodia Cantabrigiensis* (Cambridge, 1641). He reprinted the revised English ode both in 1656 and 1668; the Latin ode was not reprinted until later (in the 7th ed. in 1700). See *Abraham Cowley, A Bibliography*, ed. M. R. Perkin (Folkestone: Dawson, 1977), 79–80. His ode on Charles II's return from France was printed in 1660 and reprinted in a revised form in *Works* (1668).

[Pindar's] Invention, and the Majesty of his Style, he try'd immediately to imitate it in *English*."[2] Sprat's account is disingenuous. So also is Cowley's version of his Pindaric designs. Discussing the nature of Pindar's poetry in his 1656 Preface to *Pindarique Odes*, Cowley remarks on the peculiarities of Pindar's poetics and the difficulties of translating him into English.[3] He says nothing whatsoever about the political underpinnings of the poetry he is rendering into English. He leaves unnoted not only Pindar's connection with the tyrants of Sicily, but also the ambiguous quality of those non-hereditary rulers who ruled Sicily as Cromwell did England. In translating two odes of Pindar and in imitating Pindar's style and manner in a dozen more, Cowley professes no further intention than to introduce into English "the noblest and highest kind of writing in Verse" (Preface to *Pindarique Odes* in *Poems* [London, 1656], sig. Aaa 2^v).

We ought to be suspicious of this blandly apolitical account of Pindar, as we should also of Sprat's picture of Cowley the gentleman poet leisurely turning to reading, studying, and imitating Pindar. If, as Nethercot and most other Cowley scholars believe, the Pindaric odes were a product of Cowley's stay in Jersey in 1651 and were written between 1651 and 1655 at which point he returned to England and was imprisoned, it was hardly an apolitical time in Cowley's life.[4] Cowley was intensely concerned with the fortunes of the future Charles II, who after the disasters of the Scottish campaign and Worcester had returned to

---

[2] Thomas Sprat, "An Account of the Life and Writings of Mr. Abraham Cowley," in *The Works of Mr. Abraham Cowley* (London, 1668), sig. b2^v. For Sprat's relationship to Cowley, see Jean Loiseau, *Abraham Cowley's Reputation in England* (Paris: Henri Didier, 1931), 3–18.

[3] "I am in great doubt," Cowley tells readers in the general Preface to the *Poems*, "whether they wil be understood by most *Readers*; nay, even by very many who are well enough acquainted with the common Roads, and ordinary Tracks of *Poesie*." The difficulties Cowley attributes to Pindar's "high" and "grand" style include the many "sudden, and sometimes long" digressions, the unusual and bold figures, as well as the "various and irregular numbers" (Preface, *Poems*, sig. b^r). In the Preface to the *Pindarique Odes*, he once more makes apology for the extravagance of the original odes, which cannot be translated literally without having it appear that "*one Mad-man* had translated *another.*" Further, he goes on to expound on the "great difference of time betwixt his age and ours," and also the "difference betwixt the *Religions* and *Customs* of our Countreys, and a thousand particularities of places, persons, and manners" (sig. Aaa 2^r) These differences, Cowley says, make the task of the translator even more problematic. "Upon this ground," he tells us, he has "in these two *Odes* of *Pindar* taken, left out, and added what [he] please[d]," his aim being not so much to render what Pindar spoke, but his "*way* and *manner* of speaking" (sig. Aaa 2^v).

[4] Arthur H. Nethercot, *Abraham Cowley, The Muse's Hannibal* (London: Humphrey Milford, 1931), 135–39. Also see Jean Loiseau, *Abraham Cowley: Sa Vie, Son Œuvre* (Paris: Didier, 1931), 97–111; also Thomas Corns, *Uncloistered Virtue: English Political Literature, 1640–60* (Oxford: Oxford University Press, 1992), 252–55.

France. Cowley himself was busy throughout 1651 with expeditions to Scotland, to the Netherlands, to the Channel Islands, back to France, and finally again to Jersey where (reportedly at leisure) he fell upon the Pindarical way. Never were Cowley's or the royal fortunes lower than during Cowley's Pindaric period. We can hardly believe that politics were absent from his mind while he waited for the political winds to change and gambled on the indulgence of the Protector, when he finally returned to England during the Interregnum. In claiming that he had discovered Pindar purely by chance and that he was espousing his famous so-called obscurities simply as a new poetical method, Cowley misleads his readers, perhaps deliberately.[5]

In order to publish the *Pindarique Odes* during the Protectorate, Cowley had to make some gesture of reconciliation with the ruling powers. At the same time, however, he apparently wished to remain loyal to the Royalist cause to which he had devoted his life since he was ejected from Cambridge in 1643–1644. The translations and imitations of *Pindarique Odes* became the perfect vehicles to do both. By glossing over the politics of Pindar and by adopting a deliberately obscure style, he could have it both ways. In the general Preface to the *Poems* he claims to have accepted a political amnesty and urges his fellow Royalists that "we must lay down our *Pens,* as well as our *Arms,* we must *march* out of our *Cause* it self, and *dismantle* that, as well as our *Towns* and *Castles,* of all the *Works* and *Fortifications* of *Wit* and *Reason* by which we defended it" (sig. [a] 4ͬ). In return for the "*General Amnestie*" he and his fellow royalists received "as a *favor* from the *Victor,*" he professes to have practiced "the *Art* of *Oblivion,*" destroying all the work of his pen that had defended the cause (including, presumably, his incomplete epic on the Civil War) (sig. [a] 4ͬ⁻ᵛ). Cowley was not altogether truthful, for even though he did not finish his epic on the Civil War, he did not destroy the first three books he had completed. These "few lines" of reconciliation, addressed to Cromwell, caused Cowley some embarrassment at the Restoration, for Charles II was clearly displeased with Cowley's double-dealing.[6] His literary executor, Sprat, felt compelled to defend the poet against charges of disloyalty to the king, contending in 1668 in the "Life of Cowley" that the poet believed that it would be "meritorious service to the King, if any man who was known to have

---

[5] See Patterson, *Censorship and Interpretation.* Patterson argues that Cowley presents the Pindaric ode as "generically enigmatic, unusually dependent for its interpretation upon readers with special competence" (146). Also see S. P. Revard, "Cowley's *Pindarique Odes* and the Politics of the Inter-regnum," *Criticism* 35 (1993): 391–418.

[6] In 1659 when he returned to France Cowley had to appeal to Jermyn and to Ormonde in order to be pardoned and restored to the king's good graces. That he was never fully restored is attested by the meager rewards for service that he received from Charles II. When the Preface was reprinted in the 1668 folio of Cowley's *Works,* the offending passage describing the so-called "*Art* of *Oblivion*" was excised. See Loiseau, *Abraham Cowley,* 130–48..

followed his interest, could insinuate into the Usurpers minds, that men of his Principles were now willing to be quiet." Sprat maintained that Cowley's declaration was designed to "perswade the poor oppressed Royalists to conceal their affections, for better occasions." It is highly credible in fact, as Sprat pleads, that Cowley had used the "declaration of his peaceful intentions" to pursue his own ends, however misunderstood these ends were (sig. a^v–a2^r).[7]

If we take Sprat's defense seriously—and there is no reason why we should not—then we must re-evaluate the political intent of the 1656 volume and particularly that of the pindarics written during this very period of so-called dissembling. I believe that both Cowley's translations from Pindar and many of the pindarics that follow act out one design under the disguise and name of another, that is, that Cowley, far from having laid down his pen in the king's cause, merely pretended to have done so. His odes mark a development of the political pindaric as a tool for covert political propaganda.

1.

Cowley's book of *Pindarique Odes* opens with two loose translations or paraphrases of Pindar's Olympian 2 and Nemean 1 and proceeds with a dozen original odes in the so-called Pindaric style. Cowley's political agenda appears first of all in his choice of these two odes of Pindar for imitation and in his silence about their political underpinnings, both in Pindar's own time and later. Addressed to Sicilian men of eminence—the first to the tyrant Theron of Acragas or Agrigentum, the second to Chromius of Aetna, a nobleman close to the tyrant Hieron and the guardian of Hieron's son Deinomenes—both odes are politically charged. While praising the glories of the Sicilian city-states, Pindar's odes also allude to the political conditions that beset the tyrants Hieron and Theron, who were not only at odds with one another but also troubled with rebellion at home and danger of foreign attack. Cowley glosses over most of these problems in his headnotes. He also chooses to ignore the rich history of these two odes in antiquity and the Renaissance. Olympian 2 was one of Pindar's most popular odes and was imitated in antiquity, as in the Renaissance, as we have noted, whenever a poet wished to laud a reigning ruler, as Horace praises Augustus Caesar in *Carmina* 1.12 or Ronsard Henri II in his odes and hymns. When he chose Olympian 2 as the first of his Pindaric translations, Cowley could hardly have been ignorant of its close connections with royal encomium nor of how many other poets before him (in neo-Latin and in the vernacular) had used Olympian 2 for verses

---

[7] Sprat further contends that the declaration helped rather than harmed Charles's cause: "For certainly it was one of the greatest helps to the Kings Affairs, about the latter end of that Tyranny, that many of his best Friends dissembled their Counsels, and acted the same Designs, under the Disguises and Names of other Parties" (sig. a 2^r).

to kings, popes, and other rulers. Further, while in exile in France, Cowley could not have escaped knowledge of Pindar and his imitators in a land where political pindaric had flourished for over a hundred years and was still being practiced for encomia to noblemen.[8]

Cowley's notes to Olympian 2 and Nemean 1 are revealing both for what he tells the reader and for what he suppresses. Though he drew many notes from Benedictus's Pindar (1620), the edition of the odes he apparently used, he freely elaborates and adds notes of his own (See Figure 4.1). For example, he comments in the headnote of Olympian 2 how the ode commends Theron for his nobility, riches, hospitality, munificence, and other virtues, but consists of many digressions. In the headnote of the second ode, Nemean 1, Cowley remarks how Pindar likens Chromius, a young gentleman of Sicily, to Hercules, praising him for his person and his great endowments of mind and body. We cannot help noting that Cowley's first Pindaric translation concerns a royal subject and that his second commends a young and virtuous man. In choosing these two odes to introduce his Pindaric collection, Cowley offers us ciphers for two personages well known to his audience. The first is the powerful, munificent, but unfortunate king, Charles I, whom he served so devotedly; the second the young Prince Charles, whose virtues and promise he wishes to promote to the throne. Although in 1656 he dared not speak these names, much less praise their virtues, he could present in these Pindaric translations ciphers for the princes he admires. The agent who carried so many coded letters between King Charles and his queen now presents in his poetry a coded message to the people of England that those in the know might very easily decipher and read.[9]

Although Charles I in many ways resembles Pindar's Theron, we should not equate the English king with the Sicilian tyrant of Cowley's ode. At the time Pindar composed Olympian 2, Theron appeared to be happy and was exulting in a chariot victory in the Olympic games (476 B.C.), the most prestigious contest in the most prestigious games. If he was drawing a picture of Charles I in Pindar's Theron, it was Charles I at his height of power, the idealized Stuart monarch, who preserved the nation's traditions, just as Theron the ruler of the Sicilian city Acragas preserved its Dorian heritage. Hence, Cowley might well dub this

---

[8] It would be surprising if Cowley had not encountered Pindar's odes when he was a student at Cambridge and a close associate with the deeply learned Richard Crashaw, who would have known both the Greek originals and the neo-Latin imitations and was later to experiment with the ode style. In his Preface to the *Pindarique Odes* Cowley says that he is the first to imitate Pindar, commenting that Pindaric ode "has not been yet (that I know of) introduced into *English*" (sig. Aaa 2^v). If Cowley did not know Soowthern's or Drayton's imitations, surely he would have known Jonson's Cary-Morison ode, which had been printed in Jonson's 1640 folio. The comment is puzzling, unless Cowley is referring to the translation of Pindar into English rather than to imitation of his odes.

[9] On Cowley's activities as an agent of the king, see Sprat, "Life," sig. a^r.

ΠΙΝΔΑΡΟΥ
ΠΕΡΙΟΔΟΣ,

PINDARI
OLYMPIA, PYTHIA,
NEMEA, ISTHMIA.

IOHANNES BENEDICTVS
Medicinæ Doctor, & in Salmuriensi Academia
Regia linguæ Græcæ Professor,

AD METRI RATIONEM, VARIORVM
EXEMPLARIVM FIDEM, SCHOLIASTAE
ad verisimiles coniecturas directionem, totum
authorem innumeris mendis repurgauit.

METAPHRASI RECOGNITA, LATINA PARAPHRASI
addita, poëticis & obscuris phrasibus Græca prosa declaratis; denique
adiectis rerum & verborum breuibus & sufficientibus commen-
tarijs, arduum eiusdem sensum explanauit.

EDITIO PVRISSIMA, CVM INDICE
locupletissimo.

SALMVRII,
Ex typis PETRI PIEDEDII.

Anno M. DC. XX.
CVM PRIVILEGIO REGIS.

FIGURE 4.1
Title page of *Pindari Olympia, Pythia, Nemea, Isthmia*, ed. Iohannis Benedictus (Saumur, 1620).

Photograph by Stella Revard.

Charles, as Pindar had Theron, as "first in *Pisa's,* as in *Virtues Race*" (1.16). How-ever, although Olympian 2 congratulates Theron on his happiness and his suc-cess, it also reflects on the transitory nature of that happiness. In its digressions Olympian 2 alludes to the survival of Theron's present dynasty despite the disas-ters of the past and hints at those dangers of the present that would shortly over-whelm it. In four years' time Theron would be dead, an event Pindar might have dimly foreseen, but one which Cowley the translator clearly knew, permitting him to develop some subtle analogies between Theron and Charles. Even though Pindar lauds Theron's wealth and happiness, he also counsels patience in adver-sity and advises that even the greatest happiness does not last. He does, however, congratulate the Sicilian ruler and his people on having survived as a race against the odds. He also looks to the afterlife, where happiness lies ahead for all—that is, for all the virtuous—beyond the grave.

After its triumphant opening, Cowley's Olympian 2 recounts the "past suf-ferings of this noble Race" (3.1), the "rough ways" through which the sons of Cadmus had to pass before they could plant their noble city, Agrigentum (Acra-gas), in "*fair-fac'ed Sicilie*" (2.1–4). These sufferings include the persecution and death of Cadmus's daughters Semele and Ino, the trials of the "*innocent Parricide*" Oedipus (5. 2), and the death, at their own hands, of his wrathful sons Polyneices and Eteocles. In recounting these histories, Cowley follows Pindar closely. In his notes he explains that Pindar has told "these tragical accidents and actions of *Oedipus* and his *Sons,* in an Ode dedicated to the praise of *Theron* and his Ances-tors"—because they were "so notorious, that it was better to excuse then conceal them" (Notes, section 5). Yet, even as Cowley makes an excuse for Pindar, he also excuses the notorious tragical accidents of another family, the Stuarts: accidents which include the deaths of Mary Stuart and her grandson Charles, tragedies which neatly parallel the unfortunate death of Semele and the political misfor-tunes of Oedipus and his sons.

In Olympian 2 Pindar makes much of the fact that the sufferings of the house of Cadmus are redeemed in Thersander, the son of Polyneices and the grandson of Oedipus. Thersander was the sole survivor of a family wiped out by misfortune; he was also the reputed ancestral founder of the city that Theron rules. Now, comments the poet, Thersander lives again, both in his verse and in Theron's virtuous person. In Cowley's version of the ode Prince Charles might be covertly likened to Thersander, the surviving heir of Oedipus's family, which like the Stuarts had been hunted down by misfortune. In Prince Charles, as in Thersander, were the seeds of grace, the warrantors of continuation for the race to come.

In his translation of Olympian 2, Cowley does not pass up the opportunity to allude to the Stuarts with other covert references. As was the custom in epi-nician ode, Pindar includes praise of Theron's brother, who had won victories at Pytho and in the Isthmus, at the same time he commends Theron's victory at Olympia. Cowley expands on Pindar's reference to the brother, giving it greater

prominence than it had in the original ode. He insinuates thereby that the Stuart
virtue was found both in Prince Charles and in his brother James:

> For the *well-natur'ed* honour there
> Which with thy *Brother* thou didst share,
> Was to thee *double* grown
> By not being all thine *Own*. (5.12–15)

Renaissance editors and commentators often remarked on how close to Christian belief were many of Pindar's views on the afterlife.[10] Pindar followed the
Pythagoreans and asserted that after death the good were rewarded and the evil
punished. The injustices of earth would be righted in the afterlife. Pindar tells us
that Cadmus's unlucky daughters Semele and Ino perish on earth only to achieve
greater happiness later. Similarly, Achilles enjoys his reward in the Isles of the
Blest. In Cowley's translation the promise of immortality that concludes Pindar's
ode also applies to the Stuarts. In a Christianized context, Cowley may be touching on perhaps the most delicate question of all: the martyrdom and glorification
of Charles I. It is not too far-fetched to venture that the Achilles figure in Pindar may suggest in Cowley's translation a heroic Charles I, untimely cut off like
the Greek hero, yet attaining, as the royal martyr, the reward in heaven that was
denied him on earth. In the original ode, Pindar grants Achilles immortality because of his achievements as the military hero who killed Hector and Memnon.
Cowley drops these references; instead he describes how the divine mother Thetis, having failed to secure her son's invulnerability on earth, after death purges
his soul from wrath and endows it with a divine hardness (8.14–18).

The concluding stanzas of Cowley's translation cast light on other aspects of
the Stuart myth. In the original ode, Pindar compares the divinely-inspired poet
to the eagle at which the envious crows vainly caw and chatter. Though Cowley renders this passage precisely, he adds material of his own, commenting how
the eagle, the Jovian bird, bore Ganymede aloft: "like the sacred *Bird* of *Jove*, /
Now bears loud *Thunder*, and anon with *silent joy* / The beauteous *Phrygian Boy*"
(9.16–18). Unlike Pindar's eagle, who functions simply as an emblem for the poet,
Cowley's eagle becomes a figure of divine justice, defeating the strong and soaring above the earth, as he carries aloft the young Trojan prince Ganymede in order to confer special favor on him. Who is this "beauteous *Phrygian Boy*" whom
Jove loves? Could it be the young Prince Charles, whose right to the throne the
Jovian eagle vindicates?

In the last strophe of the original ode, Pindar joins his praise of Theron with
a brief allusion to those envious and spiteful men that grudge him praise. Cowley
alters the passage, making spiteful envy and not Theron the principal subject of
his final stanza.

---

[10] See Revard, *Pindar and the Renaissance Hymn-Ode*, 13–19.

> But in this thankless *world* the *Givers*
> Are *envi'ed* ev' en by the *Receivers*.
> 'Tis now the *cheap* and *frugal* fashion,
> Rather to *Hide* then *Pay* the *Obligation*.
> Nay worser much then so,
> It now an *Artifice* does grow,
> *Wrongs* and *Outrages* to do,
> Lest men should think we *ow*. (11.1–8)

Cowley's words have a pointed contemporary ring. Rather than merely alluding to the envy that princes such as Pindar's Theron incurred from their enemies, he seems to be delivering a lecture to those ungrateful Englishmen who have forgotten their obligation to their dead monarch. Under the veil of Pindar's poetry, he comments upon the hypocrisy and outrageous wrong that govern the Interregnum, as men transferred their allegiance from Charles I to Cromwell.

The second ode that Cowley translates, Nemean 1, features Chromius of Aetna and recounts as its myth how the great hero Heracles as an infant strangled the serpents sent to kill him.[11] Although Cowley reshapes certain details of the ode to reinforce the connection between Chromius of Aetna and Prince Charles, the ode already was perfect raw material out of which to fashion a propaganda piece for the Stuarts. It begins with a promise of renewal. Alpheus, the river god, having pursued the fleeing nymph Arethusa from Greece, finds a new breathing place in Sicily and mingles his waters with those of Arethusa, who has been transformed into a fountain. The wedding of the river god with the nymph guarantees prosperity to Sicily and also sets the tone of the ode as promising new beginnings. Having begun with the account of Alpheus's rebirth in Sicily, Pindar goes on to recount how Zeus dedicates the island to Persephone, herself reborn and returned from Hades to rejoin her mother, Demeter. In his translation Cowley emphasizes how this *island* kingdom will flourish under the goddess's protection, just as England, that sceptered isle, might also in the future revive and flourish. Nemean 1 is an ode full of future hope: a perfect foil to Olympian 2 and its lament for the past.

In his description of and address to Chromius, Cowley has deliberately shaped his translation to apply more to a youthful English prince than to Pindar's Sicilian victor:

> How *early* has young *Chromius* begun
> The *Race* of *Virtue*, and how swiftly run,
>   And born the noble *Prize* away,
> Whilst other youths yet at the *Barriere* stay? (6.1–4)

---

[11] See Hamilton's commentary on Cowley's translation of Nemean 1 in *Soliciting Darkness*, 177–80.

The lines that I have just cited Cowley interpolates into the ode, as he also interpolates that key adjective *young*, using it to describe Chromius in his headnote, in the first reference to him in the poem, and again at this juncture. His interpolations have the effect also of making clear the connection between Chromius in Cowley's translation and Prince Charles.

Young is a word Pindar never applies to Chromius, the simple reason being that the historical Chromius that Pindar addresses in the ode was not young, having served under three Sicilian tyrants and having been appointed governor of Aetna and guardian to both Gelon's and Hieron's sons. Pindar praises Chromius for his hospitality, for being a man mighty in mind and body, but not for youthful expectation. That is Cowley's addition, as is also the detailed description of Chromius's strength, beauty, and prospects of great fortune:

> *Nature* herself, whilst in the *womb* he was,
> Sow'd *Strength* and *Beauty* through the *forming Mass*,
> They mov'ed the *vital Lump* in every part,
> And carv'ed the *Members* out with wondrous art.
> She fill'd his *Mind* with *Courage*, and with *Wit*
>   And a vast *Bounty*, apt and fit
> For the great *Dowre* which *Fortune* made to it. (5.1–7)

Cowley's description better fits a young prince, courageous and witty, than an elder patron, particularly a young prince such as Charles, being groomed as a future king.[12]

In translating Pindar's ode, Cowley alludes not merely to the hopes of the young Prince Charles, but also to the hopes that dispossessed royalists cherished for him. In Nemean 1 Pindar merely tells us that hope is common to all men alike. Cowley elaborates: "Though *Happy men* the *present* goods possess, / Th'*Unhappy* have their share in *future* Hopes no less" (5.14–15). In distinguishing the happy in possession of present goods from the unhappy sharing only in future hopes, Cowley seems to allude to the ruling Puritans on the one hand and the "unhappy" royalists on the other. Without ever divulging the identity of those "happy only in hopes," he teases us to apply the description to contemporary persons and circumstances.

Upon introducing the myth of Hercules, he points still more directly at Prince Charles and his expectation of an illustrious future. Cowley takes pains in his notes to explain how the Hercules myth in Pindar's ode applies to Chromius, maintaining that it is "necessary to make a little more perspicuous" "the connexion between *Chromius* and the story of *Hercules*" (Notes to section 6). As Cowley undoubtedly knew, Hercules had been a favorite patron hero for noble

---

[12] For another view on Cowley's additions, see Robert B. Hinman, *Abraham Cowley's World of Order* (Cambridge, MA: Harvard University Press, 1960), 201–2.

houses since the time of Pindar, no less in favor with the Romans than with
their Renaissance counterparts, who, as we have noted in the first chapter, flat-
tered the nobility of France, Italy, and Spain by comparing their achievements
with those of Hercules. Although writers of religious ode might make Hercules
the cipher for Christ, as Milton had in "On the Morning of Christ's Nativity"
or Ronsard in "Hercule Chrestien," royal encomiasts tended to link Hercules
with the king or a future prince.[13] In the sixteenth century, Luigi Alamanni,
Salmon Macrin, Pierre de Ronsard, and Gabriello Chiabrera all had recounted
myths connected with Hercules to compliment their royal patrons. An ode written by Nicolas Rapin on the occasion of the birth of a son to Henri IV and his
queen had used the myth of Nemean 1 to predict a glorious future for the new-
born Louis XIII, who, like Hercules, strangled the serpents of sedition in the
cradle.[14] Moreover, this very myth was applied to Prince Charles himself in the
Oxford volume published in 1630 to celebrate his birth as Charles I's eldest son.
The Oxford poet, drawing it appears on Nemean 1, goes on to predict for the
Stuart prince a glorious future that will include the subduing of "monsters" and
"tyrants" that might afflict his state.[15] Even if Cowley did not know these specific
encomia, he would have known how often royal encomiasts had made Hercules a
political figure. Clearly, he also knew that he had to be discreet in connecting the
Hercules myth with the future Charles II. However, when he describes the infant Hercules "Wrapt in purple swadling-bands" (6.11), Cowley signals that he is
dealing with a royal child. In his translation he has altered Pindar's yellow bands
to a royal purple. Thus the Herculean infant in Cowley's translation becomes a

---

[13] Milton in "On the Morning of Christ's Nativity" alludes to the famous episode
of Hercules' strangling the serpents, most probably taking it from Nemean 1. The infant
Christ defeats the pagan gods and the snaky Typhon, just as Heracles had (226–228). In
alluding to the victory of Christ, Milton probably also refers to the hopes of a Protestant
nation, such as England, to achieve its Herculean promise and to rid the world of the Typhonic plague of Catholic domination. For a discussion of Milton's use of the Heracles
myth, see Revard, *Pindar and the Renaissance Hymn-Ode*, 241–43, and eadem, *Milton and
the Tangles of Neaera's Hair*, 87–90.

[14] See "Hymne sur la Naissance de Monseigneur Le Dauphin, 1601," "Les Vers
Mesurez de Nicolas Rapin," in *Les Oeuvres Latines et Francoises de Nicolas Rapin* (Paris:
Olivier de Varennes, 1610).

[15] See John Earles in *Britanniae Natalis* (Oxford: Iohannes Lichfield, 1630). Earles,
addressing Charles as "Magne Puer" (great boy), alludes to his accomplishments to come.
Citing the account of how Hercules, anticipating his great future, strangled serpents in
his cradle, he intimates for Charles, as for Hercules, even greater feats of arms ahead: the
subduing of the Hydra, of monsters, and of tyrants when the time comes that Charles is
mature: "Sic Herculeae primordia laudis / Iam lactantis erant; dum prima vel vbera testes
/ Virtutis bellator habet; lusitque cruorem / Serpentum, teneraque manu colla ardua pres-
sit, / Olim Hydram domiturus, & ipsos, Monstra, Tyrannos. / Tempus erit, cum, maturis
jam firmior annis, / Sperare ad patrias possis, & vincere laudes" (58).

figure for the young Charles, who will be confronted with the rebel vipers that threaten to deprive him of his right.

Pindar tells us that Hercules in strangling the snakes performed his first feat of battle. Cowley, however, makes the occasion even more warlike as Hercules quells his snaky foes:

> The *mighty Infant* seem'd well pleas'ed
> At his gay gilded foes,
> And as their spotted necks up to the *Cradle* rose,
> With his young warlike hands on both he seis'ed;
> In vain they rag'd, in vain they hist,
> In vain their armed *Tails* they twist,
> And angry *Circles* cast about,
> Black *Blood*, and fiery *Breath*, and poys'onous *Soul* he squeezes out.
> (7. 8–15)[16]

On seeing Hercules, the *"conquering Boy"* (8. 4), as Cowley calls him, the prophet Teiresias predicts from this single deed of conquest a triumphant future which includes slaying monsters on sea and land, vanquishing the hateful giant Antaeus, and meeting with the gods and giants on the plain of Phlegra.[17] To this list of conquests, our translator Cowley emphasizes a category not named explicitly in the Pindaric list: the slaying of mighty tyrants.

---

[16] The royal musician Pietro Reggio set this stanza of Cowley's ode to music as "Hercules in the Cradle" or "The Big-limb'd Babe." The song seems designed to compliment a royal patron and complements the many references in the Restoration to Charles II as a Herculean figure. Two copies of the song exist in the British Library, the first in a Restoration song-book (*Liber Caroli Morgan*, 1681), the second in an eighteenth-century song book: see BL Add. MS. 33234, fols. 17r–18v; BL Add. MS. 63626, fols. 11v–13r. (My thanks to the late Thomas Calhoun, University of Delaware, for these references.) In the university volumes produced on his return Charles II is more often compared to Apollo or Jupiter than to Hercules. However, he is characterized by one poet as the Caesar who vanquished the Hydra and the Chimaera: see *Britannia Rediviva* (Oxford: A. & L. Lichfield, 1660), sig. av. Also see *SWSTRA, Sive Ad Carolum II reducem* (Cambridge: J. Field, 1660).

[17] As Hilary Mackie has commented, Pindar combines past, present, and future in Teiresias's prophecy. From the point of view of the characters in the myth, these events are in the future. For the epinician poet and his audience, however, Teiresias's prophecy effectively brings the subject matter of the myth into the context of the present (Mackie, *Graceful Errors*, 62–63). Also see Charles Segal, "Time and the Hero: The Myth of *Nemean* 1," in *Aglaia*, 155–65. The ode moves "beyond the *chronos* of the moment (46) to the *chronos* which is the link between great moments (69), the junctures of a large design, the points where a hero realizes his inherited nature . . ." (162).

From what *Monsters* he should free
The *Earth*, the *Ayr*, and *Sea*,
What mighty *Tyrants* he should slay,
Greater *Monsters* far then *They*. (8. 9–12)

Who may these mighty tyrants be that Hercules is to slay? Cowley provides an interesting gloss in his notes, identifying them as Antaeus, Busiris, and Augias [sic] (note to section 8), the first a giant whom Hercules wrestles with and kills, the next two tyrant-kings.[18] In his tract "A Discourse on the Government of *Oliver Cromwell*" Cowley calls Cromwell both giant and tyrant (54, 58–59).[19] In his essay "Of Greatness" he describes him as the "late Gyant of our Nation," who attempted like the giants in Greek myth to scale heaven and was thrown down (*Works* [1668], 124–25).[20] Can there be any doubt which tyrant the English Hercules is to overcome?

---

[18] Once again contrast with Milton is enlightening, for Milton in both prose and poetry alludes to the story of Hercules' encounter with Antaeus. In *Areopagitica* "[Truth] and Falsehood grapple: who ever knew Truth put to a worse" (in *Complete Poetry and Major Prose*, ed. Hughes, 746); in *Paradise Regained* Christ's victory over Satan is compared to Hercules' over Antaeus (4. 564–568). See S. P. Revard, "The Politics of Milton's Hercules," *Milton Studies* 32 (1995): 217–45.

[19] [Abraham Cowley], *A Vision, Concerning his late Pretended Highnesse Cromwell, the Wicked; Containing a Discourse in Vindication of him by a pretended Angel, and the Confutation thereof by the Author* (London: Henry Herringman, 1661). In the Advertisement Cowley tells us that he wrote "A Vision" during the time of the "late Protector *Richard the Little*" and that he originally planned to write a series of three discourses, but was prevented from doing so by the "Restoration of Reason, and Right." He decided, however, to print the first of the three discourses to expose Cromwell's wickedness and to prevent any man from admiring him as a "great and eminent Person" (sigs. A2ʳ–A4ʳ). Cowley printed an earlier version of "A Discourse" under the pseudonym Ezekiel Grebner: *The Visions and Prophecies Concerning England, Scotland, and Ireland, of Ezekiel Grebner* (London: Henry Herringman, 1661 [Jan. 1660]). See Loiseau, *Abraham Cowley*, 135–36. "A Vision" was reprinted in Cowley's *Works* in 1668 as "A Discourse By way of Vision Concerning the Government of *Oliver Cromwell*" (52–78). The vision, as Cowley relates, comes upon the speaker after the funeral of the late Protector. In the verses that follow he depicts the desolation of the once "happy Isle," now "chang'd and curst" in "*Chaos*, and Confusion," which, like a "guilty, perishing Vessel," is tossed and torn until its late master, "the Royal Martyr," prays that it be saved (53–54). In another set of verses Cowley depicts Cromwell as "a great Monster," the son of Earth, who rebelled against God. This is what it means to be a tyrant, he continues, one who brings "Bloud, Confusion, Ruine, to obtain / A short and miserable Reign" (59). I quote the text from *Works* (1668).

[20] See the following verses in "A Discourse" (59): "The Son of Earth with hundred hands / Upon his three-pil'd Mountain stands, / Till Thunder strikes him from the sky." The "three-pil'd Mountain" is a reference to the three kingdoms of England, Scotland, and Ireland.

In the final stanza Cowley effects one more turn upon the Pindaric original that directs our attention to London rather than Thebes or Syracuse. Alluding to the aftermath of the battle at Phlegra, Pindar merely tells us that Hercules rested from his labors, now married to Hebe and dwelling in the house of Zeus. Cowley, however, makes Hercules the very savior of the Olympian gods:

> And that the *grateful* Gods at last
> The race of his *laborious Virtue* past,
>   *Heaven*, which he *sav'ed*, should to him give,
> Where *marry'ed* to æternal *Youth* he should for ever live;
> (9.1–4)

In sixteenth-century France, Hercules was often connected with the "victor kings" of that nation, who put down gigantic insurrections during their civil wars. Cowley follows in this tradition, but now it is not a Valois king or the Bourbon Henri IV who conquers monsters, but the future Charles II. In his note on the battle of Phlegra Cowley comments that the battle could not have been won without the assistance of the two demi-gods Hercules and Bacchus (Notes to section 8). Here, in naming both gods, Cowley may be forecasting the role that Charles's brother James was to play in assisting him to regain his throne. Cowley concludes the ode, moreover, not with Hercules in repose in heaven, but with him walking aloft in the "*Groves* of never-withering *Light*," now "frighting," as he had the monsters on earth, the constellations of the sky—"The *Lyon* and the *Bear*, / *Bull*, *Centaur*, *Scorpion*, all the *radiant Monsters* there" (9.8, 10–11).[21] Ever ready, Hercules stands prepared, as does the princely Charles, to take on new challenges.

2.

Like these two translations, many of the Pindaric imitations that follow also have covert aims and make use of Pindaric ode for political propaganda. The poems of the 1656 *Pindarique Odes* make up a carefully designed sequence and are not a mere miscellany. Cowley calls attention in his prefaces to the fact that his Pindaric odes are poetic experiments, and at first glance this appears to be so.

---

[21] See Annabel Patterson's commentary on Cowley's additions here and in the passage above: *Censorship and Interpretation*, 146–47. She appears to identify both Cowley's Hercules and his Brutus with Cromwell on the grounds that they were tyrant-slayers. She alludes to both Milton's and a French polemic's description of Hercules as a slayer of tyrants (152–53). She also cites Waller's panegyric on Cromwell (149). Waller's poem compares Cromwell and Hercules: see "Upon the Late Storme and the Death of His Highnesse, Ensuing the same," in *Three Poems Upon the Death of his late Highnesse Oliver Lord Protector of England, Scotland, and Ireland* (London, 1659).

The introductory ode, "The Praise of Pindar," is a translation of Horace's *Carmina* 4.2, and the two odes that follow, "The Resurrection" and "The Muse," seem to deal principally with Pindar's poetics. In translating Horace's ode 4.2, Cowley renders only about half of the actual ode—the innocent half! While he imitates Horace's cautionary warning about soaring aloft after the *"Theban Swan,"* he omits Horace's references to political matters and his praise of Augustus. His, he tells us, is a *"tim'orous Muse,"* which pursues like Horace's "laborious *Bee*" only *"Unambitious* tracks," content with *"Humble Sweets"* (4.5–6, 13–15) *"Unambitious,"* however, is Cowley's word, not Horace's. Further, Horace does not close his ode with the bee disporting herself in the meadows. Cowley does. While implying that he is following a poetics without a program, Cowley has begun to lay out a very definite program.

Both Cowley's preface and his prefatory pindarics—"The Praise of Pindar" and "The Resurrection"—represent Pindar as an enthusiastical, highly obscure poet, whose poetry embraces the high style and who undertakes only sublime topics in his odes.[22] In his own Pindaric imitations Cowley claims that he has adopted both Pindar's high style and also a range of subjects that would have been appropriate to the ancient poet, namely poetry, religion, and philosophy. In "The Resurrection" he undertakes both religion and poetry, beginning with an imitation of Pindar's Olympian 11 and then proceeding to describe "Pindarically" the apocalyptic last day. Cowley's true subject in this ode, despite its title and its extravagant description in section 3 of the reassembly of "scatter'ed *Atomes"* (3. 10), is not the resurrection of the dead. As the remainder of the ode abundantly makes clear, Cowley's primary object is to illustrate and then dissect the nature of Pindaric poetics. For Cowley Pindar is an untamed genius, whose verse is unpredictable and uncontrolled; his "vig'orous heat" (4. 1) is liable to carry him and any hapless imitator away. In this way Cowley excuses the difficulties, obscurities, oblique references, and subtle indirections of his own imitations by attributing them to Pindaric style rather than to Cowleian design. His *"Pindarique Pegasus"* is an unruly *"hard-Mouth'd Horse,* / Fierce, and unbroken yet," which disdains the *"servile Law* of any settled *pace"* (4. 3, 6–7, 10). It is liable to fling both writer and reader from the saddle.

Pindar was generally regarded in the seventeenth century as a difficult, obscure poet, but Cowley has exaggerated the unruliness of the Pindaric style, perhaps deliberately so. He had, as the notes to the first two translations indicate, made use of Benedictus's edition of the original odes, an edition notable for its clear exposition of the design of the odes, its lucid introductions, and its ample notes that explain Pindar's oblique allusions. Thereby Benedictus has eliminated many of the

---

[22] Hamilton argues that Cowley takes a double view of Pindar's so-called obscurity, both regarding it as a stumbling-block to understanding and embracing it as an advantage poetically: *Soliciting Darkness,* 170–94.

so-called difficulties of Pindar's style.[23] Although Benedictus acknowledges Pindar's complexity and subtlety, he insists on the basic orderliness of his odes. Unlike Benedictus, however, Cowley gives the impression that Pindar is disorderly and chaotic. He excuses him, moreover, by explaining that the disorder is simply the result of Pindar's "Enthysiastical" manner, his tendency to fall "from one thing into another" (Notes to section 1). The excuse wins Cowley, as a modern pindarist, the license to proceed as he pleases and thereby also to cloak many a potentially dangerous political reference under the veil of so-called Pindaric obscurity.

The political references in many of the odes are cautious, tentative, and contradictory. Some we might pass over, as, for example, those in the odes "To Dr. Scarborough" and "To Mr. Hobs," which seem at first appropriate to odes of praise that follow in the tradition of the familiar pindaric.[24] Both of these odes, however, are addressed to persons who were not without importance to the Royalist cause, and their genial tone and reference to matters philosophical mask some unsettling allusions to the disruptive years of the civil wars. The two odes that follow, "Destinie" and "Brutus," contain political references that it would be difficult to ignore. The opening two sections of "Destinie" use the politically-charged metaphor of life as a game of chess, supervised by angelic arbiters. In a game that pits pawns against kings, how can we fail to identify as Cromwell the "proud *Pawn*" who "still advancing higher / At top of all became / Another *Thing* and *Name*" (1.8–11)? Or can we pass over Cowley's sly identification of himself with the "losing Party" who blames his loss on "those false *Moves* that break the *Game*"? (l. 14–15)? And what about the characterization of the game as over when the "conquered *Pieces*" are brought "to their *Grave* the *Bag*" (l.16)? Can the "*Mated King*" be Charles I himself whose "*ill Conduct*" brings about his demise (1. 17), or can "*ill Conduct*" equally describe the actions towards the king as his own actions? Cowley nonchalantly presents this round of chess as a cosmic game that only gods and angels can control or understand. But might some Royalist sympathizer silently nod and understand that Cowley is alluding to the events of the previous decade?

> Some climb to *good*, some from *good Fortune* fall,
>   Some *Wisemen*, and some *Fools* we call,
> *Figures*, alas, of *Speech*, *Destiny plays us all*.
> (2.13–15)

"Brutus," the ode that follows, is a political ode that we can set beside Marvell's Horatian ode on the return of Cromwell from Ireland, for like Marvell's ode it is replete with political ambiguities. Is "Brutus" a tribute to Cromwell or to a would-be Royalist assassin of the Protector, who would remove the tyrant from

---

[23] Johannes Benedictus, ed., *Pindari Periodos* (Saumur, 1620). Benedictus also discusses Pindar's poetics and explains the regularity of Pindar's triads.

[24] A discussion of familiar ode follows in chapter 8 below.

the state as Brutus had removed Caesar? Or is it a philosophical ode that considers from a disinterested vantage point the historical Brutus, as the ode "Life and Fame" considers his contemporaries Pompey and Caesar? So ambiguous is Cowley's address to Brutus, so balanced his description of him, that we cannot be sure whether Brutus is a contemporary stand-in or simply the ancient Roman himself.[25]

In his other writings Cowley is generally favorable to the historical Brutus whom he describes as virtuous, without entirely approving his action in assassinating Caesar. In "A Discourse concerning the Government of *Oliver Cromwell*," Cowley comments, "not all the wisdom and power of the Roman Senate, nor the wit and eloquence of *Cicero*, nor the Courage and Virtue of *Brutus* was able to defend their Country or themselves against the inexperienced rashness of a beardless Boy, and the loose rage of a voluptuous Madman" (in *Works* [London, 1668], 67). Although Cowley did not accord Julius Caesar the title and position of a legitimate king, he did not regard his victory over Pompey or his assumption of leadership in the Roman state as wholly unapproved acts. Therefore we should not automatically assume that Cowley's Caesar is Charles I solely because he, like Caesar, was a leader killed after a period of civil war. As Cromwell acts the part of Caesar in Marvell's Horatian ode, he could easily also be Cowley's Caesar.

The opening encomium of the ode praises the ancient Brutus: "Excellent *Brutus*, of all humane race, / The best till *Nature* was improv'ed by *Grace*" (1. 1–2). Were not Roman republicanism so charged an issue in the 1650s and the connection between the assassins of Caesar and the parliamentarians who killed the king so generally assumed by both sides, we might simply take it for granted that Cowley is describing the position of Brutus in a pre-Christian world and nothing else. There are some problems, however, with taking the ode as a grudging compliment to Cromwell, accorded in light of the amnesty Cowley professes in the "Preface." We cannot imagine Cromwell's being entirely pleased with a poem, which, though it praises Brutus's refusal of Caesar's usurped place, dwells on his suicide—"who kill'd *Himself* rather than *serve*" (2.4)—and his defeat at the hands of "false *Octavius*, and wilde *Antonie*" (5.6). Cowley's ode, in fact, deals as much with the dangers of Brutus's principled action as with its virtue. As such, it becomes—almost— a different kind of political pindaric: a historical re-examination of issues, rather than an encomiastic address to a leader. Or perhaps this is only what Cowley wishes us to think, concealing the fact that he

---

[25] See Patterson, *Censorship and Interpretation*, 153–54. Also see T. R. Langley, "Abraham Cowley's 'Brutus': Royalist or Republican?" *Yale English Studies* 6 (1976): 41–52; James J. Keough, "Cowley's Brutus Ode: Historical Precepts and the Politics of Defeat," *Texas Studies in Language and Literature* 19 (1977): 382–91.

is writing under the guise of a new kind of philosophical ode a covert address to a contemporary would-be Brutus. [26]

As one in a sequence of odes that Cowley wrote in the period of the Protectorate after his return to England, "Brutus" makes clearest sense as an ode cautioning a would-be assassin of that "tyrant" Protector on the dangers of tyrant-killing. Although the word *tyrant* is ambiguous in this ode and could be applied equally to a man like Cromwell who had seized power by force or to a "tyrannical" king, Cowley appears to use it in the former sense. [27] If so, he is advising a fellow Royalist and would-be assassin of the tyrant Cromwell that in contemplating tyrant-killing he runs as great a risk of perishing as of succeeding. That Cowley should be cautious and ambiguous is understandable; that he should write an ode complimenting the Protector on being a "tyrant-killer," when he would, on Cromwell's death, revile him as such is entirely inconsistent with the political design of the *Pindarique Odes*. Cowley did not withdraw the Brutus ode from his 1668 *Works*, as he did the troublesome paragraph in the General Preface in which he professed conciliation. Further, the Brutus ode concludes, not by resolving the issue of what a virtuous Brutus should or should not have done, but by raising the entire question of *"Humane Virtues"* to a higher plane, testing them by applying the Christian standard of a *"God crucifi'ed"* (5.22–23). [28] Whether or not "Brutus" makes a covert political statement, the ode does stand as a different kind of political pindaric. It moves toward the kind of odes that Casimire was creating in that it debates moral issues as well as political actions.

3.

The last two odes in the 1656 collection, "The 34th Chapter of the Prophet *Isaiah*" and "The Plagues of *Egypt*," might appear at first to be only religious pindarics. [29] These Old Testament odes, like the two Pindaric paraphrases that begin the book, are, however, the most intensely political statements about the situation of the nation in the 1650s and, like the paraphrases, should be read allegorically. In the note to the first section of the Isaiah ode Cowley tells us in fact that he wants us to read these odes "Pindarically," remarking: "The manner

---

[26] For a discussion of Cowley's philosophical odes see Revard, *Pindar and the Renaissance Hymn-Ode*, 319–34.

[27] In "A Discourse" Cowley notes the multiple uses of the word *tyrant* in antiquity. He applies it to Cromwell in the sense of usurper and rebel against authority (61).

[28] The question of "tyrant-killing" did not fade away with Charles I's death on the scaffold; it continued to apply not only to a deed accomplished but also to one that might be accomplished in turn against Charles I's successor. As with most issues of the Interregnum this one too was double-edged.

[29] See Corns, *Uncloistered Virtue*, 259–65.

of the *Prophets* writing, especially of *Isaiah*, seems to be very like that of *Pindar*" (50).[30] Cowley was not alone in this observation, for some sixteenth- and seventeenth-century commentators also compared Pindar's style to the style of Psalms, Proverbs, and the Prophets, even to the point of compiling lists of comparative quotations.[31] However, Cowley has other reasons for assuming the voice of the prophet. It is significant that it is not only in these two odes that Cowley adopts the manner of the Old Testament prophet, but also in a highly charged political tract, written during the Interregnum and printed anonymously at the Restoration, entitled *A Vision, Concerning this late Pretended Highnesse Cromwell, the Wicked*. In the tract he announces his intention to write "after the manner of Prophetical Threatenings in the Old Testament" and "to denounce heavy Judgments against the three Kingdoms, and several Places and Parties within them, unless they prevented them speedily by serious Repentance, and that greatest and hardest work of it, Restitution" (sig. A2ᵛ). Whereas in the tract he directly denounces Cromwell and his government, he delivers his judgments covertly in the Isaiah ode and in "The Plagues of *Egypt*." Further, as with the Pindaric paraphrases, he translates as he pleases, omitting text here and adding there.[32]

Under the guise of versifying biblical material in a Pindaric manner, Cowley has created covert political odes that denounce Cromwellian England. Both odes use the word *Rebel* to address a proud and disobedient nation ("Isaiah" 1.12; "Plagues" 1.20). In the first ode Cowley translates the portion of Isaiah 34 in which the prophet delivers warnings to a recalcitrant Judaea; in the other he recounts the progress of the plagues that brought down Egypt. Both poems offer re-readings of biblical history from the Royalist rather than the Parliamentarian stance. The Puritan saints, who looked upon their leaders as prophets denouncing royal evil, were fond of identifying their cause with that of oppressed Israel. Cromwell was their Moses who led his people out of Egypt, away from the tyranny of a Royalist Pharaoh.[33] Cowley takes the Puritan reading of scripture and turns it on its head, identifying the Royalists as the prophets and Charles as a

---

[30] Cowley goes on to comment on this alleged resemblance: "[both] pass from one thing to another with almost *Invisible connexions*, and are full of words and expressions of the highest and boldest flights of *Poetry*" ("Isaiah," 50).

[31] Franciscus Gomarus, a noted Hebraic scholar, compares Pindaric and biblical texts, citing and analyzing in *Davidis Lyra* (1637) the meter of parallel passages in Pindar (also in Sophocles) with passages from Psalms, Proverbs, and Job. His aim was to demonstrate that Hebraic verse was constructed on the same strict principles of metrical composition as that of the best Greek writers of lyric poetry.

[32] Cowley explains, "I am forced to adde a little, and leave out a great deal to make it seem *Sense* to us" ("Isaiah," 50).

[33] Even as late as 1660 Milton in "The Ready and Easy Way" looks on Royalist oppression as Egyptian and urges the English not to "put [their] necks again under kingship as was made use of by the Jews to return back to Egypt and to the worship of their idol queen" (in *Complete Poetry and Major Prose*, ed. Hughes, 898).

princely Moses, who will lead his people from exile back to the promised land. The murmuring disobedient mob are the erstwhile Puritan saints. Cautious, of course, both in his text and in his interpretive notes, he delivers the message darkly without interpreting it for us, as he would later in his prose "Discourse" on Oliver Cromwell and in the ode on Charles's Restoration and return. Yet the message is there.

Cowley opens his paraphrase, "The 34th Chapter of the Prophet *Isaiah,*" with a direct address to the "*Rebel* World":

> Awake, and with attention hear,
> Thou *drowsie World*, for it concerns thee near;
> Awake, I say, and listen well,
> To what from *God*, I, his *loud Prophet*, tell.
> . . . .
> A dreadful *Host* of *Judgments* is gone out;
> In strength and number more
> Then ere was rais'd by God before,
> To scourge the *Rebel World*, and march it round about.
> (1. 1–4, 9–12)

Although the word *Rebel* inevitably suggests the rebel Puritans, now in control of England, in his accompanying note Cowley is careful to temper the force of the word by assuring his readers that he meant only to address human rebellion in general, not in particular. He is also cautious in interpreting the temporal contexts of the prophecy in Isaiah, remarking that commentators differ in assigning the time of its fulfillment: "some would have it to be a *Prediction* of the destruction of *Judaea* . . . the rest understand it as a *Prophesie* of the Day of *Judgement*" (50). Cowley himself would have it both ways: "The design of it to me seems to be this, first to denounce great desolations and ruines to *All Countreys*, and then to do it more particularly to *Judaea*, as which was to suffer a greater measure of them then the rest of the world; as it has done, I think, much more then any other Land under the Sun; and to illustrate these confusions by the similitude of them to those of the last Day" (50). Cowley boldly names Judaea, confidently expecting that most Englishmen will supply England in its place. While admitting that in the text there is "no Transition from the *subject* to the *similitude*," he excuses the omission as the "old fashion of writing . . . where half is left out to be supplyed by the Hearer" (50).

Here the force of Cowley's Pindaric poetics comes into play. By likening the Old Testament prophet to Pindar and Old Testament prophecy to Pindaric ode, he explains that, like the prophet and the poet, he will deliberately leave it to the audience to interpret the text. In this way Cowley tacitly tells us that we may interpret Isaiah's address freely and apply it either to a rebel Judaea or, if we wish, to the rebels in Commonwealth England. The grim message that follows seems clearly designed to warn England that the sword of God (Isaiah 34:5–6) is about to fall on a "cursed *Land*" (4.1), which does not understand that it stands on a precipice. Similarly, in the pindarics that preceded the paraphrase from Isaiah and in "The Plagues of *Egypt*," metaphors of pestilence and storm not only describe the devastation of the past civil war but also threaten a new devastation to come. A fearful storm from God assaulting men and beasts threatens to level the land; a dreadful plague hangs over all living creatures, and the destroying angel measures the ground. Already the wolves were howling in the lower rooms, and the raven and the owl (Isaiah 34:11–15) in "gilt Chambers." The "royal" lion could say to the leopard: "*Brother Leopard* come away; / Behold a Land which God has giv'en us in prey! / Behold a Land from whence we see / *Mankinde* expulsed, *His* and *Our* common *Enemie*!" (5.9–12). The unpeopling of the land, of course, need not prophesy total doom—only the end of one order and the beginning of the next. The present order, Cowley implies, has turned things upside down and a dire future is to come: "[Mankind] in the *Dens* shall lurk, *Beasts* in the *Palaces* shall raign" (6.13).[34]

Pindar was famous in his odes for conveying as much through silence and circumspection as through what he said. In Olympian 1 he is remarkably restrained in describing Tantalus's impiety; in Pythian 2 Ixion's folly is left to speak for itself; in Olympian 13 he passes over Bellerophon's doom in silence. Cowley is similarly restrained in what he withholds. He tells us nothing, for example, about how Chapter 34 fits into the larger design of Isaiah's prophetic message to Judaea. Yet, curiously enough, this grim prophecy stands between two chapters that promise deliverance to Judaea. True, Chapter 34 shows us a destroying angel measuring the ground, but Chapter 33 promises: "thine eyes shall see the king in his beauty; they shall behold a far stretching land" (33:17). It also speaks of peace and comfort: "Look upon Zion, the city of our solemnities, thine eyes shall see Jerusalem a quiet habitation" (33:20). Chapter 35, verse 4 also reassures: "Be strong, fear not, behold, your God will come with vengeance"; and verse 10 foretells: "the ransomed of the Lord shall return, and come with singing into Zion; and everlasting joy shall be upon their heads; they shall obtain gladness and joy, and sorrow and sighing shall flee away." Why did Cowley omit these lines, paraphrasing only the grim but ambiguous apocalypse of Chapter 34? Here I think he is being Pindarically subtle and sending out a twofold message: on the one hand a message of doom that the regime of the Puritan "saints" would not continue, on the other a message of assurance that Judaea would return to favor.

---

[34] For a possible gloss on this passage on "wild beasts" in government, see "A Discourse on the Government of *Oliver Cromwell*." Cowley comments: "It is upon these Principles [those of Cromwell's Protectorate], that all the great Crimes of the world have been committed, and most particularly those which I have had the misfortune to see in my own time, and in my own Countrey. If these be to be allowed, we must break up humane society, retire into the Woods, and equally there stand our Guards against our Brethren Mankind, and our Rebels the Wild Beasts" (63).

Those knowing enough would understand that Chapter 34 delivered only half of Isaiah's prophecy; the flanking chapters 33 and 35 promised fortune and favor to Judaea. As Pindar himself had astutely remarked at the end of Olympian 2 (86), the wise do not need interpreters.

There are other hints of the political allegory in the ode. Particularly provocative, as Annabel Patterson has rightly noted, is Cowley's reference to a "Sword of God" brandished above the land, its scabbard cast away (2.1–3).[35] The biblical verse says nothing about a cast-away scabbard, but Cowley notes of the scabbard, as though to underline the veiled allusion to Cromwell's unseating of Charles I: "he who draws his sword against his *Prince* should fling away the *Scabbard*" (51).[36] Further, sword and scabbard are directly applied to Cromwell in Sprat's 1659 ode on the death of Cromwell: "Thy strong and certain Remedy / Unto the Weapon didst apply. / Thou didst not draw the Sword, and so / Away the Scabbard throw" (7.4–7).[37] Sprat clearly understood the thrust of Cowley's Isaiah ode.

The Isaiah ode should be read in tandem with the final ode, "The Plagues of *Egypt*," since it too employs Old Testament prophecy and Pindaric techniques to comment on the history of the 1650s. In this final ode Cowley employs the technique of digressive myth to make his point, alluding to the "myth" of Moses' leading his people out of Egypt and narrating it, like Pindar, from several different vantage points rather than in strict chronological sequence. Without identifying him by name, Cowley shadows forth the princely Charles as Moses, making him the hero of his Pindaric narrative. "The Plagues of *Egypt*" has a double focus. Employing a central "mythic" narrative of the plagues, it indicts the Pharaoh who brings plagues upon his land and who stubbornly defies God's will; it also indicts the Israelites who submit to his authority. The opening stanza is a Pindaric apostrophe to "*Man*," content to remain captive to "*Tyrant Sin*" (1. 9). With a peculiar Pindaric indirection, Cowley lets us interpret whether "*Man*" is generic man or the English under Cromwell, who have forsaken their status as "the *choice Race*," refused the calls of "*Prophets*" and *Apostles*," and declined to come "Home to the promis'ed *Canaan*" (1.12–15). Certainly, he profits from espousing at the very beginning a Pindaric figure that could be read specifically or generally.

----

[35] Patterson, *Censorship and Interpretation*, 156. Also provocative is Cowley's note that he has omitted verses 7 through 10 that refer to the destruction of "Great *Tyrants*" ("Isaiah," 50).

[36] It is significant that Cowley attributes the saying to the Duke of Guise (during France's civil wars) and interprets it as a sign that the one drawing the sword never intends to be reconciled with his prince.

[37] "To the Happie Memory of the most Renowned Prince, Oliver Lord Protector," in *Three Poems upon the Death of his late Highnesse Oliver, Lord Protector of England, Scotland, and Ireland* (London: William Wilson, 1659), 18–19.

Is this thy *Brav'ery Man*, is this thy *Pride*?
Rebel to *God*, and *Slave* to all beside!
Captiv'ed by every thing ! and onely *Free*
To fly from thine *own Libertie*!
(1. 1–4)

In odes such as Pythian 1 Pindar likens war and civil discord to the monstrous dissonance that the giant Typhon produces pinioned under the mountain Aetna. Several places in his prose Cowley names Cromwell both a giant, whose arrogance has brought discord to England, and a rebel Pharaoh, who brought down war-like plagues on England-Egypt. Both in "The Plagues of *Egypt*" and in "A Discourse" he makes some very specific analogies between God's vengeance on Egypt and on England under Cromwell. In "A Discourse" he depicts Cromwell as both the cause of God's anger and the means for God punishing the pride of his people: "A Tyrant is a Rod and Serpent too, / And brings worse plagues than *Egypt* knew" (60). At the same time he prays that God will no longer afflict England: "Let, Gracious God, let never more thine hand / Lift up this rod against our Land" (60). In his Pindaric ode, Cowley uses the imagery of war and storm to describe the plagues that assaulted Egypt. Moses raises his hand and "all the full charg'ed *clouds* in ranged *Squadrons* move," discharging thunder, tempest, hail, and rain from the "stormy *Magazins* of the *North*" (11.7, 14). The elements fall like gunshot. When the locusts come, they come in legions. God's management of the plagues is like the management of a war: "First light *Skirmishes*" and then "The *Shock* and bloody *battel* now begins / The plenteous *Harvest* of full-ripened Sins" (14.2, 3–4). Finally, Michael raises the sword of God, "The sharpest *Sword* that ere was laid / Up in the *Magazins* of God to scourge a wicked Land" (15.13–14).

Conversely, pestilence is for Cowley a familiar metaphor for war. When he describes the battles of the civil wars in "A Discourse," he refers to rivers of blood, storms and hail, ulcerous disease: "What Rivers stain'd with blood have been? / What Storm and Hail-shot have we seen? / What Sores deform'd the Ulcerous State? / What darkness to be felt has buried us of late?" (60). Moreover, in "A Discourse" Cowley also calls the Protector (like Pharaoh) the pestilential destroyer of the land.[38] Similarly, Thomas Sprat follows Cowley in using

---

[38] There are still further connections between "The Plagues of Egypt" and "A Discourse." In a verse passage in "A Discourse" Cowley alludes to the "croaking Sects and Vermin" sent to torment the "restless Nation" and to the "armed power / of Flies and Locusts" (Exodus 8:21–24; 10:4–15), pests which devour the land (60). He hopes that "Divine Justice" will be satisfied before it brings down on England, as it had on Egypt, "the last extremity" (60). Reflecting on the "inscrutable mysteries of Eternal Providence," he tells us that God uses small means to confound the mighty, for when God wished to "correct the pride of the *Egyptians*," he did not assemble "the Serpents and Monsters of Afrique," but instead called for his "Armies of Locusts out of *Æthiopia*, and formed new

pestilence as a metaphor for civil discord in his own Pindaric ode "The Plague of Athens" (published after the death of Cromwell but before the restoration of Charles II). Praising the "incomparable Dr. *Cowley's* Pindarick way," Sprat describes the plague that beset the Athenians during the second year of the Peloponnesian War, registering in his descriptions, however, the tensions of the current political situation. He can even exclaim, after describing the horrors of plague: "Only pass by and spare the British Isle" (section xxv).[39]

In "The Plagues of *Egypt*" Cowley is sounding a warning. By narrating the devastation in ancient Egypt, he glances at the civil plagues of his own time and, as he had in the Isaiah ode, threatens an apocalypse. However, he also urges "stubborn Man"—presumably Englishmen under Cromwell—to turn from sin and repent and receive God's forgiveness and grace (2.8–13). The apocalypse is reserved for the great Tyrant-Pharaoh-Cromwell, who will be destroyed as the inevitable outcome of his resistance to God's design, and for the Egyptians who too late upbraid their "guilty *King*" (19.26). In "A Discourse" Cowley takes a moderate view, noting that God did not mean to bring England to total ruin: "It is easie to apply this general observation to the particular case of our troubles in *England*, and that they seem only to be meant for a temporary chastisement of our sins" (67). The sufferings under Cromwell were meant not to destroy the English, but to cure. Similarly, in "The Plagues of *Egypt*," Cowley comments: "God did on *Man* a Gentler *Medicine* try, / And a *Disease* for *Physick* did apply" (10.2–3). "The Plagues of *Egypt*" functions as Cowley's final coded message to the Royalists that God's purposes will work out in the end.

So subtle are the political messages of Cowley's *Pindarique Odes* that the author himself was hard-pressed to prove to Charles II that his intention in them was not to give comfort to the Protector, but quietly to harbinger Charles's own return. Taking the so-called Pindaric path, they imply rather than state, and proceed through innuendo and indirection. Hence they imitate a strain often present in Pindar, who did not always tell rulers such as Hieron and Theron exactly what was on his mind. When Charles returned from France to England in 1660, Cowley produced for him the kind of Pindaric ode that poets on the continent had been writing for triumphant kings from the time Macrin wrote for François I and Minturno for Charles V. The "ODE, Upon the Blessed Restoration and Returne of His Sacred Majestie, Charls the Second," is filled with the kind of Pindaric flourishes that Cowley employed in his translations—but now

---

ones of Vermine out of the very dust" (66–67). Cowley's phrasing here is almost a direct recollection of "The Plagues of *Egypt*": "every *Dust* did an arm'ed *Vermine* prove . . . and 'twas but just / To punish thus mans pride, to punish *Dust* with *Dust*" (7.10, 18–19). In section 8 "Armies" of insects rise, and a little further on Cowley remarks how "*Beasts* for *Mans Rebellion* dy" (10.1), employing once more that word "rebellion" to reinforce the connection between the plagues and the civil wars.

[39] See Thomas Sprat, *The Plague of Athens* (London: Thomas Childe, 1659).

employed directly and openly to compliment the returning king.[40] Just as Cowley in his version of Nemean 1 had celebrated with a portent the coming of the infant Heracles, he begins the Restoration ode by making the heavens signal with a star the prodigious wonder of Charles's birth. The Jovian eagle that in Cowley's version of Olympian 2 appeared to guarantee justice reappears as a dove returned to an England restored to peace and justice, the Augean stables of the Church having been cleansed by a restored Hercules.

As the Exodus myth was the touchstone in both the Pindaric ode "The Plagues of *Egypt*" and "A Discourse on the Government of *Oliver Cromwell*," it becomes one of the controlling myths in Cowley's ode for Charles's return to England in 1660. Cowley's Royalist reading of the Moses story makes Charles II (and not Cromwell) the leader who restores the nation to safety, guiding his people from exile across the metaphoric Red Sea of the English Channel.[41]

> How through a *rough Red-sea* they had been led,
> By *Wonders* guarded, and by *Wonders* fed.
> How many years of trouble and distresse
> They'd wandred in their fatall *Wilderness*,
> And yet did never *murmur* or *repine*;
> . . . .
> Th' *Almighty Mercy* would at last
> Conduct them with a strong un-erring hand
> To their *own Promis'd* Land.
> (8.14–18, 21–23)

Not for the last time would Charles be depicted as a Mosaic savior.

As it shares the Exodus myth with its Pindaric predecessor, the Restoration ode also shares images and symbols connected with it. In "The Plagues of *Egypt*," the serpents in Egypt's land are all under the command of the "Old Serpent" (4. 12), a title that Cowley applies both in "A Discourse" and in the Restoration ode to Cromwell. In "A Discourse" the Protector is "a mischievous Serpent," a

---

[40] First printed by Herringman in 1660, the ode was reprinted in *Works* in 1668 with a different title, "Upon His Majesties Restoration and Return," and with a slightly different text ("Verses written on several occasions" in *Works*, 16–25). I quote from the 1660 version.

[41] Parliamentarians such as Milton have so persuaded us that "Egypt" is England under the Stuarts and Cromwell the Moses who led his people from that servitude that it is a little strange at first to see Charles wear the Mosaic mantle and Cromwell assume the robes of Pharaoh. Even in the funeral panegyric for Cromwell Edmund Waller describes Cromwell as a Moses who saved his people, but did not live to see the promised land. See *Three Poems upon the Death of his late Highnesse Oliver, Lord Protector*, 31.

"*Basilick*," in his desire for the crown (59).[42] In the Restoration ode, alluding to Revelation 12:9, he conflates Cromwell with "that great *Serpent*, which was all a *Tayl*, / (And in his poys'nous folds whole *Nations prisoners* made) [4.10–11]. Yet, as he recounts in "The Plagues of *Egypt*," Moses' wand, once transformed into a serpent, challenges and destroys both the Egyptian serpents and even the great Serpent himself ("Plagues," 3.6–16, 4.1–20). By the time he writes the Restoration Ode Cowley had no need for ciphers. Throwing off the cloak of so-called Pindaric obscurity, he triumphantly employs the very imagery of his earlier ode to celebrate the returned Charles-Moses.

As Cowley covertly celebrated Prince James with his brother Charles in his translation of Olympian 2, now both are openly welcomed:

> He who has seen the double *Pair*
> Of *Brothers* heavenly good, and *Sisters* heavenly fair,
>   Might have perceiv'd (me-thinks) with ease,
> (But *wicked men* see onely what they please)
> That *God* had no intent t'extinquish quite
> The *pious King's eclipsed Right*.
> (8.5–10)

Charles I, who appeared in Cowley's Olympian 2 under the guise of the innocent parricide and the slain Achilles, now is proclaimed a martyr and the savior of the English church: "The *Martyr's blood* was said of old to be / The *seed* from whence the *Church* did grow" (9.1–2). The malice, wrongs, and outrages that Cowley complained of at the end of Olympian 2 are banished by the united forces of "King and Truth" (9.18–19). The tyrannies that Cowley alluded to only indirectly at the end of Nemean 1 are now openly named:

> No frantick *Common-wealths* or *Tyrannies*,
> No *Cheats* and *Perjuries*, and *Lies*,
> No *Nets* of human *Policies* . . .
> (9.21–23)

Moreover, the constellations that Cowley describes at the end of Nemean 1 as favoring Hercules-Charles are conflated with the star (referred to in the Restoration ode) that appeared at Charles's birth to predict his glorious future. These auspicious heavenly signs contrast with the stars, meteors, and comets that misled Cromwell, himself named a large comet:

---

[42] In "A Discourse" Cowley puns on the word *basilisk* (little king) to chastise Cromwell's ambitions: "In what oblique and humble creeping wise / Does the mischievous Serpent rise? / But even his forked Tongue strikes dead, / When h'as rear'd up his wicked Head, / He murders with his moral frown, / A *Basilisk* he grows if once he get a Crown" (59).

> Where's the *large Comet* now whose rageing flame
> So fatall to our *Monarchy* became?
> (10.9–10)

Charles is portrayed in the ode as the anti-Comet that has "frighted it away" (10. 20), just as Hercules had "frighted" the radiant monsters of the heavens.

As a complement to the story of Moses' escape from Egypt, Cowley summons up Latin and Greek exemplars to laud the returned hero-king. In Charles is combined the figures of Aeneas and Odysseus—"The *Pious Trojan*" and "The *Prudent Greek*," fitting prototypes for this "*comely Prince* of *heavenly Birth*" (13. 4–5). As the tale of Aeneas's escape from Troy was so often the chosen myth in the sixteenth century to trumpet the heroism and endurance of royal subjects, so it recurs again in Cowley's ode. Cowley tells how Charles's "*young* Virtue" was hardened by degrees, tested by loss of country, by murder of friends and kindred, by tossing at sea and on land, and by the opposition of "*angry gods*." It was only after "long *troubles* and long *wars*" sustained that he prevailed (13.11–18).

> Ere he his *fatall Birth-right* gain.
> With no lesse *time* or *labour* can
> *Destiny build* up such a *Man*,
> Who's with sufficient virtue fill'd
> His *ruin'd Country* to rebuild.
> (13.19–23)

In Cowley's hands Aeneas's story seems tailor-made to be refitted for the much-tried Stuart king, returned to repossess his own. Cowley sums it up:

> Not without cause are *Arms* from *Heaven*,
> To such a *Hero* by the *Poets* given (14.1–2).

Cowley often follows Pindar's lead in offering some philosophical reflections on the perplexing way in which human happiness is granted or withheld. Although happiness on earth is uncertain, yet it is better to experience misfortune early in life if it leads to true felicity. He gives the Pindaric aphorism a peculiarly Christian turn by remarking: "Man ought his *Future Happinesse* to fear, / If he be alwaies *Happy here*" (11.1–2). However, true felicity is what Cowley's Restoration ode proclaims, with all the Pindaric stops pulled out. Dropping the ciphers of Theron, Chromius, Oedipus, and Hercules, he introduces without cipher the true *eikon* of the returned king.

Few royal encomiasts have the tact and mastery to conclude their compliments to kings briefly and succinctly, as Pindar usually did. Cowley lets his *Pindarique Pegasus* run without reining him in. He still has more to tell of Charles's courage and his miraculous escapes; he alludes once more to biblical lore, comparing Charles and his brothers to the Judaean youths tried in the fiery furnace.

Moreover, to crown his opening allusion to the star of Charles's birth, he must like a priest "of a *Poetick* rage" predict a new Golden Age with a Messianic king on the throne (16.21–22). The temple must be rebuilt as well as the city (18.10), which Charles will do when he opens his new and *"Endlesse Parliament"* (19.21).[43]

With the exception of the Restoration ode for Charles, the Pindaric odes that Cowley produced after the Restoration are not politically motivated. Disappointed with Charles's lukewarm rewards, Cowley turned to persons other than the king for encomium and to subjects other than politics for celebration. In his ode "To the Royal Society," he assigns the role of Moses as savior of the people to the scientist Bacon rather than to a political leader.[44] For Cowley neither Cromwell nor Charles had led the English out of Egypt. The Pindaric odes of the 1668 folio not only eschew politics, but also further broaden the topics that a Pindaric ode might address, developing at the same time the ode's potential for familiar encomium as well as philosophic discourse. However, his Pindaric ode on the returning Charles II had made its impact, and, in the latter part of the seventeenth century and well into the eighteenth, royal returns and military victories brought forth odes celebrating Charles II, James II, and another conqueror, who was to cross the perilous Channel and assume the throne—William III. As Cowley left off writing political odes, the poets of the next generation—John Dryden, Aphra Behn, and a host of others—took up the mode. The political pindaric was on its way to eclipsing all other forms of occasional poetry.

---

[43] Cowley concludes the revised version of the Restoration ode with this allusion to the new parliament Charles is to open—"the *Long*, the *Endless Parliament*" (19.21)—omitting the sneer at the Rump parliament with which he had concluded the 1660 version of the ode.

[44] For a discussion of "To the Royal Society," see Revard, *Pindar and the Renaissance Hymn-Ode*, 329–34.

CHAPTER 5
STUART APOLOGETICS:
APHRA BEHN AND JOHN DRYDEN

From the time that Cowley set the tone for Charles II's reign with the pindaric of royal return to the time that Charles's reign ended with his death in 1684, the pindaric was the preferred form for addressing the restored king and members of his court. These so-called royal pindarics differ in range, tone, and intention. Some are pure poems of praise, composed to win royal favor; others have more subtle ends in mind and tell us as much about the political cross-currents of the time in which they were written as about the person whom they portend to praise. All kinds of occasions call forth these political pindarics: not just those which were politically charged, such as the thwarting of the Popish Plot, but also those which would seem to have been composed for only the most conventional occasions—royal weddings, royal births, and royal funerals.[1] Since Charles II and his consort were childless and the ostensible successor to the throne was his Catholic brother James, the Duke of York, the weddings of the Duke's Protestant daughters to Protestant princes became politically resonant occasions. When the king's death in 1684 brought James to the throne, the pindarics written to mourn the king had more work to do than simply mark the passing of one king and the succession of another. Similarly, the odes composed to celebrate James's coronation or the birth in 1688 of a Catholic prince to his queen, Mary of Modena, become political manifestos that justify the king's right. With the change of regime in 1688 the pindarics that welcome William and Mary to the throne—or in the case of Aphra Behn, the odes which decline to do so—are commentaries on the uneasy transition of power from Catholic to Protestant monarchs. Further, the pindarics written on William III's victory over James II at the Boyne or over Louis XIV at Namur are not just victory odes, but complex defenses of political policies. Even the poems on Queen Mary's death in 1694/95 that ostensibly mourn the queen also defend the Protestant cause she represented. In the latter part of the seventeenth century, Pindaric ode was a subtle and sometimes a not so subtle tool for disseminating political propaganda.

---

[1] See, for example, *A Pindarique Ode, Upon the late Horrid and Damnable Whiggish Plot* (London, 1684), published at the same year as some of the funeral odes for Charles II.

1.

The leading pindarists of the era, Aphra Behn and John Dryden, assumed the mantle from Cowley, whom they both admired and freely imitated.[2] Like him, they were staunch supporters of the Stuart monarchs, who addressed effusive compliments to Charles II, but also defended his brother James's right to succeed him. Although Dryden had written "Heroique Stanza's" in 1659 to mourn the death of Oliver Cromwell, he readily pledged his allegiance to the restored Charles II. In quick succession he composed propagandistic poetry for Charles: "Astraea Redux" (1660), "A Panegyrick on His Coronation" (1661), and later the semi-heroic poem "Annus Mirabilis" (1667), and the political satire "Absalom and Achitophel" (1681). At Charles's death Dryden's Cowleian pindaric "Threnodia Augustalis" lamented the king, but also defended the succession of the unpopular James. Aphra Behn, another accomplished Stuart apologist adept at the Pindaric mode, composed not only a Pindaric threnody for Charles II, but also a very long coronation ode for James in thirty Cowleian stanzas.[3] Behn employed pindarics again to predict and then to celebrate the birth of a Catholic prince, who would have displaced his Protestant sisters in the line of succession. Behn and Dryden probably chose the Cowleian model for their political panegyrics because it was equally useful for fulsome compliment and for political insinuation.

The flexibility of the irregular Cowleian pindaric probably accounted for its rapid acceptance with both major poets such as Dryden and Behn as well as a host of minor poets. Besides, although Milton and Jonson had employed neo-Greek triads, the triadic ode never had the currency in England that it possessed in France. With the success of the Cowleian pindaric, triadic verse virtually disappeared in England until its revival in the eighteenth century with the English translations of Pindar. One must remark, however, that the Cowleian pindaric, however irregular its metrics, deviated no more from Pindar's original odes than

---

[2] Many of the poets who wrote pindarics make no attempt to imitate Pindar, but merely imitate the Greek poet as Cowley gave him to the nation. Dryden certainly could have read Pindar in Greek, but chose in his odes to imitate Cowley's imitations rather than the original odes. Dryden also employed the Cowleian pindaric for non-political poems, such as the ode to commemorate Anne Killigrew (which we shall look at in chapter 8). He paraphrased Horace, *Carmina* 3.29 in Cowleian pindarics. He refers in "The Medal" to the Pindaric style: "Thou leap'st o'er all eternal truths in thy Pindaric way!" (l. 94). Dryden discusses Cowley's Pindaric imitations in "The Preface to Ovid's Epistles," in *The Poetical Works of Dryden*, ed. George R. Noyes (Cambridge, MA: The Riverside Press, 1950), 91. Aphra Behn did not know Greek and openly confesses her indebtedness to the Cowleian model. Of the university poets who wrote pindarics, the majority chose the Cowleian form for their English odes but retain Horatian stanzas for their Latin odes.

[3] Behn included a number of occasional pindarics in *Poems upon Several Occasions* (London, 1684). See chapter 8, and also Revard, *Pindar and the Renaissance Hymn-Ode*, 334–38.

had its Ronsardian predecessors in sixteenth-century France that had adopted Pindar's triads. Indeed, Ronsardian pindarics and Cowleian pindarics share a kind of inherent "family" resemblance, with their adoption of Pindaric figure and Pindaric myth and their use of fulsome praise for royal subjects. Hardly had Cowley printed his collection of *Pindarique Odes* in 1656 than his friend and disciple Thomas Sprat adopted the form to mourn Cromwell's death. Soon afterwards Robert Stubbes anticipated Cowley's own ode on the king's return by using Cowley's irregular verse stanzas for his own pindaric on Charles's restoration.[4] The Cowleian pindaric became a form much in favor in the commemorative volumes produced by Oxford and Cambridge Universities when after 1660 the language of these volumes began to shift from Latin to English.[5] The odes in these university volumes not only celebrate important events from 1660 to 1700, but also comment cautiously on the political significance of these events and thus continue to be important indicators of the country's political mood and poetic practice.[6]

Charles II had been on the throne for ten years when the death of George Monck, the Duke of Albemarle, furnished an occasion for political reflection on the king's accomplishments. General Monck, a popular military hero, had made possible the restoration of Charles II, and his death was an opportunity to recall the decisive event of Monck's career and to mount a good deal of pro-Royalist propaganda for Charles II. The odes in the volume Cambridge University produced are particularly resonant and full of nationalistic and religious reference. They do not miss the chance to compare this George to St. George: Monck had killed the dragon of the Commonwealth and restored the "true prince" to his throne (sig. U2^{r-v}).[7] Monck is also compared to that other dragon-killer Michael who in apocalyptic triumph prevailed against the fiery Dragon — *"the long and endless* Parliament" (sigs. Y2^v–Y3^v). The classical heroes who populated sixteenth-century royal pindarics on the continent now take their place beside some English heroes in these English pindarics. Monck is compared to Aeneas, Jason, Theseus, and Alexander (sigs. X^r, Y3^v, T3^v, T4^r); he is a Hercules who quelled the Hydra without a blow, a Perseus, who disarmed the rebellious rout

---

[4] Stubbes's ode appeared in the Oxford University collection issued in 1660 to mark Charles II's return: *Britannia Rediviva* (Oxford: A. & L Lichfield, 1660), sig. Ee2^v–Ee4^v.

[5] See *Britannia Rediviva*; also *ΣΩΣΤΡΑ, Sive Ad Carolum II reducem* (Cambridge: J. Field, 1660).

[6] University volumes mark the death of General Monck in 1670; the marriages of Princess Mary in 1677 and Princess Anne in 1683; Charles II's death and James II's accession to the throne in 1684; and the accession of William and Mary in 1689.

[7] Thomas Newcomen's pindaric on Monck's death in *Musarum Cantabrigiensium Threnodia in Obitum Incomparabilis Herois ac Ducis Illustrissimi Georgii, Ducis Albæmarlæ* (Cambridge: Joannes Hayes, 1670), sig. U^v–U3^r.

with the gorgon's head (T4ʳ). He is also the biblical strongman Samson, who metaphorically bore away the gates of the city (Y2ᵛ).[8] Seizing the occasion to summon such heroes from a mythic past, the poets remind England of that fortunate hour when Monck, wearing the armor of St. George or flexing his muscles like Hercules and Samson, re-established the institution of monarchy in England. Since this display of classical muscle comes in the wake of England's disenchantment with some of Charles's political policies, reminders that England had been saved from national chaos by the intervention of General Monck were timely.

The political tide had been turning, and England was uneasy about Charles's too close ties with France and the continued alienation of the Protestant Netherlands with the continuing Dutch naval wars. In 1674, however, Charles negotiated a treaty with the Netherlands that ended the naval wars, and at the same time the United Provinces made peace with Louis XIV. Both events signaled peace for Europe as well as a happy expectation for England, and also made possible a match in 1677 of Charles's niece Mary, his brother James's elder daughter, to the Protestant Prince of Orange. Charles II's marriage to Catherine of Braganza was childless, and James's only male heir, the Duke of Cambridge, the son of Anne Hyde, had died in 1671, leaving James's two Protestant daughters, Mary and Anne, the only conspicuous heirs. Hence the marriage of Mary to a Protestant prince appeared as a politically hopeful event for the future Stuart succession. James's unpopular wedding in 1673 to the Catholic Maria Beatrice d'Este of Modena (performed privately at Dover) called forth no commemorative volumes and no Pindaric poetry. In 1677, on the eve of Princess Mary's wedding, James's Catholic duchess, Mary of Modena, who had yet to produce a living heir, was once more pregnant and about to deliver a son, a new Duke of Cambridge. To celebrate Princess Mary's marriage to William and the pair's departure from England, a volume of mixed Latin, Greek, and English odes came forth from Cambridge University. The poets seized the occasion to congratulate Mary's uncle Charles, to whom the volume was dedicated, on his past reign and to look cautiously to the future.[9] Some poets of the Cambridge volume even combined celebration of the royal wedding with that of the recent royal birth, alluding to the "Son of *England's* Royal bloud." But the celebration of the new royal heir was premature, for the new prince lived only six weeks.

For most poets, however, the celebration of Princess Mary's marriage to the Protestant William was the main event. William was already a military leader of some renown, and his martial prowess is alluded to with comparisons to Mars

---

[8] See Judges 16:3.

[9] See Aldrovandus Everard, "On the Marriage of the *Lady Mary* to the *Prince* of Orange, and the Birth of the *Duke* of *Cambridge*," in *Epithalamium in Desideratissimis Nuptiis Serenissimorum & Illustrissimorum Principum Guilielmi-Henrici Arausii & Mariæ Britanniarum* (Cambridge: Joannes Hayes, 1677), sig. Rʳ.

and Hercules. Mary is perforce compared to Venus, wedded to a godlike Mars. The poets describe the journey of the lovers across a sea, secured by the Dutch Neptune and now safe for commerce (sig. Q^r). Mary is the treasure brought home by the Dutch burghers. The poets even recall how England once came to the assistance of the Protestant Netherlands tyrannized by Catholic Spain. William himself is praised for resisting Spain's Catholic neighbor France. As Joshua Barnes put it, the world may expect a Golden Age, now that France and Rome have failed and "True Religion" has triumphed (sig. Q3^v). In this context Mary herself is compared to her forebear, the "Great *Elizabeth*, when She / From *Spanish* yoak did set Your Countrey [the Netherlands] free" (sig. P4^v). The marriage is seen as a triumph comparable to Elizabeth's victory over the Armada.

> Then let the mighty *Spaniard* rage,
> Let *France* with force, or fraud engage;
> Let *Alba*, *Parma*, and *Turene*,
> Come from the shades agen;
> . . . .
> Joyn all mankind against this spot of land,
> Which like the earth i' th' Map does stand:
> 'Gainst their united force it shall unbroken stand
> In spight of All
> Spight of the Fates
> Englands *Elizabeth* and *Mary* shall
> Buoy up against them All,
> The sinking States.
> (R. Hill, sig. R2^{r-v})

The poets even cautiously hint at the royal fruit to come from the marriage—the much hoped-for Protestant prince.

This expectation was disappointed, for the marriage remained childless and the question of succession continued to be hotly debated, since James's marriage to Mary of Modena was also without issue. Although Charles had many illegitimate sons, notably the hapless Monmouth whose attempt on the throne had led to his exile in the Low Countries, his only ostensible heirs were his Catholic brother James and James's two Protestant daughters. In 1683 Protestant England pinned its hopes on the marriage of Mary's younger sister, Princess Anne, to another Protestant prince, George, Prince of Denmark. Coming in the wake of the Popish Plot, the conspiracy of Shaftesbury, and the rebellion of Monmouth, and immediately preceding Charles II's death in 1684, Princess Anne's marriage to a Protestant prince was looked upon as a politically significant event.

A year before the wedding of his younger daughter, James returned from an extended stay in the Hague and in Scotland, having escaped a dangerous accident at sea during his crossing. He was greeted by a pindaric of royal return, produced perhaps less to celebrate his return than to attempt to prepare the public to accept James as Charles's heir apparent. The rhetoric of the ode heroicizes James, returned from the frozen North to melt with his sunny beams "Each Frozen and Rebellious Heart" (1.10–11).[10] James's mishap at sea is depicted as a happy conquest for a conquering Caesar. At the same time, the myth of the giants' rebellion is dredged up, now to allude to Monmouth's revolt. The anonymous poet dismisses Monmouth's rebellion with mock heroic rhetoric as the antics of the "Hair-brain'd Sons of Ignorance" (4.9). The gods, sitting above, look down, smiling and indulgent, and the rebels are sent "To howle in Regions of Despair, and Flames of Discontent" (4.25). Monmouth himself as Phaethon is relegated in a digressive section to a fiery demise, the result of his own folly. Yet neither this ode nor the prologue written by Dryden to welcome the returning Duke of York eased the political tension.[11]

The subtext—unspoken and sometimes not so unspoken—of the Cambridge collection, which celebrated the wedding of Princess Anne to Prince George of Denmark in 1683, was the question of royal succession. The volume was dedicated to Charles II, and just as many odes directly address the king on political matters as congratulate the nuptial couple. Some poets remark on the uneasy political situation, the "black Designs" that threaten the state (sig. P4ᵛ), the plots that besiege the "Accursed Land! that still on Plots do'st feed" (sig. Sᵛ). One poet, William Ayloffe, openly regrets that the king has been denied a son to succeed him, and frames a Pindaric epithalamion for Anne and George that expresses the hope that the newly wed couple will produce a Protestant heir. He describes the bride and groom as an Adam and Eve about to embark on a world that will be blissfully renewed at their marriage. He also characterizes Prince George as an Apollo about to capture successfully the nymph he pursues and to crown himself with Daphnean laurel (sig. R2ᵛ, R3ᵛ). Another poet describes George as an Alpheus successfully overtaking his Arethusa (sig. Sᵛ). The mythic allusions reveal both the nation's anxieties and its hopes. The poets even characterize the prince they hope will be born of this union as a "little *Hercules*,"

---

[10] *A Pindarique Ode, On their Royal Highnesses Happy Return from Scotland After His Escape at Sea* (London, 1682). This pindaric of royal return recalls those odes of return written for James's father, Charles I, on his own return from Scotland. The Catholic Duke of York was rarely the recipient of encomiastic verse, even though his naval victories in the Dutch wars could have inspired poetry comparable to that written for Cromwell. Aphra Behn alludes to James's escape at sea and his return to court in an ode published after James's accession, "To His Sacred Majesty, King James II." See *The Uncollected Verse of Aphra Behn.* ed. Germaine Greer (Stump Cross, Essex: Stump Cross Books, 1989), 26–27, 180–81. Greer comments on James's circumstances between 1679 and 1682.

[11] See John Dryden, "Prologue to his Royal Highness, Upon his First Appearance at the Duke's Theatre since his Return from Scotland" (London, 1682). Dryden clearly alludes to Monmouth's rebellion as he greets James's return: "O welcome to this much offending Land / The Prince that brings forgiveness in his hand!" (ll. 36–37) in *The Poetical Works of John Dryden,* ed. Noyes, 132–33.

who, William Fleetwood predicts, "shall / Even Monsters in his Cradle quell; / Shall crush Ambitions Towring head, / And strike the groveling Faction dead" (sig. P3ᵛ). William Ayloffe looks abroad to identify the threatening serpents: one comes from papal Rome, the other from Calvinist Geneva (sig. R4ʳ). A Protestant prince, born into the Anglican faith, will clearly take care of both these snaky adversaries.[12] To an England uneasy over a Catholic succession, the marriage of Princess Anne to a Protestant prince seemed to promise the beginning of a new royal line.

2.

The odes that come forth in 1684 to mourn the death of Charles II are still more politically resonant, for they reflect both the nation's grief over the death of the monarch and its anxiety over the Catholic succession. Dryden and Behn, the major apologists for the Stuart cause, produce pindarics for the occasion, as do a host of lesser poets. Both universities publish commemorative volumes, the Cambridge volume abounding in Cowleian pindarics. At the same time the printer Henry Playford puts out a volume with pindarics by Aphra Behn, Francis Fane, Edmund Arwaker, and Nahum Tate. The Cowleian pindaric with its excesses and enthusiastic approach serves Cowley's poetic heirs well as they both veil and reveal their propagandistic ends. Pindar's name is used to advance the Stuart cause. What Cowley described as Pindar's "lawless" sublime would seem to authorize the extravagant lament for Charles and fulsome praise for James. Features of Pindaric ode, such as the appeal to the Muse for inspiration, are used to raise the ode to a heroic pitch. The episodic divisions of the Cowleian ode are exploited to highlight different facets of Charles's past achievements and to look forward to James's future reign. Employing the license of Pindaric "myth," poets recapitulate Charles's life, emphasizing the hardships the "exiled" prince endured in order to return and bring his people salvation.[13] Both classical and biblical allusions support the myth. The dead king is compared to Hercules, to Atlas, to Achilles, but he is just as often likened to Moses or David—the idealized Old Testament leaders—and even to Christ.

---

[12] *Hymenæus Cantabrigiensis* (Cambridge: Johannes Hayes, 1683).

[13] John Whitehall combines a reference to "*Pindarique Liberty*" with a glance backward at "the old *Chaos* of a Commonwealth," which the restoration of Charles II brought to an end: "Let them despond this day to see, / While Ye from Faction free / Enjoy your old *Pindarique Liberty*, / Whose Honours are engag'd thus much to do, / To guard the King [James], whose Sacred Life's a Guard to You" (3. 8–13) in *Miscellaneous Poems, With some Remarks on the Death of King Charles the II. And the Happy Succession of King James the II. In a Poem to the Magistracy of England* (London, 1685).

The biblical references in the pindarics on Charles II's death are particularly significant. Many poets take up the Exodus story, used by Cowley in his Restoration ode. Dryden makes the scene of Charles's return from France a Mosaic crossing of the Red Sea. Behn compares Charles to Moses, who "led the Murm'ring Crowd, / Beneath the *Peaceful Rule* of his Almighty Wand" (4.15–16) until he resigned his rule to a Joshua-James, who leads the people safe into the Promised Land. She makes James a royal prophet, on whom the dying monarch places his hand to confirm the succession (5.1–13). [14] One of the Cambridge poets also casts Charles as a Moses, who, having broken the Egyptian fetters, leads his people within the prospect of Canaan, where "*Great James*" is left, "like Joshua behind, / To perfect and compleat, what *He* so well begun" (sig. Ff3ʳ). [15] Celebrating the "Vertues of a Royal Mind, / Forgiving, bounteous, humble, just and kind" (ll. 335–336), Dryden reminds the nation in "Threnodia Augustalis" that Charles forgave the worst offenses of the rebels and went on to convey "peaceful Triumphs" on his land and to make the "drooping Arts" revive (ll. 346, 348). [16] He does not fail to exploit Pindaric sentence, as he laments the "frail Estate of Humane things, / And slippery hopes below" (ll. 399–400). He closes the Mosaic circle when he remarks that Charles, like Moses, gave his people miracles and quails and manna, but did not lead them into the promised land: "Death did his promis'd hopes destroy / He toyl'd, he gain'd, but liv'd not to enjoy / What mists of Providence are these / Through which we cannot see!" (ll. 408–411). The repeated references to Moses-Charles's failure to lead his people to the promised land are actually deft political touches, for they cast James in the role of the Joshua who is to fulfill the task left incomplete by his predecessor. If the people reject a Joshua-James, they will also be rejecting the biblical destiny that he seems to promise. By celebrating Charles as a Moses, who saved the country from the chaos of Cromwell's regime, the poets caution the nation against a return to the anarchy of the Cromwellian era and urge it to accept Charles's legitimate successor.

A quarter century earlier, eulogies had come forth on a comparable occasion: to mark the death of Oliver Cromwell and to secure the succession for Richard

---

[14] See Aphra Behn, *A Pindarick on the Death of our Late Sovereign: With an Ancient Prophecy on his Present Majesty* (London: Henry Playford, 1685).

[15] See B. Bridgewater in *Mœstissimæ ac Lætissimæ Academiæ Cantabrigiensis Affectus, Decedente Carolo II. Succedente Jacobo II Regibus Augustissimis Clementissimisque* (Cambridge: Joannes Hayes, 1684/5), sig. Ff3ʳ. The Cambridge volume contains a large section of English odes, most of them pindarics in the Cowleian style. The Oxford volume consists mostly of Latin odes.

[16] John Dryden, "Threnodia Augustalis" in *The Poems of John Dryden*, ed. James Kinsley (Oxford: Clarendon Press, 1958), 1: 442–456. "Threnodia Augustalis" is notable in that Dryden specifically names it a pindaric: *A Funeral-Pindarique Poem Sacred to the Happy Memory of King Charles II*. For commentary on Dryden, see James Sutherland, *English Literature of the Late Seventeenth Century* (Oxford: Clarendon Press, 1969), 191.

Cromwell. Curiously enough, the poems for Charles's death resemble those composed for his predecessor's funeral. In both cases the eulogists were called upon to defend a ruler who had fallen into disfavor and to assure the right of a successor who had uncertain popular support. In order to create sympathy for the dead ruler, the poets recreate or dramatize in some way the scene of his death. In "A Poem upon the Death of O. C." Marvell, like the future eulogists for Charles II, rehearses the circumstances of Cromwell's decline and death. Marvell's ode actually appeared in print for the first time in 1681, and although excised from most copies of Marvell's *Miscellaneous Poems*, apparently by royal order, the poem could have served, ironically enough, the encomiasts of Charles II as a model for the poetic representations of Charles II's demise. Poetically, Marvell creates a sense of approaching doom, as he contemplates whether Cromwell will survive or die and alludes to the storm that preceded his demise. On the day of Cromwell's death there had been a tumultuous storm, which Cromwell's detractors interpreted as divine judgment on his iniquity, but his followers as the disruption in the heavens that accompanies the fall of a great man. Marvell poignantly portrays Cromwell dead and lying in state, leaden and gray, yet still majestic, and even creates for Cromwell a kind of apotheosis, which, though restrained in comparison to the extravagance of the apotheosis imagined for Charles, yet effects his translation to Heaven.

> Despoyld of mortall robes, in seas of blisse,
> Plunging doest bathe, and tread the bright Abysse:
> There thy great soule at once a world does see,
> Spacious enough and pure enough for thee.
> How soon thou *Moses* hast and *Joshua* found
> And *David* for the sword and harpe renown'd!
> (ll. 289–294)

Marvell is also reticent in promoting Richard as Cromwell's heir, placing on his brows, instead of a diadem, a rainbow in prognostication of calm after storm: "calme peace succeeds a war; rainbows to storms, *Richard* to *Oliver* . . . He threats no deluge, yet foretells a showre" (ll. 321–322, 324). Marvell interprets the calm as a hopeful portent.

Lacking the storm that preceded Cromwell's death, Charles's eulogists make do with premonitions of one, thus endowing the occasion with a certain hyperbolic character. Perhaps looking back on the odes on Cromwell's death, Aphra Behn complains of the absence of heavenly disruption at Charles's passing: "That such a *Monarch*! such a *God* should dye! / And no *Dire Warning* to the World be given: / No *Hurricanes* on Earth! no *Blazing Fires* in Heaven!" (2.6–8).[17] Many of

---

[17] Like Behn, some Cambridge poets marvel that the passing of so great, so divine a king, whose birth was heralded by a Messianic star, should not cause a greater crack in

Charles's eulogists adopt the Pindaric "I" to render a first-person testimony, thus expressing the public grief as a private one. Behn begins, "Sad was the *Morn,* the sadder *Week* began, / And heavily the God of Day came on: / From Ominous *Dreams* my wondering Soul lookt out, / And saw a Dire *Confusion* round about" (1.1–4). Dryden in "Threnodia Augustalis" begins in a similar fashion: "Thus long my Grief has kept me dumb . . . / Tears stand congeal'd, and cannot flow; / And the sad Soul retires into her inmost Room" (ll. 1–4). Francis Fane opens his pindaric with a roll of thunder: "As *distant* Thunder in a rowling Cloud, / First murmurs *inwardly,* then roars *aloud,* / O're the amaz'd and listning Croud, / 'Till the dread Clap fright ev'ry mortal Ear, / Too *weak* Heav'ns *angry Voice* to bear; / *Such* was the sad distracting *News*" (1.1–5).[18] An anonymous pindaric on Charles's death dedicated to the Earl of Abingdon comments on the "sound" of the death proclamation: *"Alas he's dead*—the dismal sound / Like poyson'd Air / Hot Universal plagues doth it bear" (1.1–3)[19]

Narrative or digressive "myth" plays a prominent part in most of the odes on the king's passing. Thomas Flatman makes Charles a prelapsarian Adam, guarding his idyllic Eden with an angel's sword.[20] Some poets recapitulate the king's life from birth to death, others record his decline and death as though they were charting the death of a hero or god. Perhaps taking their cue from Cowley's Restoration ode, poets comment that in death, as in life, Charles had been Christ-like, a comparison that is hardly surprising, when we consider that many poems on Charles's birth compared him to the Christ child.[21] He was, after all, born of a Mary and proclaimed at his nativity by a noonday star. Alluding to the star that reportedly appeared at the king's birth ("At's Birth a Glorious Star appear'd"), an anonymous pindarist proclaims it a sign that "our Royal Babe was all *Divine,* / Good Heav'n why not *Immortal* too" (*Pindarick Ode,* 2.1, 7–8, sig. A2ᵛ). Behn likens the temporary remission of Charles's illness to Christ's Resurrection, Transfiguration, and Ascension, a conceit which Germaine Greer finds

---

nature. See, for example, Ambrose Sawyer who comments that never before did a star show a birth except for that of the "mighty Prince of Heav'n" (sig. Gg2ᵛ). Sawyer also alludes to the transports in nature at the death of Julius Caesar, contrasting them with Charles's quiet passing (*Mœstissimæ ac Lætissimæ Academiæ Cantabrigiensis Affectus,* sig. Gg2ʳ–Gg3ᵛ).

[18] Francis Fane, *A Pindarick Ode on the Sacred Memory of Our late Gracious Sovereign King Charles II* (London: Henry Playford, 1685).

[19] *A Pindarick Ode, Upon the Death of His late sacred Majesty King Charles the Second* (London, 1685), sig. A2ʳ.

[20] Thomas Flatman, *On the Death of Our Late Sovereign Lord King Charles II. Of Blessed Memory. A Pindarique Ode* (London, 1685). Flatman comments that England was an Eden while Charles lived: "Our Land (like *Eden*) flourish'd in *His* time, / Defended by an *Angels* Sword, / A terrour 'twas to those abroad, / But all was *Paradise* to those within: / Nor could th' Old Serpent's Stratagem / Ever supplant *His* well-watch'd Diadem" (3. 8–13).

[21] See *Britanniae Natalis* (Oxford: Iohannes Lichfield, 1630).

"extraordinarily miscalculated and overdone," but which in the context of the other pindarics on Charles's death is hardly exceptional.[22] Behn's ode concludes, as do many of the pindarics on Charles's death, with Charles's ascent to heaven as a god. Assuredly, in a seventeenth-century context, no less could be expected of the son of Charles I, the royal martyr.

The account of Charles's apotheosis serves a political purpose, for it both vindicates Charles's kingship and puts a seal of approval on James's. In "The Vision" Edmund Arwaker describes how a spirit comes from heaven to console the grieving Church of England on her defender's death and to assure her that although Charles has ascended to heaven James remains to assume the role of protector.[23] Several of the university poets conclude their odes with the apotheosis of Charles II. Joshua Barnes describes how the martyred Charles I is attendant in heaven to welcome one son (Charles), while looking down to bless the other son (James) as the "Hopefull Boy" (2.33). Upon his arrival in the heavenly spheres Charles tells his father that his brother is "Laden with triumphs and his People's Love" (3.10). Another Cambridge poet, Peter Nourse, describes how Strafford and Laud escort the apotheosized Charles to his father's throne, where they all four shine in saintly splendor. Barnes recounts how the gates of bliss open to receive Charles, while angels play tunes on David's lyre and remark on the parallel between King Charles and King David.[24] In still another ode Charles looks down from heaven as a bright star, the protecting Genius of the land, while James, very like the other brother of the Dioscuri, holds the earthly sway (sig. Eer).[25] As supporters of Charles I had quickly robed him in martyr's vestments, so the supporters of Charles II wished to add another Stuart saint to the list to strengthen James's cause against his detractors. A timely reminder that Charles I had been martyred — along with those other royalist heroes, Strafford and Laud — might be enough to deter extremists from inflicting a similar fate upon the last Stuart king.

---

[22] See Greer, *Uncollected Verse*, 180.

[23] Edmund Arwaker, *The Vision: A Pindarick Ode: Occasion'd by the Death of Our Late Gracious Sovereign King Charles II* (London: Henry Playford, 1685). *The Second Part of the Vision* (London, 1685) celebrates James's coronation.

[24] Joshua Barnes, "The Apothewsis of the most Serene and most Illustrious Monarch Charles the Second," in *Mæstissimæ ac Lætissimæ Academiæ Cantabrigiensis Affectus*, sig. Aa2v–Aa4v. Also see Peter Nourse, sig. Ggr. Joshua Barnes was a Greek scholar, whose later work includes editions of Greek poets; he has a Greek ode in this collection (sig. F3v–F4r). He undoubtedly knew Pindar first-hand, but seems deliberately to have taken Cowley as the model for this English ode.

[25] William Ayloffe in *Mæstissimæ ac Lætissimæ Academiæ Cantabrigiensis Affectus*, sig. Eer. Poets frequently employ the myth of the Dioscuri to link living and dead brothers. See the discussion of Ronsard's ode for Charles IX and Henry III in chapter 6 below.

Descriptions of Charles's apotheosis possess a certain epinician fervor, for the triumph of a saint, as the renowned Italian pindarist Gabriello Chiabrera had demonstrated in his Pindaric odes for Catholic saints, was analogous to the victory of an athlete.[26] The eulogists for Charles clearly have both poetic and political objectives in mind in making Charles's apotheosis into a type of epinician triumph to be celebrated with a Pindaric flourish. Milton's nephew, John Phillips, demonstrates that he had been well schooled in Pindaric techniques by his more famous uncle. His ode on Charles's death proclaims the appropriateness of Pindaric ode to celebrate kings, gods, and sons of gods, and employs more than the usual share of Pindaric devices and classical allusions.[27] In a similar fashion, the Cambridge scholar Thomas Walker makes an effort to combine threnody and epinician ode. As though Charles II were a conquering athlete who has just celebrated his last victory, he bids the king farewell as "the Darling and Delight / Of all," who "Thro' all the land in triumph rode / Whilest you did hold the easy rein, / Which gently flow'd on the swift Courser's mane" (2.1–2, 6–8). Walker also introduces a sun figure in stanza 4 that perhaps echoes the opening of Pindar's Olympian 1. As Charles's sun sinks, James's rises:

> But when another Sun appears,
> And guilds [sic] with golden rays,
> The bright, auspicious days,
> It scatters all our former fears,
> And with its genial warmth dispells
> Those vapours, which intoxicate the rude
> Unthinking and unwary crowds . . .
> (4.1–7)[28]

By depicting James as a sun-king Walker hopes to scatter the vapors of faction and treason.

---

[26] See Revard, "Milton and Chiabrera"; also see eadem, *Pindar and the Renaissance Hymn-Ode*, 264–69.

[27] See John Phillips, *An Humble Offering to the Sacred Memory of the Late Most Serene and Potent Monarch Charles II* (London, 1685). Phillips skillfully employs mythic digressions for their full propaganda effect to recapitulate the triumphs of Charles II's reign, to celebrate his Christ-like birth and death, his Herculean labors, and also his Herculean ascent to heaven. He also invokes the star of Charles's birth as a sign of his future accomplishments. John Phillips also wrote a pindaric on the death of Mary II in 1695: *In Memory of Our Late Gracious Lady, Mary, Queen of Great-Britain, France, and Ireland. A Poem* (London, 1695).

[28] See Walker in *Mæstissimæ ac Lætissimæ Academiæ Cantabrigiensis Affectus*, sigs. Aa4ᵛ–Bb3ʳ.

Classical myth plays a particularly important part in the odes on Charles's death and James's accession to the throne.[29] Like Charles, James was described as a heroic and long-suffering Aeneas, for whom the Cyclops forged an "impenetrable shield" and who was "long exercised by Fate."[30] His assumption of Charles's Herculean role, however, is still more significant. James becomes a Hercules when he takes the weight of monarchy from Charles's Atlas-like shoulders: "Our Atlas fell indeed. But Hercules was near." Ironically enough, Richard Cromwell had also been a Hercules when he lifted the burden of leadership from Oliver's Atlantean shoulders.[31] The references to James's assumption of the role of Hercules on Charles's death have an added resonance, for they hark back to Cowley's endowing Prince Charles with Herculean sinews in his translation of Pindar's Nemean 1. Throughout his reign Charles ("Our Hercules, our guardian God") was depicted as undertaking Herculean challenges: taming the Hydra-multitude, purging the senate as though it were a stinking stable, and dispensing universal benefit to all the earth.[32] On Charles's death, James must become a second Hercules if he is to be a successful monarch like his brother.

To this end Dryden recalls the Pindaric account of Hercules' killing the serpents sent to destroy him. He is assuredly telling us that James, like his brother,

---

[29] To secure James's claim to the throne, many poets emphasize his accomplishments as a soldier, comparing his deeds to those of Achilles. Henry Parke's ode in the Cambridge collection celebrates James's victories on both sea and land, specifically referring to his victory over the Belgians: "The *Belgians* did of old His floating Terrours dread, / And at th'approach of His embattl'd Navies fled." Parke even indulges a witty reference to the sea-born Venus ("the Frothy *Goddess*"), surprised to see the Mars-like James wielding the trident of Neptune (see Henry Parke in *Mœstissimæ ac Lætissimæ Academiæ Cantabrigiensis Affectus*, sig. Dd2ʳ).

[30] See Dryden's description of James's martial demeanor: "Above the rest Heroick *James* appear'd / Exalted more" (l. 128–129); "A warlike Prince ascends the Regal State" (The *Poems of John Dryden*, ed. Kinsley, 1: 430).

[31] See the collection on Cromwell's death: *Musarum Cantabrigiensium Luctus et Gratulatio* (Cambridge: Joannes Field, 1558), sig. F3ʳ. In the same collection an ode by R. Powell also exploits the Hercules and Atlas motif (sig. F2ʳ). Over twenty-five years later in the Cambridge 1684/5 collection George Stepney makes a similar claim for James II: "Which eas'd our *Atlas* of his glorious weight: / Since stronger *Hercules* Supports the State" (*Mœstissimæ ac Lætissimæ Academiæ Cantabrigiensis Affectus*, sig. Gg4ᵛ). An anonymous pindaric on Charles's death also alludes to Charles as an Atlas who passes on the earth's burden to his Herculean brother: "Your Prop, your *Atlas* is remov'd and gone" (l. 11), in *A Pindarick Ode, Upon the Death of His late sacred Majesty King Charles the Second* (London, 1685), sig. A2ʳ.

[32] *A Pindarick Ode, Upon the Death of His late sacred Majesty King Charles the Second* (London, 1685), sig. Bʳ. In a Latin poem in the 1684/5 Cambridge collection S. Hooke commends Charles as our Hercules and lists the labors that he performed for his country (*Mœstissimæ ac Lætissimæ Academiæ Cantabrigiensis Affectus*, sigs. M3ᵛ–M4ʳ).

is a leader pre-ordained from infancy to do marvelous works: "View then a Monarch ripen'd for a Throne. / Alcides thus his race began" (446–447). Strangling the serpents is a sign of his future greatness:

> And there he grappled first with Fate:
> In his young Hand the hissing Snakes he prest,
> So early was the Deity confest;
> ("Threnodia Augustalis," ll. 452–454)

Dryden has deliberately echoed Cowley's paraphrase of Nemean 1 to signal his recognition that the Hercules figure in Cowley's paraphrase is a royal cipher for the future king and also to connect James with that prophetic model. However, in shadowing forth a Hercules-James in lieu of a Hercules-Charles, Dryden moves beyond Cowley to assure us that this infant will be equal to conquering the Hydra of civil insurrection:

> And, to his Infant Arms oppose
> His Father's Rebels and his Brother's Foes;
> The more opprest the higher still he rose:
> Those were the Preludes of his Fate,
> That form'd his Manhood, to subdue
> The *Hydra* of the many-headed, hissing Crew.
> (ll. 459–464)[33]

Dryden's conflation of the Hydra and the serpents is not unprecedented. In times of political dissension, poets had described the killing of the serpents as a prologue to the conquest over the Hydra of sedition. The poets of the 1684/5 Cambridge collection have similar aims in reminding us that, like Charles, James must accomplish the same Herculean labor.[34]

---

[33] Also see John Wilson, *A Pindarique To Their Sacred Majesties, James II And His Royal Consort Queen Mary, On Their joynt Coronations* (London, 1685). In the coronation ode for James, Wilson remarks that James's early use of arms gave promise, as did Hercules', of his great future (5.8–10). Reminding his readers how Charles II rescued them from the chaos of the Cromwellian period (3.1–23), Wilson ends his coronation ode with a Pindaric sentence that at the same time reassures and warns: "*Thô the Sun Warms / At Liberty, Contract it once, it Burns*" (10.12–13).

[34] See *Mœstissimæ ac Lætissimæ Academiæ Cantabrigiensis Affectus*. In one poem Charles crushes the Hydra of rebellion (Thomas Atkyn; see R[r]); in another James performs the same feat (John Harris; see O4[v]). Moreover, when William III comes to power, he too must overcome the Hydra. See the Greek ode by Jon. Sanders in *Academiae Oxoniensis Gratulatio. Pro Serenissimi Regis Guilielmi ex Hibernia Reditu* (Oxford, 1690), sig. 8Fr. Sanders greets William as the conqueror of the triple-headed Geryon as well as the queller of the Lernean Hydra. Phillips and Smith also compare William to Hercules: see John Phillips, *Augustus Britannicus: A Poem upon the Conclusion of the Peace of Europe*

When Dryden composed the ode "Britannia Rediviva" in 1688 to celebrate the birth of Prince James, he turned once more to the story of Hercules' strangling of the serpents to argue that, like his father James and his uncle Charles, the newborn Stuart heir is a future Hercules:

> Or, if Allusions may not rise so high,
> Thus, when *Alcides* rais'd his Infant Cry,
> The Snakes besieg'd his young Divinity:
> But vainly with their forked Tongues they threat;
> For Opposition makes a Heroe Great.
> To needful Succour all the Good will run;
> And *Jove* assert the Godhead of his Son.
> (ll. 54–60)[35]

Serpent-strangling seems to have been a popular occupation for princes in times of political and religious crisis. Ronsard had attributed the Herculean feat to Charles IX and Nicolas Rapin to the future Louis XIII, the newborn son of Henri IV.[36] Dryden's verses to James's newborn heir uphold a firmly established tradition of Pindaric imitation at the same time that they reveal uneasiness about the future of the Stuart prince and his kingly father.

Dryden was not the only poet to address the crisis in the royal succession by summoning up the myth of Hercules' serpent-strangling. The very Oxford collection *Strenae Natalitiae*, published to celebrate the prince's birth, contains several poems that allude to the same myth.[37] The young Christopher Codrington, afterwards a staunch supporter in William III's wars, introduces the myth at the

---

(London, 1697), 7, and Mr. Smith, *A Pindarique Poem, Sacred to the Glorious Memory of King William III* (London, 1702), 10.

[35] *The Poems of John Dryden*, 2: 542.

[36] As we observed in chapter 2, Ronsard had also used the story of the serpents to describe the difficulties Charles IX faced: "Toutefois au besoin, sa vertu n'a failli. / Il se vit au berceau des serpens assaili / Comme un jeune Herculin, dont il rompit la force" (ll. 42–44). Ronsard also observes that this same Herculean prince had to take on the Titans, Ronsard's figure for the "heretic" Huguenots whom Charles IX tried to suppress and who were finally "vanquished" at the St. Bartholomew's Day massacre (Pierre de Ronsard, *Oeuvres Complètes*, ed. Gustave Cohen [Paris: Librairie Gallimard, 1950], 2: 475–76).

[37] "In Natalem Sereniss. Principis Walliae," in *Strenae Natalitiae* (Oxford, 1688), sig. R^r–R2^v. During a similar political crisis, the French poet Nicolas Rapin composed a "Hymne" on the occasion of the birth of the Dauphin to the French king, Henri IV. Rapin promised that the young prince, the Catholic Louis XIII, born to the erstwhile Protestant Henri IV, would strangle the serpents of sedition that had threatened his father Henri IV. See Nicolas Rapin, "Hymne sur la Naissance de Monseigneur Le Dauphin, 1601," in "Les Vers Mesvrez de Nicolas Rapin," *Les Oevvres Latines et Francoises de Nicolas Rapin Poictevin* (Paris: Oliver de Varennes, 1610), 9–12. For commentary on Rapin's *Hymne* to the Dauphin, see Jean Brunel, *Un poitevin poète, humaniste et soldat à*

conclusion of a Pindaric ode in order to dispel the fears of civil disorder. He appeals to a Goddess or Muse to preside over the young prince's nativity, an "Ayry Nuncius" to proclaim the news of the prince's birth "In loud brass which Herald-Angels use," and to oppose the Vergilian "Fama" who is also present, disseminating scandalous sedition. Codrington tries to reassure us of the prince's heroic future by comparing him to Castor, Perseus, Bacchus, and finally to the newborn Hercules:

> Young *James* already has begun,
> Earlier than *Alcides* He and Nobler Acts has done.
> Ev'n in the Womb a dreadful War
> Our Heroe manag'd from afar;
> By unseen influence strong darts he threw,
> And Factions many Headed Hydra slew.
> When the Glad Tydings first went out
> And Pious Holocausts declar'd
> The mighty things that Heaven and *James* had wrought,
> E're the warm God with amorous light
> The Infants lovely Eyes had Kist,
> The Serpents too the Tydings Heard,
> They Heard, and strait they were accurst.
> With all their Venomous Tongues they hist,
> They flung, they grin'd, they rag'd for spight,
> In vain they rag'd, they spouted Fire in vain,
> The Poison they receive again,
> And with Black Blood and Envy sweld, in thousand pieces burst.
> (5.6–23)

Codrington probably knew Nemean 1 first-hand, but it is not Pindar he echoes but Cowley and Dryden. He makes his political point still more urgent by identifying the tongues of the serpents as tongues of "rebellious" subjects who vainly attempt to bring the government down but burst with their own malice.[38] The prospects for the future are hardly optimistic, and Codrington concludes the ode by appealing once more to the Muse and indicting the wanton and lawless English nation that has been corrupted by "Luxury and Ease." He concludes in a quasi-Pindaric, quasi-Horatian fashion with a well-known aphorism: "Bounteous

---

l'époque des guerres de religion, Nicolas Rapin (1539–1608): La carrière, les milieux, l'oeuvre (Paris: Honoré Champion, 2002), 620–22.

[38] John Willis's ode in the same collection uses the Hercules story to similar effect: "So *Hercules* new-born his power show'd, / His early Victories proclaim'd the God: / Whilst dying at his feet the Serpents prove, / This mighty Infant was the Son of *Jove*. / If a new *Hydra* dares our World molest / This Prince shall crush the many headed Beast" (*Strenae Natalitiae*, sig. T2ᵛ).

Heaven has done its best, / Sit down, and be by present Fortune blest, / And to the Gods and Caesar leave the rest" (8.22–24).[39]

3.

Aphra Behn's greatest accomplishments as a Pindaric bard and a Stuart apologist came after the Glorious Revolution that expelled James II from the throne. Throughout her career Behn had praised the living Charles II, raised the Pindaric strain on Charles's death, and supported his brother James's right to reign in his stead. To celebrate James's coronation, Behn mounted an elaborate Pindaric ode in thirty sections.[40] When news of the queen's pregnancy was released, Behn penned an ode to Mary of Modena that anticipated the birth of a prince, and upon the queen's successful delivery, she wrote a second ode, which described the birth of the new prince as a messianic event.[41] But these lavishly encomiastic pindarics only hint at Behn's skill as a pindarist. With the accession of William and Mary, Behn faced a greater challenge as a Pindaric laureate in the odes she composed that address the issue of the change of regime. Although determined to remain loyal to the deposed James II, she finds it possible in the months following the accession of the new monarchs to welcome Mary, James's Protestant daughter. At the same time, despite political pressure, she declines to honor Wil-

---

[39] Later in England in 1718 to celebrate the birth of Prince George, an English poet also suggested that the new-born prince could stifle envious rumor just as Hercules had the serpents: "The Royal Babe the vip'rous Brood dismays, / And in the Cradle, like *Alcides*, slays": see Mr. Eusden, *A Poem to her Royal Highness on the Birth of a Prince* (London, 1718), 2.

[40] See A. Behn, *Pindarick Poem on the Happy Coronation of His most Sacred Majesty James II, and His Illustrious Consort Queen Mary* (London: Henry Playford, 1685). James had spared no expense to produce a memorable event in the coronation, even organizing it on St. George's Day to call forth a patriotic response. Behn's coronation ode joins celebration of James's martial achievements with celebration of the queen's virtues. They are the new Mars and Venus. Behn describes his coronation procession as though it were a victory parade: "Heav'n all open'd to survey / The *Mighty Triumphs* of the Blessed Day" (4. 2–3). She pays the Queen, Mary of Modena, special attention by describing her almost like a bride in an epithalamion and likening her to the heroic personages in Ariosto's epic romance *Orlando Furioso*, which was written for her d'Este ancestors (30.1–6).

[41] See A. Behn, *A Congratulatory Poem to Her Most Sacred Majesty, On the Universal Hopes of All Loyal Persons for a Prince of Wales* (London: Will Canning, 1688). Behn predicts: "Like the first sacred *Infant*, this will come / With Promise laden from the *Blessed* Womb, / To call the wand'ring, scatter'd Nations home" (ll. 13–15); also see A. Behn, *A Congratulatory Poem to the King's Most Sacred Majesty, On the Happy Birth of the Prince of Wales* (London: W. Canning, 1688). The two poems were printed together after the birth of the prince.

liam with an ode. Behn is unusual among contemporary poets in exploiting the potential of the pindaric to make a covert political protest. Her ode to Mary and her ode to Dr. Burnet (refusing to write for William) demonstrate how pindarics can be used not only to praise, but also to refuse to praise.

Behn's "A Congratulatory Poem to Her Sacred Majesty Queen Mary, Upon Her Arrival in England" (London, 1689) harks back to sixteenth-century ode.[42] To welcome the new queen Behn resorts to some strategies that Spenser had used in his pastoral "Aprill" (from *Shepheardes Calender*) to praise the Protestant sovereign Queen Elizabeth on her coming to the throne. She also makes use of Spenser's *Prothalamion*, a later ode which describes Spenser's disconsolate state over the lean rewards for his poetry and which employs the Pindaric "I" to deliberate questions of poetry and policy. Like Spenser, Behn was out of favor at court and was, besides, disconsolate over the fate of her former sovereign James II. At the outset of her ode Behn recreates Spenser's pastoral scene on the river Thames, describing the attendant nymphs, which Spenser also alludes to in "Aprill." Like Spenser in *Prothalamion* she conveys her distress and melancholy by setting her poem in "darkest Covert" on the banks of the Thames, fringed with "Murmering Osiers" and "bending Willows" (ll. 1–6). As Eccho repeats the poet's sighs, she hears the "raptur'd Songs" of the river nymphs that would teach Eccho a new anthem; they have caught sight of Mary approaching and greet her.[43] Just as Spenser's mood lightens when he catches sight of the two swans—the brides of *Prothalamion*—so Behn's mood changes with the appearance of Mary. The Thames, as though in Spenserian sympathy, glides along with "Harmonious Purlings" (l. 26). Spring now takes on a "Fragrant Bloom" and the Muses come to praise Mary: "The Muses all upon this Theam Divine, / Tun'd their best Lays" (ll. 36–37)—just as they had offered homage to Elisa in Spenser's "Aprill."

Spenser's "Aprill" is also important for Behn's ode in another way. Not only does it provide the model for her praise of her sovereign as "pastoral" queen, it also provides the emotional ballast that permits Behn to resolve the conflict of loyalties and accept Mary as a Protestant monarch and her rightful queen. In "Aprill" Spenser had taken pains to describe Elisa as Henry VIII's daughter—the offspring of Pan and Syrinx—legitimately descended from her royal father and ruling in his right. By assuming the reign in her father's right Elizabeth restored to England the Protestantism that her royal father and royal brother had planted there, but which her sister Mary I had displaced. Odes to Mary II often make the point that her Protestant piety was a great help to the English Church that

---

[42] See "To Queen Mary," in Greer, *Uncollected Verse*, 159–62; commentary, 220–22; also see Melinda S. Zook, "The Political Poetry of Aphra Behn," in *The Cambridge Companion to Aphra Behn*, ed. Derek Hughes and Janet Todd (Cambridge: Cambridge University Press, 2004), 46–67, here 60–63.

[43] Compare Henry Beeston's "The Queens Arrivall" which describes the "Shoale of Sea Nymphs," that accompanies Mary (*Vota Oxoniensia* [Oxford, 1689], sig. U^r).

had been threatened and weakened by James's Catholicism.[44] Herself a Catholic, Behn does not follow this bent, but she does welcome Mary II, as several other odes to Mary had, as a new Elisa, a female sovereign, who would bring to the nation the security and peace that Queen Elizabeth's reign had offered.[45] Behn's resistance at this point melts and she adds her voice to the Muses' song, realizing that she must lay aside her "Stubborn Loyalty" (l. 38) to the exiled James and accept the new sovereign Mary, James's daughter. Describing Mary as a female sovereign who rules by rightful succession from her father, Behn greets her:

> All Hail Illustrious Daughter of a King,
> Shining without and Glorious within,
> Whose Eyes beyond your scantier Power give Laws,
> Command the World, and justifie the Cause;
> (ll. 62–65)[46]

The best of the political pindarics are not just poems written to praise this or that royal patron, but poems that look at the questions of the relationship of subject to prince and ponder the responsibilities of each. Behn's poem becomes at this crucial point just that. Before she can relinquish her loyalty to the old sovereign, she must find some "New-born Reason" (l. 51) for a change that is more than mere political expediency. She has never refused to offer the reasonable obedience to a sovereign that a subject should offer, but it must be obedience that is both just and honorable: "Let me be Just—but Just with Honour too" (l. 58). Hence it is crucial for her to discover the father in the daughter before she can transfer her allegiance to Mary. She does so not only by using the analogy of Henry VIII and Elizabeth but also by exploring the mythic relationship between Jupiter and his daughter, the goddess Minerva. By associating the kingly father-god with his regal goddess-daughter, Behn can affirm how the qualities of a father can pass on to his female offspring. In Mary she discovers the royal and godly grace, charm, and natural majesty that validate her rightful claim to the throne: "You Look,

---

[44] See, for example, [Patrick] Hume, *A Poem Dedicated to the Immortal Memory of Her Late Majesty, The Most Incomparable Q. Mary* (London, 1695). Hume describes Mary as "the Pillar of the Church" (3. 21) (5), who triumphed over the "Dark Superstition" which Eliza's reign had conquered, but which had like an "Egyptian Mist" risen again to be conquered by Mary, who made the Church once more secure (10. 11–15) (11). J. D. [Samuel Cobb] says she purged the land of idols. See *A Pindarique Ode, Humbly Offer'd to the Ever-Blessed Memory of our Late Gracious Sovereign Lady Queen Mary* (London, 1694), 8.

[45] See Hume, *A Poem Dedicated to the Immortal Memory of Her Late Majesty*. Hume recapitulates the achievements of Mary's reign by comparing them to those of "fam'd Eliza" (5. 3).

[46] There is perhaps an allusion here to Psalm 45: 9–17, which describes the honor in which kings' daughters are held (esp. verse 13).

you Talk, with more than Human Grace . . . Free and Generous your Majestick Meen, / In every Motion, every Part a Queen" (ll. 77, 83–84).

Behn had a subtle purpose in using both exemplars, but particularly the former. The more that she associates the Protestant Mary with the Protestant Queen Elizabeth the more she authorizes Mary's natural right as the first female sovereign since Elizabeth to take the throne in her own right. Mary is "All that is Great and Lovely in the Sex" (l. 85); she is also by virtue of her right as her father's offspring—that is, his legitimate heir—the true queen.

> The Murmering World till now divided lay,
> Vainly debating whom they shou'd Obey,
> Till You Great Cesar's Off-spring blest our Isle,
> The differing Multitudes to Reconcile.
> (ll. 105–108)

By using that non-gendered word *offspring* Behn authorizes Mary's claim to rule and resolves her own reluctance to obey.

As "A Pindaric Poem to the Reverend Doctor Burnet" amply illustrates, the conclusion of Behn's ode to Mary is not just a clever piece of time-serving.[47] Behn's acceptance of Mary's right did not necessarily mean acceptance of William's. Dr. Burnet, the man who had been most instrumental in organizing the Glorious Revolution of 1688, had been urging Behn to write an ode in honor of the House of Nassau, thus bringing one of the strongest supporters of the Stuart cause over to the other side.[48] With the subtle turns and understated political innuendo that characterizes Pindaric ode at its best, Behn succeeds in using the medium deftly to sidestep the issue. Clearly she felt that plighting her allegiance to William would compromise her loyalty to her former patrons, Charles II and James II. It was one thing to acknowledge a daughter's accession to her father's throne, another to accept the claim of a prince with a more distant monarchical imperative. While Behn's ode to Mary consented to praise the virtues of queens, her pindaric to Burnet resists the plea "to sing of Heroes and of Kings" (l. 36). She cleverly offers a disclaimer, arguing that her voice is more suitable to sing of "Shepherds, and their humble Love" (l. 35). Her refusal to "sing of Kings" echoes the beginning of Cowley's anacreontic "Love": "I'll sing of *Heroes*, and of *Kings*; / In mighty Numbers, mighty things" ("Love," ll. 1–2 in Cowley, *Poems* [1656]). In his anacreontics Cowley had wittily refused to take up the heroic challenge, and Behn, now echoing Cowley, refuses to write a royal pindaric by pleading, as

---

[47] *A PINDARIC POEM to the Reverend Doctor Burnet, On the Honour he did me of Enquiring after me and my MUSE* by A. Behn (London: R. Bentley, 1689). The subtitle of the pindaric reveals the cautious courtesy with which Behn addresses Dr. Burnet.

[48] For commentary on the circumstances of Behn's ode to Dr. Burnet, see Greer, *Uncollected Verse*, 222–23.

Cowley and other love poets had, a penchant for lighter poetry. Moreover, the love poetry and the pastoralism of her 1684 *Poems* clearly supported her plea.

Pindaric techniques serve Behn well, not only gracefully to sidestep Burnet's request for an ode, but also to allude, while seeming to praise William, to William's and Burnet's ruthless tactics in winning the throne. By referring in her opening Pindaric figure to the Roman method of election by popular voice, Behn seems to say one thing, while hinting at another:

> When Old *Rome's* Candidates aspir'd to Fame,
> And did the Peoples Suffrages obtain,
> For some great Consul, or a *Caesar's* Name;
> The Victor was not half so Pleas'd and Vain,
> As I, when given the Honour of your Choice,
> And Preference had in that one single Voice;
> (ll. 1–6)

The passage seems innocent enough on the surface—a graceful thank-you to Burnet for asking for a poem. However, the metaphor of election of consuls and Caesars "by Peoples Suffrage" carries, as Pindar's opening figures often did, additional political freight. Although Behn ostensibly is describing the Roman method of election, covertly she is alluding to the method William used to win the crown by arguing that he was merely responding to the "Peoples Suffrage." In truth the so-called popular uprising of 1688 was organized and orchestrated by Dr. Burnet, the very Burnet whose voice Behn resists—a voice, however, that William did not ignore.

The issue raised by the Burnet ode—whether to change allegiance—is essentially that which Behn herself raised but never fully answered in her ode to Mary. In the Burnet ode, however, she constructs reasoned refusals that appear not to refuse but merely graciously to demur. At the same time Behn exposes the political craft of Burnet and the ruthless ambition of William. In so doing, Behn makes use of a metaphor from love poetry. The mistress of *The Rover* and other social comedies is playing her own game, for she acts the part of a woman who uses her wit to avoid seduction. Resisting Burnet's blandishments, she casts him in the role of the seducing rhymester and herself in that of a half-yielding maid, "Inspired with Tenderness she fears to own" (l. 23). Her "opponent," she implies, invades her weak defenses, attempting to persuade her against her will. Using the language of love, she claims she fears betrayal and distrusts love's resistless darts, thus both flattering and resisting the charming seducer. Here, as in the opening section, it is innuendo that does the work. By employing the metaphor of attempted seduction, Behn makes Burnet's request for an ode in William's honor resemble the attempt of a seducer to force a woman against her will. While she feigns pleasure in the gallantry of Burnet's request, she wins the victory of modesty and honor for herself. Her argument that her "careless Muse" is unambitious "t'enlarge her Glory" (ll. 33–34) is double-edged, for by declining glory for herself she exposes the ambition of a man all too intent on self-aggrandizement.

Behn does not develop a full-scale Pindaric digression in this ode, but the two brief passages that allude to biblical and classical stories use material that we have seen employed throughout the century in similar contexts. The first refers to the prospect of the "Promis'd Land," a reference resonant with implication both for Behn's earlier odes to Charles and James and for her ode on Mary's arrival. Behn presents herself, as she had in the Mary ode, as drawing back from the mirth and welcoming echoes of the crowds that greet the arrival of the new sovereign. She casts herself in the role of a Moses, who has been left behind (Deuteronomy 34: 1–4):

> Thus while the Chosen Seed possess the Promis'd Land,
> I like the Excluded Prophet stand,
> The Fruitful Happy Soil can only see,
> But am forbid by Fates Decree
> To share the Triumph of the joyful Victory.
> (ll. 61–65)

It is surely significant that Behn accords herself the role of Moses, so often associated in the odes on Charles's death and James's accession with Charles and now being appropriated in the William odes for William as the new conqueror and prophet. Ironically, she confers the role of a new-age Joshua on Burnet, a role, of course, granted by Behn and most other Stuart encomiasts to James when in 1684 he was about to enter the Canaan-land of his new kingship. Behn, in refusing to move from the Pisgah-sight that her Stuart master had once held, is both affirming allegiance to the elder Stuarts and refusing to share in the revised vision of the Williamites.

This passage contrasts interestingly with the Exodus passage that concludes the Mary ode. Dramatizing a different incident from Moses' career (Exodus 34: 29–30), Behn casts Mary and not herself in the role of the "Prophet of their God." Moses comes from Sinai about to deliver new commandments, descending "from the Mount with dazling brightness," "Eyes all shining with Celestial Flame." Thus appearing he dispels "Rebel Thought": the "Murmering World" ceases to debate and "Stiff-neckt *Israel*" is brought to a "Just Compliance" (ll. 105–114). In the Mary ode Behn uses the figure of Moses to sanction that very obedience to a sovereign, there Mary, that she declines in the Burnet ode to grant to William.

The classical story that Behn employs in section 5 is still more double-edged: the account of the stratagem of the Trojan horse by which the Greeks under Ulysses overcame their foes without "the Barbarous Force of Blows" but by "luckier Wisdom" (ll. 79–80, 82). Behn seems to praise the Greeks' "Wisdom and Counsel," which prevailed when military might did not, concluding, "'Twas Nobler Stratagem that let the Conqueror in" (ll. 83–85). The passage is a masterpiece of ironic praise, and demonstrates that Behn might have profited from the lessons that Cowley and Marvell had taught when faced in previous generations with similar political constraints. So ambiguous, for example, is Cowley's pindaric on "Brutus" that one hardly knows whether Cowley is praising or dispraising the man or which contemporary personage stands behind the historical Brutus. So sly are Marvell's ironies at the close of the "First Anniversary" that the recalcitrant kings of Europe find themselves praising Cromwell's accomplishments. Behn exploits both techniques, for she too is aware that there are two sides to the Troy story, though she refers only to that of the conquering Greeks. Implicitly, however, she casts herself in the role of a Cassandra grieving for her own tragedy at the same time she submits to "Fate" (Behn's own word). By casting Burnet as a wise Ulysses who spares his countrymen bloodshed, Behn seems to praise the care and counsel of his country's savior. But which country? The same counsel from Troy's vantage point was falsehood and its result ruin rather than salvation. Behn might even be recollecting Pindar's view in Nemean 7 (20–30) that the lying Ulysses was the lesser hero and only the magic of Homer's language made him appear the better. Behn has left us in the realm of double-speak as she seems to praise the duplicitous design of the Ulyssean Burnet, whose pen is more potent than his sword.

> Oh Strange effect of a Seraphick Quill!
> That can by unperceptable degrees
> Change every Notion, every Principle
> To any Form, its Great Dictator please:
> The Sword a Feeble Pow'r, compar'd to That,
> And to the Nobler Pen subordinate:
> (ll. 70–75)

Also as the ambiguous reference to the "Great Dictator" (l. 73) illustrates, Behn may be including William in her ode without ever naming him.

Behn concludes her oxymoronic discourse with Burnet in the final section of the ode, praising on the one hand his furtherance of the "great Design" and on the other maintaining her true allegiance with an ironic rhyming of "deplore" with "adore" (ll. 86–88). In the end, Behn cleverly side-steps the whole issue of praising William by asserting that only the man responsible for William's conquest has the right to immortalize it.

> 'Tis you, Great Sir, alone, by Heaven preserv'd,
> Whose Conduct has so well the Nation serv'd,
> 'Tis you that to Posterity shall give
> This Ages Wonders, and its History.

And Great NASSAU shall in your Annals live
To all Futurity.
Your Pen shall more Immortalize his Name,
Than even his Own Renown'd and Celebrated Fame.
(ll. 96–103)

Behn is fully aware that the poets of the winning side write the history, be they
Homers or Vergils or Pindars or merely Dr. Burnets. She leaves us one last ironic
gesture by her fulsome praise of Burnet as William's fitting encomiast.

Although Aphra Behn's linguistic accomplishments did not include reading
Pindar in the original Greek, she managed at second hand to grasp many of the
essential subtleties of Pindar's methods, particularly his technique of seeming
to lay down unconditional praise at the same time he assigns strict conditions
for that praise.[49] Few political odes of the sixteenth and seventeenth centuries
imitate Pindar's ironic subtleties so well as Behn's ode to Dr. Burnet—the deft
technique of using praise to reveal shortcomings. It is a curious and a fitting accomplishment that Behn in one of the final pindarics of her literary career should
finally succeed in catching the spirit of the Theban master.

4.

Pindaric ode in the late seventeenth century had no strict sectarian boundar-
ies. Whig and Tory poets—Republican and Royalist, Protestant and Catholic,
Williamite or Jacobite—were devoted to the genre. Moreover, many of the pindarists who had celebrated James II, his queen, and the new Prince James spoke
with the same Pindaric tones when they welcomed William and Mary in 1689,
composing odes for the Oxford and Cambridge volumes that came forth on this
occasion. The shift in politics results in a number of interesting Pindaric acrobat-
ics to justify the change. Edward Nicholas in an Oxford ode says that when he
sang for young James, his Muse was immature and half declined to sing; now,
however, true Pindaric inspiration has seized him:

> But hark! methinks I do already find
> The sacred rage increase within my breast,
> An unheard Extasy transports my mind

---

[49] Behn was fluent in French, if not in Greek and Latin, and two French translations
of Pindar from the early seventeenth century would have been available to her, one by
Marin in prose published in Paris in 1617, another in prose and verse by Sieur de Lagausie, published in Paris in 1626. Behn openly confesses her indebtedness to the Cowleian
pindaric, though she modestly demurs that she "never durst, like *Cowly* (*sic*), tune her
Strings, / To sing of Heroes and of Kings" (*A Pindaric Poem to the Reverend Doctor Burnet*, ll. 37–38).

And lo! my Muse and I are both possest.
(2.3–6)[50]

Just as poetic furor had moved the French pindarists of the past century, so "sacred rage" inspires this English poet as he catches sight of William, the "thrice Glorious Monarch" (2. 7).[51] Another Oxford poet, H. Downes, introduces his ode to William and Mary by proposing to probe the purpose of Pindar's "bold licentious lays" (1.1). In an exordium that itself mimics Pindar's openings, Downes suggests that Pindar would not have striven so vainly to immortalize the victors of games and races, had he had such a "bright Example" before him: "An Heroe bold, and wise, Great Prince, like thee" ((1.14–15).[52] If we pass over Downes's patent flattery, we can discover something in his argument not too far from Pindar's own: that deeds without words fade, and words themselves are often insufficient to measure the quality of heroic deeds.

Many of the Cambridge and Oxford company readily recycle the figures they had employed for James in order to praise William. William is now the conquering hero, the godlike warrior that James had been, a hero perhaps even more glorious in having effected—as the poets insist—a warlike victory without arms. Downes looks back on Cowley's "Brutus" to draw a comparison between James and William. Although mistakenly identifying the elder Brutus rather than the younger as Cowley's subject, he shows that he has learned something from Cowley about how to draw a moral indirectly by juxtaposing moralizing and narrative passages. First praising liberty as necessary to human happiness, Downes recounts how the elder Brutus faced Tarquin down, making him retreat, and so won freedom for Rome. He says nothing about William at this point, but allows his readers to draw the analogy between the Roman hero and the tyrant and between William and James.

We should not be surprised to find biblical passages side by side with classical ones. The Cambridge poet Robert Smythies summons the goddess Astraea to come to the assistance of the "Wounded Church," overcome by confusion and distress, and to bring with her Peace and Plenty and Right.[53] Smythies makes William not just the "peacefull Warriour," come as Astraea's lord to establish

---

[50] Edward Nicholas, "Ode," in *Vota Oxoniensia Pro Serenissimis Guilhelmo Rege et Maria Regina* (Oxford, 1689), sig. Z2ᵛ–Z3ʳ.

[51] See the discussion of the Ronsardian *furor poeticus* in Revard, *Pindar and the Renaissance Hymn-Ode*, 79–80, 90–93, 111.

[52] Downes, "A Pindarick Ode," in *Vota Oxoniensia*, sig. Yʳ–Y2ʳ.

[53] Robert Smythies, "On the late Happy Revolution," in *Musæ Cantabrigienses Serenissimis Principibus Wilhelmo et Mariæ* (Cambridge, 1689), sig. aʳ–a4ʳ. Particularly prominent in these odes are digressions on religion and the church. Nicholas depicts Mother Church as a sober, reverend matron, who contrasts in appearance with the Church of Rome that has kept her children in bondage (4.1–21) (sig. 2Zᵛ). Melinda Zook comments on the Jacobite reaction to William and Mary's succession. See "History's

"Order regular and true," (7.3, 8), but also the Moses to "guide us through this *Wilderness* till we to *Canaan* come" (9.9–10). We have not left Mosaic digressions behind with the odes to Charles and James; we have only changed the designees. Once more, as in the Commonwealth era, Rome is Egypt and Moses a reformed deliverer, who in the person of William cures the plagues of Egypt, crosses the Red Sea, and ushers his people into Canaan. No longer can the Stuart brothers lay claim to the Mosaic mantle. Deftly, William's Pindaric apologists, Downes and Nicholas, imitate Cowley's use of the Exodus myth in "The Plagues of *Egypt*" and the Restoration ode, even while substituting William for Charles. Beginning with an apostrophe to "lovely Albion," compassed round with foes as with waves, Downes portrays William as the "great Deliverer" who saves England from plagues (3.1–22). Nicholas names William a "second Moses, whose avenging Rod / Wav'd o're the Land does set it free / At once from Pharaohs Gods and Pharaohs slavery" (2.8–10). The very same Pindaric digressions and figures that flourished in the odes that brought in Charles II and James II now usher in the new regime of William and Mary.

5.

The next crisis for the monarchy came with the death of Mary from smallpox in December 1694 when the queen was only thirty-two years old. Mary's death once more brought up the question of succession, for William and Mary had no children, a fact lamented by Mary's eulogists.[54] William, of course, had been named sovereign in his own right, and his victory at the Boyne (1690) further secured his place as king.[55] Yet, the outpouring of odes commemorating Mary's death signaled more than the nation's grief at Mary's passing. James II waited in France at Louis XIV's side, perhaps willing to make, with his daughter's death, another effort to regain the throne by military force.[56] A burlesque dialogue printed in

---

Mary: The Propagation of Mary II, 1689–1694," in *Women and Sovereignty*, ed. Louise Olga Fradenburg (Edinburgh: Edinburgh Univerity Press, 1992), 170–91.

[54] Colley Cibber in *A Poem, On the Death of Our Late Soveraign Lady Queen Mary* (London, 1695) alludes to the lack of an heir: "Tho' Heav'n no Off-spring from her Bed design'd" (11). Hume regrets that there was no heir to be "The Son of mighty *Mars*, and Loves all-conqu'ring Queen" (13. 38) (*A Poem*, 15). Henry Purcell offered musical tributes to the late queen: see Peter Holman et al., "Henry Purcell," in *The New Grove Dictionary of Music and Musicians* (London and New York: Macmillan, 2001), 20: 604–30, here 605, 612.

[55] Oxford University printed a collection of Latin poems to celebrate William's "royal return" after victory at the Boyne. See *Academiæ Oxoniensis Gratulatio Pro Exoptato Serenissimi Regis Guilielmi ex Hibernia Reditu* (Oxford, 1690).

[56] Both universities commemorated the queen's death. The Oxford collection, *Pietas Universitatis Oxoniensis In Obitum Augustissimæ & Desideratissimæ Reginæ Mariæ* (Oxford,

1695, while holding James and the French king up to ridicule, makes clear the reality of that threat.[57] Although the odes to Mary celebrate her virtue and piety, they also call upon William to launch a campaign against the French and to recapture Namur, which the French had recently regained. James II's secret diplomacy with the French had been an unpopular part of his kingship, and with William as king the French had become the acknowledged enemy. Besides, as one poet notes, the continuing league of France with the Turks was also troublesome: "*Lewis* and *Mahomet* in Leagues Divine / Are th' only *Gemini* in our *Zodiack* shine. / *Party per pale* alone our *Coat* adorns, / We own no *Cross*, but what the *Crescent* horns."[58] The odes on Mary's death remind the nation that William and Mary had saved England from double-dealings with the French as well as from the Romish Hydra of Catholicism. As with the memorial odes for Charles II, the occasion of the Queen's passing became an opportunity to affirm William's right as king, to move him to a continental campaign against the French, and to exult in England's safety under a Protestant monarch.

With Behn dead and Dryden retired from political controversy, a host of minor poets try their hands at pindarics praising the dead Mary, comforting William, and urging him to arms.[59] The poets openly urge William to cease grieving and take up the challenge of the continental war. One exhorts him:

1695), contained no English, and mostly Latin and Greek, poems. The Cambridge volume, *Lacrymæ Cantabrigienses in Obitum Serenissimæ Reginæ Mariæ* (Cambridge: Johan. Hayes, 1694/5), included English poems, a substantial number of which were pindarics. For the English pindarics, see *Lacrymæ Cantabrigienses*, sigs. X^v–X4^r, X4^r –Y^r, Y4^r–Z^v, Z^v–Z4^v, Aa^v–Aa4^r, Cc2^v–Cc3^v. See the discussion of the Latin poems in these volumes in Revard, "The Latin Ode from Elizabeth I to Mary II: Political Approaches to Encomia," 156–69.

[57] *A Dialogue between the King of France and the Late King James, Occasioned by the Death of the Queen. Written Originally in French, at Paris* (London, 1695). The claims that the dialogue was originally written in French are, of course, spurious.

[58] See *Urania's Temple: Or, A Satyr upon the Silent-Poets* (London, 1695), 8.

[59] Included in *Urania's Temple* is an attack on the poets who did not write odes for the queen. The poet of *Urania's Temple* praises Congreve for his pastoral on the queen's death, but castigates the envy of the Jacobite faction, characterizing them as "*Night-birds* that *hoot*" and do not sing (4). He remarks on Dryden's silence, describing him as the "old *Moloch* of that *Age*" and further implies that Dryden's Catholicism kept him silent: "Sham'ed that the *Dragons-Tail* swept down the *Star*" (6). However, the intention of the poet—in spite of the abusive language—seems to have been to reconcile the two parties by Mary's death and bring the Catholic sympathizers back to the Church: "There's not one *Heretick-Line* in that whole FACE: / A *Face* that ev'n *All Churches* reconciles" (10). Another anonymous poet also comments on Dryden's silence: "Ev'n *Dryden* mourns; tho yet he does refuse / To mourn in public, and exert his Muse." See *The Mourning Poets: Or, An Account of the Poems on the Death of the Queen. In a Letter to a Friend* (London, 1695), 4.

"Weep, weep no more! Maria's softer Charms! / When War and Honour call you to your Arms."[60] Another advises:

> Enough! enough! Cease longer to torment
> Your Matchless Self, with racking Discontent;
> . . . .
> Great Britain's Safety does on *You* depend,
> Their *Lives* and *Fortunes* they to *You* Commend:
> Nay, *Belgia* too, and the *Confederates* All,
> Are to Your Interest linkt, Reciprocal: (9)[61]

An anonymous ode "By a Person of Honour" depicts William as Europe's destined savior and urges him to "return, to ALBION'S Help return" (3).[62] Patrick Hume tells Britannia itself to stop mourning and to rise and follow William into battle: "Get up, *Britannia*, th'ast no time to moan, / Get up, thy warlike *William* leads thee on." (13. 23–24).[63] Some poets depict Mary herself urging William on, like a "triumphant Goddess" or a shining star looking down from Heaven. Samuel Cobb exhorts:

> Look down, Triumphant Goddess, and some Pity show
> On us, thy subjects truly Militant below:
> Favour our Pious Cause, and let thy Beaut'ous Star
> Defend and Guide us, in our Noble WAR.
> Let Thy Star fight for us, I say,
> For Stars of Old have fought in their Battalia.
> (15. 1–6)[64]

---

[60] [John] Tutchin, *An Epistle to Mr. Benjamin Bridgwater, Occasion'd by the Death of the late Queen Mary* (London, 1694), 3.

[61] William Patridge, *A Consolatory Poem: Addressed to the Most Sacred Majesty* (London, 1695), 9.

[62] See *On the Death of the Queen, By a Person of Honour* (London, 1695). The ode casts William in the role of a Hercules: "Decreed that you should EUROPE's Saviour be, / And from fierce Monsters purge the Earth and Sea" (3). Also see [Pierre Antoine] Motteux, *MARIA. A POEM Occasioned by the Death of Her Majesty. Addrest to Three Persons of Honour* (London, 1695). Motteux urges at the conclusion: "To Arms, Heroic Prince, to Arms; / Glory, like Love, has pow'rful Charms" (12).

[63] Hume, *A Poem*, 15.

[64] [Samuel Cobb], *A Pindarique Ode: Humbly Offer'd to the Ever-Blessed Memory of our Late Gracious Sovereign Lady Queen Mary.* Written by J. D. Gent. (London, 1694), 11. Some poets depict Mary as the consort who stayed at home and governed the state, permitting William freely to take on the role of soldier and wage wars abroad; others look on her as having taken a more active interest in the war. Hume makes Mary a warlike Venus, the "Sov'reign of the Sea," who "forc'd the *French* to skulk behind the Boom" (Hume, *A Poem*, 12).

Some odes on Mary's death depict Louis XIV exulting that her death provides a brief intermission from William's challenge of his claim in the Low Countries.[65] William is urged to put Louis's exultation to an end and to teach the French a lesson, as he had taught the Irish at the Boyne: "Let *French* as *Irish* on your Triumphs wait, / . . . / Still for your Brows shall fresher Lawrels grow, / While *Thames* shall flourish, and the *Boyne* shall flow" (Tutchin, *An Epistle*, 4). Tutchin even envisions the army waiting for William's assumption of command: "Let dastard *Lewis* for a loss retreat, / All sense of Sorrow is beneath the Great, / Your num'rous Army marshall'd on the Strand / In expectation cry, will *Caesar* land? / A long, long Winter, we his absence mourn, / But sure, ye Gods! He must, He must return!" (Tutchin, *An Epistle*, 3).

As a Dutchman and England's warrior king, William had a particular interest in the Low Countries. Namur had been a site of contention between England and France (as well as between the Netherlands and France), and when William arrived on the continent in June 1695, he led a coalition of Englishmen and Hollanders to retake Namur, which Louis XIV had successfully captured in 1692. It was one of the most important campaigns of William's military career and brought forth congratulations from the very poets who in the odes on Mary's death had urged him to the campaign. It was predictable that Francis Manning should heroicize William in "A Congratulatory Poem . . . Upon His Return Home, After the Taking of Namur" (London, 1695), for Manning in a pastoral on the death of the queen had pressed England's "shepherd swain" to venture forth to challenge the Gallic lion and quell his rage.[66]

The different kind of battle over Namur was fought on the literary front with opposing pindarics by French and English poets. Nicolas Boileau-Despréaux (1636–1711), the eminent French critic who was in service to Louis XIV as historiographer and encomiast, was highly respected for his views on poetics. To celebrate the French capture of Namur in 1692, Boileau appropriated Pindar's high style and created an ode in honor of Louis XIV. Both the ode and his boast of his skill in imitating Pindar had rankled with English pindarists. Upon William's successful capture of Namur in 1695, Boileau's ode immediately became the butt of parodies, some of them in French, some in English. Attempting to dampen Boileau's wing, the English poets mocked his high flying style and his ambitious imitation of Pindar. Substituting praise of William for the praise of Louis, one English satirist replied in French, printing his metrical imitation on the page facing Boileau's original pindaric.[67] In every place that the name Louis appears

---

[65] Cibber implies that Louis is moved by fear that William will return from his grief, his rage redoubled (Cibber, *A Poem*, 13).

[66] Mr. [Francis] Manning, *A Pastoral Essay, Lamenting the Death of our Most Gracious Queen Mary* (London, 1695), 9–10.

[67] Boileau's ode is composed in a regular 10-line rhyming stanzaic pattern, which the satirist of Boileau's ode also adopts. The satirist ironically mocks Boileau's transport,

in Boileau's original, the satirist replaces it with the name William, proclaiming: "GUILLAUME a Vaincu *Louis*" (l. 10). Another ode to Boileau (also in French) parodies Boileau's ode, contesting his right to the title of the new Pindar and threatening him with the fate of Icarus: "Arrestez nouveau Pindare, / Qui d'un vol audaciuex, / Cherchant le distin d'Icare" [Halt, new Pindar, who with an audacious flight, search[es] the destiny of Icarus]. The anonymous poet advises him to curb his Pindaric Pegasus before he runs it to ground ("Ode, A Mr. Boileau" in *Vers à la Louange du Roy*, 17). Still another poet in an English ballad openly ridicules Boileau's Pindarism: "*Pindar*, that Eagle, mounts the Skies; / While Virtue leads the noble way: / *Des Preaux* [Boileau], a Vulture, only flies / Where sordid Interest seeks the Prey" (2. 1–4).[68] Poetic rivalry, as well as political spite, fuels the fight between Boileau and his satiric English attackers.

---

clipping, so to speak, his Pindaric wings. Translations of both are my own. See "Ode, de Mr. Boileau, Sur la Prise de Namur" / "Parodie, de l'Ode de Mr. Boileau, Sur la Prise de Namur," in *Vers à la Louange du Roy, Avec Une Satire contre Boileau-Despreaux & contre La Maintenon* (Londres, 1695), 4–15.

Dans ses Chansons immortèles,	In his immortal songs,
Comme un Aigle audacieux,	Like an audacious eagle,
Pindare étendant ses aîles,	Pindar extending his wings,
Fuit loin des vulgaires yeux.	Flies far from common eyes.
Mais, ô ma fidèle Lyre,	But, oh my faithful Lyre,
Si, dans l'ardeur qui m'inspire,	If, in the ardor with which you inspire me,
Tu peux suivre mes transports;	You can follow my transports,
Les Chesnes de Monts de Thrace,	The oaks of the mountains of Thrace,
N'ont rien oüi que n'efface	Have heard nothing to efface
La douceur de tes accords.	The sweetness of your favors.
(2. 1–10)(4)	

The English satirist bluntly dampens the French pindarist's wing in his line-by-line satire:

Ces actions immortèles,	These immortal actions
Du François audacieux,	Of the audacious French
Viennent de couper les aîles	Have just clipped your wings
Et faire rougir les yeux,	And made your eyes blush.
Chantez ma sincere Lyre,	Sing, my sincere Lyre,
Si, de l'ardeur qui m'inspire,	If, from the ardor which inspires me,
Vous suivez bien les transports;	You follow well these transports
Vous n'aurez rien qui n'efface	You would have nothing which would not
Celles dont aux Monts de Thrace	Efface that of the mountains of Thrace
On admiroit les accords.	One would admire the favors.
(5)	

[68] See *An English Ballad: In Answer to Mr. Despreaux's Pindarique Ode On the Taking of NAMURE* (London, 1695), 1–2. Like the French satire on Boileau's pindaric, the

The capture of Namur also brought forth some serious English pindarics, one in particular by William Congreve, who took the Cowleian ode as a poetic model. Perhaps in emulation of the *furor poeticus* of Ronsard and his followers, Congreve announces how his soul is filled with "New Fire" and soars on "new Wings" to heights unknown (l. 3–4).[69] Borrowing from both Milton and Vergil, Congreve strains to achieve a heroic effect. He opens with a Vergilian flourish: "Of Arms and War my Muse aspires to Sing" (l. 1) — and makes the Vergilian *Fama* (*Aeneid* 4. 173–188) promulgate William's fame. Although he imitates Vergil's description of the Cyclops' forge under Aetna (*Aeneid* 8. 416–24) to describe the preparations for war, he turns from Vergil to Milton when he comes to describe William's siege of Namur. Unlike other pindarists who make use of contemporary accounts of the battle in their odes, Congreve adopts as a model Milton's account of angelic warfare in book 6 of *Paradise Lost*.[70] Influenced perhaps by John Dennis's critical views on the sublime, Congreve takes for granted that the Miltonic sublime is the proper modern equivalent of the Pindaric sublime.

Although Milton's war in Heaven is often considered by modern critics a problematic aspect of his epic, it was a section of *Paradise Lost* most praised by seventeenth- and eighteenth-century critics, who deemed that it even excelled the standard of Homeric and Vergilian warfare.[71] Congreve follows Milton's mythic account by describing how the battle commences with fiery missiles hurled through the air. Then, the English and French warriors, like Milton's warring angels, imitate the giants of old by heaping Pelion on Ossa.

> When those tall Sons of Earth, did Heav'n aspire;

---

ballad parodies the ode. It reproduces Boileau's original French on the right hand page and on the left the English ballad satire.

[69] William Congreve, *A Pindarique Ode , Humbly Offer'd to the King On his Taking Namure* (London, 1695).

[70] Other pindarics on the taking of Namur focus on giving accurate, but heroic accounts of the battle, complete with names of the principal officers on each side. Francis Manning renders a heroic account of the battle, asking his Muse to rehearse the names of those who distinguished themselves in battle: see Francis Manning, *A Congratulatory Poem. Humbly offered to the King upon his Return Home, After the Siege of Namur* (London, 1695), 2–3, 7–8. Thomas Yalden uses a few more mythological flourishes, such as comparing William's descent to save Namur with Jove's descent to Semele, but his main object is to describe the action at Namur and to congratulate William on the victory: see Thomas Yalden, *On the Conquest of Namur. A Pindarick Ode* (London, 1695). Henry Denne's poem on Namur, although written in couplets, has some Pindaric flourishes. Denne praises the courage of William's officers and compares William to St. Michael leading the seraphs. Following Congreve and Dennis, Denne also borrows from Milton, making a Gallic demon whisper to Louis, as Satan had to Beelzebub in *Paradise Lost*, "Sleep'st thou, *Grand Monarch?*" See Henry Denne, *A Poem on the Taking of Namur* (London, 1695), 3, 7.

[71] For a review of the criticism, see Revard, *The War in Heaven*, 15–19.

(A Brave, but Impious Fire!)
Uprooting Hills, with most stupendous Hale,
To form the High and dreadful Scale.
(8.11–14)

This is a familiar tactic of the Pindaric poet. In order to validate the credentials of the winning side—whether Romans under Augustus, the French under Henri, or the English under William—the poet describes the opponents as rebellious and brutish giants and the victors as the Homeric gods. Accordingly, William acts the part of the god Mars and rescues Jove from his gigantic foes.

The Gods, with Horrour and Amaze, look'd down,
Beholding Rocks from their firm Basis rent,
Mountain on Mountain thrown!
With threatning hurl! that shook th' Æthereal Firmament,
Th' Attempt, did Fear in Heav'n create;
Ev'n *Jove* desponding sate;
Till *Mars* with all his Force Collected stood,
And Pour'd whole *War*, on the Rebellious Brood;
Who tumbling headlong from th' *Empyreal* Skys,
Orewhelm'd those Hills, by which they thought to rise.
(8.15–24)

As though we had missed the point, Congreve drives it home: "*Mars*, on the Gods did then his Aid bestow, / And now in Godlike WILLIAM storm, with equal Fire below" (8.25–26))

Although the source of the giants' war is classical, the language Congreve adopts to describe it is Miltonic. Congreve's readers would have understood that behind the name of Jove in Congreve's text is Milton's God and behind Mars Milton's Son of God, who in *Paradise Lost* drove the "rebellious Brood" out of heaven, sending them tumbling from the "*Empyreal* Skye." Congreve even emulates in his description of William's return after his victory Milton's account of the Son of God's triumphant return to his Father. Like the Son, who restored Heaven, William has restored to peace the landscape around Namur:

Hark, the Triumphant Shouts, from every voice!
The Skys with Acclamations Ring!
Hark, how around, the Hills rejoyce,
And Rocks, reflected *Io's* Sing!
Hautboy's and Fifes and Trumpets joyn'd,
Heroick Harmony prepare,
And charm to silence every wind,
And glad the late Tormented Air.
(11.1–8)

At the end of his ode Congreve even echoes the opening words of book 7 of *Paradise Lost* and modestly asks his Muse to descend to Earth. By moving from Vergil to Milton as his model, Congreve exalts William's warfare to a heavenly plane and raises William above Aeneas, who had been the standard to measure the Renaissance kings of the previous century, making him into a celestial hero in the Miltonic mold and also perhaps the hero of English Protestantism.

6.

Poetics as well as politics play a role in the assessment of Pindaric ode at the end of the seventeenth century. Critics of the time call into account the appropriateness of using the Pindaric form in odes such as those on the queen's death or on the king's victories. They both deplore the excesses of these odes and express dismay at the proliferation of pindarics as a literary mode. The anonymous author of *The Mourning Poets: Or, An Account of the Poems on the Death of the Queen* (London, 1695) takes it on himself to pronounce the difference between worthy and unworthy uses of Pindaric poetry. These are not new issues. French critics such as René Rapin had led the way twenty years before with a critique of Pindaric poetics. Like him, the author of *The Mourning Poets* excoriates the wildness of some pindarists, citing Samuel Cobb (who published under the pseudonym "J. D. Gent.") for using the pindaric for extravagant praise of the deceased Queen Mary as goddess and saint.

> I'll slight a Wretch, who, to exult his Theme,
> Did blest *Maria*, and her God blaspheme,
> And to adorn his Queen, his Godhead rob;
> Since *J. D. Gent.* prove only Blue-coat C——b. (10)

The sneer at Cobb's "Blue-coat" politics, however, makes it difficult to know whether this is a poetical or a political judgment on Cobb and his pindaric. Another encomiast of Mary, the pindarist 'Westley' (probably Samuel Wesley), he finds worthy of comparison with Cowley, sharing "a part of th' *English Pindar's* Flame" (7). But the highest praise is reserved for John Dennis, whom he calls "like *Pindar* . . . unutterably bold":

> Gods! With what State his daring Thoughts arise,
> While with sonorous Wings he upwards flyes,
> Till he seems lost above his darling Skies!
> . . . .
> His rapid Transports, and unequall'd Course!
> His tow'ring Muse which scorns a human Flight!
> But shines aloft, and blinds with excessive Light! (6)

Dennis is known now less as a poet than as the critic who promoted the poetics of the sublime. He had taken the occasion of Mary's death not only to write an ode commending her, but also to compose a preface to the ode that discusses Pindar's style and recommends to the modern imitator proper techniques for imitating the Greek poet. Dennis begins by quoting the French critic René Rapin, who had recommended that the ode be used, as Pindar had, only for the praise of the gods and the actions of the most glorious men.[72] Pindar's odes, says Dennis, again citing Rapin, possess a characteristic majesty—a natural elevation of style, a great spirit, a daring imagination, and an expression both noble and striking as well as pure and correct (sig. A2^{r-v}).[73] Yet for Dennis, Rapin comes a little short in his praise, not noting enough Pindar's vehemence, his impetuousness, and the magnificent sounds in his numbers: there is "something dreadful, something which terribly shakes us, at the very same time it transports us." At the same time, Dennis admits that Pindar's "affected digressions, his perpetual rambles, and his sudden and unexpected returns" cause some trouble for his readers (sig. a^r). To imitate him in English, Dennis says, one must be bold, but discreet in boldness, aiming for sublimity and magnificence, but avoiding fustian and superfluity of epithets (sig. a^r). He advises, however, against taking Cowley's way and imitating the extravagance of Pindar's digressions, commenting that though Cowley's imitations of Olympian 2 and Nemean 1 are justly admired, they suffer from wildness. Although Cowley has fire and imitates Pindar's mighty spirit, Dennis remarks, he lacks design in some of his odes, is too pointed in his wit, too loose in rhyme, and rough in his versification, and neglects Pindar's pomp and majesty (sig. a^v–a2^r). Therefore, Dennis explains, he has not taken Cowley for a model for his own pindaric. It is Milton, he affirms, who is a proper exemplar of the sublime.

> In writing these Pindarick Verses, I had still *Milton* in my Eye, and was resolv'd to imitate him as far as it could be done without receding from *Pindar's* manner. They have several great qualities common to both, and among the rest, vehemence, elevation, and a terrible Majesty; qualities which are far above me . . . (sig. a2^r)

---

[72] René Rapin, *Réflexions sur la Poétique d'Aristote et sur les Ouvrages des Poètes Anciens & Modernes* (Paris, 1674), 233–35. Thomas Rymer translated Rapin into English the same year. See Revard, *Pindar and the Renaissance Hymn-Ode*, 46–47. Dryden was also apparently indebted to Rapin, as well as Cowley, for his view that Pindar was obscure, wild, and ungovernable. See "The Preface to Ovid's Epistles," in *The Poetical Works of Dryden*, ed. Noyes, 91.

[73] See John Dennis, "Preface," in *The Court of Death. A Pindarique Poem, Dedicated to the Memory of Her Most Sacred Majesty, Queen Mary* (London, 1695). Expanding on Rapin's commentary, Dennis calls Pindar great in his designs, vast in his ideas, daring in his images, happy in his expressions, and eloquent in his discourse (sig. A2^v).

A discerning critic, Dennis judges rightly about the Miltonic sublime and also rightly (alas) about the difficulty of attaining it. While taking the design of his Pindaric poem for Queen Mary from Vergil's sixth book of the *Aeneid*—the descent into Hades—he imitates the description of Milton's Death in book 2 of *Paradise Lost* and composes a long speech for Death in the Miltonic style. Unfortunately, Dennis does not escape the fustian that he himself named as one of the dangers of imitating Pindar. As a pindaric, Congreve's poem on the taking of Namur, while certainly designed as a propaganda piece for William, succeeds better than Dennis's ode in attaining something like a Miltonic sublime.

Dennis was not the only one to criticize Cowley's imitations of Pindar. In his 1682 *Essay on Poetry* the Earl of Mulgrave, following on Boileau's and Rapin's commentaries on the proper use of the ode form, alludes to Cowley's comparison of Pindaric style to an unruly horse carrying away his rider:

> A higher Flight, and of a happier Force
> Are ODES, the Muses most unruly Horse;
> That bounds so fierce, the Rider has no rest
> But foams at mouth; and moves like one *possest*.

However, Mulgrave is not so much critical of Pindar as of Cowley for allowing his fancy to carry away his judgment:

> The Poet here must be indeed inspired,
> With *Fury* too, as well as *Fancy* fired.
> *Cowley* might boast to have performed this part,
> Had he with *Nature* joyn'd the Rules of *Art*;
> But ill Expression gives sometimes *Allay*
> To that rich Fancy, which can ne'er *decay*:
> Tho all appear in Heat and Fury done,
> The *Language* still must *soft* and *easie* run.
> These Laws may seem a little too severe,
> But *Judgment* yields, and *Fancy* governs there;
> Which, tho extravagant, this Muse allows,
> And makes the Work much easier than it shews.[74]

Samuel Wesley, although an admirer and imitator of Cowley's pindarics, also cites the dangers of the Pindaric style. Pindar's own odes, he remarks, possess "some *Sparks* of *heav'nly Fire*," but "Cowley's happy Muse" has improved the originals and made them better understood and loved. The British, he vaunts, have a

---

[74] John Sheffield, the Earl of Mulgrave, *An Essay on Poetry*, 2nd ed. (London, 1691), 13. Also see Mulgrave in *Critical Essays of the Seventeenth Century*, ed. J. E. Spingarn (Oxford: Clarendon Press, 1908–1909). Mulgrave first printed his *Essay* in 1682, drawing his critique largely from Boileau's "L'Art Poétique."

particular genius for the ode form, but, he qualifies, agreeing perhaps with Mulgrave, that the pindaric itself, while possessing "vastness" of thought and "daring Range," wants smoothness and requires "the Regulation of our Native Fire."[75]

The English critics of the *fin de siècle* often agree not only with Rapin's and Mulgrave's strictures, but also with those of a still more severe critic of Pindar's alleged wildness, Charles Perrault, who in his tractate on the Ancients and the Moderns (1688), condemned Pindar and ridiculed the Pindarism current in France.[76] An opponent of Perrault's view and one of Pindar's most vigorous defenders was the Frenchman Nicolas Boileau, whose ode on Namur had incited so many English parodies. Boileau's "L'Art Poétique" and his "Traité du Sublime" had been much admired by Restoration critics such as John Dryden, the former having been translated into English in 1683 by Sir William Soames and later revised by Dryden.[77] Supplementing the commentary of "L'Art Poétique," Boileau prefixed a discourse on Pindar to his "Ode sur la Prise de Namur," defending the ancient poet and his style against French detractors such as Perrault.[78] Pindar, Boileau declares, was one of the most ill-treated of ancient poets, ill-treated, moreover, by the mediocre spirits of his own [Boileau's] age. Boileau points out that often detractors of Pindar, such as Perrault, derived their knowledge of Pindar not from the Greek originals but from poor Latin translations. He had maintained in both "L'Art Poétique" and his "Traité du Sublime" the essential orderliness of Pindar's style. In "Réflexions Critiques sur Longin" Boileau takes the opportunity to refute Perrault's criticism by demonstrating that Olympian 1, which he presents in his own prose translation, progresses, contrary to Perrault's assertions, in a natural order and possesses a rhetorical orderliness to its design. He further asserts that though Pindar's figures may be daring, they are wholly

---

[75] Samuel Wesley, *An Epistle to a Friend Concerning Poetry* (London, 1700), 27. Wesley himself followed the Cowleian pattern in the pindaric on the death of Mary, as well as in other pindarics.

[76] For Perrault's views, see Revard, *Pindar and the Renaissance Hymn-Ode*, 46.

[77] See [Willliam Soames], *The Art of Poetry*, Written in *French* by the SIEUR de Boileau, Made *English* (London, 1683). For the original French see [Nicolas Boileau-Despréaux], *Oeuvres Diverses du Sieur D**** (Amsterdam, 1701) which reprints "Ode sur la Prise de Namur," "Discours sur l'Ode," "L'Art Poétique," "Traité du Sublime où du Merveilleus dans la Discours Traduit du Grec de Longin," "Remarques sur Longin" and "Reflexions Critiques sur Longin, Où, par occasion, on répond à quelques objections de Monsieur Perrault contre Homere & contre Pindare."

[78] Concerning Perrault's translation of Olympian 1, Boileau points out, "On sera donc assez surpris ici de voir que cette bassesse & ce galimatheas appartiennent entierement à Mr. P. qui en traduisant Pindare, n'a entenu ni le Grec ni le Latin, ni le François" ("Reflexions Critiques sur Longin," 219). (One will be then rather surprised here to see that the lowness and gibberish belong entirely to Mr. P. who, in translating Pindar, understands neither Greek nor Latin nor French). For further commentary on the Perrault-Boileau controversy, see Hamilton, *Soliciting Darkness*, 152–61.

intelligible to men of good sense. In both "Discours sur l'Ode" and "L'Art Poé-tique," he maintains that with Pindar the impression of disorder is in truth an effect of art:

> Son stile impetueux souvent marche au hazard.
> Chez elle un beau desordre est un effect de l'art.

> His impetuous style often moves dangerously,
> But with it a lovely disorder is the result of art.
> ("L'Art Poétique," ll. 197–198)

By not keeping the rules too exactly, Boileau maintains, a poet may achieve the mystery and the transport of true poetry. His own aim, he states, in composing a Pindaric ode on the taking of Namur was to rise to the challenge of depicting a great action of war in a medium appropriate to it.

Such also was Congreve's aim in both his Pindaric imitations: to celebrate in an appropriate mode two battle victories, that of William III at Namur in 1695 and of the Duke of Marlborough at Ramillies in 1706. To the latter ode he pre-fixed a discourse that, like Boileau's "Discours," argues that Pindar, far from be-ing a wild genius, was orderly in his art. At the outset of his "Discourse" he ob-serves that "there is nothing more regular than the Odes of *Pindar*, both as to the exact Observation of the Measures and Numbers of his Stanza's and Verses, and the perpetual Coherence of his Thoughts."[79] To illustrate the orderliness of the true Pindaric ode, Congreve proposed to compose a pindaric that employed Pin-daric triads rather than in the loose stanzaic structure of the Cowleian pindaric (on which he had modeled his first ode). In the "Discourse" on the ode, he not only defended his choice of triads, but also informed those readers who might be ignorant of Pindar's verse in Greek, how strophe, antistrophe, and epode func-tioned in Pindar's original odes to maintain order and also to endue the ode with variety and beauty. Although Congreve avoids attacking Cowley, whose verse he admires, he attacks those who in espousing Cowley's irregular stanzas passed off their compositions as true Pindaric odes, thus creating the impression that Pin-dar had composed irregular verses.[80] He characterizes these so-called pindarics as caricatures: "a Bundle of rambling incoherent Thoughts, express'd in a like parcel of irregular Stanza's" with "disproportion'd, uncertain and perplex'd Vers-

---

[79] See "A Discourse on the Pindarique Ode" in William Congreve, *A Pindarique Ode, Humbly Offer'd to the Queen, On the Victorious Progress of Her Majesty's Arms, under the Conduct of the Duke of Marlborough. To which is prefix'd, A Discourse on the Pindarique Ode* (London, 1706), sig. A^r–A2^v, here sig. A^r.

[80] Of Cowley's irregular pindarics, Congreve concludes, "tho' he did not imitate *Pindar* in the Strictness of his Numbers, he has very often happily copy'd him in the Force of his Figures, and Sublimity of his Stile and Sentiments" (sig. A2^v). Congreve's own pindaric on taking Namur (1695) was, as we have noted, a Cowleian pindaric.

es and Rhimes" (sig. A^r). The aim of his own ode, he states, is "towards restoring the Regularity of the Ancient Lyrick Poetry, which seems to be altogether forgotten or unknown by our English Writers" (sig. A^r).

We cannot know exactly what impact Congreve's discourse had, together with the publication of his own pindaric in regular triads. Perhaps in response to Congreve, Elijah Fenton put forth in 1707 "An Ode to the Sun" in regular triads, also in celebration of Marlborough's military victories. However, not all Pindaric poets looked on triads as the proper form for future pindarics. When he published a pindaric in 1709 celebrating Queen Anne and the Duke of Marlborough, Samuel Cobb used the Cowleian model and, perhaps in answer to Congreve, defended his choice:

> . . . whether you will call the following Lines a *Pindaric* Ode, or Irregular Stanza's, gives me no Disturbance; For however the seeming Wildness of this sort of Verse ought to be restrain'd, the *Strophe, Antistrophe,* &c. will never bear in English, and it would shew a strange Debauchery in our Taste, if it should, as may be witnessed by the servile Imitations of the Dactyles and Spondees used by Sir *P. Sidney.* (sig. A2^v)[81]

Cobb was correct in his appraisal. Triadic verse has had little currency in English, and the Cowleian pindaric—with all its excesses—continued to be the preferred mode for the pindaric well into the eighteenth century, with only a few poets taking up Congreve's challenge to write "correct" pindarics. When he translated Pindar, Ambrose Phillips chose triads for his versions of Olympian 1 and 2 and also produced in 1723 an ode in triads to lament the death of William, Earl Cowper.[82] Some twenty-five years later Gilbert West also took up the cause of triadic verse, echoing Congreve's criticism of the Cowleian pindaric and employing triads for his translations of Pindar—and in the next decades Gray and Collins attempted triadic verse.[83] But there was among English poets, as there had been among the French, no widespread espousal of triadic verse.

---

[81] Samuel Cobb, "Letter," in *The Female Reign: An Ode, Alluding to Horace, B. 4. Od. 14 . . . Attempted in the Style of Pindar* (London, 1709), sig. A2^v.

[82] See Mr. [Ambrose] Phillips, *An Ode (In the Manner of Pindar) On the Death of the Right Honourable William, Earl Cowper* (London, 1723). For Phillips's translations of Pindar's Olympian 1 and 2, see *Pastorals, Epistles, Odes, and Other Original Poems, With Translations from Pindar, Anacreon, and Sappho* (London, 1748), 117–38.

[83] Gray and Collins, however, did not imitate Congreve's political ode. They used triadic verse to praise poetry or to deal with abstract subjects. It was the Cowleian model—if not Cowleian politics—that moved Romantic writers when they took up the ode form in the nineteenth century. See also the discussion of Congreve and West in Revard, *Pindar and the Renaissance Hymn-Ode*, 5–7, 338.

7.

Samuel Cobb and William Congreve were among the last poets to write serious political odes in the "Pindaric" style and to defend these odes as authentic Pindaric compositions. The occasion for both was the victories of Queen Anne's armies under the leadership of the Duke of Marlborough.[84] By the time Cobb published "The Female Reign" in 1709, he had come a long way as a pindarist since he published the anonymous pindaric on Queen Mary's death in 1695.[85] In the preface to "The Female Reign," he specifically defends both Pindar and his own Pindaric credentials. Cobb knew and could quote Pindar, verse for verse, for he had been trained in Cambridge as a classicist. Whatever his preference for the Cowleian mode, he could not be accused of ignorance of Pindar's original odes.[86] Moreover, he had carefully observed Pindar's practices in preparation for his own imitations.

> In my Digressions and Transitions I have taken care to play always in sight, and make every one of them contribute to my main Design. This was the way of *Pindar*, to read whom, according to *Rapin*, will give a truer Idea of the Ode, than all the Rules and Reflections of the best Critics. ("Letter," sig. A2^v)

Modestly, Cobb states that he has not dived into Pindar "Head and Ears," but that, while not imitating Pindar's strophic form, he has "endeavour'd to have made my self not the greatest Stranger to his Manner of Writing; which generally consists in the Dignity of Sentiments, and an elegant variety" (sig. A2^v).[87]

---

[84] Cobb, *The Female Reign*; Congreve, *A Pindarique Ode*.

[85] Besides his ode for Queen Mary, Cobb also composed a pindaric in 1697, "Pax Redux," to celebrate William III's peace with the French. He makes a quasi-Miltonic appeal to the Muse to frame "the brave *Pindarick* Song" (3.20), describing himself as a priest who touches the sacred fires. See *Pax Redux: A Pindarick Ode on the Return of His Majesty, and the Happy Conclusion of the Peace* (London, 1697), 2. Also see Phillips, *Augustus Britannicus*, composed for the same victory.

[86] See B. Bowden, "Samuel Cobb," in *Oxford Dictionary of National Biography* (Oxford: Oxford University Press, 2004), 12: 266–67.

[87] In their respective odes both Cobb and Congreve make allusions to Pindar. Cobb strikes "the loud *Pyndaric* Strings / Like the Lark, who soars and sings" (5.5–6). However, his first digression summons up recollections of Milton, as he compares the fate of the "False *Electors*" and "Perjur'd Kings" (the Elector of Bavaria and Louis XIV) to that of Lucifer (3.1–12). Congreve includes a digression on the origin of the Orphic lyre (epode 1) and alludes to the songs of "*Spencer* sweet" and "*Milton* strong" (antistrophe 2.5). Despite his announced intention of imitating Pythian 1, Congreve fails to integrate these musical references into his ode as Marvell had in "The First Anniversary."

Both Cobb and Congreve announce that they have specific Pindaric models in mind. Congreve cites Pindar's Pythian 1, the very ode that resonated so meaningfully in Marvell's "The First Anniversary." Cobb in turn explains that he has modeled his ode on Horace's *Carmina* 4.14, rendering it "in the style of *Pindar.*" Both poets open their odes by posing Pindaric questions. Congreve invokes the poet's lyre, yoking the poet with the queen he celebrates: "what Poet wilt thou chuse / Of ANNA's Name to Sing?" (strophe 1.2–3) whereas Cobb merely asks, mimicking Horace's opening: "What can the *British Senate* give / To make the Name of ANNA live?" (1.2–3). It is hardly surprising that the principal myth for both poets is Jove's conquest of the giants, reworked to compliment Marlborough's victories at Blenheim, at Ramillies, and (for Cobb) his final victory at Oudenarde. As Pindar in Pythian 1 had drawn a parallel between Zeus's and Hieron's conquests of their enemies to celebrate Hieron's establishment of peace in Sicily, so his English imitators praise Marlborough for bringing peace to Europe. Marlborough's patrons—King William and Queen Anne—are characterized as gods, who leave their Olympian heights to punish the tyrannical French and their allies. In Cobb's account Marlborough fills the role of Hercules, who assists the gods to defeat the presumptuous giants:

> And as Gigantick Tyrants rise
> NASSAU's and ANNA's leave the Skies
> The Earth-born Monsters to Chastise;
> While Cerberus and Hydra grow
> For an Alcides, or a MARLBOROUGH. (4.16–20)

Cobb exults over the enemies of Anna and Jove as "Sure Food for Thunder"; they have been defeated and howl, like Typhon, under Aetna (14.20–24). Congreve also describes how the gods resist tyrannic power. For him Queen Anne is both Jove and Astraea, ruling above with power and descending to the earth to dispense justice when tyrannic powers threaten to overwhelm Europe: "Again *Astraea* Reigns! / ANNA Her equal Scale maintains" (epode 3.12–13). The combined power of Astraea-Anne and Hercules-Marlborough brings universal peace and drives tyranny from "*Europe*'s blissful Bound" to the "uninhabitable Zone" of the North (epode 3.1–5).

> Thus ANNA's mighty Mind,
> To Mercy and soft Pity prone,
> And mov'd with Sorrows not her own,
> Has all her Peace and downy Rest resign'd,
> To wake for Common Good, and succour Human-kind.
> (antistrophe 3.3–7)

Following the bent of his Namur ode, Congreve also casts Marlborough in the role of the avenging archangel Michael, who wields his sovereign's "sure deciding

Sword" (epode 3.14). Cobb is perhaps remembering Horace's characterization of Tiberius when he describes Marlborough as a natural phenomenon, a force of nature unleashed upon his foes. He sweeps across the land like water from a broken dike, like driving wind, and with his ally Prince Eugene, he acts the part of a *"Second Thunderbolt of War!"* as he urges the forward way (9.2). Could Cobb be recalling another force of nature, Marvell's resistless Cromwell, who also struck like lightning from heaven?

Both Congreve and Cobb take the Pindaric way in recapitulating Marlborough's former victories, as they describe the present triumph, just as though they were listing the credentials of a winning athlete. In celebrating Ramillies, Congreve recalls Blenheim:

> When Bold *Bavaria* fled the Field,
> And Veteran Gauls unus'd to yield,
> On *Blenheim's* Plain imploring Mercy, lay;
> And Spoils and Trophies won, perplex'd the Victors way.
> (antistrophe 4.4–7)

Cobb remembers how the Dyle, the Danube, and the Scheld—rivers adjoining the battlefields—were witness to previous battles, their waves made crimson by the bodies of the slain (4.8–9).[88]

Pindaric *sententiae* are not missing from these odes. "Virtue" like Pindaric metal must be tested in battle. Cobb opines: "Heroic Virtue is by Action seen, / And Vices serve to make it keen" (4.14–15); *"Virtue,"* he remarks, "as well as Gold, can pass / Thro' Walls of Stone, and Towers of Brass" (10. 3–4); and finally he asserts, *"Virtue* is a safer Way to Rise / A shorter Passage to the Skies / Than *Pellion* upon *Ossa* thrown" (14.16–18). Congreve is more reticent; "What Verse such Worth can Raise?" he queries. To "middle Vertue," he reflects, "the Poet's Art" may lend "Lustre and Life." "But Deeds sublime," he declares, "exalted high like These, / Transcend his utmost Flight; and mock his distant Praise" (antistrophe 5.3–7).

By the time Congreve and Cobb write, they can look back on a complex Pindaric tradition. Perhaps Cobb is recalling Cowley's "Plagues of *Egypt*" when he characterizes the French king as a *"Gallic Pharaoh"* (13. 15). He also remarks that Salic law did not deprive England, as it had France, of a virtuous female ruler. When Congreve recalls Hannibal's and Caesar's victories, perhaps he is remembering Marvell's praise of Cromwell's generalship. We can certainly recognize Marvell's final advice to Cromwell in Congreve's exhortation to Marlborough to persevere "Nor sheath the Terrors of thy Sword / 'Till *Europe* thou

---

[88] The Dyle is in central Belgium near the battle of Oudenarde; the Danube recalls the battle of Blenheim; the Scheld was near the battle of Dendermonde (1706). Cobb is probably glancing at *Carmina* 4.14, and Horace's summoning of the rivers to praise Caesar.

has freed /And Universal Peace restor'd" (epode 5.6–8). Though neither endowed with Marvellian irony nor possessed of Cowleian subtlety, Cobb and Congreve yet remind their readers of these poets and of the Pindaric practice, good and bad, over the past fifty years.

8.

By the end of Queen Anne's reign, the political pindaric had waned into a purely rhetorical exercise without able poets such as Marvell and Cowley or Dryden and Behn to realize the form's potential. All was lost in effusive compliment and swelling fustian. Even well-informed practitioners, such as Cobb and Congreve, demonstrate that learned imitators of Pindar can produce only perfunctory poetry. Following the rules and adapting Pindar's techniques for royal encomium simply was not enough. Hence contemporary pindarics did not long resist deflation by the wits of the age, who had begun to mock them. In "The Battle of the Books" (1710) Jonathan Swift has an all-victorious Pindar slay his feeble imitators and even render a blow that cleaved the mighty Cowley in twain. Nonetheless, Pindaric ode remained well into the eighteenth century the official form to celebrate the victories of his or her Majesty's armies, to commemorate the birth of this or that prince or the death of the monarch. When George I arrived in England to take his place on the British throne, he was perforce welcomed with pindarics.[89] However, pindarics began to be composed for lesser occasions, and so often became the butt of parody: Colley Cibber's birthday odes for the sovereign caused more laughter than wonder.[90] Nevertheless, Cibber boasted that his compositions excelled even the ancient originals. In "A Rhapsody Upon the Marvellous" he indulges his feelings on attempting the Pindaric mode: "Danger delights the Bard intrepid, / Who feels, within him, Raptures rapid / Tumbling like Torrents from the Mountain! / (Old Type of *Heliconian* Fountain.) / ... / Tho' smooth, and deep, may flow with Sense / Rage! Rage! it seems gives Excellence!"

---

[89] Pindaric odes were published in 1702 with the death of William III, and in 1714 on the death of Queen Anne. See M. Smith Gent., *A Pindarique Poem Sacred to the Glorious Memory of King William III* (London, 1702); Joseph Harris, *Threnodia Augustalis, A Funeral-Pindarique ODE, Sacred to the Happy Memory of Our Late Gracious Sovereign, Queen ANNE, &c* (London, 1714). Like Behn's funeral pindaric for Charles II, the ode for Queen Anne begins with a reflection on the sadness of the day: "Sad was the Hour, the sadder Morn began, / And heavily the God of Day came on" (1.1–2). It concludes with congratulations to King George I.

[90] The use of the Pindaric ode for birthday poems goes back at least to Matthew Prior, *A Pindarique on His Majesties birth-day ... Sung before Their Majesties at Whitehall, the fourth of November 1690* (London, 1690).

(5).[91] Cibber delivers his highest compliments to the "Prince of Lyric Poets" at the end of the ode by comparing Pindar's odes to "best Plumb-pudding" (22). Not without cause would Cibber famously be crowned by Alexander Pope in the *Dunciad* the chief of Dunces. It was left to later pindarists to rescue the ode.

---

[91] "A Rhapsody Upon the Marvellous. Arising from the first odes of Horace and Pindar" (London, 1741). Also see Boswell's account of Cibber's presentation of a pindaric to Dr. Johnson: James Boswell, *Life of Johnson*, ed. G. B. Hill (Oxford: Oxford University Press, 1979), 3: 72–73.

CHAPTER 6
THE ART OF THE FUNERAL PINDARIC:
THRENODY IN ITALY AND FRANCE

As we have seen in the previous chapters, Pindaric ode could serve both to celebrate the living and to commemorate the dead. Yet, however popular the Pindaric ode-elegy became as a type to mourn the passing of public figures of the Stuart court, neither Cowley nor his followers invented the funeral pindaric. English poets had been experimenting with Pindaric ode-elegy earlier in the seventeenth century, as both Ben Jonson's triadic Cary-Morison ode and Milton's pastoral monody "Lycidas" attest. On the continent, moreover, pindarics had long been used for funera. Benedetto Lampridio, one of the earliest Pindaric imitators, wrote a number of ode-elegies and handed down the model for the Pindaric funeral ode to later pindarists in Italy and France.

To employ Pindaric ode for laments for the dead was neither illogical nor inappropriate, and in fact has its warrant in the very nature of the ode that Pindar himself composed. In a culture where the family held a central place and where remembrance of the dead was a religious and civic duty enjoined on the living, the poet who congratulated winning athletes on their victories also had the obligation to remember deceased relatives who had won similar honors.[1] In Hellenic culture, moreover, the very heroes of myth—Heracles, Achilles, Ajax, Castor and Pollux—who so often feature in the digressions of Pindar's odes had a special status as so-called ancestors of the city-states for which Pindar composed his epinicia. These heroes had accomplished great deeds, but also had suffered calamity and death. It is not surprising, therefore, that those odes of Pindar that allude to or recount their tragedies should become models for early modern funeral odes. But before we look at these Renaissance ode-elegies, we must consider in just what way those patterns, techniques, and motifs of Pindar's own odes functioned, making it possible for later poets to adapt victory celebrations for songs to the dead.

---

[1] See Leslie Kurke, *The Traffic in Praise: Pindar and the Poetics of Social Economy* (Ithaca: Cornell University Press, 1991), 62–82.

1.

As Kevin Crotty has observed, Pindar's odes are replete with observances on the nature and conditions of human existence.[2] Pindar was a deeply religious man who reflected on defeat in the midst of victory, death in the midst of life. The summits of achievement that his athletes attained he looked upon as heights from which one might plunge into the abyss. He was keenly aware of the impermanence of human happiness, and, like most Greeks, believed firmly in the maxim that only the gods are happy. Human beings are creatures of a day, and human life the dream of a shadow, as he says at the conclusion of Pythian 8 (95–96)—lines well known to the Renaissance and paraphrased by Cowley and other imitators.[3] Pindar expresses sympathy with those who suffer, be they rulers, such as Hieron, whose illness he condoles in Pythian 3, or ordinary citizens, such as Ergoteles, the victor of Olympian 12, who had been exiled from his native Crete. The goddess Tyche (Fortune) whom he invokes in Olympian 12 confers both ill as well as good fortune. But, as Crotty has observed, Tyche is no arbitrary power, but a part of the world-wide system governed by the gods.[4]

Pindar had close ties to aristocrats in Aegina, to friends and associates in his native city of Thebes, and of course to the tyrants of Sicily who had treated him generously. Throughout his odes he intimately addresses the winning athletes and their patrons, not only congratulating them in victory, but also consoling them in sorrow. In Olympian 8 Pindar offers condolences to the boy victor, Alcimedon of Aegina, that he cannot share his victory with his dead father and uncle. Alas, he must dispatch the daughter of Hermes to Hades with the news of his victory at Olympia. Similarly in Nemean 8 he comforts the youthful athlete Deinias, whose dead father had previously won the contest in which he is now victorious. Gently Pindar tells him that while we may honor the dead, we cannot bring back the soul to the body. Such hopes are vain: "κενεᾶν δ᾽ ἐλπίδων χαῦνον τέλος" (Nemean 8.45). Pindar is also moved by national tragedy as well as by individual sorrow. In Isthmian 8 he condoles the victor Cleandros for his cousin Nicocles' death in the Persian wars that have just concluded. A heavy weight has been lifted from Hellas, which lost so many brave men. In Isthmian

---

[2] Crotty, *Song and Action*, 1. Crotty also observes that the victorious and defeated are not utterly distinct, for the high hopes of a man buoyed by victory may easily be dashed by defeat (x–xi).

[3] "As 'tis *To be*, or *Not to Bee.* / *Dream* of a *Shadow!*" (ll. 6–7) in "Life and Fame," in Cowley, *Pindarique Odes*, 39.

[4] See Crotty, *Song and Action*, 9–10. The context for Olympian 12 is important. Himera had just weathered a sea-battle that had raged off its coasts, and Pindar draws his metaphor for the vicissitudes of life from the very treachery of the seas that toss high and low the hopes of men. Pindar's principal concern is the uncertainty of human life that is at the root of the political turbulence Himera was experiencing. .

7 he comforts another young athlete, Strepsiades of Thebes, that his victory cannot be shared by his uncle of the same name, who had fallen in battle, probably at Tanagra in 457 B.C.[5] As Charles Segal has noted, "the poet's task is to reveal and create that larger perspective wherein both the grief and the joy of the individual and the family, opened to the wider frame of the city and of all Hellas, receives solace and commemoration."[6] In Isthmian 7 Pindar also glances at the growing hostilities between Thebes and Athens that would bring suffering to another generation of Thebans. An ode such as Olympian 8, the myth of which recounts the building of the fatal walls of Troy that let in the enemy, forebodes like tragedy for Aegina, which would be reduced to a tributary colony of Athens in 456 B.C., only four years after the victory the ode celebrates. Pindar closes the ode with a prayer to Zeus that Aegina may reap blessings, not sorrow, and that Nemesis not envy the city's happiness.

It is through myth, however, and through the mythic digressions of his odes that Pindar speaks most candidly about human experience. The patriarchs Cadmus and Peleus—virtuous and fortunate men, greatly favored early in life but brought to grief in old age—Pindar alludes to in Pythian 3 as examples of the precariousness of human life. The short-lived Achilles and the tragic Ajax, to whose untimely deaths he refers repeatedly in his odes, also become touchstones for tragedy. All the great heroes of the Hellenic cycles—Heracles, Jason, the Seven against Thebes, Telamon, as well as the tragic Achilles and Ajax—feature in the digressions of Pindar's odes. Whereas accounts of the great Theban hero Heracles almost always recall his triumphs, Pindar's allusions to Achilles and Ajax are usually tragic.[7] Ajax is particularly connected with the odes for Aeginetan athletes. Achilles, the greatest hero of the Hellenic world, appears in all four cycles of odes, for all Greeks claimed him as a national hero. That Achilles' death is alluded to both in the celebratory ode for Theron—Olympian 2, composed in 476 B.C.—and in the consolatory ode for Hieron—Pythian 3, composed perhaps two years later—illustrates the remarkable way in which Pindar treats the death of this hero as a touchstone for tragedy. Through allusion to Achilles and his unhappy fate Pindar might well have felt, even as he praised Hieron and Theron, that he was indirectly telling them how transitory their power was, how brief their reigns would be. He celebrates both tyrants in 476 B.C. at the zenith of their power, when both had won Olympic victories—Hieron for

---

[5] Bruno Currie argues for the relevance to Pindar of the heroization of the war dead in fifth-century Greece. See Currie, *Pindar and the Cult of Heroes*, 89–119; also see his discussion of Isthmian 7: 205–25.

[6] See Segal, "Myth, Cult, and Memory in Pindar's Third and Fourth *Isthmian* Odes," in *Aglaia*, 229–49, here 241.

[7] In Isthmian 6 Pindar describes how Heracles predicts the birth of Aias (Ajax) for his friend Telamon. In Nemean 3 he tells how Achilles, still under the tutelage of the centaur, performed youthful feats of daring.

the horse race, Theron for the chariot race. Olympians 1 and 2 became two of Pindar's most admired odes; both, while celebrating victory, veil the decline and death that was inevitably to come. In 476 B.C. Hieron was already suffering from a grievous illness and would die in 467 B.C. Theron died in 472 B.C., just four years after Pindar's triumphal ode. With the references to Achilles in Pythian 3 and Olympian 2 Pindar indirectly recognizes the mortality of both men.

As we have noted previously, both odes raise questions about the human condition. Olympian 2 lauds Theron's person, as well as the city of Acragas, settled by Dorians from Thebes, but its myth recounts the troubles of Cadmus—the tragedies of his daughters—and refers to his most unhappy descendant, Oedipus. Many critics and translators, Cowley among them, have been disturbed by the litany of woes that Pindar recites. No matter how Pindar reassures us that suffering on earth will be compensated by a blissful afterlife, we are left with an unmistakable feeling that the fatal Erynnis that hunted down Oedipus and his sons cannot easily be overcome. Sorrow seems the unfailing human lot. The tyrant of Acragas could hardly have rejoiced when Pindar told him that even men whom fate treats kindly must expect reversals.

What makes Olympian 2 so extraordinary is that Pindar does not shrink from bringing up crucial issues of mortality, fate, and human responsibility in an ode that is ostensibly a victory song for a royal patron. Nor, having raised these issues, will he be distracted from interrogating them fully. Even in praising the wealthy Theron as the "happiest of men," he questions what exactly constitutes human happiness. Is it wealth adorned with *areté*, the classical standard that a man such as Theron could understand?[8] However, wealth and virtue can hardly be called warrantors of happiness when no one can read the future and tell how long either will last to assure such "happiness." What then? The question of the afterlife necessarily impinges. Pindar posits the two realms of Hades: the first, where the good, tearless, will enjoy equal days and equal nights, and the second where the unjust will pay the penalty with heavy toil and pain. However, there is a third realm for those who have been thrice purged of injustice: the Isles of the Blest, where temperate breezes blow and golden flowers bloom. There the just make circlets of flowers for their arms, crowns for their heads. In the presence of Rhadamanthys and Cronos the heroes Cadmus and Peleus dwell, together with Achilles, brought there by his mother Thetis, who softened the heart of Zeus with her prayers.

Pindar's depiction in Olympian 2 of the happy afterlife becomes a significant model for those Renaissance poets who seek in his odes approximations of a Christian heaven. In Olympian 2 Pindar translates his heroes beyond the suffer-

---

[8] Pindar anticipates Plato in questioning how earthly standards compare with those beyond the grave. In the first book of *The Republic* a wealthy old man (much like Theron) asks Socrates how the rewards for the good and the punishments for the evil will be dispensed in the afterlife.

ing that life has brought them, but not before he investigates the fate that led to their tragic ends. Μόριμος (fated or fate-driven) is a word that could be applied to all of them, but particularly to Achilles, who, a fate-driven hero like Oedipus, acts out the tragedy he has unwittingly chosen. Pindar recalls for us Achilles' choice, alluding to the scene in the *Iliad* (1.495–527), in which Thetis, pleading for Achilles, recognizes that if Zeus honors her request it will only hasten her son's fated death. Homer's Thetis refers to her son as ὠκύμορος, but Pindar uses the word μόριμος to link Achilles to other young men who were also fate-driven: Hector, the pillar of strength for Troy, and Memnon, Dawn's son, both of whom Achilles killed. Moreover, just as Oedipus was doomed to kill his father, Achilles was destined to kill Hector and Memnon and they to die at his hand. Cadmus is also μόριμος, that is, fated to preside over the sorrows of his daughters. In this context Olympian 2 becomes an inquiry into the ways of μοῖρα or fate. By stretching the moral and eschatological dimensions of the epinician form, Pindar demonstrates that he can discuss the most important of human considerations — the dispensation of justice — in an ode that concludes by telling us that Theron's generosities are beyond number, beyond the grains of sand on the sea shore.

In Pythian 3 Pindar also interrogates the dispensation of human happiness. It is significant that Achilles appears, as in Olympian 2, in consort with Cadmus and Peleus, though from another perspective. In this ode Pindar has different lessons to teach about the intersection of divine justice and the human lot in life. Pythian 3 is, as critics have recognized, a verse letter to Hieron which, though alluding to Hieron's victories at Olympia and Delphi, has as its primary aim to offer comfort to the tyrant in his illness. Its principal hero is Asclepius (Aesculapius), the physician so honored among the Greeks that he was called the son of Apollo. Its myth focuses on Coronis, Asclepius's mother, another mortal whose blind infatuation led to her destruction. While Pindar recounts how Apollo saved Asclepius, Coronis's unborn son, from death, he also tells how Asclepius, grown greedy for reward, oversteps his art by restoring a man to life and is punished — killed by Zeus's thunderbolt. What is Pindar's point in referring to these guilty human beings? Neither the myth of Coronis nor that of her physician-son is one likely to bring comfort to the grievously ill Hieron, however Pindar may insist at the outset of the ode that he wishes that Chiron or Asclepius yet lived to cure the tyrant.

Curiously, it is the references to Cadmus and Peleus that will unlock the meaning of the ode. Like Hieron, Cadmus and Peleus were the most blessed of rulers. Both won immortal brides; both heard the Muses sing at their weddings; both were showered with gifts from the gods for their piety and probity, but both came to grief and saw their children suffer. Even though Zeus Almighty visited the bed of Semele, Cadmus witnessed his daughter struck down. Although wed to the most beautiful of goddesses, Peleus saw his only son dead and mourned by the Danaans. The same Pindar who takes these heroes to the Isles of the Blest in

Olympian 2 leaves them stricken at the funeral pyre in Pythian 3. Death, he is telling us (and implicitly Hieron also) is inevitable. Even those most favored by the gods must tread the path of sorrow, for the life of the immortal gods is unattainable. For every gift granted, the gods offer two trials. A wise man accepts the life within his grasp, for the winds of change are variable. The only comfort that Pindar leaves to Hieron is that which he as poet he can confer. The poet's lyre celebrates heroes old and young. Lycian Sarpedon died young, while Nestor was granted long life: both were celebrated through song, as Pindar now celebrates his patron Hieron.

Pindar offers the fullest elegiac celebration of the hero Achilles in Isthmian 8, the ode for Cleandros of Aegina, composed probably in 479 or 478 B.C. at the close of the Persian Wars. The ode combines celebration and dirge, celebration for Cleandros's victory in the pancratium as well as for Greece's liberation from Persian oppression; dirge for Cleandros's cousin Nicocles, a former Isthmian victor fallen in battle, and lament for other Greeks dead in the wars. It is also a lament for the terrible war just concluded, in which Pindar as a Theban bore a double burden, since his native Thebes had been allied to the Persians.[9] The ode then marks the end of a particularly stressful period in Greek history, and this is reflected in the way Pindar commemorates what would otherwise be a celebratory occasion for the men of Aegina. Pindar opens with both an exhortation to the Aeginetan youth to proclaim Cleandros's victory and a call to his own Muse, though yet stricken at heart, to celebrate. The stone of Tantalus has been lifted, and it is time, he knows, to join in song and not to dwell in sorrow:

> ἐκ μεγάλων δὲ πενθέων λυθέντες
> μήτ᾽ ἐν ὀρφανίᾳ πέσωμεν στεφάνων,
> μήτε κάδεα θεράπευε (7–9)

> and freed from great pain,
> let us not fall bereft of garlands,
> nor fail to do service to our cares.

The principal myth concerns the wedding of Peleus and Thetis, an event that averted disaster from the gods. Zeus and Poseidon had been rivals for Thetis's love, but once warned by Themis that a son born of Thetis would be more powerful than his father, the gods wisely gave the sea-nymph in marriage to the mortal Peleus. Accordingly, Thetis's all-powerful offspring, Achilles, would attain great eminence as the strongest of mortals, but would suffer an untimely death.

The averting of disaster in myth as in history does not come without suffering for human beings. Pindar's treatment of the wedding of Peleus and Thetis in

---

[9] See Laura L. Nash, *The Aggelia in Pindar* (New York: Garland Publishing Co., 1990), 13–14. Nash comments upon the relationship between epinician and dirge in this ode.

Isthmian 8 is more equivocal than it is in the other odes that allude to it, Nemeans 3, 4, and 5. As a result of the wedding, a battle hero is born, who brings saving grace to the Achaians but himself suffers early death. Like the Greeks of Pindar's time who fought at Salamis and Marathon, Achilles is the bulwark for his comrades against destruction. He severed, Pindar tells us, the sinews of Troy; he rescued Helen; he forged a safe return for the sons of Atreus. Pindar does not shrink from describing the bloody accomplishments of Achilles in battle: how he cut down Telephus, Hector, and Memnon, and sent other heroes to the house of Persephone. Yet at the same time he connects Achilles' battle accomplishments with Cleandros's athletic victories. Just as Achilles brought fame to the house of Aeacus, so Cleandros has won fame for modern Aeacids by his victory in the contests at the Isthmus. [10]

One of the extraordinary features of Pindar's mythmaking is that he can use allusive references so fluidly. He does not specifically connect Cleandros with Achilles nor with Achilles' happier father Peleus, whose joyous wedding would seem the logical event to connect metaphorically with Cleandros's happy victory. It is for us, Pindar's audience, to make the connections. So when he comes at the end of the ode to remember Cleandros's cousin Nicocles—a previous Isthmian victor—slain in the wars, he turns his audience from viewing the victorious Achilles in the living Cleandros to seeing the dead hero in Cleandros's dead cousin. Pindar accomplishes this by referring to the dirge for Achilles—a passage that contrasts remarkably with that in Pythian 3, written a few years later, in which Pindar describes how the Danaans lament their fallen comrade. Here, however, it is the Muses who stand at Achilles' bier. Not even when he was dead, Pindar tells us, did song desert Achilles. Instinctively we recall at this moment how Pindar began the ode with a reluctant appeal to the Muse to sing though his heart was heavy with grief. Song is a necessary healing part of life: the Muses make tolerable what otherwise would be intolerable. So at the conclusion of the ode, Pindar tells us how the Heliconian maidens stood close about the funeral pyre of Achilles, pouring out their polyphonous melodies. Not even in death do the Muses desert a good man.

With this simple reference to the fallen warrior Pindar makes a transition to Nicocles, another young man fallen for his comrades, whom he has included by implication in the dirge for Achilles. The Muses hasten in their chariot to remember, Pindar tells us, Nicocles' former boxing victory. So Pindar intertwines the celebration of Nicocles with that of Cleandros, two cousins from Aegina, who call to remembrance perhaps two other cousins, the greatest of mythic

---

[10] See Gregory Nagy, *Pindar's Homer: The Lyric Possession of an Epic Past* (Baltimore: Johns Hopkins University Press, 1990), 204–5. Nagy remarks not only on the links between Nicocles and Achilles, but also on the celebration of the glory of ancient heroes that is evident in the names of these two cousins: Nicocles (*kleos nikê*, glory in victory) and Cleandros (*klea andrôn*, glories of men).

heroes—Achilles and Ajax—who were also Aeacids and whose achievements Pindar had many times recalled together (Isthmian 7.30; Nemean 7.27).[11] Again Pindar is simple and direct; he merely tells us that Cleandros's victory did not disgrace that of his father's brother's son. The ode concludes, of course, with choruses of celebration, as Pindar calls back those youths whom he had summoned at the beginning of the ode to encircle Cleandros's head with myrtle and to welcome him with song. The ode pays tribute to all young men, living and dead, who did not hide their excellences and who performed deeds worthy of fame. Isthmian 8 is extraordinary for the way in which the poet deals with and balances suffering with joy, death with life. Though it is not a funeral poem for a fallen hero, though it is not a commemoration of the dead of the Persian Wars, the extent of Pindar's accomplishment is that it could have been both.

In the funeral odes that early modern poets create for fallen heroes, young and old, celebration and dirge are often movingly joined. That many poets include in their odes tributes to mythic heroes such as the great Achilles as they mourn their own dead is just another sign of Pindar's subtle but profound effect on the genre of ode-elegy in the Renaissance.

2.

Monody, the ode for a single voice, was one of the poetic forms that Renaissance poets were experimenting with in the fifteenth and sixteenth centuries, a form that has affinity with the choral odes of Pindar that they were discovering at the same time.[12] Monody was sometimes, though not always, used for a funeral song.[13] It is certainly a funeral song, however, in the brief monody that Angelo Poliziano composed for Lorenzo de' Medici. Even though he is not usually ranked as a Pindaric imitator, Poliziano knew Pindar and his odes and he uses some of Pindar's techniques in his monody. In the first stanza Poliziano adapts the invocation to the Muses and uses a striking figure reminiscent of Pindar's. He also employs short lines that replicate the pattern of short verses in the printed texts of Pindar's odes. He begins the monody by invoking a chorus

---

[11] See Segal, "Pindar's Seventh *Nemean*," in *Aglaia*, 185–227, here 213.

[12] Both Scaliger and Puttenham define monody as a funeral song. Scaliger puts it simply: "Etiam monodia dictus cantus lugubris." Puttenham goes further to call it a funeral song for a single voice: "Such funerall songs were called *Epicedia* if they were song by many, and *Monodia* if they were vttered by one alone": see J. C. Scaliger, *Poetices Libri Septem* (1581), 129; [George Puttenham], *The Arte of English Poesie* (London: Richard Field, 1589), 39. For monody as a musical term see Nigel Fortune and Tim Carter, "Monody," in *The New Grove Dictionary of Music and Musicians*, 17:5–6.

[13] See, for example, the monodies on different subjects that Pietro Crinito composed: *Poematum Libri Duo* (Paris, 1508).

of nymphs and Muses and by evoking for the dead Lorenzo the shattered laurel: "Laurus impetu fulminis, / Illa illa iacet subito" (The very laurel lies fallen after the sudden stroke of lightning). Echoing the Vulgate version of Jeremiah 9:1 ("Quis dabit capiti meo aquam et oculis meis fontem lacrimarum, et plorabo die et nocte"), Poliziano expresses his grief by depicting tears as water from an ever-flowing fountain:

> Quis dabit capiti meo
> Aquam? quis oculis meis
> Fontem lachrymarum dabit?
> Vt nocte fleam,
> Vt luce fleam.
> Sic turtur uiduus solet,
> Sic cycnus moriens solet,
> Sic luscinia conqueri.
> Heu miser, miser.
> O dolor, dolor.

> Who will pour water on my head? Who will give my eyes
> a fountain of tears, that I may weep by night, that I may weep
> by day? So the widowed turtledove, so the dying swan, so the
> nightingale invariably laments. Alas wretched, wretched!
> Oh grief, grief! (285)[14]

In the second strophe Poliziano reverses his effects: the Muses' and nymphs' choruses as well as the sound of Phoebus's lyre are mute. Although Poliziano's monody is only two strophes in length, it looks forward to the more complicated funeral odes that pindarists of the next century would develop.

As the first important Pindaric imitator, Benedetto Lampridio saw the potential in Pindar's odes for threnody as well as exultation. Some of Lampridio's funeral pindarics, such as the funera for Cardinal Sedunensis or the consolatory verses to Bembo on the death of his son, are simple dirges.[15] Others are more

---

[14] In *An Anthology of Neo-Latin Poetry*, ed. and trans. Fred Nichols (New Haven: Yale University Press, 1979), 284–85.

[15] For Lampridio's poetry see *Carmina* (Venice, 1550). The ode for the Cardinal Sedunensis praises his virtue, laments his loss to Rome, and rejoices in his translation to heaven. Lampridio makes a quasi-Pindaric aside that vice will flourish (alas) now that the cardinal is gone (fols. 10^V–11^r). The ode for Pietro Bembo is addressed to the grieving parent whom Lampridio consoles for the death of his son. The boy is snatched away to the kingdom of Pluto and Persephone, leaving behind the father bereft not only of his son, but also of song. Lampridio consoles Bembo by depicting the boy playing in a classical-Christian Elysium with his hair wreathed with flowers, listening to the songs of Linus and Orpheus. He closes with a Catullan hail and farewell (fols. 52^V–54^r). Lampridio's lament for Marc-Antonio Colonna (fol. 14^r–v), his verses to Pietro Mellini on the death of

elaborate philosophical odes that also include tributes to the dead, such as the ode, "Scilicet superbat" (fols. 40^r–44^v), composed for the doge of Genoa, which laments the death of the doge's brother, Gerolamo Adorno (1483–1523).[16] Still others, such as the odes for Vittoria Colonna and Pietro Mellini, reach beyond the occasion that prompts them and succeed, like Pindar's own odes, in being both celebratory and elegiac.

Lampridio's long ode for Pietro Mellini is exactly that: "In Petri Melini Villam, vbi ille Poetas de More Familiae coena exciperat" (On Pietro Mellini's Villa, where he received the poets for dinner according to the custom of the family). Pietro Mellini, a prominent citizen of Rome and a scion of the wealthy Mellini family, was the principal figure in one of the sodalities of poets and scholars that flourished in Rome in the early sixteenth century under Leo X.[17] To pay tribute to Pietro, Lampridio adopts the device of describing Pietro's villa as a *locus amoenus* where the Muses dwell. He not only celebrates his patron Pietro, but also, like Pindar, includes the family from which he sprang—his father, mother, and brother, and also his second wife and his prospective heir. By alluding to Pietro's recent marriage, Lampridio expresses the hope that the Mellini family will continue and thrive. Although basically a joyous ode, it contains at its center a lament for Celso Mellini, Pietro's brother, a promising poet as well as a pillar of the sodality of poets in Rome, whose sudden, early death had shocked the community of literati. The lament for Celso is as integral to this ode as Pindar's lament for Nicocles had been to the ode for Cleandros.

Celso (fols. 14^v–15^r), and his ode on Ercole Rangoni (fol. 18$^{r–v}$) offer sympathy on the deaths of close relatives or friends.

[16] The ode is almost a general lament for the human condition, of virtue unrewarded on earth, with the fate of Adorno furnishing only one particular case of this truism. Lampridio borrows a technique from Pindar and delays mention of Adorno, a friend to and patron of poets, until the end of the third epode. He not only uses illustrations from classical myth (how the double-yoked horses bore Hector away and how Camillus was sent beyond the river of Hades), but also alludes to the contemporary tragedy of an Italy devastated by war. The death of Adorno deprived Italy of a wise counselor, who served Charles V and had been attempting to forge an alliance of Genoa with Ferrara and Venice against the French.

[17] On the Mellini family see Gasparo Alveri, *Roma in ogni stato* (Rome, 1664), 2: 44–57. Alveri traces the family from the thirteenth through the sixteenth century, alluding to its ancient Roman roots. Particularly helpful is his citing of legal documents involving the Mellini—wills, marriage contracts—as well as the funeral monuments in Santa Maria del Popolo. Also see Domenico Gnoli, *La Roma di Leone X* (Milan: Ulrico Hoepli, 1938), 355–84; Carlo Cecchelli, *Le Grandi Famiglie Romane* (Rome: Reale Instituto di Studi Romani, 1946), 39–49. Also see S. P. Revard, "Lampridio and the Poetic Sodalities in Rome in the 1510s and 1520s," in *Acta Conventus Neo-Latini Bariensis*, ed. R. Schnur et al., MRTS 184 (Tempe, AZ: ACMRS, 1998), 499–507, here 502–4.

To celebrate Pietro and his villa Lampridio alludes to classical *loci amoeni*. The poets who frequent the villa are the race of Phoebus and the villa itself a veritable garden of the Hesperides, a temperate paradise like Pindar's Isles of the Blest, where no wintry blasts come and spring flowers bloom, more numerous than the sands of Libya or the waves of the Adriatic. The poet's mistress Neaera or her mythic counterpart dwells with nymphs and goddesses in this pleasurable place, and here the poets sing sweet tunes to the lyre in its praise. Venus herself would have chosen such an idyllic retreat when she carried off her lover Adonis, and here also Hylas, Hercules' favorite, might have dwelt. Despite the garden's graceful surroundings and the poetic festivities it encourages, tragedy lurks here.

Allusion to youths such as Adonis and Hylas who died young cannot fail to recall Celso Mellini, long before Lampridio ever refers directly to Pietro's dead brother.[18] But instead of alluding to Celso, Lampridio embarks on a narration of the Mellini's illustrious forebears: he cites the marriage of Mario, Celso's and Pietro's father, to the niece of Pope Innocent VIII, and the happy birth of the young man. With the mention of Celso's birth, Lampridio suddenly breaks off, overcome by the memory of loss:

> Eheu Camoenae quò rapitis, memor
> Luctum mens iterat, dolore soluor
> Rursum. Truces eheu fuistis
> Parcae nimis, semper truces. (fol. 35ʳ)[19]

> Alas, Muses, how you are carrying me away? My remembering
> Mind, brought back to sorrow, dissolves in grief,
> Alas, you are savage,
> Fates, too much so, always savage.

At this strategic point Lampridio remembers—or more appropriately signals his failure up to this point to remember—Celso's death a death, which had overwhelmed with grief the family and the literary circles in Rome. Surely, however, Lampridio's Roman audience had already recognized, as he narrated how Venus grieved for Adonis or Hercules for Hylas, that the subtext of these myths was sorrow for the dead Celso. In fact, the consolatory movement had already begun tacitly when Lampridio told how Jove consoled Venus and revived Adonis.

It now becomes apparent that the ode has all along had a dual purpose: to honor Pietro and to remember Celso. It also becomes possible now for the poet to praise Celso properly and properly to lament his death. Lampridio decries the instability of Fortune, the savagery of the Fates; he describes the gloom of the

---

[18] See Alveri, *Roma in ogni stato*, 2:51–52.
[19] A possible allusion to Horace, *Carmina* 3.25. 1–2.

Tartarean regions that may hold Celso, the fearsomeness of iron Pluto and the Furies. Lampridio laments how the harsh season has killed the early crocus, the early flowering of Celso's genius. Then, like many a poet before and after him, he looks to the return of spring that both comforts but also deludes. The young man will not return with the spring flowers. Besides these conventional elegiac motifs, there are touches that are inventively Pindaric. Lampridio recounts how the news of Celso's death came to Pope Leo, who had honored Celso previously by conferring the poetic laurel, but who had been unable to save him.[20] He remembers how Celso gave the first fruits of his wit to his country. No description of the villa as a place where the gods of poetry dwell could exclude remembrance of Celso's poetry; no celebration of Pietro, as a friend to poets and a poet himself, could fail to recollect Celso's poetic performances. Lampridio even manages to allude to the poetic festivities that took place there in such a fashion as to make them almost equivalents of winning athletic victories. Pietro is described as an Olympic victor who has managed his horses and chariot so well that he had gone twice past the turning post.

Among the myths alluded to in Lampridio's ode is the myth of Castor and Pollux, a myth that Pindar himself had so effectively employed at the end of Nemean 10. Pindar had recounted how Idas and Lynceus had ambushed Castor and wounded him grievously. Castor's brother Polydeuces pursues them and crushes Lynceus, while Zeus, defending his son, destroys Idas with a thunderbolt. Polydeuces returns to find Castor breathing out his last breath. Weeping and groaning, he calls out to Zeus to let him die with his brother, for honor dies when one is bereft of one's friends. Pitying his son, Zeus permits Polydeuces to share Castor's fate, dwelling with him half the year in Hades, but dwelling in heaven for the rest. So in Pindar's ode Zeus restores Castor to life and the ode ends.

Lampridio obviously knew Nemean 10, for he recounts how Pietro, just like Pindar's Polydeuces, calls out for Celso with a solitary voice, eager to redeem his brother when he was about to be deprived of him. Alluding to the myth, he tells too how Jupiter, when he heard Polydeuces swear that his brother was dearer to him than life, assented to honor the two. In adapting the myth, Lampridio mediates between a classical and a Christian consolation, pronouncing that Celso yet lives in Pietro, but also survives in his art. Through the grace of Apollo and the Muses, Lampridio adds, Celso has immortality in his poetry: whoever has been faithful to the altars of the Muses cannot perish. The lyre will remember

---

[20] In 1519 Celso was drowned in a flash flood, and after Celso's death the pope had a bridge constructed at the site of Celso's drowning that was posted with verses commending the young poet. Celso's death is described in Pierio Valeriano's dialogue *De litterorum infelicitate*; one of the interlocutors of the dialogue is Celso's brother Pietro. See Julia Haig Gaisser, *Pierio Valeriano on the Ill Fortune of Learned Men: A Renaissance Humanist and His World* (Ann Arbor: University of Michigan Press, 1999), 35–36, 62–65; also 39–40, 47–48, 309.

how he struck melodies—and Apollo will remember too. Whom, other than Celso, did Apollo love more?

The ode, of course, is not just a lament for Celso. At the end Lampridio returns to praise of Pietro and to celebration of his Apollonian villa. He also expresses the hope that Pietro's wife Hersilia will give birth to a new Mellini, to be named Mario for Pietro's and Celso's father. Implicit in the wish is the tacit recognition that the future child will also take the place of the dead brother, the Celso-Castor of the poem.[21] The ode concludes on a celebratory note with several witty mythic comparisons. Pietro is likened to Chiron, who in his cave extends cups of wine to his guests, but he is also likened to Ulysses who offers the Cyclops sweet drink. Finally, like a Bacchic celebrant, Pietro strikes the ground with his foot to the accompaniment of the pipe.[22] This reference to Bacchic merriment brings the ode back to its initial purpose—to celebrate Pietro and his brother and the villa where they entertained their fellow poets. It also fulfills the "Pindaric" requirement that the ode conclude with a graceful compliment to the addressee and his family.

Poetry also serves as a unifying motif in Lampridio's ode to Vittoria Colonna (fols. 54^r–57^r). Like the Mellini ode, it is both a celebration of the living Vittoria and a dirge for her dead husband, Ferrante Francesco D'Avalos, the Marchese of Pescara, an Italian military leader who had served Charles V and was victor at the battle of Pavia. At least half the ode concerns the Marchese, who had died of wounds in Milan in 1525 when Vittoria was on her way to tend him. The other half celebrates Vittoria's accomplishments as a poet and celebrator of her husband's virtues, a woman who was both poet and Muse. Lampridio's ode concerns a particularly Pindaric theme: the responsibility of the poet to redeem the memory of great men from oblivion, to preserve their glory in verse. He opens the ode by directing his song to the island of Ischia, where Vittoria holds sway, grieving, as it were, at the funeral pyre of her husband.

Although the ode laments D'Avalos' death, it also has a political subtext in commemorating the Marchese's victories in battle, cataloguing them in a cumulative sequence, almost as though they were the athletic victories of a Pindaric ode. Lampridio names the battle of Pavia as D'Avalos' crowning achievement, for at Pavia the Marchese with his brilliant tactics succeeded in defeating the French forces under François I, even as he sustained the wound that cost him his life. It is a fateful encounter, for, as Lampridio tells us, the powerful king François I had made his way across the Alps with his Gallic warriors in order to encounter D'Avalos' forces at Pavia. Lampridio in a sense recreates the battle for

---

[21] The marriage to Ersilia Caffarelli (the Hersilia of Lampridio's ode) took place in February 1521 and was the second marriage for Pietro; his first wife had died earlier. Specified in the marriage contract was that the first son should be named Mario after Pietro's father. Mario Mellini died in 1523. See Alveri, *Roma in ogni stato*, 2:51–53.

[22] A possible reference to Horace, *Carmina* 1.37. 1–2.

us, consistently employing the machinery of classical epic and keeping metaphors of war close at hand, as he describes how the forces met shield against shield and hurled their lances. He repeatedly identifies D'Avalos with Pindar's favorite hero, Achilles, describing how the Marchese's war cry resounded over the battlefield, giving comfort to friends and striking terror into the hearts of enemies. The very god of war, Mars, is astonished to see the Marchese rushing against the enemy on his swift horse. Lampridio even echoes Pindar's epic list of Achilles' victories: his slaying of Cycnus, of Memnon, of Hector. So the epinician elegy proceeds, celebrating the Marchese's accomplishments in war until Lampridio at last remembers that it is not the Marchese alone who is the subject for his lyre, but also the surviving Vittoria.

Vittoria is not only the grieving widow of D'Avalos but also the daughter of the celebrated general Fabrizio Colonna, a noblewoman sprung from one of the most important families in Rome. Only after he has distinguished her as wife and daughter, however, does Lampridio award Vittoria the proper poetic laurels. Even then he marks her as the poet-wife, whose first responsibility is to honor her dead husband, the new hero-god, and snatch his fleeting fame from the jaws of devouring Orcus. Generously, however, Lampridio says that no poet, male or female, ever more fittingly celebrated great men unless it was the *vates* who remembered the Atrides in death.

Adopting the model of the epinician ode, Lampridio celebrates Vittoria by recapitulating her excellence. Primarily, however, he uses a tactic that encomiasts employed to compliment noblewomen, be they queens, duchesses, or mere marchionesses, as Vittoria was. Vittoria is praised as a goddess, who is no less than divine in her virtue and in her beauty. She is so chaste, so modest, so gracious that she must be a companion of the nymphs, of Venus, of the Graces themselves. Lampridio equates Vittoria with the goddess of wisdom, and only at the last does he remember her status as poet and add one more title, the tenth Muse. It was a title that Phoebus reportedly had conferred on Sappho in antiquity. Just a generation before, Poliziano had used similar terms to laud the precocious Alessandra Scala, the Florentine poet-wife of Michele Marullo. In its final phrase the ode to Vittoria takes on the characteristics of a cult hymn. Employing the techniques, the devices, even the epithets usually reserved in the cult hymn for the goddess, Lampridio even bids farewell to Vittoria with the hymnic "salve" and promises like a devotee to remember her again in song.[23] In combining an epinician elegy for the Marchese of Pescara with a hymnic epinician for his Marchioness, Lampridio's ode is an extraordinary example of the manipulation for special effect of the Pindaric mode.

The poet and literary critic Antonio Sebastiano Minturno also composed a canzone on D'Avalos' death, one which was quite possibly influenced by Lam-

---

[23] See the discussion of the cult hymn in Revard, *Pindar and the Renaissance Hymn-Ode*, chap. 3.

pridio's ode to Vittoria Colonna. Although not in triads, Minturno's canzone has affinities with the contemporary pindaric, as Minturno argues in *L'Arte Poetica*, providing the theoretical justification for the kind of ode he and Lampridio had composed. Minturno argues that Italian canzone and Greek triadic ode possess similar poetic qualities and serve similar purposes. Both could address a variety of occasions and speak to great men and women. While Minturno's canzone praises the deceased Marchese, it also reflects on the poetical and political climate of Italy, declined from the golden into a silver age. The cause of such decline, he reflects, is the loss of noble personages such as the Marchese, who had been the mirror of his age. To praise the Marchese Minturno adopts the techniques of Pindar's odes and compares the Marchese's deeds to those of Hercules and Aeneas, using a chorus of Muses as well to narrate the Marchese's glorious deeds.[24] The wars in Italy in which the Marchese fell he compares, moreover, to the bloody Theban civil wars. As Minturno explains, the example of Pindar's odes helped poets to extend the range and refine the poetics of sixteenth-century poetry.

3

Prominent among the poems in the posthumous works of the talented Dutch neo-Latin poet Joannes Secundus (1511–1535) is a monody on the death of Thomas More, Henry VIII's erstwhile chancellor, the defender of the pope's authority after Henry's break with the Pope, and a martyr to the cause of Catholicism in England.[25] Secundus is usually thought of as an Ovidian elegist rather than a pindarist, but he was not unaffected by the Pindaric experiments going on in his own time. Contemporary poets and critics claimed for him the Pindaric mantle.[26] Secundus's monody for More employs odic techniques and has an intellectual range and authority that justify its placement among the Pindaric imitations

---

[24] Minturno includes the canzone for D'Avalos among his imitations of ancient lyric: see "Nella Morte del Marchese di Pescara" in *Rime et Prose del Sig. Antonio Minturno* (1559), 158–65, He refers to its Pindaric techniques in *L'Arte Poetica del Sig. Antonio Minturno*, 177. Also see Calderisi's discussion of the canzone in *Antonio Sebastiano Minturno*, 67–72.

[25] Originally attributed to Erasmus, the poem (written in hexameters) was called a "carmen heroicum" at its first printing in 1536. It does not appear in the works of Secundus until 1582: *Poetae Tres Elegantissimi* (Paris, 1582), fols. 163^v–166^r, where it is called a monody and placed at the end of the *Liber Sylvarum*. Scriverius includes it with Secundus's epitaph on More among the funera in 1619 edition and calls it a naenia. See André Blanchard, "Jean Second et ses poèmes sur l'exécution de Thomas More," *Moreana* 36 (1972): 1–32.

[26] See the discussion of the testimonia for Secundus, included in various editions of his works, in Revard, *Pindar and the Renaissance Hymn-Ode*, 151.

of the early sixteenth century. Unlike the monody that Poliziano composed for Lorenzo de' Medici, Secundus's monody is more than a funeral song. In embarking on a complex examination of human motivation, it undertakes, like Pindaric ode, to combine lyrical expression with philosophical investigation. It is also a poet's tribute to another poet, which invokes the Muses to lament the poet's fall. Plucking the poetic laurel, Secundus places it ceremonially on More's tomb in honor of laurel-bearing poets and in token of the fitness of one poet doing honor to another—"vatem canimus vates" (19).[27]

Like the pindarics of Lampridio and Minturno, Secundus's monody is both a dirge for the dead and a commentary on the age that countenanced such a sacrifice. Secundus not only laments the death of More—the humanist, the poet, and the martyr for his religion—but also decries the injustice of More's execution at the hands of Henry VIII. He indicts Henry for his crimes and laments the injustices of Fortune and the savagery of Venus and the Furies who incited Henry. Enrolling More among those martyrs who died defending justice and religion, he also remembers the recent martyrdom of John Fisher, the bishop of Rochester. While Secundus draws on both classical and contemporary traditions to frame a formal lament for the dead, he takes care to investigate intellectually the causes, both human and cosmic, for More's death.

Although Secundus eschews extended myth and uses classical machinery sparingly, he makes use of digressive techniques and includes a considerable amount of narration in the monody. He recounts More's death and his entry into heaven, and correspondingly frames a parallel narrative that predicts Henry VIII's future punishment in Hell for his bloody deed. He sets the scene by telling how the Furies rise from the shades of Erebus to spur Henry on. The king, having put away his lawful wife, shares his bed with a vile concubine, planning his new marriage. Never dignifying Anne Boleyn by name, Secundus blames her for misleading the king and exults that she too will be punished. In contrast, Catherine of Aragon is depicted as the descendant of the great Ferdinand, a woeful queen who now leads an unhappy life. Although the Furies exult at the new marriage and Venus triumphs, Secundus does not blame supernatural forces, but the king himself, who has defied law in divorcing his legitimate wife, has outraged religion in usurping the title Pontifex (properly belonging to the pope), and finally has violated all morality by condemning to death an innocent man.

Now turning to More, Secundus comments how More has ironically been undone by his own virtue: "More infelix, sic te tua virtus / Perdidit? o, aevi scelus atque infamia nostri" (Unhappy More, thus has your virtue betrayed you? O the crime and infamy of our age) (74–75). With graphic detail he describes the bloody execution: More's head falls, rivers of purple stain his breast. However, at the same moment, Secundus assures us, the kingdom of heaven opens to receive

---

[27] The poem, "Naenia, in mortem eiusdem," is cited from the version in Ioannes Secundus, *Opera quae reperiri potuerunt omnia* (Leiden, 1619), 231–36.

More's soul, while the angels sing paeans in his praise. Secundus cannot resist reminding us that the martyred More is also a poet: the inhabitants of heaven, all dressed in white, resemble the swans on the Meander as they applaud the poet.

> Quales ad vitreum Maeandri flumen olores
> Mille volant, plauduntque alis, et dulce canentes
> Caeruleum nitidis praetexunt aethera pennis (95–97).

> So to the clear stream of Maeander
> a thousand swans fly and, sweetly singing,
> flap their wings and cover the blue sky with their brilliant plumes.

Turning from this scene of celestial triumph, Secundus does not shrink from describing how the king dishonors the head of More, placing it upon a spike and delivering it as a spectacle to the mob. He condoles the grief of More's daughter Margaret who, however comforted she might be by the rewards of eternal fame that await her father, weeps as she views his bloody body. Secundus lauds her also as a poet, loved by Phoebus and included among the sorority of the Muses by Calliope.

Secundus achieves vividness by addressing a number of persons directly. He addresses the dead More with a Vergilian appellation as a fortunate old man (*Eclogue* 1.46). In contrast, he upbraids the wicked concubine Anne and warns her of future consequences. Tenderly he comfort More's weeping daughter Margaret, also addressing her directly. Finally, he calls upon the king in direct address, asking him ironically if he exults now in this so-called trophy of Venus or if he thinks thus to placate heaven: "Hocne tuae Veneri, rex ô incoeste, tropaeum / Erigis? & mollem placari sanguine Divam / Posse putas?" (124–126). Even Venus in anger turns aside from Henry, who too late mourns for his just counselor and regrets the unjust murder. With a certain Pindaric flourish Secundus invokes a classical example, that of Alexander, who succumbed to rage when heated by wine and killed his comrade Clitus, only to regret his deed and wish to follow his friend into the kingdom of the shades. Henry too will be haunted in his dreams by the ghost of the murdered man. The gods may delay punishment for such a crime, but ultimately no one escapes their justice.

Throughout the monody, Secundus has interjected brief passages of moral commentary. He at first calls into question but finally vindicates divine justice, assuring his readers that God will punish wrongdoers and will reward the good. In the final passage of the monody Secundus turns once more to More—"ô, bone vates . . . verende Senex" (O good poet . . . reverend old man [157, 161]), bidding him hail and farewell and asking him to accept graciously this poetic labor in his behalf. Almost in anticipation of More's future elevation to sainthood, he asserts that mortals owe him a divine "cultus" for having undergone a cruel death for religion—"tibi templa, tibi aras" (for you the temple, for you the altar

[160]). However, Secundus's monody, like Milton's monody "Lycidas," is essentially one poet's celebration of another. With its digressive narratives, its use of classical figures, and its moralizing addresses, it imitates Pindaric ode, broadening the model of the funeral poem.

4.

As the foremost pindarist in France and an experimenter in different types of odes, Ronsard might well have been expected to exploit Pindaric techniques in his funeral elegies and epitaphs, as he had in his hymns. Many of the same figures for whom he had composed odes and hymns he also celebrates in epitaphs: Marguerite, Duchess of Savoy; François II; Anne, Duc de Montmorency; François de Bourbon. He had, in fact, written one of his earliest Pindaric odes for François de Bourbon's victory at Cerisoles in 1544 (1.6), an ode in which he repeatedly employs Pindar's figures and echoes Pindaric *sententiae*.[28] This same ode affirms the Pindaric conviction that the lyre must not only celebrate the victories of living men, but must also remember to do honor to the dead. Ronsard goes so far as to imitate, in final antistrophe and epode, a typical Pindaric device—he announces the news of François' victory to his dead uncles Charles and Pierre. He also closes the ode with a typical Pindaric observation, that human joys are transitory and that only the gods live free from adversity. The funeral epitaph that he later wrote for François is also Pindaric, for Ronsard expresses the Pindaric sentiment that a man's deeds on earth foster his renown after death.[29] François' military accomplishments are to be his memorial. In this regard perhaps François' victory at Cerisoles and the ode Ronsard wrote for it prove to be the true Pindaric epitaph.

Ronsard frequently echoes Pindar's sentiments on the responsibility of the poet properly to memorialize the dead. His verses to René D'Urvoy (4.17), although neither an epitaph nor a triadic ode, are Pindaric and open with an adaptation of Pindar's lines from Nemean 5:

> Je n'ay pas les mains apprises
> Au mestier muet de ceux
> Qui font une image assise

---

[28] For discussion of the Pindaric elements of Ronsard's ode see Guy Demerson, "À l'origine du lyrisme de louange: la victoire de François de Bourbon à Cérisoles (I, 5)," in *Lire Les Odes de Ronsard*, ed. Dominique Bertrand (Clermont-Ferrand: Presses Universitaires Blaise Pascal, 2002), 47–62.

[29] See "Epitaphe de François de Bourbon, Comte d'Anguien," in Ronsard, *Oeuvres Complètes*, ed. Jean Céard, Danniel Ménager, and Michel Simonin (Paris: Librairie Gallimard, 1993), 2: 915–16.

Sur des piliers paresseux (4.17. 1–4).

I do not have hands set to
the silent craft of those
who make an image
seated on motionless pillars.

Like Pindar, Ronsard asserts that verse is superior to marble in memorializing the dead; its letters, though not engraved in stone, live and hence have the power to make the dead live. He also takes from Pindar the example of the great Hector, whose memory would not survive had verse not revived it and carried it through the universe. Even Achilles' plumes would be drowned—and so also a thousand other excellences and honors that the Muse guards:

C'est la Muse qui engarde
Les bons de ne mourir pas,
Et qui nos talons retarde
Pour ne devaller là bas.
La Muse l'enfer desfie,
Seule nous eleve aux Cieux,
Seule nous donne la vie
Et nous met au rang des Dieux.
(4.17.57–64)

It is the Muse who saves
good things from dying
and who delays our heels
from rushing there below.
The Muse defies Hell,
Alone lifts us to the skies,
Alone gives us life
And places us in the ranks of Gods.

Although the closing sentiments voice legitimately Pindaric claims, they also ring with the familiar Ronsardian boast—that poetry assures the immortality of the poet himself.[30]

---

[30] Epitaphs for fellow poets have a special place in Ronsard's poetry. He composed an epitaph for the fifteenth-century Florentine poet Michele Marullo, which resembles the graceful elegies that Pontano and Crinito had previously composed for Marullo. Ronsard creates the vision of the poet in the classical shades of Elysium: "Dessus les rives Elyseés, / Et sous l'ombre des Myrtes vers / Au bruit des eaux chante ses vers / Entre les ames bien priseés (Beside the Elysian shores / And under the shadow of the green myrtle, / To the sound of waters [he] sings these verses / Among the blessed souls). In this setting the Muses arrive to sing for Marullo, leading a dance to the sound of the lyre and

The most Pindaric of Ronsard's epitaphs is the one that he composed in 1574 after the death of the young King Charles IX: "Tombeau de Feu Roy Tres-Chrestien Charles Neufiesme" (2: 898–901). Rich in mythic allusions, it depicts the young prince as a Hercules, having manifested early the attributes of the Greek hero and strangled seditious serpents in his cradle: "Toutefois au besoin, sa vertu n'a failli. / Il se vit au berceau des serpens assaili / Comme un jeune Herculin, dont il rompit la force" (43–45) (Always, in need, his virtue did not fail; in his cradle he viewed the assailing serpents like a young Hercules, whose strength he employed).[31] Later this Herculean prince took on the Titans, Ronsard's name for the "heretic" Huguenots, whom Charles resisted and conquered in several battles in the 1560s.[32]

> Puis, quand la tendre barbe au menton se renforce,
> Que l'âge et la vertu s'accroissent par le temps,
> Il se vit assailli des superbes Titans,
> Qui combatoyent ce Prince en ses propres entrailles,
> Qu'à la fin il veinquit par quatres grans batailles.
> Il eut le coeur si ferme et si digne d'un Roy,
> Que combatant pour Dieu, pour l'Eglise et la Foy. (46–52)

> Then when the tender beard appeared on his chin,
> When age and virtue had come into their own,
> He was attacked by the proud Titans,
> Who combated this Prince in his own entrails,
> Which finally he vanquished in four great battles.
> He had a heart firm and worthy of a king,
> Who fought for God, for the Church, and for the Faith.

To complete the résumé of Charles's brief reign, Ronsard lists his military exploits, comparing him to Alexander, who achieved early fame but died young. Ronsard's most striking use of Pindar comes at the close of the ode when he adopts the Castor-Pollux comparison to mark the passing of one divine star and the rising of another—Charles's demise and Henri's ascent. To celebrate the succession, Ronsard, like Lampridio, echoes Nemean 10, adapting Pollux's

---

escorting the love poets of antiquity—Tibullus, Ovid, Propertius—who come in company with their mistresses—Delia, Corinna, Cynthia. As Ronsard bestows green laurels, fresh lilies and roses, he directly addresses Marullo—"Chere Ame"—and invokes the classical formula that the earth lie lightly on him. See the discussion of Marullo's influence on Ronsard in Revard, *Pindar and the Renaissance Hymn-Ode, passim.*

[31] Ronsard, *Oeuvres Complètes,* 2: 898–901.

[32] See the discussion of Charles's and Henri's wars against the Protestants in chap. 2 above. The St. Bartholomew's Massacre might be viewed as the final crushing of the Titans.

prayer to Zeus for his own address to the dead Charles. Charles may rest secure, the poet tells him, knowing that his brother reigns on earth:

> Et toy, divin Esprit, qui la France regarde,
> Qui as soin de ses maux et les prens sous ta garde,
> Comme Astre des Valois, pour tousjours luy verser
> Un bon-heur, et jamais, heureus, ne la laisser
> Resjouys loy là-haut et sereines ta face,
> Dequoy Castor, ton frere, est regnant en ta place,
> Qui par succession, est maistre de ton lieu:
> Un Dieu doit heriter à Empire d'un Dieu.
> (ll. 165–172)

> And you, divine spirit who looks after France,
> Who has care for her ills and takes her under your protection,
> As the Star of the Valois—in order to pour forth for her always
> A happiness, and always, happy, not to leave her—
> Rejoice above and serene of face,
> Just as Castor, your brother, is reigning in your place,
> Who by succession is master of your place.
> A god must inherit the empire of a god.

Ronsard places his address to Charles climactically at the end of the epitaph to affirm the eternity of rule that the brothers share and to offer consolation to France for the loss of its young "god." One hundred years later Pindar's Castor-Pollux myth served an English pindarist to compare two kingly brothers, Charles II and James, to the pair of heavenly twins, one succeeding the other:

> A faithful Pollux He, a Castor You;
> And now deceas'd are like those Brothers too.
> For two Propitious Stars in Heaven You Reign,
> You the lesser Bear, He Charles's Wain. (6)[33]

English history, like French history, afforded Pindaric apologists opportunity to remark on the tragic likenesses between its kings and the mythic twins of Pindar's Nemean 10.

5.

To conclude this overview of the Pindaric ode-elegy as it developed on the continent, I wish to look at three odes composed by two practitioners of the genre who followed in the footsteps of Ronsard. The first two odes are by Scévole de

---

[33] *An Historical Poem upon his Late Majesty King James II* (London, 1701), 1–9.

Sainte-Marthe (1536–1623), the poet-politician who was extravagantly praised by Ronsard and who composed both a dirge for Ronsard as France's premier pindarist and an ode-elegy for one of Henri III's ministers. The third ode is an ode-elegy for Sainte-Marthe himself by Daniel Heinsius, the eminent Dutch scholar, who in writing a tribute for Ronsard's French follower was staking his own claim as a would-be pindarist.

Sainte-Marthe's pindaric, "In Obitum Iacobi Fai Spressai V. CL," is, like Ronsard's ode on Charles IX, a poem produced during a era of political crisis, the uneasy period of transition from the reign of Henri III to that of Henri IV.[34] Jacques Faye, Sieur D'Espeisses (1542–1590), was one of the leading counselors of Henri III and a close associate of Sainte-Marthe himself.[35] Both were staunch supporters of Henri III and remained loyal to the royal cause when Henri III at his death named his Protestant cousin Henri of Navarre his heir. As moderate Catholics, Sainte-Marthe and Faye advocated the liberty of the French Catholic Church from Pope Sixtus V's authoritarian attempt to impose the dogmas of the Council of Trent in France. Accordingly, they opposed the fanatical Catholics of La Ligue, who rejected the future Henri IV and led a coalition of forces against him. The ode is addressed to Jacques Faye's brother Charles, himself a member of Parlement, and laments Jacques' untimely death at the crucial battle of Ivry in March 1590 just when Henri IV so much needed loyal supporters. Sainte-Marthe presents the fall of this virtuous man almost as the fall of virtue itself.

In chapter 2 we have already looked at the companion ode to this one — Sainte-Marthe's celebration of Henri IV's victory at the battle of Ivry. The exultation of the battle ode is balanced by the dirge of this lament for Faye. Both, however, refer to the national tragedy of France, oppressed with an unhappy fate. Although Sainte-Marthe laments the tragic death of the counselor, lent to France for a little time but now snatched away, he also mourns, like Pindar at the close of the Persian Wars, not one man but the thousands whom France once possessed and who now have fallen. Digressive myth serves Sainte-Marthe well, as he depicts the situation in France with Frenchmen savagely pitted against each other in war. He chooses two episodes from the *Odyssey* involving Ulysses and his comrades to dramatize the predicament of warring Frenchmen. First, he compares

---

[34] "In Obitum Iacobi Fai Spressai V. CL" in "Lyricorum Liber 1," in Scaevola and Abelius Sammarthani, *Opera Latina et Gallica* (Paris: Jacobus Villery, 1633), 78–86.

[35] Faye served Henri from the time he was Duc d'Anjou. He distinguished himself in Parlement and followed Henri to Poland and then back to France when he became king. Appointed by Henri III successively *maître des requêtes au conseil d'Etat* and *avocat-général aux parlements*, he followed Henri to Tours after the *Journés des Barricades* and on the king's death secured Tours for Henri IV. Faye died of a fever during Henri IV's siege of Paris. For Faye's biography see both Sainte-Marthe's biography included in his *Elogiorum Liber Quartus* in *Opera*, 105–7 and the biographies in *Nouvelle Biographie Générale* (Paris, 1845–1866) and *Biographie Universelle Ancienne et Moderne* (Paris, 1843–1857).

the unholy love of blood that moves the religious fanatics in France to the rapaciousness with which the Cyclops seized upon Ulysses' companions and made a feast of blood (*Ody.* 9.287–293). Next, he makes the episode in which Circe transformed Ulysses' comrades into swine (*Ody.* 10.250–261) a metaphorical description of the beastliness that has transformed the Frenchmen of his time, who have abandoned the charity and piety of their ancestors. Surely, says Sainte-Marthe, malign stars are ruling and dark night, once illuminated by Faye's presence, now prevails once more. It is hardly surprising that Sainte-Marthe harks back to France's golden age, when Faye and Michel Hospital led the government, comparing their era to the age when Augustus Caesar ruled in Rome and Vergil brought the civilizing forces of art to the state.

Like other pindarists, Sainte-Marthe uses conventional classical machinery to depict Faye's sudden, tragic demise: Orcus claims its prey, Lethe engulfs him in her tide, and the baleful goddess Nemesis rules the realm.[36] The center of the ode is devoted to a kind of biographical recapitulation, wherein Sainte-Marthe rehearses the succession of offices Faye held under his king like a list of "epinician" triumphs.[37] Faye's crowning achievement was to hold the city of Tours loyal for Henri III's successor, standing like Achilles eminent among his friends, and giving his life to the cause, just as Achilles had.[38] The ode that begins with an apostrophe to a France fallen on evil days concludes with a resigned acceptance that France has lost a glory, a light, for which the whole nation must mourn.[39]

---

[36] "An partes Nemesis suas / Hic agit, offensos scilicet vlta Deos, / Ob tot crimina criminúmque causas / Foecunda noxae quas habent haec secula? / Nam penitus pudor exoleuit: / Furta nunc fraudésque, & auara habendi / Fert quaecúnque sitis, quicquid & efferum" (epode 1.1–7).

[37] Sainte-Marthe praises Faye's Christian piety as his highest quality, testifying that his name will live through all the ages: "Nimirum insolitus dolor / Non solito vatum pectine dignus erat. / Quo res cunque cadat, profectò nunquam / Huius laboris poenitebit, si modò / Grata tibi mea sit voluptas, / Candide ô Faï, placidóque vultu / Hunc testem officij non renuas mei" (epode 9.1–7).

[38] Sainte-Marthe laments the fact that that human lives are governed by forces totally beyond human control to which human beings must submit: "Hei mihi nulla hominum generi / Tuta sors usquam fuit!" (antistrophe 8.1–2).

[39] Compare with this the ode that Paul Schede (Paulus Melissus) composed on the death of Joachim-Ernest, the prince of Anhalt-Dessau, in 1586. Melissus attempts not just to mourn the prince's death, but also to reflect on its consequences for his small duchy left to the rule of his surviving sons. With the fall of the prince, constancy, faith, and fortitude also fall and the world seems to go to wrack and ruin. Melissus connects the grief of his sons and other relatives with that of the rivers—the Elbe and the Moldau—and the forests of his native land, which shed tears for the loss of their prince. Yet to weep accomplishes nothing. It is more fitting to lead the chorus in remembrance and to anticipate future good for the country: that his virtue will revive in his sons: ("Iusta Exseqvialia in

Sainte-Marthe's funeral pindaric, "In Tumulum P. Ronsard," is a poet's tribute to a poet, which acknowledges Pierre de Ronsard as the father of the Pindaric movement in France.[40] A happier ode than the former, it honors an elder poet, who excelled in the very genre that the younger poet would now appropriate for himself. Sainte-Marthe and Ronsard were acquaintances and had exchanged verses, Ronsard having expressed esteem for the talent of his younger contemporary and Sainte-Marthe having applied the Pindaric epithet of an eagle among poets to Ronsard.[41] The ode opens by saluting Ronsard's burial place, Tours, as the glory of France and the eye of cities, a phrase, of course, that recollects Pindar's praise of the citizens of Acragas in Olympian 2.

> Quo te beatam nomine
> Praedicabo potissimùm,
> Galliae ô decus, urbium ocelle,
> Quae bellicosi nomine Caesaris
> Gloriaris ciuitas?
> (strophe 1.1–5)

> By what name shall I proclaim you
> Blessed and most powerful,
> O glory of Gaul, eye of cities,
> City which glories
> In the name of warlike Caesar?

The addressee of the ode, however, turns out to be neither Tours nor Ronsard, but Sainte-Marthe's own son Abel, an aspiring poet, who is at his side.[42] Sainte-Marthe is conscious that three generations of French poets—Ronsard, himself, and Abel—gather in one place, all sworn to the service of poetry. The revival of the Pindaric Muses that began with Ronsard must now continue in future generations with younger poets such as Abel who is just at the beginning of a life dedicated to Apollo-Cynthius. However, Sainte-Marthe celebrates Ronsard not

Obitum Ioachimi Ernesti Principis Anhaltini," in "Emmetra," in *Delitiae Poetarum Germanorum*, ed. Janus Gherus [Ranutius Gruterus] (Frankfurt, 1612), 4: 356–60.)

[40] The ode on Ronsard is featured prominently in the edition of Sainte-Marthe's and his own works that his son Abel published in 1633 after his father's death: see Sammarthani, "In Tumulum P. Ronsardi ad Abelium Filivm," in "Lyricorum Liber I," in *Opera Latina et Gallica*, 62–69.

[41] See Sainte-Marthe's epigram, "Ad Petrum Ronsardum" ("Epigrammatum Liber II," in *Opera*, 189); also the elegiac couplets on Ronsard's death, "P. Ronsardi Memoriae S." in which he had commended Ronsard for bringing the Grecian Muses to France ("Elegiae," in *Opera*, 165–66).

[42] Sainte-Marthe also wrote epigrams and odes to other leading poets of his time. See particularly the epigrams that he and Nicolas Rapin exchanged and the Pindaric ode to Rapin (discussed in chap. 8 below).

just as the Pindaric *vates*, but also as the love poet who sang to Cassandre and Marie and as the poet of the national epic, the *Franciade*. Invoking the *manes* of the great Ronsard, Sainte-Marthe metaphorically scatters choice flowers on his tomb in celebration of his place in French poetry. Yet he also poses the inevitable question, posed by poets before him and to be posed by future poets such as Milton in "Lycidas": what profit does poetry possess when the fate stands ready to "slit the thin-spun life"?

> Sed quid bonis tot profuit
> Pollere, invida si breui
> Momento haec Lachesis tulit sub Orcum?
> Nos, chare fili, quod modò possimus
> Visere hoc sacrum iuuat,
> Et busto querulas fundere naenias.
> Tu, si sepulchri cura te vlla tangit.
> (antistrophe 10. 1–7)

> But what profits it to be strong in
> so many good things, if envious Lachesis in a
> brief moment bears them under Orcus?
> Dear son, let us as best we can
> See that this sacred place may thrive
> and pour complaining songs over his grave;
> You, if any care for the tomb touches you.

The ode that begins with a tribute to France's greatest poet concludes with melancholy reflections on the future of poetry itself.

Sainte-Marthe was himself commemorated in a Pindaric ode by Daniel Heinsius (1580–1655), the important Dutch scholar, who also had Pindaric pretensions. Heinsius had praised Pindar as the Phoebus of men, the king of the Muses, in his Elegia XIV (*Monobiblos*), asking to be admitted into his company.[43] The ode on Sainte-Marthe is full of Pindaric echoes.[44] The invocation to the motherland, France ("Mater mea, Divûm genetrix"), combines two of Pindar's apostrophes: his address in Nemean 3 to the muse as mother and his appeal in

---

[43] Daniel Heinsius, Elegia XIV, "In qua inter alia de laude Pindari," "Monobiblos" in *Poemata*, ed. Nicolaus Heinsius (Amsterdam, 1649), 205–7. Also see "Elegia XII" in *Delitiae C. Poetarum Belgicorum, Huius Superiorisque Aevi Illustrium*, ed. Ranutius Gherus [Janus Gruterus] (Frankfurt, 1614), 2.2.1012–14.

[44] Heinsius's ode on Sainte-Marthe—"Ode Pindarica in obitum ampliss. viri Scaevolae Sammarthani"—was included in the volume that Sainte-Marthe's son Abel published after his father's death ("Tumulus," in *Opera Latina et Gallica* [Paris, 1633], 45–48) and was also published by Heinsius in his own works (Heinsius, *Poemata* [Amsterdam, 1649], 120–23). It pays tribute to Sainte-Marthe as a Pindaric poet and at the same time illustrates Heinsius's own poetic aspirations.

Isthmian 6 to Thebes, his nurturing mother. This kind of deliberate echoing follows Ronsard and the so-called "Pindarically inspired" verse of his school. Like them, Heinsius imbeds quotations from Pindar in his ode, while appropriating for himself the role of the Pindaric bard and priest of Apollo. Praying to be filled with the divine heat of the "Dircaean Swan," Heinsius summons the Graces to choose flowers from their garden to decorate his song and mounts Pindar's chariot of the Muses (Olympian 9.81).

Not until the antistrophe does Heinsius identify his ode as a lament: "Carmen querulum, flebile carmen, / Lugubre," a mournful song such as the unhappy mother of Itys, the nightingale, might have sung under the shadow of poplar or oak. Echoing Pindar, he cites the inexorable law of mortal life—that all must pass over to black Acheron. He vows, however, to snatch Sainte-Marthe from the "invidious tooth" of oblivion and to enroll his shade in the company of poets he has emulated—Vergil and Pindar—entrusting him to the care of the Muses he has cultivated. Heinsius concludes the ode with another Pindaric device, summoning Pindar's Echo (Olympian 14) to deliver the all-too-familiar moral that by virtue of his poetic eminence Sainte-Marthe will break the fetters of death. [45]

What we find in both Sainte-Marthe's ode to Ronsard and Heinsius's to Sainte-Marthe is a deliberate espousal of a tradition of poetic imitation that had once flourished in France under Ronsard, but which had passed its zenith. Heinsius dons the robes of the poet-priest, just as Ronsard had at the beginning of his Pindaric period; he also conspicuously joins the choruses of poets who dance under Haemus to the strains of the Theban lyre. However, as Heinsius's ode illustrates, the use of Pindaric ode to commemorate the dead had become the exercise of scholar-poets and not of poets. It remained for English poets in the seventeenth century to reinvent the genre of the funerary pindaric.

---

[45] Echo speaks: "Explicabit Echo. / 'Nata coelitum virtus, / Famae volucris laeta amplexu / Crescit, immensi patiens / Temporis, neque infames / Horret aemulos, nec ullum / Dentis invidi morsum.' / Quam tibi, perculsus virtute / Ebriusque tanta, / Auro refulgentem ut pateram, & mero, / Magni sacerdos Delii propino" (123) ("Echo shall explain: 'Virtue, born of heavenly parents, happy in the embrace of winged Fame, grows, enduring immense Time, nor does she fear the infamous envious ones nor any bite of the invidious tooth.' I, struck by and drunk with such great virtue, as a priest of the great Delian god [Apollo], raise to you this goblet shining with gold and unmixed wine").

CHAPTER 7
MELODIOUS TEARS: THE ENGLISH ODE-ELEGY

The first English poets who composed ode-elegies in the Pindaric mode could look back on earlier neo-Latin and vernacular Pindaric *funera* in Italy and France. Yet it is difficult to establish with poets such as Jonson, Milton, and Cowley which was the more forceful influence: direct knowledge of Pindar or conscious imitation of those continental forebears who had earlier espoused Pindar as a model for funerary verse. In the Cary-Morison ode and in "Lycidas" Jonson and Milton create highly original odes that appear directly to adapt Pindar's techniques for the ode-elegy. However, in their adaptations they may well be taking the cue from neo-Latinists such as Lampridio and Secundus, who composed ambitious odes that combined lament for the dead with philosophical reflection. With Cowley as well, both Pindar's original odes and continental models appear to have their impact. Yet in his collection *Pindarique Odes* Cowley made no attempt to imitate the funeral pindaric. It was Cowley's friend Thomas Sprat who first used the Cowleian pindaric for an ode-elegy on Cromwell's death. Cowley followed Sprat's lead with his own ode-elegy, "On the Death of Mrs. Katherine Philips," published in his posthumous *Works* (1668). Thereafter, as we have noted in chapter 5, the Cowleian pindaric became a popular mode for funerary poetry, so popular that in 1700 it was unremarkable that Cowley himself, the "English Pindarus," was remembered in an elaborate Pindaric ode-elegy prefixed to a reissue of his *Works*. Let us begin, however, with Jonson's and Milton's experimental odes.

1.

"To the immortal memorie, and friendship of that noble paire, Sir LVCIUS CARY, *and Sir* H. MORISON" was Ben Jonson's second attempt at a Pindaric ode, a closer and more deliberate imitation than his earlier Desmond ode. In the Cary-Morison ode Jonson chooses to render Pindar's strophe, antistrophe, and epode, englishing the terms to turn, counterturn, and stand. He also undertakes to replicate more thoroughly other structural features of Pindaric ode, including Pindar's long introductory opening figures, his allusive mythic identifications, his conspicuous moral *sententiae*, and even his run-on lines. Jonson ostentatiously

splits words, as Pindar had, and divides two strophes with Pindaric run-ons. By employing these techniques, Jonson gives the Cary-Morison ode the look of the Greek triadic ode. Yet clearly, Jonson was influenced not only by Pindar but also by continental imitators whom he no doubt knew: Lampridio, Ronsard, Melissus, Sarbiewski. and Heinsius. Jonson's library attests to his knowledge of Ronsard's pindarics and more than a few of the neo-Latin pindarists.[1]

The strongest link of the Cary-Morison ode to Pindar's original odes is subject-matter. Although Jonson's ode does not celebrate one specific event, it does celebrate two specific men—Lucius Cary and Henry Morison—young noblemen, who in social class and in aristocratic "virtue" resemble the young athletes and aristocrats whose epinician victories Pindar had celebrated. Jonson commends Cary, the living hero, as Pindar might have celebrated a patron; he introduces Morison, the dead hero, in the middle of the second triad, just where Pindar would have introduced the winning athlete. But the ode is neither an epitaph for Morison nor a congratulatory celebration for Cary, though at times it may seem both. Rather, like Lampridio's odes for Pietro Mellini and Vittoria Colonna, it is an ode of "mixed" occasion that commemorates a dead companion or loved one even as he commends the virtuous person connected intimately with him. Clearly, Jonson's intent is double: to celebrate Morison's life as the life well lived and to celebrate Cary's and Morison's friendship as the defining aspect of the lives of both men. Jonson quite consciously substitutes for athletic victory Morison's achievement of "All Offices" of life—"Hee stood, a Souldier to the last right end, / A perfect Patriot, and a noble friend, / But most a vertuous Sonne" (ll. 45–47).[2] Jonson "doubles" Morison's achievement with Cary's in that Cary too excels as patriot, son, and, of course, above all as friend. Jonson's praises of the men are not inappropriate for the Pindaric hero-athlete—"simple love of greatnesse and of good; / That knits brave minds, and manners, more than blood" (ll. 105–106).

Although we recognize that aristocratic ethics and poetic techniques form direct links between Pindar and Jonson, we must also acknowledge that Jonson's ode is as free an experimentation in Pindaric imitation as any of the other Pindaric imitations we have already examined. Jonson repeatedly takes poetic and intellectual license with the Pindaric concept and form. The opening figure is a case in point: the Infant of Saguntum who chooses, upon witnessing the horrors of life, to return to the womb and die rather than to be born. It is true that the opening resembles the Pindaric figure in its initial placement. Further, Jonson, like Pindar, uses the figure to develop intellectually the point he is making—that the long life is not necessary the good life. However, the figure, drawn

---

[1] See McPherson, "Ben Jonson's Library and Marginalia: An Annotated Catalogue."

[2] Quoted from Ben Jonson, *The Poems*, in *The Works of Ben Jonson*, ed. C.H. Herford and Percy and Evelyn Simpson (Oxford: Clarendon Press, 1947), 8: 242–47.

from Pliny (*N.H.* 7.168), rather than from Pindar, contrasts in tone, in length, and in moral with the typical Pindaric figure. Most of Pindar's figures, as well as his gnomic expressions, are brief and positive in tone. The view that life is not worth living and that it is often best not to have been born is a sentiment common in Greek tragedy, but not in Pindar. Pindar repeatedly counsels patient forbearance in the face of life's adversities. Unlike Pindar, moreover, Jonson cannot resist summing up in his typical epigrammatic style with a quip, mordant and witty. Addressing the hapless Infant, Jonson opines: "Could they but lifes miseries fore-see, / No doubt all Infants would returne like thee" (ll. 19–20).

In other instances as well Jonson often adapts Pindaric sentence for his own purposes. When Jonson asks "What is life?" he may be thinking of Pindar's famous query in Pythian 8.95–6, "τί δέ τις" (What is anyone?)[3] However, Jonson does not reply with Pindar's pithy and memorable response—man is the dream of a shadow ("σκιᾶς ὄναρ ἄνθρωπος"); instead he develops the extended example of the long-lived Stirrer, a figure worthy to have appeared in Jonson's 1616 collection of epigrams. Once more we have an instance of Jonson following Pindar, but not following him closely, but instead using Pindar's aphorism as a springboard to develop a moral of his own. The same thing is true of the ode's most celebrated image, which likens the cycles of human life to those of nature: "It is not growing like a tree / In bulke, doth make man better bee" (ll. 65–66).

Comparisons of man and nature are common in Pindar; in fact, Jonson's comparison of the tree's growth to man's life is so like Pindar's we may be surprised that Jonson didn't lift it verbatim from his Greek predecessor. In Nemean 8 Pindar likens the fame of glorious deeds in human beings to trees that shoot up when watered by dew (40). He often observes that human beings like nature are controlled by cycle. The gods grant that one generation will flower abundantly, yet another not attain its full growth. In Nemean 6 Pindar comments that the fields may lie fallow one year and produce the next (9–10). One of the fullest expansions of this idea comes in Nemean 11, an ode addressed to Aristagoras of Tenedos, an athlete who had come from an ancient family that had not recently produced an Olympian victor. Although Aristagoras had been an athlete with Olympic potential, his parents had not permitted him to compete at Delphi and Olympia. Accordingly, Pindar celebrates Aristagoras's *prytania* or installation as president of council at Tenedos and not his victory in an athletic contest. However, so outstanding was Aristagoras's potential that Pindar remarks on the paradox that it remained unfulfilled.[4] The question is not without importance to Jonson, as he considers the paradox of Morison's unfulfilled potential.

---

[3] Kevin Crotty describes Pythian 8 as an ode that lays stress on excellence as permanent and continuing (*Song and Action*, 18).

[4] Crotty observes that Nemean 11 synthesizes the description of happiness and disappointment by means of a single divine concept, *moira* (*Song and Action*, 15).

At the climax of the ode Pindar gracefully expounds this paradox by using the figure of the flowering tree. Not every generation yields men outstanding in strength; like the fields or like fruiting trees, men do not come to "abundant harvest" every year but in alternate years.

ἀρχαῖαι δ᾽ ἀρεταὶ
ἀμφέροντ᾽ ἀλλασσόμεναι γενεαῖς ἀνδρῶν σθένος·
ἐν σχερῷ δ᾽ οὔτ᾽ ὦν μέλαιναι καρπὸν ἔδωκαν ἄρουραι,
δένδρεά τ᾽ οὐκ ἐθέλει πάσαις ἐτέων περόδοις
ἄνθος εὐῶδες φέρειν πλούτῳ ἴσον,
ἀλλ᾽ ἐν ἀμείβοντι. καὶ θνατὸν οὕτως ἔθνος ἄγει
μοῖρα. (Nemean 11. 37–43)

But ancient virtue
In alternation restores strength to the generations of men.
Neither do the dark acres in succession yield harvest,
Nor do trees consent, in the circuit of years, each year
To bear flowers, sweet of scent, in like abundance,
But in alternate seasons. And so for mortal men also does
fate decree.

So for Aristagoras, whose potential was not realized in Olympian or Pythian contests, recognition must come with a future harvest.

Although Jonson's tree simile comments on human and natural cycles, it does not exactly follow the Pindaric parallel. Jonson compares the long-lived tree to the fast-dying flower, imitating a simile that was particularly common in the Renaissance funerary epigram. Vernacular and neo-Latin poets, such as Pontano and Flaminio, often evoke the fast-dying flower to mourn an untimely death, and even the young Milton in an ode composed very near the time of the Cary-Morison ode compares the untimely death of a "Fair Infant" to the fall of a flower.[5] However, at the same time Jonson's view on the limits that govern human life seems perfectly in tune with Pindar's. Long life or short life comes by divine dispensation: human beings are controlled by a mystery they cannot penetrate but which they must accept. Perfection may be achieved, however, in the brief moment: to an athlete as he grasps the victory, to the tree or flower in full bloom. But of course, such moments are evanescent. Jonson's praise of due season, Pindar's exaltation of the athlete at the moment of *kairós*, both acknowledge that human beings are only "creatures of a day."

As he bids Cary to call for wine and accept from his hand the celebratory garland, Jonson seems to be replicating the occasion of Pindaric victory. At comparable moments, Pindar recalls those men who have come before him, even

---

[5] See the discussion of Pontano, Flaminio, and Milton in Revard, *Milton and the Tangles of Neaera's Hair*, 56–61.

those who have preceded him into the halls of Hades. We have previously remarked how in Isthmian 8 and Nemean 10 Pindar comments on triumph and
tragedy. Isthmian 8 contrasts two cousins: Cleandros, who has recently won an
athletic victory, and Nicocles, a previous victor, who has died but who shares
with his living cousin the moment of renewed achievement. In the same ode Pindar also contrasts the fortunate, longer-lived Peleus with Achilles, his short-lived
son, thus reinforcing the contrast of the two cousins with different destinies. As
the mythic shadow of Achilles crosses the ode, Pindar reminds us of the inexo-
rability of mortal destiny. Similarly, Pindar's allusion to the Castor-Pollux myth
at the end of Nemean 10 points to the different destinies of men who are bound
one to another by an even closer relation.[6]

Essential to Jonson's ode is the contrast of young men of different destinies — the one taken early, the one remaining. Both Isthmian 8 and Nemean 10
furnish him important examples of these types. However, Jonson does not replicate Pindar's account of the Dioscuri with a full-fledged comparison, neither
recounting, as Pindar does, the story of Castor's death nor recording Pollux's appeal to Zeus in behalf of his brother. Rather he alludes to the Dioscuri in a fashion still briefer than Lampridio's and Ronsard's allusions in comparable odes.
Like them, he wishes to call attention to the surviving one of a pair and to console him on his loss of his other "half." Neither fully Christian nor fully classical,
Jonson's consolation goes to the heart of the myth. Exclaiming that Morison is
not dead, but lives in memory in the "bright eternall Day" (l. 81), Jonson presents
us with an afterworld somewhere between the Christian heaven and the classical
Isles of the Blessed. Like Pindar's Achilles of Olympian 2, Morison dwells in the
Muses' song, not fully transported, yet eternal "with memorie and *Ben / Jonson*,
who sung this of him e're he went / Himselfe to rest" (ll. 84–86). Jonson makes
plain that his intention in the ode is not to sing a dirge for the dead but to confer
friendship's garland; the memory is of two, not one:

> To have exprest,
> In this bright *Asterisme*:
> Where it were friendships schisme,
> (Were not his *Lucius* long with us to tarry)
> To separate these twi-
> Lights, the *Dioscuri*;
> And keepe the one halfe from his *Harry*.
> But fate doth so alternate the designe,
> Whilst that in heav'n, this light on earth must shine.
> (ll. 88–96)

---

[6] Crotty suggests that the relationship of Pollux and Castor replicates that between
friends or that between the poet and the athlete (*Song and Action*, 77–79).

As in Ronsard's and Lampridio's odic celebrations of brothers, the one expresses the absent other, just as the living brother expresses the dead: "Two names of friendship, but one Starre" (l. 98). The resolution is both Pindaric and not Pindaric. Pindar's myth has been developed, transformed, altered to express another truth. Whereas Pindar focused on the "miracle" wrought by the devoted love of one brother for the other, Jonson focuses on the paradox of a united but divided friendship.

In the course of writing this pindaric on friendship Jonson has reworked the classical ideal as well as the classical epinician form. What we have here is an updating of Pindaric *areté* to represent a Renaissance ideal of an aristocracy "that knits brave minds, and manners, more than blood" (l. 106). He adapts the myth to the Renaissance view that the friend was the copy of the other: Morison and Cary are moral twins, not actual brothers. Still further, the ancient idea of poetry conferring fame is retained and rewritten: Cary and Morison become, as Jonson expresses them, "names" for abstract moral virtue: "Nothing perfect done / But as a CARY or a MORISON" (ll. 115–116). Thus his two heroes are doing more than winning a race, even fulfilling the goal of living a life with virtue; they push beyond to become the standard for winning, the standard for measuring victory. Jonson closes with a curious metaphor; he attributes to the young "contestants" an early autumnal "harvest":

> Who, e'er the first downe blooméd on the chin,
> Had sow'd these fruits, and got the harvest in. (ll. 127–128)

As Pindar also aptly remarked, it is not every year that brings fields to harvest; but for these Jacobean contestants the early harvest brings the crops home.

2.

It is not surprising that among the earliest poetry that the young John Milton produced were Latin funeral pieces, written in commemoration of prominent elderly men connected with Cambridge University.[7] Were we not familiar with the history of ode-elegy on the continent, we might not connect Milton's early Latin verse with Pindaric ode, for in none of these Latin poems does Milton experiment, as he later does, with Pindaric strophes. Two are composed in elegiac couplets, the other two in iambics and in alcaics. However, while employing classical verse forms and now and then echoing Latin poets, these funeral pieces have a clear relationship with the neo-Latin tradition of funera that we have

---

[7] See John K. Hale, *Milton's Cambridge Latin: Performing in the Genres, 1625–1632*, MRTS 289 (Tempe, AZ: ACMRS, 2005), 127–45. Also see Revard, *Milton and the Tangles of Neaera's Hair*, 47–51.

been examining. Pindaric echoes and Pindaric techniques invade Milton's funerary odes and elegies. Milton employs odic apostrophe, digression, and mythic interlinking, and exploits in both the funera for the Bishops of Winchester and Ely the odic "I" and first-person narration. The experiments in Pindaric techniques in these early poems prepare Milton for his most accomplished funeral piece, "Lycidas," composed about ten years later to commemorate the untimely death of an alumnus of Cambridge University.

Milton's first funera are both epitaphs for the dead that commend the deceased's virtue and personal reflections on the meaning of life. Written probably during the plague year of 1625–1626, the first two ode-elegies, "In Obitum Procancellarii Medici" (On the Death of the Vice-Chancellor, a Physician) and "In Obitum Praeconis Academiae Cantabrigiensis" (On the death of the Beadle of Cambridge University), replicate the tripartite organization of the hymn-ode: an exordium, a section of interlinking mythic references, and a closing exhortation or prayer. Both apostrophize the deceased, regretting that he has fallen prey to the dark goddess, Death, and both conclude with lament and a prayer for peaceful rest.[8] Although these poems praise the virtuous life of the men they commemorate, their actual aim is to meditate on the inexorable nature of death. In his verses to the Vice-Chancellor, Milton addresses the whole human race, classically named the children of Iapetus, and remarks sadly that all human beings must obey when Death calls. Neither the heroes—Hercules, Hector, Achilles—could by strength of arm repel fate nor could the sorceresses—Circe and Medea—defeat death with their magic spells nor even the physicians—Machaon, Chiron, and Aesculapius—outwit death with skill and healing arts. His examples are classically chosen, and many of the personages named figure in Pindar's *exempla*. Chiron and Aesculapius are linked here, as they are in Pindar's consolatory ode to Hieron, Pythian 3, where Pindar has anticipated Milton in remarking that human beings cannot escape death's final reckoning. In fact, both Pindar and Milton counterpoise Aesculapius's wondrous escape from death—snatched living from his dead mother's body—with his later execution, struck down by Zeus's lightning when he tried to bring a man back from the dead. Milton even suggests that the Vice-Chancellor, like Aesculapius, angered a god—here Persephone, the queen of Hades—when he used his medical skill to save the victims of the plague. In the closing address, Milton invokes for the Vice-Chancellor this same goddess, Aetnean Proserpina, echoing perhaps Pindar's addresses to this deity in Nemean 1, Pythian 14, and again in Olympian 2.

Milton's elegy for the beadle is also odic in structure and opens with an apostrophe to the beadle, the bearer of the mace, ironically fallen prey to the

---

[8] These epitaphs could be compared with other Pindaric epitaphs, such as Melissus's pindaric on the death of the prince of Anhalt-Dessau, cited in the previous chapter. Unless otherwise noted, Milton's poetry is cited from *Complete Poetry and Major Prose*, ed. Merritt Y. Hughes (New York: Odyssey Press, 1957).

great beadle Death, who has shown no mercy to one of his own profession.[9] In its central sections Milton develops this witty paradox by alluding to other beadles or messengers, from Homer's heralds to Hermes, the classical conveyor of the dead to the underworld, whom Milton also alludes to in his ode to John Rouse. As in the ode to the Vice-Chancellor, there are allusions to Aesculapius, Coronis's son, and to the sorceress Medea, mythic references that could be either Pindaric or Ovidian. Milton regrets, as Pindar had in Pythian 3, that he lacks the power to recall men from the dead, as Aesculapius in response to the prayer of Artemis had restored Hippolytus. Neither does he possess the power to restore the beadle's youth, as Medea attempted to restore old Aeson. This ode-elegy for the beadle concludes with a collective lament. Just as Pindar appealed to an aristocratic community to join in the praise for a victor, Milton appeals to the academic community to join in the lament for the dead.

Milton's elegy for the Bishop of Winchester and his iambics for the Bishop of Ely begin with personal passages and conclude with dream-like visions. Milton tries to create a sense of immediacy by employing first-person address and recording his response on first hearing the news of the Bishops' deaths. The elegy begins with the statement of grief, "moestus eram" (1) (I am grief-stricken); the iambics with a renewed expression of grief: "My cheeks are still stained with tears." Like the previous ode-elegies, these poems meditate on death itself.[10] Milton links the two bishops' deaths and connects the death of Bishop of Winchester with the recent deaths of Protestants warring on the continent. He angrily rebukes "Savage Death" ("Mors fera" [1. 16] and the gods of the underworld, lamenting that all fall victim to death's power—the fields and oaks and flowers, and finally human beings. It is worth noting that by the time he writes "Lycidas," Milton has left off indicting Death or the gods of the underworld, but merely accuses an indeterminate blind fury who untimely "slits the thin-spun life" (1. 76).

Yet in both these early ode-elegies and in "Lycidas," Milton believes it important to vindicate the ways of the gods. In the verses for the Bishop of Ely, an aethereal voice (later identified as Ely himself) responds to the poet's complaints, explaining that death is not an enemy but a friend to man. Neither the daughter of Night and Erebus nor one of the Erinnyes, she is, like the Horae, the daughter of Jove and Themis, sent to release human beings from their bodies and to bring them into the presence of the eternal father. In Milton's early poems the consolation offered may be implicitly Christian, but it is set emphatically in classical terms. Both poems conclude with classical visions. A dragon-chariot, not unlike Medea's, conveys Ely aloft through the stars and constellations to a heavenly Olympus. Winchester is borne to a place that resembles the Isles of the Blest. Moreover, Milton's strategy in describing these voyages is not unlike Pindar's at the end of Olympian 2, for like Pindar, who is assuring Theron of Zeus's ultimate

---

[9] Hale, *Milton's Cambridge Latin*, 134–35.
[10] Hale, *Milton's Cambridge Latin*, 136–38.

justice toward human beings, Milton is presenting a beatific vision of the afterlife to counterbalance a view of the harshness of life on earth. The righteous heroes in Pindar's ode are brought after death to a paradise where ocean breezes blow, golden flowers bloom, and flowers crown their heads. The isle that Milton calls up for us is comparable: an isle beyond the Ganges, where all is radiant with light and where Favonius blows, and the earth is brilliant with color. To be sure, the imagery could be drawn from Revelation 14:13 or from *Aeneid* 6.644, as well as from Olympian 2. However, like Pindar, Milton creates a vision of the blissful isles to assure the reader that the righteous will be rewarded after death. He will employ a similar device at the end of "Lycidas."

Milton's first experiment with an extended ode, "On the Death of a Fair Infant Dying of a Cough," was written at the age of seventeen, possibly also in the plague year, 1626. In it Milton uses many of the same poetic devices to mourn the dead child that he had employed to memorialize mature men. He begins with an apostrophe to the child, addressed as a "fairest flower, no sooner blown than blasted" (l. 1), and then develops an extended myth, which recounts how this "blossom" is killed at the onset of frost. In the mythic digression the child, like the Athenian maiden courted by the North Wind, Aquilo, is inadvertently killed by her elderly suitor, Winter. Pindar often chooses a myth to congratulate a victor on his success and to assure him of the perpetuation of his family. Milton, however, uses myth here to lament the discontinuation of a family, rather than to celebrate its continuance. In Olympian 1 Pindar told how Pelops won the maiden Hippodamia by his chariot victory; Milton's myth describes the inverse. Winter takes the maiden-flower into his "cold-kind" embrace and unawares "unhous[es] [her] Virgin Soul" (ll. 20–21). Instead of celebrating success with a myth of marriage, Milton by recounting the myth of an abortive marriage marks the tragedy of death. With the use of myth Pindar heightens the celebration, Milton the mourning. Like Pindar and some of his Renaissance imitators, Milton interlocks several myths to reinforce his point. We recall how Lampridio, in the ode on Mellini's villa, had mourned the premature death of Pietro's brother Celso by recounting in sequence three myths about young men — Adonis, Hylas, and Castor — who die prematurely, only to be revived eternally. Milton uses a similar tactic in alluding next to the death of Apollo's beloved Hyacinthus, slain, like the fair flower, by a god's "unweeting hand" (l. 23) and transformed into a flower. Thereby he seems to promise that the Fair Flower, blasted by Winter, will also, like Hyacinthus, bloom again.

Milton's funeral ode, like many other funeral pieces, is philosophical and asks basic eschatological questions. Does the dead child merely lie in a "wormy bed" (l .31) or is there something eternal in her that survives? Does her soul hover above the "high first-moving Sphere / Or in the Elysian fields" (ll. 39–40), where, transformed into a goddess like Pindar's Semele, she lives in a happier heaven? Was she, perhaps, a star, shaken from Olympus; a goddess fled after the Gigantomachia; Astraea, restored to the earth; or perhaps a Christian angel, come to earth to lead human beings back to heaven? Has she now been herself translated back to heaven, where she may be better able to complete her ministries of "good"?

By posing these various and contradictory questions, Milton is using myth to bridge the chasm between the knowable and the unknowable, the certain and the uncertain. All too aware of the precariousness of the human condition, the poet posits various mythic roles for the Fair Infant in order to offer comfort and consolation to those left behind. His conclusions are philosophical, and not unlike those Pindar proposes in order to offer comfort and resolve the unknowable in his odes. Human beings must be satisfied to endure the human condition in ignorance, for human life is fraught with uncertainty. At the end of the ode, Milton turns to address the mother directly, urging her to cease from lament, to curb her sorrow, and to render back with patience what God lent. This personal touch, joined with the conventional gnomic consolation, is something the young poet might have learned from Pindar himself. Having raised those eternal and unresolvable questions about human happiness, Milton has the grace to close, as Pindar so often did, by offering the conventional wisdom of human acceptance.

"Lycidas" is another matter. Whatever its considerable debt to the tradition of pastoral eclogue and idyll, to Theocritus, Vergil, and their many Renaissance imitators, "Lycidas" is even more deeply indebted to Pindaric ode in its structure, its poetic devices, and its intellectual complexity. Odic experimentation was clearly on Milton's mind in the late 1630s when in *The Reason of Church-Government* he named Pindar's odes and Callimachus's hymns "magnific" and worthy of imitation. However, "Lycidas" is a monody, an ode for a single voice rather than for choral performance, Pindar's peculiar prerogative. Nonetheless, in "Lycidas" Milton proceeds even further in his Pindaric experimentation than he had in his early odes and elegies.[11]

With its opening exordium, invocation, central digressions, and closing epilogue, "Lycidas" has much in common structurally with the pattern of Pindaric

---

[11] "Or if occasion shall lead to imitate those magnific odes and hymns where Pindarus and Callimachus are in most things worthy" (*The Reason of Church-Government* in *Works*, ed. Patterson, 3.1: 238). Both F. T. Prince and Clay Hunt believe that the verse techniques of "Lycidas" have affinities with the Pindaric ode and came to Milton indirectly through the medium of the Italian canzone. See Clay Hunt, *"Lycidas" and the Italian Critics* (New Haven: Yale University Press, 1979); F. T. Prince, *"Lycidas* and the Tradition of the Italian Eclogue," *English Miscellany* 2 (1951): 95–105; also Prince, *The Italian Element in Milton's Verse* (Oxford: Clarendon Press, 1954). Also see James Holly Hanford, "The Pastoral Elegy and Milton's *Lycidas*," *PMLA* 25 (1910): 403–47, repr. in *Milton's Lycidas: The Tradition and the Poem*, ed. C. A. Patrides (Columbia: University of Missouri Press, 1983), 31–59. See also Nicholas von Maltzahn, "Laureate, Republican, Calvinist: An Early Response to Milton and *Paradise Lost* (1667)," *Milton Studies* 29 (1992): 181–98, noting that a contemporary, John Beale (1608–1683), refers to Milton as an "excellent Pindariste" (184).

ode. As we have previously noted, Renaissance editors and commentators included analyses of Pindar's odes in their commentaries and editions, demonstrating thereby that Pindar had organized his odes into sections that were analogous to those of rhetorical compositions. Aretius and Schmidt argue that most of Pindar's odes possess a five-part rhetorical structure: exordium, proposition, confirmation, digression, and epilogue. Both also provide diagrams of the pattern of each ode.[12] In his edition (1620) Benedictus indicates in his arguments and notes how orderly is Pindar's design for the odes.[13] If Milton had used either of these editions of Pindar, he would have learned how important it is in longer odes carefully to control the progress of parts and to integrate digression into an overall scheme.[14]

In "Lycidas" Milton coordinates two themes, which he set forth in the headnote added to the poem in 1645, seven years after its initial publication in Cambridge. His specific aims were, first, to lament the death of Edward King, a learned friend drowned in the Irish seas, and second, to predict the fall of England's corrupt clergy then in power.[15] His speaker, the uncouth swain (whom he describes only at the end of the monody), offers the official lamentation for Lycidas-King. Other speakers join in the eulogy for Lycidas, and the final speaker, Saint Peter, indicts the clergy for corruption. But Milton in the course of the monody explores and develops themes that extend far beyond those stated in the headnote. As Pindar introduced in his odes subjects seemingly extraneous to the athletic victory he celebrated, Milton takes up issues only indirectly related to the lament for King—issues such as poetic vocation, divine justice, the sympathy of the natural world to human life, and the final disposition of the human soul after death. In fact, he ranges so widely that he sometimes seems, rather like Pindar,

---

[12] See the 1587 commentary of Benedictus Aretius and Erasmus Schmidt's 1616 edition of Pindar's odes.

[13] See Revard, *Pindar and the Renaissance Hymn-Ode*, 41.

[14] Maurice Kelley and Samuel D. Atkins have proved conclusively that the copy of Pindar's odes edited by Benedictus, which the editors of the Columbia edition of Milton's Works allege contain annotations by Milton, cannot be his copy: "Milton and the Harvard Pindar," *Studies in Bibliography* 17 (1964): 77–83.

[15] "Lycidas" was first printed in 1638 in a collection of Latin and English poetry commemorating the death of Edward King, one of Milton's schoolfellows from Cambridge, who was drowned off the coast of Chester when he was on his way to Ireland to visit relatives. King had been a minor poet at Cambridge, and to commemorate him Milton joins in this pastoral lament the two vocations of pastor—the shepherd-poet and the shepherd-minister. "Lycidas" appears among the English poems that follow the Latin in *Justa Edovardo King naufrago*. It is signed only with Milton's initials, J. M. When he reprints it in his 1645 Poems as the penultimate of his English poems, he adds the headnote: "In this Monody the Author bewails a learned Friend, unfortunatly drown'd in his Passage from *Chester* on the *Irish* Seas, 1637. And by occasion fortels the ruine of our corrupted Clergy then in their height" (*POEMS of Mr. John Milton* [London, 1645], 57).

to have forgotten the aim of bestowing praise. Yet it is an essential aspect of the
odic design to use the occasion as a springboard to probe profound issues — to
investigate themes that have significance for individuals and for society at moments of victory or loss. Accordingly in "Lycidas," as in so many of Pindar's odes,
the poet seeks to discover through persistent probing how the divine shapes and
controls human life.

Pindar's methods are various. Sometimes he makes a statement or poses a
question to which the unfolding sections of the ode subtly respond. Sometimes
he calls up a mythic person or a mythic story wherein he can expansively explore the paradoxes of human existence that relate to the experience of triumph
or defeat. With victory in the athletic contest, the winning athlete and his patron are enjoying a pinnacle of human happiness, and it is the aim, of course, of
the epinician poet to congratulate them on their success. However, many of the
principal characters in Pindar's myths and digressions are less fortunate. Many
have plunged from the height of fortune into the depths of misery. The mythic
heroes that Pindar features — the tragic Achilles, the unhappy Ajax, the unlucky
Amphiaraüs — are so frequently those men initially blessed, whose lives ended
unfortunately. Thus in his mythic digressions Pindar subtly reminds his audience
that triumphal occasions, such as the victories being celebrated, are — alas — only
too transitory. Even the highest victory can veil defeat. Milton's task in "Lycidas"
is a little different, since the incident that occasions "Lycidas" — the accidental
drowning of Edward King — was, of course, tragic. Thus when Milton calls up
the tragic figures of myth, such as Orpheus, their stories seem merely to echo
or replicate Lycidas's misfortune and confirm life's unavoidable tragedies. Yet
neither poet is simply defeatist nor determined simply to bewail the misery of the
human condition. However, at the same time, he must avoid illusory comfort or
facile consolation or congratulation, knowing that the only true safety for human beings lies beyond the human realm. Thus the poet aims at the divine, be it
Christian or classical — hopeful, at last, to offer those winning words that alone
permit true victory.

Pindaric ode often begins abruptly and boldly, sometimes with a poetic image, sometimes with a striking statement that comments on poetry itself. In
Pythian 1 Pindar invokes the golden lyre, in Olympian 2 the songs that rule
that lyre, and in Olympian 7, even more strikingly, the golden bowl that brims
with song — all images connected with the poet's vocation. "Lycidas" also opens
abruptly, invoking the symbol of poetic success, the laurel crown:

> Yet once more, O ye Laurels, and once more,
> Ye Myrtles brown, with ivy never sere,
> I come to pluck your Berries harsh and crude,
> And with forc'd fingers rude,
> Shatter your leaves before the mellowing year.
> (ll. 1–5)

The implied image is the victorious crown, intertwined with Apollonian laurel, Bacchic ivy, and Venerean myrtle, a wreath that the poet inadvertently shatters when he plucks its leaves either to frame a crown for himself or to bestow one on the dead Lycidas—both actions are implicit. Laurel is the symbol both for poets and for winning athletes in the Pythian games, and myrtle, Venus's symbol, is intertwined with Bacchic ivy. However, the laurel in Milton's monody confers neither victory nor renown. Death has shattered Lycidas's triumphal crown before he could come to maturity, and untimely plucking the laurel leaves before the poet-swain could frame his own crown. The paradox is implicitly Pindaric. Throughout his odes Pindar speaks repeatedly both of the poet's responsibility to bestow the crown of praise worthily and of the difficulties attendant upon fulfilling that responsibility. In some circumstances the poet can question the appropriateness of bestowing victorious wreaths. For example, at the beginning of Isthmian 8, Pindar reflects how in a time of national mourning, after the Persian Wars, celebratory odes seem unfitting. When he himself feels anguished at heart (ἀχνύμενος θυμόν, 5–6), he hesitates to invoke the Muses. Yet at the same time in those moments of national or personal tragedy, poetry is needed all the more; gestures such as bestowing garlands of victory can become the means for healing grief and comforting those sick at heart. We must not fall "orphaned" of garlands, Pindar asserts.

The laurel must be gathered at the critical moment or καιρός. For Pindar καιρός is the moment that permits the athlete to achieve victory or the poet to reward that victory with fitting words of praise. Sometimes, however, the poet hesitates to reach for fulfillment, feeling, as Milton says in "Lycidas," that perhaps the καιρός or due season has not come or that anticipating, he disturbs it: "Bitter constraint and sad occasion dear, / Compels me to disturb your season due" (ll. 6–7). At the same time the very nature of his vocation moves the poet to expression. As Pindar repeatedly proclaims in his odes: "Who would not celebrate? Who would not sing?" With similar words Milton also takes up the task:

> Who would not sing for *Lycidas*? he knew
> Himself to sing, and build the lofty rhyme.
> He must not float upon his wat'ry bier
> Unwept, and welter to the parching wind,
> Without the meed of some melodious tear.
> (ll. 10–14)

The poet must meet the challenge: Lycidas must not remain "unwept," nor must the poetic community fail to hear appropriate poetic praise.

By invoking the Muses, the classical Muses, the daughters of Jove, Milton connects himself to the tradition of poetry to which Pindar, Hesiod, Theocritus, and Vergil belong.

> Begin then, Sisters of the sacred well,
> That from beneath the seat of *Jove* doth spring,
> Begin, and somewhat loudly sweep the string.
> (ll. 15–17)

Begin is the formal "code" word, used by the writer of the Homeric Hymns at the commencement of his hymn. Pindar employs the word *begin* (ἄρχονται) in Nemean 2.3 to connect himself to the Homeric tradition, remarking how, like the Homeric singers of old, he *begins* his song by invoking divine authority and thus establishing his credentials as a poet. It is the same word later adopted by Theocritus, Moschus, and Vergil to summon the Muses.[16] When Milton repeats the word *begin* in his invocation, he establishes his own poetic credentials and connects himself with the traditional singers of the ancient world. Their Muses are his Muses, deities who will not refuse the call to celebrate Lycidas; neither will they refuse to celebrate the poet himself when he is dead, when some gentle "muse" — some fellow poet — will favor his destined urn and bid fair peace to his sable shroud.

By naming the Muses the "Sisters of the sacred well" — the goddesses of sacred water — he is expressing a very ancient concept of poetry.[17] For poets such as Pindar and Hesiod, the Muses were deities associated with springs such as Pindar's own native Theban spring, Dirce. Pindar often describes the onset of poetic inspiration as the welling up of spring water from which he as poet is revived and nourished and his poetry sustained. For Milton there is a particular poignancy in invoking the Greek Muses by reference to their life-giving spring water. Lycidas died as the salt water of the sea overwhelmed him and the bitter waves closed over his head: Milton repeatedly reminds us of the death by water. Even the poet Orpheus, whose head was carried down the freshwater stream to the sea, was overwhelmed by water. From the welling of the Muses' water comes life and inspiration, but paradoxically from its contrary, the "whelming tide," comes death and extinction of the poet who had also so fervently invoked the Muses' welling water.

The first digression in "Lycidas" follows soon after the invocation to the Muses. Attempting to render the experience of student life that he and King would have known at Cambridge, Milton creates a pastoral idyll in which shepherds drive their flocks afield in the morning and return at night under the guidance of Hesperus which "Toward Heav'n's descent had slop'd his westering wheel" (31) — evening star and sunset remind us of the inevitable cycle of human

---

[16] The Homeric Hymns, which are usually regarded as the oldest examples of choral poetry, use the word *begin* as part of the formula to invoke the Muses or the god. See Revard, *Pindar and the Renaissance Hymn-Ode*, chap. 3.

[17] See the discussion of Pindar's Muses and their association with Milton's Muses in Revard, *Pindar and the Renaissance Hymn-Ode*, chap. 2.

life and its waning course toward the west. Milton's shepherds pursue the pastoral pastimes familiar in Theocritus' idylls and Vergil's eclogues.

> Meanwhile the Rural ditties were not mute,
> Temper'd to th'Oaten Flute;
> Rough *Satyrs* danc'd, and *Fauns* with clov'n heel
> From that glad sound would not be absent long,
> And old *Damoetas* lov'd to hear our song.
> (ll. 32–36)

Theocritean pastoral evoked a community which often joined in the kind of competitive singing that Milton here describes—a community now lost, which was sustained by song and by human fellowship. Community also held a central place in the ode, as well as in the pastoral tradition. Pindar's odes were composed for festive congregations that assembled either at the athletic site or at the victor's city-state to celebrate the victories in the games. At these festivals the poet symbolically led the choruses that offered tribute to epinician victors. In the monody Milton's shepherd swain yearns for the lost pastoral community: alone he sings to the woods and desert caves, where "all their echoes mourn" (l. 41). No fellow shepherd joins him, responds to his song, or offers sympathy or consolation. Only the memory of Lycidas's own "soft lays" survives, these also now lost to "Shepherds ear" (ll. 44, 49). The community, so often invoked by pastoral poets and by epinician bards, will be missing from Milton's monody until the mourners arrive and when the choruses of Heaven finally resume the joyous song.

One of the salient marks of Pindaric ode, often remarked on and sometimes censured by Pindar's critics, is its sudden shifts in subject and tone. At this point in the ode Milton effects just such an abrupt turn, as the swain interrupts his lament to pose the first of his odic questions: where were the protective nymphs when Lycidas drowned? Question after question dominate the central sections of Milton's monody—insistent, querulous, unsatisfied demands that follow one another. More than just a query concerning the whereabouts of protective goddesses, this first question asks perforce why a poet-shepherd favored by such deities should perish. And of course, the question is not answered but followed by another query, "Had ye been there—for what could that have done?" (l. 57). The deities of nature and the Muses, so ardently invoked as guardians of the poet, have failed. Moreover, if they failed for Lycidas, will they not fail the poet who calls upon them now?

Milton's questions resemble the questions about human life that Pindar poses in ode after ode: why are those human beings favored by the gods deserted by these same gods? why do the winds of fortune change? how do human beings deal with life when fortune turns to misfortune? As Pindar commented in Olympian 2, we can be certain only that the winds will change: no man, no matter how favored, enjoys fortune continuously. The mythic past of his own city, Thebes, gave Pindar many examples of how triumph and happiness turn to defeat and misery. In Olympian 2 he cites the case of Cadmus's daughters, Semele and Ino, and of Oedipus and his sons, once at the pinnacle of power and happiness, then struck down. He cites in Nemean 9 and many other odes the example of the Seven Warriors who attempted to conquer Thebes, only to die with the seer Amphiaraüs who predicted not only his own but also their demise. However, Pindar also takes the long view of events, reminding us in Olympian 2 that Semele will ultimately ascend to Olympus and her sister Ino to honor as a sea-nymph. In Nemean 9, he explains that in the next generation the sons of the defeated Athenian warriors will capture Thebes as victors. Adrastus, the leader of this expedition, will, moreover, become the legendary founder of the Nemean festival at which Pindar now honors both the conquered and the conquerors alike (Nemean 9.9–12).

We have often noted how Pindar deftly chooses details from myth to shape the theme and moral of an ode. By pointing to certain aspects of myth and suppressing others, he colors his narratives. In Pythian 4, he presents Medea as the prophetess who helps Jason to the fleece and who predicts future happiness for the Cyrenians and suppresses the baleful events in her future. In a comparable fashion Heracles' heroic achievements, rather than his misfortunes, are highlighted in odes in which he features. Conversely, allusions to Achilles or Hector serve in Pindar's odes only to heighten some tragic foreboding. In "Lycidas" Milton selects certain aspects of the Orpheus myth and suppresses others. For many Renaissance poets, Orpheus was simply the archetypal poet who possessed extraordinary gifts; in "L'Allegro" and "Il Penseroso" Milton alludes to his prowess in conquering Hades. In "Lycidas" Orpheus is a tragic figure, born of a Muse, who is unable to save her son. His descent from Apollo Milton leaves unnoted, even though the god later appears in the ode to respond to the swain's complaint. Milton mentions Nature's lament for her "enchanting son" (l. 59), but touches only indirectly on Orpheus's power to enchant Nature. He decries Orpheus's dismemberment at the hands of the Bacchantes, but does not tell how his "divine" head, sent to the Lesbian shore, gave the gift of poetry to the singers from Lesbos. Yet in his draft version of "Lycidas," preserved in the Trinity manuscript, Milton clearly alludes to this very detail.[18]

In Pindar's odes and in "Lycidas" a god or mythic figure often appears at strategic moments and for strategic purposes. Pindar uses the device sparingly when he wishes to arrest a moment or give it vivid realization. Sometimes he permits us to hear a suppliant's prayer to the god; other times we hear the god's speech. In Olympian 1, for example, Pelops appeals to Poseidon for the god's assistance in a very dangerous chariot competition. Pelops's prayer illustrates the

---

[18] In his draft of the poem, Milton changed "divine" head to "gory" head. See "The Trinity College Manuscript," in John Milton, *Complete Poetical Works*, ed. Harris Francis Fletcher, 4 vols. (Urbana: University of Illinois Press, 1943), 1: 381–455.

young man's sincerity, his courage, and above all his piety. Although we do not hear Poseidon's reply, we know that the god grants Pelops's request. Pelops is victorious, just as his putative descendant Hieron also has been in the Olympian contest. The entry of the divine into the human sphere marks a turning point in the young hero's life—and in the ode as well. In other odes gods descend either to help or to punish human beings. When a god speaks as Pallas Athene does in Olympian 13, human fate is changed. At Athene's urging Bellerophon bridles Pegasus and wins fame. In Pythian 3 Pindar lets us hear Apollo's voice, as he determines to intervene and save his son Asclepius from death. Similarly, in Nemean 10 another god decides the fate of his son, as Pindar presents both Polydeuces' supplication of his father and Zeus's reply. In many cases Pindar uses the dramatic speech to effect the climax of a mythic digression and sometimes also to point to the ode's moral.

Such is also the case when Phoebus Apollo, poetry's patron, appears in "Lycidas." Phoebus Apollo, as Pindar tells us in Pythian 1, holds the lyre in common right with the Muses, but in Milton's ode he appears not to celebrate poetry, but to respond to the shepherd swain's bitter complaint about poetry's meager rewards. Why should the poet serve a muse who begrudges thanks, the swain asks, and who abandons him to a blind and fury-ridden fate? We hear both the shepherd swain's angry indictment and the god's response. "*Fame* is the spur that the clear spirit doth raise," the swain complains, that which makes us "scorn delights, and live laborious days."

> But the fair Guerdon when we hope to find,
> And think to burst out into sudden blaze,
> Comes the blind *Fury* with th'abhorred shears,
> And slits the thin-spun life.
> (ll. 70, 72, 73–76)

As though responding to the protest, Phoebus appears and, touching the shepherd's ears, rejoins: "But not the praise." Repeating the word fame, Phoebus corrects the swain: "*Fame* is no plant that grows on mortal soil" (ll. 76–78).

A peculiarly classical, an almost Pindaric view of life, underlies Phoebus' speech—not inappropriately so. Throughout his odes Pindar contrasts the changeable world of men with the unvarying realm of the gods. To men seeking for fame Pindar offers nothing more permanent that the assurance that fame such as mortals achieve will be preserved in song. The Muses guard fame, but the poet knows that even fame as the world knows it is transitory. The only mortals Pindar counts happy are those few who pass on to an immortality reserved for the semi-divine heroes such as Heracles, Achilles, or Perseus. For them fame is secure, life is happy, immortality assured. Phoebus's words in "Lycidas" have more than a little in common with Pindar's view and ring with his gnomic sentence. Moreover, later in the poem, the classical god's speech on fame will be contrasted with the Christian Peter's speech on a different type of "judgment." It is significant that Phoebus does not promise immortality. Only Christ can do that. Phoebus Apollo is the sun god, but Christ is the day-star that can set and rise again. As Christ's classical counterpart, Phoebus can offer the moral assurance that the human being who strives for righteous deeds will be remembered for deeds well done. He will be honored by the "perfect witness of all-judging *Jove*," Phoebus's father-god, who "pronounces lastly on each deed." Phoebus Apollo offers us the classical assurance: "Of so much fame in Heav'n expect thy meed" (ll. 82–84). Or, as Pindar remarked in Nemean 7: Honor grows for those whose fame the god augments, even after they have died (ll. 29–30).

With the departure of Phoebus Apollo, Milton once more shifts direction abruptly, apostrophizing the "fountain *Arethuse*" and the river, "smooth-sliding *Mincius*" (ll. 85–86). Most critics regard these apostrophes simply as metonymy for the Theocritean or Vergilian pastoral that Milton imitates: Arethusa is the spring of Theocritus's Syracuse, Mincio the river of Vergil's birthplace Mantua. However, even brief mythic allusions can have subtle implications. By opening the central section of "Lycidas" with an invocation to Arethusa and closing it with an invocation to Arethusa's lover Alpheus—"Return, Alpheus" (l. 132)—Milton not only alludes to the ancient pastoral tradition, but also effects a poignant evocation of the Alpheus-Arethusa myth. Arethusa was an Arcadian nymph loved by the river god Alpheus, who rejecting him fled under the sea, emerging on the Sicilian island Ortygia, where she was transformed into a freshwater fountain just at the edge of the harbor. Alpheus pursued her undersea, also emerging in Sicily and mingling his waters with Arethusa's. Pindar, Theocritus, Moschus, and Vergil all refer to the myth, and in the Renaissance it was interpreted as a symbol, as we shall see, of transformation and resurrection.[19] In naming Arethusa at this point, moreover, Milton introduces the first of a series of water deities by whom he will attempt to redeem water, the very element that caused Lycidas's death.

Water is an important thematic image throughout "Lycidas," as Brooks and Hardy, as well as Wayne Shumaker, have made clear.[20] Milton uses the image to link his central figure, the drowned Lycidas, to the various mythic characters who appear successively in the digressive sections of the ode: the Muses whose

---

[19] For allusions to Alpheus and Arethusa see Pindar, Pythian 3. 69; Nemean 1. 1–2; Theocritus 1. 117; 16. 102–103; Moschus 3. 10, 77. Moschus recounts the myth in fragment # 6; also Vergil, *Aeneid* 3. 694–696. See J. Martin Evans, *The Road from Horton: Looking Backwards in "Lycidas"* (Victoria: University of Victoria Press, 1983).

[20] See *Poems of Mr. John Milton* (New York: Harcourt Brace, 1951), 169–86; repr. in *Milton's Lycidas: The Tradition and the Poem*, ed. Patrides, 140–56. Also see Wayne Shumaker, "Flowerets and Sounding Seas: A Study in the Affective Structure of *Lycidas*," *PMLA* 66 (1951): 485–94, repr. in *Milton's Lycidas: The Tradition and the Poem*, ed. Patrides, 129–39.

spring water inspires poets; Orpheus, the archetypal poet figuratively destroyed by water; the water deities, Arethusa and Mincius. Now Milton introduces still more mythic figures connected with water: Triton, Neptune's herald; the sea-nymphs Panope and her sisters; the river god Camus; St. Peter, the "Pilot of the *Galilean* Lake"; the river god Alpheus; St. Michael, whose mount stands on the coast of Cornwall; and finally Christ, who walked on the waves and as day-star rises from the ocean (2 Peter 1: 29), Christ who alone can offer Lycidas salvation. As he moves from one figure connected with water to the next, Milton subtly and surely transforms the destructive aspect of water back to its generative and redemptive function. Like Pindar in so many of his odes, Milton employs thematic imagery to achieve this transformation.

Pindar is famous for his use of thematic imagery to convey the message of his odes. Often he introduces an image, associates it with a character or characters, and then works a transformation, as he connects the image with different personages or concepts that he develops in the course of the ode. It is technique I have referred to as mythic or metaphoric transformation.[21] In Olympian 1 he famously apostrophizes water in the opening line of the ode, "Ἄριστον μὲν ὕδωρ" (water is best), applying it as that standard of excellence against which all else must be judged.[22] Water shines supreme as the highest of elements, purifying and upholding life, just as those contests on the banks of the river Alpheus provide a standard that enriches human life. The central myth of Olympian 1, to which I have already referred, concerns Pelops and his victory in the chariot race that assures his marriage to Hippodameia and thereby the continuation of the Dorian people from whom Hieron, the patron addressed in Olympian 1, is descended. Water appears not only as the shining element extolled at the opening of the ode, but also as the purifying element that helps, in the myth to which Pindar refers, to reconstitute the dismembered Pelops. By the waters of the ocean Pelops appeals to the sea god Poseidon, and thereafter he not only wins his chariot victory at Pisa by the waters of Alpheus, but also rests after his death in a great tomb beside the same river.

In an even more intricate way, imagery and myth work hand in hand in Pythian 12. In this ode, as Kevin Crotty has noted, Pindar deals with the

---

[21] See Revard, "Alpheus, Arethusa, and the Pindaric Pursuit in 'Lycidas'," in *Of Poetry and Politics: New Essays on Milton and his World*, ed. P. G. Stanwood, MRTS 126 (Binghamton NY: MRTS, 1985), 35–35, reworked in eadem, *Milton and the Tangles of Neaera's Hair*, 165–79.

[22] Isaac Oliver, another of the poets in the volume commemorating King, alludes to Pindar's praise of water in Olympian 1: "Had the Thebane Swan / Who lov'd his Dirce (while it proudly ran / Swell'd by his lyre) now liv'd, he would repent / The solemn praises he on water spent" (in *Obsequies to the memorie of Mr. Edward King* in *Justa Edouardo King* [Cambridge, 1638], 15). Among his water references Oliver also includes Arethusa and St. Peter walking on the waves.

contradictory character of victory, which involves both joy and sorrow.[23] Gold is the thematic image, and the story of Perseus the principal myth. At first it is not apparent why Pindar should connect Midas, the victor in a flute-playing contest, with Perseus, or narrate the stories connected with Perseus: his slaying of Medusa, his conception when Zeus took the form of a golden shower, his rescue of his mother Danaë from king of Seriphos.[24] In connecting the flute-player Midas with this hero and these events, however, Pindar is not digressing aimlessly, as he makes clear by employing the thematic image — gold — to forge a metaphoric link between Midas's flute-playing and certain events of the Perseus myth. First of all, he likens the sound of the flute to the wailing of the gorgons, who lamented the death of their sister, Medusa, even suggesting that their wailing sound inspired Athene, when she heard it, to invent the flute in order to replicate it.[25] Next, Pindar likens the golden stream that begets Perseus to the golden sound streaming from the flute. In both cases a deity, Pallas Athene or Zeus, is involved, one whose intervention radically alters human experience. Athene changes dissonant wailing to music; Zeus changes the fate of a beautiful woman by impregnating her with the hero who will rescue her.[26] On one level, Pindar is illustrating a theme he often deals with. When gods intervene in human life, miracles happen: out of deformity can come beauty, out of tragedy triumph, out of defeat victory. The flute music was born of the pain of the gorgons, Perseus from the laboring pain of his mother, and Danaë's liberation from captivity through the pain of the islanders and the king turned to stone. On another level, Pindar is simply complimenting the flute-player he addresses in his ode: joy does not come to light, he tells him, without laboring or pain. If the legend that the scholiasts hand down is true, the flute-player Midas won victory from

---

[23] Crotty regards the arguments of Nemean 11, Olympian 12, and Pythian 12 as basically the same, although the movement of Olympian 12 is different from that of the other two odes (*Song and Action*, 16).

[24] See Gildersleeve's discussion of the Pythian 12 in Pindar, *The Olympian and Pythian Odes*, ed. Basil L. Gildersleeve (London: Macmillan, 1908), 364–67.

[25] For a commentary on the art of Athene in bringing music out of dissonance, see Segal, "The Gorgon and the Nightingale: The Voice of Female Lament and Pindar's Twelfth *Pythian Ode*," in *Aglaia*, 85–104, here 95–98.

[26] As a goddess, Athene has the power to transform both human beings and things, transforming the gorgons from beautiful women to snaky-haired monsters, petrifying their beauty as they in turn petrify those who look on them. At the same time she transformed the wailing lament that came from them into lovely polyphonic music for the flute. Athene also uses her divine powers to guide Perseus, leading him to the gorgons, assisting him to kill Medusa and to use Medusa's head to liberate his mother, Danaë, from the king of Seriphos and his subjects by turning them into stone. Danaë is twice liberated, first when Zeus invades her brazen tower in the form of a stream of gold and next when Athene inspires Perseus to rescue her from the king of Seriphos. See Brumble, *Classical Myths and Legends*, 19.

apparent pain and defeat. As he was playing, his mouthpiece broke and he was forced to play upon the reeds, but nonetheless was victorious. In the end Pindar's ode reaches beyond the celebration of a flute-player or even the celebration of the origin of flute music to comment upon a universal truth: how the divine can transform human experience, bringing joy or sorrow, success or failure.

In "Lycidas" Milton works in a similar way, transforming apparent tragedy into triumph. To prepare for this transformation, Milton proceeds in the central sections of the ode to absolve the gods of the sea from responsibility for Lycidas's death. Triton comes to plead the case for Neptune, asking the waves and felon winds if they had doomed the gentle Lycidas. Aeolus attends to add to his plea, remarking that the air was calm and Panope and her sisters played on the peaceful level of the sea. If there was responsibility for Lycidas's death, it lay in the ship, which was bearing him to his destination: the "fatal and perfidious Bark, / Built in th'eclipse, and rigg'd with curses dark, / That sunk so low that sacred head of thine" (ll. 100–102). Water was the means, not the cause of death; some inscrutable fatality doomed Lycidas, a fatality connected with man, not nature.

The procession of mourners is led by the river god Camus, another water deity, who also represents the university that has lost its "dearest pledge" (l. 107). The last of these so-called figures connected with water is St. Peter, the "Pilot of the *Galilean* Lake," identified also as the keeper of the keys to heaven and the shepherd of the church (ll 109–112). As head of the church Peter is a Christian father to the shepherd Lycidas, just as Apollo as head of the poetic congregation is his poetic father. With Apollo Milton had focused on God's justice to the individual; with Peter he focuses on the individual's loss to a society that much needs him: "How well could I have spar'd for thee, young swain" (l. 113). Yet apart from this brief expression of regret, Peter avoids apology and does not defend God's apparent abandonment of the good shepherd. Instead he deals with God's vengeance on the wicked, who have failed in their pastoral responsibilities. It is the first directly political note that Milton introduces into the monody, a motif to which he called attention by adding the headnote in 1645 that he had by occasion foretold "the ruin of our corrupted Clergy then in their height." To introduce political commentary into a poem that commemorates other events is a device not unknown to Pindar or the Pindaric poets who followed him. In the turbulent fifth century B.C. it was difficult for Pindar not to glance aside at the events that were leading to the clash between Sparta and Athens. Pindar often veiled his bolder political assertions in myth. The treacherous Odysseus of Nemean 8 is often regarded as a cipher for an Athens that was beginning to strip its neighbors of political sovereignty. Similarly, the arrogant giants that Pindar's Heracles put down could be symbols for political arrogance in the ancient world. Pindar's scholiasts have thought so. If Milton had not added the headnote to "Lycidas," modern scholiasts might speculate whether St. Peter's indictment of the bad shepherds was a general or a specific rebuke for the clergy of Milton's time. The headnote resolves all doubt about Milton's intention.

Milton heightens the tone of the passage by employing dramatic speech once more. In what is the longest single speech in "Lycidas," Peter rebukes the reprobate shepherds:

> Enough of such as for their bellies' sake,
> Creep and intrude, and climb into the fold;
> Of other care they little reck'ning make,
> Than how to scramble at the shearers' feast,
> And shove away the worthy bidden guest;
> Blind mouths!
> (ll. 114–119)

It is not merely the greed of the shepherds that Peter castigates—their scrambling for benefices and rich appointments and their neglect of pastoral duties. This censure we expect. But Milton also remembers that these shepherds are also poets who badly serve the poetic craft practiced by the swain and the dead shepherd Lycidas—"the homely slighted Shepherd's trade" (l. 65). Peter derides their "lean and flashy songs" which grate on "scrannel Pipes of wretched straw" (ll. 123–124). No true poets are they, neither born to nor practicing well that ancient art. Pindar's reproach of those poets who demean the art of poetry was famous. He was the Theban eagle who soared above, and with a voice as stern as Peter's reproached the crows who cawed in vain against the divine bird of Zeus (Olympian 2. 86–88). Milton closes Peter's speech on an apocalyptic note, prophesying the punishment that awaits those who scoff at the laws of man and God: "But that two-handed engine at the door, / Stands ready to smite once, and smite no more" (ll. 130–131).

With his apostrophe to the river god Alpheus—"Return, *Alpheus*, the dread voice is past / That shrunk thy stream. Return, *Sicilian* Muse" (ll. 132–133)—Milton restores to the monody the pastoral tone and the controlling voice of the shepherd swain who had almost disappeared from it. However, the apostrophe to Alpheus also serves to refine the previous allusion to the Alpheus-Arethusa myth. Commentators looked on the myth as symbolic of resurrection, for Alpheus and Arethusa both passed through a transformative undersea journey to breathe once more in a different clime.[27] In Nemean 1.1 Pindar names Sicily the sacred breathing place of Alpheus (Ἄμπνευμα σεμνὸν Ἀλφεοῦ), where the river god attained a second life and where the poet speeds forth his songs of praise. With this briefest of references Milton implicitly links Alpheus to Lycidas, just as he had linked Lycidas to Orpheus, destroyed at the height of his poetic pow-

---

[27] For commentary on the symbolic meaning of the story, see Fulgentius, "De Alfeo, & Arethusa," in *Mythologiarum Libri III*, in C. Iulius Hyginus, *Fabularum Liber* (Paris, 1578), 294; trans. L. Whitbread, *Fulgentius the Mythographer* (Columbus: Ohio State University Press, 1971), 98–99.

ers. But here he turns a potential tragedy to good fortune. The river god, who had vainly pursued the fleeing nymph, heard a dread voice that shrank his streams. Ultimately, however, that voice gave him renewed life in Sicily and union with his beloved. With Alpheus's return Milton hints at the theme of resurrection, but he defers expanding on it here, substituting instead a flower catalogue, intended to offer consolation—"to interpose a little ease" (152). At the swain's command the Sicilian Muse bids the vales of Sicily to bring forth "Bells and Flowrets of a thousand hues," "vernal flowers" that "purple all the ground" to "strew the Laureate Hearse where *Lycid* lies" (ll. 135, 141, 151).

Confronted with the task of combining Pindaric ode, pastoral, and the Christian lament, Milton, like his fellow pindarist Benedetto Lampridio, chooses to evoke the flowers of the spring goddess Proserpina, who returned from the dead to flourish again and to console human beings who grieve. But the poet knows at the same time that to offer the flower analogy is to "dally with false surmise" (l. 153). Lycidas will not return; the laureate hearse is empty. Unlike Alpheus, Lycidas did not safely undergo the undersea journey; his body was washed far away, perhaps beyond the stormy Hebrides, visiting "the bottom of the monstrous deep" (l. 158). Having alluded to the pagan alternative of the story, Milton can now turn away from this terror to offer the Christian solution. St. Michael is only the second Christian figure to appear in "Lycidas," and like St. Peter he is not named but identified merely by epithet: the "great vision of the guarded Mount" (l. 161). Milton does not describe Michael with an apocalyptic or a militaristic demeanor, neither balancing the scales of judgment nor swinging an avenging sword. Instead he depicts him as a figure of Christian compassion, linking the angel with those classical dolphins, who so often in myth were the saviors of those lost at sea.[28] The swain's appeal to both angel and dolphins prepares us for a final turn and resolution: "Look homeward Angel now, and melt with ruth. / And, O ye *Dolphins*, waft the hapless youth" (ll. 163–164).

Until this point, the swain has offered a solitary threnody for Lycidas; now he directly addresses the company of shepherds who mourn with him: "Weep no more, woeful Shepherds, weep no more" (l. 165). The true consolation has at last begun—and Milton can move on to presenting the vision of Lycidas, redeemed in heaven. Once more we can pose a debt to Pindar, who also knew how to move deftly from the terrible to the consolatory. Olympian 2 concludes with a justly

---

[28] In his role of saving angel, Michael could be referred to a a psychopompos, a leader of the souls like Hermes. Dolphins in myth saved a number of figures, including the poet Arion whose music they admired and whom they bore safely to the shore. See J. Martin Evans, "Lycidas and the Dolphins," *N & Q*, n. s. 25 (1978): 15–17. See also Edward W. Tayler, "Lycidas in Christian Time," *Huntington Library Quarterly* 41 (1978): 103–17, condensed in *Milton's Lycidas: The Tradition and the Poem*, ed. Patrides, 303–18; and also in Tayler, *Milton's Poetry: its Development in Time* (Pittsburgh: Duquesne University Press, 1979), 45–59.

famous passage that describes the rewards that await the just soul, who will be
lightened with equal days and equal nights (Olympian 2. 41–51, 56–63). In the
Renaissance Pindar was often considered a pagan poet with close ties to Christianity. Reformed Protestants in Basel supported this view by citing odes such
as Olympian 2 that contain passages that describe the rewards of the good after
death.[29] The vision of Lycidas, redeemed in Heaven, is certainly drawn in part
from Revelation's description of the city of God.[30]

> There entertain him all the Saints above,
> In solemn troops, and sweet Societies
> That sing, and singing in their glory move,
> And wipe the tears for ever from his eyes. (ll. 178–181)

Nonetheless, the passage also has some particular affinities with Pindar's depiction of the afterlife in Olympian 2 and particularly his description of the voyage
of the good soul after death to the Isles of the Blest, where golden flowers grow
and where they entwine their hands with wreaths and are crowned by the righteous judge Rhadamanthys.

> ὅσοι δ' ἐτόλμασαν ἐστρὶς
> ἑκατέρωθι μείναντες ἀπὸ πάμπαν ἀδίκων ἔχειν
> ψυχάν, ἔτειλαν Διὸς ὁδὸν παρὰ Κρό
>   νου τύρσιν· ἔνθα μακάρων
> νᾶσον ὠκεανίδες
> αὖραι περιπνέοισιν· ἄνθεμα δὲ χρυσοῦ φλέγει,
> τὰ μὲν χερσόθεν ἀπ' ἀγλαῶν δενδρέων,
>   ὕδωρ δ' ἄλλα φέρβει,
> ὅρμοισι τῶν χέρας ἀναπλέκοντι καὶ στεφάνους
> βουλαῖς ἐν ὀρθαῖσι Ῥαδαμάνθυος . . .
> (Olympian 2. 68–75)

> Those who endured three times in either realm
> and kept their souls untainted with injustice
> travel by Zeus's road to the tower of Cronos,
> where ocean-blown breezes blow about
> the Isles of the Blest;
> flowers of gold bloom,
> some from shining trees on the shore, others the water nourishes;
> with garlands they entwine their hands, and with crowns
> their heads, according to Rhadamanthys's righteous counsels.

---

[29] For Pindar's reputation for piety, see Revard, *Pindar and the Renaissance Hymn-
Ode*, 13–19.

[30] See specifically Revelation 7:17; 4:1–4; 21:1, 4; 22:1–3.

Moreover, Pindar has not produced this glorious description of the Isles of the Blest merely to assure his patron Theron of future happiness after death.[31] The Isles are the dwelling place of those who have died before their time—young heroes like Achilles, who appears as a poignant reminder that those virtuous men who die young are assured rewards after death.

Milton's pastoral heaven has intimations of the Isles of the Blest, and Lycidas in heaven, entertained by the sweet societies, resembles both the Christian soul saved and the youthful hero rewarded.

> Where other groves, and other streams along,
> With *Nectar* pure his oozy Locks he laves,
> And hears the unexpressive nuptial Song,
> In the blest Kingdoms meek of joy and love.
> (ll. 174–177)

With "Lycidas," Milton did not seek to compose merely a pastoral elegy or a lament for the dead. In choosing the classical form of monody, he attempted to replicate the kind of ode Pindar composed in which intricate patterns are woven together, a poem which transcends the occasion it celebrates.[32]

The final frame of Milton's poem, where the poet steps forward and describes the singer of his ode—the uncouth swain—also says something about its ultimate purpose: "He touch't the tender stops of various Quills, / With eager thought warbling his *Dorick* lay" (188–189). The term *Doric* could describe either the pastoral or the Pindaric mode or both. In blending and varying his style—the various "Quills" to which he refers—Milton has created something unique in English poetry: an ode that is both classical and Christian, pastoral and epinician.

3.

Although Abraham Cowley's pindaric "On the death of Mrs. *Katherine Philips*" is a poem written by a living poet in tribute to a dead poet, it could not be more unlike Milton's monody "Lycidas." The funerary pindaric for Philips, together with his earlier pindaric "On *Orinda's* Poems," composed in the decade after

---

[31] This passage is often cited by critics as evidence that Pindar's views of the afterlife had been influenced by Pythagoras.

[32] That Milton's "Lycidas" as monody was popularly linked to Pindaric ode is evident in a later imitation designated as monody, which uses Cowley's Pindaric stanzas as its verse form. See the anonymous Pindaric monody composed by a husband on the death of his young wife: "To the Memory of A Lady Lately Deceased. A Monody" (London, 1747). The author has in mind lines from "Lycidas" when he demands, "Where were ye, Muses, when relentless Fate / From these fond Arms your fair Disciple tore" (7. 1–2).

his 1656 *Pindarique Odes* and printed in the posthumous *Works*, mark a second stage in Cowley's imitation of Pindaric ode. While the odes are governed by the Pindaric conventions he established in his earlier collection, Cowley attempts to remake the Pindaric ode into a new medium for encomium that could extend to commemoration for the dead. Among his successful pre-pindaric poems are elegies for poetic friends: "On the Death of Mr. *William Hervey*" and "On the Death of Mr. *Crashaw*," both eloquent testimonials to friendship and poetry.[33] However, he undertakes a further challenge in his odes to Katherine Philips, for in them he is addressing not a a male friend, but a woman who is neither a mistress nor a patron nor a sovereign, but a so-called "peer" in the poetic vocation.[34] In this he has something in common with Benedetto Lampridio, who in framing his Latin pindaric to the celebrated Vittoria Colonna also had to deal with the issue of Vittoria's status as a poet.

A Pindaric ode pays tribute to achievement. A funeral pindaric attempts to assess a life's achievement and must in some cases, as in Jonson's ode and Milton's monody, assess an achievement cut short by early death. Katherine Philips, like Morison and Edward King, died young, yet while Cowley laments her early demise in the second ode, he is occupied throughout both odes with a paradoxical issue: just what sort of achievement can a woman poet claim as her warrant for eternity? Cowley's first ode "On *Orinda's* Poems" addresses Philips by her poetic pseudonym of Orinda and develops (perhaps in tribute to the epinician mode) the metaphor of contest. Usually the contest of "arms" in which men and women

---

[33] See *Miscellanies* in *Poems* (London, 1656), 16–20, 29–30. Cowley employs regular strophes rather than pindarics to mourn the loss of his friends William Hervey and Richard Crashaw. Dr. Johnson commends Cowley on the naturalness of his elegiac ode for Hervey (in contrast to the so-called artificiality of the pastoral mode in Milton's "Lycidas"). However, he has some harsh comments to make about Cowley's invention of the irregular pindaric: "The Pindaric odes have so long enjoyed the highest degree of poetical reputation, that I am not willing to dismiss them with unabated censure; and surely, though the mode of their composition be erroneous, yet many parts deserve at least that admiration which is due to great comprehension of knowledge, and great fertility of fancy. The thoughts are often new, and often striking; but the greatness of one part is disgraced by the littleness of another; and the total negligence of language gives the noblest conceptions the appearance of a fabric august in the plan, but mean in the materials. Yet surely those verses are not without a just claim to praise, of which it may be said with truth, that no man but Cowley could have written them" (*Lives of the Most Eminent English Poets* [London: James Christie, 1822], 1: 45).

[34] Philips composed a pindaric in the Cowleian manner in response to an ode Cowley had written on retirement. See "Upon Mr. Abraham Cowley's Retirement" in Philips's posthumous folio, *Poems by the most deservedly Admired Mrs. Katherine Philips, The Matchless Orinda* (London, 1667). She compliments Cowley as man and poet: "For lo, the Man whom all Mankind admir'd, / (By ev'ry Grace adorn'd, and ev'ry Muse inspir'd) / Is now triumphantly retir'd. / The mighty *Cowley*" (5.13–16).

are engaged is a love contest. Traditionally, the poet—a man—assails the lady with his artillery of wit, aspiring to win her as his "prize." But what if the fellow contestant, the fellow poet, is a woman, who as a woman keeps her fort of beauty secure and as a poet engages in the same sallies of wit as the male poet, thus turning his own artillery against him? Although Cowley wittily awards Philips the victory in such a contest, he is clearly perplexed that woman should be vying with man as an intellectual competitor. Woman should be content to be fruitful like earth, Mother Cybele, since Nature has awarded her natural fecundity. Philips, however, aspires to man's sphere ("Man may be Head, but Woman's now the Brain" [1.8]), assuming cerebral fruitfulness and by producing her own literary work usurping a creative domain that is properly male. Cowley, who indulgently confesses himself a defeated competitor, takes on at the same time the responsibility of writing the epinician ode to compliment Philips on her victory.

How then, asks Cowley, must we regard this anomaly, the female poet? She is not a Muse, says Cowley, since Muses are, after all, "Female *Chimera's*" (4.2), fantasies of male brains. Neither is she properly a modern Sappho, for Sappho had a reputation for sexual promiscuity: "Ill manners soil the lustre of her Fame" (4.6).[35] Philips exists in a category of her own. However, as a female poet she is governed by the same standards that govern woman. She must shine in virtue. "Honour" is the highest thing that the female poet, or for that matter any female, possesses. By enshrining Philips in honor, Cowley deftly eliminates her as a real literary competitor and assigns her the traditional status granted women in his time—that of "goddesses" and "nymphs." In this, her virtue so excels that she easily wins a moral or "Roman" victory: "At once she overcomes, enslaves and betters Men" (4.17).

Further, he suggests that her real competition is not with men, but with other women, with the so-called amazons of antiquity who also competed with men and for whom she wins the victory. Learned Orinda is so exceptional among women that Merlin prophesied her ascendancy and foretold for her a female triumph that eluded the British queen Boadicea: "Ev'n *Boadicia's* angry Ghost / Forgets her own misfortune, and disgrace, / And to her injur'd Daughters now does boast, / That *Rome's* o'recome at last, by a woman of her Race" (5.11–14). Cowley's "literary" epinician crowns Philips with laurels as the noble exception—the virtuous literary lady.

In the pindaric on Philips's death Cowley once more permits his compliments for the woman to take precedence over his eulogy for the poet. Philips died from smallpox, and Cowley contrives Pindarically to apostrophize the "Cruel Disease" that attacked her "beauty" before it ended her life: "thy [smallpox's] Malice most of all / (Thy Malice or thy Lust) does on the fairest fall? / And in them most assault the fairest place, / The Throne of Empress Beauty, ev'n the

---

[35] The text for Cowley's odes on Philips is cited from "Verses written on several occastions," in *The Works of Mr. Abraham Cowley* (London, 1668), 2–4, 32–34.

Face?" (1.5–8). At the same time he acknowledges that the "temple" of Philips's work, like a Horatian poetic pyramid, resists death and time and remains unravaged by the disease that destroyed the body's temple. Thus it would seem that Cowley was willing to allow that the female poet should be assessed, as her male counterpart would be, by the "work" that she has left behind.

However, Cowley does not long dwell on Philips's work. When he returns to the subject of competition, he spins out compliments appropriate for female subjects. If Orinda had vied with the three goddesses for the coveted apple, she would have won the prize because Apollo is a juster judge than Paris and would have favored Orinda for the laureateship. The compliment is double-edged, for it is usual to offer noble ladies, Queen Elizabeth among them, the golden apple for beauty. Cowley is also quite willing to assure us that Philips surpasses Sappho or the Muses, whom she excels in wit and spiritual dignity, or to develop other metaphors of contest. Orinda is like a merchant ship, which eliminates all competitors and delivers her wares:

> *Orinda* on the Female coasts of Fame,
> Ingrosses all the Goods of a Poetique Name,
>   She does no Partner with her see,
> Does all the business there alone, which we
> Are forc'd to carry on by a whole Company.
> (3.16–20)

Once more Philips is being compared to female competitors, and since the works of so few female poets survive, Philips wins a victory by default: "The certain proofs of our *Orinda's* wit, / In her own lasting Characters are writ" (3.8–9).

When Cowley compares Philips to a male, it is, surprisingly, not to a poet, but to the battle hero Achilles, whose famed physical prowess is (by implication) the equivalent of Philips's intellectual toughness. Cowley had previously interpolated into his paraphrase of Olympian 2 the myth of Thetis's dipping her famous son into the Styx. Here he reshapes the myth as a compliment for Philips.

> Never did spirit of Manly make,
> And dipt all o're in Learnings Sacred Lake,
> A temper more Invulnerable take.
> No violent Passion could an entrance find,
> Into the tender Goodness of her Mind
> Through walls of Stone those furious Bullets may
>   Force their impetuous way
> When her soft Brest they hit, powerless and dead they lay.
> (4.12–19)

Tenderness and goodness, rather than Achillean passion and strength, are those qualities that win the literary lady eternal fame. But what kind of fame exactly is it that Philips has won as poet and woman? Once again Cowley sidesteps the question of Philips's skill as a poet to award the laurel to her virtue as a woman. What she has achieved in her poetry is the representation of virtuous friendship. In his earlier ode he had praised the "Honour and Friendship" that shone through her and her verses ("On *Orinda's* Poems," 4.10). Now he again lauds her supreme achievement as having told "A new, and more surprising story, / Of fair *Leucasias* and *Orindas* Glory" (5.5–6). Until the last Cowley is willing to admit Philips to full citizenship in the company of poets only by coupling her status as a poet with that as a woman. She lives as the Muse of "the glad World of Poetry and Love" (5.14). [36]

With these mythic references and fulsome compliments, Cowley attempts to remake the funeral pindaric into some new kind of epinician ode. He eschews Jonson's techniques of classical appropriation and Milton's methods of joining pastoral's consolatory mode with the pindaric's introspection. Further, he avoids both Jonson's and Milton's combination of Christian with classical apotheosis. By developing the theme of competition, he creates a secular pindaric that sets a new standard for epideictic poetry.

4.

Dryden's "To the Pious Memory of the Accomplisht young LADY, Mrs Anne Killigrew" is indebted to Cowley's pindaric on Philips both in celebrating a female poet and in espousing the epinician style to do so. [37] Composed only a little

---

[36] The question whether the celebration of "Female Wit" is an appropriate subject for the Pindaric medium is raised in 1683 in a set of three Pindaric odes. The first, "The Emulation. A Pindarick Ode," reputedly by a Young Lady, demands that women be permitted to exercise themselves in poetic as well as domestic spheres. The second is a Pindaric reply by a man who objects to the "daring Female," who complains "In *Masculine* Pindarick Strains" (1. 1–2) [6]. The third, "A Reply to the Answerer of The Emulation," is by Mr. F., who queries "Did good *Apollo* e'er deny / Charms to *Orinda's* Poetry?" (1. 2–3 [13]). Taking the example of Katherine Philips, he argues that women have the right both to compose and to be praised in pindarics. See *Triumphs of Female Wit, In Some Pindarick Odes* (London: T. Malthus, 1683). Also see the discussion of this volume in S. P. Revard, "Katherine Philips, Aphra Behn, and the Female Pindaric," in *Representing Women in Renaissance England*, ed. Claude J. Summers and Ted-Larry Pebworth (Columbia: University of Missouri Press, 1997), 227–41, here 227–28, 235–36.

[37] In "The Preface to Ovid's Epistles" Dryden discusses the techniques of Cowley's pindarics. Although he censures inaccurate translations, Dryden approves Cowley's style of imitation and freely imitates it: "A genius so elevated and unconfin'd as Mr. Cowley's was but necessary to make Pindar speak English, and that was to be perform'd in no other way than imitation." See "The Preface to Ovid's Epistles," in *The Poetical Works of Dryden*, ed. George R. Noyes (Cambridge, MA: The Riverside Press, 1950), 91.

later than Dryden's politically motivated Pindaric threnody for Charles II, the
ode to Anne Killigrew celebrates poetry at the same moment it mourns the deceased poet.[38] Anne Killigrew was a talented member of the court circle, a lady-
in-waiting to James II's wife Mary of Modena, and a budding poet and artist.
In the opening section of the ode, Dryden apostrophizes her as the "Youngest
Virgin-Daughter of the Skies" (l. 1), calling attention to Anne Killigrew's poetic status and her election to sainthood. She wears the victorious palms of the
blest and, in recognition of her status as poet on earth, has joined the choir of
the Seraphim.[39] The Catholic Dryden could well have known the poetry of Gabriello Chiabrera and Matteo Barberini, both of whom employed the Pindaric
mode to celebrate the election of virgin martyrs to sainthood. In naming Anne
as both a virgin saint and a mortal muse, Dryden places her in the category of
those martyrs engaged in epinician contests to win the ultimate "laurel" crown of
victory. Whereas Cowley has avoided comparing the poet's contest to the saint's
contest, Dryden follows Milton and Jonson in connecting them. Like them, he
claims both a Christian and a poetic stake by praising a young poet who has gone
before him to a heavenly reward.

Although Dryden makes a passing reference to Philips, who had also, like
Anne, died from smallpox, he does not follow Cowley in attempting to assess
the status of the female poet in the competitive realm of male or female poets.
He makes the same point that Cowley had when he lamented that smallpox had
deprived Anne, as it had Orinda, of life and of beauty:

> O double Sacriledge on things Divine,
> To rob the Relique, and deface the Shrine!
>   But thus *Orinda* dy'd:
> Heav'n, by the same Disease did both translate,
> As equal were their Souls, so equal was their Fate.
> (ll. 160–164)

Avoiding the question of Anne's actual achievement as a poet, Dryden makes
Anne a symbol of poetry itself in its pure and idealized state. He writes not so
much of the woman as she was but of the Pindaric idea of a woman-poet—the

---

[38] Dryden's ode was first printed in 1686, prefixed to the *Poems* of Anne Killigrew
that her father, Dr. Henry Killigrew, theologian and chaplain to James II, had printed
the year following her death. Anne's uncle was Thomas Killigrew, playwright and impre-
sario of the King's Players, the company that had performed his own and Dryden's plays.
For further information see K. B. Meyers, "Anne Killigrew," in *An Encyclopedia of British
Women Writers*, ed. Paul Schlueter and June Schlueter (Chicago and London: St. James
Press, 1988), 275-76.

[39] "To the Pious Memory of the Accomplisht young LADY, Mrs Anne Killigrew,
Excellent in the two Sister-Arts of Poësie, and Painting, An ODE," in *The Poems of John
Dryden*, ed. James Kinsley, 4 vols. (Oxford: Clarendon Press, 1958), 1: 459–65.

pure virgin nymph who remains unsoiled and undefiled. Like Milton, Dryden complains of the low state of poetry and of poets who prostitute the Muse and profane the "Heav'nly Gift of Poesy" that was meant for the "Tongues of Angels, and for Hymns of Love" (ll. 57, 61). Against them stand those who keep pure "the *Arethusian* Stream" (l. 68). Here Anne represents the inspired poet who receives the gift of poetry from heaven, in contrast to the poet who writes for pay. With the appeal to "the *Arethusian* Stream," Dryden evokes not only the Syracusan goddess-nymph of pastoral poetry, but also Milton's Arethusa, called upon in "Lycidas" to represent the apex of poetic inspiration.[40]

Although Dryden has serious concerns about the place of poetry in the post-Restoration world, his principal aim is to compose a funeral ode that, like epinician ode, would pay proper tribute to both the individual and the family. Dryden is conscientious in honoring Anne's aristocratic heritage, together with those close to her who shaped her as a poet morally and literarily, principally her theologian father and her literary uncle, Thomas Killigrew. He also remains true to his Pindaric calling by using the ode form to mention and praise Anne Killigrew's accomplishments in painting as well as the sister art of poetry.[41] Moreover, he takes care to place her with her poetic progenitors, the classical poets and especially the highest female model, Sappho, poets who shaped her "Preexisting Soul" (29).[42] Although he differs from Cowley in his treatment of Sappho and the school of female poetry, he resembles him in the emphasis he places on the way a woman's moral character shines in her verse. Also, like Jonson, Dryden makes some effort to make his subject an exemplar not just of virtue, but of aristocratic virtue as well. Anne's character, like that of the Jonsonian duo Cary and Morison, could be read in her life and in her art:

> Her Morals too were in her Bosome bred
> By great Examples daily fed,
> What in the best of Books, her Fathers Life, she read.
> (ll. 77–79)

Dryden exploits the theme of contest in a way different from Cowley. For him life resembles a contest that the hero strives to win, a domain that he seeks to

---

[40] Dryden uses some of the same machinery in his later pindaric, "AN ODE, ON THE DEATH OF Mr. Henry Purcell," a shorter, far less ambitious ode that is content merely to lament Purcell's early death, to liken him mythically to Orpheus, and to celebrate his ascent to the "Heav'nly Quire" (l. 23). See *Poems*, 2: 863–64. It was set to music by John Blow.

[41] See especially Sections V, VI, and VII of the ode.

[42] Thoughout the ode Dryden freely relates Christian to classical concepts, calling upon Epictetus in line 82, referring to the myth of the phoenix in line 135, the classical concept of stellification in line 175, and here alluding to the Platonic doctrine of the preexistence of the soul.

conquer. He puts Anne's poetic and artistic efforts in terms of "attempted" conquests. When she extends her efforts from poetry to painting, she is like a conqueror, who "to the next Realm" tries to stretch "her Sway" (l. 92). He wittily compares Anne to an ambitious general:

> (As Conquerors will never want Pretence,
> When arm'd, to justifie the Offence)
> And the whole Fief, in right of Poetry she claim'd.
> The Country open lay without Defence:
> . . . .
> All bow'd beneath her Government,
> Receiv'd in Triumph wheresoe're she went.
> (ll. 96–99, 104–105)

Dryden knows Pindar well, and he makes the digression on Anne's brother take on a peculiarly Pindaric coloring. Pindar often alludes to fathers or brothers or cousins who have died and must learn the news of their young relative's victory from a messenger to the underworld. Dryden transposes this Pindaric device by telling us how Anne's brother, still at sea and ignorant of her demise, must learn of it when he glimpses a new star among the Pleiades that represents the translated soul of his sister. The final section of the ode returns to the theme that Dryden had announced at the beginning of the ode. Dryden once more claims kinship with Anne as a Christian and as a poet. When the Golden Trump shall sound at the end of the world, he tells us, the poets shall lead the way to heaven and Anne as poetry's Muse shall be the leader of the Quire. The funeral epinician concludes with a choral triumph, with a procession of celebrants who, like the choruses of Pindaric ode that laud the victor athlete, now laud the victor poet-saint.

> There *Thou*, Sweet Saint, before the Quire shall go,
> As Harbinger of Heav'n, the Way to show,
> The Way which thou so well hast learn'd below.
> (ll. 193–195)

Dryden has tactfully avoided the question of the quality of Anne Killigrew's achievement by treating her both as a poet who died before she could reach her potential, and as a Christian saint who can represent the domain of poetry in the domain above.

5.

The three odes prefixed to the second part of the seventh edition of Cowley's *Works* (1700) are concerned with commemorating a dead poet and with assessing the place of poetry in society.[43] That two of these odes, by Thomas Flatman and Samuel Wesley, are composed in Cowley's own Pindaric form is surely testimony to its continuing popularity and to Cowley's own prestige as the inventor of a type that had become the principal medium for commemorating both the celebrated living and the celebrated dead. How easily has the crowning of the poet with poetic laurels taken the place of the crowning of the victorious athlete. How easily has the poet himself become the hero with whom an author might identify the greatest of mythic heroes. Both Flatman and Wesley take the poetic license of comparing Cowley to Hercules, first in tribute to his paraphrase of Pindar's Herculean ode, Nemean 1, and second in tribute to his invention of the English pindaric. Flatman also compares Cowley to Hercules in compliment to his early development and long career as a poet: "*Herculean Vigor* hadst thou when but young, / In riper years more than *Alcides* strong" (3.1–2). In the first section of his ode Wesley also echoes Cowley's account of Hercules' strangling the serpents: only Pindar was fit to sing of Hercules and only Cowley of Pindar because he upheld the Herculean task of his poetic predecessor. What poet now remains who could sustain these Herculean endeavors, Wesley queries:

> But who shall now the mighty Task sustain?
> And now our *Hercules* is there,
> What *Atlas* can *Olympus* bear?

By the end of the seventeenth century the funeral pindaric confidently combined Christian and classical elements, making the victory that the Christian attains in death comparable to the triumph of Pindar's successful athletes. Both attain a kind of immortality. Conversely, Wesley and Flatman contrast the earthly tomb—the splendid monument erected to commemorate a poet's earthly fame—with the everlasting immortality he enjoys in heaven. They humble themselves as celebrants and mourners before Cowley's "sacred Monument," just as Sainte-Marthe had before Ronsard's tomb. Yet, even as they moisten with tears his "wondrous Urn" (Wesley, 2.16–17), they recognize that Cowley, the

---

[43] *The Second and Third Parts of the Works of Mr. Abraham Cowley, with Additions . . . And Several Poems in Praise of the Author*, 7th ed. (London: Charles Harper, 1700), sig. a^r–a3^v. The third of these commendatory poems, though not composed in Cowleian pindarics, refers to Cowley's achievements as a Pindaric poet. Another pindaric (by Thomas Higgons), prefixed to the ninth edition, also compares the achievements of Cowley to those of Pindar: *The Works of Mr. Abraham Cowley*, 9th ed. (London Henry Herringman, 1700), sig. d3^{r-v}.

"blest Shade," has won the ultimate race: his "radiant Brow, / Encircled with an everlasting Wreath" shows him triumphant over "Disappointment, and o'er Death" (Flatman, 2.7, 12–15).

While both poets adapt the epinician ode to Christian eulogy, both also keep in mind that they are conferring a tribute on the poet that would have been appropriate not only to an athlete but also to a classical patron or a king. Wesley allots Cowley the place in his ode that Pindar would have given to Hieron or Theron, or Cowley to the king. Echoing both Cowley and Pindar, Wesley emulates Ronsard's praise of Henri II and couples Cowley's name with Jove's:

> Begin, begin, my Muse, thy noble Choir,
> And aim at something worthy Pindar's Lyre,
> Within thy breast excite the kindling Fire,
>   And fan it with thy Voice!
> COWLEY does to JOVE belong,
> JOVE and COWLEY claim my Song. (3.1–6)

Wesley uses the digressive section of his ode as a convenient place to recapitulate Cowley's career as an epinician poet. Nurtured by the Muses and educated in the lyre by his foster-father Apollo, Cowley imitated Vergil and Spenser, the best of classical and native poets, surpassing contemporaries, such as Waller, as he now outstrips any competitors that might follow him. Moreover, like Hercules, the god-man to whom he is compared at the beginning of the ode, Cowley attains a place in the Roman Olympus as a "God of Poesie," to whom others may offer tribute:

> Those who survive unhappier be,
> Yet thus, great God of Poesie,
> With Joy they sacrifice their Fame to thee. (6. 19–21)

In the odes that commemorate Cowley we find the Horatian impulse as strong as the Pindaric. Both Wesley and Flatman are eager to erect a Horatian monument to Cowley that will assure his and their own fame, a monument comparable to the marble one in Westminster Abbey that Buckingham had commissioned for the English Pindarus. It is a triumph for Cowley, if not, perhaps, for Pindar. In the chapter following we shall see how Pindaric and Horatian impulses combine in the familiar ode, a form that Cowley also brought to eminence.

CHAPTER 8
THE POETICS OF THE FAMILIAR PINDARIC

A commonplace of literary criticism, often enunciated by Renaissance critics from J. C. Scaliger on, was that Horace was the master of the familiar ode, Pindar of the high and grandiose hymn-ode. However, although pindarics were often employed for hymns and for majestic celebratory occasions, this was only one end of the Pindaric spectrum. Even at its first appearance in the fifteenth century, Pindaric ode was perceived as a heterogeneous medium, a poetic catch-all, which could be used to address persons great and small and which was equally adaptable for subjects high and low. Pindarics could be modest addresses to friends as well as trumpet blasts to kings. Hence, with the very first neo-Latin imitations of Pindaric ode, the so-called divide between Horace's familiar and Pindar's grand style began to close. So-called Horatian subjects could be treated Pindarically. Horace's bee, who sipped only from pure springs, came to consort with Pindar's melissas. On the continent the very poets who first wrote Latin pindarics, Francesco Filelfo and Benedetto Lampridio, also turned the pindaric to familiar uses. In England the poet who most ostentatiously affected Pindaric high style, Abraham Cowley, also developed the familiar pindaric. Thus, by the end of the seventeenth century, Pindaric ode had become a medium that encompassed the familiar as well as the sublime, as its mighty stanzas or triads were tuned to a more modest music.

In a good deal of the familiar poetry of the sixteenth and seventeenth centuries the poet addresses close associates who are also poets. Inevitably, with poet-friends he shares his views on poetry and takes a stance on a society that he sometimes courts and sometimes holds in contempt. Inevitably also, he must deal with upheavals in the social framework, such as the wars in Italy, the civil wars in France and England, the religious conflicts in the Low Countries and in Germany—events that impinge on him and his friends as poets. And inevitably as well, he looks back at Pindar and Horace, who function as supreme mentors and exemplars as he speaks to poet-friends not as an encomiast of princes but in his own familiar voice.

1.

Ioannes Baptista Pius of Bologna, secretary to Giulio de' Medici, remarked that Pindar teaches us to value the men of our own generation.[1] As one of the earliest neo-Latin pindarists, Benedetto Lampridio took Pius's recommendation seriously, celebrating the men of his own time, both in formal pindarics but also in intimate, sometimes sportive odes.[2] Almost all his odes were addressed to living persons, but these odes include a wide range of addressees, from popes and heads of state to private friends and other poets. Indeed, it is perhaps with the personalization of the Pindaric ode that Lampridio makes his greatest mark as a Pindaric imitator.

Lampridio's familiar odes comprise the bulk of his poetic corpus. Many of them were composed during his sojourn in Rome in the 1510s when Leo X held the pontificate and liberally encouraged poets. They are often addressed to those scholars and poets who belonged to the same poetic sodalities as he did. However, even after his removal to Padua, sometime after 1521, Lampridio continued to write poetry to his poet-friends and maintained cordial relations with the humanists that he knew at Rome, patrons of leading sodalities such as Angelo Colocci and Pietro Mellini, and Pietro Bembo, the sponsor of the Collegio dei Greci where Lampridio had taught Latin and Greek. Lampridio's odes tell us much about the literary world in Rome and throughout Italy in the period from 1510 and 1540, particularly in the 1510s when the sodalities of Mellini, Colocci, and Goritz and other literary men were flourishing before the sack of Rome in 1527 put to an end to Rome's bid to be the literary capital of Italy.[3]

---

[1] Ioannes Baptista Pius of Bologna, "Dedicatory Epistle," in *De Urbe Roma* (Bologna, 1520). Citing Homer, Pius remarks that he likes old wine, but new poets.

[2] Lampridio composed only a few perfunctory neo-Latin amatory or mythological pieces: one to Venus and the fugitive Cupid, one to the thorny roses his lady bears, and others to the lady herself, whose name is Neaera, a name dear to the hearts of neo-Latin poets from Marullus to Secundus. See Benedetto Lampridio, *Carmina* (Venice, 1550).

[3] Lampridio probably knew most of the poets of the Colocci circle. Colocci refers to Lampridio in his letters. On Colocci's association with Lampridio, see Federico Ubaldini, *Vita Angeli Colotii episcopi Nucerini* (Rome, 1673), ed. and trans. Vittorio Fanelli, *Vita di Mons. Angelo Colocci* (Vatican City: Biblioteca Apostolica Vaticana, 1969); *Atti del convegno di studi su Angelo Colocci* (Iesi: Ammistrazione Comunale, 1972). Bembo sent his son to study with Lampridio, who wrote an ode to Bembo on the son's death. See Francesco Piovan, "Lampridio, Bembo e altri," *Italia Medioevale e Umanistica* 30 (1987): 179–97. Lampridio had also made the acquaintance of Janus Lascaris, the eminent teacher of Greek and scholar, while in Rome in the 1510s, and he later addresses a long triadic poem to him after Lascaris had moved to Paris. See Stella P. Revard, "Lampridio and the Poetic Sodalities in Rome in the 1510s and 1520s," in *Acta Conventus Neo-Latini Bariensis*, ed. R. Schnur et. al., MRTS 184 (Tempe AZ: ACMRS, 1998), 499–507. Also see Sadoleto's

Not all of Lampridio's familiar odes are in so-called Pindaric triads, but even his non-triadic odes evince a Pindaric spirit. Lampridio also wrote in hexameters, iambics, sapphics, asclepiads, and other stanza forms, demonstrating considerable metrical versatility and incorporating into much of this poetry the Pindaric concepts and poetic techniques conspicuous in his triadic verse. The triadic odes to friends and patrons that run on Pindaric feet seem imbued with Horatian familiarity, and the non-triadic verses have sparks of Pindaric elevation. The ode that he wrote to Antonio Tebaldeo in iambics consoling him on the death of a friend or the stanzas to Francesco Maria Molza or Baldassare Castiglione are not less influenced by Pindar than are the triadic verses to Lazaro Bonamico or Pietro Corsi or the triadic ode to Pietro Mellini.

In adapting Pindaric verse for addresses to friends, Lampridio was being extraordinarily faithful to Pindar himself. Pindar obviously regarded the ode form just as appropriate for exchanging compliments with a friend as for commemorating the king's chariot victory. Many of Pindar's odes, even those composed for specific occasions, are actually poetic epistles to friends. Pindar often affected a warm intimate tone when writing to those friends among the aristocratic families in Thebes, in Aegina, and in Sicily. Probably the most notable examples of this kind of ode are Pythian 6 and Isthmian 2, which directly address Pindar's friend Thrasybulus, son of Theron, the ruler of Acragas. Composed while Pindar was yet a young man, they hint at the intimate friendship between the poet and the ruler's son. Assuredly, both odes were composed to celebrate the victories of Thrasybulus's father in the games at Delphi and at the Isthmus, but Pindar manages to incorporate into these odes passages that warmly address the son in familiar tones. Whereas on the one hand Pindar can praise Thrasybulus for his piety to his father and for his support of the arts, he can on the other compliment Thrasybulus's affectionate disposition to friends. He can even joke in Isthmian 2 about having to charge his friend for the ode, for Pindar was, after all, a professional poet, who relied upon the support of the aristocrats for his fees. Moreover, he also alludes to those banquets — not unlike the gatherings of Renaissance poets in Lampridio's time — at which friends celebrate poetry and friendship.[4]

One of the aims of the humanistic societies was to recreate in Renaissance Rome, Florence, Venice, and Naples the classical symposia of ancient Greece where friends assembled for conversation and wine. It is clear from his addresses to his patron, Pietro Mellini, or to his fellow poets, Corsi, Molza, or Castiglione, that Lampridio espoused the ancient ideal of aristocratic friendship. He characterizes the meetings of the sodalities in the villas about Rome as the very gathering of the gods. The inviting valleys, cool recesses, and grottos where the

---

description of the poets in Rome in the first part of the sixteenth century: Jacopo Sadoleto, "Epistola" (to Colocci) in Cod. Vat. Lat. 4103, fols. 16–17.

[4] See the discussion of Pindar's odes to Thrasybulus in Revard, *Pindar and the Renaissance Hymn-Ode*, 281–84.

poets meet resemble the *loci amoeni* of classical poetry. In such retreats, he tells
his friend Corsi, poets are free to cultivate the Muses, as Horace and Pindar had
done—far from the vulgar mob and the stir of political life, rumors of what
Spain or France were about to do.[5] Taking the lyre in hand, he asks the Pindaric question: "What young man should we praise? Who is deserving in his
virtue to be lifted to high Olympus?" The young man Lampridio plans to praise
is not an athlete or a prince, but the young Florentine poet Lorenzo Bartolini, to
whom Lampridio addressed two odes and whom Corsi had also commended.[6]
With Bartolini at his side and with Jove's favor, says Lampridio, he could attain
a Muses' Elysium.[7]

Lampridio is eager to re-establish the poet's place in society as the inheritor
of the arts of Horace, Vergil, Homer, and Pindar. In his ode to Castiglione (fol.
16 ʳ⁻ᵛ), for example, Lampridio appeals to Castiglione to remember the poets'
retreats at Mellini's villa and the Medici gardens and chastises him for his neglect of the Muses. A Tuscan beauty with dark eyes awaits a song in her honor,
hints Lampridio, exhorting Castiglione to sing and to lead the rites to Bacchus.
He intimates that when the Roman Ennius sang of war or Homer of the wily Ulysses or of the funeral ceremonies at Troy, they first steeped themselves in wine.
Wine and poetry flow freely at the meetings of the Roman sodalities, as they
had in the classical symposia. When he addresses his Florentine patron Giulio
de' Medici, cousin to Leo X and the future Clement VII, Lampridio evokes Orpheus as the proper model for the poets of Italy. Orpheus has first made his lyre
sound under his native Haemus, and so absolute was his command over the lyre
that trees followed to shade him, streams stood still, and even his Muse-mother
Calliope paused to listen to her son's music. How different is Lampridio's triumphant musician from the tragic Orpheus of Milton's "Lycidas."

After the sack of Rome in 1527 Lampridio's odes to his poet-friends turn
their notes to tragic. Like his contemporary Pierius Valerianus, who records in *De
Litteratorum infelicitate* the unhappiness of men of letters, Lampridio remembers

---

[5] Lampridio's ode to Corsi (*Carmina*, fols. 45ʳ–47ʳ) is in fact a kind of Pindaric
epistle and was composed to be dispatched to his friend in Rome. Lampridio regrets his
friend's absence and describes the pleasures of mythological retreats where golden Phoebus, in the company of goat-footed satyrs and nymphs, delights in Corsi's poetry. The
pleasant shades induce both delight and poetic composition. "Come," Lampridio urges,
"join the Bacchic throng."

[6] See Lampridius, *Carmina*, fol. 46ʳ. Odes addressed to Lorenzo Bartolini include
the following: "Quis posset ulli fidere foeminae" (fols. 39ʳ–40ʳ) and "Laurentio Bar-
tholino" (fols. 44ᵛ–45ʳ), both of which allude to Bartolini's mistress Lesbia. Also see
Corsi's introduction to his poem "De civitato Castellana Faliscorum," published in Rome
in 1525.

[7] See also the sportive little ode to Neera in which Lampridio announces to Lorenzo the "victory" of the mischievous little god Cupid (fols. 38ᵛ–39ʳ).

the happy days that are no more. Writing to Lazaro Bonamico (*Carmina*, fols. 47ʳ–48ᵛ), Lampridio employs the myth of the flood to allude to the devastation that has befallen Rome. The sombre ode is almost a reply to Bonamico's celebrated epigram on the ruin of classical Rome: "What now remains of Rome but an empty name?"[8] Yet the very myth he has chosen permits Lampridio to hope for a new beginning. He recounts how the goddess Themis advised the survivors of the flood, Deucalion and Pyrrha, to cast stones over their shoulders so as to bring new souls to life. He is perhaps remembering Pindar's use of the same myth as the centerpiece of Olympian 9. Looking backward, Pindar congratulates the Boeotian city of Opûs on its founding and on good government, and looking forward, he congratulates Epharmostos, the athlete of the hour, on his victory and looks to the future.[9] Like Pindar, Lampridio celebrates the future, hopeful that Rome's troubles are at an end. He urges his poet friend Lazaro to prophesy, as the Greeks had in their old oracles: "Speak the song which your heart knows, a song worthy of Delian laurels." A new cycle is about to start, he predicts — a happier time, if we can elude the rocks in a still dangerous ocean. Conflating Greek oracular prophecy with Christian providence, he reassures his friend that the God who once condemned the whole race to the pit of Hell may now move the earth with a nod and decree a new beginning.

In his earlier odes Lampridio had invoked the myth of the golden age to describe the happy time of Leo's pontificate. Later odes look back on this time, sometimes hoping for, sometimes despairing of the return of the golden age. His poetic letter to Francesco Maria Molza (1489–1544) expresses the hope that Jupiter will look once more with favor on the walls of old Romulus, that the lyre will sound again on the Janiculum, and that peace will be at hand. Yet he expresses these hopes timidly, not confidently.[10] Similarly, in a short triadic ode on the olive villa of Cardinal Lorenzo Pucci, Lampridio invokes Pallas, whose olive tree symbolizes the peace now conspicuously absent in Italy. Fondly recollecting

---

[8] See Bonamico's epigram: "What now remains of Rome but an empty name? / Where are your triumphal arches, your colossal statues, your pyramids, your temples of the gods? / All these things are fled. Calliope alone can live forever."

[9] For a discussion of the political paradigms of Olympian 9, see Andrew M. Miller, "*Inventa componere*: Rhetorical Process and Poetic Composition in Pindar's Ninth Olympian Ode," *Transactions of the American Philological Association* 123 (1993): 109–47.

[10] See *Carmina*, fols. 37ᵛ–38ᵛ. Lampridio addresses Molza by his poetic cognomen Furnius, adopted to compliment his lady Furnia. Regretting Molza's absence and hoping for his return, Lampridio alludes not to joyful poetic activities, but to the devastation of war. Echoing Vergil's fourth eclogue, he hopes for the coming of a golden age. Lampridio concludes with a modest wish: that he be permitted to live his brief space of life in the company of his friends. Even as late as 1522 in his pindaric to Janus Ruffus (Giovanni Ruffo Teodoli, archbishop of Cosenza), a confidant of Adrian VI, Lampridio could express hope that the golden age of Rome was not past, now that "optimus Adrianus" (the new Pope Adrian VI) had assumed the headship of the Church (*Carmina*, fols. 7ʳ–8ᵛ).

the villa that so often welcomed poets when they wished to retire from Rome, Lampridio laments the fallen city: "O Rome, how changed you are! Where can we go for the society of Thalia? Now the happy choruses are silent; Pan and his nymphs are gone, and Pallas has left the grove she once loved so much."[11] At the inauguration of Leo X's papacy in 1512, Lampridio had written an epigram predicting the beginning of the age of Pallas. It would now appear that the age of Pallas was over.[12] These familiar pindarics addressed to poet-friends succeed in giving voice to the hopes and fears of a generation of Italian poets in times of triumph and tragedy.

2.

Only in Ronsard's first book of Pindaric odes, published in 1550, do we find familiar tributes to poet-friends such as Lampridio composed for the humanist poets of Rome. Since Lampridio's pindarics, though available in manuscript, were not published until 1550, we cannot be certain whether his familiar odes functioned as models for Ronsard.[13] Addressed to his most intimate poetic associates at court—Joachim Du Bellay, Jacques Boujù, Jean Dorat, Antoine de Baïf, Jean Martin—these odes were probably composed in 1549.[14] As he compiled his first book of odes, Ronsard was still experimenting with different uses for triadic verse, and this set of odes to poet-friends differs in tone and style from the full-blown formal hymns and odes that he addressed to the king, his ministers, and the important people of the court in this collection as well as those

---

[11] See *Carmina*, fols. 12^v–14 ^{r}. In this ode Lampridio specifically remembers his poet-friends, Antonio Nerli and Paulo Bombasi, secretary to the cardinal, tragically killed by a mob during the sack when he was trying to follow the cardinal to safety. Both of these poets are named by Francesco Arsilli in *De Poetis Urbanis* as having belonged to the sodalities in Rome during this period (in *Coryciana*, ed. Blosius Palladius [Rome, 1524]). For an account of Arsilli's poem see William Roscoe, *The Life and Pontificate of Leo the Tenth* (Liverpool: T. Cadell and W. Davies, 1805), 3: 340–45. Nerli has a poem included in the *Coryciana*. Bombasio is mentioned in the Colocci papers. See *Vita di Mons. Angelo Colocci*, ed. Fanelli, 47, 163, 114–15. Bombasio was a teacher of Greek and Latin educated at Bologna, the son-in-law of Scipio Carteromachus, and a friend of Aldus Manutius and Erasmus. Valerianus remembers his death in *De Litteratorum infelicitate* (Venice, 1620), 1:22.

[12] For Lampridio's epigram on the age of Pallas, see Toscanus, *Carmina*, 1: fol. 241^r.

[13] The odes are cited from *Les Odes de Ronsard*, ed. Charles Guérin (Paris: Edition du Cèdie, 1952).

[14] For a discussion of the odes in this set, especially the final three, see Anne-Pascale Pouey-Mounou, "Quelques Arrière-Plans d'une Symétrie en Trompe-L'Œil (I. 11–14)," in *Lire Les Odes de Ronsard*, ed. Bertrand, 91–104.

that he published in 1552 and 1555. The tone is warm and personal, and Ronsard takes pains to compliment his friends on their poetry. However, a recurrent theme throughout these odes concerns, not surprisingly, the poet and his place in society. As we have often noted, Ronsard was one of the strongest proponents of the poet's "Pindaric" vocation, and this set of odes is laced throughout with references to the poet's divine status and with imbedded quotations from Pindar's odes elaborately worked into the text.[15]

The longest of the odes, that addressed to Du Bellay (1.11), contrasts in technique with the still longer triadic ode that he later addressed to Michel de l'Hospital (1.10). In it, as in the ode to the king's minister, Ronsard is concerned with poetry's place in society and attacks the gross monster Ignorance widespread throughout France. However, in the ode to Du Bellay, while referring to himself and Du Bellay as loved by the Muses, the nine "Pucelles," he eschews the elaborate mythmaking that dominates his ode to Hospital.[16] Instead, he takes a familiar tone throughout, describing himself and Du Bellay as two eagles envied by the "poètes marotiques"—mere rhymesters, the infamous crows of Pindar's Olympian 2.[17] He outlines for Du Bellay the poetic principles that he will put into practice in his later odes and hymns—that the poet must both sing the praises of the king and uphold him as he faces the storms of political life: the menacing Spanish, the hard-hearted English, the bellicose Germans. A large part of this ode is Pindaric in another way, for Ronsard addresses Du Bellay personally, referring not only to his poetry but also to his Angevin background, and including references to Du Bellay's famous uncle, the cardinal, and other relatives in the way that Pindar would have included references to the relatives of a winning athlete. Ronsard also refers directly to his own Pindaric pretensions, confidently telling Du Bellay that he does not fear the fall of which Horace had warned nor of giving his name to a sea, even though he imitates Pindar. He concludes in the same vein by borrowing a metaphor from Pindar, hoping that he may steer his own bark of poetry safely back into harbor.

In the ode that follows to Jacques Boujù (1.12), Ronsard remarks that Boujù (1515–1577), like Du Bellay, was an Angevin. One of Ronsard's first protectors at court, Boujù belonged to Madame Marguerite's intimate circle and held the post of "maître de requêtes" to the queen. Ronsard compliments him on these royal intimacies and on his status as royal poet, taking the opportunity to voice

---

[15] For a discussion of Ronsard's Pindaric vocation, see Revard, *Pindar and the Renaissance Hymn-Ode*, chap. 2.

[16] See Revard, *Pindar and the Renaissance Hymn-Ode*, 80, 84. The ode to Hospital, first published in Ronsard's collection of odes in 1552, was placed immediately before the ode to Du Bellay in the collection Ronsard reprinted in 1560. See *Odes*, ed. Guérin, 46n.

[17] Among these were Habert, Fontaine, Aneau, Carle, and Mellin de Saint-Gelais. See *Odes*, ed. Guérin, 74n.

the Pindaric thesis, afterwards expanded in the ode to Hospital, that although
Apollo inspires the Muses, they in turn inspire poets with a divine fire (1.10.
409–20). While Ronsard here alludes to his projected *Franciade* ("mon petit oeuvre"), he proposes that it will be Boujù's Muse that will enlighten the court and
drive away deaf Ignorance. Such, he says, echoing Pindar's praise of kings and
poets, is the gift that God grants to poets.

> Mais Dieu dessus les rois met
> Des richesses le sommet.
> Au poëte qui s'amuse
> Comme toi de les vanter,
> Calliope ne refuse
> De l'ouïr toujours chanter. (strophe 2.7–12)

> But God places kings
> at the summit of riches.
> For a poet like you
> who amuses himself to praise them
> Calliope never refuses
> always to be heard sing.

He seasons this aphorism with a witty personal touch, adding that if Boujù will
praise the king and the court, he himself will praise Boujù in the Dorian fashion.
It is ironic that Boujù's only known poetic work does not survive.

In his ode to Jean Dorat (1.13), his teacher and one of the first poets in
France to advocate imitation of Pindar, Ronsard pursues the theme of praise
that he had developed in the odes to Du Bellay and Boujù . Opening with a line
adapted from Nemean 4.1–2: "Le medicin de la peine / Est le plaisir" (The physician for pain is pleasure), Ronsard turns Pindar's reflections on the effects of
poetry on its hearers into a compliment for his teacher. For the so called "pain"
that Dorat the teacher experienced in guiding his pupils, Ronsard offers the rec-
ompense of praise. Further, he enrolls Dorat among the first poets in France who
attacked Ignorance, thus becoming for his pupils an oracle of the gods.

In contrast, the ode to Baïf (1.14) that follows is a *jeu d'esprit* that illustrates
the command of witty compliment that so often marks the familiar pindaric.
Commenting that the Graces never traffic in anything but honor, he confides
that he considers it friendship to conceal his friends' faults and to speak only of
their virtues. Baïf was barely seventeen when Ronsard addressed this little ode to
him. Ronsard amicably tells Baïf that although he himself composes poetry that
contrasts with Baïf's tragic strains, both pursue the Muse with honor and so will
mount to the skies and achieve immortality with their verse.

> O Baïf, la plume prompte
> À vouloir monter aux cieux,

D'un vol qui la mort surmonte,
Trompe l'enfer odieux. (Epode, 7–10)

O Baïf, the ready plume [pen]
wishing to mount to heaven
in a flight that conquers death
outwits an odious hell.

More serious in tone is the ode that concludes this group (1.15), addressed to Jean Martin (d. 1553), an elder poet and architect, who had served François I as well as Henri II.[18] As in the other odes, Ronsard takes pains to refer specifically to Martin's accomplishments as a poet, namely his translations of Italian and Latin books, making an allusion to Martin's translation of Sannazaro's *Arcadia* by referring to the Neapolitan river Sebeto. He also deals with the subject of the poet's fame and, as in the ode to Baïf, makes a point of distinguishing the fulsome praise that is false from true praise, worthy of the "golden plume." After this set of odes to intimate friends, Ronsard writes no more familiar pindarics, reserving triadic ode for more formal addresses and eventually giving up pindarics altogether.

Ronsard's few familiar pindarics to poet-friends, like so much that Ronsard did, had a disproportionately large influence on the poets who followed him. Scévole de Sainte-Marthe, who composed a Pindaric elegy on Ronsard's tomb, saluted his own poet-friends in both French and Latin pindarics. Among the addressees were the most famous humanist poets of the era: Nicolas Rapin, Pierre Pithou, Pierre Joyeux (Petrus Laetus), Joseph Scaliger, François La Mothe Le Vayer (Franciscus Pulcher Mothaeus), and above all Jacques-Auguste Thou. Sainte-Marthe composed Latin odes for all of these except Rapin, to whom he addressed a vernacular ode. The ode to Rapin is important, for it imitates Ronsard's ode to Du Bellay. Rapin was Sainte-Marthe's most intimate friend and came, as did Sainte-Marthe, from Poitiers. The ode discourses, moreover, on two typical Ronsardian themes: the divine nature of poetry and the neglect of poetry in contemporary France.[19] Enrolling Rapin among the divine poets, Sainte-Marthe describes his verse as honeyed song that comes forth from an

---

[18] For information about Martin, see Jean Guillaume et al., *Jean Martin, un traducteur au temps de François Ier et de Henri II* (Paris: Presses de l'Ecole normale supérieure, 1999).

[19] Sainte-Marthe's ode to Nicolas Rapin was reprinted in both Rapin's and Sainte-Marthe's posthumous poetry. See "Les Vers Mesvrez de Nicolas Rapin" in *Les Oevvres Latines et Francoises de Nicolas Rapin Poictevin* (Paris, 1610), sig. e^r–eij^v; Scaevola and Abelius Sammarthani, "A Nic. Rapin Grand Prevost de la Connestablie de France," in "Poesie Meslée," *Opera Latina et Gallica* (Paris: Jacobus Villery, 1633), 103–6. I quote from the latter. For Sainte-Marthe's relations with Rapin see Brunel, *Un Poitevin poète, humaniste et soldat à l'époque des guerres de religion: Nicolas Rapin (1539–1608): la carrière, les milieux, l'oeuvre, passim.*

inspired as well as a learned lyre. Rapin brings the very music of the spheres down from heaven to earth:

> Rien n'est en cest Vnivers,
> Que les nombres n'accomplissent,
> Les hauts Cieux mesme se glissent,
> Reiglez par nombres diuers:
> Et des feux la troupe ailée
> Va mesurant par compas
> En la carriere estoilée
> La cadance de ses pas.
> (Epode 1.1–8 [104])

> There is nothing in this universe
> that verse does not accomplish.
> The high heavens themselves glide,
> regulated by divers numbers.
> And of the fires the winged troop
> go measuring by compass
> in their starry circuit
> the cadence of their steps.

All this exactly fits Ronsard's concept of the Pindaric poet who burns with a sacred flame and is possessed of that "fureur" Ronsard thought indispensable for poetic composition.

Sainte-Marthe also uses this ode to inveigh against a France that does not value her own poets and refuses poetry a place comparable to that it possessed among the Latins and the Greeks. How does it happen, he asks, that France in barbarous ignorance repulses that which could most embellish her name? Despite their concerted efforts, Sainte-Marthe laments, Du Bellay, Ronsard, and Baïf all failed to establish poetry as a divine art. Hence, Sainte-Marthe concludes, it now falls to Rapin and himself to carry on that which Ronsard and Du Bellay began: to surpass the poets of Italy and to raise their two names to resound together without end.

Sainte-Marthe's Latin pindarics also follow Ronsard's familiar odes in lavishing compliments on his fellow poets. For Pierre Pithou [Petrus Pitheus] (1539–1596), advocate and scholar as well as poet, he invokes Phoebus's golden lyre and adopts terms of Pindaric praise, lauding Pithou as a man loved by men and gods, blessed with the shining dew of the Graces.[20] Yet in the era of the civil wars it was almost impossible to avoid reference to the evils of the times—the

---

[20] Pithou's collection of epigrams from ancient and modern poets (*Epigrammata et Poematia Vetera* [Paris, 1590]) was popular at the end of the sixteenth century. Ben Jonson owned a copy.

rage of Megaera and the crimes of furious men (antistrophe 1.14–17). Pithou had been a survivor of the Saint Bartholomew's massacre, a convert to Catholicism, and a supporter of Henri de Bourbon, the future Henri IV. All the more remarkable then, Sainte-Marthe proclaims, is Pithou's sang-froid, for even if he were placed where the Adriatic roars or where Mars rages, still he would be serene: "Pone Pitheum / Vbi Adria spumantior / Fremit, pone vbi Mars grauius tonat, / Semper erit quietus" (94).[21] In another pindaric to a poet-friend, Pierre Joyeux [Petrus Laetus], Sainte-Marthe confides that they live in an age when men act with blind fury and are envious of poets and their vocation.[22]

So many of Sainte-Marthe's friends were affected by the crises in *res politica* in the 1570s and 80s that it is often difficult to determine whether the primary thrust of his odes is familiar or political. Such is the case with Sainte-Marthe's epistolary ode to Joseph Scaliger (1540–1609), who left France for Leiden in 1590 because of adverse political and religious pressures ("Lyricorum Libri Duo," *Poemata et Elogia*, 102–5). Sainte-Marthe attempts to soften the bitter blow of exile, praising Batavia as the haven which possesses a man who surpasses all others in learning, He assures Scaliger that God, just like the earthly father who sends his children away from danger during a siege, has sent him from France to safe haven. He also digresses to recount the famous story told of the Greek poet Simonides. Having taken refuge in Thessaly after a tumultuous political upheaval in Athens, Simonides was miraculously saved by the intervention of the Dioscuri. The twin gods appeared and called him from the house where he was residing just before the roof collapsed killing all within. Of such value to the gods, affirms Sainte-Marthe, are those who cultivate the sacred rites of the Pierian Muses. He ends on a personal note, exhorting Scaliger to remember the friends he has left in France.

Sainte-Marthe attempts to balance poetry and politics in the longest of these familiar pindarics, addressed to Jacques-Auguste Thou (1553–1617) ("Lyricorum Libri Duo," *Poemata et Elogia*, 94–102). An advisor to Henri IV as he had been to Henri III, Thou was one of the framers of the Edict of Nantes and the author of the most important history of sixteenth-century France, *Historia sui temporis*. As a scholar and a friend to Joseph Scaliger and other eminent humanists, Thou had significant literary credentials, and Sainte-Marthe spends equal time praising Thou's accomplishments as a writer and as a statesman. The ode is full of elegant compliments: Sainte-Marthe depicts Thou as a nursling of the Muses and

---

[21] For the Latin pindarics, see Scaevola Sammarthanus, "Lyricorum Libri Duo," in Sammarthanus, *Poemata et Elogia* (Augustoriti Pictonum: Ioannes Blanceti, 1606).

[22] In the ode to Joyeux Sainte-Marthe makes a patriotic gesture as well. Perhaps alluding to Ronsard's *Franciade*, he rehearses the familiar myth of France's Trojan forebears, including a digressive account of Venus's wooing of Anchises, the birth of Aeneas, and the founding of the Trojan dynasty that would result in both Rome and Gaul. See "Lyricorum Libri Duo" in *Poemata et Elogia*, 118–23.

the Apelles of his time, the one best fit to paint his own portrait in oils if modesty did not prevent it. Yet, moving beyond compliment, he characterizes Thou as a man who had witnessed the gigantic struggles of his era, the civil wars in France, here depicted, as they so often were in the political odes of the era, through an extended account of the myth of the giants at Phlegra who challenged Jove. As a writer, therefore, Thou can speak oracles for future ages, darkly shadowing forth both the poet's and the historian's truth. Also like the divine poet Orpheus who tamed the souls of beasts, Sainte-Marthe declares, Thou could soften harsh and rebellious men and drive off the furies of war, bringing peace to France. In the end, however, this ode is a personal, not a political tribute, and Sainte-Marthe concludes by likening Thou to Vergil's old man of Hussia, who could despise the empty gifts of the world and with placid mind view the vicissitudes of Fortune. He ends with a Horatian touch that Thou knew how to temper the heaviest tasks with needful diversion, to mix the bitter and the sweet.

Sainte-Marthe's contemporary and friend, Paulus Melissus, also addressed familiar odes to humanists throughout Europe.[23] In his book of pindarics (*emmetra*), he reserves, moreover, like Ronsard and Sainte-Marthe, a section for odes to his poet-friends, among them Johann Sturm, Marc-Antoine Muret, the Italian poets Petrus Victorinus and Angelius Petrus Bargaeus, and Aldus Manutius.[24] His odes are sometimes formal encomia, sometimes more like poetic epistles. For example, the odes he sends to Joseph Scaliger in exile in Leiden have the quality of familiar letters. Like Sainte-Marthe, Melissus urges Scaliger to remember and to return to the sodality of friends in Paris, playfully telling his absent friend how his face appeared to him in a dream.[25] Melissus's odes are usually brief and lack the highly developed digressions of Sainte-Marthe's pindarics, although, like them, they are replete with mythic comparisons and compliments. He does not fail to summon the Muses or call up Apollo's golden lyre, but he possesses a particularly jovial air that is all his own. He refers to his own verse modestly and makes light of his Pindaric inspiration. He fears, he tells a friend,

---

[23] Among Sainte-Marthe's epigrams is one addressed to Melissus in which he praises his poet-friend for excelling in all kinds of verse and singing in his pindarics like the swan of Dirce. See "Ad Paulum Melissum," in "Epigrammata Lib. I," in *Poemata et Elogia* (1606), 288. Among Melissus's melic odes is an ode addressed to Sainte-Marthe with similar compliments. See "Melicorum Liber IX," in *Schediasmata Poetica* (Paris, 1586), 515–16.

[24] Melissus also addresses melic odes to most of these men. See, for example, the numerous odes to Marc-Antoine Muret, in *Schediasmata Poetica*, 16, 283, 309, 318, 326, 335, 344, and 520.

[25] See the odes to Scaliger in *Schediasmata Poetica*: "En te nunc iterum meis ocellis / Quantus quantus es, o propago Divûm, / Venerande Josephe" ("Melicorum Lib. IV," 219, ll. 1–3); "An quod susurrat Fama domestica, / Brevi futurum est, hospes ut hospitis / Desideratos ipse vultûs / SCALIGERI videam" ("Melicorum Liber IX," 555, ll. 1–4).

to mold for himself Daedalus's waxen wings or to imitate the flight of the eagle or the phoenix. Alas, both Jove and Apollo have decreed, he demurs, that in so doing he would more resemble the duck imitating the voice of the swan.[26]

Like his predecessors, Melissus neither restricts Pindaric imitation to those odes that imitate Pindar's meters nor excludes a certain Horatian jocularity from his triadic odes. In a melic ode to Joseph Scaliger, for example, Melissus borrows a metaphor from the opening of Pindar's Olympian 2 and addresses the great classical scholar as the eye of Phoebus.[27] Triadic odes and melic odes share similar mythic comparisons and poetic ornaments. For example, Melissus puns on "angelus" in both the melic and triadic odes that he addressed to Petrus Angelius Bargaeus (Pietro Angelio da Barga), and in both also alludes to Bargaeus's "starry eminence" among poets.[28] He can also summon up remembrance of classical symposia and invite his friend to a feast where the gods themselves will be present and where the lyres will sound and furor excite the poet's breast.[29] The tradition of Lampridio's Roman pindarics still survived apparently until the end of the sixteenth century.

Although some of Melissus's familiar pindarics are expansive, many make their point in a single triad.[30] Even within a triad, Melissus can, as in the odes to Marc-Antoine Muret (1526–1585) and Johann Sturm (1507–1589), develop

---

[26] "Emmetra," in *Schediasmata Poetica*, 21.

[27] "Quae vallis, aut quae te juga detinent, / Ocelle Phoebi SCALIGER" (1–2): "Melicorum Liber II," in *Schediasmata Poetica*, 118.

[28] In his Pindaric ode Melissus places Bargaeus's golden head among the golden stars with Perseus and Orion and Memnon. In his melic ode he alludes to Bargaeus as the star of the Etruscan sky, the bulwark in Italy of the Roman and Greek tongues. See "Petro Angelio Bargaeo" in "Emmetra," in *Schediasmata Poetica*, 20–22, and "Ad Petrum Angelium Bargaeum" in "Melicorum Liber V," 307–9 . For his commentary on Bargaeus's poetry, see "Melicorum Liber V and IX," in *Schediasmata Poetica*, 341–43, 526–28. Other odes offer extended compliments to Bargaeus on his verse and on his long Latin epic poem the *Syriade*, which deals with the First Crusade. Petrus Angelius Bargaeus [Angelio Pietro da Barga] (1517–1596) was an Italian scholar-poet, who wrote for the Grand Duke of Tuscany among others, edited Aristotle, and translated Sophocles into Italian. He taught Greek and was the author of eclogues, odes, and other verse in both Latin and Italian. He did not write pindarics. He includes in his collected poems a poetic epistle directed to Melissus. See Petrus Angelius Bargaeus, "Epistle VII," in Bargaeus, *Poemata Omnia* (Rome, 1585), 264–65.

[29] "Ad Petrum Angelium Bargaeum" in "Melicorum Liber V," in *Schediasmata Poetica*, 308–9.

[30] See, for example, the ode to Abel Strasburgus, which offers congratulations on a wedding ("Emmetra," in *Schediasmata Poetica*, 35–36) or the ode to Hieronymus Groslotius Lislaeus, which condoles a friend on the death of a mutual friend ("Emmetra," in *Schediasmata Poetica*, 50–51). For the odes to Muret and Sturm see "Emmetra," in *Schediasmata Poetica*, 16–18; 15–16.

something like a Pindaric digression. In the ode to Muret (16–18), he undertakes a metaphorical journey, negotiating the extremes of Scylla and Charybdis in order to arrive at Muret's distant residence in Poland. What iron pole, Melissus asks wittily, draws everything to Muret? Not only are Apollo and the Muses and the sweet-tongued Graces drawn there, but also the Atlantides, Venus, Minerva, Persuasion, and a whole troop of Sirens—all irresistibly drawn. The ode to Johann Sturm (15–16) is, if anything, still more extravagant in its praise. Sturm was, like Melissus, interested in Pindaric ode and had translated Olympian 1 into Latin in 1564. Melissus describes him as the darling of France, Italy, Germany, Britain, Spain, and Poland. In order to praise Sturm properly, he states, one must have the eloquence of Demosthenes and Cicero, the plectra of Homer or Vergil, and have tasted deeply of the Castalian spring. Only the gods can set the limit for such praise—Pallas herself must preside; Juno must shower forth wine mixed with honey. Without all these, Melissus demurs, one runs the risk of writing a prose sermon. Were such far-fetched assertions not seasoned with the poet's self-deprecating wit, they would scarcely be endurable. At the same time this kind of extravagant rhetoric is the very essence of the humanistic ode. By the end of the sixteenth century, the humanistic ode in both its Horatian and its Pindaric modes was overtaking the epigram as a favored genre of familiar poetry,. In the next century, the familiar ode in Latin gives way to the familiar pindaric in the vernacular, as Abraham Cowley and his followers explore the Horatian uses of the Pindaric ode.

3.

Before Cowley introduced the vernacular pindaric in his 1656 *Pindarique Odes*, the Latin pindaric in the familiar mode had a final flowering with the minor poet, Alexander Gil Jr., and with no less a master than John Milton. Gil was a boyhood friend of Milton's and the son of the master of St. Paul's School. In the miscellaneous collection of Latin poems entitled ΠΑΡΕΡΓΑ, published in 1632, Gil included a curious set of poems—an elegy, an epigram, and a triadic ode—which he had composed for Sir Paul Pindar, a wealthy merchant knighted by James I. The occasion for these poems was celebration of Sir Paul's substantial contribution for the embellishment of St. Paul's Cathedral.[31] Obviously inspired by Paul Pindar's name, Gil was moved to try his hand at poems in the Pindaric mode. All three poems serve to demonstrate how familiar Latin pindarics were still functioning in England (after Melissus's time) as a form of encomiastic verse. The first poem (written in elegiac couplets) combines the techniques of ode and epigram and begins by adapting the optative formula "si modo," perhaps

---

[31] Alexander Gil, ΠΑΡΕΡΓΑ, *Sive Poetici Conatus* (London, 1632), 80–82.

suggested by the opening of Pythian 3, in which Pindar wishes that Chiron were still living. Gil wishes that Pindar yet lived to honor Paul Pindar's pious deeds with laurels such as he conferred on heroes or on winners of athletic contests. Lacking the poet Pindar to honor the modern Pindar, Gil is willing to sound the Pindaric trumpet himself. The epigram that follows compares Paul Pindar's adornment of St. Paul's to Alexander's sparing of the poet Pindar's house after the siege of Thebes. In the third piece, "Ad Paulinos obambulones," Gil attempts metrically to duplicate a true Pindaric triad, its short lines typical of the usual Renaissance pindaric. Praising St. Paul's Cathedral as though it excelled both the monuments of antiquity and those of the Renaissance — even St. Peter's Basilica in Rome — Gil lauds Sir Paul Pindar as a contemporary patron worthy of Pindaric celebration: "At, fortè nostra vobis / Siquid placere possint, / Et *Pindari* labores / Imitarier, libenter / Quos promovet disertus / Episcopus, velitis" (82).[32] Gil called his ode an *epinikion*, perhaps because it describes the competition between St. Paul's and the monuments of antiquity or between Paul Pindar's labors and the poet Pindar's. Clearly, however, Gil's *epinikion* makes use of the hyperbole and wordplay characteristic of the familiar rather than the true epinician ode. Punning on Paul Pindar's name, Gil links him both with the cathedral Paul's that he has embellished and with the poet Pindar who might have praised his generosity as a patron. However modest, Gil's brief ode in praise of Paul Pindar looks forward to "Ad Joannem Rousium" and Milton's more ambitious celebration of the man John Rouse as well as the magnificent library over which he presided.

Like many humanist odes, Milton's Latin pindaric to John Rouse, the librarian of the Bodleian Library in Oxford, is part epistolary, part commendatory ode. It was sent to Rouse in 1646/47 with an accompanying volume of Milton's 1645 *Poems* to replace a lost shipment of political tracts and *Poems*.[33] Not published until 1673, the Rouse ode was one of the last poems Milton wrote in Latin, marking his final performance as a humanist poet. Written in three Latin strophes and antistrophes with a single concluding epode, the ode is, as Milton explains in his endnote, an irregular pindaric. Although Pindaric in form, it imitates not only Pindar, but also Catullus, Ovid, and Propertius, as well as those humanist poets who imitated these classical writers.

---

[32] The list of monuments includes not only St. Peter's in Rome and St. Mark's in Venice but also the temple of Diana in Ephesus: "Non *Italus* ipse *Petrus*, / Non *Venetus* ipse *Marcus*, / *Ephesina* nec *Diana*, / *Phariûm* nec alta regum / Monumenta mole *Paulum*, / Sumptu, aut decore vincent. / Cedet at ubique quicquid / Est exteri laboris: / Proque omnibus superstes / Domi forisque fama / Opus unicum loquetur" (82).

[33] See S.P. Revard, "*Ad Joannem Rousium*: Elegiac Wit and Pindaric Mode," in *Urbane Milton: The Latin Poetry*, special number of *Milton Studies* 19 (1984): 205–26, reworked in Revard, *Milton and the Tangles of Neaera's Hair*, 237–63.

Another ode dispatched to the Bodleian Library with a book of poems is, although in English and composed about ten years later, comparable to Milton's ode and inspired by the same humanistic tradition. Entitled "Mr. *Cowley's* Book, presenting it self to the University Library of *Oxford*," the ode was written on the flyleaf of the presentation copy of Cowley's 1656 *Poems* to the Bodleian and was not published until 1668 in Cowley's posthumous *Works*.[34] Milton and Cowley develop similar conceits: the book, an entity, almost a person in itself, presents itself to the library for acceptance into its eminent collection of immortal works. Milton apostrophizes the book in the opening strophe and addresses it throughout the ode in the second person. The speaker of Cowley's ode is the book itself, which first greets the Bodleian — "Hail Learnings *Pantheon!*" (1.1) and then proceeds to recommend itself and its author to the library.[35] Both odes are witty, self-conscious performances that combine a slightly pretentious seriousness with a light, casual, and deliberately unpretentious tone. In adopting the formal structure of the Pindaric ode for poems on less than formal occasions — no celebration of victory, no commemoration of a famous man, living or dead — both Cowley and Milton are following the practice of humanist poets before them. Like these poets, Cowley and Milton take for granted that epistolary odes to scholar-friends are a special sub-category and quite proper for Pindaric treatment. For Milton the learned Rouse is a humanist friend; for Cowley the library itself takes the role of the learned man. The odes sometimes swell with "Pindaric" imperatives as befit their form, but at other times murmur modestly, as they stride forth confidently in Pindaric measures and deliver a humble salute in behalf of the book, the author, and poetry itself.

Milton opens with an apostrophe to his twin-volume book ("Gemelle cultu simplici gaudens liber, / Fronde licet gemina" [ll. 1–2] [Twin-born book, rejoicing in a single cover, but with double leaves]), and then goes on to describe himself as author — a young man, not yet too much a poet, still sporting on Daunian (not Dorian) strings, with his foot barely touching the ground ("humum vix tetigit pede" [l. 12]).[36] This labored introduction suggests a debt both to Pindar and to the Roman elegists. Like Pindar, Milton begins with an elaborate figure that describes the book; but like Catullus and Propertius, he addresses the book which he is about to present to a learned friend.[37] In the antistrophe and in the strophes that follow, still addressing the book, Milton proceeds in the familiar style, almost in parody of the more formal Pindaric ode. The little book — "parvus liber"

[34] The title of the manuscript copy in Cowley's hand is "The Book, Humbly presenting it selfe to the Universitie Librarie at Oxford." The flyleaf is marked "ex dono Viri A Poëtae optimi, D. Abrahami Cowley Authoris" (shelfmark C.2.21 Art.).

[35] Cited from "Verses Written on several occasions," in *The Works of Mr. Abraham Cowley* (London, 1668), 6–8.

[36] "Ad Joannem Rousium," in *Complete Poems and Major Prose*, ed. Hughes, 46–49.

[37] See, for example, Catullus, *Carmina*, Proem 1.2; Propertius, *Elegies*, 3.1.8.

(l. 13)—becomes the hero or contestant of Milton's ode, its arduous undertaking or journey recounted in lieu of the labor or quest or contest that the athlete or the mythic hero of a Pindaric ode might have undertaken. Moreover, at the beginning of antistrophe 1 Milton addresses a Pindaric question to the book: "Quis te, parve liber, quis te fratribus / Subduxit reliquis dolo?" (ll. 13–14) (Who, little book, who seduced you by fraud from the rest of your brothers?) As though in answer to the question, Milton begins the narrative of the lost book's journey to Oxford, noting that the journey was undertaken at the request of a learned friend ("doctus amicus"), who remains unnamed until strophe 3.

In Pindaric style Milton breaks off at this point, not continuing the narration of the book's journey until antistrophe 2. At first it seems as though he is discoursing on totally extraneous matters, but these matters in true Pindaric style turn out to be far from extraneous. Milton's apparent digression expresses one of the most serious concerns of the ode: the status of poetry in a society torn by war. It is a subject that humanists before him have broached, as when Lampridio lamented the turmoil in Rome or Sainte-Marthe the upheaval of the religious wars in France. Like them, Milton also uses mythic allusions to convey the sense that poetry's sacred status is endangered. He names Oxford the birthplace of the Thames, the home of poetry, the place where the Aonian Muses have their springs and where Bacchus with his holy thyasus holds his rites. Adapting the opening lines of Pindar's Olympian 2 or Horace's *Carmina* 1.12, Milton frames a rhetorical question: "Modo quis deus, aut editus deo / . . . / Tollat nefandos civium tumultus" (l. 25, 29) (What god or offspring of a god can lift this abominable tumult from the people?) What deity, he further asks, will call back the Muses to their dwelling places, now polluted by war? Although the question is framed in a way similar to those posed by Pindar and Horace, Milton is not asking what god or what hero he should praise. Instead, he calls upon the god or god-elected man himself, asking who will pity and save his unhappy race and restore the peace of the academic community at Oxford. Only by divine intervention will the scholarly community be saved and the cult of the Muses rescued. Here Milton conflates several mythic stories, attributing to the god-elected hero the deeds of Hercules or Apollo or the Argonauts:

> Immundasque volucres
> Unguibus imminentes
> Figat Apollinea pharetra,
> Phineamque abigat pestem procul amne Pegaseo?
> (ll. 33–36)

> Who from an Apollonian quiver
> Will transfix these foul birds
> With their menacing claws,
> And who will drive Phineas's plague from the Pegasean stream?

Traditionally, Hercules, the very hero invoked by Pindar and Horace in Olympian 2 and *Carmina* 1.12, was the demi-god who killed the Stymphalian birds. Here, however, Milton conflates the unnamed demi-god with Apollo, endowing him with Apollo's quiver, and likening his deed to Apollo's purification of the shrine at Delphi with the slaying of the Python. He also glances at another mythic tale: the Argonauts' rescue of the prophet Phineas by killing the Harpies, the foul birds, which afflicted him.[38] By implication also the prophet Phineas (named in *Paradise Lost* with the blind poet-priests) is conflated with the afflicted *vates*, whose profession and very life are endangered by the civil conflict. In this context also the Thames at Oxford is linked with Hippocrene, the Pegasean stream; the fount of poetry must be purified from the foul pests of war.

The denunciation of the evils of civil war, the call for purification of the Apollonian shrine, and the anguished invocation of the god sound the most authentically Pindaric note in an ode that has up till this point been a humanist trifle in Pindaric strophes. Yet though the tone is Pindaric, the actual subject is not. Milton voices a protest, raised by many humanist poets in the sixteenth century, against those wars that make humanistic study all but impossible. Milton knows all too well that the carefree innocence of poets, so delightfully depicted in strophe 1, has not been innocently forfeited. With a deep sense of shame he indicts the men of his own race who have polluted those very springs of poetry.

When Milton returns to recount the adventures of his lost book in antistrophe 2, the book too has been fouled and polluted, fallen perhaps into a ditch or soiled by the callous hands of a bookseller intent only on profit. Only divine intervention can save it too from Lethe and carry it, winged, to the halls of Jove. At this point another "demi-god" enters the poem: Rouse himself, characterized as the metaphorical son of Apollo. With a deft stroke Milton imitates both Pindar and his humanist imitators by attaching a complimentary epithet to Rouse: "Æternorum operum custos fidelis" (l. 54) (the faithful guardian of eternal works) and linking him implicitly with Ion, who guarded the god's treasures at Delphi. This mythic identification is a dense one, for Ion, although described by Milton as the guardian of his father's treasures, was in Euripides's drama only a temple-slave at Delphi before his true identity as Apollo's son by Creusa became known.[39] Milton, however, elevates his status, also apparently conflating him with another son of Apollo, Iamus, featured by Pindar in Olympian 6. Like

---

[38] See the episodes of the Harpies in *Aeneid* 2. 225–241 and the repelling of these monstrous birds in Apollonius of Rhodes's *Argonautica* (2.187–193).

[39] See Kevin H. Lee, "Milton's Ode *Ad Joannem Rousium* and Euripides' *Ion*," *Milton Studies* 37 (1999): 1–17. Lee points out that Milton's description of Ion as the guardian of Apollo's treasures at Delphi is misleading, for Ion in Euripides's play is only a temple-slave, not a priest, and further is not recognized as Apollo's son until late in the play after a confrontation with Creusa. At the end of the play, moreover, he leaves Apollo's temple with Creusa to claim his birthright in Athens as Erechtheus's grandson. Therefore,

Ion, Iamus is obscurely born, but unlike him, he is destined to become a priest, when, after praying to Apollo and Poseidon, Apollo summons him to preside over Zeus's sanctuary at Olympia. By associating Rouse with Apollo's offspring, Milton makes Rouse take on the role of the demi-god, who will not only save Milton's little lost book but also protect the works of the Muses, so essential for humankind's future. In the antistrophe that follows, the Bodleian Library also attains, with Rouse, Apollonian status, named as the shining home of Phoebus ("Diamque Phoebi . . . domum," l. 63).[40]

In antistrophe 3 Milton finally sends his little book on its way to a secure future. Having escaped Lethean oblivion and the bookseller's hell, the book (or rather its replacement volume) confidently continues on its journey to Oxford. Milton tells it three times: you shall go ("ibis") to the pleasant groves of the Muses, to the divine house of Phoebus, and finally into the hands of a friend who will install you in true glory among the high names of Greece and Rome. On the one hand, Milton's ode is an elegant trifle, to be categorized with such odes as Melissus's odes to Sturm or to Bargaeus. How else can we describe a poem that extravagantly narrates the journey of a book from London to Oxford as though it were telling how Hercules journeyed to the ends of the earth? How else can we characterize the humanistic hyperbole that makes Rouse more than a *doctus amicus*, but a stand-in for Apollo's son, the faithful guardian of eternal works? However, Milton with these comparisons is doing more than exercising the convention of humanistic hyperbole.

Although Milton's poem functions as a humanistic epistolary ode, an elegant letter to a learned friend who would appreciate its scholarly style and language, it is also a personal ode that comments on the perilous times and on the young poet's ambitions. By recounting how his book arrives safely at the Bodleian Library, Milton is commenting on his own literary aspirations. He hopes that his poetry will be accepted into this intellectual Olympus, to share the shelves with renowned Roman and Greek works and to command, like them, a learned and discerning audience. Milton aspires, like the humanist poets who also wrote in the language of Vergil and Horace, to attain a place with the masters of the classical tongue. The epode of Milton's ode stands apart from the preceding strophes in being devoted not to the book whose adventures have ended, but to the author, who hopes that his labors have not been in vain. In closing Milton confers another mythic identity on Rouse, the kind guardian, who now is also the good Hermes who conducts the souls of the dead to their final resting place, the

---

Milton's treatment of Ion, as Lee observes, is at odds with his portrayal in Euripides's drama.

[40] As I observed in *Milton and the Tangles of Neaera's Hair*, the tribute to the Bodleian comes at a timely moment, for the Parliamentary army headed by Fairfax had just secured Oxford. One of Fairfax's first acts was to place an armed guard at the library to ensure that books would not be looted.

god who brings human beings to safe haven. Like Horace and like other humanist poets, Milton hopes that a sane posterity, exempt from malice and envy, will judge fairly how he has deserved.

Cowley's ode to his book voices similar hopes.[41] Like Milton, Cowley clung to poetry at the time of the Civil Wars when such a calling was most at risk. For him too Oxford was the "Muses Paradise"—a haven "from which may never Sword the blest expel" (1.7–8). His ode, however, often seems more like an exercise in poetic wit than an examination of the plight of poetry in time of war. From the first stanza on, Cowley unleashes a flood of far-fetched epithets, as he salutes the Bodleian library as "Learnings *Pantheon*," "Wits Illustrious Galaxy," the "sacred Ark" which contains the world's wealth that he hopes will escape the "Insatiate Times devouring Flood" (1.1–4, 11). In turn the library becomes a temple for the gods, a beneficent tree of knowledge, a bank for learning's cash, a starry heaven where authors, like stars, shine, and an institute for higher education attended by the souls of dead authors ("living University of the Dead") (1.1–13). As with Milton, the twin poles of humanistic invention and poetic fervor inform and to some degree divide the poem. Excellent Latinist that he was, Cowley was well aware that he was translating a neo-Latin tradition and practice into English. As he piles up one inventive epithet after another, he displays, as humanist poets often did, not only the cleverness but also the outlandishness of poetic hyperbole. Although in one sense Cowley was doing no more than dispatching the ode as a "cover letter" to accompany his book, in another he was, like Milton, putting in his bid for fame. During the unstable period of the 1650s that followed the ruinous civil wars, he was attempting to secure his own poetic reputation. Behind the volleys of wit is a desire to safeguard his own and others' poetry, a hope that an institution such as the Bodleian Library might be impervious to time's decay, a "Majestick Monument and Pyramide" (2.4).

Thus his description of the book's reception at the library, though clothed in typical humanistic wordplay, also gives voice to the literary ambition that such a reception signifies. For example, in section 3 Cowley rings the changes on a single word, *chain*, employing the word in a double sense. A chain may be either an honorific ornament of office, such as deacons or dignitaries wear, or the chain a book would have in a chained library, such as the Bodleian, to keep it in place. In a playful mode, Cowley quips that a chain will better please him than "all [his] own Pindarick Liberty" (3.11). To be chained at the Bodleian is truly to be free, for the book will now be bound to the mighty names at Bodley, thus granting it an even greater liberty—"a Pasport to go ev'ry where" (3.16). As Milton referred

---

[41] Both Milton and Cowley were alumni of Cambridge University, yet it is acceptance at the university library at Oxford that both allude to as a milestone in their poetic careers. Oxford still possesses Cowley's book and Milton's 1645 *Poems* and the pamphlets he sent to Rouse (and the ode itself), but at Cambridge many of Milton's works were burnt at the time of the Restoration.

to his book's arrival at the Bodleian as a translation to Olympus, Cowley suggests that his book attains at Bodley a Christianized heaven of "Patriarchs and Apostles" (4.4). For Cowley modesty and ambition go hand in hand. He calls the book an "unmalicious Sinner" (4.2) that trembles to find itself in exalted company in the bookish heaven. Gratefully accepting its place, the book declares itself and its author benefactors of predestined grace: "No labour I, nor merits can pretend, / I think Predestination only was my friend" (4.16–17).

Cowley probably held many of the same views as Milton about the status of poetry in a land that had been disrupted by war. As a poet, he suffered the vicissitudes that humanist poets such as Sainte-Marthe and Melissus spoke of. He had returned to England after a prolonged sojourn abroad in service to the future Charles II with the hope to publish his poetry. Still speaking in the person of the book, Cowley describes his own exile:

> Ah, that my Author had ben ty'd like me
> To such a place, and such a Companie!
> Instead of sev'ral Countries, sev'ral Men,
>   And business which the Muses hate,
> He might have then improv'd that small Estate,
> Which nature sparingly did to him give,
>   He might perhaps have thriven then,
> And setled upon me his Child, somewhat to live
> 'T had happier been for him, as well as me . . .
> (5.1–9)

Like Milton, Cowley places his hope in the vocation of poetry itself and in expectation that wiser readers in ages to come will value his book as "the best and noblest conversation" (5.12). At the same time he probably would have agreed with the view that Lampridio and many other hard-pressed humanist poets had sounded: that the golden society of the Muses and of congenial fellow poets has disappeared in the wake of war and was now empty memory.

4.

Several of Cowley's pindarics, both in his 1656 *Pindarique Ode*s and in his later "Verses written upon several occasions," address men of renown: Thomas Hobbes, Dr. Scarborough, and William Harvey. The philosopher Hobbes was famous as the author of *Leviathan*; Dr. Scarborough was a physician who had won fame treating the plague and other maladies during the civil wars; and William Harvey was recognized for his scientific discoveries.[42] In these pindarics,

---

[42] Scarborough was the man who stood bail for Cowley when he was thrown into prison on his return to England in the 1650s. Cowley addresses Scarborough, Hobbes,

however, Cowley does more than laud the accomplishments of the men of science who were his friends. Even as he employs the fulsome compliments and extravagant comparisons of humanist ode, thereby establishing the style and tone for the English familiar pindaric, he engages with important issues of the time. In "To Mr. Hobs" (*Pindarique Odes*, 26–29) Cowley has both a text and a subtext to exploit. In singling out the philosopher Hobbes for praise, he is also praising the new philosophy of his own time, which had finally broken the chains of Aristotelianism and had moved on into a new and independent age. In his opening figure, he contrasts the living philosophy and living soul of Hobbes with the "Vast *Bodies* of *Philosophie*" (1.1) contained in libraries that had merely passed on dead ideas.

As in the ode to his book, Cowley's ode on Hobbes piles epithet on epithet, conceit on conceit. Old philosophy he compares to a cultivated field, overworked by the Aristotelian philosophers who reaped exhausted harvests. Hobbes, the new philosopher, is the new Stagirite, who works new soil in a new field and reaps a new harvest. He further characterizes Hobbes as an explorer who goes where no one has before: "the great *Columbus* of the *Golden Lands* of *new Philosophies*" (4.8), who has left behind old empires and makes a new conquest in a new America.

> For thy learn'd *America* is
> Not only found out first by *Thee*,
> And rudely left to *Future Industrie*,
> But thy *Eloquence* and thy *Wit*,
> Has *planted*, *peopled*, *built*, and *civiliz'd* it.
> (4.10–14)

Not content to make Hobbes the philosopher who has superseded Aristotle and a philosopher-explorer who has discovered a new body of thought, Cowley casts him in the role of the philosopher-conqueror too — an Aeneas whose magnificent shield of "solid *Reason*" is a gift from heaven that repels those rebel-enemies that might contest with him and makes them admire his conquest (5.8–15). Practicing the deliberate excess of the humanistic ode, Cowley describes the breakthroughs that Hobbes has achieved in taking philosophy into a new era.

Yet Cowley is not finished with his praise of Hobbes, and to these tributes of Hobbes's accomplishments as a philosopher he adds a personal touch by describing the man himself and his volcanic personality.[43] In a final outburst of humanistic wit, he piles Pelion, as it were, on Ossa. However, in this case it is not Ossa, but Aetna. Like Aetna, Hobbes has snow on his "reverend Head," but

---

and Harvey with the familiar "thou."

    [43] Hinman argues that Hobbes had an influence on Cowley's view not only of science, but also of poetry. See Hinman, *Cowley's World of Order*, 107–23.

within "noble *Fires*" that breathe beneath the snow (6.2–3): "So *Contraries* on *Ætna's* top conspire, / Here hoary *Frosts*, and by them breaks out *Fire*" (6.9–10). Ever the humanist wit, Cowley even tries to top the concluding metaphor by citing in his footnotes analogues to his comparison in Claudian, Ovid, Tacitus, Silius Italicus, and Seneca, omitting only Pindar and his famous description of Aetna in Pythian 1.[44]

The ode to Dr. Scarborough (*Pindarique Odes*, 35–38) has a different tone. Though Cowley is no less determined to praise his friend and his accomplishments, he has to set those accomplishments in the context of the past civil wars where Scarborough labored to use his skill to avert slaughter and disease: "How long, alas, hath our mad *Nation* been / Of *Epidemick War* the *Tragick Scene*" (1.1–2). Not until section 5 can Cowley assume a genial tone and praise the doctor in humanistic terms, remarking how Scarborough takes the "*whole Apollo*" as his own, combining the healing arts with poetry: "his [Apollo's] gentler *Arts*, *belov'ed* in vain by *Mee* / Are *wedded* and *enjoy'd* by *Thee*" (5.3–4). He even wittily turns about the poetic credo, "*Ars longa, vita brevis*," into a new formula: "Thou do'est make *Life long* and *Art but short*" (5.17). Thereby he cordially wishes Scarborough the leisure to spare some hours for pleasure for himself and fellowship with his friends. Nonetheless, Cowley does not altogether dismiss the melancholy reflections on war that began the ode. Thus he concludes with a bold aphorism, worthy of Pindar: "Let *Nature*, and let *Art* do what they please, / When all's done, *Life is an Incurable Disease*" (6.17–18).

Although apparently written in the same decade as the odes to Hobbes and Scarborough, Cowley's ode "Upon Dr. Harvey" was not printed until 1668.[45] Unlike the previous odes, it does not assume the same intimacy: Cowley only once directly addresses Harvey, and then with a formal tone: "Great Doctor! th' Art of Curing's cur'd by thee" (4.14). However, he treats Harvey's outstanding contributions to anatomical science as comparable to those of Hobbes in philosophy or Scarborough in medicine, for, like Hobbes, Harvey brought science into the new age. For us the principal interest in Cowley's ode rests in its striking "Pindaric" figure at the opening and the linking myth sustained throughout the opening sections. At the outset he apostrophizes "Coy Nature" as a beauteous Virgin "injoy'd by none" (1.1–2), whom Harvey woos and eventually tames. Nature takes on the *persona* of the fleeing Daphne while Harvey becomes Apollo, the impassioned lover, who pursues scientific truth as though he were pursuing a reluctant nymph. Seeking to understand the mysteries of the circulation of

---

[44] See the notes on section # 6, *Pindarique Odes* in *Works*, 29.

[45] See "Verses written on several occasions" in *Works*, 12–14. William Harvey died in 1657; the ode appears to have been written during his lifetime, but after the publication of the 1656 *Pindarique Odes*. The ode takes account of Harvey's loyalty to Charles I, whom he served during the civil wars, and blames the wars for curtailing Harvey's career and scientific research.

the blood, he continues to track Nature as she attempts to evade him. Although Apollo was thwarted by Daphne's transformation into a tree, Harvey is not so deterred:

> But *Harvey*, our *Apollo*, stopt not so,
> Into the Bark, and root he after her did goe:
>   No smallest Fibres of a Plant,
> For which the eiebeams Point doth sharpness want,
>   His passage after her withstood.
> What should she do? through all the moving wood
> Of Lives indow'd with sense she took her flight,
> *Harvey* persues, and keeps her still in sight.
> But as the Deer long-hunted takes a flood,
> She leap't at last into the winding streams of blood;
> (1.9–18)

Through employing the analogy of Apollo's love of Daphne and casting the drama throughout as the pursuit of lover after loved one, Cowley gives vivid realization to Harvey's quest for and discovery of the principle of the circulation of the blood. As pseudo-Daphne, Nature takes her refuge in the heart, the so-called private or secret place of man, the organ which had been impenetrable to both poets and men of science alike. But at the heart itself Harvey forces Nature at last to reveal her secrets: "Till all her mighty Mysteries she descry'd, / Which from his wit th' attempt before to hide / Was the first Thing that Nature did in vain" (2.12–14). The remainder of the ode is devoted to praise of Harvey and his other scientific discoveries.[46] Cowley takes one more mythic liberty in the final section, where he compares Harvey to Jason and laments how the "Golden Fleece" of scientific discovery (5.5) was almost lost because of the devastation of the civil wars.

With his odes to the men who advanced scientific knowledge in his time, Cowley succeeds in carrying on the tradition of the familiar pindaric as a medium for praise while at the same time employing it to express his own intellectual views. In these odes, however, it is not poetry as a discipline or the Pindaric mode as its means that he defends, but, as in his ode "To the Royal Society," science and its advancement, his special cause.[47] When later seventeenth-century pindarists take up the familiar ode in the Cowleian mode, they use it, as earlier pindarists had, to defend the art of poetry, or, as in the case of Aphra Behn, both to defend poetry and to argue a feminist poetic.

---

[46] Like Hobbes, Harvey advanced the state of knowledge in his time and passed on that knowledge through his writing: "These useful secrets to his Pen we owe" (5.1). He battled for truth and purged the science of medicine from error.

[47] See the discussion of "To the Royal Society" in Revard, *Pindar and the Renaissance Hymn-Ode*, 329–34.

5.

Increasingly in the second half of the seventeenth century the familiar pindaric became the medium in which friends conversed with friends, literary critics discoursed on poetry, and poetic allies and foes settled their differences. For friends to compose complimentary verse to be prefixed to a poet's book of poetry had been standard practice in literary circles since the beginning of the sixteenth century. Often such poems were brief epigrams, but in England, from the 1660s on, encomia took on a Pindaric form and character. Sometimes such Pindaric odes or epistles were merely complimentary, but sometimes they became a medium for critical discourse. Aphra Behn, who so readily imitated Cowley's political pindarics, also takes the cue from him in the familiar ode. But it is not men of science that she addresses, but fellow poets. Two of her pindarics were prefixed to volumes of works by young writers: the playwright Edward Howard and the classicist and translator Thomas Creech.[48] While the ostensible purpose of the odes to Howard and Creech is simply to offer encouragement on the one hand and congratulations on the other, both odes afford Behn the opportunity to comment on other larger issues concerning the literary establishment in London.

Speaking as a woman poet, playwright, and translator, Behn offers an unusually insightful penetration into the male world of critics and poets. Behn was one of the first to offer comfort and advice to Edward Howard when his comedy *The New Utopia* received such a battering on the London stage that the young man publicly resolved to discontinue writing. In his preface to the edition of the play printed in 1671, Howard defends his play against its critics and includes Behn's ode with three other commendatory poems, which also offer support.[49] Behn's ode to Thomas Creech, in contrast, was composed to praise a translation of Lucretius that was warmly received. Although it too serves as a poetical preface to the young Oxford scholar's translation, Behn uses her pindaric to reflect on matters of singular interest to a woman who was also a translator. It is perhaps a testimony to the wider interests of both odes that Behn reprints them in her 1684 collection of verse.[50]

---

[48] Both Howard and Creech include Behn's pindarics among the prefatory poems in their respective volumes. See "To the Author of the *New Vtopia*," in *The Six days Adventure, or the New Utopia, A Comedy* (London, 1671), sig. a2^r–a3^r; "To The Unknown DAPHNIS on his Excellent Translation of *Lucretius*," in *T. Lucretius Carus. The Epicurean Philosopher*, 2nd ed. (Oxford, 1683), sig. d3^r–e2^r. Behn dates her poem to Creech 25 January 1682. She publishes both pindarics in the 1684 edition of her *Poems*, and they are also reprinted in the posthumous edition of 1697.

[49] Behn's poem was printed immediately after Howard's preface. Howard wrote a pindaric to Behn that she published in a collection in 1685. See *The Works of Aphra Behn*, ed. Janet Todd (London: William Pickering, 1992), 373.

[50] See "To the Honourable *Edward Howard*, on his Comedy called The New Utopia" and "To Mr. *CREECH* (under the name of *DAPHNIS*) on his Excellent Translation

The ode to Howard commences with the kind of fulsome praise that we have come to expect from the humanist ode. Although Howard's comedy had failed, Behn praises it as though it had succeeded, excelling "Beyond the Merit of the Age" and achieving a "Comick Order" so sublime in every way that it could only be compared to the plays of Jonson, the "Mighty *Ben*" (1.1, 3, 6), Indeed, says Behn, Howard even surpasses Jonson in his portrayal of character: "Your *Solymour* does his *Morose* destroy, / And your *Black Page* undoes his *Barbers* boy" ((1.11–12). Behn raises her compliments one step higher, in asserting that Howard's *Utopia* completes the design of a poetic city that Thomas More's celebrated Utopia had only roughly sketched: "*Moor* only did the Model draw, / You did Compleat that little World, and gave it Law" (1.19–20).[51] What does Behn mean by such hyperbolic praise? Although she is generous in defending a young playwright against the damnation of the poetic establishment, she has other aims apart from engaging in the debate over the merits of Howard's play. She is asserting the right of fledgling writers to belong to the Priestcraft of the Muses, to venture experimentally in their writing, and not to be rejected unfairly and driven from the sodality of writers. Behn had experienced hostility from the establishment when she herself presented works for the stage, so in defending Howard she is also speaking for herself.

Just as Cowley had defended the new science, Behn makes a passionate plea for the new poetry. Further, in so doing, consciously or unconsciously, she enrolls herself with those poets in the line of Ronsard and Cowley who adhered to a Pindaric creed of poetry and argued that the true poet must preserve himself and his craft against detractors of all sorts. The giant Ignorance that Ronsard and his poetic friends fought against still flourished in Restoration England. "Malice," as Behn tells Howard, is always ready to join with "Ignorance" to undo the writer and deprive the audience of his work (3.15–16). "Write on," she further urges, "and let not after Ages say, / The Whistle or rude Hiss cou'd lay / The mighty Spright of Poetry" (4.13–15). With the "whistle" and "hiss" Behn alludes to the catcalls of the Restoration stage, yet her words for us hark back to Ronsard's denunciation of the envious crows who caw vainly against the Pindaric eagle. Ultimately posterity, she asserts, will judge the merit of a literary work, a posterity that is not governed by envy and detraction. It is a point that Milton and Cowley had also made when they advanced the reputation of their books.

The Pindaric creed is double-edged, for it may defend the poet against detractors, but it also requires the poet's staunch devotion to the Muses in the face

---

of *LUCRETIUS*" in *Poems upon Several Occasions: With a Voyage to the Island of Love*, By Mrs. A. Behn (London, 1684), 113–18, 50–57. Todd cites a different version of the Creech ode (*Works*, ed. Todd, 25–29).

[51] In Greek Utopia or *Outopia* means "no place." In the alternate spelling *Eu-to-pia*—sometimes given to the play—it means "good place" ("Notes," in *Works*, ed. Todd, 374).

of criticism. To make this point, Behn compares the playwright to a Vestal Virgin, whose self-imposed solitude might prove for a young writer a metaphorical tomb. She warns Howard: "all your Glories unadmir'd must lye, / As Vestal Beauties are Intomb'd before they dye" (3.19–20). Behn has an ironic point to make with this comparison. First of all, the Vestal Virgins did not entomb themselves; they were entombed alive as punishment for breaking their vows of chastity, an equivalent in poetic terms to forsaking the Muses. Were a poet like a Vestal to abandon his craft in the face of criticism, the Muses would forsake him and his works would lie, justly, in oblivion. In threatening poetical entombment, Behn indicts both the establishment that rejected Howard and Howard himself.

The Howard ode also affords Behn the opportunity for a Pindaric peroration. As she reworks some metaphors introduced earlier, she urges Howard to take up his poetic craft again: "let your rich-fraught Pen, / Adventure out agen; / Maugre the Stormes that do opose its course" (4.5–7). The writer of *The New Utopia*, she wittily puns, should not despair of creating "new" worlds; the poet's own universe will set forth "More than the Universe besides can show" (4.11). She even appropriates for herself the *persona* of the Muse, a martial figure who defends the poet, just as Behn herself has defended Howard.[52] Behn reminds her audience that the true poet—male or female—never retreats nor submits in silence or gives other advantage to the foes of poetry.

> Undaunted let her [the Muse] once gain [sic] appear,
> And let her lowdly Sing in every Ear:
> ∙∙∙∙∙∙∙∙∙∙∙∙∙∙∙∙∙∙∙∙∙∙∙∙∙∙∙∙∙∙∙∙∙∙∙∙∙∙∙
> . . . thou at once maist be revengd on those
> That are thy Foes.
> And on thy Friends such Obligations lay,
> As nothing but the Deed; the Doer can repay.
> (5.11–12, 15–18)

In Behn's hands the familiar pindaric becomes the occasion for teaching some of the broader lessons about the nature of the poet and poetry.

Something of the same thing happens in Behn's poem "To Mr. *Creech* (under the name of *Daphnis*) on his Excellent Translation of *Lucretius*."[53] As in the Howard ode, Behn combines fulsome praise with playful wit as she leads up

---

[52] In another of Howard's plays, *The Women's Conquest*, the Amazons had been cast as heroic conquerors standing up for women's rights ("Notes," in *Works*, ed. Todd, 374).

[53] Although printed both in 1684 and in 1697 without numbers to divide the sections (as was usual for Cowleian pindarics), the ode to Creech is clearly divided into parts and, like Behn's other pindarics, uses alternating short and longer lines. I am indebted to Warren Chernaik for pointing out this poem to me and for his commentary on Aphra Behn. See his *Sexual Freedom in Restoration Literature* (Cambridge: Cambridge University Press, 1995).

to some serious observations about a woman poet's place in society. She begins modestly, asking for permission to present her praise and apologizing for the humbleness of her Muse and the unmanliness of her verse: "Thou great Young Man! Permit amongst the Crowd / Of those that sing thy mighty Praises lowd, / My humble *Muse* to bring its Tribute too" (ll. 1–3). As she further apologizes for the "softness" of her poetry, she alludes to Lucretius's atomic theory to justify alleged female inferiority:

> But I of Feebler Seeds design'd,
> Whilst the slow moving Atomes strove
> With careless heed to form my Mind:
> Compos'd it all of Softer Love (ll. 7–10)

She is eager, nonetheless, to present something "Worthy Divine *Lucretius*, and Diviner Thou" (l. 6), tactfully joining the poet and his translator in a single compliment.

By this time in her poetic career Behn has learned how to make indirection serve the way of direction. While her praise of Creech's translation certainly seems sincere, her profession of womanish weakness and her apology for her lack of classical education— "unlearn'd in Schools" (l. 23)—mask a protest against an educational system that excluded women from the universities. If a woman desires to read Homer and Vergil in the original languages, she finds herself at a decided disadvantage.[54]

> Till now, I curst my Birth, my Education,
> And more the scanted Customes of the Nation:
> Permitting not the Female Sex to tread,
> The Mighty Paths of Learned Heroes dead,
> The God-like *Virgil*, and great *Homers* Verse,
> Like Divine Mysteries are conceal'd from us,
> We are forbid all grateful Theams,
> No ravishing thoughts approach our Ear,
> The Fulsom Gingle of the times,
> Is all we are allow'd to understand or hear.
> (ll. 25–34)

---

[54] Women who came from aristocratic or wealthy families could be tutored in Latin and Greek. On Behn's lack of Latin see Angeline Goreau, *Reconstructing Aphra: A Social Biography of Aphra Behn* (New York: Dial Press, 1980). Although Behn published a paraphrase of one of Ovid's epistles and a translation of Cowley's *Plantarum*, she made a point of saying that she did not know Latin. Todd comments that Dryden in his preface to Ovid compliments Behn on the facility of her translation: see Janet Todd, *The Secret Life of Aphra Behn* (London: Andre Deutsch, 1996), 256.

Behn has not finished her protest about the unequal treatment of women, but in order to make a further point she launches into a discussion of the divine origin of poetry, touching briefly on Lucretius's skepticism about the gods. In antiquity poets allegedly brought direct knowledge of the gods to men, thus promoting divine worship, which, of course, as Behn was aware, Lucretius had attributed to human superstition. Playing upon this very irony, she displaces the so-called inspired poet from his favored position as a transmitter of knowledge, putting in his place a poet-translator, such as Creech, who in conveying the poet's word—now in the vernacular—to a larger audience becomes the medium for transmitting knowledge. Moreover, since the translator's audience now consists of both women and men, she suggests that the translator has placed women on a par with men, conveying knowledge to both alike. Women therefore should adore the poet-translator, Behn wryly intimates, for he has not only alleviated their ignorance, but has also granted them in the process equality with men. On the one hand, Behn's Pindaric digression seems to offer humble thanks from the "fair sex" that through the grace of the translator women may at last share in classical learning. On the other hand, her very act of giving thanks further indicts the male-dominated educational sphere for the exclusion that has made translation necessary. In Behn's hands the commendatory pindaric becomes a potent weapon of social protest.

However, Behn recognizes that a woman can take such protests only so far, for as a female poet she depends on the favor of men such as Creech to further her own reputation and career. Therefore she returns to the mode of praise, naming Oxford, as both Milton and Cowley had, as the home of the Muses. At the same time, she takes up once more the larger issue of how poetry ought to function within society. If Cowley pleaded for science as the new religion, Behn argues that poetry ought to assume that place: "Poets by Nature Aw and Charm the Mind, / Are born not made by dull Religion or Necessity" (ll. 75–76). There is a difference, she argues, between ancient superstition and a proper modern veneration of poets as the dispensers of the true knowledge.[55]

Behn puts her poetic principles to the test as she lauds Wadham College as the "Sacred Nursery" of poets (l. 65), notable for producing not only Creech but also Thomas Sprat and Rochester, referred to by their pastoral names, Thirsis and Strephon, respectively. She is attentive to the role poetry played in the Restoration era with such learned, mighty, and great men such as Sprat, Rochester, and Cowley.[56] The recently deceased Rochester, more than the addressee Creech, fills

---

[55] Behn modifies Lucretius's theory that religious worship derives from man's fear, making an analogy between it and Hobbes's notion that monarchy derives from man's desire for safety. There is a practical need, she acknowledges, for both the monarchy and the church.

[56] Sprat, at best a minor poet, is included, not so much as the author of the politically coded poem on the plague of Athens, as for his loyalty to Cowley and to Charles II

the role here of the Theocritean poet-god, the shepherd, now dead, for whom both the Muses and "Love-sick Maids" mourn, a charming hero to be contrasted with the learned Thirsis or with Daphnis. In praising Rochester with Creech, Behn once more extends the scope of her ode by evaluating those poets of the recent past and looking to the future. She devotes the final sections of her ode to the peroration, encouraging Creech to persevere as a poet and so to ensure the future of poetry as an art. Daphnis-Creech is the "Morning Star," the rising poet, in contrast to those poets who have run their race. There is also a hint of the Pindaric mode as Behn encourages Creech to complete the race, collect the laurels for the victory he has won, and move on to further poetic competition:

> Advance young *Daphnis*, as thou hast begun,
> So let thy Mighty Race be run.
> Thou in thy large Poetick Chace,
> Begin'st where others end the Race.
> (ll. 114–117)

The tradition of the familiar pindaric that Behn adapted from Cowley licensed her use of extravagant praise, seasoned with equally extravagant metaphors and figures. It was a mode she practiced to encourage not only young poets such as Howard and Creech but also lesser known memhers of the poetic establishment, both men and women.[57] It also made her the spokeswoman for poets and the craft of poetry. It is entirely possible that Behn, well versed as she was in French, was aware that in addressing familiar odes to her poet-friends she was carrying on a tradition earlier practiced by Ronsard. More certain, however, is her debt to her mentor Cowley, who had re-invented the familiar pindaric. However, in employing the pindaric for her own passionate defense of poetry, Behn brings it full circle, engaging with poet-friends and poet-foes as Ronsard had done in his own Pindaric polemics over a century before.

---

before and after the Restoration ("Notes," *Works*, ed Todd, 384). Behn applauds Sprat's loyalty to Charles II during the interregnum: "*Thirsis* who whilst a greater Plague did reign, / Then that which *Athens* did Depopulate: / Scattering Rebellious Fury o're the Plain, / That Threatn'd Ruine to the Church and State, / Unmov'd he stood, and fear'd no Threats of Fate, / That Loyal Champion for the Church & Crown" (ll. 81–86).

[57] "A Farewel to *Celladon*, On his Going into *Ireland*," her address "To *Mrs. W.* On her Excellent Verses," her pindaric "To Henry Higden Esq; On his Translation of the *Tenth Satyr* of Juvenal," to name a few others, fall within the range of the familiar pindaric. For the odes to Celladon and Mrs. W. see *Poems* (London, 1684), 13–19, 57–60. The ode to Higden on his Juvenal was not reprinted in Behn's works in the seventeenth century. It is prefixed to Henry Higden, *Satirae Singulae. A Modern Essay on the Tenth Satyr of Juvenal* (London, 1687), sig. a^r–a2^r. In it Behn comments that the nation needs a new Juvenal to cure its ills.

CHAPTER 9
THE CELEBRATION OF PLACE: THE EARLY
MODERN CITY ODE

The Renaissance city ode was in many ways the most formal and magnificent of the Pindaric structures that flourished in the sixteenth and seventeenth centuries on the continent and in England. It was comparable as a verse structure to the lavish pageants that metropolises throughout Europe often mounted to celebrate civic identity, and afforded the greatest opportunity for sweeping political utterance and for national and local celebration. Yet at the same time the city ode could be an intimate form, a place where the poet could express his personal feelings, where he could honor intimate friendships and lodge the familiar, so to speak, under the canopy of the grand. In these odes politics and poetics could join and support each other, and the poet, as he worked for his patron or lauded his native place, could at the same time acknowledge his identity as person and poet.

The city ode was a type that had roots in antiquity but had continued to flourish on its own throughout the medieval period. With the revival of ode in the Renaissance, it was connected almost inevitably with the Pindaric experiments in Latin and in the vernacular that were going on. Among the first triadic odes of that early Pindaric experimenter Benedetto Lampridio is one addressed to his birthplace, Cremona. Similarly, Lampridio's contemporary Luigi Alamanni performed a comparable feat in his vernacular *hymni*, praising the city of Genoa at the same time as he wooed his lady Pianta. Pindarists throughout Europe followed their example, creating encomiastic odes for their native places or for cities they had adopted as their own. Drayton and Spenser brought the city ode to England, and Milton in *Paradise Regained* put the city ode into the mouth of Satan, as he praised the grandest of ancient cities, Rome and Athens. In celebrating city or native land these latter-day pindarists are extending a tradition of praise that Pindar began when he celebrated the city-states of athletes who had triumphed in the Olympic, Pythian, Nemean, or Isthmian games.

1.

Three elements are found in every Pindaric victory ode without exception: the winning athlete's name, the name of the games in which he was victorious, and the name of his city.[1] The prominence of the city in the configuration of the odes of praise is not to be underestimated. Often Pindar begins an ode in fact by naming the city, considering its founder, its traditions, and the culture of its people. Isthmian 7 opens by naming Thebes, Pythian 2 by invoking Syracuse and celebrating its native gods. Other odes celebrate Athens, Acragas, Cyrene, Laomedon, and Camarina, to mention only a few. In fact, it is rare to find a Pindaric ode that does not expound with some detail on the city or state that produced the victorious athlete.[2] As Carne-Ross has commented, the athlete's city represents the continuing life of natives that pass from generation to generation.[3] Before he invokes the Graces in Olympian 14, Pindar celebrates Orchomenos, the city of the young victor, where the Graces were especially revered. He includes within his ode description of the city's abundant fertile horse-pasturing meadows and its situation by the waters of Cephisus. Similarly, in Olympian 2, immediately after invoking the hero, god, and man he would praise, Pindar proceeds to describe Theron's city Acragas visually, remarking on its splendid temples beside the river which remain to this day a wonder and a delight. With his praise of Acragas Pindar also praises those Dorian founders who were, as Pindar tells us, the eye of Sicily. In Pythian 12 Pindar invokes the city itself, describing Acragas, its acropolis and river, and naming this "house of Persephone" the most beautiful city of mortal men: Καλλίστα βροτεᾶν πολίων (Pythian 12.1–3). Pindar's famous Pythian 1 on Hieron's chariot victory at Delphi features Aetna and celebrates with Hieron's victory the founding of the city for Hieron's son. The description of the city's site, in the shadow of the mountain of the same name, is unforgettable, as is the description of a volcanic eruption on Aetna. And in Olympian 7 Pindar is so taken with the beauty of Rhodes that he recounts its origin myth, describing the island rising like a rose from the sea as the sun god Helios chooses it as his own. Other odes also have striking descriptions that bring ancient cities scenically before our eyes.

Pindar's two odes to Syracusan victors—Pythian 2 and Nemean 1—both begin with invocations to the city itself. The first, Pythian 2 (1–2), celebrates the city as the home of fighting men: "Μεγαλοπόλιες ὦ Συράκοσαι. βαθυπολέμου / τέμενος Ἄρεος" (Mighty city, Syracuse, the precinct of Ares, plunged deep in war). As he cites Ares as one of the patron gods of Syracuse,

---

[1] Most, *The Measures of Praise*, 62–63.

[2] See Christopher Carey, "Pindar, Place, and Performance," in *Pindar's Poetry, Patrons, and Festivals*, ed. Hornblower and Morgan, 199–210.

[3] See D. S. Carne-Ross, "Weaving with Points of Gold: Pindar's Sixth Olympian," Arion 15 (1976): 5–44, here 42–44.

Pindar is acknowledging the importance of war in establishing its prominence and that of its ruler, Hieron.[4] But in naming Artemis, Pindar also celebrates the city's proximity to the island of Ortygia, sacred to the goddess. The invocation of Nemean 1 gives us not just a description of Ortygia, but also an evocation of the myth of Alpheus and Arethusa that had particular significance for Sicilian Syracuse, since it pays homage to Syracuse's Dorian heritage. The two nature deities, the river Alpheus and the nymph Arethusa, were translated from Arcadia in Greece to breathe once more in the Sicilian land, just as Sicily's Dorian colonists came from Greece to Sicily to build a great city and made their Greek heritage breathe once more in the western land. It is as though Pindar were telling us that Syracuse's foundations were laid down through the power of the native gods that the Greeks brought with them. Place and the gods of place play powerful roles throughout this ode.

Isthmian 7, written for Strepsiades of Thebes, is a victory ode that celebrates Pindar's native Thebes. As he salutes "happy Thebes" (μάκαιρα Θήβα), he evokes her gods and traditions, asking which events in her history made her most rejoice at heart. Was it the arrival of Dionysus, or the descent of Zeus to Alcmene to beget Heracles, or the sowing of the dragon's teeth? Did Thebes rejoice most when her citizens overcame Adrastus of Argos or when the native Dorians translated their flourishing civilization to Sicily, colonizing it? The glory of a city is inextricably connected with the notable events in its history, and those events are marked by the specific conferral of favor by the gods. Pindar takes pains to recall those illustrious moments in the city's past at the same time he celebrates the new eminence it has attained through the victory of one of its athlete-heroes. On all these occasions the gods smiled on human beings.

Fragments of Pindar's hymns or paeans also attest to the importance of the celebration of place in his oeuvre. Paeans to Apollo make special mention of Delphi and of Apollo's birthplace Delos, and in turn Pindar connects Delos with Thebes and Athens. Paean 5, addressed to Delos from the Athenians, includes a reference to the myth that the island of Delos was formed from the body of Asteria, Leto's sister: "Δᾶλον, ἐπεί σφιν Ἀπόλλων / δῶκεν ὁ χρυσοκόμας / Ἀστερίας δέμας οἰκεῖν" (40–42) (Delos, since golden-haired Apollo gave them the body of Asteria to dwell in).[5] In this paean Pindar is clearly evoking the famous Homeric Hymn to Delos, which recounts how Leto specifically chose the sacred island as the birthing place of Apollo and Artemis. In the Homeric Hymn

---

[4] See Most, *The Measures of Praise*, 70.

[5] See Ian Rutherford, *Pindar's Paeans: A Reading of the Fragments with a Survey of the Genre* (Oxford: Oxford University Press, 2001), 251–52. Rutherford remarks on Pindar's treatment of the myth: Asteria was fleeing the embraces of Zeus when she was transformed into an island in order to be there to receive the pregnant Leto when she was about to give birth to Apollo and Artemis. Pindar accepts the folk etymology of Delos from Δῆλον (clear), when the island makes its appearance at the crucial moment.

Leto searches among the islands of the sea for that a place that would receive her, and, finding Delos, she addresses the island (her erstwhile sister), asking for refuge and promising that it will attain renown through the temple that will be built there. The island goddess responds to welcome Leto. The Homeric hymnist takes care to describe the rocky island, specifically noting Mount Cynthus and the palm tree near which Leto gave birth.

Callimachus's hymn "To Delos" carries on the tradition of the place ode, opening with a "Pindaric" question and closing with the conventional parting "χαῖρε" of the Homeric Hymns.

> τὴν ἱερήν, ὦ θυμέ, τίνα χρόνον ἢ πότ᾽ ἀείσεις
> Δῆλον, Ἀπόλλωνος κουροτρόφον; (1–2)

> At what time or when, O my soul, will you sing of
> Sacred Delos, the nurse of Apollo?

Having posed the Pindaric question, Callimachus quickly frames a clever answer. Delos, he says, is more worthy of song than the other Cyclades, for on her the lord of singers was first bathed and for her Apollo has ordained a share of song. As the centerpiece of his poetic garland, Callimachus chooses the narrative of Apollo's birth, the event that gave the "floating" island renown and fixed it in the sea. Drawing his narrative from the Homeric Hymn to Delian Apollo, he adopts the conventional language of hymn to describe the birth of Apollo: the child leaps forth; the nymphs and Eileithyia attend. Delos herself prepares a soft resting place for the god and greets him with song.

Although he remains faithful to Pindar and to the Homeric Hymn's celebration of place, Callimachus introduces his own personal voice and adds lively interpolations to the narrative. He recounts how the goddess Leto, in labor and pursued by Hera's wrath, passed by many cities that refused her a resting place until she came at last to Helicon, the Muses' hill outside Thebes. Callimachus cannot refrain from adding a witty comment. At Thebes, he notes, Apollo, although still a babe in the womb, utters his first prophecy, predicting the doom that will overtake the city that harbored within it Niobe, the impious slanderer of Leto and her twins. During the actual birth, Callimachus introduces another miraculous sign: the swans, most musical of the birds, circle the island seven times in song. Apollo's lyre is to contain only seven strings; therefore, the swans in their circling preordain this number by refraining from an eighth circling song. While adhering to the formulas of the place hymn, Callimachus extends its Homeric and Pindaric dimensions by introducing into the hymn-ode the distinctive voice and person of the poet.

2.

The Neapolitan poet Giovanni Pontano is among the earliest Renaissance poets to adapt the odic celebration of place to a celebration of his own city. Pontano's odes to Naples and to Naples's native goddess Antiniana possess some distinctive qualities of this ancient genre: a sense of civic pride, a strong religious devotion, and an eagerness to celebrate Naples's classical past and to connect the greatness of the city with its divine foundations. The native nymph Antiniana, whom Pontano invokes at the beginning of the ode to sing the praise of Naples, has more than a passing resemblance to place-nymphs such as Arethusa or Thebe ("Antinianam Nympham invocat ad cantandas laudes urbis Neapolis"). Like them she is a protective city deity, who presides over the city's natural and architectonic splendors — its towers as well as its river and seashore, its caves, inhabited by nymphs who are the sisters of the river god Sebeto, its hills and recesses sacred to Bacchus and Ceres. For Pontano Bacchus and Ceres are the deities who assure the city's prosperity and renew its climate, granting it eternal spring. The nymph Antiniana is more than a city deity for Pontano, who named her the protective goddess of his own villa, the villa *Antiniana*.[6] To honor her is a personal as well as a civic duty, and Pontano summons a pantheon of ancient gods into her company, who, together with her, confer prosperity on Naples. Jove and Minerva guarantee civic rights to Naples; Mars confers a warring spirit; the Graces and the Muses add their special gifts to Naples's cultural life. The cultivation of the arts that the Muses encourage extends the good life to all the citizens. Both poet and statesman, Pontano, like Pindar, credits the presence of the Muses as the mark of a flourishing society.

Benedetto Lampridio signals the importance of the city ode to his collection by placing first among the poems of his *Carmina* (1550) the ode to his own native city of Cremona. In it he joins a celebration of the city's past with one of a dynastic wedding that will ensure the city's continuing life.[7] When Lampridio writes of Cremona, he is not just pleasing his patrons, the Sforzas; he is also taking the occasion to confide personal reflections on the city of his birth. The affectionate tone he adopts is not too different from that Pindar assumes in praising his native Thebes. Marc-Antonio Flaminio's ode for Mantua has even closer connections to Pindar's praise of Thebes, for in it Flaminio specifically

---

[6] "Antinianam Nympham invocat ad cantandas laudes urbis Neapolis," in "Versus Lyrici," in *Opera* (Florence, 1514), fols. 144ᵛ–145ʳ. Pontano wrote several other odes to the place nymph Antiniana: "Ad Antinianam Nympham Iouis, & Nesidis filiam" and "Patvlcidem et Antinianam Nymphas alloquitur" (fols. 142ʳ–143ᵛ). See Carol Kidwell's discussion of Pontano's villa and his odes to the nymph Antiniana (Kidwell, *Pontano*, 104–7); also Maddison, *Apollo and the Nine*, 62–64.

[7] "Ad Cremonam Patriam," in Lampridius, *Carmina* (Venice, 1550), fols. 3ʳ–5ʳ. See Carol Maddison's discussion of this ode in *Apollo and the Nine*, 105–7.

echoes Pindar's Isthmian 7 and Olympian 2. He praises Mantua, as Pindar had
Thebes in Isthmian 7, as happy ("felix"), and draws from Olympian 2 Pindar's
descriptive phrase for the citizenry of Acragas, addressing Mantua as the eye of
its citizens ("ciuitatum ocelle").[8] Like Pontano, Flaminio balances his praise of
the city's monuments with his praise of its geographical situation. Imitating Vergil's description of the river Mincius, Flaminio describes the green banks along
which the river murmurs. But he also looks to its palaces, its temples, its streets,
and its imposing buildings, all evidence of the ingenuity of the people as well
as of their prowess in defending their city. Like Pindar, Flaminio regards the
happiness of the people as a sign of a flourishing city and calls peace its greatest
adornment. Mantua had given birth not only to the great Vergil, but also to his
modern counterpart, Castiglione. Flaminio transfers to these poets the place of
honor that Pindar would have reserved for the athlete or patron and Renaissance
poets for the duke or prince.

Pindar was one of Navagero's favorite poets, and his ode to Padua manifests
his influence. Aldus Manutius had dedicated the 1513 edition of Pindar's odes to
Navagero, and in the dedicatory letter he familiarly refers to the volume as "tuus
Pindarus." Following a basic odic pattern, Navagero begins with a formal invocation. He especially celebrates the men of arms and of letters who had brought
Padua distinction. Like Flaminio and Pontano, he praises the city's rural beauty,
likening its geographical situation beside its river to that of Troy, whose fate, he
comments, it also sadly shares.[9] Thus he tempers praise with regret, for the city
he celebrates with such affection had been devastated repeatedly by war. Many
of Italy's poets in their salutes to native cities had also reflected on the unhappy
consequences of war. Michele Marullo had affectionately paid tribute to his native city of Constantinople and its Hellenic past, while regretting its enslavement
by the Turks.[10] Like him and many others, Navagero celebrates glories that exist
no longer: Padua is only a shadow of what it had been in its past. Navagero brings
into sharp relief not only Padua's past glories, but also the destruction the god of
war has wrought on the city he would praise.

---

[8] See M. Antonius Flaminius, "De Lavdibvs Mantvae," in *Carmina Quinque Illustrium Poetarum* (Venice, 1558), fols. 64^v–65^r.

[9] Andreas Naugerius, "De Patauio a militibus uastato," in "Lusus" in *Carmina
Quinque Illustrium Poetarum* (Venice, 1558), fols. 22^v–23^r.

[10] See, for example, Michael Marullus, "De Fortitudine Byzantiae" and "De exilio
suo," in *Poetae Tres Elegantissimi* (Paris, 1582), fols. 23^v–24^r, 39^r–40^r.

3.

Four of the eight Pindaric hymns that Florentine exile Luigi Alamanni dedicated to François I — hymns 4 through 7 — are celebrations of place that praise Italian city-states and situate his Italian lady, Pianta, in the landscape of her native land. In a unique way, Alamanni integrates the personal and the political in the formal city-ode. He honors Pianta by describing not only her beauty but also that of Liguria, associating with her the ancient myths of the city of Genoa where she was born. Politics and poetics unite, as Alamanni pours out a personal lament for self and country at the same time he celebrates those places with which he most closely identifies. Alamanni composed these poems of exile while residing at the French court of François I, after having been banished from Florence a second time by the Medici. Nostalgically he titles his volume *Opere Toscane*, remarking how in order to celebrate Tuscany and her illustrious citizenry he has changed the Pindaric for the Tuscan lyre, "la Tosca cethra" (Hymno 4, Ballata 1.1). His aim is to raise his countrymen to the same height that Pindar had raised noblemen of antiquity, even if, he quips wittily, he risks giving his name to a sea, a consequence Horace had warned of when would-be pindarists ventured on waxen wings in over-ambitious flight.

> Deh com'alzar uorrei
> Soura 'l mortal pensiero
> Questi honorati rami;
> Che tante uolte fero
> Inuidia in cielo à i Dei;
> (Hymno 4, Contra Ballata 1, 12–16).

> Thus I wish to raise
> Above mortal thought
> These honored branches
> Which many times
> Caused envy in heaven to the gods.[11]

Among the illustrious men he celebrates is the condottiere Larcaro: "inuitto, eterno / Lume, perpetuo esempio / Alla tua antica madre" (unconquered, eternal light, perpetual example to your ancient mother) (Stanza 2, 1–3). Larcaro was a local hero of the city of Genoa, an ancestor of the lady Pianta, and a representative of the independent spirit of northern Italy.[12] In Hymn 5 Alamanni celebrates Larcaro's exploits, but he also reflects darkly and philosophically on the frailty of human endeavors, commenting how rarely human beings — poets, princes, and private persons — have the power to execute what their wills propose.

---

[11] Luigi Alamanni, "Hymni," in Alamanni, *Opere Toscane* II (Leiden, 1532), 211.

[12] See Carol Maddison's discussion of this ode in *Apollo and the Nine*, 145–47.

Come la uoglia è ingorda,
Come il potere è frale
Di nostro human disegno?
(Hymno 5, Ballata 1.1–3)

How covetous the will,
How frail the power
Of our human design?

The poet is not merely reflecting on the difficulty he experiences in carrying out the design he has proposed in the previous ode—to link praise of Pianta to the celebration of her ancestor Larcaro. He also is applying the maxim to other endeavors. Poets and princes alike must join force to will in order to complete the highest of human enterprises. In what sounds very like a Pindaric aphorism, Alamanni remarks hopefully that ill can turn to good, if will and force are not lacking.

In the digressive passage that follows, Alamanni has ample opportunity to illustrate the aphorism. He alludes to the strength that permitted Hercules to kill the Nemean lion and then to wrestle with the giant Antaeus, the son of Earth. Since Antaeus drew his strength from the earth, at first the hero and the giant were evenly matched. Fortune smiled first on one, then on the other until at last Hercules lifted Antaeus from the earth, prevailing over him. Whatever Antaeus's force, says Alamanni, he could not count on victory, for he faced the greater will of Hercules. Will joined to force conquers. The lesson would not have been lost on Alamanni's patron, François I, who had often been compared to Hercules. When he turns to Larcaro, he demonstrates again that without will force does not prevail. He tells how the condottiere, having suffered from a favorite of the king an insult that he was unable to avenge directly, used Genoa's maritime resources to enforce a naval embargo, thus winning concessions and an honorable peace. Larcaro tells the king that he has fought for honor, not for gold. Alamanni draw something very like a Pindaric moral from the story. Glory through praise, he concludes, is superior to glory through vengeance.

Hymn 6 is essentially Alamanni's lament for exile from his native Tuscany. Beginning with a recollection of Pythian 1's lyre, held by Apollo and the Muses, he celebrates the power of poetry. For Alamanni, the lyre upholds truth, calms fury, tempers flames and cold, moves mountains, and can even stop rivers or stars in their courses. It can also assuage the pangs of nostalgia for his native place. With his lyre Alamanni can celebrate Italy and his beloved Pianta, who has become a symbol for Liguria. Nostalgia for native place is a sentiment not unknown in Pindar's odes. In Olympian 12 Pindar addresses the political exile Ergoteles of Crete, and offers consolation for the loss of his native land. Alamanni might well have drawn an analogy between his case and Ergoteles'. Both achieved success in a foreign land: Alamanni in France, Ergoteles in Sicily. Pindar tells how

Ergoteles had recently triumphed in the foot race in behalf of his adopted city, Himera. Yet, as Pindar poignantly adds, he continued to feel that inner sorrow all exiles experience. Pindar consoles the victorious athlete by pointing out that though sorrow is the expected lot, sometimes joy may come unexpectedly from anguish. Pindar's moral could also apply to Alamanni. In Hymn 6, Alamanni is seeking for consolatory advice that he might give himself, some joy he might bring out of sorrow. He finds it in poetry itself, in the golden lyre he has invoked at the outset of the ode. Poetry has the power both to console and to triumph over adversity. Alamanni highlights the accomplishments of the poets Orpheus and Amphion. Orpheus with his lyre had the power to transfix Hell, and Amphion with his lyre raised the walls of Thebes. Moreover, Bacchus, Thebes' most honored son, joins these two; he is another who, as Pindar also tells us, brought joy out of sorrow.

While personal reflection and poetic celebration are important parts of Hymn 6, its principal section is devoted to celebration of the lady Pianta and her birthplace, the Ligurian city of Genoa. Like poets before him, Alamanni celebrates the city by praising the virtue, noble blood, and bravery in battle of Genoa's citizenry. He is aware, of course, that in praising Genoa, a sister city to his own Florence, he is celebrating Italy in song. Patriotic fervor for his native land has not died in him, he proclaims, though, unlike other men, he can reap few rewards from his native land. While others can look on their native land, he must bear the burden of exile, denied by a deaf heaven those desires closest to his heart.

Hymn 7 evokes a different kind of celebration of place. Alamanni creates a love song to Pianta by describing the flowering land that he associates with her—the gardens rich in plants, adorned with the Apollonian laurel that makes it ever green. His lyre is devoted to the praise of this land:

> Alto nome immortale
> Haurà Lyguria & lode,
> Ch'iui non lunge all'acque
> L'alma mia Pianta nacque.
> (Hymno 7, Stanza 2. 7–10)

> A high immortal name
> Has Liguria and praise;
> There not far from the water
> My gracious Pianta was born.

As in the previous hymn, Alamanni laments his exile, but here he expresses the pain of separation from native land through a longing for his absent lady.

Hymn 7 begins with an invocation of the sun's brilliance at midday, a description which assuredly harks back to the opening of Olympian 1. However, Alamanni transforms Pindar's invocation to water and light, paying tribute not to a prince but to his native land and to his beloved lady. For Alamanni, as for

Pindar, the sun is pre-eminent before all other lights and shines—in the absence of the moon—with golden light like the brightest of metals. The sun makes all things bright and conspicuous on earth; it dispels cold, makes the gardens green, and above all lights the beauty of Pianta. Alamanni's sun is the sun of Italy that reveals his lady's beauty and the wondrous beauty of her land—beauties which make separation all the more painful. To counter this despair, he once again calls up a Pindaric sentiment, reflecting that he must accept the inevitable philosophically: to be blessed on earth rarely belongs to the human lot. Alamanni's hymns combine personal, patriotic, philosophical, and moral reflections in order both to praise place and to express a poignant sense of its loss.

Alamanni's celebration of Genoa becomes a model for later poets. Some poets, such as Fulvio Testi (1593–1646), a contemporary of the pindarists Gabriello Chiabrera and Giovanni Ciampoli, follow him closely. Testi's ode to Silvestro Grimaldi, though in stanzas and not triads, demonstrates his awareness of Alamanni's Pindaric imitations. Like Alamanni, he celebrates the city of Genoa together with its leading noblemen and weaves a fabric of interlinking mythic references that connect the city, its statesmen, and its illustrious past.[13] In tribute to Genoa's maritime power, he cites examples both of Neptune's quelling dissent with his trident and of Jove's establishing supremacy over the gods with his thunderbolt. Moreover, like Alamanni, he celebrates the living hero Silvestro by alluding to classical types: the heroes of the Argo, who sailed by Italy; Achilles; and wise Ulysses. Silvestro also becomes, like Pindar's Hieron, a sun that outshines all in his splendor. He even echoes Pindar's apology that, in praising Silvestro, he cannot in the season of May draw honey from all the flowers, yet bestows praise modestly and well. However, he cannot resist adding, like Alamanni and a host of other Pindaric imitators, that he has heeded Horace's warning and avoided the folly of Icarus, that is, the excesses of too close imitation of Pindar.

4.

In the hands of humanist poets such as Joseph Scaliger, Ippolito and Iulio Capilupi, and Paulus Melissus the city ode becomes almost formulaic, whether composed in stanzas, triads, or hexameters. Joseph Scaliger echoes Pindar as he addresses both his adopted city Batavia and his native Verona as the eye of cities: Batavia the eye of great Belgia, Verona the eye of the world, "ocelle mundi."[14] It comes as no surprise that his contemporary Melissus dubs Nuremberg the eye of

---

[13] Fulvio Testi, "Celebra in generale le lodi della Città di Genoua, e si ristringe alle particolari del Signor Siluestro Grimaldi," in *Opere del Sig. Conte Don Fulvio Testi* (Milan, 1658), 229–32.

[14] Iosephus Scaligerus, "Ad Batauiam" and "In Veronam," in *Poemata omnia*, ed. Petrus Scriverius (Leiden: Plantin, 1615), 52, 25–27.

Europe: "Ocelle micans Europae" (strophe 1. 3).[15] Like Flaminio, Scaliger praises Verona as the flower of Italian cities, and, like Navagero, he sadly reflects on
Verona's glorious past, now eclipsed, since like Padua it has been devastated by
war. Surveys of architectural splendor as well as rural beauty dominate in many
of these odes—and in some there is nostalgia for past glory. Ippolito and Iulio
Capilupi look on Rome and Venice respectively as splendid Renaissance cities.[16]
Ippolito's ode to Rome, moreover, is full of nostalgic sentiment as well as civic
pride, for he is describing the city of his youth, to which he longs to return. As
Pontano had lauded the splendors of antique Naples, so Ippolito evokes Rome,
the city that gave civilization to the world. He describes both its natural and its
architectonic beauties: its seven hills covered with wild flowers, its warm baths,
the capitol with the temples of the gods, the palaces of the Palatine. As he evokes
these visual beauties, he calls to mind how the achievement of Rome's citizens
made the city great through enthusiasm for the arts as well as pride of arms. Inspired perhaps by his uncle's praise of Rome, Iulio Capilupi celebrates both the
beauty of Venice and its contributions in the arts of war and peace.

The odes that the German Paulus Melissus composed both for his adopted
city of Rome and for his native German city of Nuremberg combine personal and
political reflection. Melissus enthusiastically greets Rome as the seat of ancient
Caesars and modern princes: "Vrbs septicolli uertice prominens, / Antiquiorum
patria Caesarum, / Regumque sedes consulumque" (City prominent with your
seven lofty hills, home of ancient Caesars, the seat of kings and consuls).[17] As
though he were conducting a personal tour, he revisits Rome's principal monuments: its portals, the bridge over the Tiber, its fountains, as well as the celebrated view from the Janiculum. Paraphrasing both Horace and Pindar, he asks
Calliope to which monuments he should raise his lyre and sing: "Quid monumenta ducum barito leui / Cantare simis Calliope?" (sig. **3v). Yet, despite his
attention to Rome's architectural splendors and political prominence, Melissus
regards Rome principally as the city of poets both ancient and modern: Vergil,
Horace, and Ovid as well as his poet-friends, Muret, Bargaeus, and Gambara.
To praise Rome is to honor its poets as well as to exercise his own poetic vocation
in rendering that praise.

---

[15] Paulus Melissus, "Ad Inclitam Noribergam Urbem Imperii," in *Mele sive Odae ad
Noribergam et Septemviros Reipub. Norib.* (Noribergae, 1580), 5–8.

[16] Hippolytus Capilupus, "Ad Romam"; Iulius Capilupus, "De Laudibus Urbis Venetae. Cento xxix," in *Capiluporum Carmina* (Rome, 1590), 48–50, 380–81. See G. H.
Tucker, "Neo-Latin Literary Monuments to Renaissance Rome and the Papacy, 1553–
1557: Janus Vitalis, Joachim Du Bellay, and Lelio Capilupi—From Ekphrasis to Prosopopeia," in *Acta Conventus Neo-Latini Bonnensis*, ed. R. Schnur et al., MRTS 315 (Tempe: ACMRS, 2006), 81-119.

[17] Paulus Melissus, "Ode: Ad vrbem Romam," in *Melissi Epigrammata in Vrbes Italiae* (Argentinae, 1585), sig. **2r–**4r.

Melissus's triadic ode for Nuremberg imitates Pindar's praise of Acragas. As Pindar described Acragas's river and temples, so Melissus shows us the river Pegnis as it makes its way through the architectural splendor of the medieval German city. Like Pindar, Melissus points out that the happiness of the city ultimately depends on the piety of the people. Secure from evil, Nuremberg flourishes in its institutions and arts, in its schools, temples, and gardens. It rules like a queen, like an oak tree that possesses celestial vigor. Melissus's ode to Nuremberg, like Lampridio's ode to Cremona, combines praise for the city with celebration of the noble families of that city—and in an epithalamium included in a later volume, Melissus joins the praise of Nuremberg with celebration of the nuptials of one of those noble families.

In the Renaissance the city ode and the nuptial ode are often closely linked. The nuptial odes that Melissus included among the "Emmetra" of his 1586 collection could also serve as city odes. There is Pindaric precedent for this also. Although Pindar's epinician odes do not celebrate actual marriages, they do exploit epithalamic themes and sometimes also allude to those mythic marriages that had founded a city. Many of the native nymphs or goddesses of place to whom Pindar refers or whom he invokes as city patrons achieved their special status by mating with a god. They were the "brides" of Zeus or Apollo or Poseidon, and because of this they in turn became eponymous place nymphs. In Isthmian 8, for example, Pindar tells us how Zeus had favored both the nymph Thebe, the city-goddess of Thebes, and her sister-nymph, Oenopia, the city-patron for Aegina, who became the mother of the founding hero Aeacus. Apollo's choice of Cyrene made her the patron nymph of the African city of Cyrene. Her "nuptials" with the god are alluded to in Pindar's odes to Arcesilas of Cyrene. Pindar also alludes in Isthmian 8 to one of the most famous marriages of a goddess to a mortal: that of Peleus and Thetis, recounting it allusively as a specific compliment to the city of Aegina. Not surprisingly, this marriage also becomes one that Renaissance poets frequently include in their nuptial hymns. By alluding to patron city-goddesses, Renaissance poets can exploit a ready-to-hand "wedding" theme whenever a city ode changes course and becomes a wedding ode or vice versa.

Melissus's nuptial pindarics often mimic the pattern of his city odes. He includes in his epithalamia topics that the critic Julius Caesar Scaliger recommends for wedding songs: praise of the couples' and their parents' nobility, remembrance of their forebears, good wishes for the future, promise of the birth of offspring, topics which also have a place in Pindar's epinician celebrations.[18] Along with the traditional summoning of joyful maidens and youths, compliments to Erato,

---

[18] Iulius Caesarus Scaligerus, *Poetices libri septem* (Lyons, 1561), 151–55. Scaliger refers to the wedding of Peleus and Thetis as the prototype for epithalamia. He also notes that marriage songs should include exhortations to pluck the sweet fruits of marriage with kisses and close embraces and to hope that the union will be likewise fruitful—advice with which Melissus apparently concurs.

Cupid, and the Graces, and enthusiastic exhortations to seize the day, Melissus includes in the first nuptial ode of the 1586 "Emmetra" (41–43), composed for Sebaldus Welserus of Nuremberg, an allusion to the wedding of Peleus and Thetis, so important among Pindar's odes as a forecasting of the birth of the supreme hero Achilles.[19] The groom, Sebaldus Welserus, he addresses, moreover, as the flower of his country ("patriae flos"), a hero comparable to Peleus or to Achilles. The second of his nuptial odes (44–46), composed for the double wedding of the Hainzelii brothers to the Nitherti sisters, celebrates the parents of the couple and their city equally with the bride and groom. As in the previous ode classical deities—Venus and Cupid, the Graces and Muses, especially the Muse Erato—join with the appropriate civic gods to confer a blessing. The brides with their eager bridegrooms offer not only promise of a hopeful future for both families but also honor and glory for their native city.

Many of Melissus's epithalamia celebrate state events, and for these he pulls out all the Pindaric stops. Family, religion, and politics play equal roles in the ode on the marriage in 1593 of Frederick IV, the Elector Palatine, to Louisa Juliana, the daughter of William the Silent. A supporter of Henri IV of France, Frederick IV was one of the leading Protestant princes of the German league, who, educated by his Calvinist uncle John Casimir (whom Melissus invokes), had only come to power in his own right on the death of his uncle in 1592. Hence his wedding to Louisa Juliana of Orange the following year, like the marriage of William of Orange to Mary, the Duke of York's daughter, some eighty years later, became an occasion to celebrate the prince's political and military leadership. Melissus lauds the groom's military ardor as a fitting complement to his ardor for his bride. The connection of this nuptial ode with the city odes we have been examining is clear right at the outset. The ode celebrates place as well as people. The native hills, valleys, and caverns of the Palatinate resound with joy at the festivities, and the people of the Rhine and the Neckar join in, summoned to witness the wedding procession. Much is made of the classical prototypes: the weddings of Perseus and Andromeda, Atalanta and Hippomenes, Ariadne and Bacchus. Attentive to the dynastic occasion, Melissus presents himself as a Pindaric poet who takes the lyre in hand, leads the chorus, and sounds the tuba and the tympani. The wedding procession could almost double as an epinician victory procession. Melissus even refers specifically to the Pindaric metrics of his song: "Hymenaeon honorificum / Canens Erato, Pindarici / mulatur barbiti / Pandere mensuras" (strophe 4, 7–10).[20] The ode concludes with a hope for children—and indeed the eldest son of this match was Frederick V, the future husband of Princess Elizabeth,

[19] "In Nvptias Sebaldi Welseri, Patricii Avgustani et Norimbergensis," in "Emmetra," *Schediasmata Poetica* (1586), 41–43.

[20] "In Nvptias Friderici IV Electoris Palatini & Loisae-Iulianae Principia Vrania" in "Emmetra," in *Delitiae Poetarum Germanorum*, ed. Janus Gherus [Ranutius Gruterus] (Frankfurt, 1612), 4: 349–56. In 1620 the Polish poet Simon Simonides composed a

daughter of James I of England, whose marriage was also to call forth epithalamia from leading poets, including John Donne.[21] Melissus's other epithalamia also exploit Pindaric patterns, saluting family as well as place and calling upon triumphal choruses to celebrate the event.[22]

5.

Melissus was not the only sixteenth-century poet to compose wedding songs that combine salutes to family and to native place. Torquato Tasso, profiting both from his contemporaries' practice and from Pindar's example, even more fully integrates the nuptial ode and the city ode and is attentive to the political designs of both. Tasso knew and admired Pindar, although, unlike Melissus or Alamanni, he never attempted triadic verse. He regarded Pindar with Theocritus, Anacreon, and the dramatic poets of Greece among his major classical models, but took a broad view of classical imitation, employing Pindaric ode as a model for religious odes, encomiastic odes to princes, love poetry, and poetry to friends, as well as for celebratory epithalamia and canzoni in praise of place.

In the expository notes to his *Rime* Tasso is scrupulous in identifying which figures, images, devices, and even gnomic expressions he has borrowed both from classical writers such as Pindar and from Italian writers from Dante and Petrarch to Pontano and Bembo. Some of his borrowings from Pindar are surprising. Without Tasso's notes, we might overlook the debt to Pindar's Pythian 9 in the sonnet that describes how amorous persuasion unlocks the heart (1.92).[23] More noticeably Pindaric are Tasso's borrowing of metaphors or similes

---

Pindaric epithalamion in triads for the marriage of Thomas Zamoscius to Catherine, the daughter of Alexander the duke of Ostrog: see *Opera omnia*.

[21] See Heather Dubrow, *A Happier Eden: The Politics of Marriage in the Stuart Epithalamium* (Ithaca: Cornell University Press, 1990). Dubrow includes a discussion of Donne's epithalamium for the Palatine Elector and Princess Elizabeth as well as other Stuart epithalamia by Donne, Jonson, Herrick, and others. Dubrow includes a translation by Jackson Bryce of Scaliger's section on "Epithalamia" from the *Poetices*.

[22] See, for example, the nuptial odes on the marriage of George Eberhard to Sabina of Egmont and on the marriage of Ludovick Svvarsmarius to Maria of Freimonia in "Emmetra," in *Delitiae Poetarum Germanorum* 4: 360–64; 364–71. Dynastic concerns play an important part in Melissus's epithalamium for Count George Eberhard of Solms-Lich and Sabina of Egmont in 1595. Here again there are salutes to place as well as family—the nymphs of the Rhine and the daughters of Ocean are called upon to celebrate the wedding. The wedding is celebrated throughout Europe—by Belgium, Britain, France, Germany, and Scotland, who hail George, as they had Frederick, as a hero. My thanks to Sarah Bailey, former librarian of the Tower of London, for helping me to identify the persons and the date of this epithalamium.

[23] *Delle Rime del Sig. Torquato Tasso, Parte Prima e Seconda* (Brescia, 1592–1593).

for poetry, as when he compares, as Pindar had, his verses to arrows that strike (1.155) or contrasts new verses with old wine (2.43). Tasso also takes serious-ly Pindar's likening of poetry to sculpture and contrasts it with Horace's more famous pronouncement "velut pictura poesis" (2.53). For him both Pindar and Homer are authorities on myth, for in commenting on Dante's description of Ephialtes among the fallen giants in Hell, he cites Pindar's and Homer's descrip-tions of Ephialtes as a king (1.170).

In Tasso's poetry the use of Pindar extends beyond simple borrowing of phrases. For example, in the canzone "O Bel colle" (2.31–36), composed in praise of a little mountain near Ferrara and in tribute to the noble ladies of the court, Tasso combines a Pindaric celebration of place with a typical Pindaric mythic digression. [24] He begins with an invocation to the hill, which is adorned both by art and nature: "O Bel colle, onde lite / Ne la stagione acerba / Tra l'arte, e la natura, incerte pede" (2.31). There among the flowers of spring—narcissus and hyacinth—young women wander, gathering those flowers which Mother Earth brings forth in response to Father Sun. In just such a place, Tasso continues, in-troducing a digression, Venus, the mother of Cupid, in the company of Pallas, Diana, and Proserpina wandered with her nymphs and, like Ferrarese maidens, the goddesses adorned their heads with flowers. Developing the myth, he tells how Pluto, the god of the underworld, smitten by Cupid's bow, disrupted the se-renity of Nature and carried off Proserpina. As the girl cried in vain to Pallas and Diana, these goddesses grew pale and trembled, but Venus merely smiled a little smile. Although Tasso breaks the mood by introducing Pluto's disruption, he tempers it by describing the smile of Venus, who takes a different view of the pro-ceeding. Tasso good-naturedly concludes the canzone by telling his song to fly off to these gods. The canzone combines an evocation of place with a compliment to the noble ladies who adorn that place with their beauty. But it also follows, as Tasso remarks in his notes to the canzone, the practice of Greek and Latin poets in departing from its principal subject and including an extended mythic digres-sion to further adorn the canzone.

Tasso also celebrates Ferrara in the wedding song that he composed for the marriage of Cesare d'Este and Virginia de' Medici in 1586. The epithalamion has elements of the city ode, for it celebrates the reconciliation of the two city-states, Ferrara and Florence, which the union of scions of the d'Este and the Medici families attempted to effect. To honor both cities, Tasso prefaces the wedding canzone with two sonnets: the first, "Alma città" (in honor of the bride) praises Florence, the second (in honor of the groom) Ferrara; the nuptial canzone praises

---

[24] In the notes Tasso identifies borrowings from Pontano, Claudian, and Petrarch, but he also, departing from his usual practice of merely citing verbal echoes, remarks that he has imitated digressive and structural patterns common to Latin and Greek poets (2.34).

both cities.[25] To grace the wedding with glory, the Florentine river Arno shines with a special beauty, and the Adriatic pays tribute to the Tyrrhenian sea, symbolizing how Italy through the union of Ferrara and Florence will renew its ancient glory and be joined from sea to sea. Tasso concludes the song with a return to his native Ferrara and a description of how the city was adorned for the wedding.[26] With his even-handed tribute to both cities Tasso forwards the political design, subtly expressing the hope that with his dynastic marriage the conflict between Florence and Ferrara might be resolved—a hope, alas, that proved vain.

The wedding song for the Prince and Princess of Mantua (2.170–73) also has political implications.[27] In the opening section Tasso appeals to Italy ("Italia mia") to smile upon the union:

> Italia mia, che l'Apennin digiunge,
> E da mille suoi fonti
> Mille fiumi in duo mari infonde, e versa.
> Quel che parti Natura, Amor congiunge,
> Tal che non ponno i monti,
> E i gran torrenti, ond' è la terra aspersa,
> Far l'una à l'altra auersa. (1–7)

> My Italy that the Apennines divide,
> and from which a thousand springs,
> a thousand rivers flow into its two seas.
> That which Nature divides, Love joins
> So as not to place apart the mountains,
> and the great torrents, from which the earth is watered,
> to make one adverse to the other.

The union of bride and groom, Tasso proposes, is a happy omen for Italy, too often torn by rival conflicts between its city-states. The respective spouses, Tasso notes, come from opposite sides of the Apennines. Perhaps, at last, peace and concord may prevail in the land, which, though divided by "nature"—that is, by

---

[25] See *Rime*, 2:155, 156, 156–59. Edward Burman discusses the political significance of this marriage in *Italian Dynasties: The Great Families of Italy, From the Renaissance to the Present Day* (Frame, Somerset: Butler & Tanner, 1989), 44, 60.

[26] Tasso also makes other wedding songs the occasion for celebration of place. In a wedding song for Hercole Tasso and Lelia Agosta (2.168–70), Tasso salutes the gracious land ("terra gentil") of bride and groom and makes a mythic allusion to the Greek city of Thebes, which had produced the first "Hercole," and to Crete, which nourished the god Jove.

[27] See the discussion of this wedding in Virginia Tufte, *The Poetry of Marriage: The Epithalamium in Europe and Its Development in England*, University of Southern California Studies in Comparative Literature 2 (Los Angeles: Tinnon Brown, Inc., 1970), 99–101.

the Apennines—may be conjoined, as in a happy marriage, by love. Through the marriage of this couple, "two" may become one, both in the joining of spouses and in the joining of the divided land that they represent. Tasso appeals to another sense of "twoness" in the passage that follows. The husband and the wife are figured as two suns—one of valor and one of beauty—luminaries which, despite their doubleness, may shine with a single light, the one never obscuring the other. Tasso takes the occasion to allude to Rhodes, the island, celebrated by Pindar in Olympian 7, which was, like the city of Mantua, sacred to the sun. Under the auspices of the sun, says Tasso, he wishes that both Mantua and the newly wedded couple may flourish.

Almost all of the wedding songs that Tasso composed feature in some way or another the cities represented by the spouses. Some also include detailed descriptions of those cities, as, for example, the wedding canzone for Signor Matteo di Capova, Conte di Pelevo, and Signora Donna Giovanna di Tunica, which begins with an invocation to Naples (2. 176–79):

> Napoli d'alte mura antica fronte,
> Napoli, che di gloria, e d'or corona
> Impone à tanti Duci;
> Quante serene luci
> Non ha la notte all'hor, che'l velo spiega,
> Qui con Amor, ch' auolge ì cori, e lega,
> L'anime pellegrine,
> Facea ghirlande al crine,
> E allori giungendo insieme, e palme,
> Ei tessea i nodi pretiosi à l'alme.
> (4–13)

> Naples, ancient front of high walls,
> Naples, which assigned glory and the golden crown
> To so many leaders,
> How much serene light
> Does the night not possess now,
> That unfolds the veil
> Here with love, which makes the choruses turn and binds
> Pilgrim hearts,
> Makes garlands for the hair
> And, winding them together with bay and palms,
> Weaves for him precious knots for the soul.

As in the previous canzoni, Tasso organizes his song as a tribute both to the city and to the families associated with it, now joined by marriage. The groom's family, the Caspi, claimed a descent from Troy, but Tasso chooses to represent the union of families geographically rather than historically by alluding to the topography of Naples, where sea is linked to land. Choruses of Muses and Parcae, singing antiphonally, celebrate this conjoining—the choruses respond to one another, alternating their notes, while the mountains and the waters surrounding Naples also respond: "L'uno, e l'altro canoro, / E doue tace l'un, l'altro risponde, / E alternan le note, i monti, e l'onde" (20–22). Celebratory choruses, processions, and the crownings of happy celebrants are the vital ingredients of both marriage and epinician celebrations alike, and in a way this canzone is both. Tasso calls upon the sun god Apollo to accept the songs of the choruses. Apollo smiles and chases away the clouds with his light, blessing not only the choruses and the nuptial couple, but also Italy and Spain, whose adverse fortune has been changed to happiness through these nuptials. A new day dawns for all. The heroes of the Occident and the Orient are summoned to do homage, among them the Greek hero Theseus, whom Tasso puts forward as a symbol of renewed favor. Once Theseus broke faith with Ariadne, but now he affirms new faith with these nuptials. The earth and the sea that surround Naples, now united, are at peace.

Like the victory odes with which this study began, the nuptial odes often celebrate political reconciliation that hopefully will bring peace. The canzone for the wedding of the Grand Duke of Tuscany Ferrando (2.180–84) praises, as the other odes have, the flourishing Italian landscape: Tuscany with its elms, pines, and laurels as well as its rivers and fountains. But, as the digression of the canzone illustrates, Tasso is aware that the dynastic marriage of a French bride to a Tuscan husband must reflect on something beside the richness of Tuscany. France has often wooed Italy with war, Tasso tells us, but now she offers peace. The bride, though French, is descended from the Medici.[28] In recrossing the Alps and accepting an Italian husband she returns to her original Tuscan stock, mixing her Lotharingian blood with the Tuscan and thereby promoting cultivation of the arts of peace. The political resonances of this wedding song are obvious, as is Tasso's symbolism in portraying the bride as an Astraea who, returning, balances the scales of Libra, thus assuring France's concord with Italy.

6.

The political lessons of Tasso's epithalamia were not lost on the English poet Edmund Spenser. Tasso's epic poetry had been an important model for Spenser and the influence of Tasso's long heroic poem *Gerusalemme Liberata* on Spenser's *The Faerie Queene* has been well documented. However, Tasso's canzoni and epithalamia, rich in Pindaric technique and reference, were also shaping forces on Spenser's lyrical odes. Spenser was keenly aware of the Pindaric underpinnings of Tasso's experiments in the ode form, for he too had been from his earliest poems, *The Shepheardes Calender* (1579), to his later compositions, *Complaints* and

---

[28] Tasso's canzone dates from 1589 when Ferdinand I, Grand Duke of Tuscany, married Christiane de Lorraine, the granddaughter of Catherine de' Medici of France.

the *Fowre Hymnes*, an avid experimenter in different types of lyric.[29] He had also often looked to his European contemporaries for inspiration, to both Italian and French neo-Latin and vernacular poets, as well to Paulus Melissus, whom, given his residency in England in the 1580s, Spenser must have known. Spenser's *Prothalamion* is an odic experiment that attempts, like the lyrical compositions of Melissus and Tasso, to recreate a Pindaric type for a modern audience.

Prothalamion is not a Pindaric ode *per se*, but it uses, just as Melissus's odes do, many features of Pindaric ode. Written ostensibly to celebrate the betrothals of Ladies Elizabeth and Katherine Somerset, it differs remarkably, however, from the *Epithalamion* that Spenser wrote earlier to celebrate his own marriage. It is more truly an ode, written on the occasion of marriage, rather than a marriage song, for it celebrates, like Tasso's and Melissus's odes, other matters besides the coming marriages. Keenly sensitive to the geographical setting and to the political resonances of the occasion, Spenser weaves together personal, political, and topographical associations. By placing the setting of this double betrothal at London and by describing both London and the Thames, Spenser can include not only autobiographical reflections on London, the place of his own birth, but also compliments for his patron, the Earl of Essex, who was the military hero of the hour and at whose house the weddings were to take place. As he salutes the brides, a nobleman, and the city of London, Spenser incorporates formulas for praise intimately connected both with the Pindaric tradition and with neo-Latin epithalamia and city ode.

The ode begins with the evocation of place and with a personal reflection of the poet, as he walks beside the "siluer streaming *Themmes*" on a calm and sweet day, when the river banks are "paynted all with variable flowers" (ll. 11, 13).[30] His feelings, however, are at first far from celebratory. Instead of joy he feels a sense of gloom and depression because of his present situation at Elizabeth's court: "sullein care, / Through discontent of my long fruitlesse stay / In Princes Court, and expectation vayne / Of idle hopes" (ll. 5–8). His mood does not lift until he sees two swans — metaphorically the two brides — and a group of nymphs, one of whom sings a bridal song. Spenser may be remembering odes such as Melissus's "Ad Thamesim Flumen," which both describes the river and its swans and evokes the mythological story of Leda and the swan. Also, he might also be recalling Tasso's epithalamia with their mythic embellishments. Like these odes, Spenser's ode is full of mythological decoration. He refers in stanza 3 to Jove's disguise as a swan and characterizes the attendants in the bridal procession as nymphs like those who gathered flowers in Tempe and in Thessaly — who might even have been in company with Proserpina in the Sicilian meadow before her

---

[29] See the commentary on Spenser in Revard, *Pindar and the Renaissance Hymn-Ode*, passim.

[30] Quotations from *Prothalamion* are from Spenser, *Poetical Works*, ed. J. C. Smith and E. de Selincourt (Oxford: Oxford University Press, 1970), 601–2.

abduction by Pluto. Spenser includes in his wedding song references to violent sexuality, which, like Tasso, he tempers by the invocation of "faire *Venus*, that is Queene of loue, / With her heart-quelling Sonne . . . / Whose smile they say, hath vertue to remoue / All Loues dislike" (ll. 96–99). His song in praise of the double wedding also includes a song within a song, as one nymph takes the cue from Spenser himself to praise the "gentle Birdes" who approach "vnto your louers blisfull bower" (ll. 91–93). Nor does Spenser forget in the final stanza to round off his references to swan lore by describing the bridegrooms as Castor and Pollux, Jove's twins and the fruit of his encounter with Leda as a swan.

Having recounted with many a flourish the swans' progress down the river, Spenser tells how they arrive at last at "mery *London*," whereupon to signal their arrival he breaks out into what we recognize as a mini-ode in honor of the city.[31]

> . . . mery *London*, my most kyndly Nurse,
> That to me gaue this Lifes first natiue sourse:
> Though from another place I take my name,
> An house of auncient fame.
> There when they came, whenas those bricky towres,
> The which on *Themmes* brode aged backe doe ryde,
> Where now the studious Lawyers haue their bowers
> There whylome wont the Templer Knights to byde,
> Till they decayd through pride: (ll. 128–136)

While intimately connecting himself with London as his birthplace, Spenser also evokes in this strophe not only the city and its architectural structures but also its history, moving effortlessly from a description of the Inns of Court, once the dwelling of the "Templer Knights," to the description of Essex House, where the weddings are to take place: "Next whereunto there standes a stately place, / . . . therein now doth lodge a noble Peer" (ll. 137, 145). However, before complimenting this peer, the Earl of Essex, whose patronage he was seeking, Spenser adds a note of personal complaint, reflecting on the previous great lord, the Earl of Leicester, who had inhabited the palace where Essex now dwells. Once himself the great hope of England, Leicester, now dead, revives in Spenser thoughts of "olde woes" (l. 42) and those present sullen cares he referred to in the first stanza. Only with an effort does he turn away from these melancholy thoughts and turn back to celebration.

---

[31] Spenser may be recalling Tasso's allusion to the swans of the Po in his nuptial canzone for the Principe d'Urbino and Lucrezia d'Este. In this ode Tasso not only calls upon Hymen and the usual choruses of Muses and Graces and gods in attendance, but also invokes the swans of the river Po to be present and to sing the nuptial song. See Tufte, *The Poetry of Marriage*, 191.

What is interesting here is that Spenser's salute to London does not stand on its own, as so often is the case in Renaissance city odes, but is part of a more intricate structure of praise and meditation. It adheres thus more closely to the Pindaric model than many other odes of its type. With great dexterity Spenser combines the praise of place with the praise of the Earl of Essex, who assumes the role that the victorious athlete would have in a Pindaric ode. In 1596 Essex had been put in command of an expedition to Spain, where he had successfully defeated the Spanish fleet and captured Cadiz. Hailing him as "Great *Englands* glory and the Worlds wide wonder" (l. 146), Spenser endows him not only with epinician prowess but also with the *aretê* of the Greek hero Hercules. Like Hercules, Essex has sounded his name to the ends of the earth, making all respond to his person and reputation: "dreadfull name, late through all *Spaine* did thunder, / And *Hercules* two pillors standing neere, / Did make to quake and feare" (ll. 147–149). Spenser readily congratulates Essex on his "noble victorie," that "fillest *England* with thy triumphs fame" and promises "endlesse happinesse of thine owne name" (ll. 151–153). Tactfully here Spenser remembers to couple the earl's name with the queen's and to place Essex's victory in a nationalistic context: through "thy prowesse and victorious armes, / Thy country may be freed from forraine harmes: / And great *Elisaes* glorious name may ring / Through al the world, fil'd with thy wide Alarmes, / Which some braue muse may sing / To ages following" (ll. 155–160). From bridal song to celebration of city to celebration of hero, the ode has progressed at last to the lauding of Spenser's ultimate patron, Queen Elizabeth (whose uneven patronage had caused the discontent he expressed at the start of the ode). Odes of praise, whether epinician or epithalamic, dare not neglect the poet's royal sponsor. However, in the final stanza, as the grooms emerge from their Thames-side palace to receive the brides, Spenser gracefully returns to the persons and the theme of his wedding song.

Like those continental epithalamia we have looked at, Spenser's ode deftly mixes political references with dynastic celebration. But it also reserves, as Spenser looks forward to the happy future of the bridal couples and the nation, a place for the poet and his own intimate reflections as part of the scenario he describes. No poet immediately following, not even Donne in his several epithalamia or Jonson or Herrick in their marriage songs, exploits the potential of the wedding-song so fully as Spenser has nor endows it so complexly with features of the ode form as it was then developing. Daringly extending the range of the nuptial ode into Pindar's special territory of personal and political commentary, he has created an ode unique in English literature both in itself and in its character simultaneously as city-ode, wedding song, personal complaint, and political encomium.[32]

---

[32] For the use of Pindaric ode for wedding songs, see Cowley's verses for the wedding of the Duke of Buckingham to Mary Fairfax in *The Works of Mr. Abraham Cowley*, 9th ed. (London, 1700), 135–36; Aphra Behn's dialogue "A Pastoral Pindarick. On the

More modest is Drayton's ode to Coventry, but it too combines a celebration of place with a celebration of person, in this case the poet's beloved, Idea or Anne Goodere, his patron's daughter, and also includes a tribute to England's quondam queen, Elizabeth. Published first in 1606, a decade after Spenser's *Prothalamion* and not long after Elizabeth I's death and James I's accession, it was reprinted in an expanded version in 1619 as "A Hymne to His Ladies Birth-place." At first it would seem to have only marginal connection to Pindaric ode. But as I have previously argued, Drayton was a serious pindarist, who was concerned to find a new voice for the ode.[33] Moreover, he could introduce indirect political references into a light ode, as he does in "To a Virginian Voyage" and the ode on Agincourt. In his ode to Coventry he looks back nostalgically to a past era as he lauds three women: Idea, Lady Godiva, and Queen Elizabeth.

Drayton's opening apostrophe to Coventry surveys its architectural beauties — its walls, ports, and pyramids — in a manner familiar in Renaissance city ode. Like the Italian poet Alamanni, he honors the city as the birthplace of his lady, taking a special delight in linking its beauty with hers.

> Coventry, thou do'st adorne
> The Countrey wherein I was borne,
> Yet therein lyes not thy prayse,
> Why I should crowne thy Tow'rs with Bayes:
> 'Tis not thy Wall, me to thee weds
> Thy Ports, nor thy proud Pyrameds,
> Nor thy Trophies of the Bore,
> But that Shee which I adore,
> Which scarce Goodnesse selfe can payre,
> First their breathing blest thy Ayre; (ll. 1–10)[34]

Marriage of the Right Honourable the Earle of Dorset and Middlesex, to the Lady Mary Compton," in *Lycidus: Or The Lover in Fashion . . . Together with a Miscellany of New Poems. By Several Hands* (London, 1688), 134–45; and Dryden's Pindaric epithalamium "On the Marriage of the Fair and Vertuous Lady, Mrs. Anastasia Stafford, With That Truly Worthy and Pious Gent. George Holman, Esq. A Pindarique Ode," in *The Poems of John Dryden*, ed. Kinsley, 4: 1804–1806. The bride in Dryden's ode was the daughter of an executed Catholic lord, the groom a Catholic convert who had been exiled. The ode thus is not without political implication in the 1680s when the question of James II's Catholicism was being debated.

[33] See Revard, *Pindar and the Renaissance Hymn-Ode*, 305–12.

[34] "A Hymne to His Ladies Birth-Place," in *The Works of Michael Drayton*, ed. Hebel, 2: 373–74. Anne Goodere (Lady Rainsford) was the lady of the sonnet sequence Idea, the daughter of Drayton's patron, Sir Henry Goodere, to whom he dedicated the Odes. See Bernard Newdigate, *Michall Drayton and his Cicrle* (Oxford: Shakespeare Head Press, 1941), 40–48, 51.

The ode is connected perforce with the sonnet sequence to Idea and might simply be relegated to a sub-category of love poetry, did it not contain a mythic digression that endows it with political relevance to a former era, as well as the present period. In the digression Drayton has chosen to describe the semi-legendary figure Lady Godiva, lauding her as the heroine whose act of courage and defiance saved the city and guaranteed its continued freedom.

> That Princesse, to whom thou do'st owe
> Thy Freedome, whose Cleere blushing snow,
> The envious Sunne saw, when as she
> Naked rode to make Thee free,
> Was but her Type, as to foretell,
> Thou should'st bring forth one, should excell
> Her Bounty, by whom thou should'st have
> More Honour, then she Freedome gaue: (ll. 29–36)

Predictably, Lady Godiva exists as a prototype for Drayton's beloved Idea, but she also suggests a far greater personage, Queen Elizabeth, to whom Drayton takes pains to allude at this point. In her, as in Idea and Lady Godiva, the virtue of female sovereignty is illustrated, and with that virtue also the concept of freedom, especially as it encompasses notions of both generosity and liberty. By recalling "that great Queene, which but of late / Ru'ld this Land in Peace and State" (37–38), Drayton makes an indirect political statement. From the less than ideal present, he is looking back on an idealized past, where female virtue as "idea" exercised its power, securing a peace, now threatened. In three women, virtue is exemplified in person, in city, and in nation. By linking Idea to Lady Godiva and Queen Elizabeth, Drayton uses the genre of city ode to make both a moral and a political commentary on his era. As in "To a Virginian Voyage" and the ode on the Battle of Agincourt, he illustrates a theme not alien to Pindar or to an English contemporary Ben Jonson — how virtue through testing proves its worth.

7.

Pindar called Athens the bulwark of Greece (fr. 76 [46]); many Renaissance poets praised Rome as the queen of Italy. When Milton in book 4 of *Paradise Regained* put the praise of Rome and Athens into the mouth of his antagonist Satan, however, he created the most unusual example of the city ode, adapting the techniques of this Pindaric type for his own special purpose. By Milton's time particular formulas had become familiar in neo-Latin and vernacular poetry for invocations to and praise of the Renaissance city. In city ode, description of the city's unique geographical situation and of its architectural beauties had become

almost *de rigueur*. Attention also was given to its historical eminence and the
distinction of its rulers in politics and in the arts. The poet who intoned the ode
often had an intimate bond with the city he praised or with its distinguished
citizenry. Milton undercuts these formulas when he recreates two city odes and
embeds them within the narrative and dramatic fabric of *Paradise Regained*. It is
not he as poet who leads the chorus of praise for Rome and Athens, but Satan
who takes on this part, as he describes for the Son of God first imperial Rome
and then noble Athens. His verbal tour of Rome is, in fact, every way comparable
to that which the Catholic bishop-poet Ippolito Capilupi had conducted when
he systematically led his readers on a literary survey and extolled the city's beauty
and its great history. Like the neo-Latin poet, Satan takes us from the Capitol
to the Palatine mount, describing palaces, turrets, terraces, and spires, praising
pillars and roofs and the work of artificers in cedar, marble, ivory, or gold. What
we see in many ways more resembles, as critics have pointed out, the Renaissance
city than classical Rome.

> The City which thou seest no other deem
> Than great and glorious *Rome*, Queen of the Earth
> So far renown'd . . . there the Capitol thou seest,
> Above the rest lifting his stately head
> On the *Tarpeian rock*, her Citadel
> Impregnable, and there Mount *Palatine*
> Th'Imperial Palace, compass huge, and high
> The Structure, skill of noblest Architects,
> With gilded battlements, conspicuous far,
> Turrets and Terraces, and glittering Spires.
> Many a fair Edifice besides, more like
> Houses of Gods . . . (4.44–56)

Satan proceeds next to a praise of the people of Rome: the praetors, procon-
suls, legions, cohorts, and the multitudes who have come from all the corners of
the earth to celebrate Rome's pre-eminence in "Civility of Manners, Arts, and
Arms" (4.83). Satan concludes his oration by naming the regions that pay tribute
to Rome and by offering to the Son of God this great kingdom, ruled by an ab-
sentee emperor without an heir.

Having put the Renaissance city ode into the mouth of the devil, Milton changes directions and speakers and lets the Son of God deconstruct Satan's ode. The Son challenges the very premises on which this Pindaric type is
based—particularly the presumptions about praise of place and persons characteristic of the mode as practiced by so many of the neo-Latin and vernacular poets of the Renaissance. The Son of God is not impressed by Satan's extravagant
praise of Rome and its magnificence: "Nor doth this grandeur and majestic show
/ Of luxury, though call'd magnificence, / . . . allure mine eye, / Much less my

mind" (4.110–113). He refuses to value what seems only lavish consumption and superficial display; neither does he honor "so many hollow compliments and lies / Outlandish flatteries" (4.124–25). Through the person of the Son, Milton is offering a critique of the kind of encomiastic poetry that flourished in the sixteenth and seventeenth centuries as poetry of praise in the Pindaric mode. Mounting an anti-ode against Satan, the Son calls Satan's praise of Rome to account, pointing out that Satan's view of excellence fails to apply proper measure to human pursuits and human achievement. The invocation of "measure" has a particularly Pindaric resonance, as though Milton were applying through the Son a classical standard missing from Satan's appraisal of Rome. Yet whatever its so-called moral deficiencies Satan's ode for Rome exists as a superb example of a humanistic type, one on which Milton the poet has expended considerable poetic finesse.

In creating the ode for Athens and in making Satan the speaker of it, Milton tests classical and humanistic standards still more rigorously. In his encomium of Athens Satan praises not just Athens' architecture and civic glory, but its love of learning.

> behold
> Where on the *Aegean* shore a City stands
> Built nobly, pure the air, and light the soil,
> *Athens*, the eye of *Greece*, Mother of Arts
> And Eloquence, native to famous wits
> Or hospitable, in her sweet recess,
> City or Suburban, studious walks and shades;
> See there the Olive Grove of *Academe*,
> *Plato's* retirement, where the *Attic* Bird
> Trills her thick-warbl'd notes the summer long;
> There flow'ry hill *Hymettus* with the sound
> Of Bees' industrious murmur oft invites
> To studious musing; there *Ilissus* rolls
> His whispering stream; within the walls then view
> The schools of ancient Sages; his who bred
> Great *Alexander* to subdue the world,
> *Lyceum* there, and painted *Stoa* next;
> (4.237–253)

The illustrious schools of ancient learning to which Satan alludes—Plato's academy, Aristotle's Lyceum, Zeno's Stoa—are the very academies which fourteenth-and fifteenth-century Italians sought to emulate as they recovered the languages and literature of Greece and Rome. Love of learning fostered the humanistic sodalities in Naples, Rome, Florence, and Venice, Renaissance academies that by implication are also lifted up to praise with Satan's praise of Athens' schools. Milton had visited several of these academies when he journeyed to

Italy in 1638–1639 and sojourned in Florence, Rome, Naples, and Venice.[35] Their leading members in the century past had been poets such as Pontano, Lampridio, Crinito, and Marullo, who were also among the first pindarists. Those city odes of Pontano and Lampridio that we have studied set the standard for the Satanic ode Milton is creating. As he permits Satan to sound the praise of Athens and its academic sodalities, Milton is also referring tacitly to the Hellenism of the Renaissance, which fostered the culture of humanistic learning so highly valued in England and throughout Europe, a humanism that he himself had praised in his *Defensio Secunda*.[36] In naming Athens the "eye of *Greece*" (240) Milton seems to echo Pindar's praise of Acragas's citizenry in Olympian 2. But he might also just as well have been echoing the phrase as it had been espoused by Renaissance poets to praise their own cities—as Flaminio had cited Mantua as the eye of Italy and Scaliger and Melissus had so praised Verona and Nuremberg.

Like the idealized Renaissance cities lauded in the city odes, the Athens of *Paradise Regained* is praised as an idyllic place of the Muses. Its sweet recesses, studious walks and shades reflect the Renaissance love of rural retirement and studies in the midst of city life. Odes for Naples, Mantua, and Verona had dwelt on the rustic retreats of these cities that made them so conducive to intellectual life and study. Lampridio and other poets had described the rural villas, such as Mellini's villa outside Rome, where poets and philosophers thronged to cultivate the arts. Milton takes care to allude not only to Athens' philosophers, but also to the poets admired in Attic society, poets who had become the principal models for humanistic poets. Satan tells the Son, "There thou shalt hear and learn the secret power / Of harmony in tones and numbers hit / By voice or hand, and various-measur'd verse, / *Aeolian* charms and *Dorian Lyric Odes*" (4.254–257). In the extensive catalogue of ancient poets and tragedians that Satan sets forth for the Son, Milton alludes to Pindar's lyric odes as a foremost literary type. After all, Pindar was a poet highly admired by the ancients as well as by Renaissance intellectual sodalities.[37]

---

[35] See John Arthos, *Milton and the Italian Cities* (New York: Barnes & Noble Inc., 1968); also Anna K. Nardo, "Milton and the Academic Sonnet," in *Milton in Italy*, ed. Di Cesare, 489–503; also Nardo, "Academic Interludes in *Paradise Lost*," *Milton Studies* 27 (1991): 209–41; Peter Lindenbaum, "John Milton and the Republican Mode of Literary Production," *Yearbook of English Studies* 21 (1991): 121–36; also Estelle Haan, *From Academia to Amicitia: Milton's Latin Writings and the Italian Academies* (Philadelphia: American Philosophical Society, 1998).

[36] See *The Second Defense of the English People* (*Pro Populo Anglicano Defensio Secunda*) in *Complete Poems and Major Prose*, ed. Hughes, 828–30.

[37] Although Simonides and Bacchylides were also composers of lyric odes in the Dorian style, Pindar was the most famous of the three. The only poet in this catalogue mentioned by name is Homer ("Blind Melesigenes thence Homer call'd / Whose Poem *Phoebus* challeng'd for his own" [4.259–260]). Milton goes on to cite the tragedians next

Just as surely as Milton's Son of God had deconstructed the ode to the imperial city Rome, he deconstructs the ode in praise of the humanistic Athens. The ode to Rome had concentrated on the city's imperialistic accomplishments—those monuments that reflected its civil government and regal authority. The Son's critique of the ode had, in turn, focused on the politics of Rome. However, Satan's ode for Athens looks beyond its architectural beauties to focus on Greece's achievements in poetry and philosophy, intellectual achievements symbolized by the ancient city itself and its cultural inheritance in the Renaissance. Once again, the connection between the ancient city and the Renaissance cities that emulate it is implicit. So many Renaissance city odes extol the intellectual life of the city they praise; hence a critique of Athens becomes perforce a critique of the Renaissance habit of imitating the ancient Romans and Greeks and holding up classical poetry as a model for the moral and civic life of the Renaissance city. Milton's Jesus calls this standard to account. In a sweeping review of Greek literature, he dismisses ancient philosophy and poetry, criticizing it for extolling human virtue as a standard above spiritual devotion and making man rather than God the center of its study. Ancient philosophy and poetry delude the reader, he insists, referring indirectly to the myth of Ixion to prove his point:

> Who therefore seeks in these
> True wisdom, finds her not, or by delusion
> –Far worse, her false resemblance only meets,
> An empty cloud.
> (4.318–321)

The myth of Ixion occurs prominently in Pindar's Pythian 2. Describing Ixion's vain attempt to embrace the cloud image of Hera, rather than the true goddess, Pindar comments that the unwise man embraces the sweet dream of falsehood: "ἐπεὶ νεφέλᾳ παρελέξατο / ψεῦδος γλυκὺ μεθέπων ἄϊδρις ἀνήρ" (36–37). Ironically, even while he denies Pindar and Greek poetry a primacy over Hebraism and Israel, Milton has used Pindar's commentary on the vain pursuit of wisdom to underpin Jesus' critique.

It is not unexpected that Jesus should declare a preference for Hebraic poetry over the Hellenic poetry that Satan had lauded so extravagantly: "if I would delight my private hours / With Music or with Poem, where so soon / As in our native Language can I find / That solace?" (4. 331–334). However, Milton makes the Son go further in the critique. Praising the hymns and psalms of Hebraic song, he asserts that Greece learned the poetic arts from Israel, rather than Israel from Greece. To all true tastes, he says, Sion's songs excel, for they praise God aright. Although the Son of God refrains from mounting a city ode to Jerusalem,

---

(without naming them specifically), praising them for their moral teaching and "brief sententious precepts" (4.264). He ends with the praise of the orators and philosophers.

his praise of Israel and Hebraic poetry hints at what such an ode might have included. Indeed it is this third city, Jerusalem, which, with or without its city ode, triumphs over the classical cities, Rome and Athens. At the pinnacle of the temple in Jerusalem the Son of God decisively defeats Satan, achieving a victory over the devil at the same time he demonstrates how Jerusalem triumphs over Rome and Athens.[38]

Comparison of Greek and Hebraic poetry was commonplace during the sixteenth and seventeenth centuries, especially among Protestant poets, and Pindar had frequently been placed beside David, and the odes and psalms compared.[39] Although Milton himself praised Pindar as a worthy model for the ode form in *The Reason of Church Government*, he advanced Hebraic lyric poetry over Greek as a higher model.[40] This passage in *Paradise Regained* resonates with the same comparison and the same critique of Greek poetry. Yet, at the same time, we must observe that *Paradise Regained* is a short epic in the classical mode and that the odes to Athens and Rome that Milton embeds in its epic structure employ a classical form that goes back to Pindar and was one which flourished in the Renaissance as a popular lyric type. In modeling Satan's lyrical addresses to Athens and Rome on the humanistic city ode, Milton has created a poetical *tour de force*, exploiting to the fullest the poetic range and opportunities for display that this lyric type afforded while deconstructing the praise that was at its very heart.

The twin odes to Rome and Athens in *Paradise Regained* mark Milton's last espousal of a Pindaric type. In the end his relationship to Pindar's odes, as to Pindar, proves oblique. In the Rouse ode Pindarism and praise had gone hand in hand with the adoption of the Pindaric model. In *Paradise Regained*, Milton as creator of the odes stands behind both the ostensible speaker of the city ode, Satan, and his respondent, the Son of God. He permits Satan to raise in his celebration of Rome and Athens a superb architectonic and poetic type, but as man and poet he stands back from the praise that the ode mounts and does not personally embrace it. Unlike his stance in the Rouse ode or the Nativity ode, his position in *Paradise Regained* is similar to that of *Paradise Lost*. In book 4 of the epic, he employed for Satan's anti-hymn to the sun an archetypal hymn form that he both

---

[38] See Matthew 4:5–7 and Luke 4:9–12 for the account of Jesus' standing at the pinnalce of the temple in Jerusalem.

[39] See Revard, *Pindar and the Renaissance Hymn-Ode*, 12–25.

[40] See Milton's praise of the psalms in "The Reason of Church Government," *Complete Poems and Major Prose*, ed. Hughes: "But those frequent songs throughout the law and prophets beyond all these [the hymns and odes of Pindar and Callimachus], not in their divine argument alone, but in the very critical act of composition, may be easily made appear over all the kinds of lyric poetry to be incomparable" (669). Throughout his life Milton composed translations of the psalms, the most extensive group having been translated in the 1640s and 1650s and published in 1673 in *Poems, &c. Upon Several Occasions* (London, 1673).

accepted and denied.[41] Here also Milton is in a double bind as a poet, both espousing and disespousing a lyrical type of antiquity. It has often been observed that the finest tunes belong to the devil; certainly the devil's praise of Athens and Rome in *Paradise Regained* are magnificent lyrical passages widely admired, and not unjustly so. In creating them Milton manages to have it both ways. He permits his Christ to praise Israel over Athens, yet as a poet he unabashedly exercises his bent for the classical imitation and creates in Satan's city odes two of the most finely nuanced examples of a Pindaric type.

---

[41] See Revard, *Pindar and the Renaissance Hymn-Ode*, 215-18.

Epilogue

By 1700 one phase of the Pindaric revolution was coming to an end while another was about to begin. In the latter part of the seventeenth century the principal use of the pindaric in England had been for political encomium and for familiar praise. The political pindaric had almost run its course in the early 1700s. The victory odes composed for Marlborough's military triumphs on the continent signaled a last hurrah for the battle ode, even though these were not the final odes of this type to be composed. Nor did poets cease to use pindarics for other kinds of encomia, to address friends and associates or laud kings and queens. Funeral pindarics mourned the passing of Queen Anne, and pindarics greeted George I as he made his way across the Channel, just as they had welcomed Charles II years before. However, the Cowleian pindaric seemed frankly dated, and eighteenth-century poets required a more fashionable dress for their political poetry. The hyperbole of both the political and the familiar pindaric had become the target of satire. Pope turned to Horace as a model for his familiar verse. Although Congreve had tried to rescue Pindaric ode by instructing the public that what was being written in the name of Pindar bore little resemblance to Pindar's actual poetry, nothing could save the encomiastic pindaric from becoming either an exhausted poetic medium or a object for mockery.

But to say that interest in Pindar and his odes was passé would be simply inaccurate. On the continent, as German scholars asserted their eminence in classical studies, German poets followed the lead of vernacular poets in Italian, French, and English and embraced Pindaric imitation in their own language. At the same time, the English pindaric was about to metamorphose into a different kind of poetic genre. The experiments in ode that Spenser and Milton had undertaken would energize poets such as Collins and Gray and would lead them to personalize their odes. Spenser had demonstrated in "Prothalamion" and Milton in "Lycidas" that the pindaric could be a contemplative mode, where the poet could find poetic space to express both feeling and conviction. Pindar became once more a mentor for poets who were seeking to develop a new lyrical mode in which they could express their deepest emotions. His was a voice that did not merely complain, but could also raise a noble strain and command attention.

Curiously enough, this was nothing new. Pindar had been admired both in antiquity and in the Renaissance for his distinctive poetic voice. His mastery over the lyrical genre was what caught the attention of poet-admirers and poet-imitators from Horace through Cowley and what would command the attention of poets from Collins and Gray in the eighteenth century through Wordsworth and Shelley in the nineteenth. If eighteenth-century poets had turned away from Pindaric politics, it was only to rediscover Pindaric poetics. They attempted to reinvent the ancient poet through imitating his poetic voice and his soaring lyricism. Pindar was transfused to Collins and Gray more often through Milton and Spenser rather than through Cowley and his followers. Yet the Cowleian mode was too striking not to have some lasting impact. W.B. Yeats was to rediscover Cowley's discursive poetics, and to transform it in contemplative poems such as "Among Schoolchildren," "1919," and "In Memory of Major Robert Gregory." The Pindaric mode did not wither and die with the decline of political encomium at the end of the seventeenth century. Like the phoenix, it simply found the means to be born anew.[1]

---

[1] See A. P. Burnett, *Pindar's Songs for Young Athletes of Aigina* (Oxford: Oxford University Press, 2005), 1–5.

BIBLIOGRAPHY

Editions and Translations of Pindar's Odes

Pindar. *Olympia, Pythia, Nemea, Isthmia*. Ed. Aldus Manutius. Venice, 1513.

————. Ὀλύμπια, Πύθια, Νέμεα, Ἴσθμια. Ed. Zacharias Callierges. Rome, 1515.

————. *Olympia, Pythia, Nemea, Isthmia*. Ed. Jacobus Ceporinus. Basel, 1526.

————. *Olympiorum Hymni Primus et Secundus*. Trans. Menradus Moltherus. Haganoae, 1527.

————. *Olympia, Pythia, Nemea, Isthmia*. Trans. Johann Lonicer. Basel, 1528; 2nd edition, 1535; 1560 (Zurich).

————. *Olympia, Pythia, Nemea, Isthmia*. Frankfurt, 1542.

————. *Olympia, Pythia, Nemea, Isthmia*. Paris, 1558.

————. *Olympia, Pythia, Nemea, Isthmia*. Trans. Philip Melanchthon. Basel, 1558.

————. *Olympia, Pythia, Nemea Isthmia*. Ed. Henricus Stephanus. Geneva, 1560; repr. 1566, 1567 (Antwerp by Plantin), 1586, 1598 (Leiden), 1600, 1612, 1623, 1626.

————. *Opera Omnia*. Ed. Nicholas Sudor. Paris, 1582; *Olympia, Pythia*, 1575, 1576.

————. *Olympia, Pythia, Nemea, Isthmia*. Ed. Franciscus Raphelengius. Leiden, 1590.

————. *Olympia, Pythia, Nemea, Isthmia*. Heidelberg, 1598.

————. *Olympia, Pythia, Nemea, Isthmia*. Ed. Paulus Stephanus. Geneva, 1599.

————. περίοδος. Ed. Erasmus Schmidt. Wittenberg, 1616.

Les Oeuvres de Pindare. Trans. François Marin. Paris, 1617.

Pindar. περίοδος. Ed. Joannes Benedictus. Saumur, 1620.

Le Pindare Thébain: Traduction de Grec en François, meslée de vers et de prose. Trans. Sieur de Lagausie. Paris, 1626.

Ode di Pindaro. Trans. Alessandro Adimari. Pisa, 1631.

Pindar. *Olympia, Nemea, Pythia, Isthmia*. Ed. Richard West and Robert Welsted. Oxford, 1697.

Odes of Pindar. Trans. Gilbert West. Dublin, 1751.

Pindar. *The Olympian and Pythian Odes.* Ed. Basil Gildersleeve. London, 1885; 1908.

———. *Carmina.* Ed. C. M. Bowra. Oxford: Clarendon Press, 1935.

———. *The Odes.* Trans. C. M. Bowra. Harmondsworth: Penguin, 1969.

———. *Epinicia Fragmenta.* Ed. B. Snell, rev. H. Maehler. Leipzig: Teubner, 1971-1975, repr. 1989.

———. *Pindar's Victory Songs.* Trans. Frank Nisetich. Baltimore: Johns Hopkins University Press, 1980.

———. *Victory Odes: Olympians 2, 7, 11, Nemean 4; Isthmians 3, 4, 7.* Ed. M. M. Willcock. Cambridge: Cambridge University Press, 1995.

Renaissance Commentaries on Pindar

Aretius, Benedictus. *Commentarii Absolutissimi in Pindari Olympia, Pythia, Nemea, Isthmia.* [Geneva], 1587.

Portus, Franciscus. *Commentarii in Pindari Olympia, Pythia, Nemea, Isthmia.* Geneva, 1583.

Primary Texts

Academiae Oxoniensis Gratulatio. Pro Serenissimi Regis Guilielmi ex Hibernia Reditu. Oxford, 1690.

A Dialogue between the King of France and the Late King James, Occasioned by the Death of the Queen. Written Originally in French, at Paris. London, 1695.

An Anthology of Neo-Latin Poetry. Ed. and trans. Fred J. Nichols. New Haven: Yale University Press, 1979.

An English Ballad; In Answer to Mr. Despreaux's Pindarique Ode, On the Taking of NAMURE. London, 1695.

An Historical Poem upon his Late Majesty King James II. London, 1701.

An Ode Compos'd for the Publick Commencement, at Cambridge: On Monday July the 6th. 1730. At the Musick-Act. The Words by Alexander Pope Esq; The Musick by Maurice Greene, Doctor in Musick. [Cambridge, 1730].

A Panegyrick on Oliver Cromwell, and his Victories, with Three Poems on his Death. London, 1709.

A Pindarique Ode, On their Royal Highnesses Return from Scotland after His Escape at Sea. London, 1682.

A Pindarique Ode, Upon the late Horrid and Damnable Whiggish Plot. London, 1684.

A Pindarick Ode, Upon the Death of His late sacred Majesty King Charles the Second. London, 1685.

Aelian. *De Varia Historia, adiuncta est et Ode Pindari, quae inscribitur* in *Hieronem Celete.* Venice, 1550.

Alveri, Gasparo. *Roma in ogni stato.* Rome, 1664.

Alamanni, Luigi. *Opere Toscane.* Leiden, 1532.

Amaltheus, Ioannes Baptista. *Trium Fratrum Amaltheorum, Hieronimus, Ioannes Baptista, Cornelius, Carmina.* Venice, 1627.

Amaltheus, Ioannes Baptista. *Canzone di M. Giovanbattista Amaltheo, All' Illustr. et Excellent. Sig Marcantonio Colonna, General dell' Armata di Santa Chiesa Sopra la Vittoria seguita contra l'armata Turchesca.* Venice, 1572.

Arsilli, Francesco. *De Poetis Urbanis.* In *Coryciana,* ed. Blosius Palladius. Rome, 1524.

Ascham, Roger. "The Scholemaster" (1570). In *Elizabethan Critical Essays.* Ed. G. Gregory Smith. Vol. 1. Oxford: Clarendon Press, 1904.

Bargaeus, Petrus Angelius. *Poemata Omnia.* Rome, 1585.

Behn, Aphra. *Poems upon Several Occasions; With a Voyage to the Island of Love.* London, 1684.

———. *A Pindarick on the Death of Our Late Sovereign: With An Ancient Prophecy on His Present Majesty.* London: Henry Playford, 1685.

———. *Pindarick Poem on the Happy Coronation of His most Sacred Majesty James II. And His Illustrious Consort Queen Mary.* London, 1685.

———. "To the Author of the New Utopia." In *The Six days Adventure, or the New Utopia, A Comedy.* London, 1671.

———. "To the Unknown *Daphnis* on his Excellent Translation of *Lucretius."* In *T. Lucretius Carus. The Epicurean Philosopher.* The Second Edition. Oxford, 1683.

———. "To Henry Higden." In Henry Higden, *Satirae Singulae. A Modern Essay on the Tenth Satire of Juvenal.* London, 1687.

———. *Lycidus: Or The Lover in Fashion . . . Together with a Miscellany of New Poems. By Several Hands.* London, 1688.

——— *Congratulatory Poem to her Sacred Majesty Queen Mary, Upon her Arrival in England.* London, 1689.

———. *A PINDARIC POEM to the Reverend Doctor Burnet, on the Honour he did me of Enquiring after me and my MUSE.* London: R. Bentley, 1689.

———. *Poems upon Several Occasions.* London, 1697.

———. *The Uncollected Verse of Aphra Behn.* Ed. Germaine Greer. Stump Cross, Essex: Stump Cross Books, 1989.

———. *The Works of Aphra Behn.* Ed. Janet Todd. London: William Pickering, 1992.

[Boileau-Despréaux, Nicolas]. *Oeuvres Diverses du Sieur D***.* Amsterdam, 1701.

Boswell, James. *Life of Johnson.* Ed. G. B. Hill. Oxford: Oxford University Press, 1979.

Britanniae Natalis. Oxford: Iohannes Lichfield, 1630.

Britannia Rediviva. Oxford: Leonard Lichfield, 1660.

Capilupus, Hippolytus. *Capiluporum Carmina*. Rome, 1590.

Chiabrera, Gabriello. *Delle Canzoni del Signor Gabriello Chiabrera*. Genoa, 1586.

———. *Lettere di Gabriello Chiabrera Nobile Savonese*, Date in luce da Giacomo Filippo Porrata Della Compagnia de Gesù. Bologna, 1762.

———. *Canzonette, Rime, Varie Dialoghi di Gabriello Chiabrera*. Ed. Luigi Negri. Turin: Unione tipografico-editio torinese, 1952.

Cibber, Colley. *A Poem, on the Death of Our Late Soveraign Lady Queen Mary*. London, 1695.

———. *A Rhapsody Upon the Marvellous. Arising from the first odes of Horace and Pindar*. London, 1741.

[Cobb, Samuel]. *A Pindarique Ode, Humbly Offer'd to the Ever-Blessed Memory of our Late Gracious Sovereign Lady Queen Mary*, Written by J. D. Gent. London, 1694.

Cobb, Samuel. *Pax Redux: A Pindarick Ode on the Return of His Majesty, and the Happy Conclusion of the Peace*. London, 1697.

———. *The Female Reign*. London, 1709.

Congreve, William. *A Pindarique Ode , Humbly Offer'd to the King On his Taking Namure*. London, 1695.

———. *A Pindarique Ode, Humbly Offer'd to the Queen, on the Victorious Progress of Her Majesty's Arms, under the Conduct of the Duke of Marlborough. To which is prefix'd, A Discourse on the Pindarique Ode*. London, 1706.

Cowley, Abraham. *Sylva, or Divers Copies of Verses, Made upon sundry occasions by A. C.* London, 1636.

———. *Pindarique Odes*. In *Poems*. London, 1656.

[Cowley, Abraham]. *A Vision, Concerning his late Pretended Highnesse Cromwell, the Wicked; Containing a Discourse in Vindication of him by a pretended Angel, and the Confutation thereof by the Author*. London: Henry Herringman, 1661.

Cowley, Abraham. *The Works of Mr. Abraham Cowley*. London: Henry Herringman, 1668.

———. *The Second and Third Parts of the Works of Mr. Abraham Cowley, with Additions . . . And Several Poems in Praise of the Author*, 7th ed. London: Charles Harper, 1700.

———. *The Works of Mr. Abraham Cowley*. 9th ed. London: Henry Herringman, 1700.

Crinitus, Pietrus. *Poematum Libri Duo*. Paris, 1508.

Denne, Henry. *A Poem on the Taking of Namur*. London, 1695.

Dennis, John. "Preface," *The Court of Death. A Pindarique Poem, Dedicated to the Memory of Her Most Sacred Majesty, Queen Mary*. London, 1695.

Dousa, Janus. *Iani Duzae Nordovicis novorum Poematum . . . Editio*. Leiden, 1576.

———. *Odarum Britannicarum Liber, Ad D. Elisabetham, Britanniarum, Franciae, Hiberniaeque Reginam.* Leiden, 1586.

———. *Elegiarum Lib. II. Epigrammatum Lib.* Leiden, 1586.

Dousa, Janus Filius. *Poemata.* Leiden, 1607.

Drayton, Michael. *Poems By Michael Drayton.* London, 1619.

———. *The Works of Michael Drayton.* Ed. William Hebel. Oxford: Shakespeare Head Press, 1932.

Dryden, John. *Prologue to his Royal Highness Upon His first appearance at the Duke's Theatre since his Return from Scotland.* London, 1682.

———. *The Poems of John Dryden.* Ed. James Kinsley. Oxford: Clarendon Press, 1958.

———. *The Poetical Works of Dryden.* Ed. George R. Noyes. Cambridge, MA: The Riverside Press, 1950.

Du Bellay, Ioachim. *Les Regrets et Autres Oeuvres Poétiques.* Paris, 1575

Du Monin, Ian Edovard. *Les Estoiles du Ciel* (1583) printed with *L'Uranologie.* Paris, 1583.

———. *Les Novvelles Oevvres de Ian Edvoard Du Monin.* Paris, 1582?

Durant, Gilles, Sieur de la Bergerie. *Les Odes du Sieur de la Bergerie.* Paris, 1594.

Elizabeth I. *Collected Works.* Ed. Leah S. Marcus, Janel Mueller, and Mary Beth Rose. Chicago and London: University of Chicago Press, 2000.

Epithalamium in Desideratissimis Nuptiis Serenissimorum & Illustrissimorum Principum Guilielmi-Henrici Arausii & Mariae Britanniarum. Cambridge, 1677.

Eucharistica Oxoniensia in Caroli . . . regis . . . nostri e Scotia reditum gratulatoria. Oxford, 1641.

Eusden, Mr. *A Poem to her Royal Highness on the Birth of the Prince.* London, 1718.

Fane, Francis. *A Pindarick Ode on the Sacred Memory of Our late Gracious Sovereign King Charles II.* London: Henry Playford, 1685.

Favolius, Hugo. "Carmen Heroicum." In Johannes Sambucus, *De Classica ad Naupactum contra Turcas Victoria, Per D. Ianum Austriae, Class. & Marit. Praefect. Inuictiss. D. Froli V. Cae. F. parta.* Antwerp, 1572.

Felicaia, Vincenzio da. *Poesie Toscane.* Florence, 1819.

[Fisher, Payne]. *Irenodia Gratulatoria. Sive Illustrissimi amplissimique Viri Oliveri Cromwelli, & c., Epinikion.* London, 1652.

Flaminius, M. Antonius. *Carmina Quinque Illustrium Poetarum.* Venice, 1558.

Fulgentius. *Mythologiarum Libri III.* In C. Iulius Hyginus, *Fabularum Liber.* Paris, 1578.

———. Trans. L. Whitbread. *Fulgentius the Mythographer.* Columbus: Ohio State University Press, 1971.

Gil, Alexander. *ΠΑΡΕΡΓΑ sive Poetici Conatus.* London, 1632.

Gruterus, Janus [Ranutius Gherus], ed. *Delitiae CC. Italorum Poetarum Huius Superiorisque Ævi Illustrium.* Frankfurt, 1608.

————. *Delitiae Poetarum Germanorum Huius Superiorisque Aevi Illustrium.* Frankfurt, 1612.

————. *Delitiae Poetarum Germanorum.* Frankfurt, 1612.

————. *Delitiae Poetarum Belgicorum. Huius Superiorisque Aevi Illustrium.* Frankfurt, 1614.

Gomarus, Franciscus. *Davidis Lyra.* Leiden, 1637.

Habert, Isaac. *Oeuvres Poétiques.* Paris, 1582.

————. *Les Trois Livres de Meteores Avecque autres oeuures poëtiques.* Paris, 1585.

Heinsius, Daniel. *Tumulus.* Paris, 1630.

————. *Poemata.* Amsterdam, 1649.

Hesteau, Clovis. *Les Oevvres Poetiques de Clovis Hesteau.* Paris, 1578.

Hesteau de Nuysemont, Clovis. *Les Œuves Poetiques. Livres I et II.* Ed. Roland Guillot. Geneva: Librairie Droz, 1994.

Horace. *Odes and Epodes.* Ed. Charles E. Bennett. New Rochelle, NY: Aristide D. Caratzas, 1984.

Hume, Patrick. *A Poem Dedicated to the Immortal Memory of Her Late Majesty, The Most Incomparable Q. Mary.* London, 1695.

Hymenaeus Cantabrigiensis. Cambridge: Johannes Field, 1683.

Irenodia Cantabrigiensis. Cambridge: Roger Daniel, 1641.

Jamyn, Amadis. *Les Oeuvres Poétiques d'Amadis Jamyn.* Paris, 1575.

Jonson, Ben. *The Poems.* In *The Works of Ben Jonson.* Ed. C. H. Herford and Percy and Evelyn Simpson. Oxford: Clarendon Press, 1947.

Jovius, Paulus [Paolo Giovio]. *Elogia Doctorum Virorum.* Antwerp, 1557.

Lampridius, Benedictus. *Carmina.* Venice, 1550.

Lacrymæ Cantabrigienses in Obitum Serenissimæ Reginæ Mariæ. Cambridge: Johan. Hayes, 1694/95.

Le Blanc, Jean. *La Néotémachie Poetique du Blanc, Odes.* Paris, 1610.

Luctus et Gratulatio Musarum Cantabrigiensium. Cambridge, 1658.

Macrinus, Salmonius. *Carminum Libri Quatuor.* Paris, 1530.

————. *Lyricorum Libri Duo.* Paris, 1531.

————. *Hymnorum Libri Sex.* Paris, 1537.

Magny, Olivier de. *Les Odes d'Olivier de Magny.* Paris, 1559.

Malherbe, François de. *Les Oevvres de Mre François de Malherbe.* Paris, 1630.

Manning, Francis. *A Congratulatory Poem. Humbly offered to the King upon his Return Home, After the Siege of Namur.* London, 1695.

Marullus, Michaelis. *Poetae Tres Elegantissimi.* Paris, 1582.

Marvell, Andrew. *Miscellaneous Poems by Andrew Marvell.* London, 1681.

————. *The Poems and Letters of Andrew Marvell.* Ed. H. M. Margoliouth. 3rd ed. rev. Pierre Legouis and E. E. Duncan-Jones. Oxford: Clarendon Press, 1971.

Melissus, Paulus. *Schediasmatum Reliquiae.* Frankfurt, 1575.

————. *Oda Pindarica ad Serenissimam Potentissimamque Dominam Elisabetham Britanniae, Franciae, Hiberniaeque Reginam.* Augustae Vindelicorum, 1578.

————. *Mele sive Odae ad Noribergam et Septemviros Reipub. Norib.* Noribergae, 1580.

————. *Epigrammata in Vrbes Italiae. Cum Eiusdem Odis, ad Romam, Pont. Max. & Ducem Venetum.* Argentinae, 1585.

————. *Schediasmata Poetica.* Paris, 1586.

Menzini, Benedetto. *Opere di Benedetto [Menzini] Fiorentino.* Florence, 1680.

Miscellaneous Poems, With some Remarks on the Death of King Charles the II. And the Happy Succession of King James the II. In a Poem to the Magistracy of England. London, 1685.

Milton, John. *POEMS of Mr. John Milton.* London, 1645.

————. *Poems, & c. Upon Several Occasions.* London, 1673.

————. *The Works of John Milton.* Gen. Ed. Frank Allen Patterson. New York: Columbia University Press, 1931–1938.

————. "The Trinity College Manuscript." In *Complete Poetical Works*, ed. Harris Francis Fletcher, 1: 381–455. Urbana: University of Illinois Press, 1943.

————. *Complete Poetry and Major Prose.* Ed. Merritt Y. Hughes. New York: Odyssey, 1957.

Minturno, Antonio. *L'Arte Poetica del Sig. Antonio Minturno.* Venice, 1563.

————. *Rime et Prose del Sig. Antonio Minturno.* Venice, 1559.

————. *De Poeta.* Venice, 1559.

Mœstissimæ ac Lætissimæ Academiæ Cantabrigiensis Affectus, Decedente Carolo II. Succedente Jacobo II Regibus Augustissimis Clementissimisque. Cambridge: Joannes Hayes, 1684/5.

Motherus, Menradus. *Pindari Olympiorum Hymni Primus et Secundus Latinate Donati.* Haganoae, 1527.

Motteux, Pierre Antoine. *Maria. A POEM occasioned by the Death of Her Majesty. Addrest to Three Persons of Honour.* London, 1695.

Sheffield, John, the Earl of Mulgrave. *An Essay on Poetry.* 2nd ed. London, 1691.

Musarum Oxoniensium Ἐλαιοφορία, sive Ob Faedera, Auspiciis Serenissimi Oliveri, Reipub. Ang. Scot. & Hiber. Domini Protectoris. Oxford, 1654.

Musarum Cantabrigiensium Threnodia in Obitum Incomparabilis Herois ac Ducis Illustrissimi Georgii, Ducis Albæmarlæ. Cambridge: Joannes Hayes, 1670.

Musae Cantabrigienses Serenissimis Principibus Wilhelmo et Mariae. Cambridge, 1689.

Navagerius, Andreas. *Carmina Quinque Illustrium Poetarum.* Venice, 1558.

Obsequies to the memorie of Mr. Edward King. In *Justa Edouardo King.* Cambridge, 1638.

Oliva Pacis ad Illustrissimum Celsissimumque Oliverum, Reipub. Angliae, Scotiae, & Hiberniae Dominum Protectorem; De Pace Cum Foederatis Belgis feliciter sanctita, Carmen Cantabrigiense. Cambridge, 1654.

On the Death of the Queen, By a Person of Honour. London, 1695.

Owen, Corbet. *Carmen Pindaricum in Theatrum Sheldonianum in Solennibus Magnifici Operis Encaeniis Recitatum Julii die Anno 1669*. Oxford, 1669.

Patridge, William. *A Consolatory Poem: Addressed to the Most Sacred Majesty*. London, 1695.

Philelfus, Franciscus. *Odae*. Brescia, 1497.

Philips, Katherine. *Poems by the most deservedly Admired Mrs. Katherine Philips, The Matchless Orinda*. London, 1667.

Phillips, Ambrose. *An Ode (In the Manner of Pindar) On the Death of the Right Honourable William, Earl Cowper*. London, 1723.

———. *Pastorals, Epistles, Odes, and Other Original Poems, With Translations from Pindar, Anacreon, and Sappho*. London, 1747.

Phillips, John. *An Humble Offering to the Sacred Memory of the late Most Serene and Potent Monarch Charles II*. London, 1685.

———. *In Memory of Our Late Gracious Lady, Mary, Queen of Great-Britain, France, and Ireland*. London, 1695.

———. *Augustus Britannicus: A Poem upon the Conclusion of the Peace of Europe*. London, 1697.

Pietas Universitatis Oxoniensis In Obitum Augustissimæ & Desideratissimæ Reginæ Mariæ. Oxford, 1695.

Pithou, Pierre. *Epigrammata et Poematia Vetera*. Paris, 1590.

Pius of Bologna, Ioannes Baptista. "Dedicatory Epistle." In *De Urbe Roma*. Bologna, 1520.

Pontanus, Joannes. "Versus Lyrici." In *Opera*. Florence, 1514.

Pope, Alexander. *An ode compos'd for the publick commencement, at Cambridge, as it was set to music by Maurice Greene*. Cambridge, 1730.·

Prior, Matthew. *A Pindarique on His Majesties birth-day . . . Sung before Their Majesties at Whitehall, the fourth of November 1690*. London, 1690.

[Puttenham, George]. *The Arte of English Poesie*. London: Richard Field, 1589.

Rapin, Nicolas. *Les Oevvres Latines et Francoises de Nicolas Rapin Poictevin*. Paris: Olivier de Varennes, 1610.

Rapin, René. *Réflexions sur la Poétique d'Aristote et sur les Ouvrages des Poètes Anciens & Modernes*. Paris, 1674.

Ronsard, Pierre de. *Quatre Premiers Livres des Odes*. Paris, 1550.

———. *Le Cinqiesme Livre des Odes de P. de Ronsard*. Paris, 1552.

——— *Hymnes de P. de Ronsard*. Paris, 1555.

———. *Oeuvres Complètes*. Ed. Gustave Cohen. 2 vols. Paris: Librairie Gallimard, 1950.

———. *Les Odes de Ronsard*. Ed. Charles Guérin. Paris: Edition du Cèdre, 1952.

———. *Hymnes*. Ed. Albert Py. Geneva: Librairie Droz, 1978.

Sadoleto, Jacopo. "Epistola" (to Colocci). In Cod. Vat. Lat. 4103, fols. 16–17.

Sammarthanus, Scaevola [Scevole de Sainte-Marthe]. *Poemata et Elogia*. Argustoriti Pictonum: Ioannes Blanceti, 1606.

Sammarthani, Scaevola et Abelius. *Opera Latina et Gallica.* Paris: Jacobus Villery, 1633.

Sannazarius, Iacobus. *Opera Omnia Latine Scripta.* Venice: Aldus, 1535.

Sarbievius, Mathias Casimirus. *Lyricorum Libri IV. Epodon. Lib unus Alterque Epigrammatum.* Antwerp: Plantin, 1632.

———. *Lyricorum Libri IV.* Paris, 1647.

———. *The Odes of Casimire.* Translated by G. H. London: Humphrey Moseley, 1646.

———. *The Odes of Casimire, Translated by G. Hils (London: 1646).* Augustan Reprint Society Publication 44. Los Angeles: University of California Press, 1953.

Scaligerus, Iulius Caesarus. *Poetices libri septem.* Lyons, 1561.

Scaligerus, Iosephus. *Poemata omnia.* Ed. Petrus Scriverius. Leiden: Platin, 1615.

Secundus, Joannes. *Poetae Tres Elegantissimi.* Paris, 1582.

———. *Opera quae reperiri potuerunt omnia.* Leiden, 1619.

Sidney, Sir Philip. "The Defence of Poesie." In *The Prose Works.* Ed. Albert Feuillerat. Cambridge: Cambridge University Press, 1963.

Simonides Bendonski, Simon. *Opera omnia quae reperiri potuerunt olim sparsim edita, nunc in unum collecta.* Ed. Angelo Maria Durini. Varsaviae, 1772.

Smith, M. *A Pindarique Poem Sacred to the Glorious Memory of King William III.* London, 1702.

Soowthern, John. *Pandora, The Musyque of the beautie of his Mistresse Diana.* London, 1584.

Spenser, Edmund. *Poetical Works.* Ed. J. C. Smith and E. De Selincourt. Oxford: Oxford University Press, 1970.

Sprat, Thomas. *The Plague of Athens.* London: Thomas Childe, 1659.

———. "An Account of the Life and Writing of Mr. Abraham Cowley." In *The Works of Mr. Abraham Cowley.* London, 1668.

ΣΩΣΤΡΑ, *sive Ad Carolum II reducem.* Cambridge: J. Field, 1660.

Swift, Jonathan. *Gulliver's Travels.* Ed. Louis A. Landa. Oxford: Oxford University Press, 1976.

Tahureau, Jacques. *Les Premieres Poësies.* Poitiers, 1554.

Tasso, Bernardo. *Rime.* Vinegia, 1560.

Tasso, Torquato. *Delle Rime del Sig. Torquato Tasso, Parte Prima e Seconda.* Brescia, 1592–1593.

Testi, Fulvio. *Opere del Sig. Conte Don Fulvio Testi.* Milan, 1658.

The Mourning Poets: Or, An Account of the Poems on the Death of the Queen. In a Letter to a Friend. London, 1695.

Three Poems upon the Death of his late Highnesse Oliver, Lord Protector of England, Scotland, and Ireland. London: William Wilson, 1659.

Toscanus, J. M. ed. *Carmina Illustrium Poetarum Italorum.* Paris, 1576.

Triumphs of Female Wit. London: T. Malthus, 1683.

Trissino, Giovan Giorgio. *Rime.* Vicenza, 1529.

[Tutchin, John]. *An Epistle to Mr. Benjamin Bridgewater, Occasion'd by the Death of the late Queen Mary.* London, 1694.

Ubaldini, Federico. *Vita di mons. Angeli Colotii episcopi Nucerini* (Rome, 1673). Ed. Vittorio Fanelli. Vatican City: Biblioteca Apostolica Vaticana, 1969.

Urania's Temple: Or, A Satyr upon the Silent-Poets. London, 1695.

Valerianus, Pierius. *Hexametri Odae et Epigrammata.* Ferrara, 1550.

——. *Amorum Libri.* Venice 1549.

——. *De Litteratorum infelicitate.* Venice, 1620.

Vers a la Louange du Roy, Avec Une Satire contre Boileau-Despreaux & contre La Maintenon. Londres, 1695.

Vota Oxoniensia Pro Serenissimis Guilhelmo Rege et Maria Regina. Oxford, 1689.

Waller, Edmund. *The Poetical Works of Edmund Waller and Sir John Denham.* Ed. Rev. George Gilfillan. Edinburgh: James Nichol, 1857.

Yalden, Thomas. *On the Conquest of Namur. A Pindarick Ode.* London, 1695.

Secondary Texts

Albanese, Gabriella. "Le raccolte poetiche latine di Francesco Filelfo." In *Francesco Filelfo nel quinto centenario della morte*, 389–458. Padua: Editrice Antenore, 1986.

Arthos, John. *Milton and the Italian Cities.* New York: Barnes & Noble Inc., 1968.

Ascoli, Albert Russell. "Ariosto's 'Fier Pastor': Historical Meaning in *Orlando Furioso.*" In *Phaethon's Children: The Este Court and its Culture in Early Modern Ferrara*, ed. Dennis Looney and Deanna Shemek, 189-224. MRTS 286. Tempe, AZ: ACMRS, 2002.

Atti del convegno di studi su Angelo Colocci. Iesi: Amministratione comunale, 1972.

Blanchard, André. "Jean Second et ses poèmes sur l'exécution de Thomas More." *Moreana* 36 (1972): 1–32.

Boeke, Hanna. *The Value of Victory in Pindar's Odes.* Leiden: Brill, 2007.

Bowden, B. "Samuel Cobb." In *Oxford Dictionary of National Biography*, 12: 266–67. Oxford: Oxford University Press, 2004.

Bower, Thad. "Sacred Violence in Marvell's Horatian Ode." *Renaissance* 52 (1999): 75–88.

Bowra, C. M. *Pindar.* Oxford: Clarendon Press, 1964, repr. 2000.

Brill's New Pauly, ed. H. Caucik and H. Schneider. Leiden: Brill, 2003.

Brooks, Cleanth, and John Edward Hardy. "Lycidas." In *Poems of Mr. John Milton*, 169–86. New York: Harcourt Brace, 1951; repr. in *Milton's Lycidas: The Tradition and the Poem*, ed. C. A. Patrides, 140–56. Columbia: University of Missouri Press, 1983.

Brumble, H. David. *Classical Myths and Legends in the Middle Ages and Renaissance*. Westport, CT: Greenwood Press, 1998.

Brunel, Jean. *Un Poitevin poète, humaniste et soldat à l'époque des guerres de religion: Nicolas Rapin (1539–1608): la carrière, les milieux, l'oeuvre*. Paris: Honoré Champion, 2002.

Bundy, Elroy L. *Studia Pindarica*. Berkeley: University of California Press, 1986.

Burman, Edward. *Italian Dynasties: The Great Families of Italy, from the Renaissance to the Present Day*. Frame, Somerset: Butler & Tanner, 1989.

Burnett, Anne Pippin. *Pindar's Songs for Young Athletes of Aigina*. Oxford: Oxford University Press, 2005.

Burton, R. W. B. *Pindar's Pythian Odes*. Oxford: Oxford University Press, 1962.

Calderisi, Raffaele. *Antonio Sebastiano Minturno, Poeta e Trattatista del Cinquecento Dimenticato; Vita e Opere*. Aversa: Tipografia Fratelli Noviello, 1921.

Catey, Christopher. "Pindar, Place, and Performance." In *Pindar's Poetry, Patrons, and Festivals: From Archaic Greece to the Roman Empire*, ed. S. Hornblower and C. Morgan, 199–210. Oxford: Oxford University Press, 2007.

Carne-Ross, D. S. "Weaving with Points of Gold: Pindar's Sixth Olympian." *Arion* 15 (1976): 5–44.

———. *Pindar*. New Haven: Yale University Press, 1985.

Cecchelli, Carlo. *Le Grandi Famiglie Romane: I Margane, i Coppocci, i Sanguigni, i Mellini*. Rome: Reale Instituto di Studi Romani, 1946.

Chernaik, Warren. *Sexual Freedom in Restoration Literature*. Cambridge: Cambridge University Press, 1995.

Colie, Rosalie. *"My Ecchoing Song": Andrew Marvell's Poetry of Criticism*. Princeton: Princeton University Press, 1970.

Commager, Steele. *The Odes of Horace: A Critical Study*. New Haven: Yale University Press, 1962.

Coolidge, John. "Marvell and Horace." *Modern Philology* 63 (1965): 111–20.

Corns, Thomas. *Uncloistered Virtue: English Political Literature, 1640–60*. Oxford: Oxford University Press, 1992.

Crotty, Kevin. *Song and Action: The Victory Odes of Pindar*. Baltimore: Johns Hopkins University Press, 1982.

Currie, Bruno. *Pindar and the Cult of Heroes*. Oxford: Oxford University Press, 2005.

Davis, Norman. *God's Playground: A History of Poland*. New York: Columbia University Press, 1982.

Demerson, Guy. "À l'origine du lyrisme de louange: la victoire de François de Bourbon à Cérisoles (I, 5)." In *Lire Les Odes de Ronsard*, ed. Dominique Bertrand, 47–62. Clermont-Ferrand: Presses Universitaires Blaise Pascal, 2002.

Dorsten, J. A. van. "Janus Dousa: Spokesman of the Dutch Revolt." In *Acta Conventus Neo-Latini Amstelodamenis*, ed. P. Tuynman et al., 334–37. Munich: Wilhelm Fink Verlag, 1979.

Dubrow, Heather. *A Happier Eden: The Politics of Marriage in the Stuart Epithalamium*. Ithaca: Cornell University Press, 1990.

Encyclopedia of British Women Writers. Ed. Paul Schlueter and June Schlueter. Chicago and London: St. James Press, 1988.

Everett, Barbara. "The Shooting of the Bears: Poetry and Politics in Andrew Marvell." In *Andrew Marvell: Essays on the Tercentenary of His Death*, ed. R.L. Brett, 62–103. Oxford: Oxford University Press, 1979.

Evans, J. Martin. "Lycidas and the Dolphins." *N & Q* n.s. 25 (1978): 15–17.

———. *The Road from Horton: Looking Backwards in "Lycidas"*. Victoria: University of Victoria Press, 1983.

———. "Lycidas." In *The Cambridge Companion to Milton*, ed. Dennis Danielson, 35–50. Cambridge: Cambridge University Press, 1989.

Fanelli, Vittorio. "Il Ginnasio greco di Leone X a Roma." *Studi Romani* 9 (1961): 379–93.

Finley, M. I. *Ancient Sicily*. London: Chatto & Windus, 1979.

Fisker, Dorthe. *Pindars Erste Olympische Ode*. Odense: Universitetforlog, 1990.

Fitzgerald, William. *Agonistic Poetry: The Pindaric Mode in Pindar, Horace, Hölderlin, and the English Ode*. Berkeley: University of California Press, 1987.

Fletcher, Harris. *The Intellectual Development of John Milton*. 2 vols. Urbana: University of Illinois Press, 1971.

Ford, Philip. *Ronsard's Hymnes: A Literary and Iconographical Study*. MRTS 157. Tempe, AZ: ACMRS, 1997.

Fradenburg, Louise Olga, ed. *Women and Sovereignty*. Edinburgh: Edinburgh University Press, 1992.

Gaisser, Julia Haig. *Pierio Valeriano on the Ill Fortune of Learned Men: A Renaissance Humanist and His World*. Ann Arbor: University of Michigan Press, 1999.

Gerber, Douglas E. *Pindar's Olympian One: A Commentary*. Toronto: University of Toronto Press, 1982.

Gieysztor, Aleksander, et al. *The History of Poland*. Warsaw: Polish Scientific Publishers, 1968.

Girot, Jean-Eudes. *Pindare avant Ronsard: De l'émergence du grec à la publication des quatre premiers livres des Odes de Ronsard*. Geneva: Librairie Droz, 2002.

Gnoli, Domenico. *La Roma di Leon X*. Milan: Ulrico Hoepli, 1938.

Goreau, Angeline. *Reconstructing Aphra: A Social Biography of Aphra Behn*. New York: Dial Press, 1980.

Greene, Thomas M. "The Balance of Power in Marvell's 'Horatian Ode'." *ELH* 60 (1993): 379–96.

Guillaume, Jean, et al. *Jean Martin, un traducteur au temps de François Ier et de Henri II.* Paris: Presses de l'Ecole normale supérieure, 1999.

Haan, Estelle. *From Academia to Amicitia: Milton's Latin Writings and the Italian Academies.* Philadelphia: American Philosophical Society, 1998.

Hale, John K. *Milton's Cambridge Latin: Performing in the Genres, 1625–1632.* MRTS 289. Tempe, AZ: ACMRS, 2005.

Hamilton, John T. *Soliciting Darkness: Pindar, Obscurity, and the Classical Tradition.* Cambridge, MA: Harvard University Press, 2003.

Hanford, James Holly. "The Pastoral Elegy and Milton's *Lycidas.*" *PMLA* 25 (1910): 403-447, repr. in *Milton's Lycidas: The Tradition and the Poem,* ed. Patrides, 31-59.

Hauvette, Henri. *Un Exilé Florentin à la Cour de France au XVIe Siècle: Luigi Alamanni, 1495–1555: Sa Vie et Son Oeuvre.* Paris: Hachette, 1903.

Heesakkers, Chris L. "Introduction." In *Iani Douzae a Noortwyck Epigrammatum Lib. II,* 1–4. Leiden: Brill, 1976.

Hernández Núñez, Juan Carlos and Alfredo J. Morales. *The Royal Palace of Seville.* London: Scala Publishers, 1999.

Hero, A. C. "Pindar." In *Oxford Dictionary of Byzantium,* 3: 1678–79. New York: Oxford University Press, 1991.

Hinman, Robert B. *Abraham Cowley's World of Order.* Cambridge, MA: Harvard University Press, 1960.

Hirst, Derek. " 'That Sober Liberty': Marvell's Cromwell in 1654." In *The Golden & the Brazen World,* ed. John M. Wallace, 17–53. Berkeley: University of California Press, 1985.

Humiston, C. C. *A Comparative Study of the Metrical Techniques of Ronsard and Malherbe.* Berkeley and Los Angeles: University of California Press, 1941.

Hunt, Clay. *"Lycidas" and the Italian Critics.* New Haven: Yale University Press, 1979.

Huxley, George. *Pindar's Vision of the Past.* Belfast: George Huxley, 1975.

IJsewijn, Jozef. *Companion to Neo-Latin Studies.* 2 vols. Leuven: Leuven University Press, 1990–1998.

Jung, Marc-René. *Hercule dans la Littérature Française du XVIe Siècle.* Geneva: Librairie Droz, 1966.

Kelley, Maurice, and S. D. Atkins. "Milton and the Harvard Pindar." *Studies in Bibliography* 17 (1964): 77–83.

Keough, James J. "Cowley's Brutus Ode: Historical Precepts and the Politics of Defeat." *Texas Studies in Language and Literature* 19 (1977): 382–91.

Kidwell, Carol. *Pontano: Poet and Prime Minister.* London: Duckworth, 1991.

Klause, John. *The Unfortunate Fall: Theodicy and the Moral Imagination of Andrew Marvell.* Hamden, CT: Archon Books, 1983.

Knoppers, Laura Lunger. *Historicizing Milton.* Athens, GA: University of Georgia Press, 1994.

————. *Constructing Cromwell: Ceremony, Portrait, and Print, 1645-1661*.
    Cambridge: Cambridge University Press, 2000.
Kromer, Gretchen. "Homer and Odysseus in Nemean 7. 20–27." *Classical World*
    68 (1975): 437–38.
Krzysanowski, Julian. *The History of Polish Literature*. Warsaw: Polish Scientific
    Publishers, 1978.
Kurke, Leslie. *The Traffic in Praise: Pindar and the Poetics of Social Economy*.
    Ithaca: Cornell University Press, 1993.
Langley, T. R. "Abraham Cowley's 'Brutus': Royalist or Republican?" *Yale
    English Studies* 6 (1976): 41–52.
Lee, Kevin H. "Milton's Ode *Ad Joannem Rousium* and Euripides' *Ion*." *Milton
    Studies* 37 (1999): 1–17.
Lindenbaum, Peter. "John Milton and the Republican Mode of Literary
    Production." *Yearbook of English Studies* 21 (1991): 121–36.
Loiseau, Jean. *Abraham Cowley: Sa Vie, Son Œuvre*. Paris: Henri Didier, 1931.
————. *Abraham Cowley's Reputation in England*. Paris: Henri Didier, 1931.
Lowrie, Michèle. *Horace's Narrative Odes*. Oxford: Clarendon Press, 1997.
MacCaffrey, Wallace T. *Elizabeth I*. London: Edward Arnold, 1993.
————. *Queen Elizabeth and the Making of Policy, 1572–1588*. Princeton:
    Princeton University Press, 1981.
————. *Elizabeth I, War and Politics, 1588–1603*. Princeton: Princeton
    University Press, 1992.
Mackie, Hilary. *Graceful Errors: Pindar and the Performance of Praise*. Ann
    Arbor: University of Michigan Press, 2003.
Maddison, Carol. *Apollo and the Nine: A History of the Ode*. London: Routledge
    and Kegan Paul, 1960.
Maltzahn, Nicholas von. "Laureate, Republican, Calvinist: An Early Response
    to Milton and *Paradise Lost* (1667)." *Milton Studies* 29 (1992): 181–98.
McPherson, David. "Ben Jonson's Library and Marginalia: An Annotated
    Catalogue." *Studies in Philology* 71 (1974): 3–106.
McFarlane, I.D. "Jean Salmon Macrin." *Bibliothèque d'Humanisme et
    Renaissance* 21 (1959): 55–84.
Miller, Andrew M. "*Inventa Componere*: Rhetorical Process and Poetic
    Composition in Pindar's Ninth Olympian Ode." *Transactions of the
    American Philological Association* 123 (1993): 109–47.
Milosz, Czeslaw. *The History of Polish Literature*. Berkeley: University of
    California Press, 1983.
Money, David. "Aspects of the Reception of Sarbiewski in England." In *Pietas
    Humanistica: Neo-Latin Religious Poetry in Poland in European Context*,
    ed. Piotr Urbanski, 157–87. Frankfurt-am-Main, Bern, and Berlin: Peter
    Lang, 2006.

Most, Glenn. *The Measures of Praise: Structure and Function in Pindar's Second Pythian and Seventh Nemean Odes.* Göttingen: Vandenhoeck & Ruprecht, 1985.

Nagy, Gregory. *Pindar's Homer: The Lyric Possession of the Epic Past.* Baltimore: Johns Hopkins University Press, 1990.

Nardo, Anna K. "Milton and the Academic Sonnet." In *Milton in Italy,* ed. Mario Di Cesare, 489–503. MRTS 90. Binghamton: MRTS, 1991.

———. "Academic Interludes in *Paradise Lost.*" *Milton Studies* 27 (1991): 209–41.

Nash, Laura L. *The Aggelia in Pindar.* New York: Garland Publishing Co., 1990.

Neri, Ferdinando. *Il Chiabrera e la Pleiade Francese.* Turin: Fratelli Cocca, 1920.

Newdigate, Bernard H. *Michael Drayton and his Circle.* Oxford: Shakespeare Head Press, 1941.

Nethercot, Arthur H. *Abraham Cowley, The Muse's Hannibal.* London: Humphrey Milford, 1931.

Nisbet, R. G. M., and Margaret Hubbard. *A Commentary on Horace, Odes, Book I.* Oxford: Clarendon Press, 1970.

———. *A Commentary on Horace, Odes, Book II.* Oxford: Clarendon Press, 1978.

Norbrook, David. "Marvell's 'Horatian Ode' and the Politics of Genre." In *Literature and the English Civil War,* ed. Thomas Healy and Jonathan Sawday, 147–69. Cambridge: Cambridge University Press, 1990.

Patterson, Annabel. *Marvell and the Civic Crown.* Princeton: Princeton University Press, 1978.

———. *Censorship and Interpretation.* Madison: University of Wisconsin Press, 1984.

Perkin, M.R., ed. *Abraham Cowley: A Bibliography.* Folkestone: Dawson, 1977.

Pfeijffer, Ilya Leonard. *Three Aiginetan Odes of Pindar.* Leiden: Brill, 1999.

Piovan, Francesco. "Lampridio, Bembo e altri." *Italia Medioevale e Umanistica* 30 (1987): 179–97.

Pouey-Mounou, Anne-Pascale. "Quelques Arrière-Plans d'une Symétrie en Trompe-L'Œil: (I. 11–14)." In *Lire Les Odes de Ronsard,* ed. Bertrand, 91–104.

Prince, F. T. "*Lycidas* and the Tradition of the Italian Eclogue." *English Miscellany* 2 (1951): 95–105.

———. *The Italian Element in Milton's Verse.* Oxford: Clarendon Press, 1954.

Putnam, Michael. *Artifices of Eternity: Horace's Fourth Book of Odes.* Ithaca: Cornell University Press, 1986.

Quintero, Ruben. *Literate Culture: Pope's Rhetorical Art.* Newark, DE: University of Delaware Press, 2002.

Race, William H. *Pindar.* Boston: Twayne, 1986.

———. *Style and Rhetoric in Pindar's Odes.* Atlanta: Scholars Press, 1990.

Reddaway, W.F., et al., eds. *The Cambridge History of Poland*. Cambridge: Cambridge University Press, 1950.

Raymond, Marcel. *L'Influence de Ronsard sur la Poésie Française (1550–1585)*. Geneva: Librairie Droz, 1965.

Revard, Stella Purce. *The War in Heaven: Paradise Lost and the Tradition of Satan's Rebellion*. Ithaca: Cornell University Press, 1980.

———. "Pindar and Jonson's Cary-Morison Ode." In *Classic and Cavalier: Essays on Jonson and the Sons of Ben*, ed. Claude J. Summers and Ted-Larry Pebworth, 17–29. Pittsburgh: University of Pittsburgh Press, 1982.

———. *"Ad Joannem Rousium*: Elegiac Wit and Pindaric Mode." In *Urbane Milton: The Latin Poetry*, ed. James A. Freeman and Anthony Low, special number of *Milton Studies* 19 (1984): 205–26; reworked in Revard, *Milton and the Tangles of Neaera's Hair*, 237–63.

———. "Building the Foundations of the Good Commonwealth: Marvell, Pindar, and the Power of Music." In *The Muses Common-weale*, ed. Claude J. Summers and Ted-Larry Pebworth, 177–90. Columbia: University of Missouri Press, 1988.

———. "Milton and Chiabrera." In *Milton in Italy*, ed. Di Cesare, 505–20.

———. "Cowley's *Pindarique Odes* and the Politics of the Inter-regnum." *Criticism* 35 (1993): 391–418.

———. "Alpheus, Arethusa, and the Pindaric Pursuit in *Lycidas*." In *Of Poetry and Politics: New Essays on Milton and his World*, ed. P. G. Stanwood, 35–45. MRTS 126. Binghamton: MRTS, 1995.

———. "The Politics of Milton's Hercules." *Milton Studies* 32 (1995): 217–45.

———. *Milton and the Tangles of Neaera's Hair*. Columbia: University of Missouri Press, 1997.

———. "Katherine Philips, Aphra Behn, and the Female Pindaric." In *Representing Women in Renaissance England*, ed. Claude J. Summers and Ted-Larry Pebworth, 227–41. Columbia: University of Missouri Press, 1997.

———. "Lampridio and the Poetic Sodalities in Rome in the 1510s and 1520s." In *Acta Conventus Neo-Latini Bariensis*, ed. R. Schnur et al., 499–507. MRTS 184. Tempe, AZ: ACMRS, 1998.

———. "Lycidas." In *A Companion to Milton*, ed. Thomas N. Corns, 246–60. Oxford: Blackwell, 2001.

———. *Pindar and the Renaissance Hymn-Ode: 1450–1700*. MRTS 221. Tempe, AZ: ACMRS, 2001.

———. "Milton and Millenarianism: From the Nativity Ode to *Paradise Regained*." In *Milton and the Ends of Time*, ed. Juliet Cummins, 42–81. Cambridge: Cambridge University Press, 2003.

———. "The Latin Ode from Elizabeth I to Mary II: Political Approaches to Encomia." In *Britannia Latina: Latin in the Culture of Great Britain from the Middle Ages to the Twentieth Century*, ed. Charles Burnett and Nicholas Mann, 156–69. London: Warburg Institute, 2005.

Robin, Diana. *Filelfo in Milan: Writings 1451–1477*. Princeton: Princeton University Press, 1991.

Roscoe, William. *The Life and Pontificate of Leo the Tenth*. Liverpool: T. Cadell and W. Davies, 1805.

Rutherford, Ian. *Pindar's Paeans: A Reading of the Fragments with a Survey of the Genre*. Oxford: Oxford University Press, 2001.

Segal, Charles. *Pindar's Mythmaking: The Fourth Pythian Ode*. Princeton: Princeton University Press, 1986.

————. *Aglaia*. Lanham, MD: Rowan and Littlefield, 1998.

Shumaker, Wayne. "Flowerets and Sounding Seas: A Study in the Affective Structure of *Lycidas*." *PMLA* 66 (1951): 485–94; repr. in *Milton's Lycidas: The Tradition and the Poem*, ed. Patrides, 129–39.

Silver, Isidore. *The Pindaric Odes of Ronsard*. Paris: n.p., 1937.

————. *Ronsard and the Hellenic Renaissance in France. Ronsard and the Grecian Lyre*. Pts. 1–3. Geneva: Librairie Droz, 1981–1987.

Spingarn, J. E., ed. *Critical Essays of the Seventeenth Century*. Oxford: Clarendon Press, 1908-1909.

Starnawski, Jerzy. "Sarbievius (Mathias Casimirus) (Maciej Kazimierz Sarbiewski) (1595-1640)." In *Centuriae Latinae*, ed. Colette Nativel, 719–23. Geneva: Droz, 1997.

Sutherland, James. *English Literature of the Late Seventeenth Century*. Oxford: Clarendon Press, 1969.

Syfret, Rosemary. "Marvell's 'Horatian Ode'." *Review of English Studies* 12 (1961): 160–72.

Tayler, Edward W. "Lycidas in Christian Time." *Huntington Library Quarterly* 41 (1978): 103–17; condensed in *Milton's Lycidas: The Tradition and the Poem*, ed. Patrides, 303–18; reworked in Tayler, *Milton's Poetry: Its Development in Time*, 45–59. Pittsburgh: Duquesne University Press, 1979.

Thomas, Rosalind. "Fame, Memorial, and Choral Poetry: The Origins of Epinikian Poetry—An Historical Study." In *Pindar's Poetry, Patrons, and Festivals*, ed. Hornblower and Morgan, 141–66.

Todd, Janet. *The Secret Life of Aphra Behn*. London: Andre Deutsch, 1996.

Tucker, G. H. "Neo-Latin Literary Monuments to Renaissance Rome and the Papacy, 1553–1557: Janus Vitalis, Joachim Du Bellay, and Lelio Capilupi—From Ekphrasis to Prosopopeia." In *Acta Conventus Neo-Latini Bonnensis*, ed. Schnur et al., 81–119. MRTS 315. Tempe, AZ: ACMRS, 2006.

Tufte, Virginia. *The Poetry of Marriage: The Epithalamium in Europe and Its Development in England*. 2 vols. University of Southern California Studies in Comparative Literature 2. Los Angeles: Tinnon Brown, Inc., 1970.

Verdenius, W. J. *Commentaries on Pindar*. Leiden: E. J. Brill, 1988.

Wallace, John M. *Destiny his Choice*. Cambridge: Cambridge University Press, 1968.

Wilson, A. J. N. "Andrew Marvell: 'An Horatian ode upon Cromwell's Return from Ireland': The Thread of the Poem and its Use of Classical Allusion." *Critical Quarterly* 11 (1969): 325-41.

Wortham, Christopher. "Marvell's Cromwell Poems: An Accidental Triptych." In *The Political Identity of Andrew Marvell*, ed. Conal Condren and A. D. Cousins, 16–52. Aldershot: Scolar, 1990.

Zook, Melinda. "History's Mary: The Propagation of Mary II, 1689–1694." In *Women and Sovereignty*, ed. Fradenburg, 170–91.

———. "The Political Poetry of Aphra Behn." In *The Cambridge Companion to Aphra Behn*, ed. David Hughes and Janet Todd, 46–67. Cambridge: Cambridge University Press, 2004.

Zwicker, Steven N. "Models of Governance in Marvell's 'The First Anniversary'." *Criticism* 16 (1974): 1–12.

Index

Subcategories are usually listed in the order of importance. Entries with the letter "n" refer to footnotes. Page numbers and footnotes on the same page are listed only when the footnote contains additional explanatory material.